Chambers
Dictionary
of
Political Biography

Chambers

Dictionary

of

Political Biography

Editor

John Ransley

Chambers

Published 1991 by W & R Chambers Limited
43-45 Annandale Street, Edinburgh EH7 4AZ

British Library Cataloguing in Publication Data

A catalogue record for this book is
available from the British Library

ISBN 0-550-17251-3

Editorial Manager: Min Lee

Cover design by Michael Dancer

Cover illustration by John Marshall

Typeset by Pillans & Wilson Ltd. Edinburgh and London

Printed in England by Clays Ltd, St Ives, plc

Contents

Preface

This new work of reference aims at following in the tradition of *Chambers Biographical Dictionary*, which, since it was first published in 1897, has deservedly won a worldwide reputation for its comprehensiveness and accuracy.

Chambers Dictionary of Political Biography presents not only important facts but in many cases colourful insights into the lives of more than 1100 men and women who have shaped, or continue to shape, the modern political world. Those selected for inclusion have all made a significant contribution to their own countries' political development—and in several instances have exerted a profound impact on the fate of many others.

We have deliberately excluded politicians and others who, although their names may be familiar or even famous, have in perspective made only a minimal contribution to national or international government. Equally, the reader will find entries for individuals whose names may be wholly unfamiliar, but who have had a lasting influence on the world of politics.

The dictionary also presents a wide-ranging Glossary of Political Terms, which gives the correct spelling and meaning of hundreds of names and English and foreign phrases that frequently occur in the political vocabulary, as well as detailed descriptions of important events and political institutions.

Also included is a newly researched and up-to-date collection of political quotations, which reflects the humour as well as the perspicacity—or, not infrequently, deceitfulness—of historical and modern world leaders and those who comment on them.

Chambers Dictionary of Political Biography is more than an up-to-date reference work, it is unique in the scope of the information that it provides.

JOHN RANSLEY
September 1991

Political
Biographies

ABBAS, Ferhat
1899–1955

Algerian nationalist leader, born Taher, Kabylis. As a pharmacy student, he founded the Muslim Students Association in 1924, and following the defeat of the French Army in World War II drafted a manifesto for independence. In 1955 he became active in the FLN resistance movement and worked with **Ben Bella** in Cairo before founding his own provisional government in exile in 1958. When Algeria achieved independence from the French in 1962, Abbas presided over the new national assembly but was forced to resign a year later when it implemented a new constitution without consulting him, and Ben Bella became independent Algeria's first President instead. Abbas went into exile, and was rehabilitated only shortly before his death.

ABBOTT, Diane Julie
1953–

Britain's first black woman MP, born London. Educated at Harrow Girls' School and Cambridge, she worked in the Civil Service, for the National Council for Civil Liberties, and in local government; joined the Labour Party in 1981; and was elected to Westminster City Council a year later. She entered Parliament after holding a safe East London seat for Labour in the 1987 general election.

ABDULLAH IBN HUSSEIN
1882–1951

First king of Jordan, born Mecca. Prominent in the 1916–18 revolt against Turkey, he was rewarded for his pro-British stance in World War I by being made emir of the British-mandated Transjordan territory in 1921, and took the throne when the renamed country achieved independence in 1946. He annexed some of Arab Palestine on the birth of Israel two years later. An astute and cautious leader, ironically he met his death at the hands of an Arab fanatic.

ABDULLAH, Sheikh Mohammed (The Lion of Kashmir)
1905–82

Kashmiri politician. As a leading figure in the Muslim struggle to overthrow the Hindu maharajah and substitute constitional government, he was imprisoned between the wars, and on his release in 1938 founded the Muslim National Conference, and then the Quit Kashmir movement in 1946, when he was again incarcerated. A year later, he was released by the emergency administration and appointed Chief Minister, but for agreeing to Indian accession to staunch tribal infiltration, he was imprisoned for treason between 1953 and 1968. He served again as Chief Minister from 1975 until his death, when he was succeeded in that office by his son, Dr Farooq Abdullah (1937–).

ABDUL RAHMAN (Putra), Prince
1903–90

Malaysian statesman, born Kedeh. Educated at Cambridge, he was called to the Bar before returning to his home state to work as a public prosecutor. He founded the United Malays National Organisation in 1945, and became a member of the executive and legislative councils of the Federation of Malaya in 1952. He was appointed Chief Minister in 1955 and Prime Minister two years later, and, having negotiated the formation of an enlarged federation incorporating British North Borneo and Sarawak in 1964, became the first premier of Malaysia. Violent anti–Chinese riots forced his resignation in 1970.

ABERDARE, Henry Austin Bruce, 1st Baron
1815–95

Welsh politician, born Duffryn, Glamorgan. A barrister, he entered Parliament for the Liberals in 1837 and served as **Gladstone**'s Home Secretary from 1852 to 1873, then Lord President for a year. He was closely involved in framing significant educational reforms for Wales and helped to establish the University of Wales, becoming its first chancellor in 1895.

ABERDEEN, George Hamilton Gordon, 4th Earl of
1784–1860

Scottish statesman, born Edinburgh. He inherited a peerage at seven, and completed his education at Harrow under the guardianship of **William Pitt** the younger and **Henry Dundas**. He succeeded to his grandfather's earldom at 17, and as special ambassador to Vienna helped negotiate the Treaty of Tplitz that created the formidable alliance against **Napoleon**. He served as Foreign Secretary under both the Duke of **Wellington** (1828–30) and **Robert Peel** (1841–6), bringing an end to the Chinese war, and improving relations with France and the USA. As proponent of free trade, he resigned from Lord **Derby**'s Administration over the repeal of the Corn Laws in 1852, but became Prime Minister on **William Gladstone**'s resignation in 1852. His initial popularity dwindled on taking Britain into the Crimean War in 1854 and he was forced to resign a year later.

ABERDEEN, James Campbell Hamilton Gordon, 7th Earl of, and 1st Marquis
1847–1934

Scottish statesman, laird of Haddo House for 64 years. Twice Governor of Ireland between 1886 and 1915, in the interim he held the same office in Canada (1893–8). His wife, Ishbel-Maria Marjoribanks, was a leading advocate of improved rights for women and the peasantry, and made Haddo a model community that incorporated the reforms for which they campaigned. Their joint reminiscences, *We twa' (We Two)*, was published in 1925.

ABERHART, William
1878–1943

Canadian politician, born Huron County. After an early career as a clergyman and schoolmaster, he entered the Alberta legislature in 1935, and, embracing the doctrine of **Clifford Douglas**, he founded the Canadian Social Credit Party, and almost immediately became premier. His ambition to give each Albertan a monthly $5 dividend from the province's natural resources was thwarted by the federal government, but he was re-elected in 1940 and remained in office until his death.

ABRAHAM, William ('Mabon')
1842–1922

Welsh miners' leader and politician, born Cwmavon, Glamorgan. A strong advocate of sliding-scale wage agreements, whereby miners' pay was linked to the price of coal, he was probably the first trade unionist to adopt the concept of inflation-proof pay. However, the advent of collective bargaining and the 1898 miners' strike saw a fall in his personal popularity. As Labour MP for Rhondda constituencies between 1885 and 1920, he devoted himself to securing legislation to improve miners' pay and safety.

ABU–BAKR
570–634

First caliph of Islam. One of the earliest Muslim converts, he became Muhammad's chief adviser and on his death in 632 was made leader of the Muslim community. During his brief reign of two years, he suppressed political and religious revolts directed at the Medina government by the adherents of Muhammad's son–in–law, the Shiites, and set in train the subsequent Arab conquests of Persia, Iraq, and the Middle East.

ABZUG, Bella (Bella Savitzky)
1920–

American feminist and politician, born New York City. As a practising lawyer between 1944 and 1970, she frequently defended those accused of un-American activities, founded the Women Strike for Peace movement in 1961 and the National Women's Political Caucus in 1968, and won a seat in Congress in 1971. She ran unsuccessfuly for the Senate in 1976 but became mayor of New York in 1977 and is still a vigorous political activist.

ACHESON, Dean Gooderham
1893–1971

American statesman, born Middleton, Connecticut. Educated at Yale and Harvard, he practised internationally as a lawyer before joining the State Department in 1941. He was Assistant Secretary for two years from 1945, and became Secretary of State under **Harry S. Truman** (1949–53). He worked closely with **Ernest Bevin** on implementing the 1947 Marshall Plan, which provided $14 billion of reconstruction aid and loans to Europe, helped implement the 1947 Truman Doctrine on the provision of military and economic assistance to countries under threat of aggression, and was instrumental in establishing NATO in 1949. His works include *Power and Diplomacy* (1958), *Morning and Noon* (1965), and the Pulitzer prize-winning *Present at the Creation* (1969).

ACLAND, Sir Arthur Herbert Dyke
1847–1926

English reformer and politician, born Porlock. As Liberal MP for Rothertham from 1885 to 1895 and vice-president of an influential educational advisory council, he had the school-leaving age raised to 11 and abolished the payment-by-results state education system that was beginning to find favour again among many Conservatives in the early 1990s. His published works include *Handbook of the Political History of England* (1882).

ACLAND, Sir Richard Thomas Dyke
1906–

English politician. Having originally entered Parliament as a Liberal in 1931, in 1942 he resigned his party's whip on founding with the novelist J.B. Priestley the Common Wealth Party, donating his family estate to the nation in keeping with espousement of public ownership on moral grounds. When the CWP failed to capture the imagination of a war-weary and already deprived public, he served as a Labour MP from 1945, but resigned his seat 10 years later over British nuclear defence policy. His works include *Nothing Left to Believe* (1949) and *Waging Peace* (1958).

ADAMS, Gerry (Gerald)
1948–

Northern Ireland politician, born Belfast. A member of Sinn Fein, the political arm of the IRA, since his teens, he was interned during the 1970s, and was subsequently elected vice-president and president of the organisation. He was elected to the Northern Ireland Assembly at Stormont Castle in 1982, and was returned as Westminster MP for Belfast, West the following year—but has never taken his seat in the House of Commons. Though denied the 'oxygen of publicity' since the late 1980s by anti-terrorist legislation, his continuing support for nationalist extremists is evident from his attendance at IRA rallies and funerals, and at other events staged by them or in their honour.

ADAMS, Sir Grantley Herbert
1898–1971

Barbadian politician, born Barbados. After qualifying for the English Bar, he returned to the West Indies in 1924 to practise as a lawyer, became a prominent figure in Caribbean politics, and was premier of Barbados from 1954 to 1958, before being elected the first Prime Minister of the short-lived West Indies Federation (1958–62), which sought to merge seven former British colonies into a single state.

ADAMS, Henry Brooks
1838–1918

American historian, born Boston. Grandson of the sixth US President, he worked in Washington and London as a political secretary and journalist before teaching medieval and American history at Harvard from 1870. Among his many important works are the satirical novel *Democracy* and the nine-volume *History of the USA during the Administrations of Jefferson and Madison* (1870–77). He was posthumously awarded the 1919 Pulitzer Prize for his autobiography, *The Education of Henry Adams* (1907).

ADAMS, John
1735–1826

Second US President, born Quincy, Massachusetts. A farmer's son, he was a distinguished Harvard law scholar and joined the Bar in 1758. His colonialist sympathies ('No taxation without representation') caused him to decline office as Advocate-General and to oppose the Stamp Act; he was a delegate to the first Continental Congress. He sponsored **George Washington**'s appointment to commander-in-chief, and was the 'colossus of the debate' on the Declaration of Independence, which he helped to draft. After serving as chairman of 25 committees and on 64 others, he retired from Congress in 1777 but immediately became the new republic's representative in France and Holland, and, as a signatory to the 1783 peace treaty, was for three years from 1785 Minister to England. In 1787 he published his three-volume *Defence of the Constitution of the United States* and returned to America to serve as Washington's vice-president in 1789, succeeding him as the Federalists' choice in 1796. His opposition to **Hamilton**'s 1780 treaty with France lost him the 1800 presidential nomination in favour of **Thomas Jefferson**. He retired in chagrin to his home at Quincy, where he died.

ADAMS, John Quincy
1767–1848

Sixth president of the USA, son of **John Adams**, born in Quincy, Massachusetts. At 14 he became private secretary to the American envoy at St Petersburg. He was secretary to the commission for peace between the colonies and the USA, but in 1785 began to study at Harvard, and was admitted to the bar in 1790. Successively Minister to the Hague, London, Lisbon, and Berlin, in 1803 he was elected to the US senate from Massachusetts, and in 1806, boldly denouncing the right of searching ships claimed by the British government, he lost favour with the Federal party and with it his seat. In 1809 he was Minister to St Petersburg; in 1814, a member of the commission to negotiate peace between Great Britain and the USA; from 1815 to 1817 minister at the court of St James's. As secretary of state under president **Monroe**, he negotiated with Spain the treaty for the acquisition of Florida, and was alleged to be the real author of the 'Monroe Doctrine'. In 1825 he was elected president by the House of Representatives—no election having been made by the people. Failing to be re-elected, he retired to his home at Quincy, depressed and impoverished. In 1830 he was elected to the lower house of congress, where he became noted as a promoter of anti-slavery views; and he was returned to each successive congress until his death.

ADAMS, Samuel
1722–1803

American revolutionary and politician, born Boston. As a member of the Massachusetts legislature between 1765 and 1794, he organised opposition to the Stamp Act, served as a delegate to the First and Second Continental Congresses (1774–75), and was a signatory to the 1776 Declaration of Independence. He was state lieutenant-governor from 1789 to 1794, and governor until 1797.

ADDISON, Christopher, 1st Viscount
1869–1951

English politician, born Hogsthorpe, Lincolnshire. After qualifying as a surgeon and working as a professor of anatomy at Shef-field University, he was elected Liberal MP for Hoxton in 1910 and held office in the education and munitions Ministries before being made Britain's first Minister of Health in 1919. His differences with **Lloyd George** brought his resignation in 1921, when he switched his allegiances to the Labour Party. He was returned as Swindon's MP and was made agriculture minister in 1929. Ennobled in 1937, he led the Labour peers from 1940 and was appointed Leader of the Lords in 1945. His published work includes *Four and a Half Years* (1934).

ADDISON, Joseph
1672–1719

English essayist and politician, born Milston, Wiltshire. Entering the diplomatic service in 1699, he served in France, Italy, Austria, Germany and Holland, was appointed an Under-Secretary in 1705, and took his seat in Parliament three years later. After three years as secretary to the Lord Lieutenant of Ireland, he returned to England in 1710 on the fall of the Whig Government, resuming his former post on the accession of George I in 1714. He was appointed a trade commissioner in 1716 and Secretary of State a year later, but ill health forced his resignation in 1718. As a poet, critic and dramatist, his prose style—at its best in many of his articles for the *Tatler* and the *Spectator*, which he founded—served as a model until the end of the 18th century. His blank verse tragedy *Cato* (1713), which combined an appeal to the Whigs for party unity with a tirade against immorality, was hugely popular, as was his 1706 opera *Rosamond*.

ADENAUER, Konrad
1876–1967

German statesman, born Cologne. A lawyer, he served as a Centre Party member in local and provincial politics before being banned from office by the Nazis and imprisoned by them between 1934 and 1944. He was reinstated by the allies as Cologne's lord mayor in 1945, founded the Christian Democratic Union, and served as Chancellor from 1949. He was re-elected in 1953 and 1957, and held office also as Foreign Minister between 1951 and 1955. He was a strong supporter of NATO and of economic co-operation with other European nations, and nurtured better relations with France. Although his restraint during the 1961 Berlin crisis laid the foundations for German reunification, ironically the unpopularity of that approach at the time forced a coalition with the Free Democrats and his retirement in 1963.

AGNELLI, Giovanni
1866–1945

Italian industrialist and senator, born Turin. After a military education, he began making motor tricycles in 1886 and founded Fiat with a group of other investors two years later. In the early 1900s, the company diversified into manufacturing buses and military and industrial diesel engines, and made enormous profits as the main supplier of army vehicles for the 1911 war with Libya and World War I. Agnelli led industrial and business opposition to socialism and trade unionism, and acquired newspapers to propagate his policies. **Benito Mussolini** appointed him to the Senate in 1923, which further assured government protection and remunerative contracts for his company in World War II providing the basis of Fiat's post-war development as one of the world's biggest industrial conglomerates.

AGRICOLA, Gnaeus Julius
40–93

Roman soldier and statesman, born Fréus, Provence. After military successes in Britain, Asia and Aquitania, he became a consul, and as governor of Britain from 77, he brought civilization in place of hostilities, extending his influence to Scotland after the victory at Mons Graupius, Aberdeenshire, in 84. His fleet's circumnavigation identified Britain as an island for the first time, but he was eventually recalled by Domitian, who was jealous of his successes, and faded from public life. The panegyrical description of Agricola's life by his son-in-law, Tacitus, is one of the great classical biographies.

AHIDJO, Ahmadou
1924–89

Cameroonian politician, born Saroua. He entered politics in 1947 after working in a local radio station, and became Prime Minister in 1958 when the country was still a United Nations trust territory, leading it to independence in 1960. The republic's first President, Ahidjo also headed the country's only political party, the Cameroon National Union, from 1966. Complaining that his nominated successor, **Paul Biya**, would turn the country into a police state, he resigned in 1983 and went into exile in France.

AKBAR The Great (Jelal–ed–din–Muhammad)
1542–1605

Mogul emperor of India, born Umarkot, Sind. Enthroned at 13, he soon dismissed the tutor who had effectively served as head of government, and there followed years of civil war. After bringing peace to his homeland, he extended his empire to Malwa, Rajputana, Gujrat and Bengal, and in 1580 took Afghanistan. Kashmir, Sindh, Kandahar and Ahmadnagar fell to him in subsequent campaigns, making Akbar ruler of the whole of North India. He then implemented an enlightened programme of fiscal and social reforms that included the abolition of slavery, encouragement of the arts and sciences, and religious tolerance. He founded in 1582 the Din Alahi interdenominational order for scholars and theologians, resisting attempts by Portuguese missionaries to convert him to Christianity.

AKIHITO
1933–

Japanese emperor, born Tokyo. Educated among commoners in Japan and at Oxford, and married in 1959 to the first non-aristocrat to join the imperial family, Akihito—a keen cellist and amateur marine biologist—was wholly eclipsed by his father until **Hirohito**'s death in 1989, when he took the Chrysanthemum Throne and proclaimed the new Heisei era of universal peace.

ALAMÁN, Lucas
1792–1853

Mexican politician, born Guanajuato. Trained as a mining engineer, he entered the Cortes in 1820, and in the wake of the Riego Revolt that year, spoke out for independence and the monarchy. When independence was achieved the following year, he secured Vatican and French agreement to an independent Mexican royal house, and subsequently served as Minister of State to emperor Iturbide, and as Foreign Minister to Bustamante and Santa Anna. His legacies are the Mexican National Museum and the monumental work *Historia de Mexico* (1852).

ALAVA, Don Miguel Ricardo de
1771–1843

Spanish soldier and statesman. After serving under **Wellington** in the 1811 Peninsular War, he served as ambassador to the Netherlands, and as President of the Cortez forced King Ferdinand VII from the throne in 1822. He fled when the French reinstated the monarch a year later, but was rehabilitated under Queen Maria Christina, gaining appointment as ambassador to London and Paris.

ALBERONI, Giulio
1664–1752

Spanish-Italian politician, born Piacenza. After entering the priesthood, he won the favour of Philip V while serving as the Duke of Parma's agent in Spain, and was appointed a cardinal and Prime Minister in 1717. Though a liberal in home affairs, his invasion of Sardinia antagonized Britain, France, Austria and Holland and brought the destruction of the Spanish fleet. He later conspired to provoke hostilities between Austria and Turkey and a revolution in Hungary. His attempt to depose the French regent in 1719 forced Philip to remove him from office. He returned to Italy and spent most of his remaining years in a monastery.

ALBERT, Prince Consort
1819–61

Born Schloss Rosenau, Coburg. The younger son of the Duke of Saxe-Coburg-Gotha, he was educated in Brussels and Bonn, and married his first cousin, Queen **Victoria**, in 1840, becoming Prince Consort in 1857. By his patronage of the arts, science and industry (his stewardship of the Great Exhibition in 1851 both boosted British exports and funded the building of the Natural History and Science Museums and the Royal Albert Hall) he overcame the British people's initial distrust and was eventually to win their deep affection and admiration. Far from being a constitutional cipher, he was a steadying and positive influence in the monarch's handling of affairs of state, and made a substantial personal contribution to his adopted country's social and industrial development through the industrial revolution. After his death from typhoid, Victoria went into virtual seclusion on the Isle of Wight and intervened less and less in the Government of the day—even to the point of seldom attending the annual State Opening of Parliament.

ALCIBIADES
450–404 BC

Athenian statesman, born Athens. Although tutored by **Socrates**, he led a dissipated early life, particularly after his marriage to the wealthy Hipparete, and took an interest in politics only to thwart Nicias's growing power base by persuading the Athenians to form part of an alliance against Sparta. He was recalled from the 415 BC Sicilian expedition, which he instigated, to answer concocted charges of sacrilege, and subsequently plotted, with Persian support, to overthrow his enemies in Athens. His four-year command of the Athenian democratic army brought several defeats for the Spartans and the restoration of the dominion of the sea to Athens, but the ill-fated Asian expedition forced his exile. He again turned to the Persian court for help, but was assassinated by the Spartans before he could raise another army.

ALDRICH, Nelson Wilmarth
1841–1915

American politician, born Rhode Island. After a term in local politics, he was elected to Congress as a Republican in 1879, moving to the Senate two years later, where he was a ruthless defender of big business interests and promoter of high protective tariffs. He had little in common with **Theodore Roosevelt**, but compensated by dominating **William Howard Taft**. He retired in 1911. His grandson, **Nelson Aldrich Rockefeller**, became Governor of New York.

ALEBUA, Ezekiel
1947–

Solomon Islands' politician. A member of the rightist United Party, he became deputy Prime Minister in 1984 and narrowly secured Parliament's support to assume the premiership two years later when Sir Peter **Kenilorea** resigned following allegations concerning the redistribution of aid received from the French government for the repair of cyclone damage.

ALEXANDER, Albert Victor, 1st Earl Alexander of Hillsborough
1885–1965

British politician, born Weston-super-Mare. He was elected an independent MP in 1922, was appointed a Trade Secretary in 1924, and served three times as First Lord of the Admiralty between 1929 and 1946. In Britain's postwar Labour Government, he was Minister of Defence for three years, and after receiving a peerage, became leader of the Labour Opposition in the Lords in 1955.

ALEXANDER, Sir Harold Rupert Leofric George Alexander, 1st Earl Alexander of Tunis

1891–1969

Soldier and statesman, born County Tyrone. As the commander of a battalion of the Irish Guards at 24, he led World War I actions on the Western Front and at Passchendaele, Cambrai and Hazerbrouck, and between 1932 and 1939 was a staff officer with the Northern Command and in India. As the commander of a rearguard contingent in the Dunkirk evacuation, he was the last British officer in that action to leave France. His North Africa command (1942–3) brought one of the most complete victories in World War II. He subsequently secured victories in Sicily and Italy, and was made a field marshal and Supreme Allied Commander in the Mediterranean with the capture of Rome in June 1944. He became Governor-General of Canada in 1946, and from 1952 served for two years as Minister of Defence under **Winston Churchill**.

ALEXANDER THE GREAT

356–323 BC

King of Macedonia, born Pella. Tutored by **Aristotle**, he served as regent at 17 while his father, Philip II, was absent in the war against the Byzantines, and in the Chaeronea campaign was implicated in Philip's assassination. Still only 20, he crushed the Illyrians, razed Thebes, and defeated the Persians at Granicus in 334 BC. After the armies of **Darius** fell to him in Cilicia in 333 BC, he took Tyre, and was welcomed in Egypt as a liberator from the Persians. He founded Alexandria, defeated Darius again at Arbela in 331 BC, then conquered Babylon, Susa, the Persian capital of Persepolis, and Sogdiana. Meanwhile, disagreements with his generals and advisers led to a number of summary executions, and his unparalleled record of victories began to fail with huge casualties at the start of his campaign to conquer India. He retreated to Babylon with ambitions to take Arabia instead, but fell ill after a banquet— perhaps having been poisoned—and died several days later, when his body was interred in a gold coffin at a tomb in Alexandria.

ALFONSIN FOULKES, Raul

1927–

Argentine statesman, born Chascomas. A lawyer and a member of the Radical Union Party since 1945, he was imprisoned by **Peron** in 1953, but sat twice in the Chamber of Deputies during two brief periods of civilian rule between 1963 and 1976. On being elected President in 1983 with the return of constitutional government, he brought several military figures to trial for human rights abuses, reformed trade unions, and improved foreign relations, and in 1986 he was honoured for work in the sphere of civil liberties by the Council of Europe. He left office in 1989, to be succeeded by **Carlos Menem**.

ALFRED the Great

849–99

Anglo-Saxon king of Wessex, born Wantage. The youngest of King Ethelwulf's five sons, he took the throne in 871, with Wessex at risk from the Viking invaders who had already occupied the north and east of England. When the Danes invaded in 878, he took refuge in Somerset to muster his forces, then won a decisive victory at the battle of Edington. He resisted another invasion in 885, took London a year later, and signed a treaty partitioning England under Viking rule. In establishing a substantial fleet to repel further invasion, he has come to be known as the father of the English Navy. In peacetime, he promoted education and the arts, inspired the *Anglo-Saxon Chronicles*, and himself translated Latin secular works into the vernacular.

ALI, (Chaudri) Mohamad

1905–80

Pakistani politician, born Jullundur, India. After working as a lecturer, he entered government service and in 1945 became the first Indian ever to be appointed a financial adviser of war and supply. With India's partition two years later, he was appointed Pakistan's first secretary-general, became finance minister in 1951, and Prime Minister in 1955. Dwindling support among his own party colleagues and from the Moslem League brought his resignation in 1956.

ALIA, Ramiz
1925–

Albanian military and communist leader, born Shkoder. Of Muslim peasant parentage, he was a lieutenant colonel in World War II, and was president of the Labour Party before joining its central committee in 1954, serving as Education Minister and head of agitprop in 1958. He entered the Politburo in 1961 and became head of state a year later, succeeding as national leader on **Enver Hoxha**'s death in 1985.

ALLENDE (GOSSENS), Salvador
1908–73

Chilean politician, born Valparaiso. Arrested several times in his youth for his radical activities, he avoided the communists and instead helped to found the Marxist Chilean Socialist Party. He was elected to the Chamber of Deputies in 1937 and was a senator from 1945 to 1970. Between 1952 and 1964 he failed three times to achieve the presidency, but narrowly triumphed in 1970. His aspirations to achieve a socialist society within a parliamentary democracy were thwarted by business interests backed by the CIA, and in 1973 he was killed in a military coup led by **Augusto Pinochet**.

ALMIRANTE, Giorgio
1915–88

Italian politician, born Parma. After an early career as a teacher and journalist, he helped to found the postwar neo-facist Italian Socialist Movement (MSI) and won election to Parliament in 1948. He was made party secretary in 1969, leading the MSI to a decisive victory in the 1972 elections. Ill-health forced his retirement in 1972.

ALTGELD, John Peter
1847–1902

American politician, born Nassau, Germany. Raised in the USA from infancy, he served with the Unionists during the Civil War, was appointed a supreme-court judge for five years from 1886, and was elected the first Democrat governor of Illinois in 1892.

AMANULLAH KHAN
1892–1960

Afghan ruler. After assuming the throne on the assassination of his father in 1919, he led an inconclusive three-year war against the British but eventually achieved recognition of Afghanistan as a sovereign state in 1922, and became king in 1926. His zeal for immediate westernization, and his support of female emancipation in particular, provoked rebellion, and he was forced to abdicate in 1928. He went into exile in Rome a year later.

AMBEDKAR, Bhimrao Ranji
1893–1956

Indian politician, born Konkan, Bombay. Educated in Bombay, and at Columbia University and the London School of Economics, he worked as a member of the London Bar before returning to join the Bombay legislative assembly and become leader of the 60 million members of the lower castes—the 'untouchables'. As Law Minister from 1947, he was the principal author of the Indian Constitution. He resigned in 1951 and converted to the Buddhist faith shortly before his death. His works include *Annihilation of Caste* (1937).

AMBOISE, George d'
1460–1510

French prelate and statesman. As Archbishop of Rouen, he was made a cardinal and Prime Minister under Louis XII in 1498, and encouraged a split between France and Rome as part of his unsuccessful bid to secure election as Pope. His 1505 Treaty of Blois forged an alliance between France and Spain.

AMERY, Leopold Charles Maurice Stennett
1873–1955

British politician, born Gorakpur, India. After 10 years as a journalist with *The Times*, he became Conservative MP for a Birmingham constituency in 1911, holding the seat for 34 years. He held a junior Foreign Office post and was then First Lord of the Admiralty before joining **Churchill**'s wartime Cabinet as Secretary of State for India and Burma. His three-volume autobiography, *My Political Life*, was published between 1953 and 1955.

AMIN (DADA), Idi
1925–

Ugandan soldier and dictator. A soldier in the British, later Ugandan army, he successfully cultivated a friendship with premier **Milton Obote** to become commander-in-chief of the army and air force, then betrayed him by staging a coup in 1971. After dissolving Parliament and establishing a military dictatorship, he undertook a ruthless programme of revenge against his enemies, real and imagined. Over the next six years, he expelled all Ugandan Asians, many Jews, seized businesses in foreign ownership, and ordered the killing of thousands of political opponents. His attempt in 1978 to annex Kagera on the Ugandan-Tanzanian border brought an invasion by the troops of President **Nyerere** supported by Ugandan exiles and Amin's forces were defeated within six months. He fled to Libya, and subsequently found refuge in Zaire, Senegal, Nigeria and Saudi Arabia.

AMORY, Derick Heathcoat, 1st Viscount Amory

1899–1981

British politician, born Tiverton. After entering Parliament in 1945, he held a number of ministerial posts from 1951 before serving as Chancellor of the Exchequer for two years from 1958.

ANDRADA E SILVA, José Bonifacio de

1763–1838

Brazilian statesman. His early career as a professor of geology in Lisbon ended with his return to Brazil in 1819 as a member of the independence movement that in 1822 overthrew Prince Pedro I. He served briefly as Prime Minister when the Portuguese regent was made emperor, but was exiled over disputes between them over Portuguese policy.

ANDRÁSSY, Count Gyula

1823–90

Hungarian revolutionary and statesman, born Volosca. A prominent supporter of **Lajos Kossuth** in the struggle for independence between 1848 and 1849, he went into exile for 10 years but eventually achieved office as Prime Minister when the dual monarchy was formed in 1867. As Foreign Minister of Austria-Hungary between 1871 and 1879, he strengthened the German alliance to thwart the Soviet threat, thus unwittingly establishing the political framework that led to World War I.

ANDREW, John Albion

1818–67

American statesman, slavery abolitionist, born Windham, Maine. Governor of Massachusetts between 1860 and 1866, he mobilized the state during the Civil War.

ANDROPOV, Yuri Vladimirovich

1914–84

Russian politician, born Nagutskaya, Stavropol. The son of a railway official, he trained as an engineer and began work at the Rybinsk shipyard in 1930. His interest in politics developed over the next decade, and in 1940 he was charged with implementing Soviet principles in the newly ceded Karelian peninsula. After the war, in which he led a resistance movement, he won rapid promotion, and after his appointment as ambassador to Budapest in 1954, he came to the notice of **Mikhail Suslov** for his role in crushing the 1956 Hungarian uprising. Under Suslov's patronage, Andropov became KGB chief in 1957, and was made a full member of the Politburo in 1973. His unremitting opposition to reform and tough handling of dissidents throughout the 1970s marked him as **Leonid Breznev**'s natural successor in 1982, but his brief term as premier was less reactionary than many had feared, providing an opportunity for **Mikhail Gorbachev**, among others, to advance in the party hierarchy.

ANGELL, Sir Norman (Ralph Norman Angell Lane)

1872–1967

English writer and pacifist, born Holbeach. His influential work *The Great Illusion* argued that war was as disastrous economically and socially for the victor as for the conquered, and he was rewarded with the Nobel Peace Prize in 1933. He was a Labour MP from 1929 to 1931, and published his autobiography, *After All*, in 1951.

ANTALL, József

1937–

As chairman of the centre-right Hungarian Democratic Front, in April 1990—following Hungary's first free multiparty elections since 1945—Antall took his party to victory by winning 165 seats in the new National Assembly to win a clear majority, and in the coalition Government formed a month later, he headed the new Council of Ministers as premier under President Árpád Göncz.

ANTHONY, MARK (Marcus Antonius)
83–30 BC

Roman triumvir. Related on his mother's side to **Julius Caesar**, he led a dissipated youth escaping to Athens in 58 BC. He was on Caesar's staff from 54 BC. Expelled from the Senate in 49 BC for his support of **Julius Caesar**, he joined him in the Pompey and Pharsalia campaigns, and was left to rule Italy when Caesar was in Africa. When the conspirators in Caesar's assassination fled in 44 BC, Anthony was left absolute ruler, but was soon thwarted by **Octavian Augustus** and was forced into exile in Gaul. There, he raised a new army and, having formed a triumvirate with Lepidus and Cicero, he marched on Rome, killing Cicero, 300 senators and 2000 equites. After taking Italy, Anthony's forces went on to take Macedonia, and to defeat Brutus and Cassius at Philippi in Asia. There, he met Cleopatra and followed her to Egypt. He was recalled in 40 BC when war broke out between Anthony's supporters and those of Octavian, which resulted in them ruling the east and west of the Empire respectively, with Lepidus taking Africa. Although he had married Octavian's daughter while in Italy, Anthony soon returned to Egypt and Cleopatra, and his association with her and two unsuccessful campaigns against the Parthians in 36 and 34 BC led to Octavian's declaration of war on Cleopatra in 32 BC, and she, with Anthony, was defeated at the naval battle of Actium a year later. Deserted by Cleopatra's forces on his return to Egypt, and falsely informed that she had taken her own life, Anthony committed suicide in Alexandria by falling on the priceless short-sword with which he had been presented as one of the Roman Empire's greatest military leaders.

ANTHONY, Susan Brownell
1820–1906

American reformer and women's suffrage leader, born Adams, Massachusetts. Her feminist activities began at 17 as an agitator for equal pay for women teachers. An early supporter of the temperance and anti-slavery movements, she additionally championed women's rights from 1854, and in 1869 founded with Elizabeth Cady Stanton the National Woman Suffrage Association. She was arrested and tried for leading marches on New York polling stations in protest at the federal government's refusal to give women the vote. She organized the 1888 International Council of Women and the 1904 International Woman Suffrage Alliance in Berlin, and with Stanton and Matilda Joslyn Cage produced the six-volume *History of Woman Suffrage*. Her contribution to sexual equality in all races was honoured in 1978, when her face was depicted on the silver dollar, making her the first woman in history to adorn American currency.

ANTONESCU, Ion
1882–1946

Romanian general and dictator, born Pitesti. As the son of an aristocratic family, he served as a military attache in Rome and London before becoming Chief of Staff and Minister of Defence in 1937. Imprisoned in 1938 for attempting a right–wing coup, he was the Nazis' natural choice to depose King Carol and to assume the dictatorship in 1940. He was overthrown after the 1944 Russian victory, and executed two years later for war crimes.

ANTRAIGUES, Emanuel Delaunay, Comte d'
1755–1812

French politician, born Villeneuve de Berg. As a Deputy from 1789, he defended hereditary privileges and the monarch's right of veto, and served as a diplomat at St Petersburg, Vienna and Dresden. While staying in England, where he cultivated a close relationship with **George Canning**, Antraigues and his wife were murdered by their Italian servant.

APPONYI, Count Albert Georg
1846–1933

Hungarian statesman, born Vienna. His command of oratory as a member of the Diet from 1872 was rewarded with leadership of the moderate Opposition that became the National Party in 1891. In 1899, he and his supporters switched their allegiance to the Liberal Government, and Apponyi was Diet President between 1901 and 1903. A devout Catholic, as Minister of Culture from 1906 to 1910 he gave asylum to countless French

Jesuits and introduced free state education. He resigned in 1920 in protest at the peace terms imposed by the Treaty of Trianon.

AQUINO, (Maria) Corazon
1933–

Filipino politician, born Tarlac. The daughter of wealthy middle-class parents, she graduated in New York, and in 1956 married Benigno S. Aquino, who became the chief political opponent of **Ferdinand Marcos**. Her husband was imprisoned for eight years from 1972 on charges of murder and subversion, and after three further years in exile, was assassinated by a military guard as he disembarked from a plane on returning to Manila in 1983. As the leading opposition candidate in the 1986 presidential elections, Corazon Aquino led a non-violent people's campaign following accusations that Marcos's victory was the product of ballot-rigging. When the Church, military and US Administration withdrew their support for him, Marcos was forced to concede defeat and fled the country. Aquino's presidency has come under threat a number of times—most recently in 1989, when an extreme army faction attempted unsuccessfuly to depose her.

ARAFAT, Yasser (Mohammed Abed Ar'ouf Arafat)
1929–

Palestinian resistance leader, born Jerusalem. Trained as an engineer, he founded Al Fatah in 1956 and his regular articles criticizing the neglect of Palestinian refugees by the Arab regimes prompted them to collaborate in establishing in 1964 the Palestinian Liberation Organization comprising several disparate terrorist factions, though Al Fatah gained control of it within five years. Arafat's diplomatic skills secured United Nations recognition of the PLO in 1974, and he subsequently adopted a more flexible policy, accepting the principle of establishing an independent Palestinian state in any part of the disputed territory from which Israel would withdraw. In the 1980s, Arafat's influence waned in the absence of progress, with the more extreme factions within the PLO becoming more dominant—but he re-established his leadership when King **Hussein** of Jordan relinquished control of the West Bank in 1988, and enormously enhanced his international credibility by formally acknowledging Israel's right to co-exist with an independent Palestinian state. As **Saddam Hussein**'s closest ally in the Gulf crisis, he made an unsuccessful last-ditch effort—just days before the 15 January 1991 deadline for the start of hostilities—to enlist French support for a new negotiated settlement allowing a continuing Iraqi presence in Kuwait.

ARAGO, Dominique François Jean
1786–1853

French scientist and statesman, born Perpignan. After a distinguished early career as an astronomer and physicist, he took a leading part in the July 1830 revolution that overthrew Charles X, and voted with the extreme left in the Chamber of Deputies. He was a member of the 1848 provisional Government that abolished slavery in the French empire, but his political career came to an end soon after his refusal to take the oath of allegiance after **Napoleon III** proclaimed himself emperor in 1851.

ARAKI, Sadao
1877–1966

Japanese soldier and politician. An ultra-nationalist, he led a right-wing army faction and was Minister for War from 1931 to 1933, and then Education Minister for two years from 1938. After World War II he was given a life sentence for war crimes but was released a year before his death.

ARANDA, Pedro Pablo Abarca y Bolea, Count of
1718–99

Spanish statesman and general, born Sietano. He was recalled to Madrid from a posting as ambassador to Poland in 1760 and appointed Prime Minister with a brief to expel the Jesuits and the other perpetrators of uprisings, but lost power in 1773 and accepted an ambassadorial posting to France. He returned to his homeland in 1787, and briefly served again as premier in 1792 before his enforced retirement to Aragon after antagonizing Manuel de Godoy over his closeness to King Charles IV.

ARENS, Moshe
1925–

Israeli politician, born Lithuania. Educated at Massachusetts and California Institutes of

Technology, he lectured in aeronautical engineering at the Israel Institute of Technology, Haifa, and was deputy director of Israel Aircraft Industries before entering the Knesset in 1973. He served as ambassador to the US (1982–3), and was then a Minister without portfolio until 1987, when he was appointed Foreign Minister.

ARGENSON, René Louis, Marquis d'

1694–1757

French statesman. Appointed councillor to the Paris parlement in 1716, he was Foreign Minister from 1744 until falling victim in 1747 to the machinations of Madame de Pompadour.

ARIAS SANCHEZ, Oscar

1940–

Costa Rican politician, born Costa Rica. Educated in England, he started a law practice before entering politics as a member of the left-wing National Liberation Party, of which he became secretary-general. As a neutralist candidate, he was elected President in 1986, and immediately drafted a peace agreement for the region aimed at ending hostilities in Nicaragua in particular.

ARISTIDES (the Just)

530–468 BC

Athenian soldier and statesman. A commander in the battle of Marathon against the Persians, he was then chief archon, but was ostracised in 483 BC for his criticism of Themistocles' naval policy. He was rehabilitated when the Persians invaded again under **Xerxes** in 480 BC, and after being made a general, introduced radical constitutional changes, including the right of all citizens, regardless of rank, to be admitted to the archonship; and Athens, rather than Sparta, became the ruling state of the Delian league.

ARISTOTLE

384–322 BC

Greek philosopher and scientist, born Stagira. The son of a court physician, he was a tutor at **Plato**'s academy for 20 years until his mentor's death, and on failing to succeed him spent many years in Athens and Asia Minor until invited by Philip of Macedon to educate his son, the future **Alexander the Great**. He returned to Athens in 335 to found his own academy, where he taught for the next 12 years. Accused of impiety in the anti-Macedonian wave that followed the death of Alexander in 323 BC, Aristotle fled to Euboea, where he died within a year. Many of his voluminuous writings—which embraced practically every field of the social sciences, including ethics, logic, politics, rhetoric and psychology—survived in the form of lecture notes, and have had a profound influence on Western intellectual and scientific development. Among the best known are the *Metaphysics*, *Nicomachean Ethics*, *Ethics* and *Politics*.

ARMFELT, Gustaf Mauritz

1757–1814

Swedish soldier and statesman, born Finland. After taking part in the 1788-90 war against Russia, he negotiated peace and was appointed to the regency council after the assassination of Gustav III in 1792, subsequently achieving appointment as ambassador to Vienna and a command against **Napoleon** in Pomerania (1805-7). He was unpopular with Karl XIII, and was expelled in 1811 two years after the new monarch took the throne. Having previously conspired with **Catherine II** the Great, he received a ready welcome in Russia, and subsequently served Alexander I as governor of Finland.

ARMSTRONG, Robert, Baron Armstrong of Ilminster

1927–

British civil servant. After holding senior Home Office and Treasury appointments, he became principal private secretary to **Edward Heath** in 1970, subsequently head of the Civil Service and Cabinet Secretary under **Margaret Thatcher**. Even in that exalted office he would have remained relatively anonymous had it not been for his testimony during the British Government's disastrous attempt in the Australian courts in 1986 to halt publication of Peter Wright's book *Spycatcher*, when Armstrong made the famous remark that he had perhaps been 'economical with the truth'. He retired shortly afterwards, and was given a life peerage in 1988.

ARNOLD, Benedict

1741–1801

American soldier and traitor, born Norwich, Connecticut. Arnold's ambivalence and duplicitousness were evident from an early age, for he deserted soon after joining the army at 14, became a merchant, then joined the colonial forces at the start of the War of Independence. He gave distinguished service at the siege of Quebec, Lake Champlain, Ridgefield, and Saratoga, achieving the rank of major-general. Though admired by **George Washington**, he made many enemies, and was denied promotion and reprimanded for embezzlement. On assuming the command of West Point in 1780, he conspired with the British to offer its surrender, and when the plot was discovered, fled to the British lines and subsequently led actions against his former brothers-in-arms in Virginia and Connecticut. He sought refuge in England in 1781, and died there in poverty.

ARNOLD OF BRESCIA

1100–55

Italian churchman and politician. Banished for his unorthodox teachings, he went to France, where he also provoked St Bernard and was forced to seek refuge in Zurich. The 1143 insurrection against the Papal Government provided him with an opportunity to return to his homeland and to found a republic on ancient Roman lines. In 1155, Arnold's power based collapsed and he was arrested. He was hanged and his body burnt, and the ashes thrown into the Tiber.

ARRIAGA, Manoel José de

1840–1917

Portuguese statesman. An active participant in the 1910 revolution to overthrow King Manuel, in 1911 he began a four-year term as the republic's first elected President.

ARTHUR, Chester Alan

1830–86

Twenty-first US President, born Fairfield, Vermont. The son of an Irish Baptist minister, he ran a successful law practice before becoming leader of the Republicans in New York State. Implicated in a scandal involving political patronage, he was dismissed from the lucrative post of collector of customs by Hayes in 1878 but was Garfield's choice as vice-president in the 1881 election. When Garfield was assassinated a few months later, Arthur assumed the presidency, but, ironically, his unwillingness to offer posts to political friends largely contributed to his failure to win re-election in 1885.

ASHDOWN, Paddy (Jeremy John Durham)

1941–

British politician, born India. Educated in India and Ulster, he joined the Royal Marines when his parents emigrated to Australia in the 1950s, eventually serving in its equivalent of the SAS, the elite Special Boat Squadron. While stationed in the Far East, he acquired a first-class degree in Mandarin at Hong Kong University, and entered the diplomatic service in 1971. In 1976 he moved to the traditional Liberal heartland of south-west England, and overturned a large Conservative majority to become Liberal MP for Yeovil in 1983. In 1988, he succeeded **David Steel** as leader of the Liberal Democrats, and subsequent by-election successes provided evidence of his success in persuading the electorate that the LDP offered a credible alternative to Labour as the main Opposition party. Despite his military background he is not considered a hawk, but he nevertheless gave the Conservative Government his party's almost unqualified support for its stance in the 1990–1 Gulf crisis.

ASQUITH, Herbert Henry, 1st Earl of Oxford and Asquith

1852–1928

British statesman and Liberal leader, born Morley, Yorkshire. Called to the Bar in 1876, he was MP for East Fife from 1886 to 1918, and as Home Secretary (1892–95) upset many in his party by his support of the anti-Boer imperialists in the South African war of 1899–1902. With the Liberals' return to power in 1905 he became Chancellor of the Exchequer, succeeding **Campbell–Bannerman** as Prime Minister three years later. Notable reforms achieved in the early years of his administration included old-age pensions, the disestablishment of the Welsh Church, and national insurance. When the House of Lords resisted his so-called People's Budget of 1909, Asquith retaliated by calling two general elections in 1910 to re-establish his government's authority, and by introducing in 1911 legislation that greatly restricted the power of the Upper House to amend or block Money Bills or to veto Irish home rule. He briefly led the 1915 wartime coalition, but was ousted by supporters of **Lloyd George** and Conservatives disenchanted with his lack of zeal in a conspiracy from which the Liberal

Party never recovered its credibility or status as the main opposition. Asquith lost his seat at the end of the war, but returned to the Commons in 1920, and, after further disagreements with Lloyd George, assumed the leadership again between 1923 and 1926. In 1925, ironically, he was elevated to the peerage that had once tried so hard to bring down his Administration. His seven children from two marriages included Lady Violet Bonham-Carter (1887–1969) and the distinguished film director Anthony Asquith (1902–68).

ASSAD, Hafez al-
1930–

Syrian statesman, born Dardaha, Latakia. A member of the Ba'ath Party at 16, he trained as an airman in his own country and Russia, returning to the new United Arab Republic of Egypt and Syria in 1958 to command a Cairo-based fighter squadron until Syria gained independence three years later. Assad became Defence Minister and air force chief when Ba'ath party secretary Salah Jadid seized power in 1966. His refusal to obey Jadid's instructions to mount an air attack against Jordan led to a bloodless coup, and since assuming the presidency he has followed a vehemently anti-Israeli policy and, by implication, has been guilty of complicity in terrorist activities, but relations with the West improved following his meeting with former US President **Jimmy Carter** in 1987 and his active involvement in efforts to free hostages in the Lebanon. To the surprise of many, he joined the US-led coalition against **Saddam Hussein** in the Gulf Crisis of 1990–1.

ASTOR, Nancy Witcher, Viscountess
1879–1964

American-born British politician, born Danville, Virginia. The daughter of a wealthy tobacco merchant, she succeeded her husband, William Waldorf Astor (1879–1952), as Conservative MP for Plymouth in 1919, to become the first woman ever to take a seat in the House of Commons. Vehemently anti-socialist, her vigorous championing of women's rights, improved state education and temperance was rewarded with the CH in 1937, and she was ennobled in 1946. Her autobiography, *My Two Countries*, was published in 1923.

ATATÜRK, Mustapha Kemal
1881–1938

Turkish army officer, politician, and President of Turkey (1923–38), born in Salonika. He raised a nationalist rebellion in Anatolia in protest against the post-war division of Turkey, and in 1921 established a provisional government in Ankara. In 1922 the Ottoman Sultanate was formally abolished, and in 1923 Turkey was declared a secular republic, with Kemal as President. He became virtual dictator, and launched a social and political revolution introducing Western fashions, the emancipation of women, educational reform, the replacement of Arabic script with the Latin alphabet, and the discouragement of traditional Islamic loyalties in favour of a strictly Turkish nationalism. In 1935 he assumed the surname Atatürk ('Father of the Turks'). He died in Istanbul.

ATHOLL, Katharine Marjory, Duchesss of
1874–1960

Scottish politician, born Banff. The daughter of a historian, she married the eighth Duke in 1917, and after entering the Commons as a Conservative MP in 1923, she was appointed Britain's first woman Minister. As Education Under-Secretary, she resisted changes that would have given the children of poorer families less of an education, and constantly campaigned against the ill-treatment of women and children. She translated *Mein Kampf* into English as a warning of **Adolf Hitler**'s intentions, and opposed collective European non-intervention in the Spanish Civil War, publishing the best-selling *Searchlight on Spain* in 1938. For opposing the Munich Agreement she was deselected by her local Tory party, resigned her seat, and was defeated as an independent in the resultant by-election. From 1939 until her death, she worked tirelessly to assist refugees from totalitarian states. Her other published work includes *Women and Politics* (1931).

ATTLEE, Clement Richard, 1st Earl Attlee
1883–1967

British statesman, born Putney, London. As an Oxford-educated lawyer who worked alongside **John Ruskin** and **William Morris** in the slums of east London, Attlee quickly converted to socialism and began lecturing regularly at the newly–founded London School of Economics. In World War I, he was wounded and achieved the rank of major, and was elected Labour mayor of Stepney in 1919. He entered Parliament three years later and held minor ministerial posts, but joined the Opposition with the formation of **Ramsay MacDonald**'s 1931 coalition government. One of the few Labour Members to retain his seat in the following general election, in 1935 he succeeded **George Lansbury** as party leader. By refusing to enter into a coalition with **Neville Chamberlain**, he helped to assure **Winston Churchill**'s wartime premiership and achieved a huge majority in the first post-war general election to become Prime Minister himself in 1945. His vigorous programme of socialist and reformist measures included the nationalization of the Bank of England, coal, civil aviation, cable and wireless services, railways, road transport and steel; the founding of the national health service, independence for India in 1947 and for Burma a year later. Less popular among party supporters was his support for NATO, the re-arming of Germany and the development of the British atom bomb. He continued to lead Labour in Opposition when Churchill won the 1951 general election, resigning in 1955 to take a seat in the Lords. His autobiography *As it Happened* was published in 1954.

ATTOLICO, Bernardo
1880–1942

Italian diplomat, born Canneto di Bari. A lawyer by training, he began his diplomatic career in London during World War I, attended the 1919 Paris Peace Conference, and was subsequently vice-secretary of the League of Nations (1922–7). There followed ambassadorships, at Rio de Janeiro and Moscow, and in 1935 he was posted to Berlin. He became increasingly unpopular there for his suspicions about Nazi ambitions, but supported the 1939 politico-military Pact of Steel signed by **Joachim von Ribbentrop** and Italy's Foreign Minister, Galeazzo Ciano, hoping that it would act as a steadying influence on **Hitler**. His efforts to keep Italy out of the war following Germany's invasion of Poland finally exhausted his welcome, and as a direct result of pressure from Hitler he was recalled to Italy and spent the last two years of his life as ambassador to the Holy See.

AUBERT, Pierre
1927–

Swiss politician, born La Chaux–de–Fonds.

Following eight years in local politics, he joined the Neuchatel legislative assembly in 1971 and was elected a Labour member of the House of States the same year. He was Vice-President of Switzerland in 1982 and President in 1987.

AUGUSTUS, Gaius Julius Caesar Octavianus
63–14 BC

As the adopted son of **Julius Caesar** by the terms of his will, he was denied his inheritance by **Mark Anthony** on the emperor's assassination but took his revenge in the Mutina campaign, secured the consulship and his rightful property, and then joined with Mark Anthony and Lepidus in forming the triumvirate army that at first conquered Africa, Sardinia, Sicily, Gaul and Spain before defeating their opponents in Italy and the republican forces under Brutus and Cassius in 42 BC. Differences between the three leaders led to a division of the empire, with Augustus taking the western territories, consolidating his power-base in Italy, and turning Rome against Mark Anthony over his association with Cleopatra and failed campaigns in the East. After his victory in the naval battle against the Egyptians at Actium, Augustus became virtual ruler of the Roman empire, but devised in his own interests a form of federalism, and promoted traditional Roman values, the beautification of the capital, and a policy of territorial extension into northern and central Europe. But serious military setbacks in the Pannonia campaign and in Germany between AD 6 and 9, together with a disastrous personal life, compelled him to agree to the succession of his adopted son, **Tiberius**, in AD 4. Augustus is remembered best by many for his military rather than peacetime achievements, but it was his reign that nurtured and produced the generation of intellects typified by Horace, Virgil, Ovid and Livy. His autoiography is lost, but a self-written record of his achievements is inscribed on the bronze pillars of his mausoleum in Rome.

AURIOL, Vincent
1884–1966

French politician. A Socialist, he held a number of official posts from 1925, and after being imprisoned by the Vichy Government, he escaped to England to join the Free

French. He returned in 1946 to preside over two assemblies, and from 1947 to 1954 served as the republic's first post-war President.

AYERS, Sir Henry
1821–97

British-born Australian politician, born Portsea, Hampshire. He worked in the mining industry after emigrating to his new homeland in 1841, and was a member of the South Australia state legislature for 34 years from 1863. He was premier four times in 10 years, and he received the KCMG for his support of a scheme to link Australia with overseas telegraph networks. He was elected president of the Legislative Council in 1881, retiring in 1894 with the award of the GCMG. The monolithic sandstone rock in the then northern territories was named after him by the explorer William Goose in 1874.

AYLWIN, (AZÒCAR) Patricio
1919–

Chilean lawyer and politician, born Santiago. After a successful early career as a lawyer, he was elected president of the Christian Democratic Party in 1973, and as leader of the opposition coalition triggered the national plebiscite that brought down General **Pinochet** in the December 1989 elections. Power was formally transferred from the military regime to Aylwin in March 1990, but his inability to secure the two-thirds majority in Congress necessary to amend the 1980 Constitution allowed the outgoing junta to nominate almost one-fifth of the Senate's membership and thus to thwart Aylwin's efforts to lift press censorship and to abolish the death penalty. Continuing revelations about the human rights atrocities under the previous regime triggered violent demonstrations, but Pinochet still resisted attempts to remove him as commander-in-chief, which post he has vowed to retain until 1997.

AYUB KHAN, Mohammed
1907–74

Pakistani soldier and statesman, born Abbottabad. After a military education at Sandhurst, he saw action in Burma in World War II, became commander-in-chief of the Pakistan Army in 1951, and was appointed Defence Minister in 1954. He replaced President Mirza after a bloodless army coup in 1958, establishing a stable economy and

political autocracy, rooting out corruption, and introducing many other significant reforms. In 1969, civil riots and disenchantment with the presidency from both the left and right wings in the wake of disastrous crop failures forced him to leave office, and martial law was re-established. His autobiography *Friends and Masters* appeared in 1967.

AZAÑA Y DIAZ, Manuel
1880–1940

Spanish statesman. His early career as a lawyer and university lecturer changed course in 1931 when, as leader of the republican left on the fall of Alfonso XIII, he was appointed War Minister and then Prime Minister later the same year. He held office until 1933, and became premier again in 1936 for the duration of the Spanish Civil War, but was sent into exile when **Franco** achieved victory in 1939.

AZCONA DEL HOYO, José Simon
1927–

Honduran politician, born La Ceiba. As a civil engineering student, he developed a particular interest in low-cost urban housing, but his early political success as a Liberal candidate in the 1963 elections and his opportunities to implement his ideas were frustrated by successive military coups. He served in two ostensibly civilian but in fact army-controlled Administrations between 1982 and 1986, and after Gustavo Alvarez had been deposed by his own junior officers in 1984, Azcona narrowly won in the 1986 presidential elections.

AZEGLIO, Massimo Taparellu, Marchese d'
1798–1866

Italian statesman, born Turin. At first an artist and political novelist, he became a leading member of the Risorgimento movement, took an active part in the 1848 revolution, and served as Prime Minister of Sardinia from 1848 to 1852.

AZIKIWE, Nnamdi ('Zik')
1904–

Nigerian politician, born Zungeri. Educated in America, he worked as a lecturer in the US before returning to his homeland. He became interested in the nationalist movement in the

1930s and founded several newspapers to propagate his beliefs. During World War II he served as president of the Nigeria and Cameroons national council, and between 1954 and 1959 he sat in both Houses of Assembly and was prime minister of the eastern region. He was Governor-General from 1960 until 1963, when he was elected the republic's first President. He was deposed by a military coup in his absence on a visit to Britain in 1966.

BAADER, Andreas
1943–77

West German terrorist, born Munich. The son of a middle-class family, he became involved in several student protest movements in the 1960s and was once imprisoned for arson attacks on Frankfurt stores. In the 1970s, he formed with **Ulrike Meinhof** the underground guerrilla group, the Red Army Faction, was imprisoned again, but escaped and undertook a series of assassinations and terrorist attacks. In 1977 he was captured and sentenced to life imprisonment, and after the Red Army Faction failed to secure his release by hi-jacking a Lufthansa passenger plane at Mogadishu, Somalia, Baader committed suicide.

BABANGIDA, Ibrahim
1941–

Nigerian soldier and politician, born Minna, Niger state. Educated at military colleges in Nigeria, he was commissioned in 1963 and, after further training in the United Kingdom and the USA, became an army instructor and then a major-general. In 1983 he took part in the coup that deposed Shehu Shagari's Government and was made commander-in-chief by President Buhari, whom he overthrew in 1985, to assume the presidency himself.

BADOGLIO, Pietro
1871–1956

Italian soldier, born Grazzano Monferrato, Piedmont. After distinguished service in World War I, he was promoted field-marshal in 1926 and as Governor-General of Libya (1928–33) led the conquest of Abyssinia. He initially opposed Italy's entry into World War II, but eventually accepted appointment as commander-in-chief but resigned after his army's campaign in Albania, which **Mussolini**

ordered against his advice. During his brief term as Prime Minister (1943–4) following the downfall of Mussolini, he formed a non-fascist Government, negotiated an armistice, and declared war on Germany, and retired after allied forces entered Rome.

BAGAZA, Jean-Baptiste
1946–

Burundian soldier and politician, born Rutovu, Bururi province. After military training in Belgium, he was made assistant to the head of Burundi's armed forces, and in 1976 led a coup against President Micombero and was appointed President. In 1984, he became head of state when the post of Prime Minister was abolished, but was himself the victim of a coup by Major Pierre Buyoya in 1987.

BAGEHOT, Walter
1826–77

English economist, born Langport, Somerset. A mathematics graduate of University College, London, he was called to the Bar in 1852 and after working as a banker, in 1860 succeeded as editor of *The Economist* its founder, and his father-in-law, James Wilson. His *English Constitution* (1867) is still considered a standard, and *Physics and Politics* (1872) and *Economic Studies* (1880) were also influential additions to 19th-century political and economic thinking. *The Collected Works of Walter Bagehot* (1966).

BAKER, James A,
1930–

American Republican politician, born Houston, Texas. After studying law at Princeton and the University of Texas, he served in the US Marines and then worked as a corporate lawyer before entering politics as party manager for **George Bush**'s unsuccessful 1970 bid for the Senate. In 1975, he was appointed Under-Secretary of Commerce by **Gerald Ford**, and subsequently masterminded both his 1976 presidential campaign and Bush's 1979 nomination bid. He was made White House Chief-of-Staff in 1981 and Treasury Secretary in 1985, and after managing Bush's 1988 presidential campaign, was made Secretary of State. His international reputation was greatly enhanced by his Kissinger-like efforts to avoid war after the Iraqi invasion of Kuwait in August 1990, and he is seen by many as at least a desirable replacement for **Dan Quayle** as the Republicans' next vice-presidential candidate.

BAKER, Kenneth Wilfred
1934–

British politician. Educated at St Paul's School and Magdalen College, Oxford, he entered Parliament for the Conservatives on his third attempt, in 1968, and was appointed junior Minister for employment (1970–2) and for the Civil Service (1972–4). From 1974 to 1975 he was private parliamentary secretary to **Edward Heath**, and served as Secretary-General of the UN Conference on Population in 1979. He remained a back-Bencher for two years after the Conservatives' return to power, and was then made Minister for Industry and Information Technology in 1981, and for Local Government (1984–5), and Secretary of State for the Environment (1985–6). As Secretary of State for Education and Science (1986–9), he introduced controversial reforms of state schools. He was appointed Conservative Party chairman in 1989, and Home Secretary in 1990, in **John Major**'s first Cabinet, and came close to resigning over the escape of two IRA terrorists from Brixton prison in July 1991. His publications include *I Have No Gun But I Can Spit* (1980), *London Lines* (1982), and the *Faber Book of English History in Verse* (1988).

BAKUNIN, Mikhail
1814–76

Russian anarchist, born near Moscow of aristocratic descent. He took part in the German revolutionary movement (1848–9) and was condemned to death. Sent to Siberia in 1855, he escaped to Japan, and arrived in England in 1861. In September 1870 he attempted an abortive rising at Lyon. As leader of anarchism Bakunin was in the Communist International the opponent of **Karl Marx**; but at the Hague Congress in 1872 he was outvoted and expelled. He believed that communism, with its theoretical 'withering away of the state', was an essential step towards anarchism.

BALAGUER, Joaquim
1907–

Dominican Republic politician. A professor of law and ambassador to Colombia and Mexico in the 1940s, he entered politics as a member of **Rafael Trujillo**'s dictatorship, but fled to America on the president's assassination in 1961. He returned two years later to become President himself in 1966, and won re-election in 1970 and 1974. At the age of 79, he returned to power again in 1986.

BALDWIN, Stanley, 1st Earl Baldwin of Bewdley
1867–1947

British statesman, born Bewdley. Educated at Harrow and Trinity College, Cambridge, he became a Conservative MP in 1906, was made President of the Board of Trade in 1921, and succeeded **Bonar Law** as Prime Minister in 1923, shortly after bringing down the Liberal coalition with a speech that revealed his distrust of **Lloyd George**, and despite criticism of his handling, as Chancellor of the Exchequer, of the American debt. His premiership was short-lived, with Labour taking victory in January 1924, but resumed in office with a reunited party in November that year. His Government was defeated again by Labour in the 1929 election, but he served as Lord President of the Council in **Ramsay MacDonald**'s 1931 coalition, and four years later became Prime Minister again. His third term of office was notable for his disavowal of the Hoare-Laval pact ceding Ethiopian territory to Italy, a rearmament programme, and his sympathetic handling of the 1936 abdication crisis, but criticism of his failure to recognize the threat from Nazi Germany brought his resignation in 1937. Although Baldwin's competence as an international politician is questionable, he was one of the party's best-ever electoral assets, with a combination of patriotism, social consciousness, and readiness always to govern by consensus.

BALEWA Sir Abubaker Tafawa
1912–66

Nigerian politician, born Bauchi. After serving as a member of the Northern People's Congress, he entered the Federal Assembly in 1947 and served as Minister of Works and of Transport before becoming Prime Minister in 1957. He was knighted when Nigeria achieved independence in 1960, but as a reluctant federalist provoked pockets of fierce opposition to his policies, and he was assassinated in the 1966 uprising.

BALFOUR, Arthur James, 1st Earl of Balfour

1848–1930

British politician, born East Lothian. Educated at Eton and Trinity College, Cambridge, he became a Conservative MP in 1874 and was private secretary to his uncle, Lord Salisbury (1878–90), before being made Secretary of State for Scotland (1886), Chief Secretary for Ireland (1887), and First Lord of the Treasury and Leader of the Commons (1892–3). As Prime Minister, he saw the end of the South African War in 1905, introduced sweeping educational reforms in the same year, and established an imperial defence committee. The 1911 constitutional crisis brought his resignation, but in 1915 he followed **Winston Churchill** to the Admiralty, and as Foreign Secretary (1916–19) under **Lloyd George** made his famous 1917 Balfour Declaration, promising the Zionists a home in Palestine. A strong supporter of the League of Nations, he was responsible in 1921, as Lord President of the Council, for cancelling allied war debts to America.

BANDA, Dr Hastings Kamuzu

1905–

Malawian politician, born Nyasaland. After graduating in philosophy and medicine at American universities, and obtaining further honours at Glasgow and Edinburgh Universities, he practised medicine in Liverpool during the whole of World War II and then ran a successful London practice before returning to his homeland in 1958 to lead the Malawi African Congress. He was imprisoned for a year in 1959 but given an unconditional pardon the following year, became Minister of National Resources in 1961, and was made Prime Minister of Malawi (formerly Nyasaland) in 1966. As Life President since 1971, he has combined his leadership of a one-party state with pragmatic foreign policies, recognizing both the South African Government and the socialist regime in Angola.

BANDARANAIKE, Sirimavo

1916–

Sri Lankan politician, wife of **Solomon Bandaranaike**. She became premier in 1960, making her the world's first woman Prime Minister. Forced to resign on her electoral defeat in 1965, after a period in office that was plagued by economic difficulties and communal disturbances, she was premier again between 1970 and 1977.

BANDARANAIKE, Solomon West Ridgeway Dias

1899–1959

Sri Lankan (Ceylonese) statesman, born Colombo. Educated at St Thomas's College and at Christ Church, Oxford, he was called to the Bar in 1925, and on returning to his homeland joined the Ceylon National Congress and eventually became its president. In a bid to foil the growing power of the Tamils, he founded the Sinhalese Maha Sabha Assembly and the United National Party, which formed the Government between 1948 and 1956. As Leader of the House and Minister of Health in his country's first Parliament, he won for Ceylon the distinction of being the first Asian country to rid itself of malaria. In 1951 he resigned to found the Sri Lanka Freedom Party, which he took to victory in 1956 with a manifesto of nationalization, including the expropriation of foreign interests, and neutralism. He was assassinated by a Buddhist monk in 1959.

BARRE, Siad

President of Somalia. After seizing power in a military coup in 1969, he ruled ruthlessly for 21 years by using a KGB-trained secret service whose mercilessness earned itself the nickname the Backbreakers. Uprisings began in 1989 after his air force bombed two Somali National Movement-held towns. By January 1991, by which time 60000 had died and 400000 had been injured in the fighting, United Somali Congress forces led by former diplomat Muhammad Farah Aidiid, supported by SNM and Somali Patriotic Movement guerrillas, had surrounded Mogadishu. Barre responded by approving a new 25-man Cabinet supposed to be more representative of tribal factions, and promising to resign if the rebels called a ceasefire. On 26 January he fled Mogadishu.

BARROW, Errol Walton

1920–87

Barbadian politician, born Barbados. After service in the Royal Air Force between 1940 and 1947, he studied at London University and for the London Bar, and on returning to Barbados in 1950, he became active in the

Barbados Labour Party and entered the House of Assembly the following year. In 1955 he left the BLP to co-found the Democratic Labour Party, becoming its chairman in 1958. His party's success in the 1961 independence elections made him the country's first Prime Minister. He held office until the BLP was returned in 1976, but on the death of its leader, Tom Adams, in 1986, Barrow led his party to victory again with a decisive majority. He was succeeded on his own death a year later by Erskine Lloyd Sandiford.

BARTON, Sir Edmund
1849–1920

Australian jurist and statesman, born Sydney. After election to the New South Wales legislature in 1879, he led the Federation movement from 1896, headed the committee that drafted the Commonwealth Constitution Bill, and led the delegation that presented it to Westminster in 1900, to become the first Prime Minister of the Australian Commonwealth (1901–3). On leaving that office, he was a high-court judge until his death.

BARUCH, Bernard Mannes
1870–1965

American financier and statesman, born Camden, South Carolina. Educated in New York, he made a fortune from shares speculation, helped to co-ordinate US industries during World War I, and drafted the economic sections of the 1919 Treaty of Versailles. As a close adviser to several presidents and to **Winston Churchill** in World War II, he was a powerful and positive back-room political influence. He later served as a member of the American Atomic Energy Commission.

BASHIR, Omar Hassan al-

Sudanese head of state. After overthrowing the democratic parliamentary Government in 1989, he pursued a policy of self-sufficiency and disengagement from the West, which, combined with its long-held distaste for Khartoum human-rights abuses and obstruction of past relief efforts, meant that other powers were slow to respond to the drought and subsequent famine in the Sudan that

began worsening in 1990. The West's disaffection with his regime was only worsened by its pro-Iraq stance in the events that led to the 1991 Gulf War.

BATISTA Y ZALDIVAR, Fulgencio
1901–73

Cuban dictator, born Oriente province. A labourer's son, he rose to become an army colonel, and in 1933 led the coup against President Machado, to become President himself (1940–4). After losing office, he was successful in deposing President Prio in 1952, and remained as sole dictator until himself being overthrown by **Fidel Castro** in 1959, when he went into exile in the Dominican Republic.

BATMUNH, Jambyn
1926–

Mongolian politician. While working as a lecturer at the University of Social Sciences, he joined the People's Revolutionary Party Central Committee in 1952, but continued to concentrate on his academic duties and was made rector in 1967. In 1974, he was made vice-chairman of the Council of Ministers, and served as chairman of the Hural from 1974 until being made President and General Secretary of the Central Committee in 1984.

BAUDOUIN I
1930–

King of the Belgians. The elder son of Leopold III and his first wife, Queen Astrid, he took the throne in July 1951 after his father abdicated over his controversial conduct during World War II. In 1960 he took a Spanish wife, Doña Fabiola de Mora y Aragon. In 1990 he briefly stood down as king—'unfit to rule'—so that an abortion act which he opposed could be made law without requiring his consent or provoking a constitutional crisis.

BEAVERBROOK, Max (William Maxwell Aitken) 1st Baron
1879–1964

Canadian-born British newspaper proprietor and politician, born Maple, Ontario. After an early career as a stockbroker and speculator in the Canadian cement and timber industries, which made him a millionaire, he moved to England in 1910 and became a

Conservative MP the following year. He was private secretary to **Bonar Law** and became Minister of Information under **Lloyd George**, before acquiring the then almost defunct *Daily Express* in 1919 and transforming it into the world's most widely-read newspaper, and then founding the *Sunday Express* (1921) and buying the *Evening Standard* (1929). In World War II, his administrative skills were fully exploited by **Winston Churchill**, who in 1940 appointed him Minister of Aircraft Production, in which post his success in stepping up production in particular contributed significantly to Britain's subsequent air superiority, and he was Lord Privy Seal from 1943 until the Government's defeat in the 1945 election. The last of the great newspaper barons, his personal enormous loyalty to his adopted country was reflected by his occasionally over-strident newspaper campaigns, which included support for Empire free trade and for Edward VIII in the abdication crisis, and a sustained rally against Britain entering the Common Market. His books include *Men of Power* (1956) and *The Decline and Fall of Lloyd George* (1963).

BEGIN, Menachem
1913–

Israeli statesman, born Brest-Litovsk, Poland. While a law student at Warsaw University, he became head of the Betar Zionist Movement in 1931, and on the invasion of Poland in 1939 fled to Lithuania, where he was imprisoned by the Russians until 1941, when he enlisted in the Free Polish Army and was sent to British-mandated Palestine. On his discharge in 1943, he was made commander-in-chief of the terrorist Irqun Zvai Leumi resistance group, and in 1948 founded the right-wing Herut Freedom Movement, to become chairman of the party and a member of the first three Knessets. From 1973 he led the rightist coalition Likud Front that ousted the Israel Labour Party in the 1977 elections. Begin was re-elected Prime Minister in 1981, and resigned the premiership in 1983. Apart from fathering the new State of Israel through its political infancy, he made an outstanding contribution to achieving peace with the Egyptians through the 1977 Jerusalem and Camp David conferences with **Anwar Sadat**, for which both men jointly received the Nobel Peace Prize in 1978. His books include *White Nights* and *The Revolt*.

BELAUNDE TERRY, Fernando
1913–

Peruvian politician. The son of a Prime Minister, he worked as an architect before leading the Popular Action Party in the election of 1956, eventually taking it to victory in the 1963 election. As the victim of a bloodless coup in 1968 he fled to the US and lectured at Harvard, before returning to his country two years later. He was almost immediately deported, but in 1976 returned again and won the presidency in 1980.

BEN ALI, Zine el Abidine
1936–

Tunisian politician. A student of electronics at French and American military schools, he eventually rose to become head of national security, Minister of the Interior, and then Prime Minister for life under **Habib Bourgiba**. In 1987, he forced Bourgiba's retirement and assumed the presidency, immediately instituting a programme of democratic constitutional reforms.

BEN BELLA, Mohammed Ahmed
1916–

Algerian politician, born Maghnia. After distinguished service in World War II, he led the extremist independence movement from 1947 and was imprisoned, but escaped to Cairo in 1950, where he founded the National Liberation Front. The success of the FLN's long campaign against the French colonial authorities from 1954 until 1962 brought him the presidency of the new republic in 1963, but he was deposed by General Houari Boumédienne in 1965 and kept under house arrest until 1979.

BENEŠ, Eduard
1884–1948

Czechoslovak statesman, born Kožlany. A student of law and professor of sociology at Prague University, he fled his country during World War I, working in Paris with **Thomas Masaryk** on a formula for nationalism, and after the war was appointed Foreign Minister (1918-35) of the new state, and premier in 1921-2. In 1935 he succeeded Masaryk as head of state, but resigned and left Czechoslovakia in 1938. He assumed the office of President in exile in England in 1941, and in 1945 returned home to be re-elected the following year. He resigned after the 1948 communist coup.

BEN-GURION, David (David Green)

1886–1973

Israeli statesman, born Pionsk, Poland. His early interest in the Zionist movement took him to Palestine in 1906, where he worked as a farm labourer and formed the first Jewish trade union in 1915. Expelled from the country by the Turks for his support of the allies in World War I, he raised the Jewish Legion in America and fought with it in the Palestine campaign. Between 1921 and 1933 he was General Secretary of the Federation of Jewish Labour, and in 1930 was made leader of the socialist Mapai Party, which took power on the establishment of the State of Israel in 1948. In 1953 he retired as Prime Minister, but resumed the office between 1955 and 1963.

BENN, Anthony Wedgwood

1925–

English Labour politician, son of Viscount **Stansgate**. He was educated at Westminster School and New College, Oxford. A Labour MP from 1950 to 1960, he was debarred from the House of Commons on succeeding to his father's title, but was able to renounce it in 1963 and was re-elected to parliament the same year. He was postmaster-general 1964–6, Minister of Technology 1966–70, and assumed responsibility for the Ministry of Aviation in 1967 and Ministry of Power in 1969. From 1970 to 1974 he was Opposition spokesman on Trade and Industry, and on Labour's return to Government he was made Secretary of State for Industry and Minister for Posts and Telecommunications, the following year becoming Secretary of State for Energy, a post he held until the Conservative victory in the 1979 elections. Representing the left wing of Labour opinion he unsuccessfully stood for the deputy leadership of the party in 1981. He lost his seat in the general election of 1983, but returned to represent Chesterfield from 1984. He unsuccessfully challenged **Neil Kinnock** for the party leadership in 1988. Among his publications are *Arguments for Socialism* (1979) and *Arguments for Democracy* (1981).

BENTHAM, Jeremy

1748–1832

English philosopher, jurist and reformer, born London. As a child genius, he entered Queen's College, Oxford, at 12 and was admitted to Lincoln's Inn at 15, and before the age of 40 had published two major works on utilitarianism, *A Fragment on Government* (1766) and *Introduction to the Principles of Morals and Legislation* (1789), which argued that the greatest happiness of the greatest number should be the purpose of all conduct and legislation and introduced a 'hedonic calculus' to gauge the effects on society of different actions. He travelled widely in Europe and Russia, was made an honorary citizen of the French Republic in 1792, and wrote extensively on economics and penal and social reform. He founded the influential *Westminster Review* (1823) and University College, London, where his clothed preserved body remains on public view.

BENTSEN, Lloyd Millard Jr

1921–

American politician, born Mission, Texas. A law graduate of Texas University, he was a combat pilot during World War II, after which he worked as a county judge. He entered the House of Representatives in 1948 and Congress in 1971, becoming chairman of its influential Finance Committee. In the Democrats' 1988 presidential challenge, he was running mate to **Michael Dukakis**, and, as a right-winger, has since consolidated his reputation as one of his country's most even-handed elder statesmen.

BERIA, Lavrenti Pavlovich

1899–1953

Soviet secret-police chief, born Mercheuli, Georgia. Although the son of a peasant family, he attended a Baku college, where he ran a Bolshevik group, and between 1921 and 1931 worked for OGPU—the forerunner of the KGB—in the Caucasus, and was then made First Secretary of the Georgia Communist Party. In 1938, **Joseph Stalin** appointed him Minister for Internal Affairs, and he was promoted to defence vice-president during World War II. On Stalin's death in 1953 he made a bid to seize power but, after being thwarted by party and military leaders fearful of the kind of regime that his background would produce, he was arrested by Marshal **Georgi Zhukov**, tried for treason, and executed.

BERLINGUER, Enrico

1922–84

Italian politician, born Sardinia. Although he

came from a family of wealthy landowners, from his early 20s he was active in the Italian Communist Party and became its secretary-general in 1972. Under his leadership, it took more than one third of the seats in the Chamber of Deputies in 1976, and although Berlinguer's unprecedented proposal for an alliance with Catholic factions was rejected, his vision of broadly-based 'Eurocommunism' still has popular appeal.

BERNSTEIN, Carl
1944–

American journalist and author, born Washington DC. As a political writer on the *Washington Post*, he unearthed with **Bob Woodward** the Watergate cover-up after clandestine meetings with an informant who identified himself as 'Deep Throat', and their reports led directly to the resignation of President **Richard Nixon** in 1974. He received jointly with Woodward numerous journalism awards and the 1973 Pulitzer Prize for public service, and with Woodward wrote *All the President's Men* (1974), which gave a full account of their investigation, and *The Final Days* (1976), which charted Nixon's last months in office.

BERRI, Nabih
1939–

Lebanese soldier and politician, born Freetown, Sierra Leone. A graduate of law from Beirut University, he practised successfully for many years before becoming leader of the Amal—an offshoot of the Shiite nationalist movement. With Syria's backing, he developed the main military force in West Beirut and southern Lebanon, but this was later overshadowed by the successes of the Iranian-backed Hezbollah. He joined the Lebanese Government in 1984 as Minister of Justice.

BESANT, Annie
1847–1933

English theosophist, born London. After separating from her husband, a vicar, in 1873, she became vice-president of the National Secular Society and, as a close associate of Charles Bradlaugh, was an ardent proponent of birth control and socialism. Her interest in theosophy took her to India, where she became involved in politics and sat as a member of the National Congress (1917–23).

Her published work includes *The Gospel of Atheism* (1877) and *Theosophy and the New Psychology* (1904).

BEVAN, Aneurin
1897–1960

British politician, born Tredegar, Monmouthshire. One of 13 children, he received an elementary education, and followed his father in becoming a mine worker at the age of 13. By 20, he was chairman of 4000 local trade unionists, and led Welsh miners in the 1926 strike. He entered Parliament for the Independent Labour Party in 1929, then for the Labour Party itself in 1931, soon establishing a reputation for his brilliant and characteristically fiery oratory. As Minister of Health in the 1945 Labour Cabinet, he launched the revolutionary National Health Service, and as Minister of Labour in 1951 resigned when the Government proposed the introduction of NHS charges. He remained an opponent of much party policy even in Opposition, as Shadow Colonial Secretary, but by the time that he made a bid for the leadership in 1955, the influence of the Bevanite faction had waned—but he served **Hugh Gaitskell** as party treasurer and, Shadow Foreign Secretary, and became deputy leader a year before his death.

BEVERIDGE, William Henry, (1st Baron Beveridge)
1879–1963

British economist, born Rangpur, India. Educated at Charterhouse and Balliol College, Oxford, he became established as an expert on unemployment insurance as a leader writer on the *Morning Post* and the author of *Unemployment* (1909, revised 1930). After joining the Board of Trade in 1908, he was director of labour exchanges (1909–16), director of the London School of Economics between 1919 and 1937, then Master of University College, Oxford until 1945. As chairman of a Government committee, he published in 1941-2 the first comprehensive scheme of social insurance, popularly known as the Beveridge Report, which provided for benefits regardless of income, and remained at the heart of all social legislation for decades to come. He sat briefly in Parliament for the Liberals (1944–5), and was made a life peer in 1946. His numerous published works include his 1953 autobiography, *Power and Influence*.

BEVIN, Ernest
1881–1951

British politician, born Winsford, Somerset. Orphaned at the age of seven, he worked as a van boy while educating himself and became a Baptist lay preacher before entering the union movement as a paid official at the age of 30. After his brilliant defence of a 1920 pay claim, he was put in charge of forming the Transport and General Workers Union from 32 separate labour organizations and served as its general secretary (1921–40), was a leading figure in the 1926 general strike, and helped to develop the International Labour Organisation. In 1940, he joined the Cabinet as Minister of Labour in **Winston Churchill**'s wartime coalition, and as Foreign Minister and **Clement Attlee**'s closest ally in the subsequent Labour Administration (1945–51) helped conclude peace treaties with the south-east European states and with Italy, and thwarted the Soviet takeover of Berlin by securing American intervention. He was, however, an opponent of European integration, only reluctantly participating in the formation of the Council of Europe, and failed to resolve the Palestine question, which he delegated to the United Nations. He initiated the first conference of Commonwealth Foreign Ministers in 1950, but resigned through ill health in March 1951 and died a month later. As a realist (he accepted the need for Britain's nuclear deterrent), he frequently incurred the wrath of Labour left-wingers, but was greatly respected by his domestic and international political opponents. He published *The Job to be Done* in 1942.

BHATTARI, Krishna Prasad
1925–

Nepalese politician. As an opponent of absolute monarchy, he was in hiding for 12 years until 1990, when, as leader of the centrist Nepali Congress Party, he became Prime Minister in the wake of the revolution that year, which ended the uncontested rule of King Birendra. However, in May 1991, in Nepal's first multi-party elections in three decades, he offered his resignation to the king after losing his own seat in the 205-member House of Representatives to the marxist leader of the United Communist Party, Madan Bhandari.

BHINDRANWALE, Sant Jarnail Singh
1947–84

Sikh extremist leader, born Punjab. The son of a poor farming family, in 1971 he became head priest of the missionary school at which he received his education. Encouraged by Sanjay Gandhi (1946–80), the son of **Indira**, he campaigned violently against the heretical Nirankari Sikhs during the late 1970s, and in the 1980s sought a separate state of Khalistan, precipitating bloody Hindu-Sikh conflicts in Punjab. Having assembled a substantial arms cache for terrorist activities and about 500 devoted followers, he was killed by the security forces in 1984 after taking refuge in the Golden Temple complex at Amritsar.

BHUMIBOL, Adulyadej
1927–

King of Thailand, born Cambridge, Massachusetts. Educated in Bangkok and Switzerland, he was enthroned as King Rama VI in 1946 after the assassination of his elder brother, married Queen Sirikit in 1950, and has one son, Crown Prince Vajiralongkorn (1952–) and three daughters. A stabilizing influence in a country noted for its political unrest, in 1973 he overthrew, with popular support, the military administration of Field-Marshal Kittikachorn, and exercised considerable political influence as the longest-serving monarch in Thailand's history. However in February 1991 the armed forces toppled the elected government of **Chatichai Choonhaven** in a bloodless coup. The military announced a National Peace-Keeping Council to take control of the country. In March Bhumibol formally approved a new constitution and appointed a 292-member national Legislative Assembly. In May he signed into law two acts which automatically dissolved all 61 of the country's state enterprise unions.

BHUTTO, Benazir
1953–

Pakistani politician. After an education at Oxford University, where she became president of the Union, she returned to Pakistan and was placed under house arrest between 1977 and 1984 by General **Zia ul-Haq**, who had executed her father **Zulfikar Ali Bhutto**, following the 1977 coup against him. During her subsequent exile in England with her mother, she formed the Pakistan People's Party, returning to Pakistan with the lifting of martial law in 1986 and beginning her campaign for open elections. She married in 1987, and, following General Zia's death the same year, she was elected Prime Minister in 1988, taking Pakistan back into the Commonwealth in 1989. The same year she became the first head of Government in the world to bear a child while in office. Increasing friction between her Administration and the conservative presidency led to her Government being dismissed in August 1990, and soon after corruption charges were made against her, and her husband was placed in custody on related alleged criminal offences. At the start of 1991, she began a lecture tour of America and Europe, but she dismissed speculation that she was choosing self-exile in return for her husband's release.

BHUTTO, Zulfikar Ali
1928–79

Pakistani statesman, born Larkana, in British-ruled India. An aristocrat's son, he was educated in California and at Oxford University, and lectured in international law at Southampton University before returning to Pakistan and joining Iskander Mirza's Government in 1958 as Minister of Commerce. He remained in that post under President **Ayub Khan** and was made Foreign Minister in 1963. Disagreements between the two led to his resignation in 1967, when he founded the Pakistan People's Party. He was detained on several occasions before the President was forced to relinquish power in 1969, when the country was put under martial law by General Yahya Khan, who in turn handed over to Bhutto following the country's military defeat against the Bangladeshis in 1971. As President, and as Prime Minister from 1973, Bhutto implemented notable constitutional and economic reforms, but opposition to his Government grew among right-wing Islamic parties, and in 1977 he was charged with vote-rigging after his landslide victory in the first elections under the new Constitution, and was ousted by the army. In March 1978, he was executed after being found guilty of charges of conspiring to murder brought by the new military leader, **Zia ul-Haq**.

BIANCHI, Michele
1883–1930

Italian revolutionary, born Belmonte, Calabria. While a student in Rome, he worked in socialist journalism and as a labour organizer from 1905, but broke with the Chamber of Labour in Ferrara in 1912 over his vehement opposition to the Libyan War, and stood unsuccessfully for the Chamber of Deputies the following year. He was reconciled with the fascist movement during World War I, in which he served as a volunteer, and first came into close contact with **Benito Mussolini**. As a member of the new Fasci di Combattimento's central committee, he continued to work closely with labour organizations, and was instrumental in transforming fascism from a movement to a party, becoming its first General Secretary in 1921. He soon threatened to resign over compromises with non-fascist politicians that were impeding Italy's conversion to a full fascist state. Thereafter, even though he was appointed head of the Ministry of Interior in 1922, his influence waned, and he was finally forced to leave the party in 1924. As a member of the Fascist Grand Council, he was active in electoral reform and was elected to the Chamber in 1924, then, as a junior Minister between 1925 and 1929, and Minister of the Interior from 1929, he concentrated on developing the economy of his native Calabria. As one of Mussolini's closest collaborators during the early years of fascism, Bianchi was a key figure in the movement's eventual domination of Italian politics, though his contribution was more that of a brilliant administrator and tactician than as an ideologue.

BIDAULT, Georges
1899–1982

French statesman, born Paris. After working as a professor of history, he served and was taken prisoner in both world wars, and was made leader of the Mouvement Republicaine Populaire in 1945. The following year, he became Prime Minister and was re-elected in 1949, then served as deputy premier (1950-51) and Foreign Minister (1953–54). An advocate of European co-operation, his continuing popular support returned him to head the Government in 1958, but he was forced into exile in 1962 after accusations that he had plotted against **Charles De Gaulle** over the Algerian war. He returned to France in 1968 but took no further active part in politics. His autobiography, *Résistance*, was published in 1967.

(BANTU) BIKO, Steve (Stephen)
1946–77

South African black activist, born King William's Town, Cape Province. A political activist, in 1960 he founded and was first president of the all-black South African Students organization, while studying medicine at Natal University; he was made honorary president of the Black People's Convention in 1972. The following year, a ban was placed on his freedom of speech, association and movement, and he was detained without trial on numerous occasions. He died of head injuries while in the custody of the South African security police. His life was portrayed in the film *Cry Freedom* (1987).

BILLIERE, Sir Peter de la

1935–

The son of Britain's most decorated navy surgeon, he was educated at Harrow and joined the King's Shropshire Light Infantry in 1952 before being commissioned into the Durham Light Infantry. He spent nearly 20 years in the Gulf, speaks Arabic, and is personally known and liked by many leading figures in the region. He spent most of his career in anonymity as an SAS commander, when his courage under fire reached almost legendary proportions. He saw action in Malaya, Aden, Oman and Northern Ireland, before showing his brilliance as a strategist in buttressing and complementing the predominantly US forces as commander of Britain's 45 000-strong task force in the 1991 Gulf War. After the war, he was promoted from Lieutenant-general to a full general, making him equal in rank to General **Norman Schwarzkopf**, and was appointed personal adviser on the Middle East to Defence Secretary Tom King.

BIRMINGHAM SIX

Familiar collective name for the six men found guilty of the IRA bombing of the Mulberry Bush and Tavern in the Town pubs in Birmingham in 1974, in which 21 people were killed and 160 injured—together, the biggest terrorist attack in British history. The prosecution case at the 1975 trial of the accused was based mainly on confessions, which the defence claimed had been extracted after severe beatings, and one of which was shown to have been forged. The forensic evidence relied on the now discredited Geiss test for determining whether an individual has recently handled explosive substances. All six men were found guilty, and each was sentenced to 21 life sentences.

In February 1991, following their second appeal in three years, the Director of Public Prosecutions announced that he could no longer argue that the convictions were safe and satisfactory, and the following month the Court of Appeal concurred and the Birmingham Six were set free after 16 years of wrongful imprisonment. They are Hugh Callaghan (1931–), Patrick Hill (1946–), Gerard Hunter (1949–), Richard McIlkenny (1934–), William Power (1947–) and John Walker (1936–).

BISMARCK, Otto Edward Leopold von, Prince Bismarck, Duke of Lauenburg

1815–98

Prusso-German statesman, born Schönhausen, Brandenburg. After studying law and agriculture, he became a member of the new Prussian Parliament in 1847, and as an ardent royalist resisted the concept of a German empire, Austrian influence, and Prussia's demands for equal rights. He served as envoy to St Petersburg (1859) and Paris (until 1862), when he returned home as Foreign Minister and President of the Cabinet. On failing to achieve the military reorganisation and budget that he sought, he closed the Chambers and proceeded to implement his policies without their approval. When the death of the King of Denmark in 1863 led to that country's defeat by Austria and Prussia and the annexation of the two duchies, German nationalism was rekindled and, following Austria's humiliation in the seven-week war of 1866, Bismarck set about German reorganization and provoked the 1870–1 Franco-Prussian War, ultimately dictating the peace terms. As a prince and Chancellor of the new German empire, he introduced universal suffrage, codified the law, nationalized the Prussian railways, and introduced protective tariffs, but failed in his attempt to suppress the influence of the Vatican. In 1879, he formed the Austro-German treaty of alliance, which was joined by Italy in 1886, and presided over the 1878 Berlin Congress. He survived assassination attempts in 1866 and 1874, but resigned as Chancellor in 1890 (together with his son, who was Foreign Secretary) over policy disagreements with **Wilhelm II** and was given his dukedom. He was reconciled with the monarch in 1894. *Reflections and Reminiscences* (1898).

BIYA, Paul
1933–

Cameroonian politician, born Muomeka'a. A graduate of Paris University, from 1962 he was a junior Minister under President Adhidjo, before being appointed Prime Minister in 1975. He consolidated his power by abolishing the office of Prime Minister and making his own selection of Cabinet members, and survived an attempted coup by supporters of the former President to be re-elected in 1988 with more than 98 per cent of the popular vote.

BLAIZE, Herbert Augustus
1918–89

Grenadian politician, born St. George's. After practising as a solicitor, he helped to found the centrist Grenada National Party and was elected to Parliament in 1957, becoming Prime Minister in 1967. When his country achieved full independence in 1974, he led the official Opposition but following Maurice Bishop's left-wing coup in 1979, he was forced into hiding. After the US invasion of the country in 1983, he returned to lead the reconstituted New National Party, and was returned to power in 1984.

BLAKE, George
1922–

British spy. Probably the most effective traitor ever unintentionally employed by British spymasters, it is likely that he worked for the KGB almost from the start of his career with the Secret Intelligence Service in the 1940s, being responsible, on his own admission, for betraying a great many western agents. Warned by him in 1953 that the CIA had tapped into telephone cables between East Berlin and Moscow, for three years the KGB fed disinformation to the West, thus controlling its perception of the most significant aspects of Soviet military and political policy and activities. After a secret trial in 1961, he was sentenced to 42 years' imprisonment—one for each agent for whose death he was thought to be directly liable. He escaped from prison five years later and surfaced in Moscow in 1967. In interviews given at the time of the publication of his memoirs, *No Other Choice*, in 1990, he clearly revealed his disenchantment with modern communism, if not with Russia.

BLUM, Léon
1872–1950

French statesman, born Paris. A lawyer, he adopted radicalism as a result of the **Dreyfus** affair in 1899, and became the socialist leader on being elected to the Chamber of Deputies in 1919. From 1924, he was an ardent supporter of the leftist policies of **Edouard Herriot**, which in 1936 helped Blum to become the country's first Socialist Prime Minister since 1870, and was briefly premier again in 1938 as leader of a reformed popular-front Government. After his internment in Germany during World War II, he served as Prime Minister for six weeks, pending the election of the first post-war President.

BLUNT, (Sir) Anthony Frederick
1907–83

British art historian and Soviet spy. Educated at Marlborough School and in Paris, where his father was chaplain of the British Embassy, he graduated from Trinity College, Cambridge, and became a fellow there in 1932. A member of its left-wing faction, whose other members included **Guy Burgess**, **Kim Philby** and **Donald Maclean**, he was recruited as a 'talent-spotter' by Soviet intelligence, and continued to serve Moscow as a member of British Intelligence during World War II. He aided Burgess and Maclean to defect in 1951 but convinced a sceptical MI5 of his innocence, and in 1954 was appointed surveyor of the Queen's art collection. However, after Philby's defection in 1964, he made a confession in return for secret immunity from prosecution, and continued in his royal post until 1972, and as a director of the Courtauld Institute of Art until 1974. In 1979, he was identified as the Fourth Man in Andrew Boyle's book, *The Climate of Treason*, and soon afterwards his involvement was admitted in a statement by Prime Minister **Margaret Thatcher**. His knighthood, which he received in 1956, was annulled in 1979.

BOKASSA, Jean Bedel
1921–

Central African Republic politician, born Bobangui, Lobay. As a member of the French army from 1939, he was made commander-in-chief when his country achieved independence in 1963, and two years later led the coup that deposed President David Dacko. He increased his personal power by annulling the Constitution, making himself Life President, and, in 1977, proclaiming himself emperor. His ruthless regime eventually forced him into exile in 1979, but he returned for trial in 1988 and was found guilty of murder and other crimes. His death sentence was eventually commuted.

BOLIVAR, Simon ('The Liberator')
1783–1830

South American revolutionary leader, born Caracas, Venezuela. The son of a noble family, he studied in Madrid and in Paris during the Revolution, and after Venezuela's independence in 1811 fled to New Granada to raise an army. In 1813 he returned victorious to Venezuela having defeated the Spanish forces and proclaimed himself dictator. He was driven out in 1814 but returned repeatedly to harass the Spanish from his base in the West Indies. He effectively won the war in 1821 at Carabobo, and in that year was made President of Colombia, Venezuela and New Granada, and added Ecuador to the new republic in 1824, in which year also he drove the last of the royalist troops out of Peru and became dictator there. Upper Peru was renamed Bolivia in his honour but his administration was unpopular and his troops were forced to leave. On returning to Colombia in 1828, his dictatorship lost the support of the republicans there and in 1829 Venezuela broke away. In 1830, Bolivar surrendered his authority and died later the same year.

BOLKIAH, Hassanal
1946–

Sultan of Brunei. Educated in Kuala Lumpur, Malaysia, and at the Royal Military College, Sandhurst, he was appointed Crown Prince in 1961 and became sultan in 1967 on his father's abdication. He assumed the office of Prime Minister and Defence Minister when his country achieved independence in 1984. Said to be the richest man in the world, with a personal fortune estimated at $25 billion, he owns the Dorchester Hotel in London and the Beverley Hills Hotel in Los Angeles, a private fleet of aircraft, and the world's largest palace, built at a cost of $40 million. A moderate Muslim, his two wives are Princess Saleha, whom he married in 1965, and an ex-air stewardess, Miriam Bell, whom he married in 1981.

BONDFIELD, Margaret Grace
1873–1953

English trade unionist and politician, born Somerset. As an early union activist, she became chairman of the Trade Union Congress in 1923, and as Minister of Labour between 1929 and 1931 was the first woman member of a British Cabinet.

BOOTH, Charles
1840–1916

English shipowner and social reformer, born Liverpool. Although a successful businessman, the ardent radicalism that he had displayed in his youth reappeared in later life when he moved to London in 1875 and devoted 18 years to producing the prototype social survey, *Life and Labour of the People in London*, which was published in 1903. He also pioneered the concept of old-age pensions.

BOOTHBY, Sir Robert ('Bob') John Graham, 1st Baron Boothby of Buchan and Rattray Head
1900–86

British politician, born Edinburgh. Educated at Eton and Oxford, he entered Parliament for the Conservatives in 1924 and was parliamentary private secretary to **Winston Churchill** until 1929. During the war, he was a junior food Minister and served in the RAF. In 1948 he served as a founder member of the Council of Europe and subsequently as a delegate to its consultative assembly (1949–54). A rumbustious, cigar-smoking extrovert who exhibited the charisma if not the political brilliance of his mentor, Churchill, his no-nonsense style and private life (which included an affair with the wife of **Harold Macmillan**) gave him a higher public profile than his achievements really merited.

BORDEN, Sir Robert Laird
1854–1937

Canadian statesman, born Nova Scotia. He practised as a barrister before becoming a reforming leader of the Conservative Party in 1901, and Prime Minister in 1911, when he overthrew Wilfred Laurier over the US reciprocity question. Having won power mainly on nationalist policies, he was criticised for his enforcement of conscription in World War I, during which he was the first overseas premier to attend a meeting of the British Cabinet, in 1915. An architect of post-war peace, he remained premier until 1920. He subsequently represented Canada at the League of Nations, and was appointed its chief delegate to the UN General Assembly in 1930.

BORDIGA, Amadeo
1889–1970

Italian communist leader, born Resina. As a Marxist student activist at Naples University, he joined the Italian Socialist Party in 1910, but broke from the party briefly between 1912 and 1914 in protest at its electoral methods. At the outbreak of World War I, he aligned himself with the extreme left and was initially a critic of **Benito Mussolini**'s interventionism, and embraced Lenin's view that Italy should embark on a civil war against the military. In the 1919 elections, he rallied opposition to the reformists, then after forming the breakaway Partito Communista in 1921 came into conflict with the Comintern over his refusal to embrace its policies and was arrested and imprisoned, allowing for the 'Bolshevization' that he had so long opposed. After his release in 1924, he refused to stand as a Communist candidate in that year's elections, and in 1926 was arrested by the fascists and sent into exile. He was formally expelled from the party on his release in 1930, and for the next 30 years was deemed to be a 'non-person', but by the 1960s was able to witness revived interest in his philosophy by left-wing dissidents.

BOTHA, Louis
1862–1919

South African soldier and statesman, born Greytown, Natal. As a member of the Transvaal Volksraad, in 1900 he succeeded P.J. Joubert as commander-in-chief of the Boer forces during the war, and after being defeated at the critical actions at Johannesburg and Pretoria carried on guerrilla actions against the British before agreeing terms in May 1902. In 1905, he established the nationalist Het Volk movement, and, after forming a political alliance with **Jan Smuts**, was the first Prime Minister of the Union of South Africa from 1910 to 1919. He strongly supported Britain in World War I, putting down a revolt by anti-interventionist Dutch settlers led by Christiaan De Wet in 1915, and commanded a successful campaign against the Germans in South-west Africa. He died shortly after attending, with Smuts, the Versailles peace conference.

BOTHA, P. W. (Pieter Willem)
1916–

South African politician. The longest-serving member of the South African Assembly, which he entered in 1948, he oversaw a substantial strengthening of his country's armed forces as Minister of Defence between 1966 and 1980, as well as his country's controversial intervention in the Angola crisis. His attempts at constitutional reform after becoming Prime Minister in 1978, which included proposals for power-sharing with non-whites, caused several party splits and brought international criticism for their basically racist character. He became South Africa's first executive State President in 1984, but retired temporarily as National Party leader following a stroke in February 1989, and in August the same year he shook the political establishment by resigning as party leader. He was succeeded as State President by **F.W. De Klerk**.

BOTHA, 'Pik' (Roelof Frederik)
1932–

South African politician. As a member of the diplomatic service between 1953 and 1970, he represented the South African case at the International Court of Justice at the Hague (1963–6), then entered state politics and became an MP in 1970, but in 1974 again assumed a diplomatic role as South Africa's permanent representative at the United Nations (1974–7) and then ambassador to the USA. He returned to domestic politics in 1977, and as Foreign Minister in **P. W. Botha**'s 1978 Administration brought his influence as a sounding board of international opinion strongly to bear in supporting the notable reforms that were introduced at the end of the 1980s.

BOURGUIBA, Habib ibn Ali
1903–

Tunisian politician, born Monastir. After studying law in Paris, he became involved in the radical nationalist movement and between 1934 and 1954 served three terms of imprisonment under the French colonial administration. However, his comparative moderacy made him the preferred choice of the French Government as Tunisia's first Prime Minister in 1956 and President a year later, and relations improved still further after France closed its military bases in the country in 1962. In 1975, he was declared President for life, but riots by Islamic fundamentalists in 1983–4 undermined his authority, and in 1987 he was declared unfit by reason of senility by his Prime Minister, General **Ben Ali**, and deposed; Ben Ali assumed the presidency.

BRANDT, Willy (Karl Herbert Frahm)
1913–

West German politician, born Lübeck. As a fervent anti-Nazi, he fled Germany in 1933 and, after acquiring Norwegian citizenship, studied at Oslo University and worked as a journalist. On Norway's occupation in 1940 he went to Sweden, lending support to the German and Norwegian resistance movements. He returned to Germany in 1945 and having been reinstated as a German citizen three years later entered the Bundestag for the Social Democrats in 1949 and was president of the Bundesrat between 1955 and 1957. As mayor of Berlin (1957–66), he was probably the only municipal politician to achieve international fame, during the Berlin Wall crisis (1961). In 1966, he took the SPD into a coalition with the Christian Democrats and as Foreign Minister initiated a new policy of reconciliation with East Germany, which was a cornerstone of his Chancellorship from 1969 and led to the signing of the Basic Treaty in 1972. In 1974, he was forced to resign over revelations claiming that a close aide, Gunther Guillaume, had worked as an East German spy, but remained as SPD chairman, and between 1977 and 1983 headed the influential Brandt Commission on economic development in the southern hemisphere. His many published works include *The Ordeal of Co-Existence* (1963), *In Exile* (1971), *Essays, Reflections and Letters 1933–47* (1971), *People and Politics* (1978), and *World Armament and World Hunger* (1986).

BRANTING, Karl Hjalmar
1860–1925

Swedish politician, born Stockholm. Founder of the Swedish Socialist Party and of the Social Democratic Party (1889), he was made SDP leader in 1907 and was Prime Minister in 1920 and between 1921—when he won the Nobel Peace Prize—and 1925. He also served as Sweden's first representative at the League of Nations (1922–5).

BREZHNEV, Leonid Ilyich
1906–82

Russian statesman, born Dneprodzerzhinsk, Ukraine. The son of a steel worker, he joined the Komsomol (Communist youth league) in 1923 and, as an agricultural surveyor, worked on collectivisation programmes in Belorussia and the Urals during the 1920s. On joining the party in 1931, he was returned to his home town to retrain as an industrial engineer and to head the local metallurgical polytechnic. His organizational skills as propaganda chief from 1938 brought him to the attention of Ukrainian party chief **Nikita Khrushchev**, who sponsored his promotion to political commissar to the southern army during World War II and appointment as chief of the newly-ceded Moldavian republic. His achievements in that office brought him the patronage of **Joseph Stalin**, who inducted him into the Secretariat and Politburo, from which he was removed on Stalin's death in 1953. Through Khrushchev's influence, Brezhnev retained office as head of the Kazakhstan agricultural programme, and returned to the Secretariat and Politburo in 1957, only to be expelled again in 1960 when Khrushchev fell from grace. He was rehabilitated in 1963, and the following year became CPSU General Secretary after his mentor was finally ousted. As a moderate in both domestic and international affairs, he emerged as a significant figure on the world stage during the 1970s, and in 1977 was made State President. Soon after, his health deteriorated and he failed to keep control of the country's economic difficulties, for which legacy his reputation has suffered under criticism by **Mikhail Gorbachev** and other reformists.

BRIAND, Aristide
1862–1932

French socialist, born Nantes. Founder with Jean Jaurès of *L'Humanité* and of the law for the separation of church and state in 1905, he was 11 times French premier and Foreign Minister from 1925 to 1932. He shared with **Gustav Stresemann** the Nobel Prize for

Peace, and was an early advocate of a United States of Europe.

BROUGHAM, Henry Peter, 1st Baron Brougham
1778–1868

Scottish jurist and politician. As a child prodigy, he entered Edinburgh University in 1792 aged 14, and founded the *Edinburgh Review* in 1802. Aware that his liberal views were ahead of their time for Scotland, he moved to London, was called to the Bar in 1808, and entered Parliament in 1810. As a barrister, his greatest triumph was the successful defence of Queen Caroline in 1820, and, as Lord Chancellor from 1830, he was one of the greatest reformers of the courts, establishing the judicial committee of the Privy Council and the Central Criminal Court, though he was unsuccessful in his efforts to establish what is now the county-court system. In 1834, he enraged King William IV by taking the Great Seal with him on a tour and using it as the centrepiece of a house party game. He died at 90. His own three-volume *Life and Times* was published in 1871. The dignified brougham carriage was named after him.

BROWN, (Alfred) George (Lord George-Brown)
1914–85

British politician, born Southwark. After working as a union official, he was elected a Labour MP in 1945, and, as a loyal supporter of **Hugh Gaitskell**'s defence policy, was elected by the parliamentary party as deputy leader under both him and **Harold Wilson**. In the 1964 Labour Government, he remained as deputy leader and was appointed Minister of Economic Affairs, and then Foreign Secretary in 1966. One of the most colourful and outspoken figures in Labour's history, and a frequent critic of Wilson's policies, he was feted by the media more than by his own party, which he left shortly after receiving a peerage in 1970. His autobiography, *In My Way*, was published in 1971.

BROWN, (James) Gordon
1951–

Scottish politician, born Kirkcaldy. Educated at Kirkcaldy High School and Edinburgh University, where he took a first in history, he worked as a lecturer and TV journalist, and after entering local politics joined the executive of the Scottish Labour Party in 1977. After unsuccessfully contesting an Edinburgh seat for Labour in 1979, he became MP for Dunfermline in 1983. He rose rapidly in the parliamentary party's hierarchy, and has been its senior Front Bench spokesman on Treasury affairs under **John Smith** since 1987. His publications include *Scotland: The Real Divide* (1983), and *Maxton* (1986).

BROWN, John
1800–59

American abolitionist, born Torrington, Connecticut. After failing in the cattle business and land speculation, he became a self-appointed champion of black slaves, advocating the establishment of centres of insurrection as a means of bringing about anti-slavery legislation. With five of his 20 children from two marriages he participated in the Kansas border wars, and then moved to Virginia to establish a refuge for runaway slaves. His first major action was an absurdly misjudged attack in 1859 on a rifle factory in Harper's Ferry, in which most of his small band of supporters were killed or captured by troops led by Robert E. Lee. Two of his sons were killed and Brown and six other sons were tried for murder and treason and hanged. Nevertheless, the incident was instrumental in fomenting the Civil War, and 'John Brown's Body' was adopted as the marching song of the Northern troops.

BRUNDTLAND, Gro Harlem
1939–

Norwegian politician and first woman Prime Minister of Norway, born Oslo. The daughter of a Cabinet Minister, she studied medicine and qualified at Harvard as a physician, and in 1960 married the leader of the Opposition Conservative Party, Arne Olav. In 1969 she entered politics as a Labour supporter, became Environment Minister in 1974, and Prime Minister in 1981 and again in 1987. She was awarded the Third World Foundation prize in 1988 for her work on environmental issues.

BUKHARIN, Nikolay Ivanovich
1888–1938

Russian communist leader. His political activities prior to the Revolution of 1917 led to arrests, imprisonments and then exile. In 1917 he returned to become editor of *Pravda*

(1917–29), a member of the Central Committee of the Communist Party in Russia and a member of the Politburo (1924–9). Between 1926 and 1929 he was head of the Third International but was expelled from his Comintern and Politburo posts in 1929. Editor of *Izvestia* (1934) he was again expelled (1937), became one of the victims of Stalin's purges and was executed.

BULGANIN, Nikolai
1895–1975

Soviet politician, born Nizhni-Novgorod. After serving as mayor of Moscow (1933–7) and as a member of the World War II military council, he was created a marshal and succeeded **Joseph Stalin** as Defence Minister in 1946. After Stalin's death in 1946, he became vice-premier under Georgi Malenkov and premier on his resignation in 1955, though **Nikita Khrushchev** held the real power-reins as First Secretary. Both men established a precedent in making numerous state visits, but by 1958 Bulganin's authority was totally eclipsed and he remained in public office only in the nominal post of chairman of the Soviet State Bank.

BÜLOW, Prince Bernhard von
1849–1929

German diplomat and politician. After a distinguished career in the foreign service, he was Foreign Minister (1897–1900) and Chancellor (1900-9), in which offices his personal charm counted more in his relationship with **Wilhelm II** than his political skills, and he was guilty of a bad misjudgment in his threats to France in the 1905 Morocco crisis. He finally fell out of favour with the emperor after denying that he had approved an indiscreet interview given by Wilhelm to the *Daily Telegraph* that he had in fact seen. His *Memoirs*, published in 1932, provide a fascinating insight of Germany's political scene at the turn of the century, but are spoiled by his characteristic refutal of any personal responsibility for his actions.

BUNCHE, Ralph Johnson
1904–71

American diplomat, born Detroit. Left an orphan at 13 after the death of his impoverished parents from tuberculosis, he might have continued the aimless existence typical of the other young blacks in the Los Angeles district in which he was raised by his maternal grandmother, had she not insisted that he attend the University of Los Angeles. There, nurtured by the Harvard professor and black intellectual **W.E.B. Dubois**, he graduated with honours and gained a doctorate at Harvard. After further studies at Chicago Northwestern, London School of Economics and the University of Cape Town, he was made head of the political department at Howard University, Washington, and advised the Government on African affairs during World War II. He was instrumental in the drafting of the UN Charter and in planning its first General Assembly in 1946. The UN's first Secretary-General, **Trygve Lie**, recruited him to its permanent staff, and in 1948 he narrowly missed being assassinated along with Count Folk Bernadotte in Jerusalem, then successfully negotiated the armistice between Israel and the Arab states when the official mediators, convinced of the hopelessness of the task, failed to arrive, for which he was given the Nobel Peace Prize in 1950. **Hammarskjöld** appointed him Under-Secretary in his own office in 1955, and his skill and credibility again came to the fore in the violence and political chaos that was the aftermath of Congolese independence in 1960, bringing peace and order to all but Katanga—mainly because of **Lumumba**'s intractability—within two weeks. He had similar success in the 1960s with the Cyprus, Indo-Pakistan and Yemen crises. Always a pragmatist, he recognized the inadequacies and occasional impotence of the UN but was nevertheless unstintingly loyal to its aims, and as a diplomat his effectiveness and achievements in the cause of peace have probably only been surpassed in modern times by **Henry Kissinger**.

BURGESS, Guy Francis de Moncy
1910–63

British traitor. The son of a naval officer, he was educated at Eton, Royal Naval College, Dartmouth, and Trinity College, Cambridge, where his communist sympathies made him of interest to the KGB, which recruited him in the 1930s. He worked with the BBC (1936–9), wrote war propaganda, and served with MI5 (1939–41). After the war, he joined the Foreign Office and was appointed Second Secretary at the British Embassy in Washington in 1950, serving under **Kim Philby**. Recalled in 1951 for serious misconduct, he fled Britain with **Donald Maclean** later the same year and publicly resurfaced in the Soviet Union in 1953, where he spent his remaining years.

BURKE, Edmund
1729–97

British statesman and philosopher, born Dublin. Educated at a Quaker school and at Trinity College, Dublin, he entered the London Bar in 1750, but soon abandoned his legal career for literary work, publishing anonymously his *Vindication of Natural Society* in 1756 and *Philosophical Inquiry into the Origin of our Ideas of the Sublime and Beautiful* the same year. He returned to Dublin as an assistant to the Secretary for Ireland, and in 1765 became private secretary to the Marquis of Rockingham during his brief premiership. During Lord North's period in office from 1770 to 1782, Burke joined other Whigs in condemning North's actions in the American colonies and his Administration's general corruption and extravagance, publishing *Observations on the Present State of the Nation* (1769), *On the Cause of the Present Discontents* (1770), and essays on the Wilkes controversy. Also highly influential were his liberal speeches on American taxation (1774), conciliation with America (1775) and his *Letter to the Sheriffs of Bristol* (1777). His opposition to trade restrictions against Ireland and support for relaxing discriminatory laws against British Catholics cost him his Bristol seat in the Commons in 1780, but he was re-elected the same year for Malton, which he represented until 1794. The collapse of Rockingham's Government brought his appointment as Paymaster of the forces under Portland (1782-3, his last public office), but he remained a prominent and controversial public figure through his participation in the trial of **Warren Hastings** (1788). His later writings, including *Reflections on the French Revolution* (1790), *Appeal from the New to the Old Whigs*, and *Letters on a Regicide Peace*, in which he advocated the state suppression of free opinion, leaned more towards the policies of the new Conservatives than those of the Whigs that he had so long inspired.

BURNHAM, Forbes
1923–85

Guyanese politician. After studying for the London Bar, he returned home in 1949 to found the Marxist-Leninist People's Progressive Party, but the influence of extremist factions caused him to break from it in 1957 and form the moderate People's National Congress, which he took to electoral victory in 1964. He achieved his country's independence in 1966, and won the 1968 and 1973 elections, though there were allegations of ballot-rigging in both. In 1980 he introduced a new Constitution making him Executive President, and died in office.

BURNS, John
1858–1943

British politician, born London. After working as an engineer, he was elected as a Labour MP in 1892 and was president of the Local Government Board (1905) before becoming the first member of the working classes to become a Cabinet Minister, as President of the Board of Trade, in 1914. He resigned on the outbreak of World War II.

BUSH, George Herbert Walker
1924–

Forty-first US President, born Milton, Massachusetts. After service as the youngest pilot in the US Navy (1942–5), he studied economics at Yale, and subsequently made a fortune in oil-drilling in Texas before selling his interests in 1966 to concentrate on politics. He ran unsuccessfully as a Republican candidate for the Senate in 1964, but entered the House of Representatives in 1966. After a further unsuccessful bid for the Upper House, he was appointed ambassador to the United Nations (1971–3), and Republican national chairman by **Richard Nixon** (1973–4), and under **Gerald Ford** was special envoy to China (1974–5) and director of the CIA (1976). He enjoyed some success in the primaries for the 1980 presidential race, then became **Ronald Reagan**'s running mate to take the vice-presidency in 1981. During Reagan's two terms in office, he was seen as loyal and competent, particularly in the area of foreign affairs, but lacking any charisma, and his personal popularity declined in the wake of the 1987 Irangate affair. However, he soon recovered his standing and ran a brilliant 1988 election campaign in which he showed qualities of toughness and humour that the public had not seen before, giving him an easy victory over **Michael Dukakis**. In his first year in office, he soft-pedalled on the 'special relationship' that Reagan had cultivated with Britain and with **Margaret Thatcher** in particular to nurture better relations with the rest of Europe, and his standing as a statesman improved still further in the 1990–1 Gulf crisis, in which his lack of 'hawkishness' and international experience made it easier than it might have been to assemble the victorious multinational coalition forces—though he was subsequently widely condemned for his reluctance to staunch the Baghdad regime's post-war violations against Iraq's Kurdish population.

BUSTAMENTE, Sir (William) Alexander

1884–1977

Jamaican politician, born Kingston. The son of an Irish planter, he was adopted at the age of 15 by a Spanish seaman and travelled widely abroad before returning to his country in 1932 to become active in trade unionism. In 1943 he founded the Jamaica Labour Party and became his country's first Prime Minister when it achieved independence in 1962.

BUTHELEZI, Chief Mangosuthu

1928–

South African politician, born Mahlabatini. As chief of the Buthelezi tribe from 1953, he was assistant to the Zulu king, Cyprian, until 1968, and was then elected leader of Zululand in 1970. He became Chief Minister of the black homeland, KwaZulu, in 1976. Although a friend of **Nelson Mandela** since the 1950s, the readiness of African National Congress leaders to negotiate during Mandela's imprisonment with officials of the National Party created increasing dislike and distrust between their respective supporters, resulting in township clashes and some 5000 killings between 1985 and 1990. But in 1991, with Mandela again on the political scene, the two organizations entered into formal negotiations together for the first time, to achieve their common purpose of establishing a non-racist democratic political system in South Africa.

BUTLER, Benjamin Franklin

1818–93

American lawyer and politician, born Deerfield, New Hampshire. After graduating from Waterville College, Maine, in 1938, he was admitted to the Bar in 1840 and won a reputation as a criminal lawyer representing the working classes. He sat in the state legislature and Senate, and in 1861 was appointed major-general of volunteers in the Civil War, scoring a notable success at New Orleans and earning himself the title of 'Beast Butler' from Confederate soldiers. As a member of Congress from 1866, he was among the Republicans who led the reconstruction of the southern states and impeached President **Andrew Jackson**. In 1878 and 1879 his nomination for the Massachusetts governorship was endorsed by the Democrats, but he subsequently held the office for only one year, from 1882. He stood unsuccessfully for the presidency in 1884. His *Autobiography* was published in 1892.

BUTLER, Richard Austen ('Rab'), Baron

1902–82

British politician, born Attock Serai, India. Educated at Marlborough and Cambridge, and a fellow of Corpus Christi College (1925–9), he entered Parliament for the Conservatives in 1929, and after holding several junior posts became Minister for Education in 1941, and devised the famous 1944 Education Act, which restructured the secondary school system and introduced the 11-plus examination for the selection of grammar school pupils. As Chancellor of the Exchequer under **Winston Churchill** from 1951, he introduced the first emergency 'credit squeeze' Budget in 1955, becoming Lord Privy Seal and Leader of the House of Commons the same year. He was widely expected to succeed **Sir Anthony Eden** as Conservative leader and Prime Minister in 1957 but was passed over in favour of **Harold Macmillan**, and as deputy premier narrowly lost the nomination again in 1963 to **Alec Douglas-Home**. He remained in the Cabinet as Foreign Secretary until 1965, when he was made a life peer and Master of Trinity College, Cambridge, during the time that Prince Charles was an undergraduate there.

BUTT, Isaac

1813–79

Irish politician, born Glenfin, County Donegal. The son of a Protestant rector, he was educated at Raphoe and Trinity College, Dublin, and entered the Irish Bar in 1838. He took an early interest in politics and, as a Liberal Conservative, won election to Westminster in 1871, where he led the home-rule faction, but with little success.

CADBURY, George
1839–1922

English cocoa manufacturer and social reformer, born Birmingham. After taking control with his brother of the family's Birmingham-based business in 1856, and guided by his Quaker and liberal principles, he established in 1861 a new factory in Bournville as part of a 'model village' that included the unprecedented provision of decent housing for his workers. He also founded education and welfare trusts, and campaigned actively for social reform through his two London newspapers, the *Daily News* and *Star*.

CAESAR, Gaius Julius
100–44 BC

Roman general and statesman, born Rome. Born into an ancient patrician family, he led military campaigns in Asia and Spain, and as consul from 59 BC established the informal alliance with Pompey and Crassus known as the First Triumvirate. After five years as proconsul in Gaul and Illyricum, his radical reforms of the agrarian laws made him many enemies and saw his command threatened, but he won the support of the other two members of the Triumvirate in having it extended by another five years, and pre-empted any further challenge by keeping a section of his army ready to march on Rome and buying the loyalty of senators using the huge treasury accrued during the Gallic wars. However, by the late 50s his influence was waning, and Caesar sought to re-establish his authority with short campaigns to subdue risings in Britain and Germany, but in 48 BC the Senate exploited the opportunity to deny him candidacy for the consulship in his absence. Caesar then concentrated on further victories in Egypt—where he fought at Alexandra on behalf of Cleopatra, who bore his child—Greece, and Africa, and after putting down a further insurrection in Spain, and winning the loyalty of the all-important legions, in 45 BC he was proclaimed father of his country and made dictator for life and consul for 10 years. At home, he founded libraries, encouraged the formalization of Roman law, commissioned the construction of a canal through the Isthmus, and on 1 January 45 BC introduced the Julian calendar—which ended centuries of chronological chaos and survived into the 16th century. He also launched a war against the Dacians in central Europe, and was planning to attack Parthia when, on 15 March 44 BC, he was stabbed to death by a group of aristocrats, led by Gaius Cassius and Brutus, who could no longer tolerate Caesar's autocracy. However, instead of heralding an enlightened era of republican freedom, their action only served to plunge the Roman world into new civil wars that eventually brought the republic's collapse. Caesar was undoubtedly the greatest general in Roman history, and as an educated and progressive statesman, made one of the most significant contributions to his country's cultural development. And although he failed to achieve political conciliation in the later years of the republic, that was to be achieved eventually by his adopted son, Octavian (63 BC–14 AD) on becoming Emperor Augustus in 27 BC.

CAILLAUX, Joseph
1863–1944

French radical politician, born Le Mans. After serving several successful terms as Finance Minister between 1899 and 1925, as Prime Minister from 1911, he agreed terms with Germany over the Morocco crisis, but his premiership came to a dramatic end in 1914 when his wife shot dead the editor of *Le Figaro* for waging an editorial war against her husband. Her acquittal saw Caillaux's return to the political establishment, but his close association with Germany, which he had cultivated in an attempt to end World War I, brought his imprisonment in 1918. On being pardoned in 1924, he played an important role in war-debt negotiations with the USA. *Memoires* (1942–8).

CALHOUN, John Caldwell
1782–1850

American politician, born South Carolina. After an early career as a lawyer, he entered Congress in 1811, and as a nationalist was a vigorous supporter of the 1812 war against the British and of trade protection. He was **James Madison**'s Secretary of War from 1817 to 1825, and then Vice-President from 1825 until resigning seven years later over differences with President **Andrew Jackson**. He was among the leading proponents of the doctrine that states should be permitted to disregard federal laws that they considered unconstitutional or threatening to their own well-being, particularly in respect of tariffs and slavery. He served as a senator between 1832 and 1850, and was Secretary of State under **John Tyler** (1844-5).

CALLAGHAN, (Leonard) James, Baron
1912–

British politician, born Portsmouth. Educated at Portsmouth Northern Secondary School, he worked for the Inland Revenue, and after war service in the Royal Navy, entered Parliament as a Labour MP in 1945. After failing to win the party leadership on the death of **Hugh Gaitskell** in 1963, he was appointed Chancellor of the Exchequer in **Harold Wilson**'s 1964 Administration, introducing controversial fiscal measures such as corporation and selective employment taxes. He resigned in protest against the devaluation of sterling in 1967, but remained in the Cabinet as Home Secretary until Labour lost power in 1970. Labour's success in the 1974 general election put him back in the Cabinet as Foreign Secretary from 1974–6, and on Wilson's resignation in 1976, he defeated **Michael Foot** on the third ballot for party leader and succeeded to the premiership. The following year, he entered into a pact with the Liberals and other minority parties, which artificially prolonged the life of an already unpopular Government until its defeat in the 1979 election. While it would have been difficult for any successor to match Wilson's dynamism and sense of purpose, Callaghan lacked the personal charisma that might have compensated for that inadequacy. His failure to anticipate or check the growing power of left-wing extremists within his party and in trade unionism at large—whose growing influence brought the country to its knees in the 1978–9 'winter of discontent'—contributed greatly to Labour's defeat by **Margaret Thatcher**'s brand of new-look, anti-union Conservatism in 1979. He remained Opposition leader until 1980, when left-wing pressure finally forced his resignation. He was made a life peer in 1987, in which year also his autobiography *Time and Chance* was published.

CALLES, Plutarco Elias
1877–1945

Mexican political leader. After working as a schoolmaster and tradesman, he joined the 1910 revolution against **Porfirio Díaz** and was made Governor of Sonora (1917–19) and Secretary of the Interior (1920). After a four-year term as president from 1924, he founded the National Revolutionary Party, which exerted great influence over subsequent presidents until 1936, when **Lázaro**

Cárdenas wearied of his backstairs interference and had Calles deported. He lived in the USA from 1936 to 1942, when he returned to live quietly in Mexico until his death.

CALVIN, John (John Cauvin)
1509–64

French religious reformer, born Noyon, Picardy. Educated from the age of 14 at Paris University, he was intended for the priesthood but instead studied law at Orléans and Bourges. After his father's death in 1531, he returned to Paris, but under threat as a suspected Protestant, he fled to Basle two years later and promoted his doctrine of God's ascendancy over any sovereign in a letter to King Francis I and in other writings. In 1536, he moved to Geneva to organize the city's religious and political development according to strictures that included a ban on public entertainment, a requirement to dress with the utmost modesty, and the observance of strict puritan behaviour in private and public life. Not surprisingly, Calvinism's acceptance by the city's residents was short-lived, and after the Libertine riots of 1538, he was expelled from Geneva and went to Strasbourg. Three years later, he returned to organize an even stricter system of presbyterian government, under which anyone who deviated from his moral code risked being burned at the stake. However, this time his regime gained acceptance, and the industry and sobriety that it cultivated heralded a new era of unparalleled wealth for the city that lasted throughout Calvin's lifetime. After his death, the tenets of Calvinism were adopted by the Presbyterian church in Scotland and elsewhere, the Huguenots in France, the Dutch Reformed Church, and several German states. *Calvin: The Origin and Development of his Religious Thought* (1963), *Calvin* (1976).

CAMPBELL–BANNERMAN, Sir Henry
1836–1908

Scottish statesman, born Glasgow. Educated at Glasgow and Trinity College, Cambridge, he became a Liberal MP in 1868, and as Chief Secretary for Ireland from 1884, strongly supported **William Gladstone**'s policy of home rule. In 1886, he was appointed Secretary for War, and was elected party leader in 1899. When **Balfour**'s Administration collapsed in 1905, he was invited by Edward VII to form a Government, and after routing the Conservatives in a general election a month later, assembled one of the most impressive Cabinets of the 20th century, having among its members **Henry Asquith**, Edward Grey, Richard Haldane, and **David Lloyd George**. Apart from his notable and generous decision to grant self-government to the defeated Boer ex-republics, out of which grew the Union of South Africa, Campbell-Bannerman began the process of dismantling the obstructive power of the Upper House, which culminated in the passing of the momentous Parliament Act of 1911 after the Lords had blocked Lloyd George's 'People's Budget'. He died seven days after resigning in ill-health.

CANNING, George
1770–1827

English statesman, born London. Raised and educated by his uncle after the death of his father when Canning was only one year old, he attended Eton and Christ Church Oxford, and was admitted to the Bar before entering Parliament in 1794 and becoming Under-Secretary of State under **William Pitt** two years later. He was navy treasurer (1801), and as Foreign Affairs Minister from 1807 in Lord Portland's Cabinet he planned the seizure of the Dutch fleet that brought a stop to **Napoleon**'s planned invasion. His dispute with Lord **Castlereagh** over the Walcheren expedition resulted in a duel between them in which Canning was slightly wounded. As MP for Liverpool from 1812, he was a strong advocate of Catholic emancipation, and continued to support Lord **Liverpool** until resigning in 1820 in protest at the Government's action against Queen Caroline. After Castlereagh's suicide in 1822, he became Foreign Minister again, and introduced greater liberalism into Government policy, asserted British independence against the Holy Alliance, promoted commerce, and laid the foundations for the repeal of the corn laws. On Liverpool's death in 1827 he became Prime Minister in a coalition with the Whigs, but died later the same year.

CÁNOVAS DEL CASTILLO, Antonio
1828–97

Spanish statesman and historian, born Malaga. After entering the Cortes as a Conservative in 1854, he served three terms as premier (1875–81, 1884–5, and 1890–2), and took office again in 1895, but two years

later was shot dead by an anarchist while attending a festival at Santa Agueda with his wife.

CÁRDENAS, Lázaro
1895–1970

Mexican general and politician. At first a follower of **Plutarco Calles**, on becoming president in 1924 he eventually tired of his interference and had him deported, but continued Calles' policy of dismantling large estates and redistributing the land among the peasantry, to enjoy immense popularity among both the Indians and the Mexican working classes. In 1938, he came into dispute with the USA and Great Britain over his nationalization of oil fields, but had mended the rift by the time that his presidency ended in 1940.

CARDWELL, Edward, 1st Viscount
1813–86

British politician. After entering the Commons in 1842, he was Secretary of State for War under **William Gladstone** from 1869 to 1874, introducing notable army reforms that included abolition of the purchase of commissions, the development of county regiments and the reserves system, and the significant change in the command structure whereby the Minister took supremacy over the commander-in-chief.

CARNOT, Lazare Nicolas Marguerite
1801–88

French military engineer and politician, born Burgundy. After reaching the rank of captain, he entered the Legislative Assembly in 1791 and the National Convention a year later to become one of 12 members of the Committee of Public Safety that existed between 1793 and 1795. As Minister of War between those dates, he masterminded the recruitment, clothing, feeding, training and arming of more than 14 armies comprising 1 100 000 men to defend the new republic from foreign invasion. With the ending of **Maximilien Robespierre**'s Reign of Terror, he served on the Directory from 1795, but was forced to flee to Nuremberg a year later as a suspected royalist sympathizer. He returned as Minister of War when **Napoleon** took power in 1799 and brought a successful conclusion to the Italian and Rhineland campaigns. However, his disenchantment with Napoleon's self-aggrandizement caused him to resign, but the disasters that befell the French forces after their retreat from Moscow prompted his return to office, and in 1814 he became Governor of Antwerp, which he succesfully defended against the Allies. He was subsequently Minister of the Interior, but eventually died in exile.

CAROL II

1893–1953

King of Romania. After his first marriage had been dissolved, he was remarried in 1921 to Princess Helen of Greece, who became the mother of his heir, Michael. His infidelity forced him to renounce his right of succession in favour of his son, who succeeded King Ferdinand on his death in 1927. Carol was restored in 1930 after a promise (which he failed to keep) that he would give up his mistress, Magda Lupescu. At the outbreak of World War II, he first tried to appease Russia by ceding Bessarabia and Bukovina, and then switched his allegiance to Germany, but in 1940 Carol was deposed by the fascist leader **Ion Antonescu**. He lived in exile with Madame Lupescu, whom he married in 1948, in Mexico and in Portugal, where he died.

CARRANZA, Venustiana

1859–1920

Mexican politician. After the long dictatorship of Porfirio Díaz (1830–1915) that lasted from 1876 to 1911, and the murder of his successor, Francisco Madero (1873–1913), Carranza took control, and became president, later crushing the uprising led by the revolutionary leader, Zapata, with American assistance. Carranza introduced several worthwhile reforms and a new constitution, but in the 1920 rebellion led by Alvaro Obregón (1880–1928), he was murdered while fleeing to the coast.

CARRINGTON, Peter Alexander Rupert, 6th Baron Carrington (Ireland)

1919–

British statesman. Educated at Eton and Sandhurst Military Academy, he served with distinction in World War II, and his appointments in every subsequent Conservative Government under **Winston Churchill**, **Sir Anthony Eden**, **Harold Macmillan**, **Sir Alec Douglas-Home**, and **Edward Heath** included High Commissioner to Australia (1956–9), First Lord of the Admiralty (1959–63) and Secretary of Defence (1970–4). The Conser-

vatives' return to power in 1979 brought his appointment as Foreign Secretary. His early successes included independence for Zimbabwe (1980), and the reputation that he quickly won as something of a hawk, particularly in his attitude towards the Soviets, made his apparent lethargy in responding to the events that presaged the Argentine invasion of the Falkland islands even more surprising. However, Carrington was by training and nature a diplomatist, and was anyway preoccupied—as were his Foreign Office advisers—with his imminent visit to Israel in yet another British attempt to help bring peace between that country and the Arab states. Argentina's initial sabre-rattling was viewed as little more than an irritating distraction that would come to naught. However, when the invasion came on 2 April 1982, the Government found themselves on the ropes, and within days **Margaret Thatcher** was compelled—much against her personal wishes, and devastated by the loss of such an experienced Foreign Minister just at a time when she was fighting to re-establish Britain's place as a world power—to accept Carrington's resignation and to appoint Francis Pym in his place. Carrington retired from the public spotlight, but his reputation as a man of great personal integrity was left untarnished, and in 1984 he began a four-year term as Secretary-General of NATO. His autobiography, *Time and Chance*, was published in 1987.

CARTER, James Earl (Jimmy)

1924–

Thirty-ninth US President, born Plains, Georgia. After graduating from the US Naval Academy in 1946, he served as an electronics instructor in the US Navy until 1953, when he became head of the family peanut business. After sitting in the state legislature (1963–7), he was Governor of his home state from 1970 to 1974, and after winning the 1976 Democratic presidential nomination, he achieved a narrow victory over **Gerald Ford**. He has deservedly won a place in history for his part in the Panama Treaty and the reaching of the new accord between Egypt and Israel, by acting as 'honest broker' at the meeting between **Anwar Sadat** and **Menachem Begin** at Camp David in 1978. However, his country's worsening economy and the disastrous failure, on the eve of the 1980 election, of his attempt to rescue 400 US hostages held in Iran in a USAF helicopter raid brought his defeat by **Ronald Reagan**. In 1986, Carter and his wife, Rosalynn, whom he married in 1946, established the Carter Centre to promote human rights. International recognition of his work in that sphere brought him the Human Rights Award (1983) and the Albert Schweitzer Prize for Humanitarianism (1987). His books include *Why Not the Best?* (1975), his autobiography, *Keeping faith: memoirs of a President* (1982), and *Everything to Gain* (1987).

CASEMENT, Sir Roger David
1864–1916

Irish nationalist, born Dublin. After joining the British consular service, he was knighted in 1911 for exposing the exploitation of rubber workers in the Congo and Peru. While in Germany during World War I, he attempted to form an Irish Brigade of prisoners of war with which he intended to invade Ireland and end British rule. On arriving back there in a German submarine, he was arrested, tried for treason, and hanged at Pentonville prison. In 1965, the British Government allowed his remains to be reinterred in Ireland.

CASEY, Richard Gardiner Casey, Baron
1890–1976

Australian politician. A Liberal MP in the House of Representatives from 1931 to 1940 and again from 1949 to 1960, he served as Commonwealth Treasurer (1935–9) and First Minister to the United States (1940–2) before being appointed Minister of State for the Middle East by **Winston Churchill** in 1942, with a seat in the War Cabinet. From 1944 to 1946 he was Governor of Bengal, and after his return to Australia, he was made Minister of National Development (1949–51) and was Minister for External Affairs from 1951 until 1960, when he became the first Australian life peer to sit in the House of Lords. He was also made Australia's first Knight of the Garter. *Casey* (1986).

CASTLE, Barbara Anne
1911–

British politician, born Bradford. Educated at Bradford Girls' Grammar School and at St Hugh's College, Oxford, she worked in local government until the end of the war, and after entering Parliament as a Labour MP in 1945, soon won a reputation as a radical and during the 1950s consolidated her status as a favourite of the left-wing Bevanite faction. She was made party chairman in 1959, and on Labour's victory in the 1964 general election immediately entered the Cabinet as Minister for Overseas Development. As Minister of Transport from 1965 to 1968, she introduced the 70 mph speed limit and the breathalyzer testing of suspected drunk drivers, and for two years from 1968, as Secretary of State for Employment and Productivity, brought flair and a measure of success to implementing the Government's unpopular prices and incomes policy. She was Minister of Health from 1974 until returning to the Back-Benches in 1976 when **James Callaghan** replaced **Harold Wilson** as Prime Minister. In 1979, she was elected to the European Parliament, and was vice-chairman of its Socialist group until 1984. Her commitment to making the most of an apparently inexhaustible political career was typified by giving her maiden speech as a peeress at the age of 69, in 1980. Her two-volume autobiography, *The Castle Diaries*, was published between 1980 and 1982.

CASTLEREAGH, Robert Stewart, Viscount
1769–1822

British statesman, born Londonderry. Educated at Armagh and for a year at Cambridge, he became a Whig MP in the Irish Parliament in 1790 but took the Tory Whip five years later while remaining in favour of Catholic emancipation. As Chief Secretary under **William Pitt** from 1797, he promoted a measure of union, but resigned with him when Pitt's proposals were defeated. As War Minister from 1806 to 1809, he was made the scapegoat for the failed Walcheren expedition, and wounded **George Canning** in a duel to settle the dispute. In 1812, he re-established his reputation as Foreign Secretary under Lord **Liverpool**, but his diplomatic efforts, which brought 40 years of peace after **Napoleon**'s downfall, took their toll, and Castlereagh committed suicide. He is buried at Westminster Abbey.

CASTRO, Fidel
1927–

Cuban revolutionary, born Havana. The son of a wealthy sugar-planter, he studied and practised law in Havana, specializing in representing the poor in fighting the corruption and oppression that were rife under

President **Batista**, and in 1953 was sentenced to 15 years' imprisonment for his part in an unsuccessful coup. When he was released a year later under a general amnesty, he went to the USA and then Mexico to plot Batista's overthrow, and in 1956 returned to Cuba with a small band of insurgents—but was betrayed and fled to the mountains. He then waged a relentless guerrilla campaign, which gained momentum and support under an increasingly harsh police state. In December 1958 he launched a full-scale attack on Havana, and two months later, after Batista had fled the country, Castro proclaimed a new Marxist-Leninist state and began wholesale reform of Cuba's agriculture, industry, and education. Continuing resistance to his regime by the US led to the abortive Bay of Pigs invasion in 1961, and Cuba's dependence on Russian aid also gave rise to the 1962 missile crisis, when **Nikita Khrushchev** was faced down by President **John F. Kennedy** and forced to dismantle Soviet nuclear strike bases in Cuba and to recall ships carrying missiles to the country. In 1979, Castro became president of the non-aligned countries movement despite his continuing strong economic and political involvement with the Kremlin, but by the late 1980s, Cuba's status as the world's largest supplier of sugar was beginning to suffer because of the industry's outdated and unrepaired equipment. The start of 1991 ominously heralded Cuba's worst economic crisis in its 32 years of Communist rule, caused mainly by flagging economic aid and a drastic fall in basic supplies from the economically-compromised USSR—on which Cuba had come to rely for almost all the oil imports on which 90 per cent of the island's energy industry is based. Castro's failing, time-worn Stalinist economic policies were also showing their age, with Soviet insistence that future transactions between the two countries be in hard currency, at a time when Cuba's reserves had fallen to only $20 million—barely enough to run the country for a month.

CATHERINE II (Catherine the Great)
1729–96

Empress of Russia, born Stettin. After her marriage to the heir to the throne, Peter III, in 1745, she became notorious for her numerous affairs, and after her husband's accession in 1792 she was banished from the court until Peter was dethroned by a conspiracy in which Catherine's coronation was assured by her husband's murder at the hands of Gregory Orlov, one of her lovers. Under her rule, Russia expanded her territories and power, but court intrigues continued, of which the best-known is that involving Grigori Potemkin. Catherine's empire was further greatly increase by the partitioning of Poland in 1772 and by the wars with Turkey (1774), Sweden (1790) and Turkey again (1792).

CAVOUR, Count Camillo Benso di
1810–61

Italian statesman and nationalist, born Turin. Unable to reconcile his duties as a senior army officer with his liberal sympathies, he resigned his commission in 1831, and in 1847 founded the newspaper *Il Risorgimento*, which advocated representative government. On his suggestion, the king was successfully petitioned for a constitution, which was introduced in 1848. As Prime Minister from 1852 to 1859, he promoted Sardinian autonomy, and following that country's participation in the Crimean War, Cavour was able to bring the Italian question before the 1856 Congress of Paris. Two years later, he negotiated with **Napoleon III** to drive the Austrians out of Italy, but when the peace of Villafranca reversed his plans and left Venetia an Austrian domain, he resigned. However, he returned as premier in 1860 to see Victor Emanuel II declared King of Italy, with only Rome and Venetia left separate.

CEAUSESCU, Nicolae
1918–89

Romanian dictator. Born into a peasant family, he excelled at school and won admission to the Academy of Economic Studies in Bucharest. Having joined the Communist Party at the age of 15, he was imprisoned for anti-Fascist activities, and in 1945 was appointed Bucharest party secretary. Over the next 10 years, Ceausescu rose in the the party hierarchy to become secretary-general by 1965 and president of the state council in 1967. He was elected president in 1974 and was re-elected in 1980 and 1985. Ceausescu ensured both the unquestioning application of his policies and his personal survival by appointing members of his family—including his wife, Elena—to key party and governmental posts, but Romania's economy remained locked in stagnation thanks to archaic agricultural practices and a pathetically unsophisticated industrial sector. Meanwhile, Ceausescu and his family enjoyed an increasingly lavish lifestyle that included a choice of 12 palaces. In the late 1970s, his regime grew even more repressive, with its persecution of the country's Hungarian minority and the silencing of the smallest voices of dissent by Ceausescu's notorious secret police, the Stasi. After he had spurned the entreaties of **Mikhail Gorbachev** to introduce a measure of democratization, in the autumn of 1989 the people finally rose against him, and, with the support of an impoverished army, staged a bloody coup. Ceausescu and his wife were caught attempting to flee the country, and after a summary trial—at which they displayed no repentance but only arrogance—they were both executed by firing squad on Christmas Eve.

CECIL, Robert Arthur Talbot Gascoyne, 3rd Marquis of Salisbury
1830–1903

English statesman, born Hatfield House, Hertfordshire. Educated at Eton and Christ Church, Oxford, as a Conservative MP (as Lord Cranborne) from 1853 he was a staunch opponent of **William Gladstone**'s Reform Bill and continued his fight after succeeding his father as 3rd Marquis in 1868, resisting the disestablishment of the Irish Church, the Irish Land Act of 1870, and religious tests in the universities. After the 1874 election, he remained as Secretary for India, and was made Foreign Secretary from 1878 when he attended the Berlin Congress. He became leader of the Conservative Opposition on **Disraeli**'s death in 1881, and with the Conservatives back in power four years later, he began the first of three terms as Prime Minister (1885–6, 1886–92, 1895–1902) and another two as Foreign Secretary (1887–92, 1895–1900). In those offices, he exercised a firm but conciliatory foreign policy that avoided a full-scale war in eastern Europe after the Turkish massacres in Armenia, brought the Sudan under British rule again in 1896, and averted an escalation of hostilities in the Mediterranean after the Turkish invasion of Cyprus in 1897. He retired after seeing peace come to the Transvaal after the 1889–1902 Boer War.

CEREZO AREVALO, Mario Vinicio
1942–

Guatemalan politician. Educated at San Carlos University, he joined the Christian Democratic Party shortly after it was founded in 1968. The widespread political violence that blighted the country from 1974 onwards brought an end to democratic government, but in 1985, after a new Constitution had been introduced, the CDP won the congressional elections and Cerezo became his country's first civil president for 20 years.

CHAMBERLAIN, Sir (Joseph) Austen
1863–1937

British politician, born Birmingham. The half-brother of **Neville Chamberlain**, he was educated at Rugby and Trinity College, Cambridge, and spent some time in France and Germany before being elected a Liberal Unionist MP in 1892. He was appointed Financial Secretary in 1902, and was Chancellor of the Exchequer from 1903 until the Liberals were defeated in 1905, and despite being a strong candidate to replace **Arthur Balfour** on his resignation as Conservative leader in 1911, he stood down in favour of **Bonar Law**, who made him Secretary of State for India in 1915. He resigned two years later over the mismanagement of the Mesopotamia campaign, but was invited to join the War Cabinet in 1918, and became Chancellor of the Exchequer again a year later. Chamberlain was a casualty of the party split over **David Lloyd George**, but soon returned to the Cabinet as Foreign Secretary (1924–9), and received the Nobel Peace Prize for his part in the signing of the 1925 Locarno Pact. He was First Lord of the Admiralty in the short-lived 1931 National Government, and then retired, but remained an influential elder stateman.

CHAMBERLAIN, (Arthur) Neville
1869–1940

British politician, born Birmingham. The son of a former Chancellor of the Exchequer, Joseph Chamberlain (1836–1914), he was educated at Rugby and Birmingham University, and after working on the family plantation in the Bahamas, returned to Birmingham in 1897 to enter industry. He was Lord Mayor and Director of National Service (1915–16), and became an MP in 1918. His success as Minister for Health (1923–9) and as Chancellor of the Exchequer (1931–7) marked him out as **Stanley Baldwin**'s natural successor in 1937. On almost immediately finding himself confronted with the first rumblings of Germany's territorial aggression, he chose initially to follow a policy of appeasement, signing the 1938 Munich Agreement. He was soon forced to concede its worthlessness and to make preparations for war, but by May 1940, with British forces suffering a reversal of their initial success, and Chamberlain already in failing health, he surrendered the premiership to **Winston Churchill**, and died of cancer six months later.

CHAMORRO, Violetta

1919–

Nicaraguan politician. The widow of Pedro Joaquin Chamorro, whose murder in 1978 sparked off events leading to the Sandanista revolution and the overthrow of the Somozoa regime in 1979, her political career began after her husband's death. She briefly joined the junta the Sandanistas set up but left in 1980. Owner of the influential *La Prensa* newspaper, her own family of four children were split idealogically—one son ran the Sandanista party newspaper *Barricada,* one daughter was a Sandanista diplomat, one daughter took over the editorship of *La Prensa* while another son joined the contras in exile. In 1989 Chamorro stood as the candidate for the National Opposition Union (UNO) which consisted of 14 parties with widely differing ideologies. She was elected president after a decisive win over Daniel Ortega in February 1990.

CHARLEMAGNE (Carolus Magnus, Charles the Great)

747–814

King of the Franks and Christian emperor. As the eldest son of Pepin II the Short (715–68), he chose to share the Frankish kingdom with his brother Carloman, but on his death three years later became sole ruler. Between 772 and 780, he led ambitious campaigns to subjugate and Christianize neighbouring kingdoms, including those of the Saxons to the north-east, the Lombards in northern Italy, and the Moors in Spain. Charlemagne showed his displeasure with the Saxons' next rising in 782 by having 4500 of their number beheaded, but it was three years before the Saxon leader, Widukind, conceded defeat and accepted baptism. Between 780 and 800, Charlemagne added Bohemia to his empire, subdued the Turkish-Finnish nomads in the Danube basin, made his Spanish march south of the Pyrenees, and

entered Italy to defend Pope Leo III against the rebellious Romans, to be crowned emperor. In his remaining years, he consolidated his empire, which now extended from northern Spain to the Elbe, founded his capital at Aachen (Aix-la-Chapelle), and established there an academy to which many of the greatest scholars of the age were invited. Education, book-making, the arts, agriculture, industry, and the law all benefited under his patronage, and he established good relations with the West. However, Charlemagne's extraordinary empire did not long survive his death, for his sons, lacking his commitment and authority, were unable collectively to sustain an interdependent and culturally-advanced Christian federation that owed its creation as much to Charlemagne's skills as a scholar and administator as to his abilities as a great warrior.

CHARLES I

1600–49

King of Great Britain and Ireland, born Dunfermline. He overcame his childhood frailty, which forced him to crawl on his hands and knees until the age of seven, to become a skilled tilter and marksman, and he excelled as a student of theology, Having been baptized as the Duke of Albany, and made Duke of York at the age of five, he became Prince of Wales in 1616—four years after the death of Prince Henry had left him heir to the throne. In 1623, he travelled incognito to Madrid with his closest adviser, the Duke of Buckingham to seek the hand of a Spanish princess, but in the absence of an undertaking to convert to the Catholic faith, he was rebuffed by Rome. His betrothal two years later to Princess Henrietta Maria of France (1609–69), with the promise that she would be allowed freely to practise her religion and to have the responsibility for the upbringing of their children until they reached the age of 13, received a hostile reception from the growing body of Puritans, but Charles was undeterred, and three months after succeeding his father, **James I**, to the throne, he welcomed his new bride at Dover, having married her by proxy six weeks earlier. But the retinue of a bishop, 29 priests and 410 attendants that arrived with her soon tried Charles' patience, and he had them returned to France within a year. In the 12 years following the murder of Buckingham in 1628, Henrietta Maria came to exercise growing influence over the affairs of state, and it was largely at her behest that Charles dissolved no fewer than three Parliaments in the first four years of his reign, and then ruled without one for 12 years. With England now at peace with France and Spain, Charles addressed the task of refreshing his dwindling treasury with unpopular taxation of the inland counties, and of pulling Presbyterian Scotland into line with the imposition of a common prayer book. The hostility that both measures engendered forced Charles to recall Parliament in 1640, but it continued to frustrate almost his every action. Worse still, to divert hostility from the queen, he was compelled to approve the Act of Attainment, by which Parliament could not be dissolved without its consent, and to allow in 1641 the impeachment and execution of his loyal Lord Deputy for Ireland, the Earl of **Strafford**, after his secret plan to suppress the king's opponents in Ireland and England was exposed. Resentful of the power that Parliament now held, Charles went to Edinburgh in an unsuccessful bid to win over the Scottish lords. The following year, his arrival in the Chamber of the House of Commons to supervise the arrest of John Pym and four other MPs, prompted by his fear that the queen would soon be impeached, made civil war inevitable, and on 22 August 1642, the royal standard was raised at Nottingham, marking the start of more than three years of bitter fighting. The war effectively came to an end with the defeat of the royalist forces at the Battle of Naseby in June 1645, but the king spent another year trying to rally support from his refuge in Oxford before finally surrendering to the Scots at Newark on 5 May 1646. In January 1647, he was handed over to Parliament and held at Holmby House near Northampton, where he exploited his comparative freedom to negotiate a treaty with the Scots and to foment a brief resurgence of civil war. In November, he escaped to the Isle of Wight, but he and his family were soon recaptured and held at Carisbrooke Castle, until the king was returned to stand trial at Westminster. His three refusals to plead were interpreted as a silent confession, and on 30 January 1649, Charles was beheaded on a scaffold erected outside the Guildhall in Whitehall, within sight of the Parliament whose authority he had never been able to accept. On 7 February, his body was taken for internment in the vault of **Henry VIII** at Windsor. Two of his three sons were eventually to take the throne, as **Charles II** and **James II**, and he

was also survived by three daughters—the last born 10 weeks after his death.

CHARLES II

1630–85

King of Great Britain and Ireland. As Prince of Wales during the 1642–6 Civil War, he was sent to govern the west of England and saw action at the Battle of Edgehill in 1642, but when the royalist forces continued to suffer heavy defeats, he went into exile to Sicily, Jersey (where his mistresss, Lucy Walter, bore him a son, James, Duke of Monmouth), and France. Following his father's execution in 1649, Charles was proclaimed monarch by Scotland, and after arriving in Edinburgh he agreed to the Presbyterian Covenant and, despite the failure of his forces to defeat **Oliver Cromwell** at Dunbar, he was crowned at Scone on 1 January 1651. At the Battle of Worcester the following September, Cromwell's forces again triumphed and Charles fled to France and the Netherlands. Following the successful 1659 negotiations to restore the monarchy, he returned to England and, after promising a general amnesty and liberty of conscience, entered London in triumph on 29 May 1660—his 30th birthday. Despite the strongly royalist Parliament's insistence on repressive measures to quell dissent, Charles was personally inclined to favour Roman Catholicism, and under his 1663 Declaration of Indulgence, the country enjoyed peace and sound government under the chancellorship of Edward Hyde, the Duke of Clarendon. However, his promotion of the unsuccessful 1665–7 war with Holland brought Hyde's downfall, and the office of Lord Chancellor was replaced by a group of Ministers acting in concert, who thus formed the country's first Cabinet. By the late 1660s, anti-Catholic feeling was again growing in strength, partly because of the growing power of **Louis XIV** of France, but also because the Great Fire of London in 1666 was blamed by some as the product of a Catholic conspiracy. Charles had already sold Dunkirk to France for £400000 in 1662, and, having little wish to see a reprize of the old enmity, or to jeopardize an important potential source of personal income, he concluded a secret treaty whereby he undertook to become a Catholic, together with his brother (the future **James II**), and to enter into an alliance against Holland in return for an annual payment from Louis of £200,000. His second attempt to subdue the Dutch between 1672 and 1674 was barely

45

more successful than the first, but meanwhile he took a Catholic wife, Mary of Modena, in 1673. His attempt to issue a second Declaration of Indulgence to annul the penal laws against the Catholics and dissenters was rejected by Parliament, which instead passed the 1673 Test Act, which excluded Roman Catholics from sitting in Parliament or holding Government office. It was followed by repeated attempts to legislate against James's succession to the throne, or to drastically limit his powers if he did so. Mary's failure to produce an heir after four years of marriage compelled Charles to consent to the marriage in 1677 of his Protestant niece, Mary, to William of Orange (the future **William III**), and anti-Catholicism returned in the light of the fabricated account by **Titus Oates** of a Popish plot to murder the king. The next three years saw the future of the Stewart dynasty hanging in the balance, and the emergence for the first time of party distinctions—with the Whigs favouring James's exclusion, but the Tories opposed to any tampering with the succession. The Tories and Charles won the day, and the king immediately legislated for changes to borough government that effectively excluded the Whigs from power. Despite the absence of parliamentary opposition after Charles seized total power in 1681, anti-Catholic sentiment grew, and reached a peak after the 1683 Rye House plot to murder Charles and James came to light. However, James's succession was now safe,, and on his deathbed Charles finally publicly acknowledged his conversion to Roman Catholicism. He died without producing an heir, but through his affairs with Barbara Villiers, Nell Gwynne, Louise de Kéroualle, the Duchess of Portsmouth, and many others, he fathered several children, most of whom were later ennobled.

CH'EN TU-HSIU

1879–1942

Chinese revolutionary. Founder editor of *New Youth* from 1915, his sustained attacks on traditional Chinese government and society and promotion of westernization inspired the May Fourth Movement, which organized the students' rising of 4 May 1919, resulting in Ch'en's arrest. On his release, the success of the Russian revolution brought his conversion to Marxism, and in 1920 he founded the Chinese Communist Party and became its first secretary-general. However,

his failure to sustain the alliance with the nationalist Kuomintang led to his sacking by the Comintern in 1927, and two years later he was expelled from the party.

CHERNENKO, Konstantin Ustinovich

1911–85

Soviet politician, born Bolshaya Tes, central Siberia. A party member from 1931, his work as a propaganda specialist in Siberia and Moldavia brought him to the attention of regional secretary **Leonid Brezhnev**, who in 1956 appointed Chernenko as his personal assistant and sponsored his rise in the party hierarchy, culminating in his admittance as a full member of the Politburo in 1978. However, on Brezhnev's death in 1982, Chernenko was passed over for the leadership in favour of **Yuri Andropov**, but the new premier's death in February 1984 brought Chernenko's provisional appointment as leader, and in April he was confirmed as state president. He immediately sought to establish a new era of detente, but illness forced him to resign only three months after taking office, and he died the following year.

CHIANG CHING-KUO

see **Jingguo**

CHIANG KAI-SHEK

see **Jiang Jieshi**

CHICHERIN, Georgy Vasilyevich

1872–1936

Soviet diplomat. Of noble birth, he entered the foreign service but resigned on becoming politically active as a social democrat. From 1904, he lived with other revolutionaries abroad, and in 1917 he was arrested in England as a subversive, but was later freed and allowed to return to Russia in exchange for the detained British ambassador, Sir George Buchanan. As Foreign Minister from 1918, he concluded the Brest-Litovsk Treaty, which ended the German war, and while attending the 1922 Genoa Conference secretly negotiated the Rapallo Treaty, which secured recognition and trade agreements from Germany. Ill health forced his resignation in 1930.

CHILDERS, (Robert) Erskine

1870–1922

Anglo-Irish writer and nationalist, born London. Educated at Haileybury and Trinity

College, Cambridge, he worked as a clerk in the House of Commons from 1895 to 1910, then served as a volunteer in the second Boer War, and in 1903 published a bestselling spy novel, *The Riddle of the Sands*, about a German invasion of Britain. From 1910, he devoted his energies to promoting Irish home rule, and at the outbreak of World War I used his yacht to bring German arms to the Irish volunteers. Paradoxically, he served in the Royal Navy in World War II, and in 1921 entered the Irish Parliament as a Sinn Fein MP and became Minister for Propaganda. He denounced the treaty that created the Irish Free State, and after joining the IRA, was captured and ordered to be executed by an Irish military court. One of his sons, Erskine Hamilton Childers (1905–74), served as President of the Republic from 1973 to 1974.

CHIRAC, Jacques René
1932–

French politician, born Paris. After graduating from the École Nationale d'Administration, he entered Government service during the premiership of **Georges Pompidou**, and in 1967 joined the conservatives in the National Assembly. He was given ministerial responsibility for finance, agriculture and industry, and from 1974 was Prime Minister to President **Giscard d'Estaing**. Conflicts between them brought Chirac's resignation in 1976, when he established the neo-Gaullist Rassemblement pour la Republique. He was elected mayor of Paris a year later, and although he lost the first ballot for the 1981 presidential election, he went on to lead the rightist coalition during the 1981–6 Socialist Administration. Following the Socialists' defeat in the 1986 National Assembly elections, Chirac was appointed Prime Minister by President **François Mitterrand** under a unique power-sharing arrangement, but was defeated by Mitterrand in the 1988 presidential election.

CHISSANO, Joaquim
1939–

Mozambican politician, born Chibuto. After joining the National Front for the Liberation of Mozambique (Frelimo) in the 1960s, he was secretary to its leader, **Samora Machel**, and when internal self-government was granted in 1974, he was made Prime Minister, then Foreign Minister. On Machel's death in 1986, he succeeded him as president.

CHOONHAVEN, Chatichai
1911–

Thai politician. Elected in 1988 as Thailand's first Prime Minister for 12 years, he was deposed in a bloodless army coup in February 1991, and arrested at Bangkok airport on his way to present his chosen successor, Arthit Kamlangek, to King **Bhumibol Adulyadej**, the constitutional monarch. Choonhaven—who celebrated his 'twilight years' by visiting discos and riding his Harley-Davidson—ushered in a golden age of prosperity for Thailand, which he hoped would join the ranks of the four Asian 'tiger economies' of Hong Kong, South Korea, Singapore, and Taiwan. However, the appointment of Kamlangek as Defence Minister against the army's wishes brought months of friction between the military and the coalition Government, and supreme military commander Sunthorn Kongsompong finally seized power with the support of the police and the three branches of the armed services, in the 17th coup since Thailand abolished absolute monarchy in 1932. In March Choonhaven was released from military detention for a 'holiday' in Europe.

CHOU EN-LAI
see **Zhou Enlai**.

CHUN DOO-HWAN
1931–

South Korean soldier and politician, born Taegu, Kyonsang province. Trained at the Korean Military Academy, he was commissioned as a second lieutenant in 1955, and after further training at the US Army Infantry School in the 1960s, he worked with the special airborne forces group and in military intelligence. Following the assassination of President Park in 1979, he took charge of the intelligence services and investigated Park's murder. After the 1979 coup, he took control of the army, and in 1981 retired from the military to serve as president and to lead the newly-formed Democratic Justice Party. Despite his success in building the country's economy, his authoritarian rule became increasingly unpopular, and he was forced to retire in 1988.

CHURCHILL, Sir Winston Leonard Spencer
1874–1965

British statesman, born Blenheim Palace,

Woodstock. The eldest son of Lord Randolph Churchill and a descendant of one of the 17th century's greatest soldier-statesmen, John Churchill, 1st Duke of Marlborough, he was educated at Harrow and Sandhurst Military College and was commissioned in the 4th Queen's Own Hussars in 1895. He served in the 1897 Malakand and 1898 Nile campaigns, and as a London newspaper correspondent in the Boer War, was captured but escaped with a £25 reward offered for his recapture. In 1900 he entered Parliament as a Conservative MP, but crossed the Floor of the House to join the Liberal majority in 1906 to become Colonial Under-Secretary and President of the Board of Trade (1908-10), when he introduced labour exchanges. As Home Secretary (1910), he witnessed the famous siege of Sidney Street, and as First Lord of the Admiralty from 1910 began strengthening Britain's army and navy in preparation for the war with Germany that he anticipated. Having recovered his reputation after the disastrous Dardenelles expedition of 1915, **David Lloyd George appointed him Minister of Munitions in 1917. He was Secretary of State for War and Air from 1919 to 1921, but thereafter he found himself out of favour and excluded from the Cabinet. His warnings of the rising Nazi threat in the mid-1930s and his criticisms of the National Government's lack of preparedness for war went unheeded, but in 1940, Neville Chamberlain** at last stepped down and Churchill began his 'walk with destiny' as Prime Minister of the coalition that was to see the country through five of the most momentous years in its history. Churchill's highly personalized stewardship of Britain's defence and the defeat of Germany and Italy has since been criticized by some historians, but it is impossible to imagine anyone else in the role that he took upon himself—or that anyone else could have even tackled it with such stunning single-mindedness. The loyalty of the British people and the confidence of the allies was crucial in the first two years of the war, and in soon winning both, Churchill had two enormous advantages. First, he was the first premier since the Duke of **Wellington** to have first-hand experience of the killing fields: his experience of war was not confined to—and never inhibited by—the intelligence offered by his high command. Secondly, he had a brilliant mastery of oratory, which enabled him, in just the few minutes of a parliamentary statement or radio broadcast, not only to buttress the nation's resolve but to

banish any shadow of doubt, even in the darkest days of the war, that Britain would be victorious. Churchill's compassion and loathing of the scale of allied casualties made him impatient for that victory, and in the course of four years he travelled more than 150000 miles, shaped the 1941 Atlantic Charter, drew an initially reluctant American people into the battle, masterminded the strategy adopted for the Battle of Britain, Alamein and the North African campaign, and, after the enemy had been defeated, contrived with **Franklin D. Roosevelt** and **Joseph Stalin** the means of gutting Germany's historic status as an epicentre of territorial ambition. That the British electorate should have rejected Churchill in 1945 still seems astonishing, but by 1951, at the age of 77, he was Prime Minister again. Having lived through the horrors of two world wars, he was determined to prevent a third, and to that end, in the office also of Minister of Defence from 1951 to 1952, promoted with a vengeance the development of Britain's first nuclear weapons. Meanwhile, he set about reconstructing a country economically and physically ravaged by war, and when, at the age of 81, he finally relinquished the premiership to **Harold Macmillan** in 1955, its postwar recovery was nearly complete. He was the only Prime Minister ever to be honoured by the attendance of the reigning monarch at No. 10 Downing Street, when **Elizabeth II** dined there with him and his wife, Clementine (1885–1977), on the occasion of his 80th birthday. After his death the public queued for hours to pay homage to their wartime and peacetime leader as he lay in state in Westminster Hall, and tens of thousands lined the route of his funeral procession in a display of affection and respect on a scale that had not been seen since the death of **Victoria**—the queen he had once served as a young army officer. Churchill's apparently limitless energy was directed also at writing some of the finest historical and biographical works of the century. They include *Lord Randolph Churchill* (1906), *My Early Life* (1930), *Life of the Duke of Marlborough* (1933-8), *Great Contemporaries* (1937), the six-volume *History of the Second World War* (1948-54), and *A History of the English Speaking Peoples* (1956-8). In 1953, he was awarded the Nobel Prize for Literature. His son, Randolph Churchill (1911–68) was a notable journalist and author (his works include *The Rise and Fall of Sir Anthony Eden* (1953) and was a Conservative MP from

1940 to 1945. Winston Churchill's grandson, Winston Spencer Churchill (1940–), was elected a Conservative MP in 1970. He briefly held office as Minister for Foreign Affairs (1972-3), and was a highly-effective defence spokesman in Opposition (1976-9). Although he was occasionally critical of some aspects of defence and foreign policy during **Margaret Thatcher**'s premiership, the fact that he has been denied any ministerial post since the Conservatives returned to power in 1979 still seems inexplicable. He has published *First Journey* (1964), *Six Day World* (1967), *Defending the West* (1980) and his autobiographical *Memories and Adventures* (1989), *Churchill: A Life* (1991).

CITRINE, Walter McLennan, 1st Baron
1887–1983

British administrator and trade-union leader, born Wallasey. An electrician by trade, he held office in the Electrical Trade Union from 1914 to 1923, and became general secretary of the Trades Union Congress in 1926. Between 1928 and 1947 he was president of the International Federation of Trades Unions, a member of the National Coal Board, and chairman of the Miners' Welfare Commission. He was knighted in 1935 and received a life peerage in 1946, and a year later was appointed chairman of the Central Electricity Authority. He was a key figure in the postwar development of the trade-union movement and a strong advocate of enlightened worker-management structures of the kind that at last began to emerge in British industry shortly before his death.

CLARENDON, Edward Hyde, 1st Earl of
1609–74

English statesman, born Dinton, Wiltshire. As a member of both the Short Parliament of 1640 and of the Long Parliament, he criticized the unconstitutional actions of **Charles I** and was among those who demanded the impeachment of the Earl of **Strafford**. However, in 1641 he broke with the revolutionaries and followed Charles in retreat to Oxford at the end of the civil war. On the king's defeat in 1646, he joined the future monarch in Jersey, and in 1651 became chief adviser to **Charles II** in exile. Following the restoration, Clarendon was given an earldom and increased his influence by marrying the Duke of York's daughter, Anne. Under the 'Clarendon Code', the supremacy of the

Church of England was assured, but his moderation brought him into conflict with the extremists, and having incurred the wrath of his king for publicly criticizing his private life, and following the arrival of part of the Dutch fleet in the Medway, he was exiled in Rouen until his death. He is buried at Westminster Abbey.

CLARK, Joe Charles Joseph
1939–

Canadian politician, born High River, Alberta. Following his education at Alberta University and Dalhousie University, he worked as a lecturer, and in 1972 entered the House of Commons. Seven years later, as leader of the Progressive Conservative Party, he defeated **Pierre Trudeau** to become Canada's youngest Prime Minister, but lost office a year later. In 1983 he was replaced as party leader by Brian Mulroney, who appointed him External Affairs Minister in 1984.

CLEMENCEAU, Georges Benjamin
1841–1929

French radical politician, born in the Vendée. Born into a middle-class family, he followed his father in studying medicine, but in 1865 left for America to teach in Connecticut. After returning to Paris in 1868, he was elected Mayor of Montmartre and entered the Chamber of Deputies in 1876. Four years later, he founded the radical newspaper *La Justice* and his campaigns against ministerial ineptitude and the corrupt bestowing of honours finally forced the resignation of President Grévy in 1887. After losing his seat in the Chamber in 1893, he continued his ferocious attacks and took up the cause of General **Alfred Dreyfus**. He was a senator from 1902 to 1920, Minister of the Interior (1906), and Prime Minister from 1906 to 1909. He was successful in completing the final separation of Church and State, but his action in using troops to break up strikes lost him Socialist support. Government inefficiency was again the target of his newspaper tirades throughout World War I, and in a bid to restore public morale, President Poincaré appointed him premier, and as Minister for War he made the inspired choice of Marshal Foch as allied general in 1918. He was a strong critic of **Woodrow Wilson**'s idealism at the 1919 Paris Peace Conference, but in 1920 the legislature passed him over in favour of

Paul Deschanel for the presidency, and Clemenceau spent his remaining years travelling in the US and India and devoting himself to literature.

CLEVELAND, (Stephen) Grover
1837–1908

Twenty-second and twenty-fourth US President, born Caldwell, New Jersey. After working in a lawyer's office and as an attorney, he was appointed a district attorney in New York State in 1863 and sheriff of Erie County, but returned to his law practice in 1873. He revived his political career with the Democrats in 1881 as Mayor of Buffalo, and was Governor of New York State from 1883 to 1885.

COBDEN, Richard
1804–65

English economist and politician, born Heyshott, Sussex. Educated at a Yorkshire boarding school, he joined his uncle's business as a clerk in 1819, and in 1828 formed his own partnership trading in calico and fabric printing. After settling in Manchester in 1832, a visit to America and the Levant inspired his free-trade pamphlets *England, Ireland and America* (1835) and *Russia* (1836). As a prominent member of the Anti-Corn Law League, he lectured all over the country, and his contributions to parliamentary debate after entering the Commons in 1841 were acknowledged by Sir **Robert Peel** as being instrumental in securing the law's repeal in 1846. However, Cobden's devotion to his political career brought down his business, but a public subscription of £80,000 saved him from ruin. An opponent of the Crimean War (1853–6), he disputed Lord **Palmerston**'s Chinese policy, and lost his seat in 1857. However, while revisiting America two years later, Cobden was re-elected in his absence and was offered the presidency of the Board of Trade, but declined. Failing health prevented him from attending Parliament, but he subsequently arranged a commercial treaty with France (1860), gave his strong support to the Union during the American Civil War (1861–5), and strenuously opposed British intervention in the Danish question (1864). His *Speeches on Questions of Public Policy* were published in 1870. See also *Richard Cobden* (1987).

COKE, Sir Edward
1552–1634

English jurist, born Mileham, Norfolk. Educated at Norwich School and Trinity College, Cambridge, he was called to the Bar in 1578, and after holding senior offices in the judiciary, entered the House of Commons in 1589 and was Solicitor-General (1592), Speaker (1593), Attorney-General (1594) and Chief Justice and a Privy Councillor. He is famous not only for his prosecutions of the Earl of Essex (1600), Sir Walter Raleigh (1603), and **Guy Fawkes** (1605), but his steadfast opposition to every encroachment on national liberties of the Crown and Church. His independence of thought brought his brief dismissal from the Bench in 1617, but he was soon restored, only to return in 1620 as leader of the Popular Party that frustrated the court with its opposition to Spain and to monopolies. Despite being incarcerated in the Tower of London in 1621 for nine months, he prosecuted his beliefs well into the next reign as the author of the 1628 Petition of Right, and his four *Institutes* represent the earliest textbooks on modern common law.

COLLINS, Michael
1890–1922

Irish politician and soldier, born Cork. After working as a clerk in London from 1906 to 1916, he returned to Ireland and became active in the Sinn Fein independence movement, and was imprisoned in England later the same year for his part in the Easter Rebellion. On the declaration of independence, he raised funds for the movement after all revolutionary organizations had been declared illegal by the British Government, and was subsequently responsible, with **Arthur Griffith**, for negotiating the 1921 treaty that created the Irish Free State the following year. But when **Eamonn de Valera** and his supporters insisted on a fully-independent republic, civil war between the two factions broke out. Collins became head of the provisional Free State Government in 1922, but only 10 days after taking office he was killed in an IRA ambush.

COMBES (Justin Louis) Emile
1835–1921

French politician. After training for the priesthood, he became a physician and in 1885 entered politics as a senator. He was

Minister of Education from 1895 to 1906, and as premier from 1902 to 1905 introduced legislation that completed the separation of Church and State.

COMPTON, John George Melvin
1926–

St Lucian politician, born Canouan, St Vincent and the Grenadines. After graduating at the London School of Economics and being called to the Bar in 1951, he returned to St Lucia to run a law practice, and three years later joined the Labour Party and became its deputy leader. In 1961 he formed the United Workers' Party and became the country's Prime Minister when independence was granted in 1979. Another election later the same year was won by Labour, but Compton took the SLP to victory again in 1982, and again in 1987.

COMTE, Auguste
1798–1857

French philosopher and social theorist, born Montpelier. Considered to be the founding father of sociology, Comte studied at the Paris Polytechnic and made a meagre living as a mathematics tutor before coming under the influence of the social reformer **Saint-Simon** in 1818. Their friendship ended in 1824, as did Comte's marriage after only a year, and in 1826 he suffered a breakdown. Nevertheless, he completed two major works, the six-volume *Cours de Philosophie positive* (1830–42) and the *Système de Politique positive* (1851–4). Comte's theory of positivism embraced the organization and hierarchy of all branches of human knowledge and the concept of society as a basis for social planning and regeneration.

CONFUCIUS
551–479 BC

Chinese philosopher, born Lu (Shantung province). From the age of 19, he worked as a government official, and was eventually promoted to ministerial rank, but his popularity attracted hostility and eventually caused a breach with the emperor. In 497 BC he left Lu to spend 12 years wandering from court to court as a sage, but returned to Lu in 485 BC to spend his remaining years teaching and writing. After his death, his pupils collected his sayings in the *Analects*; later collections are probably derivative. Confucius taught that moral values are the basis of political and

social order, and that benevolence, reciprocity, respect and personal effort should be interpreted pragmatically with regard to individual circumstances rather than according to any abstract system of imperatives.

CONTE, Lamsana
1945–

Guinean politician and soldier. After his promotion through the ranks to become military commander of the Boke region of West Guinea, he led the bloodless coup that followed the death of President Seke Toure in 1984 and established the Military Committee for National Recovery with himself as president. His benign Administration has encouraged thousands of exiles to return to the country, and the loyalty of his army ensured that an attempt in 1985 to depose him was thwarted.

COOLIDGE, (John) Calvin
1872–1933

Thirtieth US President, born Plymouth, Vermont. The son of a farmer and storekeeper, he practised law before entering politics, and as Governor of Massachusetts (1919–20) became famous for using the militia to break the 1919 Boston police strike. He was Republican vice-president from 1921 until 1923, when he succeeded Warren Harding at the White House, and, having notably increased his country's prosperity, was returned with a huge majority in 1924 but declined to stand for a third term. His *Autobiography* was published in 1929.

COSGRAVE, Liam
1920–

Irish politician. The son of **William Cosgrave**, he was educated at St Vincent's College, Dublin, was called to the Irish Bar in 1943, and entered the Dáil in 1943. After a three-year term as Minister for External Affairs from 1954, he was elected Fine Gael leader in 1965 and was president of the Republic from 1973 to 1977.

COSGRAVE, William Thomas
1880–1965

Irish politician. After becoming active in the Irish Nationalist Movement, he was elected to the House of Commons in 1918 but did not take his seat, and following the sudden deaths of Arthur Griffiths and **Michael Collins**, he was the first president (Prime Minister) of the Executive Council of the Irish Free State from 1922 to 1932. His son, **Liam Cosgrave**, held the premiership from 1973 to 1977.

COSTA, Manuel Pinto da
1937–

Sao Tome politician, born Agua Grande. As founder of the Gabon-based Movement for the Liberation of Sao Tome and Principe in 1972, he took advantage of the military coup in Portugal two years later to return to his country and to persuade the Lisbon Government to recognize his party. He became president on Sao Tome's achieving independence in 1975.

COSTELLO, John Aloysius
1891–1976

Irish politician, born Dublin. Educated at University College, Dublin, he was called to the Bar in 1914, and from 1926 to 1932 served as Attorney-General in the Fine Gael Government. In 1948 he headed a coalition that was dominated by his party, and later that year introduced the legislation that transformed the State of Eire into the Republic of Ireland. He continued to lead his party in Opposition after **Eamonn De Valera**'s Fianna Fáil party won power in 1951, but returned as premier from 1954 to 1957, and led the Opposition again until 1959.

COTY, René
1882–1962

French statesman, born Le Havre. After practising law, he entered the Assembly in 1923 and the Senate in 1935, became Minister of Reconstruction in 1947, and President in 1953. After weathering the 1958 crisis in which the Constitution came under threat from the action of French army generals in Algeria, he promoted the return to power of General **Charles de Gaulle**, and introduced a new Constitution before stepping down in favour of de Gaulle with the birth of the fifth repulic in January 1959.

COUSINS, Frank
1904–86

British trade-union leader, born Bulwell, Nottingham. After starting work at the coalface at the age of 14, he became a lorry driver in 1938 and later joined the Transport and General Workers Union as a regional organizer. He was appointed general secretary in 1955, and in 1965 became a Labour MP. He was made Minister of Technology in 1964, but resigned his office and his seat in the Commons a year later in protest at the Government's economic policy, and returned to his former post of TGWU general secretary.

CRAXI, Bettino
1934–

Italian politician, born Milan. Educated at Milan University, in the 1950s he became active in the Socialist youth movement and worked on the party's daily newspaper, becoming chairman of the National Union of Students and a member of the party's central committee in 1957. From 1960 to 1970 he served on Milan's community council, and entered the Chamber of Deputies in 1968. He was made party general secretary in 1976, elected vice-president of Socialist International in 1977, and began a four-year term as Prime Minister in 1983. In Italy's 1991 elections, he retained considerable influence as leader of the second largest party in Christian Democrat Guilio Andreotti's coalition, pressing for decentralized government and a referendum on the establishment of a French-style executive presidency—for which Craxi proclaimed himself to be the most suitable candidate.

CRESSON, Edith
1934–

French politician. A close friend of President **François Mitterrand** for more than 25 years, and having a reputation as a fiery socialist equivalent of **Margaret Thatcher**, she became her country's first woman Prime Minister in May 1991 after the resignation of moderate premier **Michel Rocard** after three years in office.

CRIPPS, Sir (Richard) Stafford
1889–1952

British statesman and economist. Educated at Winchester and New College, Oxford, he emerged as a brilliant student of chemistry who, at 22, had a paper read before the Royal Society. He also studied law and was called to the Bar in 1913 to become the youngest barrister in the country, and soon established a reputation as the country's most brilliant advocate in patent and compensation cases. In 1930, he joined the second Labour

Government as Solicitor-General but declined to serve in the subsequent **Ramsay MacDonald** coalition, but although he came to be identified with the extreme left-wing and—as a committed Christian—with pacifism, he was later highly critical of **Neville Chamberlain**'s policy of appeasement and on the outbreak of World War II was expelled from the Labour Party but remained in the Commons as an independent. In 1940 he was appointed ambassador to Moscow, and two years later began a rapid process of rehabilitation as **Winston Churchill**'s choice of Lord Privy Seal and Leader of the House. After an unsuccessful mission to India to persuade **Mahatma Gandhi** to accept dominion status for the country, he replaced **Beaverbrook** in the key post of Minister for aircraft production for the rest of the war, and Labour's return to power in 1945, he was made President of the Board of Trade. Two years later he was appointed Britain's first Minister of Economic Affairs, and within a few weeks succeeded **Hugh Dalton** as Chancellor of the Exchequer. He successfully caught the conscience of the nation in the period of austerity that followed, to the extent that even the trade unions took the unprecedented step of adopting a self-imposed wage restraint, though he lost popularity over his decision to devalue sterling in September 1949. Ill health forced his resignation a year later. He wrote *Towards a Christian Democracy* (1945).

CRISPI, Francesco
1819–1901

Italian politician, born Sicily. A follower of **Giuseppe Mazzini**'s republican movement, he fled to France after the failure of the 1848 revolution, but returned in 1860 to accept the monarchy of Victor Emmanuel in a bid to unify the country. As a member of the Chamber of Deputies, and president from 1887, he promoted nationalism based on moral unity, abandoned Italy's traditional alliance with France in favour of the Triple Alliance with Germany and Austria, and promoted a settlement in East Africa, Somalia, and Eritrea. However, the disastrous campaign at Adowa in 1896 forced him to resign.

CROCE, Benedetto
1866–1952

Italian philosopher, historian and politician, born Pescasseroli, Aquila. After his parents

and sister perished in an earthquake on Ischia in 1883, he studied at Rome and Naples, and in the bi-monthly review that he founded, *La Criteria*, advocated a state of mind in which art, philosophy, political economy and ethics are complementary, not conflicting, elements in social development. In 1910, he became a senator, and was Minister of Education (1920–1) until **Benito Mussolini**'s rise to power forced him to resign his professorship at Naples. His later works, such as *History as the Story of Liberty*, were strongly anti-Marxian and anti-fascist, and after Mussolini's fall in 1943, Croce played a leading part in resurrecting his country's liberal institutions. His autobiography was published in translation in 1927.

CROKER, John Wilson
1780–1857

British barrister, literary critic and politician, born Galway. Educated at Trinity College, Dublin, he was admitted to the London Bar in 1822, and while practising as a lawyer, wrote several satirical dramatic works and pamphlets advocating Catholic emancipation. Two years after entering the British Parliament in 1807, he co-founded the *Literary Review*, to which he contributed more than 250 articles—including his famous attack on the work of Keats. He was rewarded with a senior Admiralty post (1809–30) for coming to the defence of Frederick, Duke of York (1763–1827) in a scandal concerning the sale of honours conducted by the duke's mistress, Mary Anne Clarke. However, his growing estrangement from Tory reform policies and disagreements with his former close friend, Sir **Robert Peel**, over the repeal of the Corn Laws caused him to leave Parliament in 1832 to resume his literary career. He co-founded the Athenaeum Club, and is credited with inventing the term 'Conservative'. His works include *Stories for Children from English History* (1817), *Essays on the Early French Revolution* (1857), and the play *On the Present State of the Irish Stage* (1804).

CROMWELL, Oliver
1599–1658

English soldier and statesman, born Huntingdon. Educated at Huntingdon Grammar School and Sydney Sussex College, Cambridge, he then studied law in London, and developed his dislike for

Charles I after first sitting in the Commons in 1628. When the king dissolved Parliament the following year, he took up farming in Huntingdon and subsequently at St Ives and Ely. He was a member of the Short Parliament of 1640 that refused the king funds for the Bishops' War, and of the subsequent Long Parliament, in which he moved the Second Reading of a Bill to introduce annual sittings. At the start of the English Civil War in 1642, he raised a troop of cavalry for the Battles of Edgehill and Gainsborough, and in 1644 he brought the war nearer to an end with a cavalry charge against royalist troops at Marston Moor. Back in Parliament, he led the independent faction that shunned reconciliation with the king, and then commanded the army that won a decisive victory over the king's forces at Naseby on 14 June 1645. Cromwell at first initially professed a willingness to negotiate terms by which the throne might be saved, but Charles' success in rallying the Scots from the Isle of Wight brought further fighting in 1648 and Cromwell resolved to rid himself of the king for ever. Charles was taken to Westminster for trial, and Cromwell's signature was among those on the death warrant that brought the king's execution on 30 January 1649. The monarchy was abolished and Cromwell declared the establishment of a Commonwealth with himself as chairman of its Council of State. He brutally brought the last vestiges of Irish resistence to an end by massacring the Catholic garrisons at Drogheda and Wexford, and between 1650 and 1651 defeated at Dunbar and at Worcester the supporters of **Charles II** who had declared him King of Scotland. Frustrated by the obstruction presented by the substantial body of royalists remaining in the Commons, Cromwell dissolved the Long Parliament in 1653 and ruled briefly as head of the Puritan Convention and then, on the implementation of a new Constitution, as Lord Protector. He reorganised the Church of England and established puritanism, brought prosperity to Scotland under his administration, and granted Irish representation in Parliament. He dissolved Parliament again in 1655 with a view to imposing regional rule under 10 major-generals in England, but the experiment failed, and after recalling the Commons in 1656 he was offered the crown. He declined to accept it, but instead won the right to name his son, Richard Cromwell, as Lord Protector. However, his relations with Parliament worsened to bring another dissolution in 1658, and Cromwell continued to rule absolutely until his death later that year. His son held the promised title of Lord Protector for just a year, but failed to emulate his father's iron grip and surrendered the office a year later. On the Restoration in 1660, Oliver Cromwell's body was disinterred from the tomb of kings in Westminster Abbey and hung from Tyburn gallows and afterwards buried there.

CROMWELL, Thomas, Earl of Essex
1485–1540

English statesman, born Putney, London. He served in the French army in Italy, worked as a clerk and wool trader, and even practised law before entering the service of Cardinal **Wolsey** in 1514 and becoming an MP in 1523. From 1525, he acted as the cardinal's chief agent in the dissolution of the smaller monasteries and helped to establish Wolsey's colleges at Ipswich and Oxford. As principal adviser to **Henry VIII** from 1530, Cromwell was made a Privy Councillor a year later, Chancellor of the Exchequer in 1533, and Secretary of State and Master of the Rolls in 1534. He devised the 1534 Act of Supremacy that made Henry head of the Church of England, and between 1536 and 1539, as Vicar-General and deputy head of the Church, supervised the destruction of the remaining important monasteries. In 1539 he was appointed Lord Great Chamberlain and made Earl of Essex, but he incurred Henry's wrath after arranging the king's disastrous, short-lived marriage with Anne of Cleves in 1640, was sent to the Tower of London, and was executed for treason with the consent of a Parliament glad to put an end to his influence.

CROSLAND, (Charles) Anthony Raven
1918–77

British politician. After war service in North Africa and Italy, he continued his studies at Oxford University and then lectured there (1947–50) before entering Parliament as a Labour MP in 1950. He held several Government posts under **Harold Wilson** between 1964 and 1970, and in 1974 started a two-year term as Minister for Environment. He made an unsuccessful bid for the party leadership in 1976, but served **James Callaghan** as Foreign and Commonwealth Secretary before dying suddenly at the age of 59. He wrote *The Future of Socialism* (1956) and *The Conservative Enemy* (1962).

CROSSMAN, Richard Howard Stafford
1907–74

Labour politician. Educated at Winchester and New College, Oxford, he became a lecturer in philosophy for the Workers Educational Association and then joined the editorial staff of the *New Statesman*. During World War II he served as an adviser on political and psychological warfare, and became an MP when Labour returned to power in 1945. At first, his middle-class background (he was the son of a judge with Conservative loyalties) alienated him from the party leadership, and he failed to gain office under either **Clement Attlee** or **Hugh Gaitskell**. However, in 1964 he was rewarded for his support of **Harold Wilson** in the leadership contest in 1963 with a Cabinet post as Minister of Housing and Local Government, and in 1966 was made Leader of the House. After two years as Secretary of State for Social Services, he returned to the *New Statesman* as editor in 1970 on the defeat of the Labour Government, but retired two years later. His three-volume diaries, published posthumously between 1975 and 1977, were notable for flouting the convention by which Cabinet discussions are never made public.

CRUICKSHANK, George
1792–1878

English caricaturist and illustrator, born London. After an early career as an illustrator of children's books, he established his reputation as a political caricaturist with his work for the *Scourge* (1811–16) and the *Meteor* (1813–14). He later brought fine colour etchings to the works of Grimm, Dickens, and Thackeray, and to the series of Harrison Ainsworth's essays that included *Guy Fawkes*. From 1835 he published *Comic Almanack*, one of the precursors of *Punch*, and applied his skills to contributing plates to pamphlets and books for the temperance movement.

CUNNINGHAM, Dr John
1939–

British politician. Educated at Jarrow Grammar School and Durham University, he worked as a lecturer and research chemist before becoming a full-time organiser for the General and Municipal Workers Union in 1968. He served as a local councillor from 1968 before entering Parliament as a Labour MP in 1970. He was private parliamentary secretary to **James Callaghan** from 1972 to 1976, and in the next Labour Government was Energy Under-Secretary from 1976 until the 1979 general election defeat. He was elected to the Shadow Cabinet in 1983, and his increasingly-important contribution as a member of the Labour Front Bench won further recognition in 1990 when he was chosen by **Neil Kinnock** to mastermind Labour's strategy for the next general election, in his capacity as Shadow Leader of the House. As a moderate, he is considered by many both inside and outside his party to be a leading contender for the leadership in the event of another Labour defeat.

CURZON, George Nathaniel, Marquis Curzon of Kedleston
1859–1925

English statesman, born Kedleston Hall, Derbyshire. Educated at Eton and Oxford University, he became a Conservative MP in 1886, and undertook an extensive world tour, which later proved invaluable in his work at the Foreign Office and in India, and provided material for the books on Asiatic Russia, Persia and the Far East that he published between 1889 and 1894. He was made Under-Secretary for India (1891) and for Foreign Affairs (1895) before being appointed Viceroy of India in 1898, aged only 39, and resigning his seat to accept a peerage. However, the pace and extent of his reforms brought friction between him and Lord **Kitchener**, who had been appointed commander-in-chief in 1902, and in 1905 Curzon was eventually compelled to resign. In 1915, he re-entered political life as Lord Privy Seal in the 1915 coalition and a member of **David Lloyd George**'s War Cabinet, and three years later was appointed Foreign Secretary. However, his ambitious plans for post-war international reconstruction brought his estrangement from Lloyd George, and even after successfully representing British interests at the 1922 Lausanne conference, Curzon's reputation for autocracy saw him sidelined by the party kingmakers, who chose **Stanley Baldwin** instead to succeed **Bonar Law** on his resignation in 1923. Curzon remained Foreign Secretary, but poor health forced his resignation a year later, and he died soon after.

CYRANKIEWICZ, Jozef
1911–1989

Polish politician born in Tarnow near Cracow. As Socialist Party secretary in Cracow from 1935, he was taken prisoner by the Germans in 1939, escaped to organize the resistance movement in Cracow, but was recaptured and sent to Auschwitz in 1941. At the end of the war, he was made party secretary-general, and served as Prime Minister from 1947 to 1952. He resumed the premiership in 1954, and held the post until 1970. He became chairman of the Council of State from 1970 to 1972 when he retired.

DACKO, David
1930–

Central African Republic politician, born M'Baiki. After six years in office as the republic's first President from 1960, his government was overthrown by **Jean Bedel Bokassa** and Dacko was placed under house arrest for several years, but in 1976 he agreed to serve his protagonist as an adviser—but with French assistance, Dacko successfully engineered a counter-coup that returned him to power in 1979. In 1981, he was re-elected for a six-year term, but was deposed again later that year by André Kolingba.

DADDAH, Moktar Ould
1924–

Mauritanian politician, born Boutilmit. A former barrister, he became a territorial councillor in 1957, and from 1958 served a 20-year term as Prime Minister of the Islamic Republic of Mauritania. He was placed under house arrest in 1978, and on leaving the country the following year was sentenced in his absence to hard labour for life.

DALADIER, Édouard
1884–1970

French politician, born Carpentras. Leader of the radical socialists from 1927, he was Minister of War and Prime Minister in the short-lived 1933 and 1934 Administrations—the latter lasting only weeks in the wake of the **Stavisky** affair. He was War Minister again in the 1936 Popular Front Government, and two years later became premier. As a pacifist, he was a signatory to the 1938 Munich Agreement, but on the fall of France he was arrested by the Vichy Government and spent the rest of the war interned by the Nazis.

DALAI LAMA (Tenzin Gyatso)
1935–

Spiritual leader and temporal head of Tibet, born Taktser, Amdo. Designated the 14th Dalai Lama at the age of two, he was enthroned in 1940 but was represented by a regency until he achieved adulthood in 1950. In that year, he took refuge in southern Tibet in the wake of an abortive anti-Chinese uprising, but then made peace with the People's Republic and was notional ruler for the next eight years. China's brutal suppression of the 1959 uprising again forced him into exile in the Punjab, and there he established a democratic alternative Government. For two decades, he resisted all attempts by the Chinese to secure his return, insisting that he would do so only if Tibet was given complete independence, but since 1988 he has advanced a compromise solution whereby Tibet would become a self-governing state in association with China.

DALHOUSIE, James Andrew Broun–Ramsay, Marquis of
1812–60

British viceroy, born Dalhousie Castle, Midlothian. He was elected to Parliament at his second attempt in 1838, and went to the Lords on the death of his father the following year. He served in the Board of Trade under both Sir **Robert Peel** and Lord **Russell**, and in 1847 was appointed India's youngest-ever Governor-General. In that office he annexed several new territories, and embarked on a massive programme of civilization that included 3218 kilometres/2000 miles of roads, the extension of the telegraph network over 6436 kilometres/4000 miles, the opening of the Ganges canal, and countrywide irrigation systems. He also successfully suppressed the suttee and thuggee movements, female infanticide, and the slave trade; brought desegregation to the Civil Service, and improved India's trading links and its agriculture, forestry and mining. He returned from India in poor health in 1856 and died four years later.

DALTON, Hugh, Baron Dalton of Forest and Frith
1887–1962

British politician, born Neath, Glamorgan. A Labour MP from 1924, he served as Minister for Economic Welfare (1940), then as President of the Board of Trade in the World War II coalition. As Chancellor of the Exchequer from 1945 in the post-war Labour Government, he nationalized the Bank of England in 1946, but resigned after Budget press leaks the following year. He received a peerage in 1960. His memoirs *High Tide and After* were published in the year of his death.

DANTON, George Jacques
1759–94

French revolutionary leader, born Arcis-sur-Aube. A founder with **Marat** of the revolutionists' Cordeliers' Club, he fled to England in 1791 but returned from exile the following year to take office as Minister of Justice in the new republic. As a member of the National Convention, he voted for the king's execution in 1793 and was among those whose opposition to the Girondists led to the moderates' downfall in 1793. As president of the Jacobin Club, he strove for domestic unity and governmental stability, but lost power to **Robespierre** in the Reign of Terror. Although he had retired from active politics, in 1794 he and his followers were arrested for conspiracy, and despite articulating a defence that won the hearts of the people for its audacity and satire, Danton fell victim to the very Revolutionary Tribunal that he had established, and was guillotined.

DARIUS I
548–486 BC

Persian ruler. Ascending to the throne in 521 BC, he suppressed several revolts while extensively reorganizing his empire's administration and economy, making the Zoroastrian faith the state religion. He expanded his territories to the Caucasus and the Indus, but was less successful in suppressing the Athenians for their part in the Ionian revolt of 499–494 BC, suffering a decisive defeat at Marathon in 490 BC. He died one year before the Egyptian revolt was quelled, while preparing a second action against the Athenians.

DAVIES, Clement
1884–1962

Welsh politician, born Llanfyllin, Montgomeryshire. Called to the Bar in 1909, he entered Parliament for the Liberals in 1929 and became leader of his emasculated post-war party in 1945. Although a man of great principle who refused several offers of office in Conservative Administrations, his equally strong reluctance to enter into any form of power-sharing served not to achieve his objective of reinforcing the Liberals' place in the political structure as a viable alternative government but rather to diminish credibility and influence still further—a trend that was not reversed until the party's renaissance in the 1980s, ironically as a consequence of the Liberal–Social Democrat pact.

DAVIS, Jefferson
1808–89

American Confederate President, born Christian County, Kentucky. After a military education at West Point, he resigned his commission and became a cotton planter, but after entering Congress in 1845, he fought with distinction in the 1846–7 Mexican War. He was a senator between 1847 and 1850 and Secretary of War from 1853 to 1857, and as leader of the States Rights Party persuaded Congress in 1860 not to outlaw slavery. The measure's subsequent rejection by the lower house and by the Democrats gave the presidency to **Abraham Lincoln** and triggered Mississippi's secession from the Union in 1861 and Davis's nomination as Confederate President for a six-year term. The ensuing Civil War brought his Government to collapse in 1865, and Davis was kept in custody for two years while awaiting trial for treason. However, he was released without trial in the 1868 amnesty, and having retired from political life wrote *The Rise and Fall of the Confederate Government* (1881).

DAWES, Charles Gates
1865–1951

American politician, born Marietta. Republican Vice-President (1925–9) under **Calvin Coolidge**, he had earlier served as a member of the commission that drew up the schedule of World War I German reparation payments to the allies. He received with **Austen Chamberlain** the Nobel Peace Prize in 1925, and was ambassador to Britain from 1929 to 1932.

DAY, Sir Robin
1923–

British barrister, journalist and broadcaster, born London. After World War II service in the Royal Artillery, he was called to the Bar in 1952 and worked for the British Council in Washington before starting a new career in journalism, joining ITN in 1955. In 1959, he moved to the BBC presenting the leading current affairs programme Panorama from 1959 to 1972. After standing unsuccessfully as a Liberal candidate in the 1959 general election, he consolidated his reputation as an acerbic and entertainingly irascible commentator and interviewer in numerous radio and TV broadcasts, and his work was honoured in 1974 with the Richard Dimbleby award for factual television. His enduring public popularity owes much to his obvious disdain for most politicians of all parties, and his bow-tie trade-mark makes him instantly recognizable even to those who cannot easily identify any other political commentator. Among all his TV confrontations, the public probably best remember the occasion when his place in society was instantly downgraded by **Margaret Thatcher** during a major TV general election interview, when she persisted in referring to him as *Mr* Day despite the fact that he had long since received a knighthood. His books include *Day by Day* (1975) and *Grand Inquisitor* (1989).

DAYAN, Moshe
1915–81

Israeli soldier and statesman, born Palestine. As a leading figure in the underground militia, he was imprisoned for two years and then released to serve in the British Army in World War II. He received a commission in the Israeli Army in 1948, and was chief-of-staff at the time of the Gaza and Sinai actions in the 1956 Suez War. He was elected to the Knesset for Labour in 1959 and was Agricultural Minister under **Ben-Gurion** until 1964. In 1966 he founded with Ben-Gurion the Rafi Party, and, while still in Opposition, was chosen to serve as Defence Minister in the 1967 Six-Day War, when the patch that he wore as a result of losing an eye in World War II served as the most instantly-recognizable trademark of any military leader since **Churchill**'s siren suit and cigar. His subsequent clearing of mined Jerusalem consolidated his popularity, though as Defence Minister again from 1969 he was unable to repeat his earlier military success, and in the wake of Israel's disastrous start to the 1973 Yom Kippur War, he was compelled to resign the following year. He rejoined the Cabinet as Foreign Secretary in 1977 and was instrumental in the negotiations that achieved the Camp David agreement which brought peace with Egypt. In 1979, he resigned over **Menachem Begin**'s inflexible approach to eventual Palestinian autonomy on the West Bank and Gaza. He died three years later, shortly after founding a new centre party. *Diary of the Sinai Campaign* (1966).

DEBRAY, Regis
1941–

French theorist, born Paris. Educated at the École Normale Supérieure, he was attracted to Latin America as a sympathetic base from which to expound his Marxist philosophies, and in the 1960s worked closely with revolutionary **Che Guevara**. In 1967, he was sentenced by the Bolivians to 30 years' imprisonment but was released in 1970 and returned to France to advise President **François Mitterrand** on Third World economies. His books include *Strategy for Revolution* (1970) and *The Power of the Intellectual in France* (1979).

DEBRÉ, Michel Jean Pierre
1912–

French statesman, born Paris. A senator from 1948, he gave his backing to **Charles de Gaulle**, and in 1958 was rewarded with his appointment as Minister of Justice, in which post he drafted the new constitution that was adopted later the same year. He was premier of the Fifth Republic from 1959 until being displaced by **Georges Pompidou** in 1962. Between 1966 and 1973 he served as Finance, Foreign Affairs and Defence Ministers, and was elected to the European Parliament in 1979.

DE GASPERI, Alcide
1881–1954

Italian politician, born Pieve Tesino, Austria-Hungary. He was a member of the Austrian Parliament from 1911 to 1916, and when Trentino was united with Italy in 1919 he sat as a member of the Italian Chamber of Deputies until it was outlawed by **Benito Mussolini** in 1925. As a co-founder of the Italian Popular Front, he was arrested, but before he could be incarcerated he found sanctuary in the Vatican, where he remained until Mussolini's downfall in 1943. He returned to active politics two years later, helping to create the centrist Christian Democratic Party, and became Prime Minister in 1945. In 1953 he resigned after finding it impossible to secure a parliamentary majority without the unacceptable compromise of Communist support, to become party secretary until his death.

DE GAULLE, Charles André Joseph Marie de
1890–1970

French general and statesman, born Lille. Drawing on his experience as an army officer in World War I, he developed a new theory of mechanised strategy that was expounded in *The Army of the Future* published in 1932, and which, although largely ignored by the French military, clearly inspired the German blitzkrieg of 1940. De Gaulle's prescience was rewarded with promotion to general and junior War Secretary the same year, but he sought refuge in England days before the signing of the French Armistice to found the Free French Army. Though largely ignored by both **Winston Churchill** and **Franklin D. Roosevelt**, he served as a focus for the resistance movement, in which he played an active role during the rest of the war. As the country's natural first choice as postwar leader, he failed to form an all-party coalition and resigned in 1946 to found a new party, Rally of French People, which took 40 per cent of the votes in the 1947 election. He relinquished its leadership in 1953, and, in the wake of the failure by successive Administrations to resolve the Algerian question, was thus free to accept office as First President of the Fifth Republic in 1958. In 1959–60, he granted self-government to all French African colonies—including Algeria, which finally achieved independence in 1962—and at home consolidated France's growing international importance by establishing its own nuclear deterrent, fostering better relations with West Germany, blocking Britain's 1962 and 1967 attempts to enter the Common Market, and recognizing the Peking Government in 1964. Despite his extensive use of the referendum, his autocratic presidential style and the growing popularity of the Left among the new young electorate created by the post-war baby boom, he won re-election in 1965 after a second vote, and recovered with an overwhelming victory in 1968 on seeking a mandate in the wake of violent student riots. However, the electorate's rejection in a referendum the following year on his proposals for Senate and regional reforms brought his resignation, and he died a year later. To the British and Americans in particular, De Gaulle epitomized Gallic obstinacy and self-interest, but it cannot be disputed that while he could not match Churchill's brilliance in wartime, he was a considerably more influential and effective, if less endearing, national leader in peacetime. His three-volume memoirs, *Mémoires de Guerre*, were published between 1954 and 1959.

DE KLERK, F. W. (Frederik Willem)
1936–

South African statesman, born Johannesburg. After practising as a lawyer in Vereeniging, he entered Parliament as a National Party candidate in 1972, and between 1978 and 1989 served in the Cabinets of both **B.J. Vorster** and **P.W. Botha**. He became Transvaal party leader in 1982, and replaced Botha as national leader and acting state president in 1989. Later the same year, he took his party to election victory, albeit with a reduced majority, promising meaningful reforms of the country's despised system of apartheid, with a view to improving its international relations. In 1990 he gave the world the greatest proof possible of his intentions by releasing **Nelson Mandela** after 26 years' imprisonment, though De Klerk's readiness also to recognize the African National Congress not only brought a hostile reaction from rightists in his own party but served to escalate tribal violence between Mandela's supporters and those of Chief **Buthelezi**'s Inkatha movement. The same year, the Government scrapped the Separate Amenities Act that provided for segregated beaches, toilets, parks and transport—and the Group Areas Act, which prohibited coloureds from living in white residential areas, was repealed the following year. In January 1991, De Klerk's adopted 24-year-old son, Willem, announced his engagement to a 22-year-old mixed-race student, Erica Adams.

DELORS, Jacques Lucien Jean
1925–

French economist and politician, born Paris. Educated at the University of Paris, from 1945 he worked for the Banque de France and many other leading financial and economic institutions before beginning his notable association with the European Community as head of the Economic and Monetary Committee in 1979, Finance Minister from 1981 to 1983, and then Minister for the

Economy, Finance and Budget (1983–4). As the Community's President and Commissioner for Monetary Affairs since 1985, he is popularly seen as the EEC's Chancellor of the Exchequer, and in that capacity was openly critical of Britain's failure to enter sooner into full membership of the European monetary system—which was only achieved in 1990—and its continuing resistance to a common currency based on a soft ecu. He will retire as socialist president of the European Commission in 1992—the year that sees the launch of the Single European Market.

DEMIREL, Süleyman

1924–

Turkish politician, born Istanbul. Trained as an engineer, he achieved high status as an expert on hydro-electric schemes, working also in the USA and Middle East, before entering politics in the 1960s. He was soon elected as president of the centrist Justice Party, now part of the True Path Party. From 1965 onwards he served three terms as Prime Minister, before the 1980 military coup outlawed political activity. He was twice kept in detention by the new regime, in 1980 and 1983.

DE MITA, Luigi Ciriaco

1928–

Italian politician, born Fusco, Avellino. As a Christian Democrat, he became a member of the Chamber of Deputies in 1963 and headed several Ministries throughout the 1970s. In 1982 he was appointed party secretary-general, and became Prime Minister in 1988 following several attempts by others to form a coalition, but his Government lasted only one year.

DENG XIAOPING

1904–

Chinese politician, born Guangan, Sichuan. After studying in France and Russia, he took part in the 1934–6 Long March, served as political commissar to the People's Liberation Army during the 1937–49 Civil War, and entered the CCP Politburo in 1955. As its head of secretariat in the 1960s, he worked closely with President **Liu Shaoqi**, but in the 1966-9 Cultural Revolution he was denounced and banished to a provincial tractor factory. Rehabilitated in 1973 by the intervention of **Zhou Enlai**, whom he had first met in Paris, he was made vice-premier, but was forced to seek refuge again following his sponsor's death in 1976. He was reinstated the following year and restored to office as party vice-chairman, state vice-premier and chief-of-staff, making him the most powerful man in the Government. Together with **Hu Yaobang** and **Zhao Ziyang** he began implementing an ambitious programme of economic reforms that borrowed from the West and were designed to broaden China's international trade. Having retired from the Politburo in 1987, he was able to distance himself from those responsible for the Tiananmen Square massacre and his reputation emerged more or less unscathed by the domestic and international recriminations that followed it.

DENKTAS, Rauf

1924–

Turkish politician, born Ktima, Paphos. Educated at The English School, Nocosia, he studied law in Lincoln's Inn, was called to the Bar, and after working in a Nicosia law practice from 1947 to 1949, was a Crown prosecutor, then acting Solicitor-General from 1956 to 1958. He was elected President of the Communal Chamber in 1960 and won re-election in 1970, and from 1975 served an eight-year term as President of the Turkish Federated State of Cyprus. In 1983 he was elected President and Prime Minister of the Republic of Northern Cyprus, and in 1991 called on UN Secretary-General **Javier Perez de Cuellar** to devise a solution to the island's split as Perez de Cuellar's last challenge before his retirement at the end of 1991.

DERBY, Edward Geoffrey Smith Stanley, 14th Earl of

1799–1869

English politician, born Knowsley Hall, Lancashire. He entered Parliament in 1830, became Chief Secretary for Ireland in the same year, and as Colonial Secretary three years later introduced legislation for the emancipation of West Indian slaves. He broke from the Whigs in 1831, declined office under **Peel**, and sat as an independent MP until resigning in 1844 to enter the Lords. By spearheading the protectionists in the Upper House who opposed Peel's repeal of the Corn Laws, Derby became Conservative leader by default, and in 1851 briefly served as Prime Minister. He became premier again in 1858 but resigned after losing a vote of confidence.

A year after becoming Prime Minister yet again in 1866, he introduced the Second Reform Act with the support of **Benjamin Disraeli**, whom he nominated as his successor in 1868.

DESAI, Shri Morarji Ranchhodji
1896–

Indian politician, born Bhadeli, Gujarat. As a member of Congress from 1930, he was twice imprisoned for civil disobedience but was made Revenue Minister in the Bombay Government in 1937. He was jailed again between 1941 and 1945 for his anti-British campaigning, but again returned to office as Revenue Minister (1946) and Home, and Chief Minister (1952). In 1956 he entered the national Government as Minister for Commerce and Industry, and was Finance Minister from 1958 until his resignation in 1963. He stood for the premiership in 1964 and 1966, but held office as deputy premier and Finance Minister under **Indira Ghandi** for two years before resigning over policy differences. In 1974 he advocated political agitation in Gujarat and began a fast, but was interned when a state of emergency was proclaimed. On his release in 1977 he was made leader of the Janata opposition coalition of four non-communist parties and became Prime Minister following elections later the same year. However, his Government fared no better in uniting India's political and religious factions and he was forced to resign in 1979. *The Story of My Life* (1979.

DE VALERA, Eamon
1882–1975

Irish statesman, born Brooklyn, New York, of Spanish-Irish parentage. After working as a mathematics teacher following his graduation from Dublin University, he joined the nationalist movement and in 1916 was sentenced to death for his part in the Easter Rebellion. The sentence was lifted on the intercession of the US consul, and he was released in 1917 to win election as a Sinn Fein candidate to the Dail, but he declined to take his seat. His further imprisonment for campaigning against World War I conscription helped his party to achieve a massive victory in the 1918 election. De Valera escaped from Lincoln prison later the same year and toured America as president of the extremist faction that refused to sit in the Westminster Parliament, and subsequently led the militants in the civil war prompted by the concessions made by **Michael Collins** in the 1921 Anglo-Irish treaty. Its approval by the Dail forced De Valera's resignation as President, but he subsequently adopted more moderate policies and took his new Fianna Fail party to victory in 1932. Over the next three years, he effectively cut all ties with Britain and established Eire under a new constitution that also provided for neutrality in World War II. The republic finally left the Commonwealth under **John Costello**'s Administration in 1948 and De Valera returned as Prime Minister in 1951, remaining in office almost continuously until his election as President in 1959.

DIEFENBAKER, John George
1895–1979

Canadian politician, born Normanby Township, Ontario. A barrister, he entered the Dominion Parliament in 1940, and became leader of the Progressive Conservatives in 1956. The following year, he led his party to victory over the Liberals for the first time in 22 years and remained in power until 1963, when his personal resignation and his party's electoral defeat followed a Cabinet split over his opposition to the deployment of American nuclear warheads. He then led the Opposition for four years before retiring from politics.

DIMITROV, Georgi Mikhailovich
1882–1949

Bulgarian politician, born Pernik. Initially a union activist, he first sat in Parliament in 1913 as a Socialist, but in 1919 helped to found the Bulgarian Communist Party, and after an abortive attempt to overthrow King Ferdinand I, he fled to the Soviet Union in 1923. As head of the Communist International's (Comintern) European section, he was accused of complicity in the burning of the Reichstag in 1933 and was returned to Moscow, where he served as Comintern's secretary-general from 1935 to 1943. In World War II, he led the resistance and became Prime Minister in 1946. His closeness to Marshal **Josip Tito** brought him into disfavour with **Joseph Stalin**, and he died while undergoing medical treatment in a Moscow hospital.

DIORI, Hamani
1916–

Niger politician, born Benin. After representing Niger in the French National Assembly (1946–51, 1956–8), as leader of the Niger Progressive Party he became Prime Minister in 1958 and the country's first President two years later. By maintaining close relations with France, his regime enjoyed a stability untypical of post-independence African states and he was re-elected in 1965 and 1970. However, party dissension led to him being deposed in 1974 in a coup led by his army chief-of-staff, **Seyni Kountche.**

DIOUF, Abdou
1935–

Senegalese politician, born Louga. He studied in Paris and worked as a civil servant before starting his political career, and in 1970 was appointed Prime Minister by President **Léopold Sédar Senghor**, whom he succeeded in 1980. In 1982, Diouf was chosen to head the informal confederation of Senegambia, and he was re-elected as his country's President in 1983 and 1988.

DISRAELI, Benjamin ('Dizzy'), 1st Earl of Beaconsfield
1804–81

British statesman and author, born London. After an early successful career as a London barrister, he found fame in 1826 with his first novel, *Vivian Grey*, and entered Parliament at his fourth attempt in 1831. The political novel *Coningsby* followed in 1844, and *Sybil* in 1846—the same year as Disraeli's famous attack on **Peel** for betraying the Tories by repealing the Corn Laws, which was largely responsible for his leader's downfall. As Chancellor of the Exchequer under Lord **Derby** from 1852, he discarded protectionism but failed to prosecute his Budget and was succeeded by **William Gladstone** in the subsequent coalition. He returned to power with Derby in 1858, but further failures to introduce reforming legislation brought his resignation, though he gained a reputation as a gifted opposition orator in the ensuing seven years of Liberal rule. As Chancellor again from 1866 in the third Derby Administration, he was at last able to pilot the 1867 Reform Bill, and became Prime Minister the following year. From the start of his 1874 Administration, Disraeli began his curious but enormously influential relationship with Queen **Victoria**, drawing her out of the recluse-like state into which she had fallen after the death of Prince **Albert** and rekindling her interest in nurturing and expanding her empire. Within a year, he had secured for Britain a half-interest in the Suez canal and made his monarch Empress of India. He initially avoided any involvement in the Turks' brutal hostilities against the Bulgarians, but with the Russians threatening Constantinople in 1878, his diplomatic skills not only averted war by achieving 'peace with honour' but added Cyprus to the British Empire. The final years of his premiership were characterized by falling world trade and higher taxation, bringing the Tories massive defeat in 1880. Disraeli died in retirement the following year, having established forever his place as the late 19th century's most remarkably resilient statesman.

DOBRYNIN, Anatoly Fedorovich
1919–

Soviet diplomat and politician, born Krasnoya Gorka. An aircraft engineer during World War II, he joined the diplomatic service in 1941 and worked at the Washington embassy from 1952 to 1955. Appointments as junior Foreign Affairs Minister and UN under-secretary followed, and he headed Moscow's American department until returning to Washington as ambassador in 1962. He became a full member of the party's central committee in 1971, and in 1986 was chosen by **Mikhail Gorbachev** as his Foreign Secretary. He retired two years later.

DOE, Samuel Keynon
1951–90

Liberian soldier and politician, born Tuzon. Having risen to the rank of master sergeant after 10 years' army service, in 1980 he engineered a coup in which President William Tolbert was killed, and replaced him as head of state. The following year he appointed himself general and commander-in-chief, and in 1984 founded the National Democratic Party, which he narrowly took to victory in elections one year later. He remained in power until he was killed in 1990.

DOI, Takako
1929–

Japanese politician, born Tokyo. After lecturing on the Japanese constitution at

Doshisha University, he entered the Diet in 1969 and since 1986 has been the leader of the Japanese Socialist Party. In 1989, he became the leader of the Upper House.

DOLLFUSS, Engelbert
1892–1934

Austrian statesman, born Texing. As leader of the Christian Democrats, he became Chancellor in 1932 and overcame the Socialist Opposition by the simple expedient of fragmenting its factions by suspending Parliament, and then reconvening it for the purpose of giving him almost absolute power. His efforts to resist the German invasion undermined by his loss of public support after he had authorized the shelling in Vienna of the homes of dissident workers, and he was murdered by the Nazis during an attempted coup.

DOUGLAS, Clifford Hugh
1879–1952

British economist. An engineer by training, he developed the economic theory of social credit, which advocated the regulated distribution of money in the form of a national dividend to overcome the lack of purchasing power— which he argued was the cause of all economic depression. His most successful follower was the Albertan premier **William Aberhart**.

DOUGLAS–HOME

see **Home of the Hirsel**

DOUMERGUE, Gaston
1863–1937

French statesman, born Aigues-Vives. Though he won election to the National Assembly in 1893 as a radical socialist deputy, he increasingly embraced rightist policies. In 1913 he served for one year as the republic's first Protestant President. He was Premier again between 1924 and 1931.

DREES, Willem
1886–1988

Dutch politician, born Amsterdam. After working as a bank clerk and civil servant, he joined the Socialist Democratic Workers Party, and after becoming its chairman in 1911, he sat in the Second Chamber from 1933 until 1940, when he played a leading role in the resistance movement. As Social Minister in 1947 he introduced a state pension, and he began a 10-year term as Prime Minister in 1948.

DREYFUS, Alfred
1859–1935

French army officer, born Milhausen, Alsace. As a captain and a member of the General Staff, in 1894 he was wrongly accused of acting as a German spy and sent to Devil's Island, but the discovery of his innocence two years later was suppressed by anti-Semitic officers. Dreyfus's case was taken up by Emile Zola, whose famous open letter indicting the authorities' prejudices and duplicity, *J'accuse*, captured the public's imagination and forced a retrial in 1899. Forged documents again produced a guilty verdict, but Dreyfus was immediately given a presidential pardon and was finally exonerated by a civilian court in 1906. Restored to his army rank, Dreyfus was honoured with the Legion of Honour for his service in World War II, and German papers published in 1930 confirmed his innocence.

DUARTE, José Napoléon
1925–90

El Salvador politician. Educated as a civil engineer in the USA, he founded the Christian Democratic Party in 1960 and became President in 1970, but two years later he was impeached and exiled to Venezuela for seven years. He regained the presidency with US backing on returning in 1980, but lost power again in the 1982 election. There followed another two years of deep political unrest, but Duarte became President again in 1984; illness brought his resignation in 1989.

DUBČEK, Alexander
1921–

Czechoslovakian statesman, born Uhrovek, Slovakia. Having spent his childhood in the Soviet Union, he joined the Communist Party in 1939 and after fighting with the patriots in World War II he began his rise through the party hierarchy to achieve the top post of First Secretary in 1968. He immediately set about implementing an extensive programme of economic and social reforms that included the abolition of censorship and the suspension of former president **Novotny** and other hardliners. Moscow reacted first by sending Russian troops into the capital, then by removing Dubček from office, to be replaced by **Gustav Husak**. Both Houses elected him President of the Federal Assembly, but he was expelled from the Presidium later the same year, and in 1970 was banished from the party. He spent the next 18 years working as a clerk, but having publicly pledged support for the reforms of **Mikhail Gorbachev**, he was given freedom to travel, and with Czechoslovakian democratization in 1990, he was feted as an honoured elder statesman and the country's greatest post-war pioneer of democratic government. He was awarded the Sakharov Peace Prize in 1989 and his book about the events of 1968, *The Soviet Invasion*, was published in 1990.

DUBOIS, William Edward Burghardt

1868–1963

American Black writer and editor, born in Great Barrington, Massachusetts. He studied at Fisk University. Tennessee, and at Harvard, where his doctoral thesis was on the suppression of the African slave trade. He was professor of economics and history at Atlanta University (1897–1910). He was co-founder of the National Association for the Advancement of Coloured People (1909), and edited its magazine. *Crisis* (1910-34). He wrote a number of important works on slavery and the colour problem, including *The Souls of Black Folk* (1903), *John Brown* (1909), *The Negro* (1915), *The Gift of Black Folk* (1935), and *Colour and Democracy* (1945). He also wrote a novel, *The Dark Princess* (1928). A passionate advocate of radical Black action he joined the Communist party in 1961, and moved to Ghana at the age of 91, where he became a naturalized citizen just before he died.

DUKAKIS, Michael Stanley

1933–

American politician, born Boston. The son of Greek immigrants, he entered the Massachusetts legislature for the Democrats in 1962, and became state governor in 1974. His autocratic style lost him the governorship in 1978, but he took the office again in 1982, promising a more consensual administration. His second term coincided with the state's emergence as a centre of US high technology and its new-found prosperity helped assure his re-election with an increased majority in 1986. He defeated **Jesse Jackson** as his party's choice as 1988 presidential candidate, but his excessively neo-liberal ticket gave **George Bush** his first term as US President.

DULLES, John Foster

1888–1959

American politician, born Washington DC. Trained as a lawyer, he was an adviser to President **Woodrow Wilson** and to the American delegation at the 1945 conference to draw up the charter of the United Nations. He served as representative to the UN's General Assembly in 1946, 1947 and 1950, and in 1953 was appointed Secretary of State, in which office he became famous for his efforts to improve US international relations, travelling more than 180 thousand miles and visiting 40 countries in his first year in that post. He was instrumental in bringing West Germany into NATO, and was a strong opponent of the Anglo-French coalition against President **Gamel Nasser** in the 1956 Suez crisis. He brought his strong Christian beliefs and sense of morality but little original thought to international affairs, but his overall contribution to at least enhancing America's reputation abroad brought him the country's highest civil decoration, the Medal of Freedom, shortly before his death from cancer in 1959. His books include *War, Peace and Change* (1939) and *War or Peace* (1950).

DURKHEIM, Emile

1858–1917

French sociologist, born Paris. After studying at the École Normale Supérieure, he taught at Bordeaux University and the Sorbonne, and in 1913 was appointed to France's first chair of sociology. He developed the theory of objective sociology, by which social phenomena are explained by reference to other social facts; and suggested that every society is subject to a powerful collective conscience that strongly influences the behaviour of its individual members. He also regarded religion as civilization's way of expressing unifying ideals.

DUVALIER, François ('Papa Doc')

1907–71

Haitian dictator, born Port-au-Prince. After a medical education, he was effective in combatting malaria on the island as public health director in 1946 and Health Minister in 1949, and opposed the military Government that came to power in the 1950 coup. In 1957, he enjoyed an overwhelming victory in the army-supervised presidential elections, only to establish a regime far more ruthless than that which had preceded it. Duvalier's 15-year presidency was characterized by ruthless suppression of all political opposition, during which he is thought to have ordered the murder of countless of his opponents by his voodoo civil militia, the notorious Tonton Macoutes, while his country's perilous economy survived only because of American aid. On his death, he was succeeded by his son, Jean-Claude ('Baby Doc').

DUVALIER, Jean-Claude ('Baby Doc')
1951–

Haitian politician, born Port–au–Prince. He succeeded his father as President-for-life at 20, and continued to use the hated Tonton Macoutes to enforce his rule. Having shown every sign of following in his father's footsteps, he was overthrown in 1986 in a military coup led by General Henri Namphrey and fled to the South of France.

EANES, Antonio Ramalho dos Santos
1935–

Portuguese soldier and politician, born Alcains. A former army officer, in 1974 he joined the dissident movement that overthrew Marcello Caetano and was briefly head of the country's television service until his appointment as chief-of-staff in 1975. He was elected President the following year.

EBAN, Abba (Aubrey Solomon)
1935–

Israeli diplomat and politician, born Cape Town, South Africa. A graduate of Cambridge, he taught oriental languages in England in the 1930s, then joined allied headquarters during the World War II. He went to work at the Jerusalem-based Middle East Arab Centre in 1944, and was appointed ambassador to the USA in 1948. In 1959 he returned to Israel, was elected to the Knesset, and until 1974 served under several Prime Ministers, most notably as Foreign Minister between 1966 and 1974. His own bid for the premiership in 1989 was unexpectedly defeated by **George Price**.

EBERT, Friedrich
1871–1925

German politician, born Heidelberg. After working as a saddler and journalist, he joined the Social Democrats and entered the

Reichstag in 1912. He was elected party chairman the next year, and after leading the Socialist majority in the 1918 revolution, he was elected the German Republic's first President in 1919.

ECEVIT, Bülent
1925–

Turkish writer and statesman, born Istanbul. A former government official and journalist, he entered Parliament for the centre-right Republican People's Party in 1957, was Minister of Labour for four years, and in 1966 was appointed party secretary. He was made chairman in 1972, and became coalition Prime Minister two years later, but resigned within months over differences with other factions in the Government. His staunch advocacy of Turkey's independence within NATO and of improving relations with Greece brought him the premiership again in 1978, but he was deposed by the military in 1980 and imprisoned twice for criticizing the new regime. He retired from political life in 1987.

EDEN, Sir (Robert) Anthony, 1st Earl of Avon
1897–1977

British statesman, born Bishop Auckland. Following distinguished World War I service, for which he received the MC, he was elected a Conservative MP in 1923. He was appointed Foreign Secretary by **Neville Chamberlain** in 1935, but resigned three years later over Government policy on fascist Italy. He returned to office in 1939 as Dominion Secretary, and, as Secretary for War from 1940, formed the Home Guard and negotiated a 20-year treaty with the Soviet Union in 1942. In 1945, he led the British delegation at the conference that established the United Nations, and on Labour's return to power, served as deputy Opposition leader until the Conservative victory in 1951, when he again became Foreign Secretary. He played an important role in the Korean and Vietnam settlements of 1954, and in negotiating with Egypt the withdrawal of British troops from Suez. He was chosen by **Churchill** to succeed him as Prime Minister in 1955, and was already fully preoccupied with the Cyprus problem, the implications of the new Soviet regime under **Nikita Khrushchev**, and the death-penalty abolition crisis when, in June 1956, Egyptian military forces seized the Suez Canal. In November, against the advice of Lord **Louis Moutbatten** and **Dwight D. Eisenhower**, Eden ordered British troops to retake the canal in an Anglo-French action ahead of the invading Israeli forces, confident of victory despite the threat of Russian intervention. In the face of bitter criticism from the US Government and United Nations, desertion by many senior members of his Cabinet, including **Harold Macmillan**, and the catastrophic effect on the economy—with 15% of Britain's gold and dollar reserves exhausted within three weeks—Eden was compelled to cancel the action on 3 December. Widely condemned for both decisions and suffering from failing health, Eden resigned in January 1957, to be succeeded by Macmillan. He received an earldom in 1961. His three volumes of memoirs were published between 1960 and 1965.

EDWARD VIII

1894–1972

King of Great Britain and Ireland, born Richmond, Surrey. The eldest son of **George V**, he served in the Royal Navy and in the British Army in France in World War I before succeeding to the throne on his father's death in 1936. His wish to marry a twice-divorced American, Wallis Simpson (1896–1986), provoked a constitutional crisis, with the British and Dominion Governments refusing to accept her as queen, even in a morganatic marriage. Despite **Stanley Baldwin**'s exhaustive efforts to persuade the king of his duty to his country, Edward announced his abdication in a radio broadcast on 11 December 1936. He was given the title Duke of Windsor and married Simpson in June 1937 in France, to which they returned after the war to live the rest of their lives. Edward served as Governor of the Bahamas from 1940 to 1945. There is some speculation about the Duke's pre-war and even wartime association with the Fascists, and it has even been suggested that **Adolf Hitler** offered Edward the throne in the event of a German victory, if he would publicly support the Nazi cause.

EINSTEIN, Albert

1879–1955

German-Swiss-American mathematical physicist, born Ulm, Bavaria. Educated at Munich, Aarau and Zurich, he took Swiss nationality in 1901 and achieved fame with the publication from 1905 of his theories of relativity, receiving the Nobel Prize in 1921. Further work on gravitation and the speed of light resulted in him being offered special professorships in Zurich and Prague. He was director of the Kaiser Wilhelm Physical Institute in Berlin from 1914 until 1933, when **Adolf Hitler**'s rise to power prompted him to move to America to lecture. In 1940, he wrote to President **Franklin D. Roosevelt** warning him of the implications of Germany's developing the atom bomb, though he was unsuccessful in persuading the President to initiate or escalate America's nuclear development program until the Japanese attack on Pearl Harbour. However, the effects of the A-bomb dropped on Hiroshima in 1945 caused Einstein to campaign actively for the international limitation of atomic weapons. In 1952, he declined an invitation to succeed **Weizmann** as President of Israel. His non-technical works included *Why War* (1933).

EISENHOWER, Dwight David

1890–1969

American general and thirty-fourth US President, born Denison, Texas. A graduate of West Point, he was chief military assistant under General MacArthur and groomed by General George C Marshall for command of the allied campaign in French North Africa in 1942. His success there brought his appointment as Supreme Commander of Operation Overlord, the cross-Channel invasion of 1944. There was some criticism of his strategy in that campaign, in not advancing to take Berlin, which allowed Russia to emerge as Europe's leading military power, but his reputation remained largely intact, and in 1950 he was appointed Supreme Commander of NATO's land forces. Two years later, he was the Republicans' triumphant victor over **Adlai Stevenson** in the presidential elections, brought an end to the war in Korea, and won re–election in 1956. His largely successful terms in office owed more to his military objectivity and emphasis on the rehabilitation of Europe than to his political sophistication.

EISNER, Kurt

1867–1919

German politician, born Berlin. Having led the successful 1918 Bavarian revolution, he was appointed the new republic's first President in 1919, but was assassinated in Munich later the same year.

ELIOT, Sir John
1592–1632

English statesman, born Port Eliot, Cornwall. A parliamentarian from 1614, he broke with Buckingham in 1625 and was instrumental in securing his impeachment. His denouncement of taxation helped to force the Petition of Rights from **Charles I** in 1628, but his continued criticism of the monarch brought his incarceration, in 1629, in the Tower of London, where he died three years later.

ELIZABETH I
1533–1603

Queen of England and Ireland. The daughter of **Henry VIII** and his second wife, Anne Boleyn, she was brought up in the Protestant faith and survived several early intrigues against her to take the throne in 1588 on the death of **Mary I**. Elizabeth immediately repealed her half-sister's Catholic legislation and gave full force to the Church of England. The forced abdication and imprisonment of **Mary Queen of Scots** led to Elizabeth being excommunicated by Rome and to increasing suppression of her Catholic subjects from the 1560s, which inevitably produced numerous plots against her and led to Mary's execution in 1587. England's support of the Dutch rebellion against Spain, and Elizabeth's unspoken patronage of the activities of Sir John Hawkins and Sir Francis Drake in seizing Spanish possessions in the New World, prompted Philip II to launch his disastrous Armada in 1588—the last invasion of the British Isles attempted during Elizabeth's reign. The cost to the taxpayers of the numerous military expeditions that she sanctioned brought famine and social unrest in the 1590s and the enactment in 1597 of the Poor Law, which placed on parishes a duty to provide for the most needy. Despite extensive voyages of discovery by Drake and Sir Walter Raleigh, Elizabeth's only real colony remained Ireland, the exploitation of which by English settlers provoked the 1597 rebellion under Hugh O'Neill. Although Elizabeth had numerous romances, she never married, content in the knowledge that her heir-apparent, **James VI** of Scotland, would succeed her as Protestant monarch, which he did, as James I of England, on her death in 1603.

ELIZABETH II (Elizabeth Alexandra Mary)
1926–

Queen of Great Britain and Ireland and Head of the Commonwealth. On the death of her father, **George VI**, in February 1952, she was proclaimed queen and was crowned in June 1953. In the first years of her reign, she benefited enormously from the coaching of **Winston Churchill**, and showed her gratitude and personal affection for him by being the first British monarch ever to dine at No. 10 Downing Street on the occasion of his retirement as Prime Minister in 1955. She has kissed hands with more British premiers than any other monarch, and, apart from Churchill, is thought to have favoured **Harold Wilson** most. As Head of the Commonwealth, she remains greatly respected in most of her territories, and even by those countries that have long since achieved independence. Through her weekly audiences with the Prime Minister of the day, she has not flinched from offering advice on every aspect of her nation's domestic and international affairs, and many premiers have discovered to their peril that they should never underestimate her knowledge and understanding of the minutiae of their Administrations' difficulties and shortcomings. In recent years, she has increasingly expressed her concern about the effect of Government policies on the more vulnerable sectors of society, and it is widely thought that relations between her and Britain's first woman Prime Minister became strained during the final years of **Margaret Thatcher**'s premiership. Her abdication is rumoured almost annually, but her continuing excellent health and stamina, and the great love that her subjects still have for her, suggest that she will remain on the throne until the end of the century.

ELLIOT, Walter
1888–1958

Scottish politician. A Conservative MP from 1918, he held office as Secretary of State for Scotland (1936–8) and Minister of Health (1938–40), and wrote and broadcast widely on political topics. His wife, Katharine (1903–90), was created Scotland's first life peeress, Baroness Elliot of Harwood, in October 1958.

EMPSON, Sir Richard
1460–1510

English politician. Appointed Speaker of the

House of Commons in 1491, he subsequently acquired the offices of High Steward of Cambridge University and Chancellor of the Duchy of Lancaster. He became infamous for his oppressive practices when, during the reign of **Henry VII**, he was reponsible for collecting taxes and other moneys due to the Crown, and was beheaded by **Henry VIII** for tyranny and treason. His name is sometimes invoked by modern day politicians as a warning to Chancellors of the Exchequer against introducing oppressive fiscal measures.

ENGELS, Friedrich
1820–95

German socialist, born Barmen. Resident mainly in England from 1842, he used his experience of his father's Manchester cotton factory in writing *Condition of the Working Class in England* (1844), and while in Brussels the same year, met **Karl Marx** and worked with him on drafting the first Communist Manifesto, published in 1848. They both returned to Germany, where Engels fought with the revolutionaries in the unsuccessful Baden uprising of 1849. On the death of his father, he sold his interest in the business and supported Marx financially for the rest of his life. Following Marx's death in London in 1883, Engels devoted the rest of his life to translating his colleague's writings, including the second and third volumes of *Das Kapital* (1885, 1894).

ERHARD, Ludwig
1897–1977

German economist and politician, born Fürth, north Bavaria. As a student and then teacher of economics at Nuremberg, he was unable to apply his education in the 1930s because of his refusal to join the Nazi Party, but immediately after World War II he was appointed professor of economics at Munich, and served as Bavaria's Minister for Economic Affairs before being appointed economic director for the American and British zones of occupation in 1947. He entered the Bundestag for the Christian Democrats in 1949, and as Finance Minister under **Konrad Adenauer**, his policies of social free enterprise were instrumental in bringing about post-war West Germany's economic miracle. He began a three-year term as Adenauer's successor as Chancellor in 1963.

ERSHAD, Lieutenant-General Hossain Mohammad
1930–

Bangladeshi soldier and politician, born Rangpur. After officer training in East Pakistan, he rose to the rank of colonel during the 1971 Civil War, and as a major-general from 1975, he was deputy chief-of-staff to the Bangladeshi army until 1978, then chief-of-staff. His next promotion was to lieutenant-general in 1979. In 1983 he seized power and governed first as chief martial law administrator, then Prime Minister, becoming President in December 1983. He was re-elected President in 1986, but faced increasing pressure for a return to civilian government. In December 1990 he lost the support of the army and was forced to step down.

ES–SA'ID, Nuri (Nouri Said Pasha)
1888–1958

Iraqi politician, born Kirkuk. During training for the Turkish army he fled to Egypt when his pan-Arab activities became suspect, and he fought against the Turks in World War I. In 1921 he was appointed Iraq's first Chief of General Staff, and became Defence Minister a year later. He was Prime Minister several times from 1930 onwards, and died at the hands of extremist assassins after the 1958 coup of **Abdul Karim Kassem**.

EVATT, Herbert Vere
1894–1965

Australian jurist and politician, born East Maitland, South Australia. A lawyer, he sat in the New South Wales State Assembly, and was a High Court Justice from 1930 to 1940, when he entered the Federal Parliament for Labour. As Minister of External Affairs (1941–9), he frequently visited Britain and represented his country in **Winston Churchill**'s war Cabinet, and was elected President of the UN General Assembly in 1949. From 1951 he headed the Labour Opposition, but a party split between social reformists and the Catholic faction, which gave priority to suppressing communism, prompted him to relinquish the leadership in 1960. He continued to give public service as Chief Justice of New South Wales until his retirement in 1962.

EYADEMA, (Étienne) Gnassingbe
1937–

Togolese soldier and politician, born Pya, Lama Kara. Following extensive foreign service in the French army, he was made commander-in-chief of his own country's army in 1965, and two years later led the bloodless coup that overthrew President Nicholas Grunitzky. He has banned all political parties other than the Togolese People's Assembly, which he founded, and, having survived several attempts to depose him, has begun to introduce a measure of democracy.

FAISAL II (Faisal Ibn Ghazi Ibn Faisal el Hashim)
1935–58

King of Iraq, born Baghdad. Succeeding to the throne at the age of four on the accidental death of his father, Ghazi, in 1939, he was educated at Eton and then ended the regency of his uncle, Emir Abdul Illah, by taking the throne in 1953. In the wake of the 1956 Suez crisis, he pledged continuing support for Egypt, but disagreements between the two states led him in 1958 to form a new federation with King **Hussein** of Jordan to counter the United Arab Republic and Syria. Perhaps preoccupied with threats further afield, he failed to detect the extent of public discontent with his own reign, and in July 1958, Faisal, his entire household, and his Prime Minister were murdered in the military coup led by **Abdul Kassem** that transformed Iraq into a republic.

FAISAL, Ibn Abdul Aziz
1905–75

King of Saudi Arabia, born Riyadh. Having served as his country's representative at the United Nations for several years, in 1958 he became virtual ruler despite the fact that his brother, Saud, remained on the throne until abdicating in 1964. His enlightened reign saw not only the emergence of Saudi Arabia as one of the world's great oil powers but the intelligent application of its huge new wealth to the benefit of the country's social infrastructure. Nevertheless, inter-family rivalries led to him being assassinated by his nephew in 1975.

FAKUDA, Takeo
1905–

Japanese politician and financier. He entered Government service in the Ministry of Finance in 1929, where he remained until 1950, entered the House of Representatives in 1952, and served three terms as Finance Minister (1965–6, 1968–71, 1973–4). He became Deputy Prime Minister in 1974, simultaneously holding office as director of the Economic Planning Agency, before beginning his two-year term as Prime Minister in 1976. He was also twice president of the Liberal Democratic Party (1966–8, 1976–8).

FALKENDER, Marcia Matilda, Baroness Falkender (née Marcia Williams)
1932–

British political worker and Labour peeress. After reading history at Queen Mary College, London, she joined the administrative staff at Labour Party headquarters, but she quickly assumed greater responsibilities in the research department and came to the notice of **Harold Wilson**, who recruited her as his private and political secretary in 1956. After Wilson's 1964 general election success, Falkender played a vital role in overturning a Whitehall and City establishment used to more than a decade of sympathetic Tory rule, overhauled No. 10's creaking administration, and devised a new open-door policy that encouraged Ministers to maintain a dialogue with the Prime Minister outside the Cabinet room. The process is brilliantly and often riotously described in her book *Inside No. 10* (1972). She was made a life peer in 1974.

FANFANI, Amintore
1908–

Italian politician. A former professor of political economics, he is notable not so much for the brilliance of his premierships as a Christian Democrat but for their number. He first became Prime Minister in 1954, and held that office again in 1954, 1958–9, twice between 1960 and 1963, and in 1982–3. He held the presidency of the Italian Senate from 1968 to 1973, then became Prime Minister again in 1980–1, 1983, and 1987.

FAROUK I
1920–65

Last King of Egypt, born Cairo. Educated at English public schools and at the Royal

Military Academy in Woolwich, London, he took the throne in 1937, dismissed Prime Minister Nahas Pasha, and busied himself with devising a somewhat idiosyncratic programme of economic development and land reform. His prevarication as Axis troops threatened Egypt in 1942 prompted the British to insist on Pasha's reappointment, and Farouk's new-found postwar freedom from tiresome matters of state and his huge personal wealth allowed him to indulge his extravagant tastes and preference for a playboy lifestyle. His subjects' disaffection finally manifested itself with the 1952 army coup engineered by General **Mohammed Neguib** and Colonel **Gamal Nasser**, leading to Farouk's abdication and the founding of the Egyptian republic. He first fled to Italy, and died in exile in Monaco.

FAWCETT, Dame Millicent

1847–1929

English suffragette and educational reformer, born Aldeburgh, Suffolk. The younger sister of Elizabeth Garrett Anderson—the first woman to practise medicine in England—she became active in the suffrage movement after her marriage to the political economist Henry Fawcett. She led the National Union of Women's Suffrage Societies from 1897 until 1918, but disapproved of the militant tactics adopted by the followers of **Emily Pankhurst**. She also campaigned for women to be permitted to enjoy higher standards of education, and founded Newnham College, Cambridge, in 1871. She wrote *Political Economy for Beginners* (1870) and *The Women's Victory—and After* (1920).

FAWKES, Guy

1570–1606

English conspirator, born York. Of Protestant parentage, he developed his fervent Catholicism while still a schoolboy, having been taught about **Henry VIII**'s ruthless subjugation of the Catholics 40 years earlier, and appalled by the persecution of his Catholic friends. In 1592, he fought with the Spanish in the Netherlands, and in 1603 rode to Spain in a fruitless attempt to persuade the king to raise an army against his Protestant homeland. The following year, Fawkes secretly returned to London to join the small group of conspirators, led by Robert Catesby, who devised a plan to blow up the

Chamber of the House of Lords during the State Opening. The plot was supposedly discovered with only hours to spare before its execution, and Fawkes and seven other conspirators were beheaded. There is, however, strong evidence to suggest that they were merely pawns in an elaborate hoax, engineered by the state to discredit Rome.

FEATHER, Victor Grayson, Baron Hardie

1908–76

British trade union leader, born Bradford. Educated at Hanson Grammar School in his home town, he became a trade unionist on getting his first job at a local store at 14, and became shop steward a year later and branch chairman at 21. He joined the headquarters staff of the Trades Union Congress in 1947, and as assistant secretary from 1947 to 1960 travelled widely in Europe and in India and Pakistan, helping to establish new labour organisations. He succeeded George Woodcock as General Secretary in 1969, and proved adept at balancing the demands of more extreme unions in the TUC with the realities of life under a rightist Conservative Administration, exemplified by the Industrial Relations Act of 1972, which imposed strict controls on the circumstances in which a union's membership could take disruptive action. His ingenious response was to form with employers an independent body to arbitrate in labour disputes, thus pre-empting many of the Act's provisions. He retired in 1973, became president of the European Trade Union a year later, and was ennobled in 1974.

FERDINAND I

1503–64

Holy Roman Emperor. The second son of Philip I, King of Castile, and younger brother of the emperor Charles V, he was made ruler of the family estates in Germany in 1521, and married Anna, daughter of the Bohemian and Hungarian monarch, Ladislas II, the same year. He subsequently took the throne of Bohemia in 1527, while leaving inviolate the Hapsburg possessions, but a rival claimant with Turkish support denied him the Hungarian throne. He achieved conciliation between the Roman Catholics and Protestants, and became emperor on Charles' abdication in 1558.

FERRARO, Geraldine Anne
1935–

American politician, born Newburgh, New York. Of Italian Catholic parentage, she was educated at Fordham University and New York Law School, and headed a successful practice from 1961 to 1974. She entered municipal politics as a Democrat in 1974, and from 1978 headed a Supreme Court bureau for the victims of violent crime. She was elected to the House of Representatives in 1981, and was later chosen by **Walter Mondale** as the first woman to run as vice-presidential candidate. Her reputation was damaged by newspaper reports about tax avoidance by her husband, businessman John Zaccaro, and she retired from politics after the Democrats' defeat in the 1984 election.

FITT, Gerard, Baron Fitt
1926–

Northern Ireland politician, born Belfast. After working as a merchant seaman for 12 years, he became active in local politics, and in 1962 was elected to represent an Eire seat in the Northern Ireland Parliament. In 1972, he founded the Social Democratic and Labour Party, which he represented at Westminster for nine years, but then resigned as its leader to take the Labour Whip again. Unflinching in his opposition to sectarian violence both by republicans and loyalist extremists, he has himself been the subject of at least one attempt on his life. His conciliatory stance led to the loss of his Belfast seat in the 1983 general election, and he was made a life peer the following year.

FITZGERALD, Dr Garrett
1926–

Irish politician, born Dublin. The son of a former External Affairs and Defence Minister in the Irish Free State, he was educated at Belvedere College, University College, and King's Inns, Dublin, and lectured at the former in political economy from 1959 to 1973, when he was elected to the Dail for Fine Gael in 1969. He held office as Foreign Affairs Minister for four years from 1983, was elected party leader, and subsequently served two terms as Prime Minister (1981–2, 1983–7). He was an architect of, and a signatory to, the 1985 Anglo-Irish Agreement, but his party's popularity continued to wane, and he resigned the leadership in 1987.

FIVE, Kaci Kullmann
1950–

Norwegian politician, born Oslo. She was deputy chairman of the Conservative Party from 1977 to 1981, when she first entered the Storting, and vice-chair of the parliamentary party until her appointment as Minister of Trade and Shipping in 1989, in the right-wing coalition that collapsed in 1990. In April 1991 she was elected leader, in the expectation that she would breathe new life into the main opposition party after five years of decline under three elderly male leaders. Her election made her Norway's third female political leader, with Mrs Gro Harlem Brundtland, Labour Prime Minister, and Centre Party chief Ms Anne Enger Laghnstein.

FLATHER OF WINDSOR, Baroness
(Shreela Flather)
1938–

Britain's first Asian woman life peer, created 1990. Born in Lahore, she attended University College, London, and was called to the Bar in 1962. After working as a teacher, she entered politics in 1976 as the first female member of an ethnic minority in Britain to be elected a councillor, and has since served on numerous advisory committees concerned with prison reform, housing, social services, and ethnic rights. She was a member of the Commission for Racial Equality from 1980 to 1986, in which year she was elected Mayor of Windsor and Maidenhead. In 1987, she was chosen as UK delegate to the European Community's economic and social committee.

FOOT, Michael Mackintosh
1913–

British statesman and journalist, born Cornwall. After graduating from Oxford, where he was president of the Union, he joined the left-wing weekly magazine *Tribune* in 1937, gaining promotion through its editorial ranks until assuming the editorship in 1955. He served concurrently as acting editor of the London *Evening Standard* (1942–4) and as a political columnist on the pro-Labour national daily newspaper *Daily Herald* (1945–55). In 1960, he entered Parliament as MP for the Welsh constituency of Ebbw Vale, and eventually joined the Cabinet as Employment Secretary (1974–6), becoming deputy party leader in 1976. He replaced

71

James Callaghan as party leader in 1980, but he proved no match for **Margaret Thatcher** in her second general election contest in 1983—for despite being a man of undoubted political integrity, his rather detached air and characteristically dishevelled appearance did little to impress voters in the first election to rely heavily on exploiting the media, and TV in particular, to sway the electorate. He resigned as party leader shortly after Labour's defeat—but far from retreating quietly to the Back Benches, he continued to contribute frequently to parliamentary debate, impressing even the newest and bluest Tory MP with what was, after all, a mere shadow of his once great mastery of rhetoric. In 1990, he announced his intention not to stand at the next election, and that he had no wish to take the seat in the Lords that he would almost certainly have been offered. His published work includes *Guilty Men* (1958), *Debts of Honour* (1980), *Loyalists and Loners* (1980), *The Politics of Paradise* (1988), and a two-volume biography of **Aneurin Bevan** (1962, 1973).

FORBES, George William

1869–1947

New Zealand statesman. As leader of the United (formerly Liberal) Party, he became Prime Minister in 1930, but the country's parlous economy compelled him a year later to enter into a coalition with the Reform Party, but their combined efforts did little to counter the Depression and he resigned in 1935.

FORD, Gerald R(udolph)

1913–

Thirty-eighth President of the USA, born Omaha, Nebraska. Educated at the University of Michigan and Yale Law School, he saw wartime service with the US Navy before establishing his own practice in 1946. In 1949, he entered the House of Representatives for the Republicans, and first came to the notice of a wider public in 1963, as a member of the Warren Commission that investigated the assassination of **John F. Kennedy**. He was Leader of the Lower House between 1965 and 1973, in which year **Richard Nixon** invoked the 25th Amendment for the first time in history, to nominate Ford as America's fortieth Vice-President. He automatically assumed the presidency on Nixon's resignation in 1974 over the Watergate scandal, and while his motive in granting his predecessor a pardon was to bury the affair, his action only served to prolong the furore. He survived two assassination attempts in 1975 to stand as presidential candidate in his own right the following year, but was defeated by **Jimmy Carter**. His wife recovered from a well-publicized alcohol problem to found the Betty Ford Clinic, which pioneered the use of counselling as a long-term cure for addictive conditions.

FORREST, John, 1st Baron Forrest of Bunbury

1847–1918

Australian explorer and politician, born Bunbury, Western Australia. After a successful early career in government service, he was made surveyor-general in 1883, and was then appointed Western Australia's first premier (1890–1901). In the first Commonwealth ministry, he served as Minister of Defence (1901–3), and held various other offices until achieving in 1918 the distinction of being the first Australian politician to be raised to the British peerage. He died on the sea voyage back from England, after taking his seat in the Lords for the first time.

FOX, Charles James

1749–1806

English statesman, born London. Educated at Eton and Hertford College, Oxford, he entered Parliament for the Liberals at 19, and served Lord North's Administration as a Lord of the Admiralty and Commissioner of the Treasury. An opponent of British coercion during the American War of Independence, he was made a Secretary of State on the fall of North's Government in 1792, and formed a coalition with his political mentor a year later, but it collapsed when the Lords rejected Fox's India Bill. With **William Pitt** taking power, Fox led a formidable Opposition that benefited not least from his brilliance as an orator, and which exploited to the full his opponent's discomfiture over the antics of the regency and the trial of **Warren Hastings**. He brought a degree of moderation to Pitt's policy towards the French Revolution, and was a leading opponent of the war with France, eventually securing peace after returning to office in 1806 on Pitt's death. To him would have fallen also the kudos of abolishing the slave trade, but he died shortly before his Bill was due to go before Parliament.

FRANCO (BAHAMONDE), Francisco Paulino Hermenegildo Teodulo ('El Caudillo')

1892–1975

Spanish dictator, born El Ferrol, Galicia. After commanding the Spanish Foreign Legion in Morocco, he was made chief-of-staff in 1935, and a year later was sent to govern the politically unstable Canary Islands. At the outbreak of the Spanish Civil War, he returned to Morocco to raise an army of Legionnaires and Moorish troops, and on returning to Spain led, with German and Italian help, the forces that, three years later, overthrew the Republican Government. He then established a single-party state under the control of his Falange Party, and in World War II contrived to maintain Spain's neutrality, refusing **Adolf Hitler** permission to launch an attack on Gibraltar from Spanish territory. He remained indisputably in control of his country's affairs for the next two decades, but the growth of its tourist industry from the 1960s and Franco's decision to allow the US to establish air bases there in return for economic aid not only brought Spain new prosperity but its people an awareness of their isolation from mainstream Europe, and regional opposition eventually compelled Franco to encourage a more liberal Cortes and to nominate as his rightful successor **Juan Carlos**, who assumed the restored throne on Franco's death.

FRANKLIN, Benjamin

1706–90

American statesman and scientist, born Boston, Massachusetts. The 15th of his parents' 17 offspring, at 12 he was apprenticed as a printer on the newspaper, the *New England Courant*, owned by one of his brothers, James, and took over its running when his brother was imprisoned by the Speaker of the Assembly for his editorial attacks on the Administration. From 1724, Franklin worked in London for two years before returning to Philadelphia to found his own successful printing company. He entered public service in 1736, holding successively the offices of clerk of the Assembly and postmaster-general. In 1746, he began his famous experiments with electricity, in which he identified positive and negative currents, defined the true nature of lightning, and introduced the use of conductors to protect buildings from lightning damage, for which

work he was elected a Fellow of the Royal Society. He also identified the course of the Gulf Stream and conceived the use of thermometers to navigate it, and defined the solar heat-absorbing characteristics of different colours. In 1747, politics again became dominant in his life, and he was sent to England to protest at the taxation of the colonies without a reciprocal right of representation. When negotiations collapsed, he returned to the USA to participate in the events that resulted in the Declaration of Independence on 4 July 1776. Later that year he was sent to cultivate ties with the French, and was successful in persuading them to enter into an alliance and to supply armaments for the ensuing war. After Britain's recognition of American independence in 1785, Franklin remained in Paris as US envoy for two years, and subsequently served three terms as president of Pennsylvania state. He retired from public life in 1788, having also helped to draft the American Constitution.

FRASER, John Malcolm

1930–

Australian politician, born Melbourne. After graduating from Oxford University, he became in 1955 the House of Representatives' youngest MP, and went on to hold senior office in Liberal Administrations as Army Minister (1966–8), Defence (1969–71) and Education and Science (1968–9, 1971–2). He became party leader in 1975, to serve as caretaker premier for a month during the constitutional crisis of that year. He continued as Prime Minister in the subsequent Liberal-National Country coalition formed in December 1975, until Labour's victory—only the second in 33 years—in 1983. He retired from politics shortly afterwards, to take up farming in West Victoria.

FRIEDAN, Betty (Elizabeth)

1921–

American feminist and writer, born Peoria, Illinois. Educated at Smith College, she was transformed from a housewife to a bestselling author overnight with the publication in 1963 of *The Feminine Mystique*, which reappraised the role of American women and analyzed their frustration at their submissive role in society. Benefiting from the new climate of equality that had arrived under the Democratic Government of **John F. Kennedy**, she founded the National Organization for

Women in 1966, and led the Women's Strike for Equality in 1970. The success of her campaigns was largely due to their absence of stridency, as the avoidance of competing aggressively with the hitherto dominant sex was fundamental to her teachings. Her books include *It Changed My Life* (1977) and *The Second Stage* (1981).

FRIEDMAN, Milton
1912–

American economist, born New York. His education in Chicago and New York was followed by eight years at the National Bureau of Economic Research (1937-45), and during his professorship at Chicago University from 1946 to 1983, he developed and refined his monetarist and free-market theories, which contradict those of **John Maynard Keynes** in postulating that a country's economy, and hence its inflationary tendencies, can be effectively ordered by controlling its money supply. In Britain, his notions were enthusiastically adopted by **Margaret Thatcher** on coming to power in 1979, but their appropriateness to the UK, and their viability within the European monetary system in particular, was increasingly called into question with the unification of Europe, Britain's impending entry into its exchange-rate mechanism, and the prospect of the single European market in 1992. The recipient of the Nobel Prize for Economics in 1976, he served as an adviser to **Ronald Reagan**'s Administration between 1981 and 1988. His books include *Capitalism and Freedom* (1962), and *Inflation: Causes and Consequences* (1963).

FUCHS, Klaus Emil Julius
1911–88

German-born British physicist and spy, born Frankfurt. As the son of a pacifist Protestant churchman, he was brought up to embrace a creed known as Christian Communism, and was a brilliant scholar at Kiel and Leipzig Universities. He fled to Britain to escape the Nazis in 1933, and on his release from internment in 1942, he became a British citizen and quickly established his credentials to be chosen to study atomic theory in America, as part of Britain's own nuclear weapons development programme. In 1946, he was appointed head of theoretical physics at Harwell, but in 1950 was put on trial accused of serving as a Russian spy for six years. He was stripped of British citizenship and imprisoned, and on his release in June 1959 he went to East Germany and worked at its nuclear research centre until his retirement in 1979.

FULBRIGHT, James William
1905–

American politician and lawyer, born Sumer, Missouri. After studying at Oxford as a Rhodes scholar, and at George Washington University law school, he entered the House of Representatives for the Democrats in 1942, where he promoted American membership of the United Nations. He went to the Senate in 1944, where he sponsored an international exchange scholarship scheme, and in 1954 distinguished himself as a memorable opponent of the anti-communist witch hunts conducted by **Joseph McCarthy**. A constructive and courageous liberal, he pioneered more liberal attitudes to communist China and Cuba, and decried American involvement in the Vietnam war. His books include *Old Myths and New Realities* (1965) and *The Arrogance of Power* (1967).

GADDAFI, Colonel Muammar
1942–

Libyan soldier and politician. Born into a nomadic family, he was largely self-taught in his early childhood, but by the 1950s he was sufficiently educated to win a university place, only to abandon his studies to enter a military academy in 1963. In 1968, he secretly formed the Free Officers Movement, which overthrew King Idris the following year, when Gaddafi became chairman of the Revolutionary Command Council, promoted himself to its highest rank, and assumed the post of commander-in-chief of the armed forces. He soon embarked upon a policy of complete nationalism by expelling foreigners and closing British and US air bases while encouraging a revival of Islamic fundamentalism. His harbouring of international terrorists, patronage of pro-Palestinian outrages in the West, and active support of other anarchic activities—which included the training of IRA terrorists and the supply of arms to the organisation—eventually triggered the US bombing of the Libyan capital with British approval in 1988. In declaring his unqualified support of Iraq's invasion of Kuwait in 1990, he was alone among leaders of other Arab states seeking a solution to the

Palestine question, and Gaddafi found himself increasingly isolated after the UN's announcement at the end of the Gulf War that it would not entertain his formal participation in any future negotiations on the issue.

GAIRY, Sir Eric Matthew
1922–

Grenadian politician. In 1950 he founded the country's first political movement, the left-of-centre Grenada United Labour Party, and was a member of the Legislative Council (1951–2, 1954–5) before being appointed Minister of Trade in 1956 and Chief Minister and Minister of Finance in the Federation of the West Indies (1967–74). He became Prime Minister in 1974, but was ousted five years later by the left-wing leader Maurice Bishop.

GAITSKELL, Hugh Todd Naylor
1906–63

British politician, born London. Educated at Winchester School and New College, Oxford, he joined the socialist movement during the 1926 general strike, and on leaving university joined the Workers Educational Association and lectured in economics to Nottinghamshire miners. In 1938 he became reader in political economy at the University of London, and seven years later entered Parliament. He was given a junior portfolio the following year, and in 1947 was made Minister for Fuel and Power. Following his appointment as Minister of State for Economic Affairs, he became in 1950 the youngest Chancellor of the Exchequer since **Arthur Balfour**. His decision to introduce National Health Service charges prompted the resignation of **Aneurin Bevan** as Health Minister, which was the beginning of a long feud between Gaitskell and the party's left wing. After defeating Bevan to succeed **Clement Attlee** as party leader in 1955, he bitterly opposed Prime Minister **Anthony Eden**'s handling of the 1956 Suez fiasco, worked at softening Labour policy from one of outright nationalization to the development of a shareholder state, and narrowly won the support of the 1961 Labour Party conference in reversing its decision a year earlier to make unilateral nuclear disarmament official party policy. Gaitskell was also a keen European, and in his final years in office strongly supported Britain's entry into the EEC. He wrote *Money and Everyday Life* (1939).

GALBRAITH, John Kenneth
1908–

Canadian-born American economist, born Ontario. Educated at Toronto, California and Cambridge Universities, he emigrated to the USA in 1931, and in 1939 was appointed assistant professor of economics at Princeton University. He was professor of economics at Harvard (1949–75), during which period he served as an economic adviser to **John F. Kennedy**, and, from 1961 to 1963, as ambassador to India. His large and influential body of works includes *American Capitalism: the Concept of Countervailing Power* (1952), *The Affluent Society* (1958), *The Age of Uncertainty* (1977), *A History of Economics* (1987), and his autobiography, *A Life in our Times* (1981).

GALTIERI, Leopoldo Fortunato
1926–

Argentine soldier and politician, born Caseras, Buenos Aires. After entering the National Military College, he was commissioned in 1945 and, as a lieutenant-general by 1979, joined the junta that in 1976 had deposed Isabel Peron, who had succeeded her husband, **Juan Peron**, on his death. He succeeded General Viola as head of state in 1981, and when the country's economy continued to worsen and to threaten Galtieri's position, he sought to retrieve his popularity by ordering the invasion of the Falkland Islands (Malvinas), whose sovereignty had long been disputed between Argentina and Britain. However, the Argentine occupation was soon ended by British forces, and the following year Galtieri was court-martialled for negligence and sentenced to 12 years' imprisonment.

GAMBETTA, Lon Michel
1838–82

French politician, born Cahors. As a lawyer, he became popular for his leftist views and after being elected a deputy in 1869, was among those who proclaimed the republic in 1870 following **Napoleon III**'s surrender. As Minister of the Interior of the Government of National Defence, he escaped by balloon to Tours, and was dictator of France for five months, continuing to send forces against the Germans even when Paris capitulated. However, his decree disenfranchising the royalty was rejected by his colleagues, and he resigned and went to Spain in 1871. On his return to France, he was re-elected, and after the fall of the commune became head of the republicans. When the pro-monarchist Duc de Broglie took office in 1877, civil war seemed inevitable, but was averted by Gambetta and President MacMahon. After a brief imprisonment for sedition, Gambetta won re-election and MacMahon resigned. As president of the Chamber of Deputies from 1879, he formed a Cabinet, but after its refusal to accept his proposals for proportional representation in 1882, he resigned and died a few months later from a gunshot wound, though whether he was murdered or died by his own hand is not clear.

GANDHI, Indira
1917–84

Indian politician, born Allahabad. The daughter of **Pandit Nehru**, she was educated in India and at Somerville College, Oxford, and after becoming actively involved in the independence movement, joined the Congress in 1950 and became party president in 1959. She was made Minister of Information in 1964, and two years later became Prime Minister on the death of **Lal Shastri**. After allegations of corruption were made against her in 1975, she declared a state of emergency that lasted for two years, and in the 1977 general election her party was defeated and she lost her parliamentary seat. After she was acquitted of all charges in 1978, she formed her own Indian National Congress (I) Party, and returned as Prime Minister following the 1980 election. In October 1984, she was assassinated by members of her own Sikh bodyguard following the storming of the Golden Temple at Amritsar and the massacre of 3000 Sikhs.

GANDHI, Rajiv
1944–91

Indian politician, the eldest son of **Indira Gandhi**. Educated at Shiv Nikentan School, Delhi, University of London, and Trinity College, Cambridge, he worked as a pilot for Air India from 1972 to 1981, when, on the death of his younger brother, Sanjay, he inherited his parliamentary seat as an MP for the Congress Party founded by his mother. He was elected general secretary of the party in 1983 and president in 1984, in which year, following the murder of his mother, he also became Prime Minister. He began a cam-

paign of modernizing his country's industrial infrastructure, but was implicated in a bribery scandal in 1987 and was heavily defeated in the general election held two years later. On 21 May 1991, while new elections that seemed certain to return him as leader of 800 million Indians after 18 months in the political wilderness were still under way, the 48-year-old leader was killed by a bomb hidden in the clothing of a woman who handed him a bouquet as he was about to address a rally near Madras. The assassination, thought to be the work of a Sri Lankan Tamil guerrilla group, brought to an end a dynasty that had ruled India for most of the years since it gained independence in 1947.

GANDHI, Mohandas Karamchand (Mahatma Gandhi)
1869–1948

Born Porbander, Kathiawar, the son of a Chief Minister and a strict Hindu, he was married at 13 and after continuing his education studied law in England and was called to the Bar in 1891. After working as a lawyer in India and in South Africa from 1893 to 1914, he led peaceful demonstrations by fellow countrymen who objected to registering as aliens and forced the Transvaal Government to recognize monogamous marriages celebrated according to Indian rites, and subsequently secured better conditions for Indian labourers. In 1915 he returned to India to campaign for the 'untouchables' in the caste system, and when the British Government refused to grant independence, he embarked on his long struggle for self-rule, using the passive tactics that had proved so successful in South Africa. However, acts of violence by some of his followers brought Gandhi's imprisonment in 1922 under a six-year sentence, but he was released early in poor health. After becoming president of the National Indian Congress Party in 1924, he launched a new campaign of civil disobedience, and was jailed again in 1930, but the British authorities were forced to release him when his fasting threatened his life. Between 1935 and 1941, Gandhi went into virtual retirement, and although he gave his moral support to Britain in World War II, refused any further involvement on the ground that India had not been consulted. After reviving his campaign for self-rule, he was imprisoned between 1942 and 1944, and on his release contributed to the negotiations that brought India's independence in 1947. He continued to preach against partition and to promote unity between Hindus and Moslems, but a year after the establishment of the Congress Government under **Pandit Nehru**, he was assassinated by a Hindu fanatic while attending a prayer meeting.

GARCIA, Perez Alan

1949–

Peruvian politician, born Lima. He read law at the Catholic University, Lima, and then continued his studies in Guatemala, Spain and France before returning to his country and winning election to the National Congress in 1978 as a moderate left-winger. Four years later he was appointed secretary-general, and in 1985 succeeded **Fernando Belaunde Terry** in the first democratic elections of a civilian president.

GARIBALDI, Giuseppe

1807–82

Italian patriot, born Nice. After working as a seaman, he joined the Young Italy movement of **Giuseppe Mazzini** and was condemned to death for his part in attempting to seize Genoa. After escaping to Brazil, he fought with the guerrillas against Brazil, and was taken prisoner, but after winning his freedom returned to Italy during the 1848 revolution. He served with the Sardinian army against the Austrians and commanded the defence of Rome against the French. After living in exile, he returned to 1854 to run a farm, but again took up arms against the Austrians in the 1859 war of liberation. In 1860, at the head of the 1000-strong force of Red Shirts, he took Sicily and Naples, but was unsuccessful in liberating Rome from papal rule in 1862 and 1867.

GAVIRIA, César

1947–

President of Colombia since August 1990, he gave immediate priority to smashing the country's all-powerful drug cartel, by promising not to extradite to the US drug-traffickers who surrendered. The policy enjoyed immediate success, with the surrender in January 1991 of Jorge Luis Ochoa, deputy head of the infamous Medellin cocaine cartel and the arrest of other figures such as Deny Muñoz, head of the cartel's hit squad, and accused of murdering more than 40 policemen.

GAYOOM, Maumoon Abdul

1937–

Maldivian politician. Educated at the Al-Azhair ur Cairo, he lectured on Islamic studies at the American University in Cairo from 1967 to 1969, and at Nigeria University from 1969 until returning home in 1972 to run the Government shipping and telecommunications agencies. He was appointed under-secretary to Prime Minister Ahmed Zaki in 1974, and subsequently held a number of diplomatic and ministerial posts before succeeding Ibrahim Nasir as president and Minister of Defence in 1978. He was re-elected in 1983, and after taking office again in 1988 foiled an attempted coup with the assistance of Indian paratroopers.

GEMAYEL, Amin

1942–

Lebanese politician. A lawyer by profession, he supported his brother, **Bachir Gemayel** in the 1975–6 Civil War, and on Bachir's assassination as president-elect in 1982 took office in his place. Although he adopted more moderate policies, they failed to achieve peace in Lebanon and in 1988 his presidency came to an end.

GEMAYEL, Bachir

1947–1982

Lebanese soldier and politician. After joining, at the age of 11, the militia of the Phalangist Party founded by his father, Pierre Gemayel, he continued his education and studied law, and worked briefly in a Washington law firm before returning home as the party's political director in East Beirut. He was among those who led the Christian militia in the 1975–6 Civil War, and after eliminating all possible rivals, and adopting a policy of non-intervention by the Israelis and other foreign powers, he was elected president in 1982. But having already escaped two attempts on his life, he was killed in a bomb explosion, and his brother, **Amin Gemayel**, took office in his place.

GENGHIS KHAN

1167–1227

Mongol conqueror, born Deligun Bulduk. He succeeded his father as Mongol chief at the age of 13 and spent six years subjugating hostile tribes, including the Turkish Uigurs, from whom the Mongols derived their civilization, alphabet, and laws. In 1211, he overran the empire of North China, and in 1217 annexed the Khanate empire from Lake Balkhash to Tibet. He expanded the Mongol territories still further in 1218 by conquering the empire of Khwarezm, and from 1225 masterminded expeditions that penetrated as far north as southern Russia and the Crimea, and eastward, to conquer practically the whole of North China between 1217 and 1223. Genghis Khan was not only a brilliant strategist but an able and progressive administrator, who formed his territories, which extended from the Black Sea to the Pacific, into a system of states that survived long after his death.

GENSCHER, Hans-Dietrich
1927–

German Foreign Minister, born Halle. Having joined the Hitler Youth Movement, he fought in the army during World War II and after the partitioning of the country remained in East Germany to study law at Leipzig University. The increasing repression of the communist regime caused him to flee to West Germany in 1952, and in 1959 he became secretary-general of the Free Democratic Party. He was subsequently appointed Interior Minister (1969–74) and party chairman, Deputy Chancellor and Foreign Secretary in 1974. As party chairman, he masterminded the FDP change of allegiance from the Social Democratic Party to the Christian Democratic Union that brought down **Helmut Schmidt**'s Government in 1982. As a proponent of a stronger Europe, he played a key role in Germany's reunification in 1990. However, at the beginning of 1991, the reputation of Europe's longest-serving Foreign Minister began to suffer as a result of the initial paucity of Germany's military and financial support in the Gulf War. He was also tainted by his closeness to **Mikhail Gorbachev**, which, although invaluable only months earlier in achieving German reunification, then served to compromise him in the wake of the violent Russian suppression of the pro-independent Baltic states.

GEORGE III
1738–1820

King of Great Britain, born London. After succeeding to the throne in 1760, he began his term as Britain's longest-reigning monarch (before Victoria) determined to reconcile all classes of his subjects, albeit at the cost of his relations with the first Prime Minister under his reign, William Pitt (the elder). The Earl of Bute was the next to submit to his king's displeasure over the treaty reached between France and Spain, and **George Grenville**'s introduction of the Stamp Act presented George with his first taste of the growing resentment of the American colonies at British rule, which was to continue through the Administrations of Rockingham, Chatham and Grafton. It was not until George was 10 years into his reign that he found, in Lord North, a premier whom he could respect, but the king's insistence on making no concessions to the American rebels delayed the reaching of a peace treaty after the War of Independence until 1783. George had meanwhile seen Rockingham, Shelburne and Portland come and go as his chief minister, and in 1783 made the inspired decision to instal **William Pitt** (the younger) as the head of a Tory Government that lasted 18 years, and which saw the dismantling of the Whig power base that the king had so despised. However, when Pitt achieved union with Ireland in 1801, George refused to assent, and on Pitt's resignation, Addington held the premiership until the start of the war with France, when Pitt resumed office. On Pitt's death in 1806, by which time the king was beginning to show signs of mental instability, **William Grenville** became Prime Minister and then Perceval, Portland and Grenville again, but the king's illness meant that he played an increasingly smaller part in the affairs of state, and by the time that the Prince of Wales was appointed regent in 1811, George was hopelessly insane and took no further role in the affairs of state.

GEORGE V
1865–1936

King of Great Britain, born Marlborough House. After serving in the Navy and travelling extensively throughout the empire, he was created Prince of Wales in 1901 and succeeded his father, Edward VII, in 1910. He reigned during one of the most significant and turbulent periods of British history, encompassing as it did the Union of South Africa (1910), World War I (1914–18), the Sinn Fein rebellion (1916), Irish Free State settlement (1922), election of the country's first Labour Governments (1924, 1929), the Statute of Westminster (1931), and the emergence of Nazi Germany in the mid-

1930s. He was the originator in 1932 of the monarch's Christmas Day broadcast to the Commonwealth. In 1893, he married Princess Mary (1867–1953), and their five children included **Edward VIII**, who abdicated before his coronation, and **George VI**, who reigned from 1936 to 1952.

GEORGE VI
1895–1952

King of Great Britain, father of **Elizabeth II** and Princess Margaret (1930–), born Sandringham. Educated at Dartmouth Naval College and Trinity College, Cambridge, he took part in the Battle of Jutland (1916), became an air cadet, and joined the RAF in 1918. In 1920 he was appointed Duke of York and married Lady Elizabeth Bowes-Lyon in 1923. On the abdication of his brother, **Edward VIII**, in 1936, he reluctantly took the throne, and during World War II inspired the nation by visiting all the theatres of war and becoming the first monarch to make regular radio broadcasts to the people. On the gaining of Indian independence in 1947, he substituted his title of Emperor of India for that of head of the Commonwealth, and although his health was failing him, he continued to follow an exhausting programme of overseas visits and domestic duties, including the opening of the 1951 Festival of Britain, until his death from coronary thrombosis.

GHEORGIU-DEJ, Gheorghe
1901–65

Romanian politician. After joining the Communist Party in 1930, he was imprisoned three years later for his part in a railway strike, and on his release in 1944 was appointed party secretary and Minister of Communications. In 1945 he was instrumental in deposing the coalition Government of Nicolae Radescu (1874–1953) and establishing a communist regime in which he was Prime Minister from 1952 to 1955 and president from 1961 until his death.

GILLRAY, James
1757–1815

English caricaturist, born London. After studying art and printing, he worked as a successful engraver, producing between 1779 and 1811 some 1500 humorous and acutely observed caricatures of the leading figures and social manners of his time, of which those

that lampooned the French, **Napoleon** and **George III** are particularly good examples of his work. He went insane four years before his death.

GIOLITTI, Giovanni
1843–1928

Italian statesman, born Mondovi. After an early career as a lawyer, he entered politics to become Prime Minister five times between 1892 and 1921. Having failed to keep Italy out of World War I, when hostilities ended he redoubled his endeavours to introduce vast schemes of social reforms, which included universal suffrage.

GISCARD D'ESTAING, Valéry
1926–

French politician, born Koblenz, Germany. After serving in the liberation movement during World War II, for which he was awarded the Croix de Guerre, he graduated from the École Nationale d'Administration and worked in the Ministry of Finance from 1952 to 1954. In 1956, he entered the National Assembly as a conservative Independent Republican, and was appointed Finance Minister by **Charles de Gaulle** in 1962. He left office over policy disagreements in 1966, but returned to the same post when **Georges Pompidou** became president in 1969. Following Pompidou's death in 1974, he narrowly won the presidency and embarked on a series of liberalizing reforms, but his inability to stabilize the economy brought his defeat by **François Mitterrand** in the 1981 presidential election. He was re-elected to the National Assembly in 1984 as leader of the centre-right Union for French Democracy, which he founded in 1978.

GLADSTONE, William Ewart
1809–98

British statesman, born Liverpool. The son of a Liverpool merchant and MP of Scottish ancestry, he was educated at Eton and Christ Church, Oxford, and in 1832 was elected as a Tory to the reformed Parliament. In 1834 he was made junior Lord of the Treasury by **Robert Peel**, then colonial Under-Secretary. On the Tories' return to power in 1841, Gladstone was made vice-president of the Board of Trade and Colonial Secretary in 1843, but resigned his seat over free-trade differences with his sponsor, the Duke of Newcastle. After the Corn Law question was resolved, Gladstone returned to the Commons in the 1847 general election, but by then had become acutely aware of social inequality at home and abroad—citing the dreadful conditions under which Neapolitan political prisoners were held by King Bomba. By the time of Peel's death in 1850, Gladstone began to establish his reputation as a great orator—particularly in the debate on **Benjamin Disraeli**'s 1852 Budget. In the subsequent first coalition under Lord **Aberdeen**, Gladstone was appointed Chancellor of the Exchequer, but briefly left office when **Russell** gave way to Lord **Palmerston** at the start of the Crimean War. He returned as Chancellor in 1850, but by the time of the 1865 general election his political transformation was complete, and it was as a Liberal that he became Leader of the House under Russell, who was Prime Minister again after the death of Palmerston. His Administration lost power in 1866 when a Bill proposing minor electoral boundary reforms was defeated by the Conservatives with cross-party support, but the Fenian insurrection served to return the Liberals to power in 1868, with Gladstone as Prime Minister. In his first Administration, he disestablished the church of Ireland (1869), abolished religious tests for universities, established the basis of Britain's first structured national education system, and introduced the secret vote. However, a Bill intended to enhance university prospects for Irish Catholics failed to win support, and when the Catholics joined with the Conservatives in voting against it, Gladstone tendered his resignation. When **Disraeli** refused to accept responsibility Gladstone remained in office, but his weak handling of foreign affairs and public discontent with the Liberals' attitude to trade unions prompted him to dissolve Parliament in 1874, when Disraeli returned to power. For the next six years, Gladstone renewed his studies of theology and Homer, but when Parliament was again dissolved in 1880 over the Tories' antipathy to Turkish atrocities in the Balkans, Gladstone undertook, at the age of 71, an exhausting campaign that concentrated on the Conservative stronghold of Midlothian, and the Liberals were swept back into power. In his second Administration, Gladstone extended the franchise to farm labourers, but his overwhelming preoccupation during that and his next two terms in office was Irish home rule and his relationship with **Charles Parnell** and the Irish Parliament. The issue was eventually to split the party, and after Gladstone's home-rule Bills of 1886 and 1894 were both defeated, he retired. On his death four years later, he was buried at Westminster Abbey. Although at times unbearably pompous—which accounted for Queen **Victoria**'s indifference towards him—Gladstone achieved many lasting constitutional and social improvements, a legacy which afforded the Liberals parliamentary dominance well into the 20th century. His son, Herbert Gladstone (1854–1930), became governor of South Africa in 1910.

GODOLPHIN, Sidney, 1st Earl of
1645–1712

English statesman, born Helston, Cornwall. After service as a royal page, he entered Parliament in 1668, and in 1684 was made head of the Treasury and given a baronetcy. Following **William III**'s landing in 1688, Godolphin remained loyal to **James II**, on whose behalf he started negotiations with William, and when James took flight, Godolphin voted for a regency. Nevertheless, William initially reinstated him at the Treasury as first commissioner, but Godolphin lost office in 1696 when the king replaced his Tory Ministers by Whigs. When Anne succeeded to the throne, she made him her sole Lord High Treasurer in 1702, and he was given an earldom four years later. Godolphin's able management of the state purse financed the expeditions of the Duke of Marlborough without increasing the public debt by more than £1 million annually. However, he eventually succumbed to the machinations of Robert Harley, who dismissed Godolphin on becoming Prime Minister in 1710.

GOEBBELS, Joseph
1897–1945

German Nazi politician. The son of a factory foreman, he was excused service in World War I because of his club foot. He continued his studies at eight different universities, and was among the founder members of the National Socialists, becoming head of the Berlin party in 1923. After **Adolf Hitler**'s rise to power, he was made Head of Propaganda in 1933, in which post his personal gift for oratory and his ability to stage-manage spectacular public demonstrations contributed enormously to the growth of the Nazi movement. At the height of World War II, Hitler virtually ceded the running of the country to Goebbels to concentrate on directing his military efforts. Unlike many of Hitler's cohorts, Goebbels was loyal to his Fuhrer to the end, poisoning himself and his family shortly after Hitler had taken his own life. *The Goebbels Diaries* (1965).

GOERING, Hermann Wilhelm
1893–1946

German Nazi politician and marshal, born Rosenheim, Bavaria. After army service on the western front in World War I, he was transferred to the air force in 1915 to become a highly-decorated pilot, and, already harbouring anti-Semitic attitudes because of his mother's remarriage to an ennobled Jew, he joined the National Socialist Party in 1922, and was given command of **Adolf Hitler**'s storm troops, the Brownshirts, five years later. After the failure of the 1923 Munich putsch, he went into exile, but returned in 1928 as one of 12 Nazi deputies to the Reichstag. He became president of the assembly in that year, and when Hitler took power in 1933, Goering joined his Government, was made a general, and served as Minister for Prussia, where he founded the Gestapo, and began establishing concentration camps to contain anyone whose politics, race or religion were considered suspect. He was later appointed Air Minister, then War Minister in 1938 with the rank of field marshal, when he responded to the signing of the Munich Agreement by ordering a five-fold increase in the Luftwaffe. At the start of World War II, he was charged with responsibility for the economy, given the specially-created title of Reich Marshal and named as Hitler's successor. However, the Luftwaffe's defeat in the Battle of Britain and Hitler's realization that Goering's war preparations had been inadequate lessened his influence, and with the liberation of Normandy in 1944, realizing that his disgrace might soon take a more tangible form, he plotted to oust Hitler but was betrayed and sentenced to death. After managing to escape, he was captured by US troops, and when the Nuremberg trials began in 1946, he was the principal defendant. Condemned for guilt 'unique in its enormity', he was sentenced to death, but poisoned himself a few hours before he was due to be executed.

GOLDWATER, Barry Morris
1909–

American politician, born Phoenix, Arizona. Of Jewish-Polish descent, he was educated at Staunton Military Academy, Arizona, and the University of Arizona, and after joining the army reserve in 1930 was transferred in 1940 to the USAF, in which he served as a ferry pilot and instructor during World War II. He was chief of staff of the Arizona National Guard from 1945 to 1952, meanwhile establishing a successful clothing business. In 1953 he became Republican Senator for his home state, and, being on the right wing of the party, supported **Joseph McCarthy**'s witch hunts and was critical of President **Eisenhower**'s Administration, particularly in respect of its intervention in state economies. In 1964 he contested the presidency but was heavily defeated by **Lyndon Baines Johnson**. He returned to the Senate in 1969 and became chairman of the Armed Services Commission before retiring in 1986.

GONZÁLEZ MÁRQUEZ, Felipe
1942–

Spanish politician, born Seville. After studying law and entering that profession, he joined the then illegal Spanish Socialist Workers Party in 1962, and was its secretary-general by the time that the party was made legal in 1977 as a result of his moderating influence. In 1982, the party formed the first left-wing Government since the socialist coalition of 1936, and in 1986 Gonzalez was returned to serve another term as Prime Minister.

GORBACHEV, Mikhail
1931–

Soviet statesman, born Privolnoye, North Caucasus. The son of peasant farmers, he was secretly baptized, and after excelling at school he won a place at Moscow University to study law in 1950. After his marriage to a philosophy student, Raisa (1933–), he worked for the Communist Party in Stavropol and was appointed regional agriculture secretary in 1962. He became Stavropol party leader in 1970, and having attracted the notice of **Yuri Andropov** was brought into the CPSU Secretariat as Agriculture Secretary in 1978. He was promoted to full membership of the Politburo in 1983, and took overall charge of the country's economy when Andropov became head of state later that same year. Following the death of **Konstantin Chernenko** in 1985, Gorbachev became party leader, introducing a new generation of progressive technocrats into the Moscow bureaucracy to give effect to his swingeing programme of economic reform. A strong critic of the hard-line legacy of **Leonid Brezhnev**, he introduced the words 'glasnost' ('openness') and 'perestroika' ('restructuring') into the international vocabulary as he strove to encourage open criticism of Moscow's failings and to revitalise the Soviet economy. Meanwhile, he made unprecedented efforts to enhance East-West accord through his meetings with **Ronald Reagan** and other world leaders and the signing of an arms limitation treaty in 1987. However, by the end of the 1980s, Gorbachev's encouragement of German reunification and Moscow's lessening of its grip on the affairs of the Soviet republics, with its ramifications for the Soviet economy and its food supplies in particular, saw his popularity spiralling downwards everywhere but in the West, which acknowledged his enlightened leadership by awarding him the Nobel Peace Prize in 1990. But after he tightened the Kremlin's grip as the Baltic states increasingly agitated for independence, he was strongly denounced not only by the West but by left-wing reformists led by **Boris Yeltsin**, at the same time suffering an increasingly uneasy relationship with the reactionary Red Army, which in January 1991 ignored his instruction to serve only as a stabilizing occupation force in Lithuania, gunning down street demonstrators. However, the underlying and unprecedented regard in which he was held by the West, and the threat of the withdrawal of the international aid on which the Soviet economy is becoming increasingly reliant, helped to stabilize his position, and in April 1991 he reached a new accord with Yeltsin and his supporters, with the promise of taking a more cautious approach to the management of the Soviet economy, establishing a separate police force not controlled by the Kremlin, and of eventually granting self-government to the Baltic states. On 19 August, the day before several Soviet Republics were due to sign the new Union Treaty, he was held under house arrest in the Ukraine while a State Emergency Committee headed by Prime Minister **Yanayev** seized control. The failure of the coup was due in large part to the opposition of Yeltsin and the Russian parliament, and Gorbachev faced a power struggle when he resumed the presidency.

GORBUNOVS, Anatolijs

As the moderate nationalist President of Latvia, he followed Lithuania and Estonia in declaring in 1990 his intention to return his country to its pre-World War II status, to become independent of the Soviet Union. In January 1991, after Soviet troops arrived in Vilnius and Riga in the aftermath of the Lithuanian suppression, he secured from **Mikhail Gorbachev** a pledge that if a national referendum willed it, the process of establishing Latvia as an independent state could begin.

GORIA, Giovanni
1943–

Italian politician, born Asti, Piemonte. After being appointed provincial secretary of the Christian Democratic Party, he was elected to the Chamber of Deputies in 1976 and held a number of ministerial posts in the coalitions led by his party before being made Treasury Minister in 1982. In the aftermath of the 1987 constitutional crisis, in which the Socialists withdrew their support, Goria managed to form another coalition, which he led until it collapsed in 1988.

GORMLEY, Jo (Joseph), Baron Gormley
1917–

British miners' leader, born Ashton-in-Makerfield. After an elementary education at St Oswald's Roman Catholic School in his home town, he began work in the mines at the age of 14, later entering local politics and winning election to the executive council of the National Union of Mineworkers in 1957. He was appointed north-western regional secretary in 1961, and joined the Labour Party's national executive two years later. In 1971 he became general secretary and served as a member of the Trades Union Congress general council from 1973 to 1980. Throughout his term as general secretary, he worked unceasingly to improve miners' conditions and to prevent the rundown of the British coal industry, while strongly denouncing the unofficial actions of militants led by **Arthur Scargill**, in their attempts to use strike tactics to bring down the Conservative Governments of **Edward Heath** and **Margaret Thatcher**. When he retired as NUM general secretary in 1982, the constructive and realistic approach that he had taken to industrial relations was acknowledged with the award of a life peerage. His autobiography, *Battered Cherub*, was published the same year.

GOTTWALD, Klement
1896–1953

Czechoslovakian politician, born Deduce, Moravia. After serving with the Austro-Hungarian army in World War I, he joined the Communist Party and was appointed secretary-general in 1927. As an opponent of the 1938 Munich Agreement, he was invited to Moscow towards the end of World War II to be groomed for eventual office, and in 1945 was chosen to head the provisional Government. He became Prime Minister the following year, but when his party faced defeat in the 1948 elections, he staged a coup that kept him in office, and continued to head a total dictatorship until his death five years later.

GOULED APTIDON, Hassan
1916–

Djiboutian politician, born Djibouti City. While serving as a representative of French Somaliland in France, he became increasingly active in the independence movement and in 1967 founded the African People's League for Independence. When Djibouti achieved self-government in 1977, he became the country's first President, later merging the APLAI with others to form the country's only political entity, the People's Progress Party. His policy of neutralism in a war-torn region of the continent has ensured his continuing popularity, and in 1987 he was re-elected for a final six-year term.

GOW, Ian
1937–90

British politician. Educated at Winchester School, he later studied law, and after army service as a commander of the 15th/17th Hussars (1956–62), he practised as a solicitor. He entered Parliament for the Conservatives in 1966, and served as parliamentary private secretary to **Margaret Thatcher** after his party's 1979 election victory, then as Minister of Housing (1983–5) and Treasury Minister, until resigning in 1986 in protest at the Anglo-Irish Agreement. His continuing fierce condemnation of IRA activities and of any relaxation of Britain's obligation to the Province, together with his continuing closeness to Thatcher, who frequently sought his informal counsel, singled him out as a prime IRA target, and he was killed by a car bomb during the parliamentary summer recess in 1990. His local standing as a constituency MP saw him returned for his Eastbourne constituency even when national voting trends took their toll on safer seats, but in the by-election caused by the outrage, the Liberal Democrat candidate, David Bellotti, overturned Gow's legacy of a 16000 Conservative majority.

GOWON, Yakubu
1934–

Nigerian soldier and politician, born Garam, Plateau state. Baptised a Christian in a Muslim state, he received military training in Nigeria and at Sandhurst Military Academy, and between 1963 and 1966 rose from the rank of adjutant-general to commander-in-chief. The ethnic and tribal difficulties that had continued after the country achieved independence eventually prompted Gowon to stage a military coup, and to assume the presidency, and he eventually brought the civil war to an end in 1970. Five years later, he was ousted in a bloodless coup while visiting Kampala, and, after pursuing academic studies in Britain, settled in Togo.

GRAMSCI, Antonio
1891–1937

Italian politician and theoretician, born Ales, Sardinia. Born into poverty, he nevertheless made the most of his elementary education to win a place at Turin University, where he proved to be a brilliant student. He helped to found a left-wing newspaper in 1919, and promoted workers' councils, but having grown disenchanted with moderate socialism, in 1921 he helped to establish the Italian Communist Party, which he represented at the Third International in Moscow the following year. After entering Parliament, he became party leader, and in 1926, four years after **Benito Mussolini** took power, the party was banned and Gramsci was imprisoned for the rest of his life. In prison, he completed some 30 notebooks of political reflections, which were published in 1947 as *Lettere del carcere*, and which are regarded as one of the most significant political texts of the 20th century.

GRANDI, Count Dino
1895–1988

Italian politician and diplomat, born Mordano, Bologna. After studying law he took part in the fascists' 1922 march on Rome, and from 1929 to 1932 served as **Benito Mussolini**'s Foreign Minister. As ambassador to London from 1935, he failed to convince Mussolini of the likely extent of British reaction to Italy's invasion of Abyssinia in 1935. He was recalled to Rome after the formation in 1939 of the Berlin-Rome axis and appointed Minister of Justice. In 1943, he moved the motion in the grand council that forced Mussolini's resignation, and after fleeing to Portugal was sentenced to death in his absence. He later sought exile in Brazil, and after returning to Italy in 1973 wrote two acclaimed works, *The Foreign Policy of Italy 1929–32*, and *My Country*.

GRANT, Bernie (Bernard Alexander Montgomery)
1944–

British Member of Parliament, born Georgetown, Guyana. Educated at St Stanislaus College, Georgetown, Tottenham Technical College, and Heriot-Watt University, he worked as an analyst in Guyana before moving to Britain in the early 1960s, where he found employment as a railway clerk and, from 1969 to 1978, as a telephonist. He was then appointed an area officer with the National Union of Public Employees (1978–83), and worked as a development officer for the Black Trade Unionists Solidarity Movement (1983–4), before entering local government service in Newham, east London, in 1985. He was elected to Haringey council in 1978, and led the Labour majority from 1985 to 1987, when he was elected MP for Tottenham. In 1985, whilst a prospective Parliamentary candidate for the Labour party, he received all-party condemnation both in and out of Parliament, when he was reported as having said that he would not condemn the actions of the youths in the Broadwater Farm housing estate riot, in which a young police constable was hacked to death. However, he subsequently stated during a council debate that the kind of violence associated with the death of PC Blakelock was 'inexcusable'. He is founder and chairman of the Parliamentary Black Caucus, which promotes greater parliamentary representation of the ethnic minorities.

GRANT, Ulysses Simpson
1822–85

American soldier and 18th US President, born Point Pleasant, Ohio. After graduating from West Point Military Academy in 1843, he fought in the 1846-8 war with Mexico, and was promoted to the rank of captain in 1853. He resigned from the army the following year to farm in Missouri, but on the outbreak of the civil war in 1861 he took up his uniform again and enjoyed a number of early military successes, including the capture of Vicksburg, Mississippi, in 1863. After vanquishing the Confederates in Tennessee, he was promoted to lieutenant-general and given command of the Union forces. His strategy sent William Sherman to Atlanta while he led the offensive across the Potomac to Richmond, and after a 10-day battle, General Robert E. Lee surrendered his entire army on 9 April 1865. Grant was appointed a full general the following year, but he relinquished the rank on being elected Republican president in 1868 and again in 1872. His two Administrations saw the granting of suffrage without regard to race, colour or previous servitude, and the peaceful settlement of the Alabama claims. When he failed to be nominated for a third term, he became a partner in a banking house, only to be robbed by two of its partners of his entire fortune. Shortly after starting work on his autobiography in an attempt to provide for his family, he was diagnosed as suffering from cancer, and shortly before his death Congress restored him to the rank of general so that his dependants would qualify for an army pension.

GRATTAN, Henry
1746–1820

Irish statesman, born Dublin. Educated at Trinity College, Dublin, and at the Middle Temple, London, he was disinherited by his father for his fervent support of the nationalist, Henry Flood (1732–91), and deserted law for politics to become an MP in the Irish Parliament in 1775. When Flood accepted a Government appointment, Grattan succeeded him as leader of the independent cause and campaigned vigorously for the removal of restrictions on Irish trade. When that was achieved in 1779, Grattan concentrated on achieving legislative independence, and in 1782 secured the abolition of all claims by the Parliament at Westminster to legislate for Ireland. Unsuccessful in his attempt to defeat the Act of Union, he sat in the House of Commons until his death.

GREER, Germaine
1939–

Australian feminist and author. Educated at Melbourne University and Oxford University, it was while she was lecturing in English at Warwick University (1969-83) that she published in 1970 her controversial and highly influential book, *The Female Eunuch*, which attacked male domination of society and women's place in marriage as a legalized form of slavery. She has since written *The Obstacle Race* (1979), *Sex and Destiny: the politics of human fertility* (1984), and a study of her father, *Daddy, We hardly knew you* (1989).

GRENVILLE, George
1712–70

English politician. After studying at Eton and Oxford University, he entered the House of Commons in 1741, and in 1762 was appointed Secretary of State and First Lord of the Admiralty. During his term as Prime Minister (1763–5) he infuriated the American colonists by the introduction of the Stamp Act, which fuelled the discontent that culminated with the American War of Independence, and continued the persecution of the radical essayist and parliamentarian **John Wilkes**.

GRENVILLE, William Wyndham, 1st Baron
1759–1834

English statesman. The son of **George Grenville**, he studied at Eton and Oxford, and became an MP in 1782. He served as Paymaster-General (1783), Speaker (1789), and Home Secretary (1791), before becoming Foreign Secretary under his cousin, **William Pitt**, in 1791. He resigned two years later, together with Pitt, over the refusal of **George III** to accept Catholic emancipation. In 1806 he formed the Government of 'All the Talents', which, before it was dissolved in 1807, abolished the slave trade.

GREY, Charles, 2nd Earl
1764–1845

English politician, born Fallodon, Northumberland. Educated at Eton and King's College, Cambridge he joined the Whig Opposition in Parliament in 1786, and wasted little time attacking the Government of **William Pitt** for its domestic and foreign policies and its union with Ireland in particular. On the Whigs' return to power in 1806, he became First Lord of the Admiralty, and as Foreign Secretary on the death of **Charles Fox**, piloted the abolition of the African slave trade. After succeeding his father to the earldom in 1807, he withdrew from doing battle in the Commons, but after the 1830 general election returned as Prime Minister of the new Whig Administration. He introduced his first Reform Bill a year later, and after its defeat and the dissolution of Parliament, he returned even more resolved to secure its provisions. When the second Bill was carried by the Commons but rejected by the Lords, there were violent demonstrations, and Grey piloted a third attempt that reached its Second Reading in the Lords but collapsed when Ministers resigned over its disenfranchisement clauses. After the Duke of **Wellington** failed to form a Government, Grey returned as premier and persuaded William IV to create a sufficient number of new peers to guarantee the legislation's adoption in the Upper House. His Bill finally received royal assent in June 1832, and Grey continued to lead the reformed Parliament, extending his earlier anti-slavery measures to the colonies. However, a Cabinet split over reform of the Church of Ireland made Grey's position untenable, and he resigned in 1834.

GRIMOND, Jo (Joseph), Baron Grimond of Firth
1913–

British politician, born St Andrews, Scotland. The son of a jute manufacturer, he was educated at Eton and Balliol College, Oxford, and after continuing his law studies was called to the Middle Temple Bar in 1937. In World War II, he served with the Fife and Forfar Yeomanry, winning promotion to the rank of major, and in 1945 first contested Orkney and Shetland for the Liberals, and was secretary of the National Trust for Scotland (1947–9) before successfully fighting the seat again in 1953. His lengthy term as party leader, in succession to **Clement Davies** (1884–1962), from 1956 saw a doubling in the number of Liberal seats at Westminster and the party's re-emergence as a political force, rather than remaining a relic of the Edwardian era that had survived only because of the Liberal tradition in Scotland and south-west England, and he contributed greatly to the new spirit of confidence in its ability to serve as a moderating influence in what had become virtually one-party Opposition. After he relinquished the leadership to **Jeremy Thorpe** in 1967, he remained in the Commons for six years before accepting a life peerage. He remained an influential figure in the party's development under **David Steel**, and has lived to see its growing popularity with the electorate, despite the diffusion of its appeal that occurred while it dallied with, and then absorbed, Labour's breakaway Social Democrats in the late 1980s—reflected in the renamed Liberal Democratic Party's string of national and local government election successes at the start of the 1990s. Among his works are *The Liberal Future* (1959), *The Referendum* (1975), *The Common Welfare* (1978), *Memoirs* (1979), *A Personal Manifesto* (1983), and *Britain—A view from Westminster* (1986).

GRIVAS, George Theodorou
1898–1974

Cypriot terrorist leader, born Cyprus. Having joined the army in his youth, he commanded a division in the 1940–1 Albanian campaign and led a resistance movement during the German occupation. In December 1945, he founded an extreme anti-communist nationalist movement, EOKA, and nine years later directed its activities at ending British rule on the island. When his secret diaries, revealing the extent of his planned campaign, were discovered in 1954, a reward of £10000 was offered for his capture. He left the island after the 1959 partition was agreed, and on his arrival in Greece was proclaimed a national hero and made a general in the Greek army. He was in Cyprus again between 1964 and 1967, and after being recalled to Greece, returned secretly to the island in 1971 and headed a new wave of terrorism for EOKA until his death.

GROMYKO, Andrei Andreevich
1909–89

Russian statesman, born Minsk. Born into a peasant family, he studied agriculture and economics at the Soviet Academy of Sciences and became a research scientist there. On the outbreak of World War II, he joined the Washington embassy, and as ambassador to the US from 1944 attended the Teheran, Yalta and Potsdam conferences. In 1946 he was admitted as a deputy to the Supreme Soviet and appointed deputy Foreign Minister and permanent representative to the UN Security Council, in which capacity he used his power of veto on no fewer than 25 occasions. He began a one-year term as ambassador to London in 1952, and from 1957 to 1985 was Foreign Minister. As a product of the Stalin era, and a disciple of **Nikita Khrushchev**, he epitomised in Western eyes the uncompromising Soviet diplomat, but in the 1970s Gromyko adapted to the new spirit of détente and made a more positive contribution to East-West relations. In the last two years of his life, he continued as a member of the Politburo in the ceremonial post of president of the USSR.

GROSZ, Karoly
1930–

Hungarian politician, born Miskolc. After working as a printer and newspaper editor, he joined the ruling Hungarian Socialist Workers Party in 1945, and in 1961 moved to Budapest to work in its propaganda department. He was appointed deputy head in 1968 and head in 1974. From 1984 to 1987 served as Budapest party chief, and having been admitted to the Politburo in 1985, was appointed Prime Minister in 1987. Shortly after being made party leader in 1988 in succession to **Janos Kadar**, he relinquished the premiership, but remained influential in Hungary's move to socialist pluralism and away from Kremlin influence, which eventually brought its independence from Moscow.

GUEVARA, (Ernesto) 'Che'
1928–67

Argentine revolutionary leader. A graduate of medicine from the University of Buenos Aires, he joined **Fidel Castro**'s communist revolutionary movement in Mexico in 1955, and after playing a leading role in the 1956–9 Cuban revolution, held a number of Government posts under Castro's patronage. In 1965, he left Cuba to continue his guerrilla activities in South America, and was captured and executed in Bolivia two years later after fomenting anti-Government demonstrations. His romantic if undeserved image as an idealistic champion of the underprivileged saw his adoption by the left-wing youth movement of the 1960s, when his poster adorned a million student bedrooms. He wrote *Guerrilla Warfare* (1961) and *Reminiscences of the Cuban Revolutionary War* (1968).

HABYARIMANA, Juvenal
1937–

Rwandan soldier and politician, born Gasiza, Gisenji prefecture. After military training he joined the National Guard and rose rapidly to the rank of major-general and army chief by 1973. In the same year, he exploited the disorder caused by the resumption of tribal hostilities between the Tutsi and Hutu to stage a bloodless coup against President Gregoire Kayibanda and establish a military regime. He subsequently founded the National Revolutionary Development Movement as his country's only legal political movement, and has promised a return eventually to constitutional government.

HADRIAN (Publius Aeligus Hadrianus)
76–138

Roman emperor, born Rome. After a childhood spent in Spain with his colonist family, through the patronage of his father's cousin, the future emperor Trajan, he served as a tribune, praetor, provincial governor and consul before being proclaimed emperor by the army in 117. Three years later, he began a lengthy tour of his empire, including Gaul, Germany, Britain (where he ordered the building of Hadrian's Wall), Spain, Mauritania, Egypt, Asia Minor, and Greece. After returning to Rome in 126, he put down a major revolt in Judaea (132–4) caused by his ban on circumcision, which he considered inhumane, and then devoted himself to reorganizing his army and acting as a patron of the arts.

HAIG, General Alexander Meigs, Jr
1924–

American soldier and public official, born Philadelphia. Educated at West Point, the Naval War College, and Georgetown University, he joined the US Army in 1947, served in Korea (1950–1) and Vietnam (1966-7), and was promoted to general in 1973. In **Richard Nixon**'s Administration he served as deputy to **Henry Kissinger** in the National Security Council and was made White House Chief of Staff in 1973 at the height of the Watergate scandal. In 1974 he

returned to military duty and was NATO's Supreme Allied Commander, Europe from 1974 to 1979. He served briefly as **Ronald Reagan**'s Secretary of State (1981–2) before resigning over policy differences, and ran unsuccessfully for the Republican party's presidential nomination in 1987.

HAIG, Douglas, 1st Earl Haig of Bemersyde
1861–1928

Scottish soldier and field-marshal, born Edinburgh. Educated at Clifton, Oxford University, and the Royal Military College, Sandhurst, he was commissioned in the 7th Hussars and saw active service in Egypt and South Africa before being posted to India, returning to England in 1911 as GOC Aldershot. At the start of World War I, he led the 1st Corps of the British Expeditionary Force to France and became commander-in-chief in December 1915. For the next two and a half years, with British forces contained by the sea, the Swiss border, and the Germans' interior lines, Haig found himself compelled to wage a war of attrition on the Western front that cost the lives of two million British soldiers, with 600000 lost at the battle of the Somme (1916) and 245000 at Passchendaele (1917) alone. His breakthrough came when Marshal Foch took Marne and Haig was able to break through the Hindenburg line in September, forcing Germany to sue for peace the following month. In 1919, he was given command of the home forces, a gift from the nation of £100000, and an earldom, and soon after he founded the British Legion for the care of ex-servicemen.

HAILE SELASSIE
1891–1975

Emperor of Ethiopia (Abyssinia). In 1916, he led the revolution against Lij Yasu to become Prince Regent, and after ascending the throne of Abyssinia in 1930, he quickly set about the westernization of his country to make it, in relative terms, one of the most progressive of the East African states. When the Italians conquered his country in 1936, he fled to England and remained there until Abyssinia was retaken by British forces in 1941. In the early 1960s, he helped to found the Organisation of African Unity, to serve as a league of African nations, and established a Parliament, but by the late 1960s, the poverty that beset his country was giving rise to growing resentment at his rule, and the famine of 1973 provided the spur to mutiny among the armed forces, who deposed the emperor in 1974 in favour of the Crown Prince. Haile Selassie and several other members of his family were placed under house arrest, and he died the following year.

HAILSHAM, Quintin McGarel Hogg, 2nd Viscount

1907–

English jurist and statesman, born London. Educated at Eton College and Christ Church, Oxford, he became a fellow of All Souls in 1931 and was called to the Bar in 1932. He entered Parliament as an MP in 1938, and after succeeding to the title in 1950 was made First Lord of the Admiralty (1956–7), Minister of Education (1957) and Lord President of the Council (1957–9, 1960–4). He was Conservative Party chairman from 1957 until 1959, when he was appointed Minister for Science and Technology, and was made Secretary of State for Education and Science in 1964. In the 1963 leadership crisis, he renounced his peerage for life and re-entered the Commons, serving as Opposition Home Secretary from 1966. In 1970 he was given a life peerage as Baron Hailsham of St Marylebone, and was Lord Chancellor (as his father had been) in every Conservative Government between 1970 and 1987. In 1978, he saw his wife, Mary, killed in a horseriding accident while they were visiting Australia. Since his retirement from the country's highest constitutional office, he has continued to speak frequently on judicial matters in debates in the Lords. He wrote *The Case for Conservatism* (1947), *The Conservative Case* (1959), and *The Door Wherein I Went* (1975). In his autobiography, *A Sparrow's Flight* (1990), he describes the deep religious convictions that guided his years in power and consoled him in his personal tragedies. His son, Douglas Hogg (1945–), was elected the MP for **Margaret Thatcher**'s home town of Grantham when the Conservatives returned to power in 1979, and was appointed Minister for Trade and Industry in 1989. Douglas's wife, Sarah, a former journalist, was appointed head of No. 10's economic policies unit after **John Major** became Prime Minister in 1990.

HALL, Gus (Alvo Gus Halberg)

1916–

American communist leader. Of Finnish descent, he worked as a lumberjack in Michigan and as a steel-worker in Ohio before being appointed as National Secretary of the Communist Party of the United States of America in 1940. He was jailed for eight years during the 1950s as the consequence of the anti-communist purges led by Senator **Joseph McCarthy**.

HAMILTON, Alexander

1757–1804

American statesman, born Nevis, West Indies. As an early campaigner against British colonialism, he fought in the American Civil War as a captain of artillery, and became **George Washington**'s aide-de-camp in 1777. Policy disagreements between them led to Hamilton's resignation in 1781, but he continued to serve in the army and distinguished himself at Yorktown. After the war he studied law and practised successfully in New York, and as a Senator from 1782 took part in the negotiations that paved the way for the 1787 Philadelphia convention. He was the author of 51 out of the 85 issues of *The Federalist*, and as Secretary of the Treasury from 1789 he did much to restore the country's economy. He resigned that office in 1795 but continued to lead the Federal Party until he was killed in a duel with a political rival, Aaron Burr.

HAMMARSKJÖLD, Dag Hjalmar Agne Carl

1905–61

United Nations Secretary-General, born Jönköping, Sweden. After lecturing at Stockholm University in the early 1930s, he joined the Bank of Sweden and was its chairman from 1941 to 1948. He was then appointed Foreign Minister (1951–3) and served as a delegate to the Council of Europe and the UN General Assembly until his appointment as UN Secretary-General in 1953. He was instrumental in sending a UN emergency force to Sinai and Gaza in 1956, reconciling the Middle East states (1957–8), and installing UN observers in the Lebanon (1958). There has been speculation that his death in an air crash while flying to Ndola in Northern Rhodesia to arrange a truce in the Congo was an act of sabotage. He was posthumously awarded the Nobel Peace Prize.

HAMMOND, Eric Albert Barratt
1929–

British trade union leader. After becoming active in trade union affairs and local politics in his early 20s, he rose from shop steward of the Electrical, Electronics, Telecommunications and Plumbing Union to its General Secretary in 1984. An opponent of traditional restrictive union practices, he outraged the movement in the mid-1980s by reaching agreements with newspaper proprietors weary of overmanning that resulted in smaller numbers of EETPU members undertaking tasks that previously had been the province of SOGAT '82 and NATSOPA print workers, which led to the EETPU being expelled from the Trades Union Congress in 1988.

HANNIBAL
247–182 BC

Carthaginian soldier. After notable service in Spain, he was appointed commander in 221 BC and his victory over the whole country by 218 BC allowed him to embark on the Second Punic War. After skirting the Pyrenees with a force that included elephants, he took Rhone and defeated the Gauls, and managed the unbelievable feat of taking his army across the Alps in only 15 days. Thousands perished in the cold, but after pressing the Taurini, Ligurian and Celtic tribes into his service, he fragmented the Roman army at Lake Transimene (217 BC) and Cannae a year later. His losses made a march on Rome untenable, and he chose to consolidate his army in southern Italy. In 203 BC, his brother, Hasdrubal, attempted a crossing with reinforcements from Spain, but was killed in the Battle of Metaurus. In 203 BC he was recalled to Africa to counter a Roman invasion led by Scipio, but his army was massacred at Zama and the war came to an end. In peacetime, Hannibal attempts at introducing political reforms forced him into exile, first to the court of Antiochus II at Ephesus, and then to that of Prusias, King of Bithynia. But realizing that demands from the Romans for his surrender could not long be resisted, he poisoned himself.

HANSARD, Luke
1752–1828

English printer, born Norwich. After joining the staff of the House of Commons printers, he became acting manager in 1774, and in 1798 succeeded the business's sole proprietor. From 1774 until 1889, Hansard and his descendants printed all parliamentary reports, and today's *Official Report*, containing the verbatim record of each day's proceedings on the Floor of the House and in its Standing Committees, is still popularly named after him.

HARALD V
1937–

King of Norway, born Oslo. Like his father, **Olav V**, he was educated at Oslo University, a military academy, and at Oxford. He served briefly in each of the country's three armed services, and in 1968 took the then unprecedented step of marrying a commoner, Sonja—a shopkeeper's daughter—after strenuous efforts by his father to obtain Cabinet approval. As Prince Regent, he effectively served as monarch after the king suffered a stroke in 1990, and he formally succeeded to the throne (the pomp of coronation having been discarded since 1957, in a pledge to the Constitution) on Olav's death at the age of 87 in January 1991.

HARDIE, (James) Keir
1856–1915

Scottish socialist and founder of the Labour Party, born Holytown, Lanarkshire. After working in the coal mines from childhood, his championship of miners' rights led to his victimization and dismissal, and he moved to Cumnock to work as a journalist. In 1886 he left the Liberal Party to join the newly-formed Scottish Labour Party, and in 1888 he was defeated as Britain's first Labour candidate, but won a London constituency in 1892, and scandalised the House—whose Members then wore tail-coats and top hats—by taking the oath dressed in a tweed suit and with a cloth cap under his arm. In 1893, he founded the Independent Labour Party, and later founded and edited the *Labour Leader*, which in 1903 became the party's official periodical. He was chairman of the movement until 1900, when he was re-elected by a Welsh constituency, and then led the parliamentary party until 1911. He was chairman of the renamed Labour Party in 1913–14. As well as being a staunch supporter of the suffragette movement, he was a lifelong pacifist, and after denouncing the Boer War, he lost his seat in the Commons in 1915 after opposing Britain's involvement in World War I.

HART, Gary
1936–

American politician, born Ottawa, Kansas. After becoming involved in the Democratic Party while a student at Yale University, he worked as a member of **John F. Kennedy**'s presidential campaign staff in 1960 and then moved to Denver to establish a law practice. After managing **George McGovern**'s unsuccessful 1974 bid for the White House, he entered the Senate the same year, where he gained a reputation for his advocacy of realistic liberal reforms that combined social and environmental improvements with improved economic efficiency. In 1980 he sought the presidential nomination for himself, but was narrowly defeated by **Walter Mondale**. He retired from the Senate to concentrate on his next bid for the presidential nomination, but in 1987 he withdrew from the race when his wholesome, family image was besmirched by newspaper reports that he was conducting an affair with a young model, Donna Rice.

HASSAN II
1929–

King of Morocco, born Rabat. Educated at Bordeaux University, he became head of the army and on succeeding to the throne in 1961 also assumed the office of Prime Minister. After rioting in Casablanca in 1965, he suspended Parliament and established a dictatorship, and despite implementing some constitutional reforms in the early 1970s, he has retained supreme political and religious authority. From 1976 to 1988 he maintained a large army on the western Saharan frontier to prevent the incursion of Polisario guerrillas. In 1984, unrest in the larger centres of his kingdom compelled Hassan to establish a form of coalition government under a civilian Prime Minister.

HASTINGS, Warren
1732–1818

English administrator in India, born Churchill, Oxfordshire. Educated at Westminster, he held several public offices for the East India Company before being appointed its first Governor-General in 1773. His first action was to bring to trial two Bengali finance Ministers on charges of embezzlement, but the case collapsed, to the delight of his bitter enemy, Sir Philip Francis, who served as a member of his council.

Nevertheless, he was successful with many important administrative and judicial reforms, as well as improving the country's trade wealth (not least by organising its opium revenue) to the benefit of his employers. The enmity between Hastings and Francis led to a duel being fought between them, in which the latter was injured, and, humiliated, he resigned office in 1780. Four years later, Hastings himself relinquished the governorship and returned to England, where he found himself subjected to a parliamentary inquiry over his conduct during the Mahratta war and his connivance in the forfeiture of property belonging to the Dowager-Princess of Oudh. He was impeached at the Bar of the House of Lords, but at the end of his trial, which started in 1788 and comprised 145 sittings over seven years, Hastings was acquitted of all charges but had been reduced to poverty by the expense of conducting his defence. The East India Company supported him in his retirement at his ancestral seat of Daylesford, Worcestershire, which he had purchased on his return from India, and he passed his remaining years as a country gentleman, having been made a Privy Councillor by the Parliament that had tried to break him, and having received several honours from the City of London.

HATTERSLEY, Roy
1932–

British politician, born Sheffield. Educated at Sheffield City Grammar School and Hull University, he worked as a journalist and National Health Service executive, served as a Labour city councillor for Sheffield from 1957 to 1964, and was elected to Parliament for a Birmingham constituency in 1963. In 1966, he was appointed private parliamentary secretary to the Social Security Minister, and was Under-Secretary of State, Department of Employment for a year from 1968, when he became Minister of Defence Administration. After the election of a Conservative Government in 1970, he was Opposition spokesman on Foreign Affairs, Defence, and Education. In 1976 he joined the Cabinet as Secretary of State for Prices and Consumer Protection and from 1974 to 1976, was Minister of State for Foreign and Commonwealth Affairs. Since the Conservatives' return to power in 1979, he has served as chief Opposition spokesman on the Environment (1977–80), and Home and

Treasury affairs (1980–3, 1983–7), and was appointed Shadow Home Secretary under **Neil Kinnock** in 1987. He has been Labour Deputy Leader since 1983. His career as a journalist is reflected in his frequent contributions to *The Guardian, Punch* and numerous other publications. His books include *Nelson: A Biography* (1974), *Goodbye to Yorkshire* (1976), *Politics Apart* (1983), the autobiographical *Yorkshire Boyhood* (1986), *Choose Freedom: The Future for Democratic Socialism* and *Economic Priorities for a Labour Government* (1987), and a critically acclaimed novel, *In the Quiet Earth* (1991).

HAUGHEY, Charles James
1925–

Irish statesman. Educated at University College, Dublin, he was called to the Irish Bar in 1949 and worked as a chartered accountant before entering the Dàil for the Fianna Fail Party in 1957, becoming its leader two years later. He was appointed Minister of Justice, of Agriculture and of Finance, but was dismissed from the Cabinet in 1970 over economic differences with Prime Minister **Jack Lynch**, and was subsequently acquitted of conspiracy and illegally importing arms. In 1979, he succeeded Lynch as premier for two years. He returned to power in 1982 but was defeated nine months later after losing a vote of confidence. Since his re-election in 1987, his Government has failed to make much headway in improving the Irish economy, and despite his personal condemnation of IRA terrorism, the Irish judiciary's frequent refusals to extradite individuals suspected of carrying out killings and bombings on the mainland have incensed Westminster. However, at the start of the 1990s, and much to the chagrin of many Ulster loyalists, Haughey adopted a more conciliatory attitude to the Northern Ireland problem, which paved the way for the initiatives by Secretary of State Peter Brooke that resulted in June 1991 in the first round-table discussions between the Province's Catholic and Protestant leaders.

HAVEL, Vaçlav
1936–

Czechoslovak dramatist and politician, born Prague. Educated at the Academy of Dramatic Art in Prague, he worked at the Prague Theatre as a stagehand before becoming its resident writer from 1960 to 1969. Considered a subversive, he was frequently arrested, and in 1979 he was imprisoned for more than four years. As the country's democratization movement gained momentum, he was imprisoned again briefly in 1989, and later that year, with the collapse of communist rule, he was elected President. His dramatic works include *The Garden Party* (1963), *The Conspirators* (1970), and *Temptation* (1987).

HAWKE, Robert James Lee
1929–

Australian trade union leader and politician, born Bordertown, South Australia. Educated at the University of South Australia and Brasenose College, Oxford, he worked for the Australian Council of Trade Unions, and was its president for 10 years from 1970 before becoming a Labour MP in 1980. After the Liberal Government's defeat in the 1983 general election, just one month after he was made party leader, Hawke took the premiership, and in 1987 Labour slightly increased its majority in the House of Representatives but failed to win control of the Senate.

HEALEY, Denis Winston
1917–

British politician, born Keighley, Yorkshire. Educated at Bradford Grammar School and Balliol College, Oxford, where he studied modern languages, he joined the Labour Party in 1936 and during World War II rose to the rank of major in the Royal Engineers. In 1945 he unsuccessfully stood for Parliament as a Labour candidate, but was elected in 1952, and after serving as a member of the Shadow Cabinet from 1959, he was Secretary of State for Defence from 1964 to 1970. In Opposition, he was Labour spokesman on Foreign Affairs (1970–2) and on Treasury matters (1972–4). During his term as Chancellor of the Exchequer from 1974, he presented more Budgets than any previous holder of that office, but was blighted by sterling's vulnerability, which—despite his stringent fiscal measures and the warning that he would tax the rich 'until the pips squeak'—he did little to resolve. After the Conservatives regained power, he was defeated for the leadership by **Michael Foot**, but was Deputy Leader until 1983, and Labour's chief spokesman on Foreign Affairs from 1981 to 1987, when he resigned from the Shadow Cabinet. He continued to make characteristically acute and witty speeches on the economy and foreign affairs, but in 1990 announced his decision to leave the Commons at the next general election. His books include *NATO and American Security* (1959), *The Race Against the H Bomb* (1960), *Labour, Britain and the World* (1963), *Labour and a World Society* (1985), and *Beyond Nuclear Deterrence* (1986). An accomplished photographer, a collection of work was published as *Healey's Eye* in 1980. His wife, Edna (1918–), a successful and esteemed biographer, has written *Lady Unknown: the life of Angela Burdett-Coutts* (1978) and *Wives of Fame* (1986).

HEATH, Edward Richard George
1916–

English politician, born Broadstairs, Kent. Educated at Chatham House School and Balliol College, Oxford, he served in the Royal Artillery in World War II and was mentioned in dispatches, and became a Conservative MP in 1950. He was a junior and then Chief Whip between 1951 and 1959, and Minister of Labour (1959–60), and, as Lord Privy Seal from 1960 to 1963, led Britain's negotiations to join the Common Market. He was Secretary of State for Trade and Industry from 1963 until the Conservatives lost power in 1964, when he became Opposition spokesman on economic affairs. In 1965 he was elected party leader and took his party to victory in the 1970 general election. His premiership was dogged by industrial disputes and the repercussions on the British economy of spiralling oil prices, and in the wake of the 1973 miners' strike, which forced industry to close two days a week because of power shortages, his Government was defeated when Heath sought an electoral mandate for his policies in 1974. A year later, he was defeated by **Margaret Thatcher** after **William Whitelaw** withdrew from the contest and gave her his support. His bitter criticisms of Thatcher's policies in almost every sphere since the Conservatives returned to power in 1979 at first isolated him from much of the party, but his views became increasingly influential again as the appeal of Thatcher's policies began to wane at the end of the 1980s, leading to her replacement by **John Major** as party leader and premier in November 1990. Heath's undiminished international credibility was evident from his meetings with **Saddam Hussein** before and after the 1991 Gulf War, which were instrumental in securing the release of British hostages and prisoners. He has resisted attempts to move him to the Lords, and, on the retirement of Sir Bernard Braine at the next general election, he will become the Father of the House as its longest-serving current Member of Parliament. A lifelong bachelor, he is an authority on classical music and has frequently conducted major concerts for charity. He is also an expert yachtsman, and, after winning the 1969 Hobart Ocean race, captained the British crew for the Admiral's Cup in 1971 and 1979. His books include *Old World, New Horizons* (1970), *Sailing: a course of my life* (1975), *Music: a joy for life* (1976), *Travels: people and places in my life* (1977), and *Carols: the joy of Christmas* (1977).

HEGEL, Georg Wilhelm Friedrich
1770–1831

German philosopher, born Stuttgart. After studying theology at Tübingen, he taught in Berne and Frankfurt, but his work as a lecturer at Jena came to an end when the university was closed following **Napoleon**'s victory. He then worked as a newspaper editor in Bamberg and as headmaster of Nuremberg gymnasium. In 1807 he published *The Phenomenology of Mind*, which dealt with the human intellect's progression from reason, spirit and religion to absolute knowledge. In *Science of Logic* (1812, 1816), he explored the process of logical argument and the evolution of ideas and historical movements. He resumed his university career at Heidelberg in 1816, and a year later published his *Encyclopaedia of the Philosophical Sciences*. Later works, such as *Philosophy of Right* (1821), present his political philosophy and reproduce his most significant lectures on the traditions of philosophy, art, and history, many of which exerted great influence on groups as diverse as Marxists, idealists and existentialists. In 1816, he became a professor at the University of Berlin, where he met his death in a cholera epidemic at the age of 60.

HENG SAMRIN
1934–

Cambodian (Kampuchean) politician. Having served as a commissar in **Pol Pot**'s brutal Khmer Rouge regime (1976–8), he fled to Vietnam after leading an abortive coup and established the Kampuchean People's Revolutionary Party. He took power with Vietnamese patronage in 1979, but, following Vietnam's withdrawal of its troops, his influence dwindled, and in recent years the country has effectively been under the control of its moderate and conciliatory Prime Minister, Hun Sen.

HENLEIN, Konrad
1898–1945

German politician. After leading the Sudeten German Youth Movement from 1923, he was made Gauleiter when **Adolf Hitler** seized the territory from Czechoslovakia in 1938, and from 1939 to 1945 was civil commissioner for Bohemia. At the end of the war, he committed suicide after being captured by American soldiers.

HENRY VII
1457–1509

King of England, born Pembroke Castle, Wales. The father of **Henry VIII**, he took the throne in 1485 on the death of Richard III at the Battle of Bosworth Field and consolidated his ambition to return peace and prosperity to England by his marriage to Elizabeth of York. His emphasis on expanding the nation's trade was shown by his peace settlement with France and his readiness to fund a mercantile fleet. The marriage of his heir to Catharine of Aragon cemented an alliance with France and thwarted French aspirations, and the longstanding enmity with Caledonia came to an end on the marriage of his daughter, Margaret Tudor, to James IV of Scotland. After being widowed in 1503, Henry planned to remarry so as to further his grand design, but did not find another wife that suited his tastes or his strategy before his death six years later.

HENRY VIII
1491–1547

King of England, born Greenwich. The second son of **Henry VII**, he was an exemplary scholar who took a particular interest in the arts, and his accession in 1509 was welcomed as much by intellectuals such as John Colet and Thomas More as by the people, who immediately warmed to their handsome and accomplished new monarch and rejoiced at his marriage to the Spanish pricess Catharine of Aragon seven weeks after he acceded to the throne. Henry consolidated his popularity when he led the English forces that joined those of Spain in the Holy League's invasion of France in 1512, and with his successful defeat of the Scots at the Battle of Flodden a year later. However, the Spanish alliance ended in 1525 with the defeat of Frances I by Charles I. Fearing the implications of this for the security of the English throne, Henry now sided with the French. Even more preoccupied with his wife's inability to provide him with a male heir (for only **Mary Tudor** had survived infancy) and infatuated with Anne Boleyn, niece of Thomas Howard, 3rd Duke of Norfolk, in 1528 he asked Pope Clement VII to have his marriage annulled. The Roman curia's rejection of Henry's request brought the downfall of his long-serving chief minister, Cardinal **Wolsey**, who was stripped of office in 1529 and died while awaiting trial for treason. Henry's next ploy was to put pressure on Rome by accusing the whole body of the English clergy of treason and then pardoning it only after enacting a tribute of £118000, demanding recognition of his status as protector and supreme head of the Church, and withdrawing payments to the Pope—actions that brought a request by Thomas More to be relieved of his office as Chancellor. In 1533 the king married Anne, and the following year he ruled that all bishops should be appointed only with the approval of the Crown, broke all ties with Rome, and proclaimed himself head of the Church of England. More and Bishop Fisher, having refused to swear to the king's new status, were executed in 1535, and in 1537 Henry ordered the publication of the *Bishop's Book* with which, through its promotion of orthodox doctrines, he sought to disarm his opponents by asserting that his quarrel was only with the Pope Clement VII, not the Church of Rome. In 1535 his ambitious Lord Privy Seal, **Thomas Cromwell,** accepted with alacrity the additional title of vicar-general and the task of reporting on the state of the monasteries for the guidance of Parliament. Henry used Cromwell's findings to legislate immediately for the suppression of all monasteries having a revenue of under £200 a year, and within a year the measure was extended to them all, with their land and revenues passing to the Crown and to individuals in the king's favour. The same year saw the natural death of Catharine and the ending of Henry's 1000-day marriage to Anne Boleyn, with her execution for alleged infidelity. The day after her execution, Henry announced his betrothal to one of Anne's ladies-in-waiting, Jane Seymour and married her 10 days later. In 1537 Henry was at last presented with a male heir, the future Edward VI. Jane died 12 days later and the king's next wife, Ann of Cleves, was virtually forced on him by Cromwell, with a view to buttressing Henry's throne with the support of Protestant Germany. However, such was the king's distaste for his plain new bride that he consented only on the understanding that the marriage would be short-lived, and six months later required Parliament to annul it. Cromwell's reputation never recovered from the episode, and as he was anyway now detested by both Parliament and the people, Henry had no further use for his services and he was executed without trial in 1540 on a charge of high treason brought by the Duke of Norfolk. Norfolk's niece, Catherine Howard, married Henry the same year, but he soon tired of her and within two years had her beheaded after Thomas Cranmer, Archibishop of Canterbury, had persuaded Catherine to admit to premarital affairs. Catharine Parr, widow of Lord Latimer, became Henry's sixth, and last, wife in 1543, and was the only one to survive him. For the last four years of his life, Henry was preoccupied less with the bedchamber than the intrigues of the French in Scotland, which eventually benefited from his 1546 peace treaty with Francis I. Before taking to his death bed, Henry added Norfolk's son, Henry Howard, to his list of political executions—and Norfolk himself only avoided the same fate because Henry died days before the Duke was due to be executed. 'Bluff King Hal' is usually portrayed as either a licentious monster or a tormented and misunderstood ecclesiastical reformer. Probably a little of both, he was adored by the majority of his subjects all his life.

HERMANNSSON, Steingrimur
1928–

Icelandic politician. After training as an electrical engineer in the USA, he worked in industry and was director of his country's National Research Council from 1957. He became chairman of the Progressive Party in 1979, becoming Prime Minister at the head of the 1983–7 Independence Party coalition. He briefly served as Foreign Minister under Thorsteinn P. Isson before resuming the premiership in 1988.

HERRIOTT, Édouard
1872–57

French radical socialist statesman, born Troyes. After working as a professor in Lyons, he became a senator in 1912, and as leader of the Radical Socialist Party in the Chamber of Deputies from 1919 to 1942 held office in several coalitions between the wars. In 1942 he was imprisoned by the Vichy Government and renounced his Legion of Honour when it was conferred on German collaborators. After the war, he was reinvested and was president of the National Assembly from 1947 to 1953, when he was made Life President. Although a supporter of the League of Nations, he opposed any European defence policy that meant German rearmament. He wrote *Madame Récamier* (1904) and *Beethoven* (1932).

HESELTINE, Michael (Ray Dibdin)
1933–

British publisher and politician, born Swansea. Educated at Shrewsbury School and Pembroke College, Oxford, where he was president of the Union in 1954, he completed his national service as an officer in the Welsh Guards, and was a millionaire at 26 from his property redevelopment and magazine publishing companies, which he started with a £1000 legacy. He contested Gower in 1959 and Coventry, North in 1964 before entering Parliament as Conservative MP for Tavistock in 1966. He was made junior Minister for Transport (1970), and the Environment (1970–2) and Minister for Transport and Shipping (1972–4) and, in Opposition from 1974 to 1979, as MP for Henley, was his party's spokesman on industry (1974–6), and shadow Environment Secretary (1976–9). On the Conservatives' return to power in 1979, he was Secretary of State for the Environment until 1983, in which year he was appointed Defence Secretary. In 1986, he resigned in protest at the sale of the British helicopter manufacturer, Westland, to a US rather than a European company, the case against which **Margaret Thatcher** had not permitted him to put to the Cabinet. In November 1990, Thatcher's unpopularity among many MPs because of her intransigence over European monetary union and derogation of British parliamentary powers to Brussels not only brought the resignation of deputy premier Sir **Geoffrey Howe** but triggered Heseltine's long-expected challenge for the party leadership. In the first ballot on 20 November, Thatcher secured less than the 15 per cent majority needed for an outright win and announced her resignation. In the next ballot, Heseltine came second to **John Major**, who appointed him Environment Secretary in his new Cabinet with a brief to give priority to reforming the highly unpopular poll tax, and in April 1991 Heseltine announced that it would be scrapped by 1993 in favour of a council tax based on property values. He is the author of *Reviving the Inner Cities* 1983), *Where There's a Will* (1987), and *The Challenge of Europe* (1989).

HESS, Rudolf (Walter Richard)
1894–1987

German politician, born Alexandria, Egypt. Educated at Godesberg, after active service in World War I he joined the Nazi Party in 1920, while a student at Munich University, and took part in the abortive Munich putsch three years later. Following his imprisonment—where it is said that **Adolf Hitler** dictated *Mein Kampf* to him—Hess became deputy leader in 1934 and Hitler's successor-designate after **Hermann Goering** as Fuhrer. In May 1941, on the eve of Germany's invasion of Russia, he flew a plane to Eaglesham in Scotland in a bizarre attempt to negotiate Anglo-German peace. He was temporarily imprisoned in the Tower of London and then placed under psychiatric care until the end of the war. In 1944 he was returned to Nuremberg to face trial and sentenced to life imprisonment in Spandau jail, guarded by British, American and Russian soldiers. Requests by humanitarian organizations in Britain and America to have him released on compassionate grounds were ignored by Moscow, and after 1966 Hess was Spandau's sole remaining prisoner. After his death was reported in 1987, uncorroborated but plausible claims that Hess had been smuggled out with secret Anglo-American connivance years before were dismissed by his son.

HEUSS, Theodor
1884–1963

German politician, born Brackenheim, Württemberg. After studying at Munich and Berlin and editing a political journal, he was appointed professor at the Berlin College of Political Science (1920–33), and sat in the

German Parliament from 1924 to 1928, and again from 1930 to 1932. As the author of two books critical of **Adolf Hitler** in the early years of his rise to power, Heuss was forced into temporary retirement in Heidelberg, where he continued to write criticisms of the Nazi regime under a pseudonym until the end of World War II. In 1946, he helped to found the Free Democratic Party and to draft the new federal constitution. In the penultimate year of his 10-year term as President from 1949, he became the first German head of state to visit Britain for more than 50 years. His autobiography, *Vorspiele*, was published in 1954.

HINDENBURG, Paul von Beneckendorf und von
1847–1934

German soldier and president, born Posen. After his education at Wahlstatt and Berlin cadet schools, he fought at the battle of Königgrätz (1866) and in the Franco-Prussian War (1870–1), rising to the rank of general in 1903. He retired from the army in 1911 but was recalled at the outbreak of World War I and won decisive victories against the Russians at Tannenberg (1914) and the Masurian Lakes (1915). He was less successful on the western front and was forced to retreat in 1918. Nevertheless, he was considered a national hero and held the presidency from 1925 to 1934. After defeating **Adolf Hitler** for the office in 1932, he saw him made Chancellor in 1933, but was able to suppress Hitler's attempts to overthrow constitutional government until his death.

HIROHITO
1901–89

Emperor of Japan. After making the first visit by a Japanese prince to the West in 1921, he ascended the throne in 1926 after his father suffered a mental breakdown. After an initial period of liberalizing rule, the court became influenced by intrigues and secret societies, which Hirohito did little to contain, yet he approved a rapid escalation of Japan's military strength and the invasion of Manchuria in 1932 and the war against China from 1937. After Japan's declaration of war on the USA in 1941, the Japanese military displayed both incredible tenacity and extreme cruelty in its handling of POWs, and their sacrificial loyalty to their divine leader was typified by the action of the kamikaze air crew who suicidally piloted their planes at US warships. With no sign of Japanese surrender on the mainland, the war was only brought to an end by the dropping by the USAF of atomic bombs on Hiroshima and Nagasaki in August 1945, leading to Hirohito's unprecedented broadcast to his people, in which he renounced his divinity and surrendered to General **Douglas MacArthur**. After the war, Hirohito remained monarch but relinquished most of his powers in favour of constitutional government. On his death in 1989, there were widespread demands by organizations representing British and American ex-prisoners of war that his state funeral should not be dignified by the attendance of senior figures from those countries, but, as a gesture of reconciliation, Britain was represented by Prince Philip and the USA by Vice-President **Dan Quayle**.

HISLOP, Ian David
1960–

British writer and editor. Educated at Ardingly College and Magdalen College Oxford, he joined the staff of *Private Eye* in 1981 and was appointed deputy editor in 1985, succeeding **Richard Ingrams** as editor a year later. He regularly contributes book reviews and articles on current affairs and the arts to several other publications, as well as being a member of the *Spitting Image* scriptwriting team. He has edited several *Private Eye* spin-off books, and is the author of *Battle for Britain* (1987).

HITLER, Adolf (Adolf Shicklgrüber)
1889–1945

German dictator, born Braunau, Upper Austria. Educated in Linz and Steyr, his father's ambitions for him to enter government service were undermined when Hitler deliberately failed his exams so that he might realize his ambition of becoming a great artist. After his father's death, he attended a private art school in Munich but failed twice to enter the Vienna Academy and was encouraged to train as an architect. In the pre-war years, he made what income he could from his amateurish sketches and odd jobs, dodged military service, and in 1913 moved to Munich. After volunteering for a Bavarian regiment in 1914, he rose to the rank of corporal and was recommended for the Iron Cross for his service on the western front. In 1919, while acting as an army

informer, he became interested in the fledgling National Socialist German Workers Party, on whose activities he was meant to spy, and joined the group, which by 1920 had become properly established. In 1923, the strength of its support was sufficient to encourage Hitler to lead with **Herman Goering** an attempted putsch against the Bavarian Government, but the putsch was unsuccessful, Goering was badly injured, and Hitler was gaoled for nine months. During his internment, he dictated *Mein Kampf* to **Rudolf Hess**, and after his release cultivated relationships with the industrialist Alfred Krupp and other right-wing members of the establishment to help build his National Socialist Party in preparation for his 1932 bid for the presidency. Hitler was unsuccessful, but by the following year **Paul Hindenburg** could no longer afford to ignore Hitler's growing power base and influence and appointed him Chancellor, in a vain attempt to contain his ambitions. Hitler immediately exposed the futility of that ploy, discarding the moderate policies of Vice-Chancellor Franz von Papen, and, after conspiring in the burning of the Reichstag building in 1933, denounced it as a communist plot and used the incident as an excuse to call a general election, in which the National Socialists achieved a bare majority. Hitler immediately assumed absolute power, crushing a threat to his leadership in 1934 by ordering the murder of Ernst Röhm and hundreds of other disenchanted Nazis by the SS under the direction of Heinrich Himmler and Reinhard Heydrich. Hindenburg's death later that year left the way clear for Hitler to realize his long-nurtured territorial aspirations by discarding the Treaty of Versailles, rearming Germany, sending his troops into the Rhineland in 1938, and establishing with **Benito Mussolini** the Rome-Berlin axis. The rest of Europe stood by, and **Neville Chamberlain** even acquiesced, when later that year he seized the Sudeten—the largely German-populated territory of Czechoslovakia—and then Bohemia, Moravia, and Memel from Lithuania. It was only when Hitler moved on Poland in August 1939, after it had refused his request to surrender Danzig and to allow free access to East Prussia, that Chamberlain was compelled to acknowledge his naivety and, on 3 September, to declare war on Germany. Hitler's aggression showed itself no less on the domestic front, with the relentless persecution by the Gestapo of political and other 'undesirables'—particularly the Jews, Catholics, members of minority faiths, and suspected communists—and their internment in concentration camps and subsequent slaughter by the hundreds of thousands. Having signed a pact of convenience—for both parties—with Russia, and given it half of Poland, Hitler was able, in 1940, to send his forces into Denmark, Norway, Holland, Belgium, and France. However, the Luftwaffe's defeat in the Battle of Britain (August–September 1940) and the cost to German air power forced Hitler to concentrate on the land war to the east and in Africa. Over the next two years—despite America entering the war in December 1941—the German army marched into Romania, Yugoslavia, Greece, Russia, and—with Italian support—into North Africa as far as Alexandria. But October 1942 saw a sudden change in the Führer's fortunes, with Field Marshal Montgomery's victory over General Erwin Rommel at El Alamein, the German retreat from Leningrad, and its forced withdrawal from North Africa because of British and American attacks, a month later. Sicily, Italy, and Normandy were liberated soon after, and the attempt on Hitler's life by members of the high command in July 1944 signalled that many senior Nazi officers knew that the war was lost. Hitler rallied with V1 and V2 attacks, but the successful raid by the Norwegian resistance on the 'heavy water' plant at Telemark had already truncated the development of any more sophisticated long-range weapons, and when the Ardennes counter-offensive of December 1944 failed, Germany itself tasted invasion. After retreating to his command bunker under the Berlin chancellory, only a few hundred yards from the Russian lines, Hitler's megalomania began bordering on insanity as he furiously planned future strategies for non-existent armies. In the final days, he married his mistress since the 1930s, Eva Braun, in the presence of his chief minister **Joseph Goebbels**, who then administered poison to himself and his family. When Hitler's bunker was unearthed during the demolition of the Berlin Wall in 1990, there was no evidence to disprove contemporary reports that Hitler and his wife committed suicide the day after their marriage, on 30 April 1945, and that their bodies were then burned to prevent them being publicly mutilated. Hitler's legacy was the 30 million service men and women and civilians killed during actions on land, in the air, and at sea, throughout Europe, North Africa, and Britain, and in the gas ovens of Belsen, Dachau, Auschwitz and Ravensbrück; and the partitioning of his adopted homeland and the hugh expansion of communist control into eastern Europe that was to last 35 years.

HOARE, Samuel John Gurney, 1st Viscount Templewood
1880–1959

British politician. Educated at Harrow and New College, Oxford, he became an MP in 1910, and held Colonial Office appointments in Russia and Italy, and as Secretary of State for Air (1922–9) was a passenger on the first civil air flight to India. In 1931 he was appointed Secretary of State for India, helped draft its constitution, and piloted the India Bill through the Commons in 1934. As Foreign Secretary in 1935, he made a memorable speech to the League of Nations on collective security, but resigned later that year over Cabinet policy in respect of Italy's invasion of Abyssinia. He was made First Lord of the Admiralty in 1936, and during the war was Lord Privy Seal, Secretary of State for Air again, and ambassador to Spain. His strong opposition to capital punishment was argued in *The Shadow of the Gallows* (1952), and an autobiographical work, *Nine Troubled Years*, was published in 1954.

HOBBES, Thomas
1588–1679

English philosopher, born Malmesbury. Educated at Magdalen Hall, Oxford, he travelled extensively as a family tutor and made the acquaintance of Francis Bacon and Ben Johnson in England, Galileo in Florence, and Descartes and Gassendi in France. After his introduction to Euclidean geometry while in his 40s, he worked on a broader application of its argument that the universe in motion, rather than at rest, is the natural state of things. Because of the patronage that he had enjoyed under many royalists, at the start of the Civil War he was forced into exile in France, where he tutored the future **Charles II**. After he was allowed to return to England in 1651, he published his greatest political work, *Leviathan*, but his sketches of the Civil War, *Behemoth* (1680), were suppressed, and he spent his final years writing verse translations of the *Iliad* and *Odyssey*.

HO CHI MINH (Nguyen Van Thann)
1892–1969

Vietnamese Communist leader, born Annam. The son of a mandarin, between 1915 and 1923 he worked as a ship's cook in the US Navy, as a chef in London, and as a photographic assistant in Paris, where in 1920 he founded the French Communist Party. From 1923 until 1930 he lived in Moscow, Bangkok, Canton, Shanghai and Hong Kong, where in 1930 he organized the Indochinese Communist Party. On his return home in 1941, he founded the Vietnamese Independence League, and in 1945 was declared President by the Japanese of the newly-independent republic. In an attempt to reimpose its rule, France established a puppet state in South Vietnam under Bao Dai, and continued to wage war against the north until 1954. Following the partitioning of North and South Vietnam at the 17th parallel, Ho Chi Minh began his long campaign, with Chinese assistance, to overthrow the south. Despite huge US military intervention between 1963 and 1975, Ho Chi Minh's Vietcong retained the initiative, and forced a ceasefire in 1973, four years after his death. The Civil War continued until 1975, when Saigon fell and was renamed Ho Chi Minh City.

HO HSIANG-NING
1880–1972

Chinese revolutionary and feminist, born in Canton. Educated in Hong Kong and Japan, she married fellow revolutionary Liao Chung-k'ai in 1905 and was an active advocate of links with the communists and Russia. Her husband was assassinated in 1925, and when two years later **Jiang Jieshi** (Chiang Kai-shek) broke with the communists, she returned to Hong Kong and was an outspoken critic of his leadership. She returned to Peking in 1949 as head of the overseas commission. Ho Hsiang-Ning was one of the first Chinese women to cut her hair short and publicly to advocate nationalism, revolution, and female emancipation.

HOLKERI, Harri
1937–

Finnish politician, born Oripaa. A political activist in his teens, he joined the youth league of the centrist National Coalition Party in 1959 and served as its information, research and national secretary between 1962 and 1971. He was elected to Helsinki city council in 1969. A year later he entered Parliament, and he became Prime Minister in 1987.

HOLT, Harold
1908–67

Australian politician, born Sydney. After studying law at Melbourne University, he joined the United Australia Party, later the Liberal Party, and sat in the House of Representatives from 1935. He succeeded **Robert Menzies** as Prime Minister in 1966, and during the Vietnam War strongly supported the USA with the slogan, 'All the way with LBJ.'

HOME OF THE HIRSEL, Baron Alexander Frederick Douglas-Home
1903–

Scottish politician, born London. After his education at Eton and Christchurch College, Oxford, he became Conservative MP for Lanark in 1931 and served as Parliamentary Private Secretary to **Neville Chamberlain** from 1937 to 1939. On his father's death in 1951, he succeeded to the peerage and was made Secretary of State for Commonwealth Relations, Leader of the House of Lords and Lord President of the Council (1957–60), and Foreign Secretary (1960–3) under **Harold Macmillan**. As his party's surprise choice as leader to succeed Macmillan in 1963, he was obliged to renounce his seat in the Lords and was re-elected to the Commons later that year. Although a man of enormous political integrity and ability, his rather distant manner and aristocratic image did not serve him well in comparison with the streetwise and charismatic Labour leader, **Harold Wilson**, and the Conservatives lost the election by only 20 seats. The following year, he was replaced as party leader by **Edward Heath** under a new selection procedure that Douglas-Home had sponsored, and in 1974 returned to the Lords as a life peer.

HONECKER, Erich
1912–

East German politician, born Neunkirchen in the Saarland. A miner's son, he joined the German communist movement in 1929 and was imprisoned for his anti-fascist activities between 1935 and 1945. At the end of World War II, he entered the Volkskammer and was admitted to the Politburo and Socialist Unity

Party as a candidate member in the 1950s, gaining full membership in 1958. He became party chief in 1971, and head of state following **Walter Ulbricht**'s death in 1973. Although he encouraged a degree of East-West détente, he was regarded as one of the most inflexible of the communist bloc's leaders, but his hitherto close relationship with Moscow deteriorated after **Mikhail Gorbachev**'s rise to power, especially when he ignored the Russian leader's advice to soften his regime. When the mass exodus of East Germans in 1989 finally triggered democratization and German reunification in September 1990, Honecker left office a broken man and was admitted to a Russian hospital.

HOOVER, John Edgar
1895–1972

American security services chief, born Washington DC. After the premature death of his father, he worked to help support his family while studying law at evening classes and graduating from George Washington University. He joined the Justices Department, becoming assistant Attorney-General in 1919 and Assistant Director of the Federal Bureau of Investigation in 1921. Three years later, he began a term as its director that only ended on his death 48 years later. He won acclaim for his campaigns against gangsterism in the interwar years and for tracking down communist sympathizers after World War II, but in his later years in office he was criticized for abusing his power by persecuting liberal and civil-rights activists, and had a notably stormy relationship with Attorney-General **Robert Kennedy** during the presidency of his brother, **John F. Kennedy**.

HOUPHOUËT-BOIGNY, Felix
1905–

Ivory Coast politician, born Yamoussoukro. After studying medicine in Dakar, Senegal, he ran a law practice and then entered the French Constitutional Assembly in 1945 and sat in the National Assembly from 1946 to 1959. He became President when his country achieved full independence from the French in 1960. As a pragmatist, he has maintained links with South Africa, and has won justifiable praise for making the Ivory Coast one of the most economically stable of the African democracies.

HOWE, Sir (Richard Edward) Geoffrey
1926–

British politician, Port Talbot, Glamorgan. He was educated at Winchester College and Trinity Hall, Cambridge, and after serving as a lieutenant with the Royal Signals (1945–8) was admitted to the Bar in 1952, and became active in the Conservative movement in the early 1950s. After twice unsuccessfully contesting a Welsh seat, he entered Parliament for an English constituency in 1964 but lost it two years later. He returned to the Commons in 1970, when he was appointed Solicitor-General. He was then Minister for Trade and Consumer Affairs (1972–4), and Opposition spokesman on Treasury affairs until 1975, when he lost to **Margaret Thatcher** in his bid for the party leadership. On the Conservatives' return to power in 1979 he was made Chancellor of the Exchequer, and was Foreign Secretary from 1983 until 1989, when he was demoted to Leader of the House (and given the titular office of deputy Prime Minister) following policy disagreements with Thatcher over European monetary union. A year later, he resigned in protest at her continuing intransigence, and his highly critical speech to the House in October 1990 heightened the party split that contributed to Thatcher's decision to stand down three weeks later. In 1991, he announced his decision not to continue as an MP after the next general election.

HOXHA, Enver
1908–85

Albanian politician, born Gjinokaster. Educated in France, he worked as a school teacher and in 1941, founded the Albanian Communist Party as a rallying point for the nationalist guerrillas who formed the bulk of the resistance to German and Italian occupation during World War II. He became Prime Minister in 1944, and, after deposing King Zog two years later, became head of state assuming also the offices of Foreign Minister and Supreme Commander of the Armed Forces. In 1954, a year after the death of **Joseph Stalin**, he took the new title of First Secretary and instituted a swingeing programme of nationalization and collectivization that nevertheless remained independent of the Soviet and Chinese models. By the time of his death, Albania was the poorest country in Europe.

HOYTE, (Hugh) Desmond
1929–

Guyanese politician, born Georgetown. After studying at London University and the Middle Temple, he taught in Grenada from 1955 to 1957 and then practised as a lawyer in Guyana. Two years after he joined the socialist People's National Congress, his country achieved full independence and he was elected to its National Assembly. He held office in a number of Ministries before becoming Prime Minister under President **Forbes Burnham**, and then President on Burnham's death in 1985.

HUA GUOFENG (Hua Kuo-feng)
1920–

Chinese politician, born Hunan province. He fought in the liberation war of 1937–49, and, after studying agriculture, rose in the party hierarchy to become a member of the Central Committee in 1969 and of the Politburo in 1973. Two years later, he was appointed Minister for Public Security, and was chosen to succeed **Zhou En-lai** as Prime Minister in 1976 and became party leader on **Mao Zedong**'s death later that same year. In his first two years in office, he made notable advances in modernizing his country's economy and improving relations with the West, but he was gradually eclipsed by **Deng Xiaoping** and replaced as Prime Minister and party chairman by **Zhao Ziyang** and **Hu Yaobang** in 1980 and 1981 respectively. He was ousted from the Politburo in 1982, but remained a member of the Central Committee.

HUDDLESTON, Ernest Urban Trevor
1913–

English Anglican missionary. Educated at Lancing College and Christ Church, Oxford, he went to Johannesburg as a missionary in 1943, where he remained until 1958, when he became novice master of a Yorkshire community. From 1960 to 1968 he was Bishop of Massasi, Tanzania, and of Mauritius, and Archbishop of the Indian Ocean from 1978 to 1983. He has written extensively on universal brotherhood and racial problems. His books include *Naught for your Comfort* (1956), *God's World* (1966) and *I Believe* (1986).

HUME, Cardinal (George) Basil
1923–

English Benedictine monk and cardinal, born Newcastle-upon-Tyne. Educated at Ampleforth College, St Benet's Hall, Oxford, and Fribourg University, Switzerland, he was ordained in 1950 and returned to Ampleforth as senior modern language master two years later. He was magister scholarium of the English Benedictine Congregation (1957–63) and Abbot of Ampleforth from 1963 until being made a cardinal in 1976. He wrote *Searching for God* (1977) and *In Praise of Benedict* (1984).

HUME, David
1711–76

Scottish philosopher and historian, born Edinburgh. After graduating from Edinburgh University, he practised law but then entered commerce before moving to France in 1734 to write his first important work, *A Treatise of Human Nature*, which he published anonymously in England in 1740. His theories of the artificiality of the principles of justice and political obligation were expounded in his *Treatise*, which was not well received, but his popular later work *Essays Moral and Political* (1742) provided the financial security necessary to continue his writing. His *Enquiry concerning human understanding* (1748) was widely influential, as was *Dialogues concerning Natural Religion*, which he wrote in 1750 but did not publish until 1759. In 1752 he became keeper of the Advocates Library in Edinburgh, and then achieved enormous fame with *Political Discourses* (1752) and his five-volume *History of England* (1754–62). From 1763 to 1765 he served on the staff of the British Ambassador to Paris, where he was feted by the French court and literary society. He returned to London in 1766, became Under-Secretary of State for the Northern Department in 1767, and went into retirement in Scotland a year later.

HUME, Joseph
1777–1855

Scottish radical politician, born Montrose. A student of medicine in Edinburgh, he was appointed assistant surgeon with the East India Company in 1797 and held a number of important posts during the 1802–7 Mahratta War. He returned to England a wealthy man in 1808 and was an MP from 1819 to 1855. He brought his commercial experience to the advocacy of savings banks and freedom of trade with India, but also campaigned for the abolition of flogging in the British Army, imprisonment for debt, forced recruitment by the British Navy, and many other reforms. He also opposed attempts by the Orange lodges to give the throne to the Duke of Cumberland on the death of William IV.

HUMPHREY, Hubert Horatio
1911–78

American politician, born Wallace, South Dakota. Educated at Minnesota University and Louisiana University, he became mayor of Minneapolis in 1945 and was elected to the Senate for the Democrats in 1948. He campaigned vigorously for civil rights, but as Vice-President from 1964 under **Lyndon B. Johnson** he was criticized for supporting America's continuing involvement in the Vietnam War. In 1968, he won the first round for the presidential nomination, but the subsequent party split and general disillusionment with Democrat policies helped to return the Republicans to power under the leadership of **Richard Nixon**.

HURD, Douglas Richard
1930–

English politician. The son of Baron Hurd, he was educated at Eton and Trinity College, Cambridge before joining the diplomatic service in 1952. After posts in Peking (Beijing), New York and Rome, he joined the Conservative party research department in 1966. Moving into active politics he became private and then political secretary to **Edward Heath** (1968–74) and then held a number of junior posts in **Margaret Thatcher**'s government (1979–84). Resignations by senior cabinet ministers from 1984 fortuitously made Hurd's progress suddenly rapid, from Northern Ireland Secretary (1984–5) to Home Secretary in 1985 and, unexpectedly, Foreign Secretary in 1989. As Foreign Secretary he played a key role in redefining the UK's role in the new Europe. He unsuccessfully contested **Michael Heseltine** and **John Major** for the Conservative party leadership in 1990. Major confirmed his position as Foreign Secretary and Hurd won widespread respect for his handling of the Gulf crisis in 1990–1.

HUSAK, Gustav
1913–

Czechoslovak politician, born Bratislava. After studying law at Bratislava Law Faculty, he joined the resistance movement in World War II and later worked for the Slovak Communist Party before being imprisoned in 1951 for his political activities. After his rehabilitation in 1960, he taught at the Academy of Sciences (1963–8), and became First Secretary of the SCP and deputy premier in 1968. In 1969, following the 'Prague Spring' and Russian invasion of the previous year, he replaced **Alexander Dubcek** as Moscow's nominated premier and was charged with overhauling the party and establishing a new federalist constitution. Although initially regarded as a puppet premier, he implemented a degree of reform with the approval of **Leonid Brezhnev**, and by the time of his retirement in 1987 he was held in considerably more esteem by the West than when he first took office.

HUSSEIN, ibn Talal
1935–

King of Jordan. Educated at Victoria College, Alexandria, and at Harrow and Sandhurst Military College, he succeeded his father in 1952 on his retirement from the throne because of mental illness. After his 1955 marriage to Princess Dina was dissolved, he married an English woman, Princess Muna, in 1961, and a year later she gave birth to an heir, Abdullah. He has steered a careful course between placating nationalist neighbour states—for example, by his dismissal of the British general, Glubb Pasha, in 1956—and cultivating good relations with the West. The Iraqi coup of July 1958 brought an end to his federation with that country. In 1972 he divorced Princess Muna and married Alia Baha Eddin Toukan, who was killed in an air crash five years later, and in 1978 married Lisa Halaby. In the 1990–1 Gulf crisis, he went to extreme lengths to mediate between Western leaders and **Saddam Hussein**, not least because Iraq is the biggest customer of Jordanian exports, and in the wake of the 1991 War was faced with the problem of continuing to accommodate the thousands of refugees to whom Jordan had opened its borders at the start of the crisis.

HUSSEIN, Saddam

1937–

Iraqi dictator, born al-Auja, near Takrit. The son of a landless peasant family, he lived in Baghdad with his uncle, a teacher, from the age of 10, but left school almost illiterate and was rejected by the army on his first attempt to enter it in 1953. He then attended law school, but neglected his studies after joining the then fledgling radical nationalist Ba'ath Party, which sought a single pan-Arab state. After participating in an abortive coup in 1957, he fled to Egypt, and two years later took part in the attempted assassination of General Abdul Karim Qassim, who two years earlier had overthrown the Iraqi monarchy. He spent the next two years in hiding in Syria, and in 1961 entered Cairo University's faculty of law, but failed to graduate. After Qassim's murder by Ba'ath separatists in 1963, Hussein joined the new regime as an interrogator, and the following year was appointed to the party's regional command. He was made deputy Secretary-general in 1966, and a year later effectively seized control under the nominal presidency of President Bakr, whom he forced to resign in 1979 as self-appointed commander-in-chief, head of government, and chairman of the Revolutionary Command Council. His immediate ordering of the execution of his rivals, real or imagined, marked the start of a brutal dictatorship in the guise of nationalism, which grew even more extreme after the attempted assassination in 1979 of his deputy premier, Tariq Aziz, by members of the Shiite Muslim revolutionary al-Daawa movement, membership of which he then made punishable by death. In 1982, two years after he started to wage war against Iran, Hussein was almost captured, and his subsequent attempt to agree a ceasefire was rejected by **Ayatollah Khomeini**, with the result that hostilities continued until his decision to end the offensive, after his army had suffered huge casualties, making him the target of several assassination attempts in 1988. Having temporarily suspended his territorial ambitions, he directed his aggression at the Kurdish population, 5000 of whom were massacred, some by poison gas, in 1988 alone. The legacy of economic chaos and political instability left by the Iran-Iraq War and his pointless persecution of the Kurds prompted another attempt on Hussein's life in December 1989, for which 19 senior army officers were summarily exe-

cuted. In July 1990, after accusing Kuwait and the United Arab Emirates of undermining Iraq's economy by over-producing oil, Hussein moved 30000 troops to the Kuwaiti border, and in August ordered them to invade. His action brought UN sanctions and Security Council approval of the installation in Saudi Arabia of US defence forces. Fearing an attack on Baghdad, Hussein moved British and American hostages to key installations, and declared that Kuwait was his country's 19th province. Despite the increasing build-up of American and British forces in Saudi Arabia, the significant restoration of diplomatic relations between Britain and Iran, and the setting of a UN deadline for military action, Hussein remained intransigent, but in December made the surprising decision to release all hostages. Later the same month, he refused to meet with US Secretary of State **James Baker**, but strived to maintain his credibility with other Arab states by allowing showpiece visits by several leading European political figures, including **Edward Heath** and **Kurt Waldheim**, and announcing that Israel would be the first target of his counter-attack if the allied forces moved on Baghdad. On January 3, 1991, Hussein allowed Tariq Aziz, now Foreign Minister, to attend talks in Geneva instigated by **George Bush**, but following their breakdown and a fruitless last-minute meeting in Baghdad between Hussein and UN Secretary-General **Javier Perez de Cuellar**, USAF and RAF began bombing Baghdad short before midnight on 16 January, starting the world's 7423rd recorded armed conflict. Hussein retaliated, as he had promised to do, by ordering the launch of Scud missiles targeted at Tel Aviv and Haifa, as well as at the allies' military base at Dahran in Saudi Arabia. After the apparent defection of large numbers of his air force and the capture of the Qaruh island on 24 January, Hussein showed his displeasure by executing several senior members of his command, and triggered an environmental catastrophe by pumping oil into the Gulf. After an initial victory over US troops at Khafji on 30 January, the town was retaken, and Hussein's increasingly haywire strategy, already crippled by the bombing of vital communications headquarters, neared collapse with the US naval bombardment of his key troop positions in Kuwait. Hussein's announcement on 12 February that he was seeking Soviet intervention in ending the war, and on 15 February that he intended to withdraw from Kuwait came to naught, and following further mass executions of civilians in Kuwait, the coalition forces launched their Operation Desert Storm ground offensive on 24 February. Hussein's remaining and highly demoralized forces in Kuwait offered little resistance and surrendered in huge numbers, and in a broadcast on 26 February, Hussein announced the withdrawal of his troops and that Kuwait was no longer part of Iraq. Hussein was immediately confronted with a civil war as his army retreated through southern Iraq, but managed to contain the uprising there, and, in a carbon copy of his actions after the end of the Iraq-Iran conflict, sought to pre-empt any Kurdish action to bring him down by ordering air attacks on the Kurds' centres of population. That action, and the deaths and starvation among the hundreds of thousands of Kurdish refugees who fled to the Iranian and Turkish borders, left the West wondering whether the UN Security Council's approval only of the liberation of Kuwait had gone far enough. Meanwhile, Hussein continued to maintain an iron hold on Iraq from his highly-fortified headquarters in Takrit, and made no response to hints by President Bush in April 1991 that the US would be agreeable to Hussein being granted immunity from prosecution for war crimes provided that he went into exile. In accordance with the terms of the peace treaty agreed at the end of the Gulf War, a special UN delegation were sent to oversee the destruction and removal of all non-conventional weapons stocks. Initially the Iraqis refused to disclose all its nuclear sites, but when a resumed air offensive was threatened by the allies the Iraqis supplied the necessary information.

HU YAOBANG
1915–89

Chinese politician, born Hunan province. As a member of the Red Army from 1929, he took part in the Long March (1934–6) and held office under **Deng Xiaoping** before leading the communist youth league from 1952 to 1967. He was disgraced during the 1966–9 cultural revolution, but was rehabilitated in 1976 and, with Deng Xiaoping's patronage, was admitted to the Politburo in 1978. He became party leader in 1981 but was dismissed in 1987 for his liberalism and failure to control student unrest. Fears that his death in April 1989 would mark a new era of hard-line leadership under **Zhao Ziyang**

triggered huge demonstrations, which culminated with the Tiananmen Square massacre in June, in which at least 3000 were killed and 12000 injured when student barricades were stormed by the People's Liberation Army.

IBARRURI GOMEZ, Dolores ('La Pasionaria')
1895–1989

Spanish writer and politician, born Gallarta. Working first as a maid and then a journalist, she joined the Socialist Party in 1917, wrote for the workers' press, and then helped to found the Spanish Communist Party in 1920 and the anti-fascist Women's League in 1934. She was elected to the Cortes in 1936, and during the Civil War was famous for her rousing speeches exhorting the people to confront the fascist forces. She found refuge in the Soviet Union when **Franco** eventually seized power in 1939, and when she returned to her homeland in 1977 at the age of 81, she was immediately re-elected to the National Assembly.

IBN KHALDUN
1332–1406

Arab historian and politician, born Tunis. He held several different offices in Spain, but abandoned politics in 1375, travelled extensively, and then moved to Cairo where he pursued an academic and judicial career. He produced the monumental Arab history *Kitab al-ibar*, but his most influential and provocative work is *Meqaddimah*, in which he advanced the theory of cyclical social development whereby peoples gain civilisation, are corrupted by their own success, and are in turn superseded by another ascendant culture.

IBN SAUD, Abdul Aziz
1880–1953

King of Saudi Arabia, born Riyadh. Raised in exile in Kuwait, he was recognized by the British after succeeding his father as Sultan of Nejd and liberating his family's territories from the Rashidi rulers in 1921, whereupon he established a puritanical Muslim society. He implemented a far-reaching programme of administrative and social reforms, one of the most important of which was the provision of safe passage for pilgrimages to Mecca, which he achieved by dethroning King Hussein of Hejaz and annexing his domain. He proclaimed himself King of Saudi Arabia in

1932, and negotiated shrewdly with American companies after oil was discovered in his country in 1933, adding hugely to his personal wealth and that of his tribal sheiks. He took a neutral stance in the World War II, and on his death was succeeded by the Prime Minister—his son, Saud Ibn Abdul Aziz (1902–69).

ICHIKAWA, Fusaye
1893–1981

Japanese feminist and politician. A co-founder of the New Women's Association in 1920, she campaigned successfully for the right of her sex to attend political meetings, and from 1924 advanced the cause of women's suffrage after witnessing the growth of the movement in the USA during a three-year stay in that country. As post-war leader of the New Japan Women's League, she secured the vote for women in 1945. As a member of the Diet from 1952, she spent much of the next two decades agitating vigorously against bureaucratic corruption and legalized prostitution. She lost her seat in 1971 but was returned in both the 1975 and 1980 elections.

ILIESCU, Ion
1930–

Romanian politician, born Oltenita, Ilfov. Educated at Bucharest Polytechnic and in Moscow, he joined the Communist Youth Union in 1944 and the Communist Party in 1953, and from 1949 to 1960 served on its central committee. In 1965 he began a three-year term as head of party propaganda, and as a member of the central committee again from 1968 held office as First Secretary and Youth Minister (1967–71), and First Secretary of Jassy County (1974–9). In 1984, he withdrew from office to take up the directorship of a technical publishing company, but in the wake of the 1989 revolution and the execution of **Nicolae Ceausescu**, he became president of the National Salvation Front in December that year, and, two months later, of its successor, the Provisional Council for National Unity. In May 1990, he was elected president and resigned his party posts. Discontent with the economic situation resulted in protests against his government at the end of 1990 and early in 1991.

INGRAMS, Richard Reid
1937–

British writer and publisher, born London. Educated at Shrewsbury School and University College, Oxford, in 1962, at the age of 25, he founded with Peter Cook, William Rushton and other members of the new-wave of young satirists, and edited, the satirical fortnightly *Private Eye*, which has always been mercilessly impartial in lampooning politicians and other establishment targets, as well as serving as a springboard for notable exposés of corrupt practices by powerful figures that the established media shied away from instigating. He became chairman in 1974. The periodical and its contributors have been the subject of several successful libel actions, and has more than once owed its survival to the loyalty and generosity of its readers. In 1986, Ingram relinquished the editorship to **Ian Hislop**. Ingram is the author or co-author of numerous spin-off and other books, including *Dear Bill: the collected letters of Denis Thatcher* (1980), *The Best of Dear Bill* (1986), *You Might As Well Be Dead* (1986), and *England: An Anthology* (1989).

INÖNÜ, Ismet (Ismet Paza)
1884–1973

Turkish soldier and politician. Following distinguished World War I service, he was made **Kemal Ataturk**'s chief of staff for the war against the Greeks (1919–22), and, as the first premier of the new republic from 1923 to 1927, he transformed Turkey into a modern state and assumed the presidency unopposed on Ataturk's death in 1938. He led the Opposition from 1950, and after becoming president again in 1961 he survived numerous assassination attempts and an attempted army coup, but was forced to resign in 1965 when his minority administration was no longer able to govern effectively.

IRIGOYEN, Hipólito
1850–1933

Argentine politician, born Buenos Aires. Leader from 1896 of the Radical Civic Union Party that campaigned for electoral reform, he was one of the first to benefit from the improved democratization that it helped to secure, serving as first Radical President from 1916 to 1922. He was re-elected in 1928 but deposed by the military in 1930.

ISAACS, Sir Isaac Alfred
1855–1948

Australian politician, born Melbourne. A lawyer, he was made Attorney-General of Victoria, helped draft the federal constitution in 1897, and was a member of the federal Parliament from 1901 to 1906. Between 1906 and 1930, he sat as a High Court justice and Chief Justice, and in 1931 became the first Australian to hold office as Governor-General.

ISMAIL PASHA
1830–95

Khedive of Egypt, born Cairo. Viceroy from 1863, the granting to him by the Ottoman Sultan of the right to maintain an army and to conclude treaties effectively made him sovereign from 1872, when he undertook a huge programme of rebuilding and development, largely from the proceeds of the country's cotton crop, the value of which had risen sharply as a result of American shortages during the Civil War. He commissioned the Suez Canal but in 1875 could not sustain the project and sold his interest in it to the British for £4 million. His failure to introduce a constitutional government brought further European interference in Egypt's affairs in 1879 and he was deposed by the Sultan, to be succeeded by his son.

ISOCRATES
436–338 BC

Athenian pamphleteer, born Athens. After studying under Gorgias and **Socrates**, he worked briefly and unsuccessfully as an advocate, and then turned to teaching oratory. Many of his writings, such as the *Symmachicus* and the *Panathenaicus*, were meant to serve as model speeches, but were widely circulated as instructional or argumentative constitutional texts, thus becoming the first ever political pamphlets. He advocated the unity of all Greece against the Persians, but that ambition was thwarted by the victory at Chaeronea by Philip II of Macedonia in 338 BC.

JACKSON, Andrew ('Old Hickory')
1767–1845

Lawyer, military leader, and seventh President of the USA, born Waxhaw, South Carolina. As a barrister and Nashville public prosecutor, he helped frame the constitution of Tennessee, which he represented in Congress from 1796, and as a senator from the following year. In the War of Independence, he commanded 2500 men in the successful action at Alabama in 1813, which he followed with a decisive victory at Horseshoe Bend the following year. He went on to take the British base in Spanish Florida and subsequently became the territory's first governor. He was re-elected to the Senate in 1824 and achieved the presidency for the Democrats in 1828. His political practices were far less honourable than his military record, being characterized by the reward of high office for political favours. In his second term, his ambition to annex Texas from Mexico was thwarted by the anti-slavery faction, but he had the satisfaction of seeing it join the Union in the last year of his life.

JACKSON, Jesse
1941–

American clergyman and politician, born Greenville, North Carolina. After being ordained a Baptist minister in 1968, his ministry soon embraced the cause of black human rights and his association with **Martin Luther King** was followed by his founding of a campaign in 1971 to promote black economic advancement. In the 1984 race for the Democratic presidential nomination, he developed a 'rainbow coalition' of minority and pressure groups to take one fifth of the convention's votes, and doubled his support in the 1988 contest to come second to **Michael Dukakis**. Clearly intent on becoming the USA's first black President, he has not been slow to associate himself with any event of international importance, though in the prelude to the 1991 Gulf War, he was derided by the media for exploiting his minimal involvement in the return of the first British hostages from Baghdad.

JAGAN, Cheddi Berrat
1918–

Guyanan politician, born Port Mourant. After qualifying as a dentist in Chicago, he returned to his homeland and entered local politics before his election as a member of the majority People's Progressive Party in 1953. Fearful of the colony's fate under the Communist-inspired Administration, the British Government suspended the country's constitution, removed Jagan and his Ministers from office, and imposed military control. The following year, Jagan was briefly imprisoned, but in 1955 he won re-election as party leader, and the PPP returned to power in 1957. He was appointed Minister of Trade and Industry in the resultant executive council, though his power and that of his colleagues was subject to the British Governor's extensive powers of veto. Between 1961 and 1964 he eventually won effective control of his country's affairs as the first Prime Minister of British Guiana, now Guyana.

JAKES, Milos
1922–

Czechoslovakian politician, born Ceske Chalupy. Trained as an electrical engineer, he joined the Communist Party in 1945 and subsequently studied in Moscow. He supported the 1968 Soviet invasion and later oversaw the purge of reformists. He joined the secretariat in 1977 and Politburo in 1981, and in 1987 replaced **Gustav Husak** as party leader. A close friend of **Mikhail Gorbachev**, his deliberately slow restructuring of Czechoslovakia's political regime is designed to avoid the kind of counter-productive confrontation that has created difficulties for the Baltic states and other republics that have been impatient to break from the Soviet Union.

JAMES VI and I
1566–1625

King of Scotland from 1567, **James I** of England from 1603 the son of **Mary, Queen of Scots**, and Henry, Lord Darnley. Born in Edinburgh Castle, he was baptized Charles James at Stirling Castle. On his mother's forced abdication in 1567 he was proclaimed king, as James VI. He was placed in the keeping of the Earl of Mar, and taught by George Buchanan. A civil war between his supporters, the 'king's men' and those of his mother, the 'queen's men' lasted until 1573 and saw three successive short-lived regencies, of Moray, Lennox and Mar. A measure of stability emerged after 1572 during the regency of James Morton, who laid down some of the foundations for James's later personal reign. Morton fell briefly from power in 1578, recovered, but was arrested and executed in 1581, largely at the instigation of Captain James Stewart, created Earl of Arran, and James's cousin, Esme Stuart, made Duke of Lennox. Suspicion of these two royal favourites combined with

ultra-Protestantism to induce a coup, the Ruthven Raid (1582), when the king was seized. Although presbyterian ministers were not involved, the General Assembly by approving 'this late work of reformation', stamped a life-long suspicion of the aims of the kirk in the young king's mind. Within ten months James had escaped and a counter-coup orchestrated by Arran was instituted. In 1584 a parliament reiterated the primacy of the crown over all estates including the church; within days more than a score of radical ministers had fled into exile in England along with some of the Ruthven lords. The exiles returned by the end of 1585 and Arran was displaced from power, but the assertion of royal power, now under the guiding hand of the Chancellor, John Maitland of Thirlestane (1543–95), continued. The execution of Mary, Queen of Scots in 1587 drew a token protest from her son, but it was not allowed to disturb the league recently concluded with England (the Treaty of Berwick, 1586) or James's English pension. In 1589 he went to Denmark, where he married the Princess Anne of Denmark (1574–1619) and she was crowned queen in May 1590. The early 1590s saw a careful playing-off of Roman Catholic and ultra-Protestant factions against each other and by 1596 a new stability resulted. A mysterious presbyterian riot in Edinburgh in December 1596 heralded the beginning of a long campaign by the crown, first to influence the General Assembly and latterly to introduce bishops into the kirk; this was completed by 1610 despite bitter opposition, expecially from Andrew Melville, who was imprisoned in the Tower of London for five years. On the death of **Elizabeth** of England (1603), James ascended to the throne of England as great-grandson of James IV's English wife, Margaret Tudor. Although he promised to visit Scotland once every three years, he next returned in 1617. A joint monarchy thus became absentee monarchy, although the king's political skill and knowledge allowed him to govern Scotland 'by his pen'. James who went to England as an acknowledged, successful and learned king, was at first well received by his English subjects. But the dislike of this scheme for a 'perfect union' of his two kingdoms, distrust of some of the crown's financial devices, and resentment of royal favourites accelerated and made more acrimonious the recasting of the relationship between crown and parliament that inevitably followed the end of a long reign such as that of Elizabeth. The death of the king's eldest son, Henry, Prince of Wales (1612) devolved the succession on his second son, the future **Charles I**, who became closely attached to the king's new favourite, Buckingham. It was James' vision of bringing peace to a war-torn Europe as much as their escapades in Spain which brought renewed friction with the House of Commons after 1621. James died at Theobalds. His achievements as king of England are still a matter of acute dispute, but he is widely recognized as one of the most successful kings of Scotland, where politics and society were transformed during his long reign. This calculating tough-minded and talented scholar-king ill deserves the half-truth so often ascribed to him as 'the wisest fool in Christendom'.

JAMES VII & II
1633–1701

King of Great Britain and Ireland. The second son of **Charles I**, and brother of **Charles II**. He was born at St James's Place, London, and was created Duke of York. Nine months before his father's execution in 1649 he escaped to Holland, served under Turenne (1652–5), and in 1657 took Spanish service in Flanders. At the Restoration (1660) James was made lord high admiral of England, twice commanding the English fleet in the ensuing wars with the Dutch. In 1659 he had entered into a private marriage contract with Anne Hyde, daughter of the Earl of Clarendon and the year after her death in 1671 as a professed Catholic, he himself became a convert to Catholicism. In 1673 parliament passed the Test Act, and James was obliged to resign the office of lord high admiral. Shortly after, he married Mary of Modena, daughter of the Duke of Modena. The national ferment occasioned by the Popish Plot became so formidable that he had to retire to the continent, and during his absence an attempt was made to exclude him from the succession. He returned at the close of 1679, and was sent to Scotland to take the management of its affairs; this period saw the beginnings of a remarkable cultural renaissance under his patronage. Meanwhile the Exclusion Bill was twice passed by the Commons, but in the first instance it was rejected by the Lords, and on the second was lost by the dissolution of parliament. During this period James spent much of his time in exile but after defeat of the bill he returned to England, and in direct violation of the law

took his seat in the council, and resumed the direction of naval affairs. At the death of Charles II in 1685 James ascended the throne, and immediately proceeded to levy, on his own warrant, the customs and excise duties which had been granted to Charles only for life. He sent a mission to Rome, heard mass in public, and became, like his brother, the pensioner of the French king. In Scotland, parliament remained loyal, despite renewed persecution of the Covenanters; in England the futile rebellion of Monmouth was followed by the 'Bloody Assize'. The suspension of the Test Act by the king's authority, his prosecution of the seven bishops on a charge of seditious libel, his conferring ecclasiastical benefices on Roman Catholics, his violation of the rights of the universities of Oxford and Cambridge, his plan for packing parliament, and numerous other arbitrary acts showed his fixed determination to overthrow the constitution and the church. The indignation of the pepole was at length roused, and the interposition of William, Prince of Orange, James' son-in-law and nephew and the future **William III**, was formally solicited by seven leading politicians. William landed at Torbay, 4 November 1688, with a powerful army, and marched towards London. He was everywhere hailed as a deliverer, while James was deserted not only by his ministers and troops, but even by his daughter the Princess Anne (later Queen Anne). The unfortunate king, on the first appearance of danger, had sent his wife and infant son to France; and, after one futile start and his arrest at Faversham, James also escaped and joined them at St Germain. He was hospitably received by **Louis XIV**, who settled a pension on him. In 1689, aided by a small body of French troops, he invaded Ireland and made an ineffectual attempt to regain his throne. He was defeated at the battle of the Boyne (1690), and returned to St Germain, where he resided until his death. He left two daughters—Mary, married to the Prince of Orange, and Anne, afterwards queen—and one son by his second wife, James Francis Edward Stewart. He had several illegitimate children—one of them, Marshal Berwick.

JARUZELSKI, Genral Wojciech
1923–

Polish soldier and politician, born Lublin. A distinguished military career led to his appointment as chief of general staff in 1965 and as Minister of Defence in 1968. He joined the Politburo in 1971 and became Prime Minister and party leader following Pinkowski's resignation in 1981. Faced with increasing agitation for economic and labour reforms led by **Lech Walesa**, he declared martial law with the aid of Soviet troops and outlawed Solidarity, whose leaders were then put on trial. Martial law was lifted the following year, and in the then liberalizing shadow of Moscow, Jaruzelski was forced to resign as premier in 1985, as a precursor to the establishment of a democratic government, but he retained the increasingly impotent office of President after Walesa's election as Prime Minister in 1990.

JAWARA (Alhaji), Sir Dawda (Kair abu)
1924–

Gambian politician, born Barajally. A graduate of Glasgow University, he enjoyed a meteoric rise after entering politics in 1960, becoming Prime Minister only two years later. He retained the premiership when Gambia became fully independent in 1965, and assumed the presidency when it declared republic status in 1970. He served two further five-year terms, survived an attempted coup by Senegalese confederationalists in 1981, and was again re-elected in 1982 and 1987.

JAY, John
1745–1829

American jurist and politician, born New York. A lawyer, he was a delegate to both continental congresses and drafted the constitution of New York State in 1777, subsequently serving as its chief justice. Elected congressional president the following year, he was then sent to France as one of the commissioners charged with negotiating with Britain the Treaty of Versailles under which American independence was formally recognized. He next served as Foreign Secretary (1784–9), and while holding office as chief justice of the Supreme Court, he concluded the 1794 convention with Britain known as Jay's Treaty, which though favourable to the States was denounced by the Democrats as a betrayal of France. He was Governor of New York from 1795 to 1801.

JEFFERSON, Thomas
1743–1826

Lawyer and third President of the USA, born Shadwell, Virginia. Two years after being admitted to the Bar, he was elected to the House of Burgesses and played a prominent role in the first Continental Congress of 1774, not least in drafting the Declaration of Independence that was signed on 4 July 1776. As governor of Virginia from 1779 to 1781, he formulated the state's constitution, and in Congress successfully promoted decimal coinage. Following four years in France, he was made Secretary of State by **George Washington** in 1789, and, as the only Republican in the Cabinet, was acknowledged as his party's leader. He retired from politics in 1794, but was recalled to serve as Vice-President three years later, and became President in 1800, winning re-election for a second term in 1804. Under his Administrations, the French territories in the Mississippi basin were purchased in 1803, Ohio was admitted to the Union, and the slave trade was abolished in 1808. In retirement, he helped to found the University of Virginia in 1825.

JENKINS, Roy Harris, Baron Jenkins of Hillhead
1920–

British politician and author, born Abersychan, Wales. His election as a Labour candidate for a London seat in 1948 made him that Parliament's youngest MP, and he represented a Birmingham constituency from 1950 to 1976. As a private Member, he introduced legislation that gave greater protection to authors, publishers and printers against prosecutions for obscenity. In **Harold Wilson**'s first Government, he was Minister of Aviation, a liberal Home Secretary, and from 1967 Chancellor of the Exchequer. During his three years in that office, his stringent fiscal policies, exemplified by his 1968 Budget, brought the Labour Administration back from the brink of collapse, and he is retrospectively viewed as one of the greatest Chancellors of the century. In opposition, he was deputy leader from 1970 to 1972, and with Labour's 1974 election victory he returned to the Home Office for two years, resigning as an MP in 1977 to accept the presidency of the European Commission. In 1981, his growing disillusionment with Labour over its economic policies and anti-Common Market stance prompted him to form the Social Democratic Party, of which he became joint leader with **David Owen** in 1982. He won Glasgow, Hillhead for the SDP in a by-election the same year, but lost the seat in 1986 and received a life peerage the following year. His extensive literary credits include acclaimed biographies of **Attlee**, **Asquith** and **Truman**. His memoirs *A Life at the Centre*, was published in 1991.

JIANG JIESHI (Chiang Kai-shek)
1887–1975

Chinese general and statesman, born Fenghwa, Zhejiang. While undergoing military training in Tokyo, he was converted to the nationalist cause by **Sun Yixian** (Sun Yat sen), fought in the 1911 revolution, and was made head of the Whampoa Military Academy, which trained Kuomintang officers on the Russian model. In 1926, he took command of the army, and within two years had achieved Chinese unification, while also resisting Communist infiltration and reducing the influence of the Kuomintang. During his presidency of the republic from 1928 to 1931, he consolidated the nationalist regime, but was unable to contain the left-wing splinter groups that were eventually to bring his downfall. A head of the executive from 1935 to 1945, his role as commander-in-chief in the war against Japan was at the cost of neglecting to suppress right-wing elements in the Kuomintang, and the split with the Communists was intensified. In 1948 the Kuomintang fell victim to the Communist advance and Jiang was forced to withdraw to Formosa (Taiwan) with the remnants of the nationalist army, where he sought to rebuild his forces with US assistance. He also introduced wide-ranging social and economic reforms that helped to establish the stability and prosperity of Taiwan. On his death at the age of 87, he was succeeded by his son, Jingguo. His autobiography, *Summing up at Seventy*, was published in 1957.

JIANG QING (Chiang Ch'ing)
1914–91

Chinese politician, born Zhucheng, Shandong province. After studying drama and literature, she became a stage and film actress, but by 1936 abandoned that career to study Marxist-Leninist theory, and became the third wife of Communist leader **Mao Zedong** in 1939. In the 1960s, she emerged as one of the hated Gang of Four that led the Cultural Revolution (1965–9), and on Mao's death in 1976 she was arrested and imprisoned for her part in the attempted militia coups in Shanghai and Beijing. In 1980, she was put on trial for subversion and for authorizing the detention and torturing of her political enemies and sentenced to death, though her execution was later suspended. She committed suicide after being temporarily released for medical treatment.

JIANG ZEMIN
1926–

Chinese politician, born Yangzhou, Jiangsu province. A former electrician and automobile engineer, he served with the diplomatic service in Moscow from 1950 to 1956, and during the 1960s and 1970s was an industry and power Minister. As mayor of Shanghai from 1985, and although a party loyalist, he won a reputation as a cautious reformer and was admitted to the CCP's Politburo in 1987. Following the 1989 Tiananmen Square massacre and the dismissal of **Zhao Ziyang**, he was elected party leader, and has since made strenuous efforts to retrieve China's former progressive image, not least through his advocacy of a westernized economic strategy and stronger trading links with the USA and Europe.

JINGGUO (Chiang Ching-kuo)
1910–88

Taiwanese politician. The son of **Jiang Jieshi**, he studied in the Soviet Union during the 1930s, returning to China with a Russian wife in 1937. After the defeat of Japan in 1945, he held a number of posts before fleeing with his father and the defeated nationalist Kuomintang forces to Taiwan in 1949. He was appointed Defence Minister in 1965 and Prime Minister in 1972. In 1975, he was made nationalist leader on the death of his father, and in 1978 was made state president. The highly successful programme of post-war economic recovery that had begun under Jiang Jieshi was further developed by Jingguo, and in the later years of life he initiated a new era of political liberalization and democratization, which was continued by his successor, Lee Teng-hui.

JOHN, Patrick
1937–

Dominican politician. Chief Minister from 1974 in succession to Edward LeBlanc, he became his country's first Prime Minister when it achieved independence in 1978, but his autocratic premiership brought his banishment from the Assembly and his replacement by Eugenia Charles as Prime Minister in 1980. The following year he was acquitted after his alleged involvement in a plot to overthrow his successor, but in 1985 fresh conspiracy charges were brought against him and he was sentenced to 12 years' imprisonment.

JOHNSON, Lyndon Baines
1908–73

Thirty-sixth President of the USA, born Stonewall, Texas. At first a teacher and political secretary, he entered the House of Representatives as a Democrat in 1937, and, after decorated service in the US Navy, joined the Senate in 1948 and as its leader from 1953 was adept at using procedural tactics to thwart the Republicans. Having himself failed to secure the presidential nomination, he was made Vice-President by **John F. Kennedy** in 1960. After the President's assassination in Dallas, Texas, in November 1963, Johnson took the oath while being flown to Washington aboard Air Force 1, and was returned with a huge majority in 1964. He put through Congress several constitutional reforms promised by Kennedy, notably the 1964 Civil Rights Bill, and himself initiated several worthwhile community care and educational provisions, such as the Medicare health programme for the elderly. However, his escalation of his country's involvement in the Vietnam War, which produced only mounting casualties among young US servicemen, brought him increasing unpopularity with the electorate (typified by the anti-war protestors' famous chant of 'LBJ, LBJ—how many kids have you killed today?') and he declined his party's presidential nomination for the 1968 election.

JOSEPH, Sir Keith Sinjohn, Baron Joseph
1918–

British politician, born London. A barrister before entering Parliament for the Conservatives in 1956, he was Secretary of State for Social Services (1970–4) and then for Industry (1979–81) before serving a sensitive and controversial five-year term as Education Secretary, during which his rightist policies had the effect of limiting both the resources available to state schools and parental choice. A deeply intense and introspective man, he

unwittingly presented an image of dark genius, which, combined with the influence that he appeared to wield over **Margaret Thatcher**, as a close friend and political adviser, was seen by his enemies both inside and outside the party as being redolent of Rasputin—thus earning him the sobriquet of The Mad Monk. He was given a life peerage in 1987.

JOUBERT, Piet (Petrius Jacobus)
1834–1900

Afrikaans soldier and statesman, born Cango, Cape Colony. At first a farmer, he then studied law and was elected to Parliament in 1860, achieving office as Attorney-General in 1870 and as acting President in 1875. In the first Boer War (1880–1), he successfully commanded the Transvaal forces, negotiated the 1881 Pretoria Convention, and returned to politics as Vice-President in 1883. He was given command again in the second Boer War (1899–1902) but ill-health forced his resignation within a year of the start of the war and he died soon afterwards.

JINNAH, Mohammed Ali
1876–1948

Pakistani statesman, born Karachi. Having qualified as a barrister in London, he ran a successful practice in Bombay and was elected to the legislative council and National Congress, and subsequently became president of the Muslim League, through which he achieved co-existence with the Congress Party with the 1916 Lucknow Pact. An opponent of **Ghandi**'s campaign of civil disobedience, he resigned from Congress over its preoccupation with Hindu interests and secured safeguards for the Muslim minority at the 1931 London conference. He continued to campaign for partition despite conciliatory efforts by both Ghandi and Sir **Stafford Cripps** to maintain Indian unity, and in August 1947, in the last year of his life, Jinnah finally realized his ambition with the coming into existence of the Dominion of Pakistan by a British Act of Parliament, with him installed as governor-general of the new Muslim state.

JOHN PAUL II (His Holiness Pope Karol Jozef Wojtyla)
1920–

Pope since 1978, born Crakow, Poland. The

son of an army sergeant, he was active in the resistance movement in World War II, and secretly studied theology, leading to his ordination in 1946. He was made Archbishop of Cracow in 1964 and became a cardinal in 1967. In 1978, his election as Pope brought him the distinction of being the first non-Italian in 450 years to be chosen to serve as the spiritual leader of the world's 600 million Roman Catholics—and the youngest since Pius IX (1792–1878) to achieve the papacy at 46. John Paul's sense of humour and worldliness, and his courage in travelling widely to address huge gatherings despite an assassination attempt in 1981, have endeared him to many millions of non-Catholics. He has also established his place as the most politically-aware Pope of this century, and strenuously advocated reconciliation of the peoples and religious factions involved in the 1991 Gulf War.

JUAN CARLOS I

1938–

King of Spain, born Rome. The son of Alfonso XIII, he spent his childhood in Italy and in Spain, and in his teens was the subject of an agreement between his father and General **Franco** that he should take precedence as pretender. After serving a two-year term in the armed forces, he was formally named by Franco as the future king in 1969 and took the throne on the head of state's death in 1975. Despite his restraint in effecting a gradual restoration of democracy, he has twice been the target of assassination attempts.

JUGNAUTH, Sir Aneerood

1930–

Mauritian politician. After qualifying as a barrister in London in 1954, he returned to his homeland and joined the pre-independence legislative council in 1963. In 1970, two years after full independence was achieved, he co-founded the socialist Mauritius Militant Movement but soon after established the breakaway Mauritius Socialist Party, and became Prime Minister in a coalition of the two parties that took victory in the 1982 election. The following year he reformed the MMP as the republican Mauritius Socialist Movement, and while success in transforming Mauritius into a republic within the Commonwealth continued to evade him, he was re-elected in 1983 and 1987 as the head of an MSM-dominated coalition.

KADAR, Janos

1912–89

Hungarian politician, born Kapoly, south-west Hungary. A member of the then illegal Communist Party since 1932, he served with the underground during World War II and narrowly escaped capture by the Gestapo. He was made Minister for Home Affairs when the communists took control in 1948, and after being imprisoned for three years for supporting liberal policies of the kind being pursued in Yugoslavia by **Josip Tito**, returned to senior office in 1956 as a member of **Imre Nagy**'s anti-Stalinist Government. On the outbreak of the revolution in October of that year, he first aligned himself with the anti-Stalinists, but then established a pro-Moscow puppet Government and, with Soviet help, crushed the uprising. He lost the premiership in 1965, but remained influential as First Secretary of the Central Committee, permitting some economic reforms to improve living standards while remaining loyal to the Soviet Union. He relinquished the leadership in 1988 to serve in the titular post of party president, but shortly before his death in 1989, he was expelled from the central committee.

KAGANOVICH, Lazar Moiseyevich

1893–1991

Russian politician, born Gomel. After joining the 1917 revolution, he was made secretary of the Ukrainian central committee, and in 1928 was promoted to Moscow party secretary. During the 1930s, he was a willing participant in forced collectivization and, as **Joseph Stalin**'s brother-in-law, helped organize the purges of 1936–8. He was made deputy premier in 1947, but was expelled from the Council of Ministers four years after Stalin's death in 1953 and sent to manage a Siberian cement works. The last prominent survivor of the Stalin era, he eventually retired in obscurity in Moscow.

KAGAWA, Toyohiko

1888–1960

Japanese social reformer. After converting to Christianity, he attended the Presbyterian College in Tokyo and Princeton Theological Seminary in the USA, and on returning to his country worked in the slums of Kobe. In 1918 he helped to found the Federation of Labour, and in 1921 the Farmers Union and a system of agricultural collectives. After World War II he helped to promote women's suffrage and democratization. His early autobiography, *Before the Dawn*, was published in 1920.

KAIFU, Toshiki
1932–

Japanese politician. After entering the House of Representatives for the first time in the 1960s as a Liberal Democrat, he was re-elected five times and served as Labour Minister, and between 1974 and 1976 in a number of other senior posts under Takeo Miki. He was subsequently appointed deputy Cabinet Secretary, then chairman of the party's Diet policy committee, and was Education Minister from 1976 to 1977 and again from 1985 to 1986. He became Prime Minister in 1989. In the 1991 Gulf War, even Japan's minimal 5.5 billion yen contribution was fiercely criticized by dissenters in his own party, as well as by the Japan Socialist Party—the majority faction in the Diet's upper house—for not being made conditional on its use only for peaceful purposes.

KALDOR, Nicholas, Baron Kaldor of Newnham
1908–86

Hungarian-born British economist, born Budapest. Educated in Budapest and at the London School of Economics, he taught at the LSE from 1932 to 1947, and during World War II worked on both the British and American strategic bombing surveys. In 1947 he was made research and planning director of the Economic Commission for Europe, and while professor of economics at Cambridge University from 1966 to 1975 he was economic adviser to Labour Governments under **Harold Wilson** and **James Callaghan**. He wrote *An Expenditure Tax* (1955), which advocated expenditure taxes as opposed to income tax, and *The Scourge of Monetarism* (1986).

KAMENEV, Lev Borisovich
1883–1936

Soviet politician, born of Jewish parentage in Moscow. An active revolutionary from 1901, he was exiled to Siberia in 1915, and after being liberated in the 1917 revolution joined the Central Committee. He was expelled as a Trotskyist in 1927 but readmitted a year later. After his further expulsion in 1932, he was shot dead after being arrested with **Grigory**

Zinoviev for allegedly conspiring against **Joseph Stalin**. In 1988 he was posthumously rehabilitated by the new Russian leadership under **Mikhail Gorbachev** after the Soviet Supreme Court found him innocent of any crimes, together with his wife, Tatyana, who was executed after a show trial in 1937.

KANARIS, Constantine
1790–1877

Greek naval officer and statesman, born on the Isle of Ipsara. As a merchant captain, he provided his own ships in the fight for Greek independence from Turkey in 1822–4, and after being rewarded with senior commands entered the Senate in 1847. Between 1848 and 1877 he served three terms as Prime Minister, and played an active role in the 1863 revolution that gave the throne to George I.

KAPP, Wolfgang
1858–1922

German revolutionary, born New York. After working as a civil servant and director of the Prussian agricultural banks, he founded the German Fatherland Party in 1917, sat in the Reichstag from 1918, and in 1920 led a monarchist putsch against the Weimar republic. After seizing Berlin, he proclaimed himself Chancellor, but was thwarted by a general strike in protest at his actions. Having fled to Sweden, he returned to Germany in 1922, was arrested, and died awaiting trial.

KARAMANLIS, Konstantinos
1907–

Greek politician. After running a law practice, he held several minor official posts before being invited by King Paul to form a Government in 1955. He retained the premiership almost continuously for eight years, during which period Greece signed a treaty of alliance with Cyprus and Turkey. He went to live abroad after his defeat in the 1963 elections, but returned to become Prime Minister again in 1974 and to supervise the restoration of civilian rule after the collapse of the military regime. He was President of Greece from 1980 to 1985.

KARMAL, Babrak
1929–

Afghan politician, born Kabul. After

studying law and political science at Kabul University, he was imprisoned for anti-Government activities during the 1950s, and in 1965 formed the Khalq Party, and in 1967 the Parcham Party. In 1977, the two merged to form the banned People's Democratic Party, with Karmal as deputy leader. After briefly taking office as President and Prime Minister in 1978, he was forced into exile in eastern Europe, returning in 1979 after the Soviet invasion to become head of state. His rule was fiercely opposed by the mujahedeen guerrillas, and in 1986 he was replaced as party leader and President by **Najibullah Ahmadzai**.

KASAVUBU, Joseph
1910–69

Congolese politician. After working as a teacher and civil servant in the colonial Belgian administration, he secured UN support in his struggle for power against **Patrice Lumumba** after independence in 1960, eventually triumphed in the civil war, and replaced General **Sese Mobutu**'s caretaker military Government. He survived the many challenges to his Government that followed, but was finally deposed in the 1965 Civil War by Mobutu, whom he had appointed commander-in-chief.

KASSEM, Abdul Karim
1914–63

Iraqi soldier and revolutionary, born Baghdad. A career soldier, he had risen to the rank of brigadier by 1955, and three years later led the coup that overthrew the monarchy and brought about the execution of King **Faisal II**, Prime Minister Nuri Es-Sa'id, and his uncle, Prince Abdul Ilah. As self-appointed head of state he suspended the Constitution and established a left-wing military dictatorship that became increasingly isolated from other Arab states. He survived one attempt on his life, but failed to suppress the 1961–3 Kurdish uprising and was killed in a coup led by Colonel Salem Aref, who reinstated constitutional government.

KAUNDA, (David) Kenneth
1924–

Zambian politician, born Lubwa. Educated in Lubwa and Munali, he worked as a teacher before founding the Zambian African National Congress in 1958 to agitate for Northern Rhodesian independence, but he was soon imprisoned for his activities and the organization was banned. He was elected president of the United National Independent Party in 1960, and chairman of the Pan-African Freedom Movement in 1962, and was appointed Minister of Local Government and Social Welfare for Northern Rhodesia the same year. He played a significant role in negotiating independence, which was granted to the new state of Zambia nine months after he became President of the Lusaka Government in January 1964, in elections that were the first to offer universal adult suffrage. He served as chairman of the Organisation of African Unity in 1970 and 1987. He is the author of *Black Government* (1961), *Zambia Shall be Free* (1962), *A Humanist in Africa* (1966), *Humanism in Africa* (1967) and *Kaunda on Violence* (1980).

KEKKONEN, Urho Kaleva
1900-86

Finnish statesman, born Pielavesi. A law graduate of Helsinki University, he fought against the Bolsheviks in 1918, and after entering Parliament held several ministerial posts between 1936 and 1944. He was four times Prime Minister before being elected President in 1956. His premiership was characterized by a conciliatory attitude to the Soviet Union that was not at the expense of his neutrality and credibility among the Scandinavian countries. He supported Finland's entry into the European Free Trade Association in 1961, and in 1975 hosted the 35-nation Conference on Security and Cooperation in Europe, which led to the step-down in Soviet, American and European nuclear arsenals that was achieved in the late 1980s, and was awarded the Lenin Peace Prize in 1980. His popularity was such that special legislation was passed to enable him to remain in office until 1984, but he resigned in poor health in 1981. He wrote *Neutrality: The Finnish Position* (1970).

KELLOGG, Frank Billings
1856–1937

American jurist and statesman, born Potsdam, New York. After practising law in Minnesota, he sat in the Senate (1917–23) and was appointed ambassador to London in 1923. As Secretary of State from 1925, he drew up with **Aristide Briand** the 1928 pact that outlawed war and became the legal basis for the Nuremberg trials, and for which he received the Nobel Peace Prize in 1929. From 1930 until 1935 he sat as a judge in the Permanent Court of Justice at the Hague.

KELLY, John
1931–91

Irish jurist and politician, born Dublin. After an early career as a barrister and academician, he entered the Dáil for Fine Gael in 1969, serving as Chief Whip and a junior Foreign Minister before becoming Attorney-General for just 48 days under **Liam Cosgrave** in the 1973 coalition. As Industry and Commerce Minister in the short–lived 1981 Administration formed by **Garrett Fitzgerald**, Kelly found it impossible to work with Labour members of the Cabinet and became increasingly distrustful of his own party leader's socialist inclinations. He refused a Cabinet post in Fitzgerald's subsequent 1982–7 coalition, but as a Back-Bencher consolidated his reputation as one of the Republic's most honest and articulate, if occasionally idiosyncratic, politicians. He retired from the Dáil two years before his death.

KENILOREA, Sir Peter
1943–

Solomon Islands politician, born Takataka, Malaita Island. After qualifying as a teacher in New Zealand, he joined the Civil Service in 1971 and then entered politics as leader of the Solomon Islands United Party. In 1976 he was made Chief Minister, and became Prime Minister following the granting of independence in 1978. His opposition to decentralization led to his resignation in 1981, but he returned three years later to lead a coalition Government. He resigned in 1986 following allegations that he had accepted a secret gift of French finance to repair cyclone damage to his home village, but he remained in the Government as Foreign Minister and Deputy Premier.

KENNAN, George Frost
1904–

American diplomat and historian, born Milwaukee, Wisconsin. After graduating from Princeton University in 1925 he worked in US foreign service listening posts in the USSR and in World War II served in legations in Berlin, Lisbon and Moscow. In 1947 he was appointed director of policy planning, and his policy of strategic containment was adopted by Secretary of State **Dean Acheson**, to whom he was principle adviser from 1949 to 1952, and by **John Foster Dulles**. After serving as US ambassador in Moscow (1952–3) he was professor of history at Princeton's Institute for Advanced Study, and revised his views in favour of US disengagement from Europe. He wrote *Realities of American Foreign Policy* (1954), *Russia Leaves the War* (1956), and *The Nuclear Delusion* (1982).

KENNEDY, Edward Moore
1932–

American politician, born Brookline, Massachusetts. The son of **Joseph Kennedy**, he was educated at Harvard and Virginia University Law School and entered the Bar in 1959, succeeding his brother, **John F. Kennedy**, as Democratic senator for his home state in 1962. In 1969, he became the youngest majority Whip ever in the US Senate, and by 1979 was a leading candidate for the presidential nomination. He withdrew from the race following renewed attention by the media to the controversial incident in 1969 when a young campaign worker, Mary Jo Kopekne, was drowned after the car in which they were travelling together after leaving a party crashed off a bridge on Chappaquidick Island. He has remained, however, an influential backstairs Senate figure and a member of several of its important committees. His publications include *Decisions for a Decade* (1968), *In Critical Condition* (1972), and *Our Day and Generation (1979)*.

KENNEDY, John F(itzgerald)
1917–63

Thirty-fifth US President, born Brookline, Massachussets. The son of **Joseph Kennedy**, he studied at Harvard and in London, and worked at the embassy there, during which he published in 1940 *While England Slept*—a thesis on Britain's unpreparedness for war. As a US Navy torpedo boat commander in World War II, he was awarded the Purple Heart, and he entered the House of Representatives for the Democrats in 1947 and the Senate in 1952. His 1956 book, *Profiles of Courage*, won the Pulitzer Prize. In 1960, he became the first Catholic and the youngest ever President of the USA in the closest contest since 1916, and began implementing a radical programme of social reform headed by desegregation in schools and universities and civil rights. Even those who thought that he brought little but glamour and a social conscience to the White House could not fail to be impressed by his masterful and statesmanlike handling of the 1962 Cuban missile crisis, and by his ability in 1963 to negotiate a partial nuclear test ban with the Soviet Government that he had humiliated less than a year earlier, which served to expunge memories of the 1961 Bay of Pigs fiasco, when US troops had attempted to invade Cuba. Kennedy was naturally adored by young Americans, who saw him as the perfect leader in the liberalizing Sixties, but he was also much admired by international statesmen, including **Harold Macmillan**, the last of the great Edwardian Conservative statesmen, whose background and policies could not be more different from those of the young President. After less than three years in office, Kennedy was mortally injured by rifle fire as he was being driven in a motorcade through Dallas, Texas. The alleged assassin, **Lee Harvey Oswald**, was himself shot dead two days later by nightclub owner Jack Ruby, as he was being moved under heavy police escort. The controversy surrounding Kennedy's assassination has continued through the years, despite the finding by a commission chaired by **Earl Warren** that Oswald had acted alone, the most popular theories being that Kennedy was the victim of a Castro-inspired Mafia hit, or of a CIA disenchanted with his liberal policies and the interference in its affairs by his brother, **Robert Kennedy**, in his role as Attorney-General. What is certain is that John F. Kennedy brought a wondrous combination of style, statesmanship and humanitarianism to the Oval Office that had not been seen since the days of **Franklin D. Roosevelt**, and which has yet to be emulated. *The Making of the President* (1961), *J.F. Kennedy and Presidential Power* (1972).

KENNEDY, Joseph Patrick
1888–1969

American businessman and diplomat, born Boston. The son of a Boston publican of Irish descent, he was educated at Harvard and made his fortune from the stock market and speculation in the 1930s. As a supporter of **Franklin D. Roosevelt** and a generous contributor to the Democratic Party, he was appointed ambassador to Britain in 1938, but resigned in 1940, believing that a Nazi victory

was imminent. His nine children from his marriage to Rose Kennedy in 1914 included **John**, **Robert** and **Edward Kennedy**.

KENNEDY, Robert Francis
1925–1968

American politician, born Brookline, Massachussets. The son of **Joseph Kennedy** and younger brother of **John F. Kennedy**, he was educated at Harvard and Virginia University Law School, served with the US Navy during World War II, and, after being admitted to the Massachusetts Bar in 1951, successfully prosecuted several union leaders as a member of the House Committee on Improper Activities from 1957 to 1959. After masterminding his brother's presidential campaign, he made the most of his office of Attorney-General from 1961 to 1964 to draft and implement the President's civil rights legislation. Having entered the Senate in 1965, he offered his candidacy for the 1968 presidential race, but, after winning the Californian primary, he was shot by a 24-year-old Jordanian-born immigrant, Sirhan Sirhan, as he left victory celebrations at a Los Angeles hotel, and died the following day. Sirhan was sentenced to the gas chamber in 1969, but remains in death row.

KENNEY, Annie
1879–1953

British suffragette, born Yorkshire. Having started working in Yorkshire mills at the age of 10, she befriended **Emmeline Pankhurst** in 1905 and, directed by Christabel Pankhurst from France, served as an extreme militant from 1912, for which she received several prison sentences. She continued to assist Pankhurst in her work during World War I, and retired in 1918 after the granting of women's suffrage. Her *Memories of a Militant* were published in 1924.

KENT, Bruce
1929–

British cleric and peace campaigner. Educated in Canada and at Brasenose College, Oxford, where he read law, he was ordained into the Catholic Church in 1958 and was a cleric in Kensington (1958–63) before being appointed a secretary to the Archbishop of Westminster (1964–6) and chaplain to the University of London (1966-74). He continued to work as a chaplain and parish priest in London, eventually being made a monsignor, while becoming increasingly actively involved in the Campaign for Nuclear Disarmament, of which he was made General Secretary (1980) and vice-chairman (1985). He resigned his ministry on being made the organization's chairman in 1987.

KENYATTA, Jomo

1889–1978

Kenyan politician, born Mitumi. An orphan, he was educated at a Scottish missionary school and started work as a farm hand before joining the Kikuyu Central Association in 1922 and becoming its president. He visited Britain in 1929, and again from 1931 to 1944, studying for a year at London University. After three visits to Russia, he returned to Kenya to found the Pan African Federation with **Kwame Nkrumah**, worked on the land, and married an Englishwoman in 1942. From 1946 he led the Kenya African Union Party, which advocated extreme nationalism, and headed the offshoot Mau Mau terrorist organisation. In 1952, he was sentenced to seven years' hard labour for his activities, but was released in 1958 and sent into exile in the northern territories, then to his home village. In 1961, he was elected an MP and president of the dominant KANU faction, became Prime Minister in June 1963, and retained the premiership after Kenya was granted independence in December that year. In December 1964 he became President of the republic. One of the most instantly recognizable of African leaders, with his trade-mark tribal hat and fly-stick, Kenyatta has, despite his earlier well-earned reputation as a ruthless terrorist leader responsible for the deaths of countless whites and dissenting tribesmen during the Mau Mau campaign, earned worldwide respect for his moderate and progressive rule over his one-party republic.

KEREKOU, Mathieu

1933–

Benin soldier and politician, born Natitingou. After receiving his military training in France and joining the army of what was then Dahomey, he took part in the 1967 coup that removed his country's civilian Government, but declined to take office in the subsequent regime and instead rose to the rank of army deputy chief. However, in 1972 he used the military to depose Justin Ahomadegbe, and established the National Council of the Revolution, renamed his country Benin, and embarked on a policy of enlightened socialism. Once social and economic stability returned, he dissolved the NCR and installed a civilian Administration. Kerekou was elected President in 1980 and again in 1984, and in 1987 resigned from the army as a gesture of his commitment to genuine democracy. In 1991, he announced his abandonment of Marxism and his intention to stand in open elections to be held that year.

KERENSKY, Alexander Feodorovich

1881–1970

Russian revolutionary leader, born Simbirsk. After studying law in Leningrad, he joined the Socialist Revolutionary Party in 1905 and sat in the Duma from 1912. In 1917, he took a leading part in the revolution and between March and July was appointed Minister of Justice and for War, and Prime Minister. He insisted on Russia's participation in World War I and crushed a military revolt in September, but two months later was deposed by the Bolsheviks and fled to France. In 1940 he went to Australia, and then to America, where he taught at Stanford University from 1956. He wrote *The Prelude to Bolshevism* (1919), *The Catastrophe* (1927), *The Road to Tragedy* (1935) and *The Kerensky Memoirs* (1966).

KERR, Sir John Robert

1914–

Australian lawyer and administrator, born Sydney. After graduating from Sydney University he was admitted to the New South Wales Bar in 1938 and after war service was made a QC in 1953. He held a number of senior judicial appointments before being made Chief Justice of New South Wales in 1972 and Lieutenant-Governor the following year. A year after he was appointed Governor-General of the Commonwealth of Australia in 1974, he made constitutional history by dismissing the Prime Minister **Gough Whitlam** when the coalition Opposition refused to pass his Budget unless the premier called federal elections and the banks declined to release funds to allow the machinery of government to operate. Kerr then invited Opposition leader **Malcolm Fraser** to head an interim Administration and to call an immediate election, which, by returning Fraser, vindicated Kerr's actions. In 1977 he relinquished the governorship to become Australia's ambassador to UNESCO, but the ensuing controversy caused him to resign before taking up the appointment. His book, *Matters of Judgment*, was published the same year and updated in 1988.

KEYNES, John Maynard, 1st Baron
1883–1946

English economist, born Cambridge. Educated at Eton and King's College, Cambridge, he worked at the India Office (1906–8), lectured, and as a member of a Royal Commission on Indian finance published his first book on the subject. In World War I, he was an adviser to the Treasury, but resigned as a representative at the Versailles Peace Conference in protest at the harsh economic terms imposed on Germany in the draft treaty, explaining his reasons in *The Economic Consequences of the Peace* (1919), which he wrote at the suggestion of **Jan Smuts**. In 1923 he was made editor of the Liberal periodical *Nation*, and strongly denounced **Winston Churchill**'s restoration of the gold standard in 1925. The unemployment crisis prompted his two great works, *A Treatise on Money* (1930) and *General Theory of Employment, Interest and Money* (1936), which challenged the Treasury view that unemployment was unavoidable, and were influential in formulating **Franklin D. Roosevelt**'s New Deal economic policy. As a Treasury adviser again during World War II, he proposed the international clearing union, played a prominent role in drafting the Bretton Woods agreement (1944–6), helped establish the International Monetary Fund, and contributed to the abortive negotiations for a continuation of American lend-lease. He also wrote *Essays in Persuasion* (1931) and *Essays in Biography* (1933).

KHALID, ibn Abdul Aziz
1913–82

King of Saudi Arabia. The fourth son of the founder of the Saudi dynasty, he took the throne in 1975 after the assassination of his brother, King Faisal, and as a moderate and stabilizing ruler, gained international respect during one of the most volatile periods in modern Middle Eastern history. He was influential in bringing an end to the 1975–6 Lebanese War, and in ending Saudi Arabia's dispute with the other members of the Organization of Petroleum Exporting Countries. pr

KHAMA, Sir Seretse
1921–80

Botswanan politician, born Serowe, Bechuanaland (now Botswana). The nephew of the chief regent of Bamangwato from 1925, he was educated in Africa and at Balliol College, Oxford, and in 1948 married an Englishwoman while studying for the London Bar. In 1950, he and his uncle were banned from Bamangwato. On being allowed to return in 1956, he became active in politics and was restored as chief in 1963. He became Bechuanaland's first Prime Minister in 1965, and President of Botswana in 1966.

KHOMEINI, Ayatollah Ruhollah
1900–89

Iranian religious and political leader. As a Shi'ite Muslim bitterly opposed to the pro-Western regime of the Shah of Persia, **Mohammed Reza Pahlavi**, he was exiled from 1964 in Turkey, Iraq and France, returning to popular acclaim in 1979 after the collapse of the Shah's Government to become head of state with the support of the Islamic Revolution Party. Under his leadership, Iran underwent a turbulent period of change that imposed strict observance of Islamic traditions and principles and a total rejection of western influence. In 1989, Khomeini urged Moslems worldwide to execute his fatwah (death sentence) on the British author **Salman Rushdie**, whose newly-published novel *The Satanic Verses* was held to blaspheme Islam. On his death in June 1989, he was succeeded by Ayatollah Khamenei, who encouraged greater moderation and took the initiative in restoring normal diplomatic and trade relations with the West.

KHRUSHCHEV, Nikita Sergeyevich
1894–1971

Soviet politician, born Kalinovka, near Kursk. Being without the benefit of any formal education and virtually illiterate, he worked as a shepherd boy and locksmith, but after joining the Communist Party in 1918 and fighting in the civil war, he rose rapidly in the party hierarchy and in 1939 was made a full member of the Politburo and the Presidium of the Supreme Soviet. In World War II, he organized guerrilla warfare in the Ukraine and took charge of reconstructing devastated territory, then turned to reorganising Soviet agriculture. On the death of **Joseph Stalin** in 1953 he became First Secretary of the All- Union Party, and at the 20th Congress in 1956 denounced Stalinism and the personality cult. The following year he removed from high office his three strongest rivals for the premiership—Molotov, Kaganovich and Malenkov—and while he frequently travelled abroad, his purpose seemed mainly to denounce every country of the West that he visited. His efforts to decentralize the Soviet economy—which were never seriously repeated until **Mikhail Gorbachev**'s rise to power—alienated the entrenched bureaucracy and his colleagues' distrust of his aggressive, personalized leadership, saw him sent into obscure retirement in 1964. Under the liberalizing influence of Gorbachev, Khrushchev has been rehabilitated to some extent, with the text of his formerly secret speech to the 1956 Congress, in which he denounced Stalinism, being officially published in 1989. An 'autobiography' of dubious provenance, *Khrushchev Remembers*, was published in the West in 1970.

KIESINGER, Kurt Georg
1904–88

German politician, born Ebingen. After practising as a lawyer from 1935 to 1940, he joined the National Socialists and during World War II worked at the Foreign Office as a Nazi propagandist. At the end of the war he was imprisoned, but released in 1947 and exonerated by a German court the following year. He was a member of the Bundestag from 1949 until 1958, when he became Minister-President of his native Baden-Württemberg. He was then president of the Bundesrat (1962–3), and in 1966 he succeeded **Ludwig Erhard** on his resignation as Chancellor over West Germany's worsening economy. Sharing **Konrad Adenauer**'s vision of European unity, he formed with **Willy Brandt** a coalition between the Christian Democratic Union and the Social Democrats, and in 1969 relinquished the chancellorship to Brandt while remaining an influential member of the Bundestag until his retirement in 1980.

KIM DAE JUNG
1924–

South Korean politician, born Mokpo, Cholla. As a Roman Catholic, he was imprisoned by communist troops during the Korean War, and thereafter rose steadily in national politics, but after challenging General **Park Chung-Hee** for the presidency in 1971 was a target for persecution and was imprisoned from 1976 to 1978 and again from 1980 to 1982. He then went into exile in the United States, and on his return to South Korea in 1985 successfully led an opposition campaign for democratization. Kim's popularity among fellow Chollans and blue-collar workers further alienated him from the military and business elite, and in the 1987 presidential election he was defeated by the Government's nominee, **Roh Tae Woo**.

KIM IL SUNG, Marshal
1912–

North Korean soldier and political leader, born Pyongyang. After founding the Korean People's Revolutionary Party in 1932, he led a long struggle against the Japanese and, having established the new Workers Party of Korea in 1945, proclaimed his country a republic in 1948. He was premier until 1972 and then President, and remained in power after being re-elected in 1982 and 1986 on his policies of isolationism and the development of a Stalinist political-economic system. His son, Kim Jong II (1942–), is his designated successor.

KIM YOUNG SAM
1927–

South Korean politician, born Geoje, South Kyongsang province. Educated at Seoul National University, he was elected to the National Assembly in 1954 and in 1974 founded the opposition New Democratic Party and was elected its president. His credible opposition to the regime of **Park Chung-Hee** led to him being banned from all political activity, and in 1983 he staged a 23-day hunger strike against the restrictions placed on him. In 1985 Kim was officially unbanned, and he immediately founded the New Korea Democratic Party, which he reconstituted as the Reunification Democratic Party in 1987, in which year he came second to the Government's candidate, **Roh Tae Woo**, in the national elections.

KING, Martin Luther, Jr
1929–1968

American clergyman and civil rights campaigner, born Atlanta, Georgia. The son of a Baptist pastor, he studied at a seminary in Chester, Pennsylvania, and read theology at Boston University before establishing the first black ministry in Montgomery, Alabama, in 1955. He came to international prominence during the Alabama bus boycott, and in 1957 founded the Southern Christian Leadership Conference, which co-ordinated non-violent civil rights activities throughout the USA. In 1963, he led a huge black rights march on Washington, and in 1964 received an honorary doctorate from Yale, the Kennedy Peace Prize, and the Nobel Peace Prize. During a visit to Memphis, he was shot dead at his hotel by a white man, James Earl Ray, who was arrested in London the following year and returned to Memphis, where he was sentenced to 99 years' imprisonment. Martin Luther's widow, Coretta Scott King (1927–), carried on his mission through the Martin Luther King Jr Centre for Social Changes in Alabama.

KING, William Lyon Mackenzie
1874–1950

Canadian statesman, born Kitchener, Ontario. After studying law in Toronto and winning a fellowship in political science at Harvard, he worked in the Civil Service. He entered Parliament for the Liberals in 1908 and was made Minister for Labour a year later. In 1914, he became director of industrial relations at the Rockefeller Foundation. In 1919 he was made party leader and served three terms as Prime Minister between 1921 and 1948. His belief that the dominions should be autonomous within and equal to the British Empire was embodied in the 1931 Statute of Westminster, and having opposed sanctions against Italy over her invasion of Abyssinia, on the eve of World War II he wrote to **Benito Mussolini**, **Adolf Hitler** and the President of Poland urging them to agree peace terms. Once Poland was attacked, he immediately declared war on Germany, but initially opposed conscription. In 1940–1 he signed agreements with **Franklin D. Roosevelt** that integrated the two countries' economies, and represented Canada at the 1945 conferences that established the United Nations.

KING-HALL, (William) Stephen (Richard)
1893–1966

British political writer and broadcaster. Educated at Lausanne, Osborne and Dartmouth, he saw action with the Royal Navy at Jutland in World War I and afterwards joined the Admiralty, in which he served as an intelligence officer to the Mediterranean fleet, and as a commander from 1928. In 1929 he joined the Royal Institute of International Affairs, and broadcast and wrote extensively on current affairs. In 1939 he entered Parliament as a National Labour MP, and sat as an Independent from 1942 to 1945. He founded the Hansard Society in 1944. He wrote *Western Civilisation and the Far East* (1924), *Imperial Defence* (1926), and *Our Own Times* (1934). He was made a life peer in 1966.

KINNOCK, Neil Gordon
1942–

British politician, born Tredegar, South Wales. The only son of a miner and steelworker and of a district nurse living in the constituency that **Aneurin Bevan** had represented since 1929, he was educated at Lewis Grammar School, Pengam, became a Labour Party activist while still in his teens, and in 1961 won a place at University College, Cardiff, to study history and industrial relations. He soon gained a reputation as a forceful orator at meetings of the Socialist Society, and in 1965, in his final year, was elected president of the students' union. On graduating, he joined the Workers Educational Association as a tutor and organiser, and was among those who fought attempts by **Harold Wilson**'s Labour Government in the late 1960s to curb union powers. On marrying Glenys Parry, a teacher whom he had met at university, in 1967, the couple moved to a village in the Bedwelty constituency, for which he was successful in being appointed prospective parliamentary candidate in 1967 after the sitting Labour MP announced his decision not to stand at the next general election. After Wilson announced a snap election in June 1970, and despite the Conservatives' success in ousting the Government, Kinnock, then aged 28, held the traditionally Labour seat with a majority of 22000. He was barracked throughout his maiden speech in the Commons for breaking with tradition by addressing a controversial issue—the problems of the National Health

Service—rather than offering the usual bland round-tour of his constituency that is conventionally the content of a new MP's first contribution in the Chamber. The brashness and range—and length—of Kinnock's speeches during his first years in the House irritated as many Labour as Conservative members, but with experience, he moderated his barnstorming style to one more attuned to the subtleties of parliamentary debate, frequently directing his fire at the Labour Government that was in power between 1974 and 1979. However, although he was one of the earliest members of the Campaign for Labour Party Democracy formed by **Tony Benn** and other left-wingers in 1973 to combat Wilson's somewhat autocratic style of policy-making, he took little part in its activities, preferring to take independent action such as his 1975 vote against Wilson's proposed increase in the Civil List, which required his resignation as parliamentary private secretary to **Michael Foot**. His street credibility among the party left was still further enhanced by an astonishingly effective appeal for funds at the traditional *Tribune* rally at the Labour Party Conference later the same year. After Wilson relinquished the premiership to **James Callaghan** in 1976, the new leader made several attempts to persuade Kinnock to accept a post in his Government but without success, partly because of Kinnock's strong personal hostility to legislation to create separate assemblies for Scotland and Wales, which, ironically, was piloted by Michael Foot in his new post as Leader of the House of Commons. Kinnock was vindicated when, nearly two years later, a referendum produced only a tiny Scottish majority in favour of devolution and the proposal found favour among only one in 10 of Welsh voters. In the second half of the 1970s, Kinnock directed his energy to cultivating the party's grass roots, which had the effect of creating a positive reaction in the parliamentary Labour Party, which placed him fourth out of 34 candidates for the Shadow Cabinet. But before he had a chance to exploit his tremendous popularity within the PLP and at constituency level, Callaghan, struggling with a hopeless economy and humiliated by the referendum result, went to the country in May 1979 and suffered the greatest electoral swing since World War II and the party's lowest vote since 1931, with the Conservatives, benefiting from **Margaret Thatcher**'s dynamic style of leadership, winning 339 seats against Labour's 251. At 37,

Kinnock at last accepted a post in the Shadow Cabinet as junior education spokesman. He retained that brief after **Michael Foot** replaced Callaghan as party leader in 1980, and was one of his staunchest supporters when an attempt was made to remove Foot in 1982—for which loyalty Foot privately decided that he would reward Kinnock by publicly favouring him as his successor. By 1983, Labour's internal strife, typified by the party's inability to contain the excesses of Militant Tendency and the Bennites, and Callaghan's deliberately damaging attack on Labour's defence policy, did nothing to reverse its fortunes, with Labour's showing in the general election on 9 June even worse than in 1979, with the loss of another 20 seats—including that of Tony Benn. Within days, Kinnock, who had been returned by the new Islwyn constituency with a 14000 majority, was receiving the voting pledges of the country's most powerful union leaders under a new electoral system of selecting a new leader involving the PLP, unions and constituencies. At the party conference in October, he took 71 per cent of the vote against Roy Hattersley's 19 per cent, Eric Heffer's 6 per cent, and Peter Shore's 3 per cent. Kinnock had little more than three years to transform the Labour Party and rid it of the discontented and disruptive factions that had dogged it since the 1960s, so it was hardly surprising that he managed to improve the party's strength in the Commons by only 20 seats in the June 1987 general election. But by the end of the 1980s, the resoluteness with which he had tackled the task of improving Labour's image was producing concrete results, with the party getting a much improved showing in opinion polls, and everyone from **George Bush** to leading figures in the City hedging their bets and putting out the welcome mat for Kinnock and senior members of his Shadow Cabinet for the first time. During the Conservatives' 1990 leadership crisis and the Government's humiliating U-turn over the poll tax in April 1991, Kinnock showed himself in top form and exploited their embarrassment to the full—but he was shrewd enough to drop adversarial politics for the duration of the 1991 Gulf War, with the result that with the next general election on the near horizon, opinion polls were frequently showing Labour ahead of the Conservatives. His publications include *Wales and the Common Market* (1971), and *Making it our Way* (1986).

KIRK, Norman Eric
1923–74

New Zealand politician, born Waimate, Canterbury. While working as an engine driver, he became involved in local, then national Labour politics, to become party president in 1964. From 1965 to 1972 he led the Labour Opposition and became Prime Minister in 1972 at one of the most difficult times in the country's history, with its parlous economic state exacerbated by the repercussions on its farming industry of Britain's entry into the Common Market. He died in office in 1974 and was succeeded by his Finance Minister, Wallace Rowling.

KIRKPATRICK, Jeane Duane Jordan
1926–

American academic and diplomat, born Duncan, Oklahoma. Educated at Columbia University and Paris University, she worked as a researcher for the State Department (1951–3) and then at Trinity College and Georgetown University, Washington, becoming professor of government at the latter in 1978. Her hawkish, anti-communist defence views, which were untypical of most academics of her generation, and her advocacy of a new Latin-American and Pacific-orientated diplomatic strategy, led in 1981 to her appointment by President **Ronald Reagan** as permanent representative to the United Nations. On relinquishing that post in 1985, having formerly been a Democrat, she joined the Republican Party.

KIROV, Sergey Mironovich
1888–1934

Soviet politician. An early associate of **Joseph Stalin**, he was secretary of the Leningrad Communist Party from 1926, and was made a member of the Politburo in 1930. His murder by an unknown assassin triggered the first Stalinist purge, in which more than 100 suspected opponents of the leader's regime were executed after show trials.

KISSINGER, Henry Alfred
1923–

American diplomat, born in Fürth, Germany. Emigrating to America in 1938, he entered national politics in 1968, while still a Harvard professor, as national security adviser to **Richard Nixon**. His tireless efforts as a mediator in the Vietnam peace negotia-

tions brought him the Nobel Peace Prize in 1973 and the new office of Secretary of State, and he went on to improve détente with China and the Soviet Union, paving the way for Nixon's historic visits to Peking and Moscow. His special style of shuttle diplomacy came to the fore again in the Arab-Israeli negotiations from 1973 to 1975, as well as in the Angola and Rhodesian crises. He declined to continue as Secretary of State under the new **Carter** Administration in 1977 but remained a powerful and influential figure in world diplomacy, and in 1983 was chosen by President Reagan to head a bipartisan commission on Central America. **Bush** was the fourth American President grateful to benefit from his advice, albeit unofficially, during the 1990 Gulf crisis and the subsequent war.

KNUT, Sveinsson (Canute the Great)
c.995–1035

King of England, Denmark and Norway. After defeating Edmund at the Battle of Ashington in 1016, he shared power with Edmund until his death a month later, and then ensured his own rule by banishing or executing all possible claimants to the throne. After inheriting the Danish throne in 1018, he overthrew Olaf II of Norway and reigned there also from 1030. As King of England, he ruled firmly but beneficially, showing reverence for the English Church and its saints. The popular legend about his attempt to turn back the tide wholly misinterprets what was in fact a demonstration to his courtiers that only God could control the elements. Following his death and interment at Winchester Cathedral, his younger son, Harold I Knutsson, ascended the English throne, but that of Norway was taken by Magnus I Olaffson, who also inherited Denmark on the death of Knut's son, Hardaknut.

KOESTLER, Arthur
1905–1983

Hungarian-born British author, born Budapest. During his education in Vienna, he adopted the Zionist cause, then worked on a collective farm in Palestine from 1926 until becoming scientific editor with a German newspaper group. His communist beliefs brought his dismissal, but he soon became disenchanted with the party after travelling in Russia, and resigned from it in 1938. While reporting the Spanish Civil War for a London newspaper he was imprisoned under sentence of death by **Francisco Franco**, and was also jailed by the French in 1940. After escaping from the occupation, he went to London and was briefly imprisoned there before joining the Pioneer Corps. After the war, he gained a reputation as an author of political and humanist works. His prodigious output of essays, autobiographical writing and novels includes *Spanish Testament* (1938), *Darkness at Noon* (1940), *Scum of the Earth* (1941), *Arrival and Departure* (1943), *Promise and Fulfilment* (1949), *The God that Failed* (1950), *Reflections on Hanging* (1956), *The Act of Creation* (1964), and *The Ghost in the Machine* (1967). A selection of his non-fiction, *Bricks to Babel*, was published in 1980. Three years later, he and his wife committed suicide together when he became terminally ill.

KOHL, Helmut
1930–

German politician, born Ludwigshafen. After studying law at Frankfurt and Heidelberg Universities, he worked in the chemical industry, and having joined the Christian Democrats after the war, became chairman for the Rhineland state parliament in 1956 and Minister-President in 1969. In 1976 he entered the federal Parliament in Bonn and ran as Christian Democratic Union/Christian Social Union candidate for the Chancellorship. Although **Helmut Schmidt** kept office through a coalition with the Free Democrats, Kohl headed the largest parliamentary group. In 1980 he was replaced as CDU/CSU leader by **Franz-Joseph Strauss**, and despite his failure to replace Schmidt, the collapse of the coalition in 1982 saw Kohl installed as interim Chancellor and his victory in the following year's elections. In 1987, after being cleared the previous year of any involvement in the Flick bribes scandal regarding illegal party funding, he was re-elected Chancellor. In January 1991, six weeks after united Germany's first national elections, he announced a coalition Government that, while keeping CDU/CSU dominance in the key defence and labour and social affairs Ministries, reflected the strength of the vote for the Free Democrats, with the FDP's **Hans Dietrich-Genscher** remaining as Foreign Secretary. However, by April his party lost control of Kohl's own Rhineland home state to the Social Democrats for the first time since World War II, ending the controlling CSU and FDP coalition in the Bundesrat.

KOLLONTAI, Alexandra Mikhaylovna
1872–1952

Russian revolutionary and feminist, the world's first female ambassador. After renouncing her middle-class upbringing, she was exiled to Germany in 1908 for her activities as a member of the Russian Social Democratic Party and then travelled widely in the USA, promoting Socialism and urging America's non-participation in World War I. She returned to Russia after the revolution and was appointed commissar for public welfare, in which post she advocated social reforms such as collective child-care and easier divorce. Between 1923 and 1945 she served as Minister to Norway and Mexico and ambassador to Sweden, and was instrumental in the negotiations that ended the Soviet-Finnish War in 1944. Her works included the controversial collection of short stories *Love of Worker Bees* (1923), whose themes included sexuality and women's place in society. Her 1926 autobiography has never been published in Russia.

KOSCIUSZKO, Tadeusz Andrezei Bonawentura
1746–1817

Polish soldier and patriot, born Sionim, Lithuania. After military training in France, he fought for the colonists in the American War of Independence from 1775 until 1783, achieving the rank of brigadier-general. He returned to Poland in 1784, and when Russia invaded in 1792, he held Dubienka for five days with 4000 men against a force of 18 000 Russian soldiers. After the second partition of Poland in 1794, he headed the national movement in Cracow and was appointed dictator and commander-in-chief. He saw action again against the Russians at Warsaw, but was defeated by their superior numbers, and was wounded and taken prisoner. Two years later, after Emperor Paul of Russia restored his liberty, he travelled to England, America and France, where he settled as a farmer. In 1806 he refused to support **Napoleon**'s plan for the restoration of Poland, and after retiring to Switzerland was killed when his horse rode over a precipice.

KOSSUTH, Lajos
1802–1894

Hungarian revolutionary leader, born Monok, near Zemplin. After qualifying as a lawyer, he sat in the Pressburg Diet and was imprisoned for publishing an illegal journal. On his release in 1840 he edited another extreme Liberal publication, and in 1847 returned to the Diet as opposition leader. After the French Revolution of 1848, he called for independent government, and in 1849 started planning for war against the Habsburg dynasty with the support of the National Assembly. However, having failed to secure the intervention of the western powers and to avoid a party split, he resigned his dictatorship and, after the defeat at Temesvr in August 1849, he fled to Turkey and was imprisoned there. British and American intervention brought his release in 1851, and from 1852 he lived in England. On the outbreak of the Franco-Italian war in 1859, his efforts to incite a Hungarian uprising against Austria with the support of **Napoleon III** were frustrated by the Villafranca Treaty, and he attempted to foment further hostilities against Austria in 1866. When his country was reconciled with the Habsburgs in 1867, he retired from active political life to Turin, refusing to avail himself of the amnesty declared that year. Between 1880 and 1882 he published three volumes of *Memories of my Exile*, and had completed a work on Hungarian history at the time of his death.

KOSYGIN, Alexei Nikolayevich
1904–80

Soviet politician, born and educated in Leningrad. On his election to the Supreme Soviet in 1938, he held a number of industrial posts and served on the Central Committee (1939–60) and Politburo (1946–52). After a year as chairman of the state economic planning commission, he was appointed first deputy Prime Minister in 1960, and in 1964 succeeded **Nikita Khrushchev** as premier. His attempts at modest economic reforms and decentralisation were blocked by the party conservatives and the bureaucracy, and he died soon after resigning in poor health in 1980.

KOUTCHE, Seyni
1931–87

Niger soldier and politician. After military training in France, he continued his service with the French army in his own country before it achieved independence in 1960 under the presidency of Hamani Diori. The severe drought of 1968–74 increased general discontent with Diori's regime and Koutche staged, as commander-in-chief, a coup that replaced it with military government. His intention was to restore the country's economy and then return it to civilian rule, but before he could realize that ambition, he died while undergoing surgery in Paris.

KRAG, Jens Otto
1914–78

Danish politician. After serving as Minister of Foreign Affairs from 1958 to 1962, he became leader of the Social Democratic Party and was Prime Minister from 1962 to 1968 and again from 1971 for a year. In 1972, he took Denmark into the Common Market, but after a referendum later that year showing that more than one third of the electorate was against EEC membership, he resigned and was succeeded by Anker Jorgensen.

KRENZ, Egon
1937–

German politician. Educated at Putbus Teacher Training Institute and Moscow University, he joined the Freie Deutsche Jugend in 1953 and then the Socialist Unity Party in 1955, holding several posts in both between 1957 and 1964. In 1967 he was appointed Secretary-General of the Ernst Thälman Pioneer Organisation, and was chairman from 1971, in which year he also entered the Volkshammer. He was FDJ First Secretary from 1974 to 1983, continued his membership from 1969 of the Council of National Front, served as a candidate member of the SED central committee from 1971 to 1973, and was appointed Secretary in 1989. Having been admitted to the Politburo as a candidate in 1976, he became a full member in 1983, and its General Secretary in 1989, in which year he was elected Head of State.

KRISHNA MENON, Vengalil Krishnan
1896–1974

Indian politician, born Calicut, Malabar. Educated at the Presidency College, Madras, and at London University, he worked as a history teacher and a barrister in London, and in 1929, as secretary of the India League, served as the spokesman for his country's nationalist movement. When India was made a dominion in 1947, he was appointed High Commissioner, and in 1952 led the Indian delegation to the United Nations, bringing **Pandit Nehru**'s influence to bear on international problems as leader of the uncommitted

Asian bloc. As Defence Minister from 1957 to 1962, he came into conflict with Britain over the Kashmiri question.

KRUGER, Stephanus Johannes Paulus
1825–1904

South African soldier and politician, born Colesberg, Cape Colony. After the British annexation of the Transvaal in 1877, he led the revolt that brought independence and was elected president in 1883, when he immediately had to grapple with the social and political problems caused by the influx of Uitlanders (non-Boer settlers) on the discovery of gold in the Rand. His insistence that they should not be granted civil rights led to the Civil War, in which Kruger briefly took some part before leaving for England in the hope of securing British support for his cause. On failing to do so, he settled in Switzerland, where he died after publishing *The Memoirs of Paul Kruger* in 1902.

KUCAN, Milan
1941–

Slovenian politician. As the communist leader of what has long been the most liberal of the Yugoslavian republics—a legacy of its pre-World War I status as part of the Habsburg empire—and long-resolved to end the Belgrade regime's control of his country, Kucan ignored pressures by Serbia's hardline leader **Slobodan Milosevic** to bring a halt to the emergenge of opposition politics towards the end of the 1980s. In 1990, in Yugoslavia's first free elections since the war, Kucan was re-elected as non-party President, and on 24 June 1991 announced his country's independence from the republic, in common with Croatia's leader, **Franjo Tudjman**. Milosevic retaliated by ordering federal army units into both countries and air attacks on Slovenia's airport and military and communications centres, marking the start of a civil war that seem certain to result in the most dramatic changes in Yugoslavia's political and physical boundaries since its transformation into a communist state by Marshal **Josip Tito** in 1943.

KUN, Béla
1886–1937

Hungarian revolutionary, born Transylvania. After working as a journalist, he served in the army and was taken prisoner in Russia, and in 1918 founded the Hungarian Communist Party. In 1919 he organized the Budapest revolution and established Hungary as a Soviet republic. On failing to secure popular support, he fled to Vienna and then to Russia, where he is believed to have been murdered in a Stalinist purge.

KURCHATOV, Igor Vasilevich
1903–60

Russian physicist, born eastern Russia. As director of nuclear physics at the Leningrad Institute from 1938, and of the Soviet Atomic Energy Institute by the end of World War II, he undertook important studies of neutron reactions and was instrumental in the development of Russia's first atomic bomb in 1949, thermonuclear device in 1953, and the world's first nuclear power plant in 1954. He was made a member of the Supreme Soviet in 1949.

KUZNETS, Simon Smith
1901–85

Russian-born American economist and statistician, born Pinks, Ukraine. After emigrating to the USA in 1922, he studied at Columbia University and at the National Bureau of Economic Research, and was professor of economics at Pennsylvania (1930–54), Johns Hopkins (1954–60) and Harvard (1960–71). He developed a unique approach to his subject that combined indisputable facts with creative and original thought, typified by his theory of a 20-year cycle of economic growth. He wrote *National Income and its Composition 1919–38* (1941), and was awarded the Nobel Prize for economics in 1971.

KYPRIANOU, Spyros
1932–

Cypriot politician, born Limassol. Educated at the Greek Gymnasium and at the City of London College, he was called to the London Bar and founded and became first president of the Cypriot Students Union. In 1952 he was appointed secretary to Archbishop **Makarios**, and returned with him to Cyprus in 1959. He was Foreign Minister from 1961 to 1972, and in 1976 founded the Democratic Front. He succeeded Makarios as President on the archbishop's death in 1977 and was re-elected in 1978 and 1983. In 1988, he suffered a surprise defeat by the independent candidate **Georgios Vassilou** and left office without realizing his ambition of finding a peaceful solution to the island's partitioning.

LAFAYETTE, Marie Joseph Paul Yves Roch Gilbert Montier, Marquis de
1757–1834

French reformer, born Chavagnac Castle, Auvergne. After sailing to America in 1777 to support the colonists, he was given a command by **George Washington**, and after briefly returning to France, was back in Virginia for the battle of Yorktown in 1779. On his return to France in 1787, he was summoned to the Assembly of Notables, and sat in the States-General and the National Assembly of 1789. Following his appointment as commander of the armed citizenry, he formed the National Guard, but his moderation and advocacy of progressive reforms—including the abolition of all titles and class privileges—made him despised by the Jacobins, who were unrelenting despite his military successes in the actions at Philippeville, Maubeuge and Florennes. He eventually fled to Austria, where he was imprisoned until **Napoleon Bonaparte** secured his release in 1797. From 1818 to 1824 he aligned himself with the extreme left in the Chamber of Deputies, and led the Opposition from 1825 to 1830, when he took part in the Revolution and commanded the National Guard. In 1824, he revisited America at the invitation of Congress, which voted him a gift from the nation of $200 000 and a township. He then withdrew from public life to live a quiet retirement until his death in Paris 20 years later.

LAFFITTE, Jacques
1767–1844

French financier and statesman, born Bayonne. After making a personal fortune as a Paris banker, he was appointed governor of the Bank of France in 1814 and entered the Chamber of Deputies in 1817. His house served as the headquarters of the 1830 revolution, which he funded largely out of his own pocket, and he briefly held office in the Cabinet formed in November that year. In 1837, he founded a discount bank, and six years later was elected president of the Chamber of Deputies.

LAFONTAINE, Oskar
1943–

German politician, born Saarlois. Educated at Bonn University, as regional leader of the Social Democratic Party from 1977 his radicalism saw him dubbed 'Red Oskar' and the 'Ayatollah of the Saarland'. However, he adopted more moderate policies after his election as minister-president of the state assembly in 1985, and in 1987 he was appointed a deputy chairman of the SPD's federal organization.

LANDSBERGIS, Vytautas
1932–

Lithuanian politician. On becoming president when Lithuania declared its independence from Moscow in March 1990, he was immediately confronted by economic sanctions imposed by Moscow, but his Government's struggle to survive the attempted intimidation benefited greatly from the sympathy increasingly being shown towards demands for independence among the Baltic states by **Boris Yeltsin**. Although the Latvian and Estonian leaders had thereby learnt the lesson of adopting a lower-key approach to their dealings with the Kremlin, Landisbergis refused to countenance any back-tracking, and his Government's continuing intransigence resulted in Russian troops occupying Vilnius and seizing several public buildings in January 1991 on the pretext of rounding up Lithuanian conscripts to the Soviet army who had refused to report for duty. The subsequent killing of demonstrators in Vilnius in an unauthorized show of strength by Red Army soldiers was publicly condemned by **Mikhail Gorbachev**, but the incident increased fears in the West that he was losing control of the military.

LANGE, David Russell
1942–

New Zealand politician. After studying law at Auckland University and qualifying as a solicitor and barrister, his work in the cause of the underprivileged saw his election to the House of Representatives in 1977. He rose rapidly in the Labour Opposition to become deputy leader in 1979 and head of the party in 1983. A year later, he took Labour to a decisive general-election victory with a campaign fought largely on his party's non-nuclear defence policy—which he immediately implemented on becoming Prime Minister, ignoring strong criticisms from the West and from the USA in particular. He secured a further term in the 1987 election, but ill health and party disputes prompted his resignation in 1989.

LANSBURY, George
1859–1940

British politician, born Lowestoft. After taking an early interest in improving the conditions of the poor, he entered the Commons as a Labour MP in 1910, but resigned two years later to seek re-election as a supporter of women's suffrage. On failing to be returned to Parliament, he founded the *Daily Herald*, which was adopted as Labour's official newspaper when he eventually returned to Parliament in 1922. In 1921, as mayor of a London borough, he was jailed for refusing to increase its rates. As the first commissioner of works from 1929, he increased the number of London's public parks and opened the Serpentine lido. He was party leader from 1931 to 1935, when, as a pacifist, he resigned over labour's hostile response to the Italian invasion of Ethiopia, but remained an MP until his death. The actress Angela Lansbury (1925–) is his daughter

LASKI, Harold Joseph
1893–1950

English political scientist and socialist, born Manchester. Educated at Manchester Grammar School and New College, Oxford, he lectured at McGill University (1914–16), Harvard (1916–20), Amherst (1917) and Yale (1919–20), and in 1926 joined the London School of Economics as professor of political science, where he won a large following for his pragmatic brand of Marxism. However, his strong belief in political freedom led him to conclude, after the downfall of the Labour Government in 1931, that some measure of revolution in Britain was necessary. He was elected Labour party chairman in 1945. He wrote *Authority in the Modern State* (1919), *A Grammar of Politics* (1925), *Liberty in the Modern State* (1930) and *The American Presidency* (1940).

LASSALLE, Ferdinand
1825–64

German writer and revolutionary, born Breslau. After studying in Paris and Berlin, he took part in the 1848 revolution, when he met **Karl Marx**, and was imprisoned briefly for sedition before settling in the Rhine country for several years. In 1848, he returned to Berlin, and after publishing *System der erworbenen Rechte* (1861), founded in Leipzig a working-man's association, which was the forerunner of the Social Democratic Party, to agitate for universal suffrage. He subsequently extended his campaign to the Rhineland and Berlin, and his highly critical attack on Liberalism, *Capital or Labour*, argued that European development would depend on a democracy of labour and that political interests should take second place to social considerations. He was killed in a duel for the hand of the woman he loved.

LAURIER, Sir Wilfrid
1841–1919

Canadian statesman, born St Lin, Quebec. After a successful early career as a barrister, he was made Minister of Inland Revenue in the Liberal Government, was elected party leader in 1891, and assumed the premiership in 1896—thus becoming the first French-Canadian and the first Roman Catholic to be Prime Minister. In 1911, Laurier was defeated on the question of commercial reciprocity with the United States, but he remained party leader. During World War I, his party split over conscription, which Laurier opposed while strongly supporting his country's involvement in the war.

LAVAL, Pierre
1883–1945

French politician, born Châteldon (Puy-de-Dôme), Auvergne. Largely self-educated, he qualified as a lawyer in Paris and in 1914 entered the Chamber of Deputies, first as a socialist, but from 1927 he sat as an independent senator. After holding a number of portfolios, he was twice Prime Minister (1931–2, 1935–6). An advocate of peace with Germany, he served as deputy in the despised Vichy regime of Marshall **Henri Pétain**, and as Prime Minister from 1943 to 1944 openly collaborated with the Germans. On the liberation of France, he fled to Germany, then Spain, but returned in 1945, and after being brought to trial and found guilty of treason, he was executed.

LAW, Andrew Bonar
1858–1923

British statesman, born New Brunswick, Canada. Already a successful iron merchant in Glasgow, he entered the Commons as a Unionist MP in 1900, and following the Conservatives' two election defeats in 1910, he was chosen in 1911 to succeed **Balfour** as party leader on the Opposition Benches. On the forming of the wartime coalition, he was appointed Colonial Secretary (1915–16), a member of the War Cabinet and Chancellor of the Exchequer (1916–18), Leader of the House (1916), and Lord Privy Seal (1919). Although he retired in 1921, he was recalled to serve as Prime Minister in October 1922, when the Conservatives withdrew from the coalition, forcing **David Lloyd George** to resign, but resigned seven months later after being diagnosed as suffering from inoperable cancer. He died later the same year.

LAWSON, Nigel
1932–

British politician, born London. Educated at Westminster School and Christ Church, Oxford, on completing two years' service as a sub-lieutenant with the Royal Navy (1954-6), he became a journalist on *The Financial Times*, and was City editor of *The Sunday Telegraph* from 1961 to 1963. He then contributed a column to *The Financial Times* and regularly broadcast for the BBC before taking up the editorship of *The Spectator* in 1966. From 1970 he wrote for *The Sunday Times*, *The Times* and the *Evening Standard*, and, having already served as a special adviser to Sir **Alec Douglas-Home** and to Conservative Party headquarters, he entered Parliament in 1974. He served as Opposition spokesman on economic and Treasury affairs from 1974 until the Conservatives returned to power in 1979, when he was made Financial Secretary to the Treasury. He was Secretary of State from 1981 to 1983, when he was appointed Chancellor of the Exchequer. Lawson's six years of piloting the nation's economy embraced one of its greatest booms this century, bringing to the task a degree of flair and self-confidence that had not been seen since the Chancellorship of **Roy Jenkins**. Though at first one of **Margaret Thatcher**'s closest Cabinet colleagues, by the late 1980s they had become increasingly estranged over Lawson's advocacy of lower interest rates to cure industrial stagnation and of Britain's full membership of the European monetary system, in which he had the support of Foreign Secretary Sir **Geoffrey Howe**, himself a former Chancellor. His sudden resignation in October 1989 (when he was replaced by **John Major**) over Thatcher's increasing interference in his portfolio marked the beginning of a party split that widened over the following year—and which, shortly after Howe's own resignation from the Cabinet

saw Thatcher dropped as party leader in November 1990. In 1991, Lawson announced his intention to retire from the Commons at the next general election. He has written *The Coming Confrontation* (1978), *The Power Game* (1979), and *The New Conservatism* (1980).

LE DOC THO (Phan Dinh Khai)
1911–

Vietnamese politician, born Ninh province. A member of the Communist Party from 1929, he was exiled by the French in 1930, and on his release seven years later became head of the Nam Dinh revolutionary movement. After being re-arrested and imprisoned from 1939 until the end of World War II, he worked as an organizer for the Vietnamese party and joined its Politburo in 1955. For his efforts to secure peace at the 1968–9 Paris conferences, he was awarded the 1973 Nobel Peace Prize jointly with **Henry Kissinger**, but declined to accept. He retired in 1986.

LEE KUAN YEW
1923–

Singaporean politician, born Singapore. After studying law at Cambridge and qualifying as a barrister, he returned to Singapore in 1951 to practise. In 1954, he founded the moderate anti-communist People's Action Party, and a year later joined the Singapore Legislative Assembly. He became the country's first Prime Minister in 1959, since when he has stewarded his country's economic development to great effect. His son, Brigadier-General Lee Hsien Loong (1952–), is viewed as his possible successor.

LEE TENG-HUI
1923–

Taiwanese politician, born Tamsui. After receiving his education at universities in the USA and Japan, he taught economics at the National Taiwan University, and became city mayor in 1979. As a member of the ruling Kuomintang Party and a protégé of **Jiang Jieshi** (Chiang Kai-Shek), he was appointed vice-president in 1984, and became state president and party leader on Jiangs's death in 1988. Taiwan's first island-born leader, he has significantly accelerated the pace of liberalization and 'Taiwanization'.

LENIN, Vladimir Ilyich (Vladimir Ilyich Ulyanov)

1870–1924

Russian revolutionary, born Simbirsk (Ulyanov). Born into a middle-class family (his father was a school inspector, and his maternal grandfather was a doctor), his older brother, Alexander, had already been hanged, in 1887, for conspiring to assassinate Tsar Alexander III by the time that Lenin entered Kazan University to study law. It was not long before he was expelled for subversive activities, and in 1889 he moved to St Petersburg (Leningrad) University. His part in organising the illegal Union for the Liberation of the Working Classes brought his arrest and exile to Siberia for three years. On his release, he went to Switzerland, where he edited a political newspaper and helped to found with other dissidents the Social Democratic Party, to serve as the spearhead of a revolution against Tsarism. The concept of a professional core of party activists advocated in his 1902 publication, *What is to be done?*, was adopted by the party's Bolshevik majority at its 1903 London congress, but resisted by the moderate Mensheviks. Lenin returned to Russia shortly after the failed 1905 rising, but left again two years later, and over the next decade worked at ensuring the Bolsheviks' dominance over the moderates, bringing his own interpretation to the works of **Karl Marx** and **Friedrich Engels**, and directing the establishment of the Russian communist underground. The first 1917 revolution, in which Germany connived to undermine the Russian war effort, deposed the tsar, and it was with German help also that, the following month, Lenin was smuggled back to St Petersburg to set the seal on the most momentous event in Russian history. By November, the Red Army had defeated the core of resistance (though fighting with the White Army continued until 1921), and Lenin was proclaimed president of the Council of People's Commissars. For the next three years, he grappled with the task of implementing communist principles and of establishing total state control over the country's economy, but by 1922—already weakened after being shot in an attempt on his life in 1918, and now suffering the aftermath of a stroke— Lenin was forced to concede the impracticality of quickly implementing so radical a policy and allowed a measure of free enterprise to return. Shortly before he died, Lenin wrote a note urging **Joseph Stalin**'s removal from the post as party secretary-general, but it was suppressed, and **Leon Trotsky** was defeated for the leadership after Lenin's death on 21 January 1924. His embalmed body was placed in a crystal casket in a mausoleum in Red Square, and St Petersburg was renamed in his honour. Lenin remained a revered figure in Russian history not only as the father of the modern Soviet Union but as a man whose key motivation was the furtherance of Marxist principles for the benefits that they could bring to his people, rather than a hunger for personal power. However, following the failed attempt to depose **Mikhail Gorbachev** as president, and the denunciation of the Communist Party by **Yeltsin** and his supporters, many of Lenin's statues and portraits were removed from their positions of honour.

LEOPOLD II

1835–1909

King of Belgium, born Brussels, the son of Leopold I (1790–1865). As a monarch with territorial ambitions, in 1885 he became king of the Congo, which was annexed to Belgium in 1908, and at the same time improved his country's traditional vulnerability by restructuring its military and establishing a network of border fortifications. He was popular with his subjects, who under his rule saw commerce and industry flourish, particularly during the later part of his reign. He was succeeded by his nephew, Albert (1875–1934).

LE PEN, Jean-Marie

1928–

French politician. After graduating in law in Paris, he served as a paratrooper in Indo-China and Algeria during the 1950s, and in 1956 entered the National Assembly as a right-wing Poujadist. During the 1960s, he became associated with the extreme right-wing Organisation de l'Armée Sécrète, and in 1972 founded the National Front. Over the next decade, it emerged as a new fifth force in French politics, to take 10 per cent of the vote in the 1986 National Assembly elections, but Le Pen was unsuccessful in his bid for the presidency two years later.

LESSEPS, Ferdinand, Vicomte de

1805–94

French diplomat and canal-developer, born Versailles. After holding diplomatic posts in

Lisbon, Tunis, Cairo and other capitals, he realized the potential for a Suez canal and, after negotiating a concession with the Egyptian Viceroy, supervised its construction between 1860 and 1869. The following year, he started work on the Panama canal, but the project was abandoned. Lesseps and four other directors were tried for embezzlement and mismanagement, but Lesseps' sentence of five years' imprisonment was eventually reversed. He wrote *Histoire du canal de Suez* (1875–9) and *Souvenirs de quarante ans* (1887).

LEVER, Harold, Baron Lever of Manchester
1914–

British politician, born Manchester. Educated at Manchester Grammar School and Manchester University, he was called to the London Bar in 1935, and in 1950 began an uninterrupted 29-year career as a Labour MP. Following Labour's 1966 election victory, he was made Under-Secretary of the Department of Economic Affairs, but as one of **Harold Wilson**'s most trusted and competent parliamentary colleagues, was soon promoted to the Cabinet as Financial Secretary (1967–9) and Paymaster-General (1969–70). After Labour's defeat in the 1970 election, he served as Shadow Cabinet spokesman on economic affairs, and as chairman of the powerful all-party Public Accounts Committee (1970–3), until Labour's return to power in 1974, when he began a five-year term as Chancellor of the Duchy of Lancaster. He received a life peerage in 1979.

LIE, Trygve Haldvan
1896–1968

Norwegian lawyer, born Oslo. After becoming an MP, he was appointed Minister of Justice and of Shipping before fleeing to Britain with other members of the Norwegian Government in 1940, where he acted as Foreign Minister until the end of the war. In 1946, he was elected UN secretary-general, but resigned in 1952. He served as Minister for Industry (1963–4) and for Commerce and Shipping until his death. He wrote *In the Cause of Peace* (1954).

LIGACHEV, Yegor Kuzmich
1920–

Soviet politician. Trained as an engineer, he joined the Communist Party in 1944 and in 1957 was made party chief of the new science-based city of Akademogorodok, where he gained a reputation for his commitment to flushing out official corruption. He was called to Moscow by **Nikita Khrushchev** in 1961, but after the premier was replaced four years later, he was posted to western Siberia for 18 years to serve in a minor capacity. When **Mikhail Gorbachev** came to power in 1985, Ligachev was brought back to Moscow and made a member of the Politburo and initially served as deputy leader, but by 1988, Ligachev's conservatism had caused a rift, and he was demoted to agriculture secretary. However, he remains an influential member of the party machine and is still viewed as a serious rival for the leadership.

LI HONGZHANG (Li Hung-chang)
1823–1901

Chinese statesman, born Hofei, Nganhui. After serving as a secretary in the Imperial army during the 1853 Taiping rebellion, he was appointed a provincial judge, and in 1862 governor of Kiangsu—out of which, in conjunction with General Charles ('Chinese') Gordon, he drove the rebels in 1863. After securing the governorship of Chih-li in 1872, he was made senior grand secretary, and used his new power to found the Chinese navy and to promote a native mercantile marine. On the outbreak of war with Japan in 1894, his efforts as supreme commander in Korea were frustrated by the incompetence and cowardice of his officers, and when the Chinese were despatched from Korea, he was recalled to Peking to be stripped of office. His refusal would normally have brought his immediate execution, but the growing Japanese threat compelled the emperor to reinstate Li, who finally brought the war to an end in 1895—albeit at the cost of ceding Taiwan and reparations of £35 million. His aspirations of strengthening his power base took him to Europe and America in 1896, but he fell from power in 1898 after he was discovered to have entered into secret talks with Russia.

LILBURNE, John
1614–57

English pamphleteer and Puritan, born Greenwich. After serving a two-year term of imprisonment for importing Puritan literature in 1638, he joined the parliamentary army in the Civil War and rose to the rank of lieutenant-colonel before resigning over the

Covenant. He then campaigned ceaselessly for the extreme Levellers, the extreme faction of the Puritans, and was imprisoned on several more occasions for pamphleteering against **Cromwell**'s autocratic rule and for greater liberty of conscience.

LI LISAN (Li Li-san)

1896–1968

Chinese politician. After receiving his education in France, he founded a branch of the Chinese Communist Party in Paris in 1921, and after returning to China was made party leader in 1929. In 1931, having failed to foment a proletarian revolution in the cities, he fled to Moscow, but in 1936 was imprisoned there as a Trotskyist. Following his return to China in 1945, he was appointed Minister of Labour (1949-54), and then served as political adviser to **Lin Biao** until 1956, when he was demoted from the higher tiers of the party machine on admitting to 'leftist opportunism'. However, he retained his place on several important committees until retiring a year before his death.

LIN BIAO (Lin Piao)

1908–71

Chinese soldier and politician, born Wuhan, Hubei province. After graduating from Whampoa Military Academy, he joined the communist fight against the Kuomintang and became commander of the North-East People's Liberation Army in 1945. In 1959 he was appointed Defence Minister, and survived the 1966–8 Cultural Revolution to become deputy to **Mao Zedong**. In 1969 he was made party vice-chairman and was formally designated as Mao's successor, but in 1971, fearing another purge, he formulated Project 571 a plan to have Mao assassinated during a train journey from Shanghai to Peking and to seize power in a military coup. However, the plot was uncovered and while fleeing to the Soviet Union, Lin was killed when his plane crashed over Outer Mongolia.

LINCOLN, Abraham

1809–65

Sixteenth US President, born Hedgenville, Kentucky. Born into a pioneering family that eventually settled in south-west Indiana in 1816, he was encouraged in his education by his stepmother, and when the Lincolns moved to Illinois in 1830, Abraham worked as a shop clerk in New Salem. After an unsuccessful early attempt to win election to the legislature for the Whigs, he bought his own store, and when its failure left him in debt, he became village postmaster and deputy county surveyor while studying law. In 1834 he at last realized his ambition to enter the legislature, and from 1846 sat in Congress. For the next few years, having married in 1842, Lincoln devoted the greater part of his energies to developing his law practice, but when the repeal of the Missouri Compromise by Stephen A. Douglas in 1854 reopened the question of slavery in the territories, Lincoln entered fully into the controversy and was soon showing his power of oratory. When the Republican Party was organized in 1856 to exploit the Democrats' split over the issue, Lincoln became its leader in Illinois and was nominated by the state for the vice-presidency. The 1858 electoral battle between Lincoln and Douglas seized the imagination of the nation, and despite Lincoln winning a majority of the popular vote, he lost the election, whose outcome was decided by the Illinois legislature. At the Republicans' 1860 convention, Lincoln gained his party's presidential nomination after three ballots, and triumphed in the November election with 40 per cent of the vote, largely because of the continuing Democratic split. In his first inaugural address, by which time South Carolina had left the Union, and the six gulf states had formed the Confederate States of America, Lincoln spoke of the futility of secession and made clear that he expected the nation's laws to be observed by all states. But not even his oratorical skills and conciliatory efforts could prevent the impending conflict and on 12 April 1861, the Civil War began with the Confederate attack on Fort Sumter in Charleston harbour. Lincoln assembled a force of 75000 militia and 65000 regulars and proclaimed a blockade of the southern ports, but the Confederacy countered by putting 100000 men in the field and soon won control of 11 states. On 22 September 1862, following the routing of the Union army at Bull Run and other defeats, Lincoln made his famous proclamation of freedom for slaves in the rebellious states. Union victories under General **Ulysses S. Grant** at Vicksburg and Gettysburg in 1863, and the general's policy of attrition, finally bought an end to the war and General Robert E. Lee surrendered at Richmond on 9 April 1865. Two months later, Lincoln was unanimously nominated for a second term, and in the election trounced the Democratic candidate by taking more than two thirds of the popular vote and all but 21 of the 233 electoral votes. On Good Friday, 14 April 1882—a month after making his second inaugural address, in which he made his memorable speech about the significance of war—Lincoln was shot by a deranged actor from the south, John Wilkes Booth, as he watched a performance of *Our American Cousin* at Ford's Theatre in Washington, and died the following morning. His wife, Mary, already suffering mental illness following the death of three of her four sons, deteriorated further after her husband's assassination and was adjudged insane in 1875, but declared competent a year later. There are several editions of Lincoln's *Collected Works*.

LINI, Walter Hadye
1942–

Vanuatuan priest and politician, born Pentecost Island. After studying for the Anglican priesthood in the Solomon Islands and New Zealand, he joined the New Hebrides National Party, later the Vanuaaku Pati, became chief minister in 1979, and Prime Minister when Vanuatu achieved independence in 1980. His strict adherence to a policy of non-alignment and to the implementation of socialist principles brought his re-election in 1983 and 1987, and saw him survive a challenge to his rule in 1988.

LI PENG
1928–

Chinese politician, born Chengdu, Sichuan province. The son of a radical communist writer, Li Shouxun, who was executed by the Kuomintang in 1930, he was adopted by **Zhou En-Lai** on his mother's death in 1939 and trained as a power engineer. In 1981, he was appointed Minister with responsibility for the power industry, became deputy-premier in 1983, and after joining the Politburo in 1985 was appointed Prime Minister in 1987. In May 1989, Li Peng imposed martial law to counter widespread student agitation triggered by the failure of the leadership to honour promises made by party chief **Zhao Ziyang** to implement a measure of liberalizing reform. His refusal to make any concessions prompted the peaceful student occupation of Tiananmen Square, and Li Peng's action in using army units to bring the demonstration violently to an end, with the loss of more than 3000 lives, earned him international condemnation.

LIU SHAOQI (Liu Shao-ch'i)
1900–71

Chinese politician, born Yinshan, Hunan province. After leaving school, where one of his fellow pupils was **Mao Zedong**, he continued his studies in Changsa and Shanghai, where he learned Russian, and went to Moscow in 1921 to complete his education. Having joined the Communist Party, he returned to China to work as a labour organizer in Shanghai, and as a member of the Politburo from 1934, became its foremost expert on party structure and wrote *How to be a Good Communist* (1939). He was subsequently appointed party secretary (1949), and as chairman of the People's Republic of China from 1958, his power was second only to that of Mao Zedong. As an advocate of a freer market economy, he was denounced as a bourgeois renegade during the 1966-9 Cultural Revolution, stripped of office, and banished to Hunan province, to be replaced as Mao's nominated successor by **Lin Biao**. He was posthumously rehabilitated a decade after his death in detention.

LIVERPOOL, Robert Banks Jenkinson, Earl of
1770–1828

British statesman. Educated at Charterhouse and Christ Church, Oxford, he entered the Commons as a Tory MP in 1791, and as Foreign Secretary from 1801 until the Government fell, he negotiated the unpopular Treaty of Amiens. When **William Pitt** returned as Prime Minister in 1804, having resigned three years earlier over the king's rejection of Catholic emancipation, Liverpool was made Home Secretary. On Pitt's death in 1806, he declined to form a Government, and continued as Home Secretary until being appointed Secretary for War and the Colonies in **Spencer Perceval**'s new Administration. After Perceval was assassinated at the House of Commons in 1812, Liverpool formed a Government that was considered reactionary in its foreign policies and repressive at home, but which nevertheless saw Britain safely through the last stages of the Napoleonic wars, and which was to last for nearly 15 years. In 1827, after successfully reconciling the old and new Toryism to his country's economic and commercial advantage, he was struck down with apoplexy, dying a year later.

LIVINGSTON

American political dynasty descended from the fifth Lord Livingston, guardian of **Mary Queen of Scots**, which began when Robert (1654–1728) settled in Albany in 1673. Of his grandsons, Philip (1716–78) was a signatory to the Declaration of Independence, William (1723–90) was governor of New Jersey, and William's son became a Supreme Court justice. His great grandson, Robert R. Livingston (1746–1813) first practised law, entered Congress in 1775, helped draft the Declaration of Independence the following year, and was until 1801 chancellor of New York State. His part in negotiating the cession of Louisiana enabled Robert Fulton to construct the first steamer, and he introduced to America the use of sulphate of lime as a manure, and merino sheep. Another great-grandson of the first Robert, Edward Livingston (1764–1836), sat in Congress from 1795 to 1801 and was New York district attorney and mayor before having to surrender his office and property after federal funds had been misappropriated by one of his subordinates. He recovered from his misfortune to run a successful practice in New Orleans. During the second war with England he was aide-de-camp to General Thomas ('Stonewall') Jackson, and while a member of Congress again from 1822 to 1829 contributed significantly to the Louisiana criminal code. After his election to the Senate in 1829, he was made Secretary of State, and from 1833 served as Minister to France.

LIVINGSTONE, Ken (Kenneth)

1945–

British politician, born London. Educated at Tulse Hill Comprehensive School and Phillipa Fawcett College of Education, he worked as a technician at the Chester Beatty Cancer Research Institute from 1962 until devoting himself to a political career. After joining the Labour Party in 1969, he worked as a London regional executive (1974–86) and served as a Lambeth and Camden local councillor from 1971 to 1978. In 1973, he was elected to the Greater London Council, the capital's strategic planning authority, and was appointed transport spokesman in 1980. When Labour won control of the GLC the following year, Livingstone staged a remarkable overnight coup with the support of the Labour group's strong left-wing faction, in which he successfully deposed the moderate leader-designate,

Andrew McIntosh (1933–)—who was compensated with a life peerage in 1982—and his closest allies became chairpersons of the most important committees. Livingstone transformed the GLC from being a significant but largely administrative element in the capital's political infrastructure into an instrument of left-wing policies and a key weapon in the party's barracking of national Conservative policies. His flair for exploiting the media (even if it fell short of suppressing the revelation that he kept pet newts) ensured that he hit the headlines with as much regularity as members of the Shadow Cabinet. When his success in constantly frustrating Conservative education, housing and transport policies, and enraging reactionaries by his patronage of ethnic and other social minorities, began to be emulated to equally devastating effect by other Labour-controlled municipal authorities, the Government were stung into introducing in 1986 legislation to dismantle the highest tier of Britain's regional political administration. The following year, Livingstone won election to Parliament, but, as something of an embarrassment to a leadership anxious to distance itself from the party's left-wing image of the early 1980s, and having further alienated himself by displaying strong pro-Republican sympathies in debates on the Irish question, he has failed to gain the Shadow Cabinet post for which he once seemed pre-ordained. Nevertheless, the grudging admiration that he won from Londoners of all political persuasions for his success in putting London's infrastructure on the political map, and his refusal to soften his style (in Who's Who, he identifies his London club as the Lesbian and Gay Centre), even at the cost of personal advancement, could still see him follow in the footsteps of previous bad boys of the Labour Back-Benches who have eventually risen to positions of real power in the party.

LI XIANNIAN

1905–

Chinese politician, born Hubei province. He worked as a carpenter before serving with the Kuomintang (1926–7), and after joining the Communist Party in 1927, he founded the Oyuwan People's Republic in Hubei. He took part in the Long March (1934–6) and was a commander in the war against Japan and the subsequent civil war. In 1956, he was admitted to the CCP Politburo and secretariat, but was disgraced during the 1966-9 Cultural Revolution. Under **Zhou Enlai** he was rehabilitated and became Finance Minister in 1973, then served as state president under **Deng Xiaoping** from 1983 to 1988.

LLOYD-GEORGE of DWYFOR, David Lloyd George, 1st Earl
1863–1945

British statesman, born Manchester. Of Welsh parentage, he was taken to Criccieth, Caernarvonshire, at the age of two on the death of his father, where he was brought up by his mother and her brother, Richard Lloyd, from whom he acquired his religion, radicalism, and fervour for Welsh nationalism. After studying law, he started work as a solicitor in 1844, and five years later won in a by-election the Caernarvon constituency that he was to represent for 55 years. He quickly established his place on the left wing of the Liberal party through his support of the Boers in the 1899–1902 South African War, and when the Liberals returned to power in 1906 he was appointed President of the Board of Trade in **Henry Campbell-Bannerman**'s new Administration. When **Herbert Asquith** became premier in 1908, Lloyd George became Chancellor of the Exchequer, and wasted little time creating a new welfare state that provided for old age pensions (1908), and national insurance (1911). His 1909 Budget, with its proposals for graded income tax, triggered the most significant constitutional crisis in modern parliamentary history. Though it passed easily through the Commons, the Conservative majority in the House of Lords, still smarting from their election defeat, seized on the opportunity to frustrate the new Government by refusing to give the Finance Bill their approval. The battle was resolved by Asquith's twice seeking a mandate from the electorate the following year, and by the passing of the Parliament Act 1911, which removed the power of the Lords to delay any Money Bill and restricted their stalling any other type of legislation to a maximum of two years. Although a pacifist by nature, when Germany invaded Belgium in 1914, Lloyd George saw a parallel between the latter country's struggle and the Welsh nationalist cause, and accepted the challenge of applying his considerable abilities to the new offices of Minister for Munitions (1915) and Minister for War in 1916 after the death of Lord Kitchener, in which year he also succeeded Asquith as coalition premier. While he used all his skills of oratory to rally the country, as **Winston Churchill** was to do in World War II, his relationship with Britain's military leaders frequently became strained, not least because of Lloyd George's abhorrence of the cost of the conflict in human lives. His contribution to the negotiations that produced the Treaty of Versailles were, typically, notable for his insistence on the rehabilitation of the smaller countries that had suffered under German occupation. However, the 'khaki' election that immediately followed the end of the war left the Liberals without a majority in the Commons, and when in 1922 the Conservatives voted to end the coalition, Lloyd George was forced to resign. As Leader of the Opposition, he applied himself to mending the Liberal split caused partly by his own complete dominance over party policy, and to rebuilding its campaign funds through his skilful management of the *Daily Chronicle* and other investments. The party closed ranks temporarily to fight the 1923 election, but it was not until the 1926 General Strike that it was fully reunited. Nevertheless, the electorate, disenchanted with the party's long period of internal strife, returned only 59 Liberals in 1929, but over the next two years, what little was left of the popularity collapsed to give them only a handful of seats at Westminster, and Lloyd George resigned as leader. In semi-retirement at his agricultural estate at Churt, Lloyd George wrote his six-volume *War Memoirs* (1933–6) and *The Truth about Peace Treaties* (1938). In the mid-1930s he visited Germany and admitted to being much impressed by **Adolf Hitler**, but on the outbreak of World War II, he condemned **Neville Chamberlain** for his policy of appeasement and urged co-operation with Russia. Perhaps the greatest political compliment paid to him was the invitation he received from **Winston Churchill** in 1940 to join the War Cabinet, but Lloyd George's health was already failing, and he accepted the post of ambassador to Washington instead. After he returned to Britain, he was created an earl shortly before his death.

LODGE, Henry Cabot
1850–1924

American senator, historian and biographer, born Boston. After working as assistant editor of the *North American Review*, he pursued a political career from 1878, and after entering the Senate in 1893, campaigned vigorously against the League of Nations. His grandson, Henry Cabot Lodge (1902–85), succeeded him as a senator in 1936, served as America's delegate to the UN (1953–60), and was ambassador to South Vietnam (1963–4, 1965–7).

LONGFORD, Francis Aungier Pakenham, 7th Earl of
1905–

British politician. Educated at Eton and New College, Oxford, where he gained a first in modern greats, he worked as a lecturer before joining Conservative Party headquarters as a research assistant in 1930, then returned to lecturing at Christ Church, Oxford. After being forced to resign his 1940 army commission because of ill health, he was personal assistant to Sir **William Beveridge** (1941–4), and between 1947 and 1965 held office in Labour Governments as Chancellor of the Duchy of Lancaster, Minister of Civil Aviation, First Lord of the Admiralty, Lord Privy Seal, and Secretary of State for the Colonies. In 1964 he became Leader of the House of Lords, and was Lord Privy Seal from 1966 to 1968. However, Longford's distinguished public and ministerial service over nearly three decades has been eclipsed by the famous campaigns against sexual liberalism (which won him the sobriquet 'Lord Porn') and for prison reform that the earl (a Catholic convert) has conducted since the 1960s—the latter embracing his much-criticized attempts to secure the release of Myra Hindley (1942–), who was sentenced to life imprisonment in 1966 for her part in the multiple Moors murders, and his prison visits to the homosexual mass murderer Dennis Nilsen (1948–) on compassionate grounds. His numerous works on the prison system, politics, and religion, and his notable biographies, include *Abraham Lincoln* (1974), *Kennedy* (1976), *Nixon* (1980), *Ulster* (1981), *Pope John Paul II* (1982), *Eleven at No. 10*, (1984), *One Man's Faith* (1984), *The Search for Peace* (1985), *Saints* (1987), *A History of the House of Lords*, and *Punishment and the Punished* (1991).

LONSDALE, Gordon Arnold (Konon Trofimovich Molody)
1924–

Soviet spy, born in Canada. Posing as a Canadian businessman, he engaged in espionage activities in Britain from 1954, and did untold damage to the effectiveness of its intelligence network during a period that encompassed the height of the Cold War with Russia. After his arrest and trial in 1961, he was sentenced to life imprisonment, but was returned to Russia in 1964 in exchange for a British agent, Greville Wynne.

LOUIS I (the Pious)
778–840

King of Aquitaine. The sole surviving son of **Charlemagne**, Holy Roman Emperor in the West, his reign was notable for its reforms of the Church, in which he collaborated with Benedict of Aniane, and for the raids of the Norsemen in the north-west territories. However, the consequential proliferation of hereditary countships and of offices of favour caused a decline in the imperial authority, and after Louis I's death, his sons' disputes among themselves for supremacy of the empire only served to cause its disintegration.

LOUIS XIII
1601–43

King of France. He was only nine years old when his father, Henri IV, was assassinated and his mother became regent, and at 14 he entered into an arranged marriage with Anne of Austria, but it was not until 1638 that the union produced an heir, the future **Louis XIV**. In 1617, Louis exiled his mother to the provinces and took the throne, but his experience and youth, combined with his timid character, ill-prepared him for his early attempts to subdue the Huguenots and the German Protestants. On being appointed the king's chief minister in 1624, Cardinal Richelieu exploited his monarch's ineffectual rule and, after banishing Louis' second, Spanish wife, Marie de Medici, Richelieu realized one of his king's earlier aspirations by bringing down the Huguenot stronghold of La Rochelle in 1628, but supported the German Protestants to prevent the domination of Europe by the Habsburgs. He encouraged Louis to lead a successful campaign against Spanish territorial ambitions in Italy, and although Richelieu was becoming increasingly the subject of intrigues by those jealous of his influence, he continued to enjoy his monarch's complete support. In peacetime, Richelieu went on to establish the centralized administration and systematic patronage of the arts that are associated with Louis' reign, but which were almost totally the product of Richelieu's initiatives. After the latter's death in 1643, Louis sought the counsel of another trusted Minister, Jules Mazarin, who on the king's death a few months later became the favourite of his widow, and was her lover by the time that Marie became regent for Louis XIV.

LOUIS XIV (The Sun King)
1638–1715

King of France, born St Germain-en-Laye. After his succession, at the age of only five on the death of his father, **Louis XIII**, the kingdom was under the government of his mother and of her lover, Jules Mazarin, who, between 1643 and 1651, successfully frustrated the aspirations of noblemen who had incited street violence in a bid to take power. On Mazarin's death in 1661, Louis—now married to the Infanta Maria Theresa of Spain—assumed the office of Chief Minister. He immediately set about reforming his country's economy (not least by raising taxes to fund the 32-year construction of Versailles and of other palaces) and industry, sacking corrupt members of the court and appointing competent Ministers in their place. As War Minister, he ordered the creation of a navy and remodelled the army to become the most formidable fighting force in Europe. On the death of his father-in-law in 1665, Louis laid claim to part of the Spanish Netherlands, resulting in the 1667–8 War of Dutch Devolution, which provoked a triple alliance between Britain, Holland and Sweden, but bribed **Charles II** with the 1670 Treaty of Dover to support his second war against the Dutch from 1672, which was only brought to an end when the future **William III** opened the sluices and then secured an honourable peace in the 1678 Treaty of Nijmegen. On his private remarriage after Maria Theresa's death in 1683, Louis came under the Catholic influence of his second wife, the Marquise de Maintenon, and sanctioned the bloody persecution of Protestants and the French Huguenots, which had the intended effect of their fleeing to Holland and England. William III and the Dutch joined forces again to stifle French expansionism, but Louis' military might brought victories at Mons, Steenkirk and Neerwinden between 1691 and 1693, while his navy saw off an Anglo-Dutch fleet off St Vincent in 1693. However, it was not enough to protect France's territorial gains, most of which Louis was forced to cede under the 1697 Treaty of Ryswick. When Philip V

took the Spanish throne on the death of Charles II in 1700, the prospect of a powerful alliance so alarmed the other European powers that they removed the nearest threat by inflicting crushing defeats on the French army at Blenheim (1704) and Ramilles (1706). Peace finally returned in 1713, but two years later Louis XIV died, bringing an end to the longest reign in European history, and leaving his country practically bankrupted by the costs of war. His only son, Louis, had died in 1711, and his grandson, the Dauphin, a year later, so the throne passed to his great-grandson, the five-year old **Louis XV**.

LOUIS XV
1710–74

King of France. On succeeding his grandfather, **Louis XIV**, at the age of five, he was served as regent first by Philip, Duke of Orléans, and on his death in 1723 by the Duke of Bourbon whom—after marrying Maria Leczinska, daughter of the deposed King of Poland—Louis replaced by his former tutor, Cardinal de Fleury, in 1726. Fleury proved a capable governor until his death in 1743 at the age of 90. Louis soon endeared himself to his subjects by his part in the war of the Austrian succession, but he lacked Louis XIV's interest in politics and administration, preferring to consolidate the royal autocracy and to concentrate on defending his throne from the orthodox Catholics, and the heavy losses suffered under his command in the Battle of Fontenoy only increased his distaste for warfare. His private life also began to impinge on affairs of state, with his chief mistress, Mme de Pompadour (1721–64), asserting increasing influence over government policy. After eight uneventful years, France again found herself taking up arms in the Seven Years War, but in 1761, the king's new Foreign Minister, the liberal Duke of Choiseul, a friend and ally of Mme de Pompadour, brought an end to hostilities by forging a permanent alliance with Spain, and assured the nation's future defence by rebuilding its weakened navy. The duke saw the 1763 Treaty of Paris between Britain, India and America as posing another threat, but the peace-loving Louis negotiated secretly to avoid further hostilities, while Choiseul contrived to absorb the Duchy of Lorraine and Corsica into France in 1766 and 1770 respectively. The duke also involved himself in domestic affairs, and, despite his king's reservations, forged an alliance with the Parlements to ensure the suppression of the French Jesuits. Mme de Pompadour died in 1764, the Dauphin the following year, and the queen in 1768, but Louis found a new mistress in Mme du Barry (1741–93), while the succession—and continuing harmony with the empire—was assured by his grandson, the future **Louis XVI**, and his marriage in 1770 to Marie Antoinette (1755–93), youngest daughter of the Empress Maria Theresa. However, Mme du Barry, jealous of Choiseul's influence and power, persuaded Louis to dismiss his long-serving and loyal Minister, and the subsequent abandonment of his many planned reforms incurred the wrath of the Parlements, compelling Louis to curb their power by establishing a replacement for the magistracy comprised of royal nominees, which lasted until the king's death. Louis' last years saw deceptive calm at home and peace abroad, but the antiquated autocracy he inherited remained.

LOUIS XVI

1754–93

King of France. After becoming Dauphin on the death of his father (the only son of **Louis XV**) in 1715, he married Maria Antoinette (1755–93), youngest daughter of the Empress Maria Theresa, in 1770, and took the throne in 1774. Although confronted by the problems of an empty Treasury, huge state debts, and already excessive levels of taxation, Louis nevertheless managed to ease some of the fiscal burden on his subjects and to introduce other reforms, although a plan for special taxation of the privileged classes to strengthen the economy in the aftermath of the country's involvement in the American War of Independence failed in the face of strong opposition from the aristocracy. In 1788, Louis dissolved all the parliaments when other fiscal reforms failed to win their approval, and ordered the Treasury to make no cash payments except to the army. However, Louis could not ignore for ever the need to restore a representative legislature, and in 1789 he convened a meeting of the state assembly, which had been in abeyance since 1614, and under its new title of the Constituent Assembly, it addressed the task of drawing up a new Constitution. But when its Deputies soon presented demands for political independence and equal rights, the king retaliated by sacking his Chief Minister,

deploying troops throughout the nation, and dissolving the Ministry, and 12 July 1789 saw the start of the French Revolution—with rioting in Paris, the storming of the Bastille two days later, and the spread of violent demonstrations to the provinces. An exodus of princes and noblemen followed the Assembly's declaration on 4 August of the ending of manorial and feudal rights, while Louis remained at Versailles and attempted to effect a reconciliation by feigning republican sentiments. However, on 5 October, the royal family was forced to return to Paris, where the Assembly reconvened. That marked the start of two years of almost farcical duplicity, with Louis delaying any meaningful concessions to the republicans, while at the same time making several attempts to escape with his family. In 1792, a year after the Assembly had been replaced by the Legislative Assembly, Louis was compelled by the Girondists to sanction the doomed war against Austria, and after the Prussian advance into Champagne under the Duke of Brunswick, the Assembly dissolved itself to reappear as the National Convention, which proclaimed the birth of the republic. Louis was brought to trial for numerous acts of treason, and on 21 January 1793, he was guillotined in the Place de la Revolution—thus bringing to an end the 1025 years of royal rule that had begun with **Charlemagne** in 768.

LOUIS-PHILIPPE

1773–1850

King of the French, born Paris, the eldest son of the Duke of Orléans (1647–93). After renouncing his title, as his father had done, he joined the National Guard, and in the wars of the republic was forced to flee to Austria and Switzerland, where he worked for a time as a teacher. In 1796 he went to the USA and in 1800 to London. Nine years later he married Marie Amlie, daughter of Ferdinand I, and on the restoration, recovered his estates, regained his popularity in Paris, and after the 1830 revolution, accepted the crown as the elect of the sovereign people. Under his rule, the middle classes prospered, the franchise was limited to the aristocracy, and corruption blossomed among the bourgeoisie. Louis-Philippe reacted violently to the consequent agitation for electoral reform, stifling the press and compelling the judiciary to subject the most outspoken of his opponents to summary trial. Prince Louis

Napoleon twice attempted to exploit the unrest by assuming the part of pretender, in 1836 and 1840, and after the Duke of Orléans' death in 1842, republicans, socialists and communists united in an effort to bring Louis-Philippe down. Despite his efforts to divert his subjects' aggression with his campaign in Algeria, he continued to receive the condemnation of the Deputies, and in February 1848 the populace rose against him—with the complicity of the regular army, national guard and municipal police—and he was forced to abdicate and flee to England, eventually to die in exile two years later at Claremont.

LOVETT, William
1800–77

English reformer. From humble beginnings as a London cabinet-maker, he educated himself to become by 1836 the founder of the London Working Men's Association, which devised a six-point charter, including provisions for male suffrage and voting by ballot, that marked the beginning of the Chartist movement. Although an advocate of reform by non-violent means, Lovett became inadvertently involved in the Birmingham chartists' riots in 1839, and while serving a year's imprisonment wrote *Chartism: a New Organisation of the People*, which was published on his release. However, his continuing emphasis on moral protest rather than political action caused his estrangement from the movement's extremists, and in his later life he concentrated on promoting better education for the working classes.

LOW, Sir David (Alexander Cecil)
1891–1963

British political cartoonist, born Dunedin, New Zealand. After working for several newspapers in New Zealand, he moved to London and joined the *Star* in 1919, and then the *Evening Standard* in 1924. His famous creations included the reactionary Colonel Blimp, whose name passed into the English language, and his interpretation of the TUC as a powerful but occasionally doltish workhorse. He worked for the *Daily Herald* from 1950, and *The Manchester Guardian* from 1953. His volumes of collected cartoons include *Lloyd George & Co* (1923), *A Cartoon History of the War* (1941), *Low's Company* (1952) and *Low's Autobiography*.

LUBBERS, Rudolf Franz Marie
1939–

Dutch politician, born Rotterdam. After graduating from Erasmus University, Rotterdam, he joined the family engineering business, but became politically active in the 1960s, and by 1973 had become Minister of Economic Affairs. In 1982, at the age of 43, he was elected Prime Minister of the Christian Democratic Appeal coalition.

LU HSUN
see **Lu Xuh**

LUMUMBA, Patrice Emergy
1925–61

Congolese politician, born Katako Kombe, Kasai province. After working as a post office clerk, he started his own business in Leopoldville, and in 1958 founded the National Congo Movement. When independence was granted in 1960, Lumumba became the new republic's first Prime Minister, but was immediately confronted by tribal warring over his extreme anti-Belgian attitudes. Within months, he had lost control of overall government, though he managed to maintain a power base in Stanleyville with communist support. In December 1960 he was arrested on the order of the central Administration and flown to Katanga. The circumstances in which he died shortly after arriving there were never satisfactorily explained, but it is believed that he was executed.

LUSINCHI, Jaime
1924–

Venezuelan politician, born Clarines, Anzoategui state. While studying medicine, he joined the Democratic Action Party and after being expelled from the country for his political activities, between 1952 and 1958 he spent some time in Argentina, Chile and the USA. On the return of democratic government to Venezuela, Lusinchi returned to enter the new Parliament, and became party leader. In 1984 he succeeded the Christian Social Party leader, Luis Herrera, as president, but the austerity that accompanied Lusinchi's efforts to grapple with the country's collapsing economy lost him his popular support, and in the 1988 election he was defeated by the Democratic Action Party's leader, Carlos Andres Perez.

LUTHULI, Albert John
1898–1967

South African resistance leader. The son of a Zulu Christian missionary, he was educated at an American mission school near Durban and worked as a teacher for 15 years before his election as tribal chief of Groutville, Natal. His anti-apartheid activities led to him being deposed, but in 1952 he was elected president-general of the African National Congress, and over the next 10 years devoted himself to the cause of non-violent resistance. In 1960 he was awarded the Nobel Peace Prize for his unswerving commitment to non-violent opposition despite the provocative measures imposed by the South African Government and the growing impatience of black African extremists. A five-year ban on his travelling outside Natal prevented him being installed as rector of Glasgow University in 1962, and the order was renewed for another five years in 1964. He wrote *Let My People Go* (1962).

LUXEMBURG, Rosa
1871–1919

German revolutionary, born Zamość, Poland. As a convert to communism while still in her teens, she became a member of the Polish underground and by the mid-1890s had founded the Polish Social Democratic Party, later Polish Communist Party. In 1898 she moved to Berlin to help to found the German Communist Party, and at the outbreak of World War I formed with the anti-militarist social democrat, Karl Liebknecht (1871–1919), the Spartacus League—for which she spent the remainder of the war in prison. After her release in 1919 she took part in an abortive uprising, and was murdered, together with Liebknecht, by army officers in Berlin.

LU XUN (Lu Hsun)
1881–1936

Chinese writer, born Shaohsin, Zhejiang. After working as dean of studies and principal of Shaohsin Middle School, in 1913 he was appointed professor of Chinese literature at Peking University and University for Women, and later dean of the College of Arts and Letters at Sun Yixian (Yat-Sen) University, Canton. His first published work was *Diary of a Madman* (1918), and his most successful, *The True Story of Ah Q* (1921), was translated into several languages. The 26 short stories that he wrote between 1918 and 1925 were collected in *Cry and Hesitation*.

LVOV, Prince Georgi Evgenievich
1861–1925

Russian politician. The liberal head of the provisional Government that was formed after the March 1917 revolution, he left Russia when he was replaced by **Alexander Kerensky** five months later.

LYNCH, John (Jack)
1917–

Irish politician, born Cork. Educated at Cork Monastery School and University College, Cork, he entered public service in the Department of Justice in 1936, and having continued his legal studies, was called to the Bar in 1945 and worked in a legal practice. In 1948, he began a 23-year term as a member of the Irish Parliament for Fianna Fail. He was Minister for Education (1957–9), for Industry and Commerce (1959–65) and for Finance (1965-6), before being appointed party leader in 1966 and becoming Taoiseach (Prime Minister) the same year. He was Opposition leader from 1973, following Fine Gael's election success under **Liam Cosgrave**, until Fianna Fáil took power again in 1977, when he resumed the premiership for another two years. He resigned in 1979, to be succeeded by **Charles Haughey**.

LYONS, Joseph Aloysius
1879–1939

Australian statesman, born Stanley, Tasmania. After graduating from Tasmania University he worked as a teacher, but in 1909 entered the House of Assembly as a Labour MP, and after being appointed Minister of Education and of Railways (1914–18) was Prime Minister from 1923 to 1929. In the federal Parliament he served as Postmaster-General, Minister of Public Works and Treasurer, but left his party in 1931 after a policy row and founded the United Australian Party, which he led to power to become Prime Minister again from 1932 until his death.

MACAULAY, Thomas Babington, 1st Baron Macaulay
1800–59

English author, born Rothley Temple, Leicestershire. Educated at private schools in Cambridge and Hertfordshire, and at Trinity

College, Cambridge, where he twice won the Chancellor's medal for English verse, he was called to the Bar in 1826, and thereafter combined his legal career with poetry, contributing to the leading magazines of the day. In 1830 he entered the House of Commons, and applied his great skill as an orator in the Reform Bill debates. In 1834, he began a four-year term as legal adviser to the Supreme Council of India, and in 1839 returned to Britain and to Parliament as MP for Edinburgh. He was Secretary of War under Lord **Melbourne**, and although he was re-elected in 1846, lost his seat in the general election a year later. In 1852, Edinburgh again returned him to the Commons, from which he retired four years later. The first two volumes of his *History of England*—which enjoyed unprecedented popularity for a historical work—were published in 1848, and the next two in 1855. The unfinished fifth volume appeared in 1861. In 1849 he was elected Lord Rector of Glasgow University, and he received a peerage in 1857. He was buried at Westminster Abbey.

MacDONALD, (James) Ramsay

1866–1937

British politician, born Lossiemouth. After working as a teacher in Scotland, he moved to London to study science, but ill-health forced him to pursue a career in political journalism instead. As a leading member of the Independent Labour Party from 1893, he subsequently served as secretary (1900–11) and leader (1911–14, 1922–31) of the Labour Party that succeeded it, and became a Labour MP in 1906, but his pacifist views lost him the leadership in 1914 and his seat in the 1918 election. On returning to the Commons in 1922, he again became party leader, and took his party to victory in 1924 to form Britain's first Labour Administration, but held office as premier in the minority Government for only 10 months, the Conservatives having exploited the Zinoniev affair—which centred on a letter said to prove Communist influence on the Administration—to bring down MacDonald's Administration. He became Prime Minister again in 1929, but the country's worsening financial crisis compelled him to appoint a predominantly Conservative-controlled Cabinet to run the National Government, but was able to assert Labour's dominance after its success in the 1931 election. He was Lord President from 1935 until his death.

MacGREGOR, John (Roddick Russell)

1937–

British politician. Educated at Merchiston Castle School, Edinburgh, St Andrews University, and King's College, London. Between 1963 and 1964 he worked on the current affairs weekly *New Society* and as special assistant to Prime Minister **Alec Douglas-Home**, then as a researcher at Conservative Party headquarters until 1965. From 1965 to 1968 he worked in the private office of then Opposition leader **Edward Heath**, and became an MP in 1974. He was an Opposition Whip from 1977 until the Conservative's 1979 election victory, when he served as a Government Whip for two years until being appointed Under-Secretary of State for Industry. He joined the Cabinet as Minister of State for Agriculture, Fisheries and Food from 1983 to 1985, and again from 1987 to 1989 (after serving two years as Chief Secretary to the Treasury). He weathered the egg salmonella and mad cow disease controversies, and won **Margaret Thatcher**'s special admiration for his success in achieving much-improved terms for British farmers under the EEC's common agriculture policy. MacGregor's low-key but effective style brought him promotion to the key role—as Britain's state schools prepared for sweeping changes in their funding and examination systems—of Secretary of State for Education and Science. On Sir **Geoffrey Howe**'s resignation in 1990 as Lord President of the Council and Leader of the House of Commons in protest at Thatcher's resistance to European monetary union, MacGregor was chosen to take his place, and in that role soon showed his value both as an even-handed manager of parliamentary business and a steadying, impartial influence during the parliamentary party's November 1990 leadership crisis. His reappointment in **John Major**'s first Cabinet therefore came as no surprise.

MACHEL, Samora Moises

1933–86

Mozambican politician. After his education at a Roman Catholic mission school was cut short by his brother's death in a mining accident and the need to help support his family, he worked as a hospital nurse and in 1963 joined the Frelimo movement, to become leader of the liberation troops fighting for independence from Portugal. When independence was granted in 1975, he

139

became Mozambique's first president, but was killed in a plane crash near the South African border in 1986.

MACKAY, James Peter Hymers, Baron Mackay of Clashfern
1927–

Scottish jurist and Lord Chancellor, born Scourie, Sutherland. The son of a railway signalman, he was educated at George Heriot's School and Edinburgh University, and taught mathematics at St Andrews University. In 1948, he began studying at Cambridge University for a research degree, but developed an interest in law and after graduating was admitted to the Bar in 1955. He was subsequently appointed a QC, specializing in tax law, and entered the House of Lords as Lord Advocate for Scotland on the Conservatives' return to power in 1979, but resigned in 1985 and joined the Cross-Benchers as a Lord of Appeal. Following Lord Havers', resignation after a brief term as Lord Chancellor, in 1987 Mackay was appointed to the most senior office in the British constitution, ranking as it does only second to that of the monarch and above that of Prime Minister. Mackay's refreshing pragmatism, reflected in his vigorous promotion of legislation that radically simplified basic litigation and lowered its cost, predictably brought howls of protest from the legal establishment. He is demonstrably guided—as was his most distinguished recent predecessor, Viscount **Hailsham**—by his strong but liberal moral beliefs. In 1989, he was expelled by the fundamentalist Free Presbyterian Church of Scotland—which holds that as Rome teaches that saints or priests can be mediators, Roman Catholics cannot be Christians—for attending two Catholic requiem masses.

MACLEAN, Donald Duart
1913–83

English traitor, son of Liberal cabinet minister, Sir Donald Maclean. Educated at Gresham's School and Trinity College, Cambridge, at the same time as **Anthony Blunt**, **Guy Burgess** and **Kim Philby**, he was similarly influenced by communism. He joined the Diplomatic Service in 1935, serving in Paris, Washington (1944–8) and Cairo (1948–50), and from 1944 acted as a Russian agent. After a 'nervous breakdown' in 1950, he became head of the American Department of the Foreign Office, but by 1951 was a suspected traitor, and in May of that year, after Philby's warning, disappeared with Burgess to Russia. He was joined in 1953 by his wife Melinda (b.USA 1916) and children, but she left him to marry Philby in 1966. Maclean became a respected Soviet citizen, working for the Foreign Ministry and at the Institute of World Economic and International Relations.

MACLEOD, Iain Norman
1913–70

Scottish politician. Educated at Fettes College and Conville and Caius College, Cambridge, he fought in France during World War II, and after working as a member of the Conservative Party secretariat, he entered Parliament in 1950. He was Minister of Health (1952), and of Labour (1955–9), before being appointed Secretary of State for the Colonies in 1959, in which office he made a notable contribution to the granting of independence to many African colonies. From 1961 to 1963 he was subsequently Chancellor of the Duchy of Lancaster and Leader of the House of Commons and party chairman, then edited *The Spectator* for two years, returning to the Cabinet as Chancellor of the Exchequer in 1970. As one of the most popular figures in his party, and a brilliant orator, he was considered a leading contender for the premiership, but died suddenly at the age of 57.

MACMILLAN Sir (Maurice) Harold (1st Earl of Stockton)
1884–1986

British statesman, born Birch Grove House, Chelwood Gate, East Sussex. The son of Maurice Crawford Macmillan, a member of the British publishing dynasty, and of Helen Macmillan, the daughter of an Indiana doctor, he was educated at Eton and at Balliol College, Oxford. While on active service with Grenadier Guards for the duration in World War I he was wounded three times, and served as ADC to the Governor-General of Canada from 1919 until retiring from the Army a year later. He was Conservative MP for Stockton-on-Tees from 1924 to 1929 and again from 1931 to 1945, and in the wartime coalition was Parliamentary Secretary to the Ministry of Supply (1940–2), Under-Secretary of State for the Colonies (1942), and Resident Minister at Allied Headquarters in North-West Africa from 1942 to 1945, then Secretary for Air briefly until Labour's victory in the first post-war general election (in which he was returned as Conservative MP from Bromley). On the Conservatives' return to power in 1951, he was appointed Minister of Housing and Local Government, and subsequently held office as Minister of State for Defence (1954–5) and Secretary of State for Foreign Affairs (1955), and was Chancellor of the Exchequer from December 1955 until Sir **Anthony Eden**'s sudden resignation in January 1957, when Macmillan succeeded him at No 10. The start of Macmillan's six-year premiership coincided with the ending of Britain's post-war austerity and the heralding of a consumer-led economic boom (summed up in his famous phrase of the 1957 general election campaign, 'You've never had it so good'); Britain's acceptance of its declining role as a colonial power; and a partial defrosting of Anglo-Soviet relations. But at the beginning of the 1960s, a different and unsettling domestic and international picture began to emerge. At home, inflation was rife, prompting the highly unpopular 1961 wages freeze; Macmillan's 1959 Moscow visit to **Nikita Khrushchev** failed to achieve the new détente that the British Prime Minister sought with the eastern powers and the country's worsening economic crisis compelled Macmillan in 1962 to dismiss no fewer than seven of his Cabinet Ministers in his 'night of the long knives'— though the audacity of his action at least earned him the sobriquet of 'Supermac' by the cartoonists of the day. But there were triumphs too that year, with Macmillan acting the wise uncle to America's new young Democratic president in the Cuban missile crisis, and thereby helping **John F. Kennedy** to defuse an episode that was the West's closest brush with a nuclear war. Macmillan's final year as Prime Minister was, typically, a mix of advances and setbacks. he played a key role in that year's nuclear test ban treaty, but failed to neutralize **Charles de Gaulle**'s domination of central European policy, particularly in thwarting Britain's entry into the Common Market. In any event, after 12 years of Conservative rule, and in the immediate aftermath of the **John Profumo** affair, the party's hold on the electorate was beginning to weaken. In October 1963, Macmillan announced his resignation, almost inexplicably ignored **Rab Butler**'s suitability as his successor, and left **Alec Douglas-Home** to suffer the slenderest defeat by Labour in the election that followed a few months' later. In contrast to most of his successors,

Macmillan declined to stand again for his safe seat and immediately retired from active politics. It was not until 1984 that he at last agreed to accept an earldom. His memorable maiden speech in the Lords, almost exactly 60 years after he entered Parliament, was one of the first to be televised, allowing a new generation a glimpse of the unique blend of compassion, political acuteness and drollness that were characteristic of the last of the great Edwardian statesmen. His numerous books included *Planning for Employment* (1935), *The Middle Way* (1938, reissued 1966), *Economic Aspects of Defence* (1939), and his six-volume memoirs: *Winds of Change* (1966), *The Blast of War* (1967), *Tides of Fortune* (1969), *Riding the Storm* (1971), *Pointing the Way 1959–61* (1972), and *At the end of the Day 1961–63* (1973); and *Past Masters* (1973).

MADISON, James
1751–1836

Fourth US President, born Port Conway, Virginia. After entering the Virginian convention in 1776, he became a member of the Continental Congress in 1780, and in 1784 of the state legislature. In the 1787 convention that drafted the federal constitution, he was a contributor, with **John Jay** and **Alexander Hamilton** to the *Federalist*, and was chief author of the Virginia Plan, which acknowledged the constitutional status of slaves for the first time. As an opponent of centralization of government, he became leader of the Jeffersonian Republican Party, and when **Thomas Jefferson** assumed the presidency in 1801, Madison became Secretary of State. As president from 1809, he promoted the 1812 war of neutral rights with Britain and tariff protection. He retired in 1817 at the end of his second term.

MAGINOT, André
1877–1932

French politician, born Paris. After entering the Chamber of Deputies in 1910, he was Minister of War from 1922 to 1924, and again from 1926 to 1931, when he ordered the construction on the Franco-German border of the famous Maginot line of fortifications that comprised concealed weapons, underground stores and living quarters. However, in World War II, the German strategy of invading through Belgian made the scheme redundant, and its name has since become a euphemism for a useless form of defence.

MAJOR, John

1943–

British politician, born London. Educated at Rutlish Grammar School, he later studied accountancy by a correspondence course and after qualifying worked for Executive Standard Bank in the UK and overseas from 1965 to 1981. A member of the Conservative Party since 1960, he entered active politics as a Lambeth borough councillor in 1968, and served as chairman of its housing committee from 1970. After twice failing to win election to Parliament as Conservative candidate for St Pancras, North in the February and October 1974 general elections, he entered the Commons as Member of Parliament for Huntingdon as one of the intake of young new MPs who gained a place on the Back-Benches as a result of **Margaret Thatcher**'s 1979 landslide victory over Labour. He served as parliamentary private secretary to two Home Office Ministers from 1981 to 1983. After a two-year term as a Government Whip, he became Under-Secretary of State for Social Security (1985–6), Minister of State for Social Security and the Disabled (1986–7), and Chief Secretary to the Treasury under the chancellorship of **Nigel Lawson** (1987–9). In July 1989, he served for barely three months as Secretary of State for Foreign and Commonwealth Affairs before returning to the Treasury as Chancellor of the Exchequer. In 1990, growing criticisms by several leading party figures—including Lawson and another former Chancellor and Foreign Secretary, Sir **Geoffrey Howe**—combined with the Conservatives' plummeting popularity—encouraged another former Cabinet Minister, **Michael Heseltine**, to stand against Thatcher in the usually routine election of party leader. When the Prime Minister failed to secure the necessary majority in the first round of voting, she resigned the leadership, leaving Heseltine to fight Foreign Secretary **Douglas Hurd**, with Major adding his name to the candidates as a late outsider. However, after Thatcher let it be known that he was her preferred candidate, Major's appeal as a compromise candidate proved irresistible, and he won the ballot, to become Britain's fortieth Prime Minister. Within days, Major was finalizing the UK's entry into the European exchange rate mechanism, and had charged Heseltine—whom he had appointed Secretary of State for the Environment—with the task of scrapping the poll tax. He soon established his international capability with his presentation and promotion at home and abroad of Britain's active role in the Gulf War. His Treasury experience allowed him to work positively with his new Chancellor of the Exchequer, Norman Lamont. Eight months into his premiership, he signalled a less combative approach to industrial relations by hosting the first visit to No 10 by a delegation of trade unionists in a decade. However, the country's deepening recession, disappointing by-election results, and Labour's improving showing in the opinion polls prevented Major from calling the expected June 1991 general election.

MAKARIOS III (Mihail Christodoulou Mouskos)

1913–77

Cypriot Orthodox archbishop and first president of the Republic of Cyprus, born Paphos. After his ordination in 1946, he was elected bishop of Kition in 1948 and became archbishop and primate two years later. As the political leader of the Enosis movement that agitated for the end of British rule and union with Greece, he was exiled to the Seychelles in 1956 for his suspected collaboration with EOKA guerrilla forces. He later lived in Athens, but after independence was granted in 1959, he returned as head of state. Opposition to his leadership from the Turkish Muslim minority, Enosis extremists and even his fellow bishops prompted several attempts on his life, and in 1974 a short-lived coup saw him deposed as president for a year. On his death, the posts of primate and head of state were separated, bringing to an end a Byzantine tradition that under Makarios had become a political anachronism.

MALAN, Daniel François

1874–1959

South African politician, born Riebeek West, Cape Province. After studying at Victoria College, Stellenbosch, and Utrecht University, he returned to South Africa to become a cleric with the Dutch Reformed Church, but after 10 years abandoned that career to become editor of the Nationalist newspaper, *Die Burger*. He entered Parliament in 1918 and in the 1924 Nationalist Government was Minister for the interior, of education, and of public health, introducing legislation—including the adoption of Afrikaans as the official national language—aimed at consolidating the nationalist cause.

He was Leader of the Opposition from 1934 to 1939 and again from 1940 to 1948, when he became Prime Minister and Minister for External Affairs. He immediately set about imposing national apartheid with the creation of white, black and coloured zones—which, while being widely denounced abroad, met with only non-violent civil disobedience in South Africa itself. He resigned the premiership in 1954, having established a system of segregation that was to endure for another quarter of a century, until it began to be dismantled by **F.W. de Klerk**.

MALCOLM X (Malcolm Little)
1925–65

American black nationalist leader, born Omaha, Nebraska. The son of a radical Baptist minister, he spent his childhood in Lansing, Michigan, and Boston, and in his teens began a life of petty crime that brought him several terms of imprisonment. While in jail in 1952, he was converted to the Black Muslim sect led by Elijah Muhammad, and on his release the following year adopted the name Malcolm X and travelled the country promoting the movement. He was initially vehemently opposed to integration and advocated black separatism and the use of violence in self-defence. However, after visiting Mecca in 1964, he adopted a new creed that combined orthodox Islam and African socialism with anti-colonialism and racial solidarity. The change triggered a bitter feud between the various factions among his followers, and in 1965, he was assassinated by Black Muslim extremists while attending a rally in Harlem.

MALIK, Jacob Alexandrovich
1906–80

Soviet politician, born in the Ukraine. As one of **Joseph Stalin**'s favourite protégés, he was ambassador to Japan from 1942 to 1945, and was appointed deputy Foreign Minister in 1946. In 1948 he succeeded **Andrei Gromyko** as the Soviets' chief delegate to the United Nations, and was ambassador to Britain from 1953 to 1960, when he served a further term as deputy Foreign Minister. He was Soviet ambassador to the United Nations from 1968 to 1976.

MALTHUS, Thomas Robert
1766–1834

English economist and clergyman, born Dorking. A fellow of Jesus College, Cam-bridge, from 1793, he became a curate at Albury, Surrey, in 1797, and a year later published anonymously his *Essay on the Principle of Population*, in which he challenged the works of Jean-Jacques Rousseau and other political philosophers, arguing that their assertions of the perfectablity of man were nullified by the natural tendency for the population to grow faster than the means of subsistence, and advocated positive action to reduce the birth-rate by birth control or the encouragement of abstinence. He also wrote *An Inquiry into the Nature and Progress of Rent* (1815).

MANDELA, Nelson
1918–

South African lawyer and politician, born Umtata, Transkei. The son of the Chief of the Tembu tribe, he was educated at the University College of Fort Hare and the University of Witwatersrand and began practising law in Johannesburg in 1952. As national organizer of the multiracial African National Congress (ANC), he initially promoted non-violent civil disobedience and a negotiated solution to the end of white subjugation, and in 1955, drew up with the Pan-Africanist Congress (PAC) the freedom Charter calling for equal political rights for all racial groups. Mandela's approach hardened after 67 blacks were massacred by police in 1960 during a demonstration at Sharpeville against the notorious pass laws that controlled freedom of movement, and the international outrage and further protests that followed prompted the Government, with National Party leader Dr **Hendrik Verwoerd** as Prime Minister, to outlaw the two organizations. The establishment by both the ANC and PAC of military wings outside South Africa brought Mandela's arrest, and in 1962 he was sentenced to five years' imprisonment. Further charges of treason and incitement to murder were brought in 1963 and despite a memorable four-hour defence speech he was sentenced to life imprisonment in 1964. Sent to Robben Island and then later to Poll-smoor, he retained his aura of authority, persuading fellow prisoners to retain their ideals and remaining a potent symbol of black resistance. By 1988 the president, P.W. Botha, had embraced a new moderacy, and within a year had legislated for the appointment of black Cabinet Ministers and an extension of representation outside the homelands—but he still refused all requests to release Mandela, now aged 70 though he was given improved conditions after his health deteriorated. At the start of 1989, the Government were rocked by a corruption scandal involving two Ministers, and Botha called a general election for September, stepping down two months before. Acting State President **Frederik de Klerk** took the National Party to victory again, and within weeks accelerated the neglected programme of reforms. In February 1990, he unbanned the ANC and other political organizations and ordered Mandela's release. Nearly 26 years of imprisonment had done nothing to diminish Mandela's dignity and charisma, and in his role as deputy ANC leader, he embarked on a gruelling schedule of nationwide appearances and meetings with international politicians. Within a year, he reached an accord with Inkatha and he saw the Government's abandonment of the last vestiges of apartheid. In July 1991, at the ANC's first public congress in 30 years, he succeeded Oliver Tambo as ANC president, and declared his intention to secure full democratic representation of his people by the end of the decade.

MANDELA, (Nomzano) Winnie
1934–

South African civil rights activist, born Bizana. After her marriage to **Nelson Mandela** in 1958, she became active in his work for the African National Congress, and after its banning in 1960, served several terms of imprisonment for her political activities. She was kept in Brandfort from 1977 to 1985, out of the public eye. In 1985 she returned to Soweto and became involved in the militant politics of the township. Throughout Nelson Mandela's 26 years' incarceration, she campaigned ceaselessly for black rights on his behalf and for his release. In May 1991, after a 44-day trial, she was released on bail pending an appeal after being given a six-year sentence for complicity in the kidnapping and assault of suspected police informers by members of her bodyguard from the so-called Mandela United Football Club—but was cleared of any part in the murder of a 14-year-old activist, 'Stompie' Moeketsi. Many were surprised when she was appointed head of the ANC's department of social affairs.

MANLEY, Michael Norman
1923–

Jamaican politician, born Kingston, the son of **Norman Manley**. After service with the Royal Canadian Air Force in World War II, he studied at the London School of Economics (1945–9) and worked as a journalist before returning to Jamaica and becoming leader of the National Workers Union in the 1950s. He sat in the Senate for the National People's Party—which had been founded by his father—from 1962 to 1967, then in the House of Representatives, and in 1967 was appointed party leader. As Prime Minister in 1972, he embarked on a radical socialist programme that distanced him from the US, and despite rising unemployment won re-election in 1976. His party suffered heavy defeats in the 1980 and 1983 elections, but since his return to power in 1989, he has followed more moderate policies.

MANLEY, Norman Washington
1893–

Jamaican politician, born Kingston. After studying law, he was called to the Bar and rose to become a distinguished QC, successfully defending in 1938 his cousin and political opponent, the trade-union activist **Alexander Bustamente**, against a charge of sedition. In the same year, Manley founded the People's National Party, which he took to victory in the 1955 election. His long term as Prime Minister saw the granting of Jamaican independence in 1962, and in 1969 he handed over the party leadership to his son, **Michael Manley**.

MANNERHEIM, Carl Gustav Emil, Freiherr von
1867–1951

Finnish soldier and statesman, born Askainen. As an officer in the Russian army from 1889, he fought in the Russo-Japanese War (1904–5) and in World War I. On Finland's declaration of independence following the Russian revolution in 1917, he was made supreme commander and regent and successfully suppressed the Finnish Bolsheviks. After being defeated for the presidency in 1919, he retired into private life, but at the outbreak of the Russo-Finnish Winter War of 1939, he was recalled as commander-in-chief, organized the Mannerheim defences, and became marshal in 1942. He was president for a year from 1944.

MAO ZEDONG, (Mao Tse-tung)
1893–1976

Chinese communist leader, first Chairman of the People's Republic of China, born

Shaoshan, Hunan province. The son of a peasant farmer, he was educated at Changsha, then enlisted in the revolutionary army in the 1911 rebellion against the Manchu dynasty. As a student and library assistant at Beijing (Peking) University from 1918, he spent hours reading the works of **Sun Yixian** (Sun Yat-sen), **Karl Marx** and other revolutionary thinkers, and in 1921 co-founded the Chinese Communist Party (CCP). From 1924 he returned to the revolutionary army with responsibility for organizing new guerrilla units, and after being appointed head of propoganda under Sun Yixian, promoted the alliance with **Jiang Jieshi**'s Kuomintang, though it was to last only until 1927, when the nationalist leader turned on the communist, forcing Mao to retreat to south-eastern China. There, he established in 1931 the Chinese Soviet Republic in Jiangxi province, but in 1934 was forced to flee the territory with the advance of Kuomintang forces and began with his army the famous 9600 km/6000 ml long march to safety in Shaanxi in the north. The two factions agreed a truce during the war with the Japanese (1937–45), but at the end of the war hostilities between them resumed, and within four years Mao triumphed and was proclaimed Chairman of the People's Republic of China. Mao abandoned his earlier devotion to the Soviet model and in 1958 initiated the industrial revolution known as the Great Leap Forward. The forced establishment of communes that was central to its success were widely unpopular, and within a year Mao had stepped down as his country's leader, while remaining party chairman. In that capacity, he launched the Cultural Revolution (1966–9), whose targets were bureaucracy, corruption—real or imagined—and all aspects of traditional Chinese (let alone western) culture. Countless thousands of political dissidents—as well as historians, teachers, authors, poets and even painters—were imprisoned for their 'non-conformist' attitudes, and the people were expected constantly to remind themselves of the thoughts of Chairman Mao, which were encapsulated in the official little red book that almost every Chinese child and adult was expected to carry. In his final years, Mao's total sway over the Chinese nation remained undiminished, and he enjoyed playing the wider role of international statesman, hosting visits by leading Western political figures as a way of antagonizing Moscow. His death at the age of 83 was followed by a power struggle briefly won by the Gang of Four, whose members included Mao's widow, **Jiang Qing**.

MARAT, Jean Paul
1743–93

French revolutionary, born Neuchâtel, Switzerland. After studying medicine at Bordeaux, Paris and Holland, he practised in London and Paris, and was appointed physician to the Comte d'Artois, later **Charles X**, until 1786. With the growth of the revolutionary movement, he joined the Cordelier Club, and in 1789 founded the revolutionary newspaper *L'ami du peuple*, which incited the 'sans-culottes' violently to pursue their cause. He was twice forced to flee to London, but with the success of the revolution, he was elected to the Convention in 1793 as a Paris deputy. He was briefly arrested at the instigation of the Girondins, but on his release contrived their downfall with the assistance of **Robespierre** and **Danton**. He was killed while in his bath by Charlotte Corday.

MARCHAIS, Georges
1920–

French politician. A miner's son, he joined the French Communist Party in 1947, and as its general-secretary since 1972, he strengthened his policy of achieving its aims by democratic means by entering into a union with the Socialist Party. However, when that made little headway, he broke with the Socialists in 1977 and adopted a manifesto that was close to the Moscow line. After Marchais unsuccessfully contested the presidency in 1981, the FCP contributed Ministers to **François Mitterrand**'s Administrations until 1984.

MARCOS, Ferdinand Edralin
1917–89

Filipino politician. Educated at the University of the Philippines, his early political activities saw him accused but acquitted of murdering one of his father's political opponents in 1939, and during World War II, he served in the resistance and, after being captured by the Japanese, survived internment in the notorious Bataan camp. At the end of the war, he entered the House of Representatives, and between 1959 and 1966 was a senator, first for the Liberals and then for the Nationalists. He was elected president in 1965 and re-elected in 1969, but growing unrest over the country's failing economy led to his imposition of martial law in 1972. Thereafter, he ruled as virtual dictator until 1986, when his regime, and his family's incredibly lavish lifestyle, came to an end with the success of the campaign led by **Corazon Aquino**. Marcos and his wife, Imelda, went into exile in Hawaii, and after his death two years later, Imelda was put on trial in America on charges of embezzlement involving huge sums from her country's treasury.

MARKIEWICZ, Constance Georgine, Countess
1868–1927

Irish nationalist and first British woman MP, born London. After studying art at the Slade School in London and at Paris, she married Count Casimir Markiewicz in 1900. Following their move to Dublin in 1903, she joined Sinn Fein in 1908, and after she had established a close friendship with Maude Gonne MacBride, her husband went to the Ukraine in 1913 and never returned. For her active part in the 1916 Easter Rebellion, she was sentenced to death but won a reprieve in the 1917 general amnesty. The following year she became the first woman to be returned to the House of Commons, for a Dublin constituency, but refused to take her seat. She was elected to the first Dàil Eireann in 1919 and made Minister for Labour, and served two further terms of imprisonment, before returning to the Dàil in 1923.

MARSHALL, Alfred
1842–1924

English economist, born London. Educated at Merchant Taylors' School and St John's College, Cambridge, he was principal of University College, Bristol (1877), and lecturer on political economy at Balliol College, Oxford (1883) before becoming professor of political economy at Cambridge (1885–1908). His *Principles of Economics* (1890) still serves as a standard text book. He also wrote *Industry and Trade* (1919), and *Money, Credit and Commerce* (1923).

MARSILIUS OF PADUA
1275–1342

Italian political theorist and philosopher, born Padua. As rector of the University of Paris from 1313, he lectured on natural philosophy and undertook medical research, and then became actively involved in Italian politics. His *Defensor Pacis* (1324) argued against the temporal power of the clergy and the Pope and advanced a form of government based on popular consensus and natural rights. On its publication, he was obliged to return to Paris, and after being excommunicated by Pope John XXII, he remained under the protection of Louis of Bavaria in Munich until his death.

MARTENS, Wilfried
1936–

Belgian politician. Educated at Louvain University, he served as a Government advisor before being appointed Minister for Community Problems in 1968. In 1972, he became leader of the Dutch-speaking Social Christian Party, and in 1979 became Prime Minister of the first of six coalition Governments.

MARTI, José
1853–95

Cuban writer and patriot. Exiled at 16 for associating with activists for Cuban independence from Spain, he lived in Mexico, Guatemala, Spain and the USA, and gained a reputation as a distinguished author and poet. In America, he organized a new revolutionary movement and abandoned his career as a writer to take part in the 1895 uprising, but within weeks was killed at the Battle of Dos Rios.

MARY, Queen of Scots
1542–87

Queen Consort of France (1559–60), daughter of James V of Scotland by his second wife, Mary of Guise, born at Linlithgow Palace, Scotland. Queen of Scotland at a week old, her betrothal to Prince Edward of England was annulled by the Scottish parliament, precipitating war with England. After the Scots' defeat at Pinkie (1547), she was sent to the French court and married the Dauphin (1558), later Francis II, but was widowed at 18 (1560) and returned to Scotland (1561). Ambitious for the English throne, in 1565 she married her cousin, Henry Stuart, Lord Darnley, a grandson of Margaret Tudor, but disgusted by his debauchery, was soon alienated from him. The vicious murder of Rizzio, her Italian secretary, by Darnley and a group of Protestant nobles in her presence (1566) confirmed her insecurity. The birth of a son future James VI, failed to bring a reconciliation. While ill with smallpox, Darnley was mysteriously killed in an explosion at Kirk o' Field (1567); the chief suspect was the Earl of Bothwell, who underwent a mock trial and was acquitted. Mary's involvement is unclear, but she consented to marry Bothwell, a divorcee with whom she had become infatuated. The Protestent nobles under Morton rose against her; she surrendered at Carberry Hill, was imprisoned at Loch Leven, and compelled to abdicate. After escaping, she raised an army, but was defeated again by the confederate lords at Langside (1568). Placing herself under the protection of Queen **Elizabeth**, she found herself instead a prisoner for life. Her presence in England gave rise to countless plots to depose Elizabeth and restore Catholicism. Finally, after the Babington conspiracy (1586) she was brought to trial for treason, and executed in Fotheringay Castle, Northamptonshire.

MARY I
1516–58

Queen of England, born Greenwich, the daughter of **Henry VIII** and Catherine of Aragon. After being forced by her father to sign a declaration that his marriage to her mother had been unlawful, Mary withdrew from public life rather than acknowledge the new Church, but on her father's death in 1553, she became entitled, by means of her father's testament and a parliamentary settlement, to take the throne. The Duke of Northumberland's attempts to have Henry's will set aside in favour of his daughter in law, Lady Jane Grey, met with violent public opposition, and he was executed. On taking the throne, Mary slowly reintroduced the old religion and reinstated the bishops, but cautiously stopped short of acknowledging papal supremacy. Mary's determination to marry Phillip of Spain brought the first rift with her subjects, and the 1554 Wyatt rebellion prompted her to remove her possible rivals by ordering the execution of Lady Jane and her father and having the future **Elizabeth I** incarcerated in the Tower of London. After her marriage to Philip later the same year, Mary reached an accord with Rome whereby Parliament voted for reconciliation with the Holy See while securing the realm's absolution from papal censures. Her

place now secure, Mary was content to play a passive role in the persecution of Protestant opponents to her reign that earned her the sobriquet of Bloody Mary. Nicholas Ridley and Hugh Latimer were burned at the stake in 1556, and Thomas Cranmer the following year, and more than 300 others met a similar fate. But Mary's reign was to last only another two years, and she died without producing an heir.

MARX, Karl
1818–83

German social, political and economic theorist, born Trier. Raised as a Protestant after his Jewish father, a lawyer, had converted his faith to avoid anti-Semitism, Marx studied at Bonn University (1835–6) and at Berlin University (1836–41), where he associated with the followers of **Georg Hegel** and other revolutionary thinkers, and from 1842 worked on a liberal newspaper in Cologne before it was suppressed by the authorities. During his subsequent stay in Paris, Marx developed the still fledgling doctrine of communism in his writings, which argued the alienation of man under capitalism, and that it could only be defeated by revolution. Political pressure saw him decamp to Brussels in 1845 where, with **Friedrich Engels**, he drafted and published in 1848 the *Communist Manifesto*, which concludes with the famous exhortation, 'The workers have nothing to lose but their chains. . . Workers of all lands, unite!' After the 1848 Paris revolution, he returned to Cologne to edit another radical publication, but when that was closed after a year, he took refuge with his family in London. There, Marx spent weeks on end researching in the Reading Room of the British Museum, eventually publishing the first volume of *Das Kapital* in 1867. Another two followed, posthumously, in 1884 and 1894. It brought together all the strands of Communist ideology in denouncing superficial values and the exploitation of the working class, and predicting the replacement of the capitalist system by a self-supporting classless society. Having supported the First International from its inception in 1864, Marx saw its disintegration in 1872 in the aftermath of the split by the anarchist supporters of **Mikhail Bakunin**. He remained in London until his death, and was buried at Highgate cemetery.

MASARYK, Jan
1886–1948

Czechoslovak diplomat and statesman, born Prague. The son of **Thomas Masaryk**, he worked in the diplomatic service from 1925 to 1938, and, as ambassador to London during World War II, did much to promote his country's cause through his diplomatic activities and a series of radio broadcasts. In July 1941 he was made Foreign Minister in exile, and in 1945 returned to Prague with his father's successor, **Benes**, in the hope of checking communist influence in the post-war coalitions. On 19 March 1948, he was killed when he fell from an open window in his office at the Foreign Ministry, but doubt has always surrounded the official explanation that he was thought to have committed suicide in protest at the Stalinization of his homeland.

MASARYK, Thomas Garrigue
1850–1937

Founder-President of Czechoslovakia, born Hodonin, Moravia. After lecturing in philosophy at Prague University from 1882 to 1914, he became active in nationalist politics, and as a member of the Vienna Parliament (1891–3, 1907–14) made his famous exposé of documents forged by the Habsburg authorities in a bid to discredit the Slav minorities. In 1914, he fled to London, and as chairman of the Czech National Council, agitated for a new Europe based on national self-determination. In 1917 he went to Russia to form the Czech Legion among prisoners-of-war, and later to the USA, where in 1918 he won recognition from **Woodrow Wilson** as his country's leader in exile. At the end of the war, he returned to his country as president-elect but took little active part in politics, though he was among the first to warn of the Nazi menace. He retired in 1935.

MASIRE, Quett Ketumile Joni
1925–

Botswana politician. After an early career as a journalist, he became involved in politics as a member of the Bangwaketse Tribal Council and Legislative Council, and in 1962 co-founded, with **Seretse Khama**, the Botswana Democratic Party. He was deputy prime minister from 1965, becoming vice-president a year later when his country achieved independence. On Khama's death in 1980 he was elected president, and has continued his predecessor's policy of non-alignment, to make Botswana one of the most politically-stable of the African states.

MATTEOTTI, Giacomo
1885–1924

Italian politician, born Fratta Polesine, Rovigno. After graduating from Bologna University in law, he worked as a regional organizer for the Socialists and was elected to Parliament in 1919. Following a speech in the Chamber of Deputies on 30 June 1924, in which he denounced Fascist intimidation and violence during the April elections, Matteotti was kidnapped on his way to Parliament, beaten, and murdered. When public outrage reached a pitch that threatened to bring down the Government, **Benito Mussolini** went through the motions of dismissing a number of subordinates and appointing a moderate Minister of the Interior, and pre-empted the Opposition's calls for his dismissal by persuading the king to maintain a passive role in the affair. However, by the end of June the Opposition deputies withdrew from the Chamber, but Mussolini again protected his position by forming a new Cabinet that included a number of them. But the furore continued throughout the summer and autumn, and on 20 November Mussolini was compelled to announce that fascism's revolutionary phase had ended and that moderate rule had replaced it. However, that declaration antagonized both extremists and the militia, and after the publication in December of information that directly implicated Mussolini in Matteotti's murder, he was confronted by a delegation of 33 militia consuls who demanded immediate action against the anti-Fascists. Mussolini blinded Parliament with his most important public speech, on 3 January 1925, in which he professed to take complete personal responsibility for all political, moral and criminal activity since he took office, and promised a further statement—which many expected would contain his resignation—in 48 hours. However, within days he unleashed a fresh wave of Fascist violence directed at all suspected of opposing him.

MAUROY, Pierre
1928–

French politician. After an early career as a teacher, he became involved in trade unionism and socialist politics, and helped to develop the new French Socialist Party in

1971 and to encourage the unification of the left-wing factions. In 1973, he was elected to the National Assembly and was appointed prime minister by **François Mitterrand** in 1981. However, his attempt to deal with an ailing economy by reflation was unsuccessful, and he was replaced by Laurent Fabius in 1984. A leading figure in the party's traditional left wing, he became its first secretary in 1988.

MAURRAS, Charles
1868–1952

French journalist and critic, born Martigues (Bouches-du-Rhône). After studying philosophy at Paris, he established a reputation as an avant-garde journalist, and after visiting Greece fell under the influence of its culture and, appalled by the persecution of **Alfred Dreyfus**, lost sympathy with republicanism and promoted his belief in the value of the monarchy in *Trois idées politiques* (1898) and *Enquête sur la monarchie* (1901). His later essays, including *Action française* (1908) and *Les Conditions de la victoire* (1916–18), and his highly critical articles in *Figaro*, finally brought his imprisonment. Having supported the reviled Vichy Government during World War II, he was tried and sentenced to life imprisonment when France was liberated, and remained in prison until 1952, when he was released on medical grounds shortly before his death.

MAXTON, James
1885–1946

Scottish politician, born Glasgow. After graduating from Glasgow University he worked as a teacher. A staunch pacifist and conscientious objector, he was imprisoned for attempting to foment a strike of shipyard workers during World War I. After joining the Independent Labour Party, he became its chairman in 1926, and was an MP from 1922 until his death.

MBOYA, Tom
1930–69

African nationalist leader, born Kenya. Educated at Holy Ghost College, Mangu, he worked as a sanitary inspector, and in 1951 joined **Jomo Kenyatta**'s Kenya African Union, becoming its treasurer two years later. When the party was outlawed, he briefly served as secretary of the Kenya Federation of Labour, but the shortcomings of the 1954 Constitution saw his return to political activism as one of the leaders of the pro-independence movement. In 1960, he achieved significant constitutional concessions at the London Conference, and after the emergence of the KAU later that year as Kenya's chief political movement he was appointed its general secretary. He subsequently served as Minister of Labour (1962–3), and of Justice (1963–4), and five years after being made Minister of Development and Planning in 1964, he was assassinated by tribal extremists in Nairobi.

McCARTHY, Joseph Raymond
1909–57

American politician, born Grand Chute, Wisconsin. Educated at Marquette University, Milwaukee, he qualified as a lawyer and served as a state circuit judge, and after service in World War II, and contrary to the Constitution, was elected a senator in 1945. He defied a Supreme Court ruling to take his seat, and in 1950, having established his right-wing credentials by accusing the State Department, in the wake of the Fuchs and Hiss spy trials, of harbouring 205 prominent communists, he was re-elected with a huge majority. As chairman of the House Committee on Un-American Activities from 1953, he became notorious for his televised 'witch- hunts' in which hundreds of innocent people, from minor officials to Hollywood movie stars, were mercilessly interrogated as suspected members of a communist conspiracy bent on undermining the American way of life. He was brought down the following year when, after being accused of financial irregularities by the Democratic majority in the Senate, he countered with an attack on President **Dwight D. Eisenhower** that lost him the remaining vestiges of his Republican support.

McGOVERN, George Stanley
1922–

American politician, born Avon, South Dakota. After service in the USAF in World War II, he was professor of history and of government at Dakota Wesleyan University, won election to the House of Representatives as a Democrat (1956–61), and entered the Senate in 1963. As a radical liberal, he was chosen as the Democrats' presidential candidate to fight **Richard Nixon** in 1972, but suffered the most crushing election defeat in American history, largely due to his wholly unsuccessful attempts to negotiate with Hanoi. In 1984, he failed to secure a second nomination, with his party favouring **Walter Mondale** instead, but in January 1991, he announced his intention to stand for the 1992 nomination.

MAZZINI, Giuseppe
1805–72

Italian patriot and republican, born in Genoa. Trained as a lawyer, he became an ardent liberal, founded the Young Italy Association (1833) and, expelled from France, travelled Europe advocating republicanism and insurrection. In 1848 he became involved in the Lombard revolt, and collaborated with **Garibaldi** in attempting to keep the patriot struggle alive in the Alps. In 1849 he became one of the triumvirate governing the Roman Republic, overthrown after two months by French intervention. During the events of 1859–60 he and his supporters worked strenuously but vainly to make the new Italy a republic. He died at Pisa.

MEHEMET 'ALI (Mohammed Ali)
1769–1849

Viceroy of Egypt, born Albania. After fighting with the Turkish forces in Egypt against the French, he remained in command of Albanian troops and in 1805 emerged as pasha (viceroy). He became supreme leader in 1811 after ordering the treacherous massacre of the semi-independent Mamluk beys, then invaded Arabia, suppressed the Wahabis—followers of an extreme Muslim sect—and seized Mecca and Medina. With warfare at an end, Mehemet confronted the task of modernizing the economy by establishing agricultural monopolies and new industries, and used part of the proceeds to build a new army with which he conquered the Sudan (1820–30) and came to the aid of his former Turkish adversaries in suppressing the Greek independence movement. However, the Turks, fearful of Mehemet's growing military power and influence, sought British assistance in forcing his son, Ibrahim, to withdraw from Syria, but Mehemet was mollified by the granting of a hereditary title. However, in 1848 he went insane, and after briefly succeeding him as the head of the khedival dynasty, Ibrahim died later the same year.

MEINHOF, Ulrike Marie
1934–76

West German terrorist, born Oldenburg. After becoming involved in left-wing politics as a student at Marburg University, she became a respected journalist, and in 1961 married the communist activist Klaus Rainer Röhl, but the union ended in 1968. After interviewing **Andreas Baader** in prison, she was converted to the use of violence in achieving radical social change, and in 1970 she helped Baader to escape. While in hiding, they formed the Red Army Faction terrorist movement. She was arrested in 1972, and in 1974 was sentenced to eight years' imprisonment. She committed suicide two years later.

MEIR, Golda (Goldie Mabovich)
1898–1978

Israeli politician, born Kiev, Ukraine. Following her family's emigration to Milwaukee, USA, when she was eight years old, she married there at 17 and after becoming involved in the Zionist movement, she settled in Palestine in 1921. She entered local Labour politics seven years later, and between 1929 and 1946 served on the Federation of Labour's executive and secretariat. At the outbreak of World War II, she joined the War Economic Advisory Council, and in 1945 was appointed head of the Jewish Agency for Palestine. When the State of Israel was created in 1948, after a one-year term as ambassador to Russia, she became a member of the Knesset and was appointed Minister of Labour (1949–56), then Foreign Minister (1956-66). In 1967 she founded the Israeli Labour Party, and two years later was elected Israel's first woman Prime Minister, holding office until her resignation in 1974. Her autobiography *My Life* was published in 1975.

MENDERES, Adnan
1899–1961

Turkish statesman, born Aydin. After studying law, he chose to become a farmer instead, and in 1932 entered politics—at first in opposition to, then in the ruling party of, the father of modern Turkey, **Kemal Atatürk**. In 1945 he helped to found the new Democratic Party, and became Prime Minister when it took power in 1950. He was re-elected in 1954 and 1957 but deposed in the army coup of 1960. After being put on trial together with 500 other members of the Democratic Administration, he was sentenced to death and hanged.

MENEM, Carlos
1935–

Argentine politician, born Anillaco, La Rioja province. While studying law, he became active in **Juan Peron**'s Justice Party, founding its youth league in 1955, and in 1963 was elected provincial president. He became governor of La Rioja in 1983 and was re-elected in 1987, and two years later defeated the Radical Union Party candidate for the presidency. Although his campaign exploited popular sentiment over his country's continuing claim to the sovereignty of the Malvinas (Falklands Islands), on assuming office he declared a willingness to resume diplomatic relations with the UK, and by 1990, he had achieved a measure of success in that regard, to the benefit of Argentina's traditionally perilous economy. However, in January 1991, his eight-man Cabinet resigned at his request to allow a ministerial reshuffle following a corruption scandal involving the granting of an import licence to a US firm, in which the the premier's economic adviser (and brother-in-law) was alleged to be implicated.

MENGISTU, Mariam Haile
1937–

Ethiopian soldier and politician. After training at Holetu Military Academy, he was enlisted in the Ethiopian army, and having risen to the rank of colonel, took part in the 1974 coup that deposed **Haile Selassie**, and three years later overthrew the subsequent military regime. Despite Ethiopia's perilous economy, ceaseless guerrilla fighting in Eritrea, and frequent droughts throughout the 1970s and 1980s, Mengistu managed to retain power with help from Russia and then the West. In 1987, he sanctioned the return of one-party civilian rule under the Marxist-Leninist Workers Party, with himself as president. In May 1991, as an alliance of rebel groups closed in on the capital, Addis Ababa, Mengistu fled the country and his Government fell.

MENZIES, Sir Robert Gordon
1894–1978

Australian statesman, born Jeparit, Victoria. Educated at Melbourne University, he practised as a barrister, became a King's Counsel in 1929, and entered the Victoria Parliament in 1928. He was deputy premier from 1932 to 1934, in which year he joined the House of Representatives and was appointed Attorney-General. On the death of **J.A. Lyons** in 1939, Menzies succeeded him as leader of the United Australia Party and became prime minister shortly afterwards. A party split brought his resignation in 1941, when he founded an anti-Labour coalition, the Liberal Party, which he led for the next 25 years. During his record term as Prime Minister from 1949 to 1966, he maintained strong political links with Britain and cultivated a close economic and military alliance with the US. From 1965 to 1978, he served as **Winston Churchill**'s successor as Lord Warden of the Cinque Ports.

METAXAS, Yanni
1870–1941

Greek politician, born Ithaka. After his military training, he fought in the 1897 Thessalian action against the Turks, then studied military science in Germany and returned to help reorganize the Greek army prior to the 1912-13 Balkan Wars, becoming chief of the general staff in 1913. As a royalist and a supporter of King Constantine's policy of neutrality in World War I—he was exiled, together with the king, by the pro-British republican leader **Eleutherios Venizelos** in 1917, but was allowed to return after Constantine's abdication following the Turks' defeat of the Greek army in Asia Minor. He subsequently formed the Party of Free Opinion, and on the failure of Venizelos's 1935 attempt to bring down the restored monarchy, Metaxas became deputy prime minister, and prime minister in 1936. As head of a military dictatorship, his efforts to strengthen the country's economy and armed forces proved providential in the Italian invasion of 1940–1.

METTERNICH, Prince Clemens Lothat Wenzel
1773–1859

Austrian statesman, born Coblenz. After studying at Strasbourg and Mainz, he joined the diplomatic staff of the Hague embassy, and then served as Austrian Minister in Dresden, Berlin, and Paris. In 1807 he concluded the treaty of Fontainebleau, and two years later was made Foreign Minister. In 1811, he was compelled to declare war against France, was made Prince of the Empire, then at the Vienna Congress, played a leading role in structuring the new German federation, while opposing Prussian influence, and in protecting his country's interests in Italy. From 1815, he concentrated on inhibiting all popular and constitutional aspirations at home, and encouraging their resistence abroad, and as such was largely responsible for provoking the movement that brought the 1848 French revolution, which had repercussions throughout Europe and eventually brought down his own Government. Metternich fled to England, and in 1851 retired to his castle on the Rhine. He died in Vienna eight years later. His self-laudatory *Autobiography* was published in translation from 1880 to 1883.

MIDSZENTY, Cardinal Jozsef
1892–1975

Hungarian Roman Catholic prelate, born Mindszent, Vas. He was primate of Hungary from 1945 and cardinal from 1946, and two years later was charged with treason by the Communist Government and sentenced to life imprisonment. After his temporary release following the 1956 rising, he was granted asylum in the American legation in Budapest, where he remained as a voluntary prisoner for 14 years. In 1971, he went to Rome and was asked to resign by Pope Paul VI over his criticisms of Vatican policy towards Hungary. Midszenty spent his last years in a Hungarian religious community in Vienna. His *Memoirs* were published in 1974.

MIHAILOVICH, Draza
1893–1946

Serbian soldier. After distinguished service in World War I, he rose to the rank of colonel in the Yugoslav army, and following the German occupation in 1941, headed the Chetniks mountain guerrilla movement. In exile from 1943, he was appointed Minister of War, but when **Tito**'s communist resistance grew dominant, he switched his allegiance to the Germans and Italians. After the war, he was captured and executed for collaborating with the occupation powers.

MILOSEVIC, Slobodan
1941–

Serbian politician, born Pozarevac. Educated at Belgrade University, he joined the Communist League in 1959, was active in student affairs, and entered government service as an economic adviser to the mayor of Belgrade in 1966. From 1969 to 1983 he held senior posts in the state gas and banking industries. He was appointed president of the Serbian League of Communists in 1984, and his election to Belgrade City Committee two years later served as the springboard for his successful 1988 bid for the presidency. As a hardline party leader in the pre-perestroika mould, he won immediate popularity by disenfranchising the Albanian majority in Kosovo privince, and in the absence of any strong reformist candidate to oppose him, survived the anti-Moscow wave in the republic's 1990 multi-party elections that removed the communist leadership in Croatia and Slovenia. however, Milosevic's continued efforts to dominate the affairs of the more liberal republics, and his action in appropriating £875 million of federal reserves to buttress Serbia's ailing economy without the consent of any of them, prompted Croatia and Slovenia to declare their independence on 24 June 1991. Milosevic initially tried to mend the split by assenting to the appointment of a Croatian, Stip Mesic, as state president, but when that ploy failed, he sought to regain control of the two republics, and to safeguard the 70000 Serbs in Croatia, by force, taking Yugoslavia to the brink of a full-scale civil war. Eventually he was forced to acknowledge Slovenia's independence in the hope that he could keep Croatia, with its large Serbian minority, as part of Yugoslavia.

MINTOFF, Dom(inic)
1916–

Maltese politician, born Cospicua. He served as general secretary of the Labour Party (1936–7) before continuing his education at the University of Malta and Hereford College, Oxford, where he graduated in engineering science, then worked as an engineer in Britain (1941–3) and as an architect in Malta. In 1945 he joined the Council of Government formed to prepare for Malta's first stage in its move to self-government two years later, when he became Minister of Works and deputy prime minister. He resigned in 1949, but became prime minister again in 1955 and began negotiations with Britain to achieve full independence. The talks broke down in 1958, and following demonstrations over the transfer of the island's dockyard to a commercial concern, the British Government suspended the Maltese Constitution. Mintoff resigned to found the Maltese Liberation Movement, of which he became leader in 1962. The country was granted full independence two years later, and Mintoff became Prime Minister in 1971. Three years later Malta became a republic within the Commonwealth.

MIRÓ, Dr José Cardona
1903–74

Cuban politician, born Havana. The first Prime Minister of **Fidel Castro**'s revolutionary Government and later one of its most bitter critics, Miró studied at Havana and Rome universities, and was among the academics who in exile engineered the movement against **Fulgencio Batista**'s ruthless military dictatorship and his eventual downfall in 1958. But Castro stripped Miró of the premiership after only 45 days, appointing him ambassador to Spain and then to Washington. Instead of taking up the latter post, Miró found political asylum in the Argentine embassy in Havana, and then formed the Cuban National Revolutionary Council in exile in Miami—calling for an uprising against Castro and his replacement by an elected Government with Miró as provisional president. In the Bay of Pigs fiasco, he felt that Kennedy had betrayed his support by not committing sufficient forces to the adventure and failing to order a second invasion. He subsequently resigned his leadership of the CNRC and moved to Puerto Rico, where he worked as a professor of law until his death.

MITCHELL, James Fitzallen
1931–

St Vincent and the Grenadines politician. After training and working as an agronomist between 1958 and 1965, he became a hotel proprietor, then became active in politics as a member of the St Vincent Labour Party. In the Administration formed when internal self-government was introduced in 1969, he was trade Minister until 1972, then prime minister as head of the People's Democratic Party. After founding the New Democratic Party in 1975, he became premier again in 1984, five years after his country achieved full independence.

MITTERRAND, François Maurice Marie
1916–

French statesman and author, president of France (1981–). Born in Jarnac in South West France, the fifth child of a stationmaster, he attended the University of Paris during the mid 1930s, studying law and politics and immersing himself in French literature. During World War II he served with the French forces (1939–40), was wounded and captured, but escaped (on the third attempt) in December 1941 from a prison camp in Germany and became a network commander in the French resistance. He has been awarded the Legion d'Honneur, the Croix de Guerre and the Rosette de la Resistance. He was a deputy in the French national assembly almost continuously from 1946, representing the constituency of Nievre (near Dijon), and held ministerial posts in 11 centrist governments between 1947 and 1958. A firm believer in the democratic traditions of Republican France, which he now saw to be under threat, he opposed **de Gaulle**'s creation of the Fifth Republic in May 1953 and, as a result, lost his Assembly seat in the November 1958 election. He became radicalized, leaving the Catholic church during the early 1960s, and began to set about building up a strong new, left-of-centre anti-Gaullist alliance, the 'Federation of the Left'. After returning to the national assembly in 1962, he performed creditably as the Federation's candidate in the 1965 presidential election against de Gaulle and in 1971 became leader of the new Socialist party (PS). He proceeded to embark on a successful strategy of electoral union with the (then important) Communist party which brought major gains for the Socialists, establishing them as the single most popular party in France by 1978 and in May 1981 was elected president, defeating **Giscard d'Estaing**. As president, Mitterrand initially introduced a series of radical economic and political reforms, including programmes of nationalization and decentralization. However, deteriorating economic conditions after 1983 forced a policy U-turn and in the March 1986 election the Socialists lost their National Assembly majority. This compelled him to work with a prime minister, **Jacques Chirac,** drawn from the opposition 'right coalition'. However, despite being forced to concede considerable executive authority to Chirac in this unique 'co-habitation' experiment, the wily Mitterrand, nicknamed 'the fox', outmanouevred his young rival, comfortably defeating Chirac in the presidential election of May 1988. Following fresh national assembly elections in which the conservative parties lost their majority, the moderate socialist,

Michel Rocard, was appointed prime minister in a new left-of-centre administration. After Rocard's resignation in May 1991, he was replaced by **Edith Cresson**. During the Gulf crisis of 1990 Mitterrand tried to find a diplomatic settlement but when this failed he demonstrated his commitment to the Atlantic alliance by sending French troops to the area.

MOBUTU, Sese Seko Kuku Ngbendu Wa Za Banga (Joseph Dsir Mobutu)
1930–

Zaïrean soldier and politician. He rose quickly through the ranks to become commander of the Belgian army at the age of 30, joined **Patrice Lumumba**'s Congolese National Movement Party, and when independence from Belgium was granted in 1960 continued as commander-in-chief, with Lumumba as prime minister and **Joseph Kasavubu** as president of the new Republic of Congo. However, the new Administration's ineffectual handling of dissidents in Katanga province prompted Mobutu to seize power, but five months later he returned control of the country to a civilian Government. He took power again as president after the 1963–5 civil war, introduced a new Constitution, and in 1971 renamed the country Zaïre. He was successful in repelling invasion from Shaba (formerly Katanga) in 1977, but another incursion the following year, which resulted in the massacre of Europeans in Kolwezi, required the intervention of Belgian and French forces to restore peace to the region.

MODROW, Hans
1928–

German politician, last East German head of state, born Jasenitz. After serving his apprenticeship as a locksmith, he served in the German army from 1942 until the end of the war, and from 1949 was active in the Socialist Unity Party (SED), taking office as a member of East Berlin city committee (1953–61) and city council (1953–71). He entered the Volkskammer in 1958, and in 1967 was made head of agitation and propaganda. he was elected First Secretary for Dresden in 1973, and to the party's central committee. In 1989, as demonstrations for a more liberal regime and the exodus to West Berlin continued, Modrow's reputation as a liberal and his personal popular support brought his appointment as Prime Minister of a new East German Government pledged to reform and free elections. Shortly after his meeting with West Germany's Chancellor **Kohl** in December 1989, Modrow announced a four-point plan to reunify Germany, and within months, hardliners such as **Erich Honecker**, **Egon Krenz** and Willi Stoph had resigned or been arrested. Modrow headed the new GDR coalition formed in April 1990, and following unification of the two Germanys on 3 October 1990, was one of five prominent former East German politicians who were sworn in as Ministers without Portfolio of the new federal Government.

MOHAMMED AHMED
1848–85

Egyptian Mahdi (Muslim messiah), born Dongola. After entering the civil service, he operated as a slave trader, and then began a relentless and successful campaign against Egyptian rule in the Sudan. In 1883 he proclaimed his own capital of El Obeid and later that year his forces defeated Hicks Pasha and the Egyptian army. On 26 January 1885, the Mahdi took Khartoum in the action in which General Charles Gordon was killed, and Mohammed died six months later. *Mahdism* (1891), *Mahdi of Allah* (1931), *The Mahidiya: history of Anglo-Egyptian Sudan* (1951).

MOI, Daniel Arap
1924–

Kenyan politician, born Rift Valley province. Born into a poor farming family, he was educated at the Mission School, Kabartonjo, and the Government African School, Kapsabet, and from 1946 to 1956 worked as a teacher. After entering the House of Representatives in 1963, he served as Minister for Local Government (1963–4), and for Home Affairs (1964–7), and in 1967 was appointed vice-president by **Jomo Kenyatta** as his nominated successor. He was provincial president of the Kenyan African National Union from 1966, and after becoming KANU president and head of state on Kenyatta's death in 1978, he purged the army, launched an ambitious plan to develop Kenya's economy and infrastructure, and pre-empted political opposition by proclaiming KANU as the country's only legal party. He was re-elected head of state in 1983 and 1988.

MOLLET, Guy Alcide
1905–75

French politician, born Flers, Normandy. Already a member of the Socialist Party, he worked as an English master at Arras Grammar School from 1923 until the outbreak of World War II, during which he captained a resistance group and was held prisoner for two years, and in 1946 was elected party secretary-general, joined the Constituent Assembly and was a member of the transitional Administration headed by **Léon Blum** pending the election of France's first postwar president. In 1949, Mollet served as a delegate to the Council of Europe and became its president in 1955. After becoming prime minister in 1956, he survived the Suez crisis but finally lost office the following year after staying in power longer than any French premier since the war. After supporting **Charles De Gaulle**'s successful bid for the presidency in 1958, he served in his Government for a year before being elected a senator of the French Community.

MOLYNEUX, James Henry
1920–

Northern Ireland politician, born Seacash, Killead, County Antrim. Educated at Aldergrove School, Country Antrim, he served in the RAF from 1941 to 1946, and was a vice-chairman of hospital and mental-health management committees before becoming active in politics as secretary of the South Antrim Unionist Association (1964–70) and vice-president of the Ulster Unionist Council from 1974. In 1970 he entered the House of Commons as an Ulster Unionist MP, and from 1974 to 1977 served as leader of the Ulster coalition there. He was a member of the Northern Ireland assembly from 1982 to 1986. As Deputy Grand Master of the Orange Order and a close political ally of **Ian Paisley**, he played a leading role in the 1991 efforts by Northern Ireland Secretary Peter Brooke to initiate new negotiations between loyalist leaders and the British and Irish Governments to bring peace to the Province.

MOMOH, Joseph Saidu
1937–

Sierre Leone soldier and politician, born Binkolo. After attending military schools in Ghana, Britain and Nigeria, he was commissioned in 1963, and rose to the rank of major-general in 1983. Two years later, on the retirement of President Siaka Stevens, Momoh was nominated as his successor by the All People's Congress—the country's only legal political party. Since taking office, Momoh has dissociated himself from his predecessor's policies, pledging to fight corruption and establish economic stability.

MOLOTOV, Vyacheslav Mikhailovich
1890–1986

Russian politician, born Kukaida, Vyatka. Educated at Kazan High School and Polytechnic, he joined the Bolsheviks in 1905, and in 1912 became a disciple of **Lenin** and a regular contributor to the newly-launched Communist newspaper *Pravda*. In the March 1917 rising, he headed the party's central committee, and after the successful October revolution, was made a member of the military council that engineered the coup against **Alexander Kerensky**. In 1921, Molotov was appointed party secretary and the youngest candidate-member of the Politburo, and seven years later was given responsibility for heading the Five-Year Plan. He entered the international political arena as Foreign Affairs Commissar from 1939, and after initially signing a non-aggression pact with Germany, went to London in 1942 to put his name to a 20-year alliance with Britain. He was **Joseph Stalin**'s chief adviser at the Teheran and Yalta conferences, and in 1945 served as the Soviet Union's representative at the San Francisco conference that gave birth to the United Nations, and at the Potsdam Conference. He was the author of the pacts that bound the republics to the Kremlin, and also won notoriety for his persistent 'Niets' in exercising his right of veto in numerous UN debates. When Georgi Malenkov succeeded Stalin in 1953, Molotov was reappointed Foreign Secretary and adopted a more conciliatory attitude, but he gradually fell from favour and in 1956 was demoted to a junior post, and in 1957, accused by **Nikita Khrushchev** of sabotaging peace, was posted to Outer Mongolia until 1960.

MONCKTON, Walter Turner, 1st Viscount Monckton of Brenchley
1891–1965

English lawyer and statesman, born Plaxtol, Kent. Educated at Harrow and Balliol College, Oxford, he was called to the Bar in

1919. As Attorney-General to the Prince of Wales, later **Edward VIII**, from 1932, he was his close advisor in the 1936 abdication crisis. He served as director-general of information in the wartime coalition, and was an MP before receiving a peerage in 1957, after which he held office in Conservative Governments as Minister of Labour (1951-5), and of Defence (1955-6), and Paymaster-General (1956-7).

MONDALE, Walter Frederick
1928–

American politician, born Ceylon, Minnesota. Educated at public schools in Minnesota and at Macalaster College, and Minnesota University, he studied law, completed his army service (1951-3) and was admitted to the Minnesota bar in 1956. He then ran a private law practice, and from 1960 to 1969 was state Attorney-General. He entered the Senate for the Democrats in 1964, successfully partnered **Jimmy Carter** in the 1976 elections to serve as his Vice-President from 1977 to 1981, but failed in his own bid for the White House in 1984. His publications include *The Accountability of Power: Towards a Responsible Presidency* (1976).

MONNET, Jean
1888–1979

French statesman, born Cognac. After entering Government service in 1914, he gained a reputation for his mastery of economic and financial affairs, and in 1947 was appointed commissioner-general in charge of an ambitious programme to modernize his country's economy and infrastructure. In 1951, he was awarded the Prix Wateler de la Paix, and served as president of the European Coal and Steel Authority from 1952 to 1955. In 1956 he was elected president for the Action Committee for the United States of Europe.

MONROE, James
1758–1831

Fifth US President, born Westmoreland County, Virginia. After serving in the war of independence, he was elected to the Virginian legislature and, in 1783, to Congress. From 1785, despite his promotion of state autonomy, he served as chairman of the committee that prepared for the framing of the American Constitution, and as a member of the Senate from 1790 to 1794, fought **George Washington** and his federalist sup-

porters and was sent out of harm's way as envoy to Paris. He was recalled in 1796, and after a three-year term as state governor from 1799, helped to negotiate with France the Louisiana purchase. He returned to diplomatic duties in London and Spain, and in 1811 returned to Virginia for a further term as governor and to serve as Secretary of War. In 1818 he was elected president, and his candidacy for a second term from 1820 won almost unanimous support. His Administration saw the recognition of the Spanish-American republics, and his famous declaration—known as the Monroe Doctrine—of the immunity of US territories from further colonization. He left office in 1825 in deep debt, depending in his remaining years on the charity of his relatives.

MORE, Sir Thomas, Saint
1478–1535

English scholar and statesman, born London. Educated at Oxford, he completed his legal studies at New Inn and Lincoln's Inn, and after three years as reader in Furnival's Inn, spent four years in the Charterhouse devoting himself to prayer and religious studies. In the closing years of the reign of **Henry VII**, he entered Parliament, and when **Henry VIII** came to the throne, and under the patronage of Cardinal **Wolsey**, he achieved increasingly high office, becoming Treasurer of the Exchequer (1521), Chancellor of the Duchy of Lancaster (1525), and Speaker of the House of Commons. On Wolsey's fall from favour in 1529, More accepted—much against his wishes—the Lord Chancellorship, and although intolerant of those holding contrary religious opinions and remaining loyal to the concept of papal supremacy, he promoted domestic theological reform and reorganization of the clergy. Henry's growing estrangement from Rome brought More's resignation as Lord Chancellor in 1532, and when Henry appointed himself head of the Church two years later, More's refusal to acknowledge his king's new status led to his imprisonment in 1534, and a year later he was brought to trial for high treason and beheaded. The husband of More's devoted daughter, Margaret, later wrote a notable biography, and More himself published *Utopia* (1516, translated 1556), and *History of King Richard III* (1513). He was memorably portrayed by the British actor Paul Schofield in the film *A Man for All Seasons* (1966), based on Robert Bolt's stage play.

MORO, Aldo
1916–1978

Italian politician. Twice Christian Democrat prime minister (1963–8, 1974–6) and Foreign Minister from 1970 to 1972, he was one of a number of moderate Italian politicians and other public figures who were kidnapped and murdered by the extreme left-wing Red Brigade terrorist organization during the 1970s.

MORRISON, Herbert Stanley, Baron Morrison of Lambeth
1888–1965

British politician, born Lambeth, London. After attending a state school, he furthered his education by reading books while working as an errand boy and shop assistant. A co-founder of the London Labour Party, he became its secretary in 1915, and after entering the London County Council in 1922, he became its leader in 1934. His was the concept of a strategic authority for the capital's infrastructure, which he began to realize by co-ordinating its public transport network. In 1923, he was elected to Parliament, and in **Winston Churchill**'s wartime Cabinet served as Home Secretary and Minister of Home Security. In the postwar Labour Administration, he held unprecedented influence as deputy prime minister, Leader of the Commons and Lord President of the Council, and in 1951 served briefly as Foreign Secretary before Labour's election defeat. He then became deputy leader of the Opposition, and in 1955 was defeated by **Hugh Gaitskell** for the party leadership. He was created a life peer four years later. He wrote *How London is Governed* (1949), *Government and Parliament* (1954), and his *Autobiography* (1960).

MOSHOESHOE II (Constantine Beregent Seeiso
1938–

King of Lesotho. Educated at Oxford, he was declared chief of the Basotho people in 1960 and proclaimed king when the country gained its independence six years later. His tendency to interfere in Government resulted in his twice being placed under house arrest, and in 1969 he was sent into exile in Holland. However, after pledging that he would take no further part in his country's politics, he was allowed to return a year later.

MOSLEY, Sir Oswald Ernald, 6th Baronet
1896–1980

British politician. After becoming a Conservative MP in 1918, he crossed the Floor of the House to join the Labour Benches in 1924, but from 1929 sat as an Independent and served for a year in **Ramsay MacDonald**'s National Government, resigning over its failure to tackle unemployment. In 1931 he founded the New Party, and in 1932 the neo-Nazi organization, the British Union of Fascists, whose followers, the Blackshirts, provoked violent demonstrations by staging anti-Semitic marches through the traditionally Jewish east end of London. He was detained during World War II, and on his release in 1948 formed the Union Movement, whose advocacy of European economic homogeneity was embodied in Mosley's book, *Europe: Faith and Plan* (1958). His second wife, Diana Mitford, whom he married in 1936, was the sister of Unity Mitford (1914–48), who won notoriety as a popular member of **Adolf Hitler**'s social circle.

MOUNTBATTEN, Louis Francis Victor Albert Nicholas, 1st Earl Mountbatten of Burma
1900–79

British naval commander and statesman, born near Windsor. The younger son of Prince Louis Mountbatten (1854–1921) and a great-grandson of Queen **Victoria**, he was educated at Osborne and Dartmouth Royal Naval Colleges, and in World War I served with distinction on HMS *Lion* and HMS *Elizabeth*, and in World War II commanded a destroyer flotilla from 1939 to 1941, when he was made chief of combined operations. From 1943 he was supreme allied commander, south-east Asia operations, until the end of the war, and in 1947, as **Clement Attlee**'s inspired choice as Viceroy of India, brought dignity to the hitherto shambolic transfer of British rule. He was Fourth Sea Lord and commander of the Mediterranean fleet from 1952 to 1955, then First Sea Lord (1955–9), and Chief of Defence Staff (1959–65). His colourful circle of close friends included the Duke of **Windsor** (formerly **Edward VIII**) and Noel Coward, and he served as a valued confidante to Prince Charles during his adolescence. In 1979, as a symbol of both British governance and of the monarchy, he was killed by an IRA bomb while sailing near his holiday home in County Sligo, Ireland.

MUBARAK, Hosni
1928–

Egyptian politician, born Cairo. After serving as a pilot and flying instructor in the Egyptian air force, he rose to the rank of commander-in-chief, and after the 1973 war with Israel became deputy president. On the assassination of **Anwar Sadat** in 1981, he assumed the presidency, and has continued his predecessor's policy of pursuing good relations with Israel while maintaining credibility with anti-West Arab states. During the 1991 Gulf War, he was the Arab leader most critical of **Saddam Hussein**, and reasserted his credentials with Israel by strongly denouncing the Iraqi missile attacks on Tel Aviv and Haifa that Hussein hoped would win him the support of the Arab world against the western coalition.

MUGABE, Robert Gabriel
1924–

First Prime Minister of Zimbabwe. After improving his elementary education by correspondence courses, he became a teacher in 1942, and while working in Ghana came under the influence of **Kwame Nkrumah**'s radical nationalist movement, and joined the National Democratic Party, then the Zimbabwe African People's Union (ZANU). After escaping from detention for his political activities, he co-founded with **Ndabaningi Sithole** the Zimbabwe African National Union (ZANU), and after 10 years of detention from 1964 to 1974, he went to Mozambique to organize guerrilla strikes against Rhodesia. He took part in the Lancaster House negotiations that finally brought independence in 1980, when Mugabe was invited to form a Government after ZANU won more than 50 seats in the election later the same year. Large numbers of white Rhodesians left the country fearing a black backlash and persecution under Mugabe's Marxist-inspired regime, but their fears proved largely unfounded, and Mugabe served as Prime Minister with moderation until 1987, when Parliament granted his request to merge the offices of head of government and head of state to make him the country's first president. A year later, ZANU and ZAPU merged to make Zimbabwe a one-party state under Mugabe's leadership.

MUJIBUR RAHMAN (Sheikh Mujib)
1920–75

Bangladeshi politician, born Tungipana. After being expelled from Dacca University for his political activities, he co-founded in 1949 the Awami People's League to campaign for autonomy for East Pakistan, became its leader in 1953, and took the party to electoral success in 1970. After the war with Pakistan and the founding of the independent state of Bangladesh, he became the country's first Prime Minister. He initially displayed political tolerance, but increasing opposition to his rule led to other parties being outlawed, and Mujibur ruled as head of a socialist one-party state until 1975, when he and his wife were assassinated in a military coup.

MULDOON, Sir Robert (David)
1921–

New Zealand politician, born Auckland. After infantry service in World War II, he qualified and worked as an accountant and entered Parliament as a National Party (Tamaki) MP in 1960. He was made junior finance Minister in 1962 and was Minister of Finance from 1967 until 1972, when he was elected leader of the Opposition. He led his party to victory in the 1975 election, and was Prime Minister until 1984, when he resigned as party leader. He became Shadow Foreign Minister in 1986. He wrote *The Rise and Fall of a Young Turk* (1974), *Muldoon* (1977), *My Way* (1981), and *The New Zealand economy: a personal view* (1985).

MULRONEY, (Martin) Brian
1939–

Canadian politician, born Baie Comeau, Quebec province. The son of an Irish immigrant, he was educated at St Francis Xavier University, Nova Scotia, and studied law at Laval University, Quebec City, then practised as a lawyer in Montreal. His growing influence in the Progressive Conservative Party, was not, however, sufficient to dislodge **Joe Clark** in his 1976 bid for the leadership, and for the next seven years he devoted his energies to the presidency of a US-owned ore company. He eventually replaced Clark in 1983 as the party's first leader from Quebec in 90 years, and in 1984 led the Conservatives to a landslide victory over the Liberals. He immediately instigated a radical programme of reform that served to settle disputes between the provinces and central Government and to establish a free-trade agreement with the US. He was decisively re-elected in 1988.

MURRAY, Len (Lionel), Baron Murray of Epping Forest

1922–

British trade union leader, born Shropshire. Educated at London University and New College Oxford, he joined the economic staff of the Trades Union Congress in 1947, was assistant general secretary from 1969 to 1973, and, as general secretary from 1973, was prominent in promoting among the TUC's member unions the 'social contract' to limit wage increases that was an important element in the Governments of **Harold Wilson** and **James Callaghan**. His relationship with central Government was less happy from 1979 when the Conservatives returned to power, while at the same time he came under attack from left-wing leaders for his moderacy. He retired in 1984 and was given a life peerage the following year.

MUSEVENI, Yoweri Kaguta

1945–

Ugandan soldier and politician. Educated at Dar-es-Salaam University, he was appointed to the personal office of **Milton Obote**, and when Obote was overthrown by **Idi Amin** in 1971, Museveni went into exile in Tanzania, where he formed the Front for National Salvation, which eventually seized power in 1979. Museveni served as Defence Minister under two provisional presidencies, but when Obote returned to office in 1980, he became estranged from his former protegé and retained power only by the continuing presence of Tanzanian forces. When they withdrew in 1982, the country was plunged into a state of near-civil war, until Museveni assumed the presidency in 1986, promising national reconciliation.

MUSSOLINI, Benito

1883–1945

Italian dictator, born Predappio, near Forli, Romagna. The son of a blacksmith, he first worked as a teacher, but in 1902 went to Switzerland, where he developed his revolutionary beliefs, and in 1904 returned to Italy. After brief imprisonment for his activities, he edited a socialist publication from Trento, then in Austria, and, following a further short term of imprisonment, became editor of the influential nationalist newspaper *Avanti* in 1912. He became estranged from the socialists over their neutral stance in World War I, and founded *Popolo d'Italia* to publicize his belief that only by supporting the Allies could Italy retrieve the disputed Austrian territories. Mussolini fought and was injured in the war, and in 1919 he founded *Fascio di Combattimento* ostensibly to serve the interests of neglected ex-servicemen, but really to promote the extreme form of nationalism to which he was by then committed. The groups of fascist Blackshirts whose creation he encouraged were turned to his advantage against the Communists, and in 1921 he exploited his growing personal popularity to win election to the Chamber of Deputies, and the following year his Blackshirts marched on Rome and Mussolini became *Il Duce* ('the leader'). He first mollified **Giovanni Giolitti**, then replaced him under the eyes of a king, Victor Emmanuel, who was more concerned with his own security. Under Mussolini's dictatorship, the people suffered their worst poverty for 10 years, Abyssinia fell, Italy sided with **Franco** but lost her natural allies, and the country became involved in a world war that was to prove disastrous in both the short and long terms. After the allied landings in Sicily in 1942, even Mussolini's own Fascist Council turned on him, and he had to be rescued by German paratroops and taken to northern Italy in a doomed attempt to re-establish his authority. When that failed, he tried to flee the country with his mistress disguised as a German soldier, but was caught and unmasked by a member of the Italian resistance, summarily executed, and his corpse mutilated by the people after it was hung upside down in a public square in Como. A translation of his *Autobiography* was published in 1928, and memoirs of his wife, Rachele, *My Life with Mussolini*, in 1959.

MUZOREWA, Bishop Abel Tendekayi

1925–

Zimbabwean clergyman and politician. Following his ordination in 1953, he was consecrated the first black bishop of the United Methodist Church in 1968, and in 1971 was elected president of the African National Council (ANC), which sought an internal settlement of the Rhodesian problem. In 1975 the ANC split into a conciliatory faction led by Muzorewa, and the militant movement headed by **Joshua Nkomo**. During the 1979 transition to independence, Muzorewa served as nominated Prime Minister, but his moderacy counted against him in the 1980 elections that followed the granting of full independence, and his party was overwhelmingly defeated in the contest for seats in the new Parliament by those of Nkomo and **Robert Mugabe**.

MWINYI, Ndugu Ali Hassan
1925–

Tanzanian politician, born Zanzibar. Educated at Mangapwani School and Dole School, Zanzibar, and at Zanzibar Teacher Training College and Durham University, England, he worked as a teacher and head teacher, and joined the Ministry of Education in 1964. He was appointed Minister of State in the presidential office in 1972, and was later Minister for Health (1972–5), Minister for Home Affairs (1975–7), ambassador to Egypt (1977–81), and Minister for Natural Resources and Tourism (1982–3). He became vice-president to **Julius Nyerere** in 1984, and succeeded Nyerere as president in 1985.

NADER, Ralph
1934–

American lawyer and consumer activist, born Winsted, Connecticut. Educated at Princeton and Harvard Law School, he entered the Bar in his home state in 1959, and in 1965 established himself as a devastating campaigner against corporate neglect of consumer interests with his book, *Unsafe at any Speed*, and its damning indictment of the Corvair car manufactured by General Motors, who were subsequently ordered to pay him $300000 damages for harassment. He went on to establish a national network of consumer groups, lobbied successfully for consumer protection legislation, and also inspired new laws on pollution, food safety, and public access to official information. In 1980, he became head of the Public Citizen Foundation. His other books include *The Menace of Atomic Energy* (1977) and *Who's Poisoning America?* (1981).

NAGY, Imre
1895–1958

Hungarian politician, born Kaposvar. As a conscript in the Austrian army in World War I, he was captured and sent to Siberia, whence he escaped in 1917 at the height of the Russian revolution. He became a Soviet citizen a year later, and on returning to his homeland a year later, he was appointed to a minor post in the revolutionary Government, but fled to Russia after the counter-revolution, where he remained throughout World War II. He was then installed as agricultural minister in the provisional Government, and in 1947 was elected Speaker of the Hungarian Parliament. As Prime Minister from 1953, he pursued more liberal political and social policies, resulting in his removal two years later by the Rakosi regime. Its collapse in 1956 saw his return to office, and promises of free elections and a lessening of Soviet control, but they failed to quell the revolution and his appeals to the West to resist the Russian occupation failed and he was replaced by a puppet premier, **Janos Kadar**, and executed. In 1989, the Hungarian Supreme Court declared him innocent of any crimes against the state, and his remains were reinterred with honour in Budapest.

NAHAYAN, Sheikh Zayed bin Sultan al-
1918–

Emir of Abu Dhabi. At first a governor of the eastern province of Abu Dhabi, one of the seven Trucial States on the southern shores of the Persian Gulf, and of the Gulf of Oman, in 1969 he deposed his brother, Sheikh Shakhbut, and assumed the throne. When the states chose to become the federation of the United Arab Emirates in 1971, Nahayan became president of its Supreme Council, to which office he was unanimously re-elected in 1986.

NAIDU, Sarojini
1879–1949

Indian feminist and poet, born Hyderabad. Educated at Madras, London, and Cambridge, she became known as the nightingale of India as the author of three volumes of lyric verse between 1905 and 1915. She lectured widely on feminism and campaigned for the abolition of purdah, and in 1925 became the first president of **Gandhi**'s Indian National Congress. She was imprisoned several times for civil disobedience, and took a leading part in the negotiations that led to her country's independence in 1947, when she was appointed governor of the United Provinces, now Uttar Pradesh.

NAJIBULLAH, Major General

1947–

Afghan politician, born Paktia province. Educated at Habibia Lycée and Kabul University, he became active in the Moscow-inspired People's Democratic Party of Afghanistan (PDPA) in the mid-1960s, and was twice imprisoned for his political activities. After King Mohamed Zahir Shah was deposed in a military coup and abdicated in 1973, he rose rapidly in the party hierarchy, and as a member of the PDPA's central committee, played a key role in the negotiations that led to the 1978 treaty of friendship with the USSR that served as a pretext for the Russian invasion the following year, when he was made Information Minister. He was admitted to the Afghan politburo in 1981, and became President in 1987. Strong guerrilla resistance by the members of the National Islamic Front continued, and insistence by the Russian army, in the wake of continued attacks by Pakistani mujaheddin guerrillas on the Kabul-Soviet border, that Najibullah's regime should continue to be funded despite the USSR's own economic difficulties was a factor in the resignation in December 1990 of Foreign Minister **Eduard Shevardnadze**. In 1991, the United Nations renewed its call for elections in mujaheddin-controlled territories with a view to replacing Najibullah's regime with a democratically-elected Government.

NAKASONE, Yashiro

1917–

Japanese politician, born Taksaki. Educated at Tokyo Imperial University, he joined the Ministry of Home Affairs in 1941, served as a lieutenant-commander in World War II, and entered the House of Representatives in 1947 for the conservative Liberal Democratic Party (LDP). Between 1959 and 1982, he held office as Minister of Science and Technology (1959–60), Transport (1967–9), Defence (1970–1), Trade and Industry (1972–4), and Administration (1980–2). He was party secretary-general from 1974 to 1976, and as Prime Minister from 1982, his programme of domestic economic liberalism combined with an aggressive attack on export markets further improved his country's wealth and made him one of the most popular politician for decades and the first LDP leader since the 1960s to win re-election for a second term. He retired in 1987, and was subsequently named in connection with the Recruit-Cosmos insider-trading scandal.

NAPOLEON I (Napoleon Bonaparte)

1769–1821

Emperor of France, born Ajaccio. He left Corsica to learn French and to pursue a military education in Brienne and Paris, and on the outbreak of the revolution returned to his homeland to help overthrow the royalist Government, then returned to the mainland. His command of the artillery at the siege of Toulon (1793) saw him promoted to brigadier general, but on the fall of **Robespierre**, Napoleon was briefly imprisoned. Barras appointed him second-in-command to suppress the 1795 Paris uprising, and his success gave him the command of the army in Italy, where he swiftly despatched the Austrians with inspired actions at Arcola, Rivoli, and Mantua. Returning to France, Napoleon was offered the command of the army of England by a Directory intent on neutralizing his power, but instead he began planning to conquer Egypt, and in 1798 a fleet of 30000 ships left Toulon, took the surrender of Malta by way of an excursion, and skilfully twice eluded Nelson. Cairo fell quickly, but the British admiral virtually destroyed the invader's fleet on the Nile soon after, cutting off the army's means of retreat. Despite the debacle, Napoleon found his way back to Paris in 1799 and applied himself to domestic victories; overturning the now unpopular Directory and proclaiming himself ruler of France. His administrative masterworks included local government centralization, the creation of the Bank of France, legal reform, the construction of many new roads and bridges, and the modernization of the country's ports—all of which were motivated by his new military ambitions, fuelled by the return of the French army from Egypt in 1802. He again went to war with Austria (while finding time to be crowned Emperor by the Pope in 1804), and having assembled his forces at Boulogne to invade England, turned them about to take Austerlitz, Jena and Friedland instead between 1805 and 1807, to subdue the coalition of Austria, Prussia and Russia—with the latter becoming a close ally. Napoleon's hitherto faultless judgment deserted him in the 1808 Spanish and Portuguese campaigns, where the Duke of **Wellington** scored resounding victories in the Peninsular War, and despite the drain that it made on his resources, Russian unrest caused by the Emperor's trade restrictions against Britain compelled him to invade in 1812, with the burning of Moscow achieved only at the cost of most of Napoleon's best infantry. A year later, he had to retreat from Germany, and with the allies following him across the Rhine, and Wellington driving up from Spain, the little general was forced to abdicate in April 14 and to seek refuge in Elba. When the allied leaders met at the Congress of Vienna a month later to settle their territorial claims, news came to them that Napoleon had escaped, and he was Emperor again for 100 days with the support of his old marshals, troops, and the populace at large. He was finally defeated by Wellington at Waterloo on 18 June, abdicated a second time, surrendered to the British, and was exiled to St Helena. On his death in 1840, his body was brought to Paris to be reinterred with great pomp and ceremony at the behest of **Louis Philippe**, whose antecedents Napoleon had so long reviled.

NAPOLEON III, Charles Louis Napoleon Bonaparte

1808–73

Emperor of France, born Paris. The third son of the King of Holland, he was brought up in Switzerland, and became head of the dynasty in 1832 on the death of the only son of **Napoleon I**. After an abortive action against the French in Strasbourg in 1836, he sought refuge in America, and after returning home on his mother's death the following year, he was expelled to England at the insistence of the French. In 1840, he made another attempt to bring down the French throne at Boulogne, was captured, and sentenced to life imprisonment. He escaped in 1846, and returned to London to plan another action, but the 1848 revolution saw him recalled to Paris as a deputy in the new Assembly. His disaffection with its rival factions brought his resignation only two days later and he returned again to London, only to be brought back to Paris in September to enjoy a huge victory over Genral Cavaignac for the presidency. Soon finding himself at odds with the majority of the deputies, he took command of the army, and placed those loyal to him in the posts of greatest power, and in the face of continuing opposition in the Assembly, dissolved the Constitution in 1851 and imprisoned or deported his most vocal political enemies. The public reacted with nothing but approval for his actions, more than seven million of whom voted for his re-election as president for a ten-year term. He broadened his appeal and consolidated his immunity by restoring the imperial title (though only for his own benefit), controlling the press, reassuring the bourgeoisie, and courting the clergy to win over the peasantry. In 1860, he won further popularity by annexing Savoy and Nice, regulating the price of bread, and entrusted Baron Haussmann with the complete remodelling of Paris. At the same time, he expanded international trade through important exhibitions and commercial treaties. His foreign policies enjoyed equal success, typified by the victory at Lombardy against Austria in 1859 and the 1857–60 Chinese expedition. Napoleon astutely acknowledged the changing priorities of the electorate, dismissing hardliners such as Prime Minister Rouher, and liberalizing the Constitution, though at the cost of waning support from the army. He engineered a distraction by declaring war against Prussia in 1870, on the pretext of putting Leopold of Hohenzollern on the Spanish throne, but after early minor successes, the French infantry, which numbered only 270000 men, was overwhelmed by Prussia's 500000-strong army, and defeats at Weissenburg, Spicheren, Mars-la-Tour, Gravelotte, and Sedan in August forced Napoleon, with only 83000 men remaining, to surrender on 1 September. He was confined until the signing of a peace treaty the following year, when he joined his wife in exile in Chislehurst, Kent, where he remained until his death. His son, Eugene (1856–79), was killed while serving with the British Army in the 1879 Zulu campaign.

NASSER, Gamal Abdel

1918–70

Egyptian soldier and statesman, born Alexandria. Disenchanted by the corruption and inefficiency of King **Farouk** as a result of his experiences as an army officer in the 1948 Palestine campaign, Nasser nurtured army support to engineer the 1952 coup that removed Farouk and replaced him with General **Mohammed Neguib**, but the latter's dictatorial aspirations caused his own downfall two years later, with Nasser assuming both the presidency and premiership in 1954. Soon after becoming his country's elected President in 1956, he signalled his intention to develop a new Arab empire across North Africa by announcing Egypt's expropriation from the British of the Suez Canal, which prompted Israel's invasion of the Sinai peninsula, the doomed intervention of

Anglo-French forces, and threatening noises offstage by Russia. Nasser's military defeat was transformed into a political victory, and he went on to consolidate his new standing in the Arab world by creating in 1958, by federation with Syria, the United Arab Republic, which formed the United Arab States on joining with Yemen a year later. Nasser's attempts to smash the Baghdad pact and to liquidate the Middle East's remaining sovereign states started successfully in Iraq, but were thwarted by Anglo-American intervention in Jordan and the Lebanon, and his ambitions suffered a further setback when Syria withdrew from the UAR and its union with Yemen in 1961, but recovered to some extent when the UAR formed joint presidency councils with Iraq and Yemen in 1964. Heavy losses among Egyptian forces in the 1967 Six-Day War prompted Nasser to resign, but he was persuaded to resume the presidency of the UAR almost immediately, to remain in office until his natural death three years later.

NE WIN (Maung Shu Maung)
1911–

Burmese politician. Educated at Rangoon University, he was active in the anti-British nationalist movement of the 1930s, and in World War II was chief-of-staff of the collaborationist army that was formed after the Japanese invasion. Following Burma's independence in 1948, he held several senior military and Cabinet posts, and served as caretaker premier from 1958 to 1960. He was installed as chairman of the revolutionary council that ruled the country after the 1962 coup, and became President in 1974. Although he left that office in 1981, he remained a dominant force in his country's affairs as chairman of the ruling Burma Socialist Programme Party, which embraced isolationism and an amalgam of Marxism, Buddhism and Burmese nationalism. He was forced to resign as party leader in 1988 following riots in Rangoon triggered by the country's continuing economic decline.

NEAVE, Airey
1916–79

British Army intelligence officer and politician, born London. Educated at Eton and Merton College, Oxford, he joined the Territorial Army a year after graduating in jurisprudence, and was wounded at Calais in the 1940 retreat and taken prisoner. He escaped from a Polish P.O.W. camp but was recaptured and sent to the maximum security prison at Colditz Castle, from which he was the first British officer ever to escape, in 1942. He managed to return to London, bringing with him valuable intelligence information, and set himself the task of establishing new underground movements and training air-crews means of escape in occupied territory. By the end of his war service, he had been honoured with the MC, DSO and TD, Croix de Guerre, and US bronze star. In 1943, Neave entered the Bar, and as a lieutenant-colonel served charges on many of the leading war criminals who stood trial at Nuremberg. He entered Parliament for the Conservatives at his third attempt, in 1951, and held several junior Government posts, survived a heart attack in 1959, and developed his interest in science and technology as governor of Imperial College (1963–71) and in the plight of the elderly and refugees. He was prominent in the group that deposed **Edward Heath** as party leader in 1975 and replaced him with **Margaret Thatcher**, who rewarded Neave by appointing him head of her private office and, on the return of a Conservative Government in 1979, giving him a Cabinet post as Secretary of State for Northern Ireland. As an opponent of power-sharing and of the withdrawal of British forces from the Province, and because of his personal closeness to the Prime Minister, Neave was picked by the INLA as their first target of the new Administration, and in March 1979 he was killed when a bomb fixed under his car was detonated as he drove out of the House of Commons car park. His books include three describing his wartime experiences, *They Have Their Exits* (1953), *Saturday at MI9* (1969), and *The Flames of Calais* (1975).

NEGRIN, Juan
1901–1984

Spanish politician, born Madrid. As a professor at Madrid University, he became a leading socialist activist, and on the outbreak of the Spanish Civil War he was appointed Prime Minister, which post he held until the republicans' defeat in 1939, when he went into exile, first in France and then in England.

NEGUIB, Mohammed
1901–

Egyptian soldier and statesman. As an army general, he led the 1952 coup against King

163

Farouk I and assumed the offices of commander-in-chief and Prime Minister, then abolished the monarchy the following year and proclaimed himself President of the new republic. His deputy, Colonel **Gamal Abdel Nasser**, deposed him in 1954.

NEHRU, Jawaharlal
1889–1964

Indian statesman, born Allahabad. The son of a wealthy and distinguished lawyer who had led the nationalist Swaraj party, Nehru was educated at Harrow and Trinity College, Cambridge, entered the London Bar in 1912, and then returned home to practise in Allahabad High Court. As a member of Mahatma Gandhi's Indian Congress Committee, he was imprisoned by the British in 1921 and spent 18 of the next 25 years in gaol. In 1928, he was chosen from the ICC's socialist wing to become National Congress leader, and in World War II resisted with others **Stafford Cripps**'s offer of dominion status in return for India's support of allied efforts. When India achieved independence in 1947, Nehru became its first Prime Minister and Foreign Minister. As democratic leader of the first republic within the Commonwealth, he often served as a go-between for the great powers during the cold war of the 1950s, initiated his country's industrialization, reformed its states on a linguistic basis, and showed moderation in his approach to the Pakistan problem. His daughter **Indira Gandhi** was Prime Minister from 1971 to 1977, and again from 1980 until her assassination in 1984. Nehru's many published works include *Soviet Russia* (1929), *India and the World* (1936), and *Independence and After* (1950).

NENNI, Pietro
1891–1980

Italian politician, born Faenza, Romagna. A socialist activist from his teens, he was banished by the fascists in 1926 and went to Spain, where he served as political commissar of the Garibaldi Brigade in the Civil War. He returned to his homeland in 1944 to become Secretary-General of the Italian Socialist party, and was vice-premier in **De Gasperi**'s 1945–6 coalition, and Foreign Secretary until 1947. His pro-Soviet party broke with the Communists in 1956, and in 1963 he became deputy Prime Minister again in the centre-left four-party coalition. In 1966, he achieved his ambition of uniting the two factions as the

United Socialist Party, which enjoyed overall gains in the 1968 election. However, the socialists lost ground to the communists and, against Nenni's advice, withdrew from the coalition. He served as Foreign Minister in the resultant coalition, but resigned a year later.

NERO
37–68

Roman emperor, born Antium. Adopted by his mother's second husband, Claudius, he was proclaimed by the Praetorian Guard his successor as emperor on Claudius's death in 54. His tyranny, extravagance and debauchery made him the target of many intrigues, which he countered by poisoning Claudius's natural son, Britannicus, and murdering his mother, Agrippina, and his wife, Octavia. When two-thirds of Rome burned to the ground in 64, he made a scapegoat of the Christians and had many put to death, then plundered the provinces to meet the cost of rebuilding the city and constructing a magnificent palace for himself on the Palatine hill. Another conspiracy against Nero in 65 failed, and Nero took his revenge by having Seneca murdered, and himself killing his pregnant wife, Poppaea. When Claudius's daughter, Antonia, refused to marry Nero, he had her executed and married instead Statilia Messallina, after making her a widow by his own hand. In 68, the Praetorian Guard could tolerate his excesses no more, and supported the Gallic and Spanish legions that installed Galba as emperor, with Nero saving himself from certain execution by taking his own life.

NESSELRODE, Count Karl Robert
1780–1862

Russian diplomat, born Lisbon. The son of the Russian ambassador to Portugal, he won the confidence of Emperor Alexander I and played a major role in negotiating the Peace of Paris, and, as one of the most active participants in the Holy Alliance, contributed to the suppression of the Hungarian revolutionaries in 1849, while continuing to improve détente with the western powers.

NGO DINH DIEM
1901–63

Vietnamese statesman, born Annam. The son of a mandarin and himself a Roman Catholic, Diem worked as a civil servant before becoming Minister of the Interior in 1933, and continued to hold senior posts until he was forced into exile in 1950 after refusing to support **Ho Chi Minh** and Bao Dai. In 1954, he returned to South Vietnam as Prime Minister, masterminded Bao's fall from power, and succeeded him as President in 1955. As hostilities with the North escalated, and although almost wholly dependent on American support for his country's economic survival, he refused to be counselled by the US on his handling of the war and after causing further unrest by embarking on a campaign against militant Buddhists, he was murdered by dissident army officers.

NGUYEN PHU DOC

1924–

Vietnamese diplomat, born Hanoi. Educated at Hanoi University and Harvard Law School, he was appointed permanent observer to the UN in 1964, and special adviser on foreign affairs to President **Nguyen van Thieu** in 1968. In the last year of the Vietnam war, he served as an envoy to Thailand, Khmer Republic, Laos, Indonesia, and the USA. He was Foreign Minister when the peace treaty with the North was signed in 1973, and subsequently served as ambassador to Belgium (1973–5). He is remembered best for his active participation in the series of peace conferences held between 1966 and 1969, the Paris Conference of 1968, and for his part in drafting the 1973 Paris Agreement.

NGUYEN VAN LINH

1914–

Vietnamese politician, born North Vietnam. A member of the anti-colonial Thanh Nien movement (later Communist Party) since his teens, most of his political activity was centred on the south, where he won a reputation as a pragmatic reformer. He was admitted to the party's Politburo in 1976, but suffered a temporary setback in the early 1980s when he lost favour to the conservative element. He was readmitted to the Politburo in 1985, and became party leader a year later. His leadership has brought a new phase of economic liberalisation and improved relations with the West, typified by his phased withdrawal of Vietnamese forces from Kampuchea and Laos.

NGUYEN VAN THIEU

1923–

Vietnamese soldier and politician, born Ninh Thlian. Educated at a Catholic school and at the National Military Academy in Hú, he served in the National Army from 1948 to 1954 and then in the Republican Army from 1954, taking command of the 1st Infantry Division in 1960, and 5th Infantry Division in 1962. The following year, he was made Armed Forces Chief of Staff, and became deputy premier and Minister of Defence in 1964, and head of state in 1965. In 1967, as the war against the Vietcong escalated and American involvement increased, he became President of the Republic of Vietnam, and in 1973 was a signatory to the peace treaty that formally ended hostilities, although fighting between North and South did not end until 1975 with the fall of Saigon (now Ho Chi Minh City), when Thieu first took refuge in Thailand, and then retired from public life in Surrey, England.

NICHOLAS II (Nikolai Alexandrovich)

1868–1918

Last Tsar of Russia. The son of Alexander III, he took the throne in 1894, and began his reign with some promising initiatives, as the instigator of the 1898 Hague Peace Conference and the architect of an alliance with France and of a new period of détente with Britain. However, public support started to wane as a result of the disastrous 1904–5 war with Japan, which saw the destruction of the Russian fleet, and the massacre of anti-monarchists in the Bloody Sunday demonstrations of 1905. Despite a nod in the direction of democracy with the establishment of an elected duma (Parliament) in 1906, he resisted its authority, and his reputation also suffered by the tsarina's fixation with **Rasputin**, who was suspected of being a German agent. Nicholas fared little better as commander of the Russian armies from the start of World War I, and continuing unrest at home fomented the 1917 revolution and forced his abdication. Nicholas, his wife, Alexandra, and all their children were taken to Siberia by the revolutionary guard in August 1917, and the following July were executed by their Bolshevik guards, who probably feared that the end of the war might bring international pressure for the restoration of the monarchy. In 1929, a German citizen, Anna Anderson, announced herself to be one of the tsar's daughters, Anastasia—a claim that she maintained until her death in 1983.

NICHOLSON, Joseph Shield
1850–1927

British economist. Educated at King's College, London, and Trinity College, Cambridge, he was professor of political economy at Edinburgh University from 1880 to 1925, winning a reputation as one of the country's foremost and most pragmatic authorities on economic policy. He was the author of numerous works on the subject, of which the most important and influential was *Principles of Political Economy* (1893).

NIMERI, Gaafar Mohammed al-
1930–

Sudanese soldier and politician, born Omdurman. Educated at the Sudan Military College, Khartoum, he continued his army training in Egypt and developed a close affinity with **Gamal Abdel Nasser**, which encouraged him in 1969 to lead the coup that removed Sudan's civilian government and replaced it with a Revolutionary Command Council. In 1971, he became President under a new Constitution and was twice re-elected, but his regime lost popularity in the 1980s by its imposition of regional policies and strict Islamic law, and while on a trip to America in 1985, Nimeri was himself deposed by an army coup led by General Swar al-Dahab.

NIXON, Richard Milhous
1913–

Thirty-seventh President of the USA, born Yorba Linda, California. Born into a middle-class Quaker family of Irish descent, he practised briefly as a lawyer before and after war service with the US Navy, and entered the House of Representatives for the Republicans in 1946. Marked out early in his political career as a forceful orator and a deft stategist, he consolidated his reputation as a leading member of the House Committee on Un-American Activities in 1950 and was elected to the Senate a year later. As Vice-President from 1953 under **Dwight D. Eisenhower**, he adopted an unusually high profile, and his travels to meet world leaders included a notable confrontation with **Nikita Khrushchev** in Moscow in 1959. As the Republicans' candidate in the 1960 presidential race, he narrowly lost the election to

John F. Kennedy—not least because of his abysmal performance in TV debates with the telegenic Democrat, in which Nixon came over as a shallow and shifty individual, giving rise to his political rivals' famous campaign slogan, 'Would you buy a used car from this man?' He was defeated again in the 1962 elections for the governorship of California, and declined to run for the presidency in 1964, but finally triumphed over **Hubert Humphrey** in 1968, largely because of the Democrats' policy split over Vietnam. As President from 1969, he made the first visit ever by the holder of that office to China, began winding down the US commitment in Vietnam, and began thawing Soviet relations, to win a landslide victory over **George McGovern** in 1972. In his determination to serve a second term, he had apparently acquiesced in a number of activities by his staff to undermine the Democrats' campaign, which included a break-in at their Washington campaign headquarters at the Watergate hotel. When the full extent of the scandal became known, seven of Nixon's associates were indicted, and the production of apparently doctored tape recordings of his conversations with them led to the President being named by a Grand Jury as an un-indicted conspirator and his threatened impeachment, which resulted in him taking a place in the history books as the first US President ever to resign, in August 1974, though he was given a full pardon by **Gerald Ford** on the latter's taking office a month later. Nixon retired from public life, but re-emerged in the 1980s as something of a rehabilitated sage, winning recognition as the architect of the new era of improved relations with China and the Soviet Union. His books include *Six Crises* (1962), *The Real War* (1980), *No More Vietnams* (1986), and *Victory without War* (1988). His Memoirs were published in 1978, and his autobiography, *In the Arena*, in 1990.

NKOMO, Joshua Mqabuko Nyongola
1917–

African nationalist and Zimbabwean politician, born Matabeleland. He spent much of his early political life travelling the world to publicize the Rhodesian problem, and was a member of the African National Congress from 1952 until its banning in 1959. As president of the Zimbabwe African People's Union from 1961, he was frequently gagged by Government restrictions, but as a moderate eventually reached agreement with Rhodesian premier **Ian Smith** in 1975 on the founding of a constitutional conference, and the following year formed with **Robert Mugabe** the ZAPU-ZANU Popular Front to secure black majority rule. His efforts were rewarded in 1980 with a Cabinet post in Mugabe's first Government, but differences between the two and increasing tribal-based hostilities between ZAPU and ZANU supporters, brought Nkomo's dismissal in 1982, and he left the country amid fears that he would be assassinated. He returned to Zimbabwe several months later at Mugabe's invitation to rejoin the Cabinet, and in 1988 his party was reformed as the ZANU Popular Front under Mugabe's leadership, with Nkomo content in his new role as an elder statesman.

NKRUMAH, Kwame
1909–72

Ghanian politician, born Ankorful. Educated at Achimota College, Lincoln University, Pennysylvania, and the London School of Economics, he returned to his homeland in 1949 to found the nationalist Convention People's Party, and a year later was imprisoned for inciting strikes, but was elected to Parliament while still in gaol. On his release in 1951 he became virtual Prime Minister as leader of the Assembly, and was formally elected premier in 1956. The following year, he became the first Prime Minister of a newly-independent Ghana within the Commonwealth. He campaigned vigorously against white domination, and, after Ghana became a republic in 1960, he reinforced the Pan-African movement by promoting the 1961 Charter of African states. However, domestic equilibrium eluded him, and his country's parlous economic state triggered vigorous opposition and several attempts on his life. He continued to enforce his will by controlling the judiciary and winning the 1964 referendum on a one-party state—though a large question mark hung over the secrecy of the ballot and the validity of the result. His inability to retrieve his early popular support led to him being overthrown in a military coup in 1966 during his absence on a visit to China, and he subsequently became Ghana's head of state. His books include *Towards Colonial Freedom* (1946), *The Autobiography of Kwame Nkrumah* (1957), and *Consciencism* (1964).

NOEL-BAKER, Baron Philip John
1889–1982

British politician. Educated at Cambridge, he competed successfully for his country in athletic events from 1912, and captained the British Olympic team that year and again in 1920. In World War I, he commanded a Quaker ambulance unit, and served on the secretariat of the 1919 Peace Conference and of the League of Nations from 1919 to 1922. He was a professor of international relations at London University from 1924 until his election to Parliament for Labour in 1929, and on losing his seat two years later worked as Dodge Lecturer at Yale University. He returned to the Commons in 1936, and held several junior ministerial posts before entering the Cabinet as Secretary of State for Air (1946–7), Commonwealth Relations (1947–1950), and Minister of Fuel and Power (1950–1). His lifelong commitment to the peace movement brought him the Nobel Peace Prize in 1959 for his book *The Arms Race*, and a life peerage in 1977. His son, Francis (1920–), was a Labour MP from 1945 to 1950, and again from 1955.

NORIEGA, General Manuel Ities Morena
1940–

Panamanian soldier and politician, born Panama City. Educated at Panama University and a military college in Peru, he was commissioned in the National Guard in 1962, and became head of intelligence in 1970 and chief of staff in 1982, in which capacity he was effectively head of state, and enjoyed considerable support from the US in aiding CIA activities against left-wing elements. However, his regime's human rights abuses and his personal alleged close involvement in drug trafficking led in 1988 to a Grand Jury indictment. He survived an attempted coup in October 1989, but surrendered to American troops ordered into the country by President **George Bush** two months later, after taking refuge in the capital's Vatican embassy, and was taken to the US to stand trial.

NORTH, Colonel Oliver
1943–

American soldier, born San Antonio. Educated at the US Naval College, Annapolis, he was decorated with a Silver Star and Purple Heart after being wounded while leading a counter-insurgency platoon in the

Vietnam War. He worked as an army instructor and security officer before being appointed deputy director of the National Security Council by President **Ronald Reagan** in 1981, in which post he initiated a number of controversial actions, including the 1983 mining of Nicaraguan harbours and the 1986 bombing of Tripoli. Implicated in the Irangate scandal, involving the supply of arms to Iran in exchange for American hostages, and the operation of a secret slush fund to aid the Contra guerrillas in Nicaragua, he was forced to resign in 1986, and was subsequently found guilty, in 1989, of 12 charges against the state, for which he received a three-year suspended gaol sentence and was fined $150000.

NOVOTNY, Antonin
1904–75

Czechoslovakian politician, born Letnany, near Prague. A bricklayer's son, he helped to found his country's Communist Party in 1921, and on his release in 1945 after four years in a Nazi concentration camp, he rose rapidly in its hierarchy, and was among those who engineered the Soviet takeover of the Czech Government in 1953. He became First Secretary, and virtual dictator, that year, and President from 1957. But his loyalty to Stalinism eventually brought economic stagnation, which his adoption of more conciliatory policies from 1962 failed to correct. In 1967 he was forced to resign as First Secretary in favour of **Alexander Dubcek**, and as President a few months later.

NU U (Thakin U)
1907–

Burmese politician. A graduate of Rangoon University, he worked as a teacher before becoming active in nationalist politics as a member of the Dobhama Asiayone ('Our Burma') organization in the 1930s, bringing his imprisonment by the British at the start of World War II. In 1942, during the Japanese occupation, he was released to serve in a puppet Government, but in 1945 formed the Anti-Fascist People's League that collaborated with the British against the Japanese, and when Burma achieved independence in 1948, he became its first Prime Minister. Apart from two brief periods out of office (1956–7 and 1958–60), he remained premier until 1962, when regional opposition to his Administration saw it overthrown by General Ne Win. He was imprisoned until

1966, and on his release lived in Thailand and India, organizing exiled opposition groups. In 1980, he returned to Burma, and formed the National League for Democracy in 1988.

NUJOMA, Samuel Daniel
1929–

Namibian President, born in Ongandijern. Educated by Finnish missionaries, he was co-founder in 1958 of the South- West Africa People's Organization (SWAPO), which aimed at peacefully bringing an end to South Africa's economic domination of his homeland, but he was exiled two years later, establishing a provisional headquarters for his party in Dar es Salaam. Returning to Namibia in 1966, he was again arrested and expelled. Compelled to abandon his policy of achieving independence without violence, he formed the People's Liberation Army of Namibia based in Angola, whose guerrilla tactics prompted South Africa to acknowledge in 1976 the principle of ultimate independence, and in 1985 to instal a sham transitional Government, though the UN recognized only SWAPO as the true representative of the Namibian people. South Africa finally capitulated in 1989, and Nujoma became the new state's first elected President the following year.

NYERERE, Julius Kambarage
1922–

Tanzanian politician, born Butiama, Lake Victoria. After qualifying as a teacher at Makerer College, he took a master's degree in history and economics at Edinburgh University, and worked as a teacher in Dar es Salaam, where in 1953 he formed the African Association. The following year, he left the profession to found the nationalist Tanganyika African National Union, of which he became president, and joined the Committee of the UN General Assembly in 1956. He served briefly as a member of the Tanganyika Assembly before resigning in protest in 1957, but returned a year later after new elections. In 1960, he was made Chief Minister, and became premier a year later when Tanganyika was granted internal self-government. He left office in 1962 to reform his political base, and was elected President later that year after Tanganyika had become a republic. In 1964, he negotiated the union of Tanganyika and Zanzibar as the republic of Tanzania, and since 1977 has led the Chama cha Mapinduzi (Revolutionary Party) formed from the mainland's TANU and the former Zanzibar Afro-Shiraz Party. Nyerere's moderate Administration was thwarted in its attempt to establish a form of socialism based on rural values due to economic difficulties that were exacerbated by the 1978-9 war against the Ugandan dictator **Idi Amin**, and he relinquished the presidency in 1985 while remaining as party leader. In addition to political works that include *Essays on Socialism* (1969) and *Freedom and Development* (1973), Nyerere's early academic training has been applied to producing Swahili versions of Shakespeare's works, including *Julius Caesar* and *The Merchant of Venice*.

OASTLER, Richard
1789–1861

English reformist, born Leeds. An early campaigner against slavery and child labour, his advocacy of fairer employment conditions for all led to 1847 legislation imposing a 10-hour working day. On opposing the new poor laws, he was dismissed from his post as an estates steward and spent four years in the debtors' prison.

OATES, Titus
1649–1705

English conspirator, born Oakham. A former naval chaplain who claimed to have learnt Jesuit secrets while posing as a convert, in 1678 he made allegations of a Vatican plot to murder **Charles II** and massacre English Protestants. The outcry that followed was exploited by Lord **Shaftesbury**, and 35 Catholics were executed for treason. Oates was eventually discredited and imprisoned for life in 1685. He was released on the accession of **James II** but was never again recognized at court and died a pauper.

OBOTE, (Apollo) Milton
1924–

Ugandan politician, born Kampala. After working as a labourer, clerk and salesman, he was elected to the legislative council in 1957, and founded the Uganda People's Congress in 1960. When Uganda achieved independence in 1962, he was made the nation's first Prime Minister under Mutesa II. The king's opposition to a one-party state led to a coup in 1966, with Obote declaring himself president of the new republic. Himself deposed by **Idi Amin** in 1971, he was exiled in Tanzania

until Amin was overthrown in 1979, and Obote resumed the presidency a year later. He remained in power until 1985, when domestic and external pressures triggered a coup by **Basilio Okello**, forcing Obote again into exile, in Zambia.

O'BRIEN, (Donal) Conor (Dermod David Donat) Cruise
1917–90

Irish historian and politician, born Dublin. Born into a strongly-nationalistic family, he was a brilliant graduate from Trinity College and by the 1950s was producing outstanding analytical writing, such as *Parnell and his Family* (1957). His first-hand experience of the 1960 Congo crisis produced the autobiographical narrative *Katanga and Back* and the play *Murderous Angels*. He was elected to the Dáil as a Labour MP in 1969, but lost his seat four years later because of his strong opposition to IRA violence in Ulster. He was later editor-in-chief of *The Observer*.

O'BRIEN, William Smith
1803–64

Irish nationalist, born County Clare. As Conservative MP for Ennis and then County Limerick between 1825 and 1835, and although a Protestant, he supported Catholic claims as a supporter of **Daniel O'Connell**'s Repeal Association. Eventually becoming disillusioned with O'Connell's opposition to the use of force, he founded his own Irish Confederation in 1847, and as a participant in a minor uprising the following year, he was sentenced to death, but was then transported to Tasmania instead. He was released in 1854, gained an unconditional pardon two years later, and eventually returned to Ireland but took no further part in politics.

O'BRIEN, William
1852–1928

Irish nationalist, born Mallow, County Cork. After working as a journalist, he was a nationalist MP from 1883 until 1898, then founded the United Irish League in 1898 and was imprisoned for two years. On his return to Parliament as MP for Cork, he led the independent nationalists until 1918, retiring from politics when Sinn Fein won a landslide victory. His books include *Evening Memories* (1920) and *The Irish Revolution* (1923).

O'CONNELL, Daniel ('The Liberator')
1775–1847

Irish nationalist, born Cahirciveen, County Kerry. After early success as a lawyer, he formed the Catholic Association in 1823, and was returned as MP for Clare in 1828 but was unable to take his seat until 1830, after the passing of the Catholic Emancipation Bill. As MP for Dublin from 1832, he led a group of 45 repealers, but was compelled to reduce his agitation for reform under the subsequent benign Administrations, but in 1840 formed the Repeal Association, and the movement regained its momentum, though a huge public meeting planned in October 1843 had to be abandoned when **Wellington** ordered 35000 troops into Ireland. O'Connell was subsequently found guilty of sedition, but the sentence was set aside by the House of Lords after he had spent 14 weeks in prison. With the growing strength of the Young Ireland Movement from 1846, his refusal to embrace violent revolutionary tactics, and the diffusion of political activity caused by the potato famine, O'Connell's influence soon waned. He left Ireland in 1847, and died soon after, in Genoa.

O'CONNOR, Feargus Edward
1794–1855

Irish chartist, born Connorville. An MP from 1833, he resigned soon after following disputes with **O'Connell** over his conservative attitude to social reforms, but was re-elected in 1837 to pursue universal suffrage and voting by secret ballot, exemplified by the 'monster petition' to Parliament of 1848. However, support for the movement declined, and O'Connor went insane in 1852.

O'CONNOR, T(homas) P(ower)
1848–1929

Irish journalist and nationalist, born Athlone. After working on newspapers in Dublin and London, he was elected to Parliament and from 1880 until 1929 sat in the Commons first as a Parnellite MP for Galway in 1880 and then for a Liverpool constituency. He was made a Privy Councillor in 1924, and eventually became Father of the House. He founded a number of newspapers and journals, including the London *Star* (1887) and the radical *TP's Weekly* (1902).

OGLETHORPE, James Edward
1696–1785

English soldier and colonist, born London. After early service in the 1717 war against the Turks, he entered Parliament in 1722, where he campaigned vigorously against press gangs and prison conditions. He obtained a charter to found Georgia as a refuge for imprisoned English debtors and refugee Austrian Protestants, and accompanied the first settlers there in 1733. He successfully defended Georgia against Spanish invasion a year later, but in 1743 was recalled to England to answer chances of incompetence and was later implicated in the 1745 Jacobite rebellion. He was acquitted, but his military career was left in ruins and he failed to win re-election to Parliament in 1754.

O'HIGGINS, Bernardo
1778–1842

Chilean revolutionary, born Chillán. The son of the Irish-born viceroy of Chile and Peru, he joined a plot to free Chile from Spanish rule while receiving his education in England, and developed a revolutionary movement on his return to the country in 1802. After partial success in the 1810 revolution, he was made commander-in-chief, and, with the help of Argentine revolutionary forces, finally took control of the country in 1817. He proclaimed independence the following year and took office as President, but was much less of a success as a dictator than he had been as a liberator and was deposed in 1823, when he retired to Peru.

O'KELLY, Sean Thomas
1882–1966

Irish statesman, born Dublin. A pioneer of the Sinn Fein movement and of the Gaelic League, he was imprisoned after fighting in the 1916 Easter Rising, but won election to the first Dáil in 1918. He was Speaker from 1919 to 1921, and as an opponent of the Irish Free State became prominent in **de Valera**'s Fianna Fáil Party, serving under him between 1932 and 1945 as Local Government Minister and as Finance and Education Minister. He was President of the Irish Republic from 1945 to 1959.

OLAV V
1903–91

King of Norway, born in Norfolk, England, the great grandson of Queen **Victoria** and son of Princess Maud, daughter of Edward VII. His father, King Haakon, was the first head of the restored monarchy after Norway broke from Sweden in 1903. Olav was educated at Oslo military academy and at Oxford, and took a Swedish princess, Martha, as his wife in 1929. Evacuated with his father by a British cruiser after the 1940 German invasion, the whole family was reunited in Washington, where they spent the remaining war years. On his father's return to the throne in 1945, Olav supervised German disarmament and the prosecution of collaborators, and he became king on his father's death in 1957. In 1962, he made the first state visit to Edinburgh for 150 years, by way of expressing gratitude for the help given to the many members of the Norwegian resistance movement who had been based in Scotland during World War II. He lived simply in the style of the Norwegian court, as befitted a largely social democratic society. He spent the whole of his 30 years as monarch without a consort, his wife having died two years before he took the throne. He was succeeded by his son, **Harald V**.

OLDENBARNEVELT, Johan van
1547–1619

Dutch statesman, born Amersfoort. A leading figure in the struggle for independence from Spain, he offered the throne to **Elizabeth I**, and as the most influential member of the subsequent republican government he made alliances with England and France in 1596 and eventually signed a 12-year truce with Spain, in 1609. However, the resultant continuing religious differences made him many enemies, and he was falsely accused of corruption and treason and executed.

OLLENHAUER, Erich
1901–63

German politician. After taking refuge in Czechoslovakia during the 1930s on the rise to power of **Adolf Hitler**, he spent World War II in England, and eventually returned to his homeland to lead the German Social Democratic Party in 1952. An opponent of **Konrad Adenauer**'s support for the western alliance, he was replaced in 1960 by **Willy Brandt**.

O'NEILL, Terence Marne
1914–90

Northern Irish statesman. After wartime service in the Irish Guards, he entered the Northern Irish Parliament (Stormont) in 1946 and held a number of junior and senior posts in several Government departments before becoming Prime Minister in 1963. His acceptance in 1969 of civil rights for the Roman Catholic minority forced his resignation. He was given a life peerage the following year. *Ulster at the Crossroads* (1969), *The Autobiography of Terence O'Neill* (1972).

OPPENHEIMER, Robert J(ulius)
1904–67

American nuclear physicist, born New York. Educated at Harvard, Cambridge and Zurich, he worked as a physics professor in the USA in the 1930s, and in 1942 joined the Manhattan Project to develop America's first nuclear weapon. Stunned by the consequences of his work with the dropping of the first atom bombs on Hiroshima and Nagasaki, he resigned in 1945 but continued to serve as a Government adviser. He campaigned vigorously for joint control with the Soviets of atomic energy and a halt to development work on the hydrogen bomb, and in 1953 he returned to lecturing after being denied further participation in secret research for his alleged left-wing associations.

ORLANDO, Vittorio Emmanuele
1860–1952

Italian politician, born Palermo. A professor of law, he entered the Chamber of Deputies in 1897, was made Minister of Justice in 1916, and became Prime Minister a year later after his country's humiliating defeat by Austro-German forces at Caporetto in World War I. His failure to win at the 1919 Paris peace conference territorial concessions promised in return for Italy's alignment with the allies brought unpopularity and two failed attempts to form a coalition, and in 1921 he pledged support to **Benito Mussolini** in an attempt to retain constitutional government. The growing power of the fascists forced his resignation in 1925, and despite his refusal to swear allegiance to the regime, he publicly supported its part in the Ethiopian war and the king's dismissal in 1943. In 1944, he re-entered the Chamber of Deputies, and served as the Constituent Assembly's first post-war premier in 1946. He failed to win election in 1948 but was appointed a senator for life for services rendered to the nation.

ORTEGA (SAAVEDRA), Daniel
1945–

Nicaraguan politician, born Libertad, Chontales. An activist against **Anastasio Somoza**'s regime from his teens, he joined the Sandinista National Liberation Front in 1963 and became its national director in 1966. On his release after serving a seven-year jail sentence for guerrilla bank raids, he led the coup that deposed Somoza in 1979 and established a provisional government. He became President in 1985, and contrived to remain in power, despite the efforts of the US-backed counter-revolutionary Contras, until 1990, when he was compelled to hold elections and was defeated by **Violeta Chamorro**.

ORWELL, George (Eric Blair)
1903–50

English novelist, born Motihari, Bengal. After police service in Burma in the 1920s, he lived briefly in Paris, and while working as a shopkeeper in England published his first two novels in 1935 and 1936. After fighting and being wounded in the Spanish Civil War, he developed his socialist beliefs in *The Road to Wigan Pier* (1937), an attack on middle-class socialism, and two further books, and then worked as a war correspondent for the *Observer* and the BBC before publishing his brilliant satire of Communist ideology, *Animal Farm*, in 1945. His view of a Stalinist, totalitarian state in which 'Big Brother is watching you' was portrayed in *1984*, published in 1948.

OSWALD, Lee Harvey
1939–63

American assassin, born New Orleans. A former US Marine, he defected to the USSR in 1959 and took a Russian wife, but, claiming to be disillusioned with his adoptive country, he was allowed to re-enter the USA in 1962, though he continued to associate with Communist fringe groups. Shortly after the assassination of **John F. Kennedy** as he was driven in a motorcade through Dallas on 22 November 1963, Oswald was arrested, but was himself shot dead by nightclub owner Jack Ruby as he was being transferred to another jail two days later. Although the Warren Commission found that Oswald had acted alone, and that the slaying was the work of a psychopath and without political motivation, the true circumstances surrounding the most famous assassination of the 20th century, and the identity of all those responsible, remains a topic of undiminished speculation nearly three decades later.

OWEN, Dr David Anthony Llewellyn
1938–

British politician, born Plympton. After an early career as a doctor, he entered Parliament for Labour in 1966, held office as a junior Health and Foreign Minister, and in 1977 was appointed the youngest Foreign Secretary for more than 40 years. Disillusioned with Labour policies in subsequent Administrations and in Opposition, he was one of the breakaway Gang of Four senior Labour MPs who in 1981 founded the Social Democratic Party, replacing **Roy Jenkins** as leader in 1983 after its poor showing in that year's general election. The SDP's further lack of success in the 1987 election brought its eventual merger with the Liberals, and Owen resigned to head a tiny, reconstituted SDP. As a man of principle, he has remained popular with the electorate, and the reformation of Labour policies under **Neil Kinnock**, particularly in respect of foreign affairs, has led to frequent speculation that he may return to his former party. His books include *Face the Future* (1981), *A Future that will Work* (1984) and *Time to Declare* (1991).

OWEN, Robert
1771–1858

Welsh social and educational reformer, born Newtown, Montgomeryshire. Having started work at 10, he was at 19 the manager of a cotton mill, and by 1800 had prospered enough to be able to purchase the mills and manufacturing village at New Lanark in Scotland. There he developed a model industrial community that offered unparalleled housing and working conditions, founded the first day-nursery and playground for his workers' children and introduced evening classes and a co-operative shop. His attempts to establish similar communities elsewhere, including Indiana, were unsuccessful, and in 1828 he relinquished his interests in New Lanark after disagreements with his partners. The rest of his life was spent campaigning for disparate causes, including spiritualism. In the 1970s, New Lanark was restored to make it a living community again and it was honoured with a European award for social conservation in 1988. Owen's *A New View of Society* (1813) argues that character is formed by social environment.

OXENSTIERNA, Axel
1583–1654

Swedish politician, born Uppsala. As Chancellor to Gustavus II of Sweden from 1612, he masterminded his Protestant monarch's triumphant sweep through Germany in the Thirty Years War, and after his death in 1632 became regent to Gustavus's daughter, Queen Christina, and further enhanced Sweden's territorial gains. Subsequent increasing interference in state affairs brought Christina's abdication in 1653 and her mentor died soon after.

ÖZAL, Turgut
1927–

Turkish statesman, born Malatya. After an early career in government service and with the World Bank, he joined the personal staff of Prime Minister **Bülent Ecevit** in 1979, and a year later served as deputy to his successor in the new military regime, Bülent Ulusu. With the return of a degree of constitutional democracy in 1983, he founded the Islamic, rightist Motherland Party and won a narrow victory in the elections the same year, to become Turkey's first civilian President for 30 years. He retained power in the 1987 election. In recent years, he has strived to improve his country's lamentable reputation for human rights abuses and to secure its admission as a member of the European Community. In the 1991 Gulf War, despite strong domestic criticism, he allowed Turkish bases to be used by the USAF in mounting attacks on Iraq and the occupation forces in Kuwait.

PADEREWSKI, Ignace Jan
1860–1941

Polish pianist, composer, and politician, born Kurylowka, Podolia. A musical prodigy who played the piano from the age of three, Paderewski studied at Warsaw, Berlin and Vienna, and taught at the Warsaw Music Institute and at the Strasbourg conservatory before embarking on an exhausting series of concerts as a virtuoso in Europe, the USA, Australia, New Zealand and South Africa, donating much of the income from his performances to the cause of Polish nationalism. From the 1880s, he also established a reputation as a composer, his most popular works being his piano concerto (1888), and the opera *Manru* (1901). From 1910, he campaigned vigorously for his country's

independence, and while in America during World War I persuaded **Woodrow Wilson** to incorporate Polish nationalism in his famous Fourteen Points. He was rewarded by his countrymen for his patriotism by being chosen as their first Prime Minister in 1919. He returned to the concert stage a year later, but after going into exile following the German occupation of 1939, he was appointed President of the provisional Government that was established in Paris in 1940, before dying in Switzerland a year later.

PAENIU, Bikenibeu
1956–

Tuvaluan politician. One of the new generation of Tuvalu's non-party political system, he defeated **Tomasi Puapua** in the general election of 1989. At that time he declared that his administration would seek to promote a greater sense of national identity in the country, and reduce Tuvalu's dependence on foreign aid. His new cabinet included Naama Latasi, the first woman to serve in Tuvalu's parliament since the country was granted independence in 1979.

PAHLAVI, Mohammad Reza
1919–80

Last Shah of Persia, born Teheran. Following his succession to the throne in 1941 on the abdication of his father, his first two marriages ended in divorce after both failed to produce a male heir, but his 1960 marriage to Fara Diba, the daughter of an army officer, produced the Crown Prince Reza (1960–), another son, and two daughters. The early years of his reign were notable for a move away from despotic rule and the introduction of many worthwhile reforms, including the removal of martial law after 16 years in 1957, votes for women, and compulsory education—albeit at the cost of rioting by religious groups. The 1960s were marked by sporadic violent demonstrations and the assassination of a prime minister, leading to the imprisonment and torture or execution of countless dissidents. But by the late 1970s, it was apparent that the shah and his Government had lost their grip on Iran's worsening economic situation, acute social inequality, and the growing anti-western feeling fomented by strict fundamentalists, who particularly resented US influence. When fundamentalists, intellectuals, communists and human-rights activists combined to secure the return of the country's spiritual leader, **Ayatollah Khomeini**, in 1979, and following further violent political rioting in which more than 10000 died, the shah left the country, to be replaced by a revolutionary Government led by Khomeini. While the ex-shah was in America undergoing medical treatment, revolutionaries occupied the US embassy in Teheran and held many of its staff hostage for more than a year, in an unsuccessful attempt to have the ex-shah returned to Iran for trial. He eventually retired to Egypt at the invitation of President **Anwar Sadat**, and remained there until his death.

PAINE, Thomas
1737–1809

English-born American revolutionary and writer, born Thetford, Norfolk. Born into a quaker family, he followed his father in becoming a corset-maker at the age of 13 and then served in the Navy and worked as a teacher. In 1771 he became an exciseman, but was dismissed after leading a demonstration for better wages. On moving to London, he met **Benjamin Franklin**, who financed his passage to America, where he settled in Philadelphia and established himself as a radical journalist. After the outbreak of the American Revolution (1775–83), he published *Common Sense* in 1776, which advocated immediate independence. During his service in the continental army, he published as a series of pamphlets his work on the colonial cause, *The American Crisis* (1776–83), and was secretary to the Congress committee on foreign affairs from 1777 to 1779. Visits to France and England followed, during which he published *Dissertations on Government* (1786) and his most celebrated work, *The Rights of Man* (1791–2), which was designed to serve as a rebuke to **Edmund Burke**'s *Reflections on the Revolution in France*, and advocated the overthrow of the British monarchy. Indicted for treason, he escaped to Paris, where he took French citizenship and became a deputy in the National Convention (1792–3). As a Girondist, he displeased **Robespierre** by opposing the execution of the king, had his citizenship rescinded, and was imprisoned. When the Reign of Terror ended, he won his release by pleading that he was an American. Shortly before his arrest, he had published the first part of his condemnation of accepted religion, *The Age of Reason*, and completed the second part in prison and published it on gaining his freedom. With this, Paine took radicalism too far even for former close friends such as **George Washington**, and although he returned to American in 1802, he never regained his former popularity as a constructive free-thinker. He died in virtual poverty on the small farm in New Rochelle that New York state had bestowed on him many years before.

PAISLEY, Reverend Ian Richard Kyle
1926–

Northern Ireland clergyman and politician, born Ballymena. Educated at Ballymena High School, South Wales Bible College, and the Reformed Presbyterian Theological College, Belfast, he was ordained by his Baptist minister father in 1946 and founded his own denomination, the Free Presbyterian Church of Ulster, in 1951. From 1966 he published the *Protestant Telegraph*, and in 1969 entered the Northern Ireland Parliament as Protestant Unionist MP for Bannside, becoming leader of the Opposition in 1972. After co-founding the Democratic Unionist Party, he sat in the Northern Ireland Assembly for the DUP from 1973 to 1975, as a member of the Constitutional Convention from 1975 to 1976, and again in the National Assembly from 1982 to 1986. Since 1970, he has been MP for Antrim North in the House of Commons and leader of the Democratic Unionists there, though he resigned briefly in protest at the Anglo-Irish Agreement. As a member of the European Parliament since 1979, he staged a well-publicized one-man protest there against the choice of the Pope as a guest speaker in 1988. As the Province's most vociferous opponent of Irish unification, he is the greatest source of inspiration to, and object of fanatical devotion from, Ulster loyalists. Although occasionally engendering the distrust of moderate leaders of both the Protestant and Catholic communities, he has won praise for his impartial handling of his constituents' problems regardless of their religion. His publications include *History of the 1859 Revival* (1959), *Christian Foundations* (1960), *The Massacre of Bartholomew* (1974), *America's debt to Ulster Kidd* (1982), and *Those Flaming Tennents* (1983).

PALME, (Sven) Olof Joachim
1927–86

Swedish politician, born Stockholm. Educated at Stockholm University and

Kenyon College in the USA, he joined the youth league of the Social Democratic Labour Party in 1949 and entered the Riksdag in 1956. He held a number of ministerial posts from 1963, and after serving as secretary to Prime Minister Tag Erlander, succeeded him in 1969. Despite the loss of an overall parliamentary majority two years later, he managed to implement a number of significant constitutional reforms, but in 1976 his Government fell over proposals to increase funding of the welfare system by higher taxation. He led a minority Government again from 1982, but four years later was shot dead while walking home with his wife.

PALMER, Geoffrey Winston Russell
1942–

New Zealand politician. After graduating from Victoria University, Wellington, he taught law in America and New Zealand before entering the House of Representatives for Labour in 1979. He was appointed Attorney-General in 1984, and after becoming deputy Prime Minister in 1989, succeeded to the premiership on the resignation of David Lange.

PALMERSTON, Henry John Temple, 3rd Viscount
1784–1865

English statesman, born Westminster. Educated at Edinburgh and Cambridge Universities, he was elected MP for Newport, Isle of Wight, in 1807, but from 1811 represented Edinburgh for 20 years, until he lost his seat for supporting the Reform Bill. He entered the Admiralty as a junior Minister, then became Secretary for War under five Prime Ministers between 1809 and 1928, including **George Canning** and the Duke of **Wellington**. He withdrew from the Tory Party in 1828, but was offered the Foreign Office in the Whig Administration of Earl **Grey** two years later, and in that office helped to secure Belgian independence and the Spanish throne for Isabella II, and sought an alliance with Austria and Turkey to check Russian ambitions in the East. He left office when the Whigs were defeated, but returned as Foreign Minister under Lord **Russell**. Worsening relations between Britain and Spain, and with Greece after the celebrated Don Pacifico affair—over the claim of a Gibraltar Jew living in Athens to British citizenship—culminated in a vote of censure

against Palmerston in the House of Lords in 1850 but it was defeated by the Commons. However, his remarks to the French ambassador in 1851, when he expressed his approbation of **Napoleon III**'s coup d'état, compelled Russell to secure his resignation, but a few months later, Palmerston brought down the Government over the Militia Bill. He refused office under the Earl of **Derby**, but rejoined the Cabinet as Home Secretary in Lord **Aberdeen**'s 1852 coalition, and assumed the premiership when it fell in 1855. His Administration was returned with an increased majority in 1857 after he sought a mandate following **Cobden**'s motion on the Chinese war, but lost office a year later over the Conspiracy Bill. In June 1859 he again became Prime Minister, to be confronted by the ramifications of the American Civil War, Napoleon III's war with Austria, and the Austro-Prussian War with Denmark. Although Palmerston's tendency towards liberalism and the ready use of force created difficulties in his relationship with Queen **Victoria**, he enjoyed immense public popularity—not least because it was his policy to serve as the head of a nation rather than of a political party, and in that he achieved a greater degree of parliamentary consensus than any other British premier in peacetime.

PANDIT, Vijaya Lakshmi
1900–

After a private education, she entered Government service in 1935 and was Local Government and Health Minister (1937-9), and as a member of the Opposition was imprisoned in 1940 and 1941 for her nationalist campaigns. On the Congress Party's return to power, she led her country's delegation to the United Nations from 1946 to 1948, and was president of the Assembly in 1953-4. She was ambassador to the USA and Mexico from 1949 until re-entering Parliament in 1952, and from 1954 until 1961 was envoy to Britain and Ireland. She returned to Parliament in 1964. She wrote *The Evolution of India* (1958), and her memoirs, *The Scope of Happiness*, were published in 1979.

PANKHURST, Emmeline, née Goulden
1857–1928

English suffragette, born in Manchester. In 1879 she married Richard Marsden Pankhurst (d.1898), a radical Manchester barrister who had been the author of the first women's suffrage bill in Britain and of the Married

Women's Property Acts of 1870 and 1882. In 1889 Mrs Pankhurst founded the Women's Franchise League, and in 1903, with her daughter Christabel Harriette (1880–1958), the Women's Social and Political Union, which fought for women's suffrage with extreme militancy. She was frequently imprisoned and underwent hunger strikes and forcible feeding. She later joined the Conservative party. She wrote her autobiography in *My Own Story* (1914). Her daughter Estelle Sylvia Pankhurst (1882–1960), was also a suffragette.

PAPADOPOULOS, Georgios
1919–

Greek soldier and politician, born Eleochorion, Achaia. After army training in the Middle East, he fought in Albania against the Italians before the German occupation, during which he served as a member of the resistance and was then appointed a colonel in the Greek army. In 1967, he led a coup against King Constantine II to establish a military dictatorship, and following the abolition of the monarchy in 1973, was appointed president under a new republican constitution, but was himself ousted by the army later the same year. The following year he was arrested and convicted of high treason, but the death sentence passed on him was commuted.

PAPANDREOU, Andreas George
1919–

Greek politician. The son of a former Prime Minister, **George Papandreou**, he was educated at Athens University Law School and Harvard, lectured in the USA and Canada, and took US citizenship in 1944 before returning to Greece in 1961 as director of the Centre for Economic Research and adviser to the Bank of Greece. After resuming his native citizenship, he became active in politics and was imprisoned and then exiled following the military coup led by **Georgios Papandreou** in 1967. On returning to his country in 1974, he re-entered national politics and as founder of the Pan-Hellenic Liberation Movement, later renamed the Pan-Hellenic Socialist Movement, he led the Opposition from 1977 until becoming his country's first socialist Prime Minister in 1981. In 1989, following a heart attack and public ridicule over his association with a young air stewardess following his divorce, he failed to form a new Government and resigned.

PAPANDREOU, George
1888–1968

Greek politician, born Salonika. After practising as a lawyer, he entered politics and held Government office in several left-wing republican Administrations between 1923 and 1925, during the period that the monarchy was temporarily suspended. Following the German occupation, he fled the country in 1942, but after returning two years later as head of a coalition was removed by the army, which was suspicious of his socialist credentials. He remained an influential figure in national politics, and after founding the Centre Union Party in 1961, returned as Prime Minister (1963, 1964–5). In 1965, he resigned over constitutional differences with King Constantine II, and after the military coup of 1967 was placed under house arrest until his death. His son, **Andreas Papandreou**, continued his political fight to become the country's first socialist Prime Minister in 1981.

PARETO, Vilfredo
1848–1923

Italian economist and sociologist, born Paris. After working as a professor of economy at Lausanne from 1893, he wrote a number of works on the subject that embodied a uniquely mathematical approach. His sociological treatise, *The Mind and Society* (1916), anticipated some of the principles of fascism.

PARK CHUNG-HEE
1917–79

South Korean soldier and politician, born Sangmo-ri, Kyonsang province. Educated at a Japanese military academy, he fought with the Japanese during World War II, and after joining the South Korean army in 1946, reached the rank of major general, and in 1961 deposed the civilian Government of Chang Myon in a bloodless coup. As founder of the Democratic Republican Party, he was elected president in 1963, and implemented a highly successful programme of export-led industrial development that achieved annual growth rates of as much as 20 per cent during the 1960s and 1970s. However, increasing resistence to his authoritarian rule led to the re-imposition of martial law in 1972 and necessitated emergency measures in 1975. After four more precarious years as head of state in charge of a worsening economy, he was assassinated in 1979 by the head of his security services.

PARKINSON, Cecil
1932–

British politician, born Carnforth, Lancashire. Educated at the Royal Lancaster Grammar School and Emmanuel College, Cambridge, he entered commerce as a management trainee and worked as an accountant before becoming active in local politics and winning election as a Conservative MP in 1970. Two years later, he was appointed parliamentary private secretary to the Minister for Aerospace, **Michael Heseltine**, was an Opposition Whip from 1974 to 1976, and shadow spokesman on trade from 1976 until the Conservatives returned to power in 1979, when he was appointed Trade Minister. He was then Paymaster-General and Conservative national chairman (1981–3), Chancellor of the Duchy of Lancaster (1982–3), and Secretary of State for Trade and Industry (1983). In 1983, he resigned from the Cabinet and as party chairman following the disclosure that his personal parliamentary secretary, Sarah Keays, was carrying his child. She gave birth to a daughter later that year, though in his entries in *Who's Who* and in *The Parliamentary Yearbook*, he continues to acknowledge only his three daughters by his 1957 marriage. Always a close confidante of **Margaret Thatcher**, she invited him back to the Cabinet in 1987 as Secretary of State for Energy, and he was Transport Secretary from 1989 until surrendering office in the Cabinet reshuffle that followed **John Major**'s election as party leader and his succession to the premiership in November 1990. In 1991, Parkinson announced his intention to leave the Commons at the next general election.

PARNELL, Charles Stewart
1846–91

Irish politician, born Avondale, County Wicklow. The son of a Protestant landowning family who had purchased an estate in Ireland under **Charles II**, and whose grandfather, Sir John Parnell, had been Irish Chancellor, he entered Parliament in 1875 as a home rule supporter for County Meath, and soon became renowned for his ingenious use of parliamentary procedure to obstruct Government business. As president of the Irish National Land League, he raised £70000 in the USA to help rehabilitate Irish agriculture in the wake of the potato blight, and became chairman of the Irish parlia-

mentary party in 1880. The rise in agrarian crime that followed his policy of boycott led to Parnell and 34 other Irish MPs being ejected from Westminster and imprisoned, but Parnell was released after undertaking to denounce the assassination of the Chief Secretary, Lord Frederick Cavendish, in Dublin, and other criminal activities in return for Government moderation over rent arrears. In 1886, Parnell and his 85 fellow Irish MPs used their vote to help introduce **William Gladstone**'s home rule Bill, and although they were successful in bringing down the first Government of Lord **Salisbury**, they failed to secure the legislation because of defections by Liberal MPs. When Salisbury took the issue to the country later the same year, he was returned with a Unionist majority of more than 100, throwing Parnell into an alliance with Gladstone. In 1889, Parnell was cleared of complicity in Burke's murder and other organized outrages following the publication in *The Times* of letters purportedly written by him, and, his character restored, he was given the freedom of the city of Edinburgh the same year. After he had been cited as co-respondent in the 1890 O'Shea divorce action, with costs awarded against him, Parnell was removed as party chairman after pressure from Gladstone and he returned to Dublin. Shunned by the Church and with a dwindling group of close supporters, his influence and popularity with the electorate soon waned, and in the 1892 general election, by which time Parnell had died suddenly in Brighton, five months after his marriage to Mrs O'Shea, 72 anti-Parnellites were returned against only nine members of his faction.

PARRI, Ferrucio
1890–1982

Italian resistance leader and politician, born Pinerolo. After a university education, he worked as a teacher from 1914 before joining the army, in which he gave distinguished service in the trench warfare along the Alps. In 1919, he returned to teaching, but his active opposition to fascism brought his dismissal. In 1926, after helping the ageing socialist leader Filipino Turati (1857–1932) to escape from Italy, he was imprisoned for four years, and again from 1930 to 1932. Despite continuous police surveillance, Parri resumed his fight against fascism, and after the collapse of **Benito Mussolini**'s regime in 1943, he emerged as leader of the politica and military resistance in the north of the country, later helping to plan allied military strategy. On his return to Rome in 1945, he was arrested and spent two months in a German prison and was then moved to Switzerland, but gained his release when the Germans started negotiating their surrender in Italy. In June 1945, he became the country's first postwar Prime Minister, but his Government, pressured by the parties of both the left and the right, fell in November the same year. Nevertheless, he continued his campaign for Italy's political and economic reconstruction as a member of the Constituent Assembly from 1946 and after entering the Senate in 1948, and actively supported his country's membership of NATO. His efforts to work for European unity and to reconcile Italy's various leftist parties continued through the 1950s and 1960s, and he devoted his final years to historical research on resistance movements. His memoirs, *Scritti, 1915–75*, were published in 1976.

PASSY, Frédéric
1822–1912

French economist and author, born Paris. After entering the Chamber of Deputies in 1881, he founded the International Peace League in 1867, and joined the International Peace Bureau in Bern in 1892. In 1901, two years after leaving the Assembly, he shared the Nobel Peace Prize with Jean Dunant. He wrote *Mélanges économiques* (1857), *L'Histoire du travail* (1873) and *Vérités et paradoxes* (1894).

PASTERNAK, Boris Leonidovich
1890–1960

Russian poet and novelist, born Moscow. After studying law at Moscow University and philosophy at Marburg, he worked as a librarian after the Revolution, and published his first collection of verse in 1912. His political poems, *The Year of 1905* (1927) and *Lieutenant Schmidt* (1927), on the Potemkin mutiny, were followed by several notable short stories. During the Stalin era, he worked as an official translator into Russian of Shakespeare, Goethe and others. After misinterpreting the extent of the 'new liberalism' that was heralded when **Nikita Khrushchev** came to power, he caused a furore with *Doctor Zhivago*, which was banned in the Soviet Union, and after being expelled from the Soviet Writers Union, was compelled to refuse the Nobel Prize in 1958—the year in which a translated edition of his controversial work was published in the West. He lived the rest of his life in obscurity in the Soviet Union, where his works continued to be produced only in secret editions until they were at last acknowledged during the early years of **Mikhail Gorbachev**'s presidency.

PATTEN, Chris (Christopher Francis)
1944–

British politician, born London. Educated at St Benedict's School, Ealing, and Balliol College, Oxford, he joined the staff of the Conservative Party's research department in 1966, and was seconded to the Cabinet Office and Home Office (1970–2) before being appointed personal assistant to the then party chairman, Lord **Carrington** (1972–4). He was director of research from 1974 before being returned as MP for Bath in 1979, when he was made private parliamentary secretary to the Leader of the House, then to the Secretary of State for Social Services (1981–). He was made junior Northern Ireland Minister in 1983, Minister of State for Education and Science in 1985, and Minister for Overseas Development from 1986 until joining the Cabinet as Secretary of State for the Environment in 1989. Considered one of the most astute and ambitious of the 1979 intake of 'Thatcher's babies', he was replaced as Environment Secretary by **Michael Heseltine** in **John Major**'s first reshuffle on becoming Prime Minister in November 1991, and appointed to the key post of party chairman, charged with engineering a Conservative victory in the next general election. He published *The Tory Case* in 1983.

PAVLOV, Vladimir Yakovlevich
1923–

Soviet Prime Minister, born Mosalsk, Kaluga. Educated at Moscow Railway Engineering Institute, he worked as a railway engineer from 1941 to 1949. He then became active in the party organization, eventually gaining promotion to a senior post in the Komsomol, and became a deputy to the Supreme Soviet in 1966. He served as ambassador to Hungary (1971–81) and to Japan (1981–5). After his appointment as Prime Minister in January 1991, Pavlov showed himself to be a candid realist in his task of reconciling the reformist factions, and constructively applied his diplomatic experience as intermediary— though one favouring the western coalition—in the prelude to the 1991 Gulf War.

PAZ ESTENSSORO, Victor
1907–

Bolivian politician and economist. Educated at the University Mayor de San Andres, he entered politics in the 1930s, and in 1942 founded the centre-right National Revolutionary Movement. After choosing exile in Argentina in 1946 when one of the country's many military dictatorships took power, he returned in 1951 to bid for the presidency, and although not successful at his first attempt, took victory in elections the following year. As one of his country's most enlightened and reformist heads of state, he introduced a swingeing programme of democratic political reform until leaving office in 1956, but was re-elected to serve again from 1960 to 1964 and in 1985, at the age of 77.

PEACOCK, Andrew Sharp
1939–

Australian politician, born Melbourne. Educated at Scotch College, Melbourne, and the University of Melbourne, he practised law before entering Parliament as a Liberal MP in 1966. He was appointed Army Minister (1969–71), and Minister for External Territories until 1972, and on the Liberals' return to power served as Minister for Foreign Affairs (1975–80), and for Industrial Relations. In 1981, he resigned as Minister for Commerce and Industry over policy differences with Prime Minister **Malcolm Fraser**, and unsuccessfully challenged him for the Liberal leadership a year later. Nevertheless, he resumed his earlier portfolio, and eventually succeeded Fraser as head of the party after the Liberals lost the 1983 general election.

PEARSE, Patrick Henry
1879–1916

Irish writer, educationalist and nationalist, born Dublin. After joining the Gaelic League in 1895, he became editor of its journal and lectured in Irish at University College, Dublin. In 1908 he founded a bilingual school at Ranelagh and later moved to Rath Farnham. From 1915 he was active in the Irish Republican Brotherhood, serving as commander-in-chief of the insurgents in the 1916 Easter Rising, and was proclaimed president

of the provisional Government. After the uprising had been quelled, he was court-martialled and shot. He wrote numerous poems, short stories, and plays, in English and Irish.

PEARSON, Lester Bowles
1897–1972

Canadian politician, born Newtonbrook, Ontario. Educated at Toronto and Oxford Universities, he was a history lecturer before entering public service in 1935 as a first secretary with the Canadian High Commission in London. On his return to Canada in 1941 he was appointed Under-Secretary of State for Foreign Affairs, and as ambassador to Washington in 1945 represented his country at the conferences that drew up the UN charter. He was president of the UN General Assembly in 1952–3, and for his work while Foreign Secretary from 1948, was rewarded with the Nobel Peace Prize when he retired from that office in 1957. From 1958 he led the Liberal Opposition and was Prime Minister from 1963 to 1968. He published *The Four Faces of Peace* in 1968.

PEEL, Sir Robert
1788–1850

English statesman, born Bury. After inheriting the fortune made by his father, a mill-owner and MP, while a child, he was educated at Harrow and Christ Church, Oxford, and himself became a Conservative MP in 1809. He was made a junior Minister for the colonies (1812) and for Ireland, but was forced to resign in 1818 having displayed strong anti-Catholic attitudes. In 1822 he rejoined the Cabinet as Home Secretary, but again left office in 1827, together with the Duke of **Wellington**, over efforts to achieve Catholic emancipation by **George Canning**'s Conservative-Whig coalition. As Home Secretary (1829) in the Government formed after Canning's death, he established the London police force. He later lost his seat, but was returned to the Commons in 1833, a year after the Whig Government had passed the famous Reform Bill. When **William IV** dismissed the Whig Prime Minister Lord Melbourne in 1834, he sent for Peel to form a new Administration, but as he was in Rome, **Wellington** was invited temporarily to assume the office that he had relinquished four years earlier, but was replaced by Lord Melbourne the following year. In the general election following the death of George IV, the Conservatives returned to power, but Peel's resumption of office was delayed by Queen **Victoria**'s refusal to part with her ladies of the bedchamber—all Whigs. Peel led the Conservatives to victory again in 1841, to thwart Whig attempts at free trade, and continued his vendetta against **Daniel O'Connell** by having him tried for sedition—though the sentence was quashed by the House of Lords. Ironically, the famine that followed the potato blight in Ireland created a necessity for 'cheap corn', and Peel, now replaced by the future Earl of **Derby**, secured the repeal of the Corn Laws with the support of **William Gladstone** and other eminent Tories. Peel's almost maniacal opposition to Irish emancipation forced his retirement when he was defeated over the Irish Protection of Life Bill of 1846 and the Whigs came to power under Lord **John Russell**, and he died four years later in a riding accident. *Memoirs* (1857), *Private Letters* (1820).

PERCEVAL, Spencer

1762–1812

British politician. Educated at Harrow and Trinity College, Cambridge, he practised as a lawyer before becoming a Conservative MP in 1796 and Solicitor-General under **William Pitt** in 1801. As Chancellor of the Exchequer from 1807 and a close confidante of **George III**, with whom he shared strong opposition to Catholic emancipation, he was effectively head of the Government, and became premier on the death of the Duke of Portland in 1809. Three years later, he achieved the dubious distinction of being the first British Prime Minister to be assassinated, when a deranged bankrupt stabbed him to death in the Central Lobby of the House of Commons. Some time elapsed before the Prince Regent invited Lord **Liverpool** to succeed Perceval—which has since served as a salutary reminder to subsequent holders of the office that, as a Prime Minister has no specific departmental responsibilities, a Government can constitutionally function indefinitely without one.

PEREIRA, Aristedes Maria

1923–

Cape Verde politician, born Boa Vista island. After working as a radio telegraphist, he won promotion to head of Guinea-Bissau's telecommunications service, and became active in politics, establishing the Independence of Portuguese Guinea and Cape Verde Party in 1956. Following his country's independence in 1975, Pereira became its first president and won re-election in 1981 and 1986.

PERES, Shimon

1923–

Polish-born Israeli politician. After emigrating to Palestine with his family in 1934, he was raised in a kibbutz but later studied at New York and Harvard universities. When the new state of Israel was created in 1948, he was made head of naval services, then was director-general of the defence ministry from 1953 until his election to the Knesset in 1959. He was Minister of Defence from 1974 until 1977, when he became party chairman, leading the Labour Opposition until entering into a power-sharing agreement with the consolidation party, Likud, under **Ytzhak Shamir**, which made him Prime Minister from 1984 to 1986, with Shamir assuming the premiership thereafter. After the inconclusive 1988 general election, Peres rejoined Shamir in a new coalition.

PÉREZ DE CUÉLLAR, Javier

1920–

Peruvian diplomat, born Lima. Educated at the Law Faculty of Lima University, he joined the Foreign Ministry in 1940, and after entering the diplomatic service in 1944 was posted to France, the UK, Bolivia, and Brazil. In 1946 he was a member of the Peruvian delegation to the United Nations, and returned to Peru to become Foreign Minister from 1961 to 1963. He was then ambassador to Switzerland (1964–6), Foreign Office permanent under-secretary and secretary-general (1966–9), and ambassador to the USSR and to Poland (1969–71). He was made Peru's permanent representative to the UN in 1971 and joined its Security Council in 1973, then served as the organization's special envoy to Cyprus (1979–81) and as ambassador to Venezuela (1978–9). In 1979 he returned to the UN as under-secretary-general for special political affairs, and was appointed as **Kurt Waldheim**'s successor as Secretary-General in 1982. His quiet, unassuming manner and his achievements—among which the most notable were his part in ending the 1982–8 Iran-Iraq War and concluding independence for Namibia in 1985—made him one of the UN's most effective representatives, though he was obviously bitterly disappointed by his failure to mediate successfully to prevent the 1991 Gulf War.

PERICLES
490–429 BC

Athenian statesman. Born into a noble family of thinkers, he became a radical opponent of the ruling oligarchy led by Cimon with the support of the Spartans, and in 460 BC contrived to take power from its conservative council and to have Cimon ostracized. His successful expeditions and programme of colonialism served to increase the naval supremacy of Athens, as did the peace treaty that he concluded with the Persians and the Delian League, and later with the Spartans—all of which he achieved with the purpose of ending mutually-destructive wars. In 444 BC, an attempt was made by the aristocracy to overthrow him with accusations that he had squandered public money on patronage of the arts—including the building of the Parthenon—but he survived to lead the Athenians in victory again in the Samian war of 439 BC. But not content with the massive territorial gains he had already made, he induced the Assembly to form an alliance with Corfu against Corinth, which provoked the Peloponnesian War that lasted from 431 to 404 BC, eventually causing the collapse of the Athenian empire. Pericles died in the great plague of 430 that took the lives of a quarter of the population.

PÉRON, Juan Domingo
1895–1974

Argentine soldier and politician, born Lobos, Buenos Aires. After joining the army in 1913, he took part in the 1943 army coup that deposed the pro-Axis President Ramon Castilio, and, with his gift for stirring public oratory, soon emerged as the new regime's most effective instrument for securing popular support. As Secretary of Labour, he secured huge union support by imposing minimum wages, while at the same time adroitly cultivating the right-wing by advancing the careers of young officers in his joint capacity as under-secretary of war, while the loyalty of a third important faction, the lower-class members of the *descamisados* paramilitary who were the equivalent of **Adolf Hitler**'s blackshirts, was secured by his wife, Evita (**Maria Eva Duarte de Péron**). By 1945, such was Peron's enormous popularity with the masses that senior army and navy officers engineered his imprisonment, but were forced to release him after thousands gathered at public meetings demanding his release. A year later, he was elected president, and immediately set about establishing a corporatist dictatorship. Political opposition was brutally suppressed by torture and summary execution, and despite Peron's attempts to revitalize the economy by nationalizing foreign-owned enterprises and other forms of state intervention, he succeeded only in alienating the Church and a large number of the military, middle class and unions—and in 1955 was deposed and fled the country, though the army was unsuccessful in replacing the civilian Government with martial law. Nevertheless, the Peronist bedrock of support so carefully nurtured by Juan and Evita during their early years in power consolidated itself over the next decade, and in 1966 the military took power to prevent a Peronist Party electoral victory. But a free presidential election was eventually allowed, the victorious Peronist candidate stood down in favour of the party's former leader, and in 1973 Juan returned to head his country for just one more year before dying in office, to be succeeded by his third wife, Isabelita.

PÉRON, Maria Eva Duarte de ('Evita')
1919–52

Born into poverty in Los Toldos, Buenos Aires, she began her stage career touring small towns with third-rate repertory companies, and after eventually becoming established as a leading actress with a Buenos Aires radio station, was able to enter the social circles of the capital's high society, where she met **Juan Péron**. After her marriage to him in 1945, she agitated for the poor and women's suffrage, and used part of the donations she elicited from the wealthy to gain control of newspapers to promote her cause—and Juan's—even more vigorously. Although physically unprepossessing and no great beauty, she employed her theatrical training to the full in making emotion-charged public speeches that leant heavily on recollections of her childhood poverty, and which won for her the adoration of hundreds of thousands of underprivileged Argentinians. Her death at the age of 32 prompted huge displays of public mourning and devastated her husband, who refused to have her interred and kept her preserved remains in a glass coffin at the presidential palace until he was deposed and forced to leave the country three years later.

PÉTAIN, Henry Philippe Omer
1856–1951

French soldier and marshal of France, born Cauchy-à-la-Tour. As a junior officer, he was considered by his superiors unfit to rise above the rank of major, but after promotion to temporary brigadier in 1914, he was given a command two years into World War I and his brilliant defence of Verdun in 1917 made him a national hero. He was made marshal on Armistice Day, restored order after the 1926–8 Moroccan revolt, but as Minister for War (1934) argued vigorously for the doomed Maginot Line defence system. In 1939 he was appointed ambassador to Spain, and on the collapse of the French Government the following year was appointed Prime Minister at the age of 84 and immediately sought terms with the Germans, in the belief that France would only be regenerated through suffering. However his Vichy Government came to be reviled as a tool of collaboration, and on the liberation of France, Petain was found guilty of treason, but because of the service that he had given to his country in World War I, the death sentence passed on him was commuted to life imprisonment.

PHILBY, 'Kim' (Harold Adrian Russell)
1911–88

British double agent, born in Ambala, India, son of Harry St John Philby. He was educated at Westminster and Trinity College, Cambridge, where, like **Guy Burgess**, **Donald Maclean** and **Anthony Blunt**, he became a communist. Already recruited as a Soviet agent, he was employed by the British Secret Intelligence Service (MI6), from 1944 to 1946, as head of the anti-communist counter-espionage. He was first secretary of the British embassy in Washington, working in liaison with the CIA, from 1949 to 1951, when he was asked to resign because of his earlier communist sympathies. From 1956 he worked in Beirut as foreign correspondent for *The Observer* and the *Economist*, obtaining the posts with the help of the British foreign office, until 1963, when he admitted the truth and disappeared to Russia, where he was granted citizenship. In 1968 he published *My Silent War* (1968). His third wife, Eleanor, joined him in Russia (1963) but returned to the West (1965).

PHOMVIHANE, Kaysone
1920–

Laotian politician, born Savannakhet province. Educated at Hanoi University, he saw action with the anti-French forces in Vietnam after World War II, and joined the exiled Free Lao Front nationalist movement in Bangkok in 1945. After later switching his allegiance to the North-Vietnamese-backed Pathet Lao Party and becoming its leader in 1955, he successfully directed guerrilla resistance to the rightist regime, to become Prime Minister of the new People's Democratic Republic of Laos in 1975, as well as general-secretary of the Lao People's Party. After initial attempts to realize a radical socialist programme of industrial nationalization and rural collectivization, Phomvihane embarked on a revised policy of economic and political liberalization.

PIECK, Wilhelm
1876–1960

East German politician, born Berlin. A carpenter by trade, he helped found the Spartacus League in 1915 and three years later the German Communist Party that, under his leadership, engineered the abortive Spartacist uprising in Berlin. With the emergence of the Weimar Republic, he was elected as a communist member of the Reichstag in 1928, but fled to Moscow when **Adolf Hitler** came to power, and in 1935 became secretary of the Comintern. Ten years later he followed the Red Army into Berlin and in 1946 founded the dominant Socialist Unity Party. From 1949, he served as the last president of the German Democratic Republic—the office being abolished on his death.

PIERCE, Franklin
1804–1869

Fourteenth US President, born Hillsborough, New Hampshire. After studying law and being admitted to the Bar in 1827, he served as a member of the state legislature from 1829 to 1833, and then entered Congress as a Democrat and supporter of **Andrew Jackson**. After becoming a senator in 1837, he was made party leader and strongly advocated the annexation of Texas, with or without slavery. Following the Whigs' victory of 1846, he saw action as a brigadier-general in the Mexican War, and on his return to political life was nominated for the presidency against the Whigs' choice, Scott Winfield, and took office. His Administration was notable for achieving reciprocity of trade with the British American colonies, the treaty with Japan, the repeal of the Missouri Compromise and the passing of the Kansas-Nebraska Act, which led to the Civil War and the unpopularity of which forced his retirement from politics in 1857.

PILSUDSKI, Józef
1867–1935

Polish marshal and statesman, born Zulw. As an activist for Polish independence, he was imprisoned several times, and on his return from five years' exile in Siberia in 1887, formed the Polish Socialist Party and edited underground publications. After further imprisonment in Warsaw and St Petersburg, he escaped to Cracow and in World War I fought with other dissidents on the side of Austria. He disbanded his force in 1917 on realising the threat to his country of Austro-German domination, and in 1918, with Poland now a republic, he became provisional president. In 1919, his attempt to establish the country's frontiers was defeated by the Bolshevik army, and the following year he went into retirement, but became Prime Minister again after engineering a coup in 1926. He resigned the premiership in 1928, but as Minister of War effectively remained the most influential member of the Government. The constitutional reforms that Pilsudski introduced during his years in power preserved a dictatorship until after his death.

PINDLING, Sir Lynden Oscar
1930–

Bahamanian politician. Educated at Nassau Government High School and London University, he practised as a lawyer, was elected leader of the Progressive Liberal Party in 1956, and entered the House of Assembly a year later. As Prime Minister from 1969, he led his country to full independence within the Commonwealth four years later. His party returned to power in the 1977, 1982 and 1987 elections, but Pindling's laudable achievements in the area of human rights have been somewhat overshadowed by investigations into alleged administration involvement in drug-trafficking.

PINOCHET UGARTE, Augusto
1915–

Chilean soldier and politician. After joining the army in 1933 at the age of 18, he became a training instructor at the Academy of War in 1954 and had won promotion to deputy director by 1964. In 1973, he was made commander-in-chief, and soon after led a CIA-backed coup in which the Marxist president, **Salvador Allende**, was shot dead at his palace. As head of a so-called provisional Government, Pinochet crushed all political opposition and became virtual dictator, and despite growing discontent with his regime and an attempt on his life, he announced his intention to remain in office for another eight years. However, a 1988 plebiscite in which he sought a mandate to remain in power only served to confirm his enormous unpopularity, and in 1990 he relinquished the presidency.

PITT, William (Pitt the Younger)
1759–1806

English statesman, born Hayes, Middlesex. As a sickly child, he received most of his early education at home, but graduated from Pembroke Hall, Cambridge at the age of 17 and was called to the Bar in 1780. He entered Parliament as a member of Lord North's Opposition in 1781, became Chancellor of the Exchequer and Leader of the Commons at 23, and declined the premiership on the resignation of Lord **Shelburne** in 1783, but accepted it the following year after the fall of the Duke of Portland's Administration, to become the country's youngest-ever Prime Minister. Though ridiculed for his inexperience by **Charles James Fox**'s Opposition, Pitt's Government survived for 17 years, during which he cemented good relations with America, reduced the national debt, reformed Parliament, and reorganized the East India Company. He also abolished public hangings at Tyburn and lifted the ban on Roman Catholics entering the army and the Bar. In 1800, he left office briefly in protest at the king's opposition to his successful attempt to achieve union with Ireland, but returned four years later to meet the threat from **Napoleon Bonaparte**, and learned of Britain's victory at the Battle of Trafalgar shortly before his death at the age of 46.

PLATO
428–348 BC

Greek philosopher, born Athens. The pupil of **Socrates**—whose execution in 399 BC by the restored democracy Plato described in *Apology*, *Crito* and *Phaedo*—and the teacher of **Aristotle**, he travelled widely in Greece, Egypt and the Greek cities of southern Italy, returning to Athens in 387 BC to found the academy that became a famous centre for philosophical, mathematical and scientific research. Although he devoted the majority of his life to academic consideration of human values, in 367 and 361 BC he returned to Sicily to persuade Dionysius II to train as a philosopher-statesman, but was unsuccessful. His writings comprise some 30 philosophical dialogues and his biographical *Letters*, of which only the seventh and eighth are thought to be genuine. In *The Republic*, which remains one of the most compelling and influential works in the history of philosophy, Plato describes a utopian political state ruled by philosopher-kings. His later works, including the *Parmenides*, *Theaetetus* and *Sophist*, arouse great interest and argument among modern philosophers and contain some of Plato's most persuasive and original work.

PLUMMER, (Arthur) Desmond, (Herne), Baron Plummer of St Marylebone
1914–

British politician, born London. Educated at Hurstpierpoint College and the College of Estate Management, he served in the Royal Engineers during World War II, and after resuming his career in commerce, entered politics as a local councillor in 1952. He was subsequently a member of the London County Council, and later of the Greater London Council, which was the capital's strategic planning authority until it was abolished, together with the other municipal authorities, by the Conservative Government in 1986. He was leader of the Conservative majority from 1967 to 1973, and remained to head the Opposition for a year before being succeeded by **Horace Cutler**. He received a life peerage in 1981.

PODGORNY, Nikolai Viktorovich
1903–83

Russian politician, born in the Ukraine. After working as a mechanic, he retrained as a food technologist and through his successful stewardship of regional agricultural policy, came to the attention of **Nikita Khrushchev**, who sponsored his admission to the Politburo in 1960. As President of the USSR from 1965 to 1977, he introduced a number of liberalizing domestic reforms and improved Soviet relations with the West.

POINDEXTER, Rear-Admiral John Marlan
1936–

American naval officer and statesman, born Washington, Indiana. Educated at the US Naval Academy and California Institute of Technology, where he obtained a doctorate in nuclear physics, he was appointed head of naval operations in 1974 and deputy head of educational training in 1978. In 1981 he joined President **Ronald Reagan**'s National Security Council, becoming National Security Adviser in 1985. In November 1986, he was obliged to resign together with his assistant, Lieutenant-Colonel **Oliver North**, over the Irangate scandal, which revolved around the illegal supply of arms in return for American hostages held in Iran and the secret funding of pro-US Contra rebels in Nicaragua. He retired from the US Navy the following year.

POL POT (Saloth Sar)
1926–

Kampuchean (Cambodian) politician. After working on a rubber plantation, he joined **Ho Chi Minh**'s anti-French resistance movement during the early 1940s and joined the Indo-Chinese Communist Party in 1946. During the 1960s and early 1970s, he led the pro-Chinese Khmer Rouge in guerrilla warfare against the Governments of Prince Sihanouk and his successor, Lieutenant General Lon Nol, whom he overthrew in 1976 to assume the premiership. Under Pol Pot's brutal regime, more than 2.5 million Kampucheans lost their lives, and when it was overthrown by Vietnamese troops in 1979, Pol Pot resumed his role as military leader of the resistance. Despite his official retirement in 1985, he remains an influential and feared figure within the movement.

POLLITT, Harry
1890–1960

British communist leader, born Droylesden, Lancashire. After starting work in a cotton mill at the age of 12, he joined the newly-formed Independent Labour Party at 16 and after finding employment at a boilermakers, became shop steward at 21. In 1924 he joined the staff of the National Minority Movement, and four years later was appointed secretary of the Communist Party of Great Britain. He was imprisoned for seditious libel in 1925, and during the Spanish Civil War helped to found the British battalion of the International Brigade. He resigned as secretary in 1956 to become party chairman. His autobiography, *Serving My Time*, was published in 1940.

POMPIDOU, Georges Jean Raymond
1911–74

French statesman, born Montboundif, Auvergne. After working as a teacher, he served with the resistance in World War II, then worked as an administrator and was appointed director-general of Rothschild's bank in 1954. He entered the National Assembly in 1953, and on **Charles De Gaulle**'s return to power three years later he headed his personal staff and was made Prime Minister in 1962. However, his mentor resented Pompidou's growing influence after his expert handling of the 1968 political crisis, and dismissed him. Pompidou comfortably won the presidency following De Gaulle's resignation a year later, and by the time that he left office in 1974, had done much to reverse the illiberal and isolationist policies that had typified his predecessor's presidency.

POPOV, Viktor Ivanovich
1918–

Soviet diplomat. Educated at the Moscow Institute of History and Philosophy, he joined the Ministry of Foreign Affairs in 1954, and served as an envoy in Vietnam (1960–1) and Australia (1967–9) before being made a roving ambassador and representing the USSR at the United Nations. As ambassador in London from 1980 to 1986, he cultivated improving detente after an initial period of Soviet hostility to the new Conservative Government under the 'Iron Lady' **Margaret Thatcher**.

PORRITT, Jonathon (Espie)
1950–

British environmental campaigner. The son and heir of a baronet, he was educated at Eton and Magdalen College, Oxford, and worked as a teacher for the Inner London Education Authority from 1975 to 1984, from 1980 as head of English and drama at Burlington Danes School in west London. After developing an interest in environmental matters, he joined the newly-formed Ecology Party and stood unsuccessfully as one of its candidates in the 1979 and 1984 British general European Parliament elec-

tions. He was appointed to its council in 1978 and was chairman in 1979-80. Director of the Friends of the Earth from 1984 to 1990, he left in 1990 to concentrate on writing and broadcast journalism. He wrote *Seeing Green—the Politics of Ecology* (1984), *Friends of the Earth Handbook* (1987), and *The Coming of the Greens* (1988).

POWELL, Colin
1945–

US soldier and Chairman, Joint Chiefs of Staff, born Harlem. The son of Jamaican immigrants, he received an elementary education before joining the US Army in 1963, and rose through the ranks, winning a Purple Heart and Bronze Star during the Vietnam war, to become the first US commander never to have attended West Point Military Academy. He served as National Security Adviser to **Ronald Reagan**, and in the prelude to the 1991 Gulf War was given charge of Operation Desert Shield as supreme commander of all US air and land forces, answering directly to George Bush. Although he tended to be eclipsed in media terms during the height of the conflict by his second-in-command, General **Norman Schwarzkopf**, his brilliant press briefings at the beginning of the campaign did much to consolidate public support for the actions of the coalition forces. Given **Dan Quayle**'s stature in the Republican Party and in the eyes of the American public at large, Powell is strongly tipped to succeed **George Bush** at the White House, to become the first-ever black occupant of the Oval Office.

POWELL, (John) Enoch
1912–

British politician and scholar, born Stechford, Birmingham. Educated at King Edward's School, Birmingham, and at Trinity College Cambridge, he was a Fellow there from 1934 to 1938, and then worked as a professor of Greek at Sydney University until enlisting as a private in the Royal Warwickshire Regiment at the start of World War II. He was commissioned in 1940 and by 1944 had risen to the rank of brigadier. After the war, he joined the Conservative Party and was elected as MP for Wolverhampton in 1950. He was junior housing Minister from 1955 to 1957, and Financial Secretary to the Treasury from 1957 until resigning, together with Peter Thorneycroft, a year later over policy differences. He accepted office again under **Harold Macmillan** in 1960 as Minister for Health, but resigned again three years later—this time in protest at the selection of **Alec Douglas-Home** as Macmillan's successor—and was never again to hold a Government post. He caused a furore with his 1968 'rivers of blood' speech on race relations—not least because he was known as a man of enormous intellect. Although he was branded a racist by the understandably alarmed leaders of ethnic minorities, in retrospect it seems likely that his quoting of Virgil was only a natural, if miscalculated, device for a classicist to employ in emphasizing his genuine concern about the effect of immigration on Britain's social infrastructure, which the Government eventually acknowledged with its 1986 immigration control legislation. His vehement opposition to Britain's entry to the Common Market caused him to resign his seat in 1974, but he returned to the House of Commons later that year as an Ulster Unionist MP. After losing his seat in the 1984 general election, he retired from public life. His numerous academic and political works include *The History of Herodotus* (1939), *Change is our Ally* (1954), *Great Parliamentary Occasions* (1960), *Freedom and Reality* (1969), *Common Market: THE CASE against* (1971), *Still to Decide* (1972), *No Easy Answers* (1973), *Joseph Chamberlain* (1977), and *Enoch Powell on 1992* (1989).

PREMADASA, Ranasinghe

1924–

Sri Lankan politician, born north Colombo. Educated at St Joseph's College, Colombo, he joined the Ceylon Labour Party and then the United National Party in 1950 and became deputy mayor of the municipal council in 1955. After entering Parliament in 1960, he was Chief Whip (1965–8, 1970–7), Minister for Local Government (1968–70), and Leader of the House (1977–8) before becoming Prime Minister in 1978. During his 10 years as premier, he implemented an extensive housebuilding programme and made great efforts to alleviate the poverty of his people. As President since 1988, he has been preoccupied with mounting civil unrest from the Tamils in the north and the Sinhalas in the south, and with deteriorating relations with India.

PREM TINSULANONDA, General

1920–

Thai soldier and politician, born Bangkok. After training at the Chulachomklao Royal Military Academy, Bangkok, he rose from the rank of sub-lieutenant in 1941 to become commander-in-chief of the Royal Thai Army in 1977. In the military Government of General Kriangsak Chomanam (1977–80) he was deputy Minister of the Interior, and was Defence Minister from 1979 until being made Prime Minister in 1980. After relinquishing his army office, he headed a series of civilian coalition Governments, survived attempted coups in 1981 and 1985, and proved deft at assuaging key business figures and military leaders in building his country's economy and security, to produce annual growth rates of more than 9 per cent throughout the late 1980s. He retired from office in 1988.

PRICE, George

1919–

Belize politician, born Belize City. Educated in Belize and the USA, he served as a city councillor from 1947, and in 1950 founded the left-of-centre People's United Party, which campaigned for independence. When Belize achieved a degree of self-government in 1954, Price was appointed Prime Minister, and held office until full independence was granted in 1981. In 1984, the PUP's 30 years of uninterrupted rule were ended by the United Democratic Party's success in a general election, but Price returned to power in 1989.

PROFUMO, John Dennis

1915–

British politician. The son of a baronet, he was educated at Harrow and Brasenose College, Oxford, was mentioned in dispatches while serving with the 1st Northamptonshire Yeomanry in World War II, and was promoted to brigadier by 1945. He was Conservative MP for Kettering from 1940 to 1945, and re-entered the Commons as MP for Stratford-upon-Avon in 1950. Between 1952 and 1958 he held several junior ministerial appointments before being appointed Minister of State for Foreign Affairs in 1959. After entering the Cabinet as Secretary for War in 1960, he had an affair with a 19-year-old nightclub dancer, Christine Keeler (1942–), while she was having a relationship with an attaché working at the

Russian Embassy. When the story broke in 1963, Profumo made a personal statement to the Commons in which he denied any impropriety, but when further newspaper revelations showed him to have lied, he resigned from the Cabinet and as an MP—not because of his affair and its possible security implications, but for deceiving the House. The incident nearly brought down the Government of **Harold Macmillan**, not least because the security services had apparently kept him in ignorance of Profumo's indiscretion for reasons of their own, and Macmillan relinquished the premiership soon after. Profumo subsequently devoted himself to community work for the underprivileged, and in 1975 was awarded the CBE for charitable services.

PROUDHON, Pierre Joseph
1809–1865

French journalist and socialist, born Besançon. Born into poverty, he became a printer's compositor in order to complete and extend his education, and then started his career as a publisher. After moving to Paris, he issued *Qu'est-ce que la propriété?*, which introduced his famous paradox that all property is theft, and in 1842 was tried for his revolutionary opinions, but was acquitted. During the 1848 revolution he was elected to the Assembly but the extreme views that he advocated in his newspapers—including the thesis that anarchy is but the culmination of social progress—brought him imprisonment and exile in Geneva. He soon returned to Paris to surrender himself to the authorities, was again jailed, and while in prison published *Confessions d'un révolutionnaire* (1849), *Actes de la Révolution* (1849), and *La Révolution sociale démontrée par le coup d'état* (1852). He was released in 1852 but was soon sentenced to a further three-year term, which was quashed after he went to Belgium and received an amnesty. In emphasizing the social necessity of liberty, equality and justice, and the development of a mature, self-controlling society in which the confines of law and government can be dispensed with, he is viewed as a forerunner of Marx. Certainly his body of work, which runs to 33 volumes of political argument and a further 14 volumes of letters, provides a unique record of advanced 19th-century socialist thinking.

PUAPUA, Dr Tomasi
1938–

Tuvaluan politician. After studying at the Fiji School of Medicine and graduating from Otago University, New Zealand, he worked as a doctor and became active in politics, and was elected Prime Minister in 1981, holding that office until he was defeated in the 1989 general election by Bikenibeu Paeniu. While cultivating international links to advance his country's economy, he was an outspoken critic of French nuclear tests on Mururoa Atoll in French Polynesia.

QUADROS, Janio
1917–

Brazilian statesman. He worked as a teacher and lawyer before being appointed governor of Sao Paulo in 1955, and served a seven-month term as President in 1961 before resigning and seeking exile. He eventually returned to his country, was rehabilitated, and became mayor of Sao Paulo in 1985.

QUAYLE, J Danforth ('Dan')
1947–

American politician, born Indianopolis. After practising as a lawyer for three years, he entered the House of Representatives as a Republican in 1977 and became senator for Indiana in 1981, but was virtually transparent until announced as the surprise choice of running mate for **George Bush** in the 1988 election. Accusations that he lied about his military record, and that his wealthy family had kept him from being sent to Vietnam, blighted the presidential campaign, but the **Reagan** legacy and Bush's personal popularity ensured Quayle's survival. During Quayle's vice-presidency, his sometimes ill-chosen remarks and actions have served as a constant source of material for critical commentators, and for comedians.

QUBOOS, bin Said
1940–

Sultan of Oman, born Salalah. The fourteenth member of the ruling Albusaid dynasty, after an education in England that was completed at Sandhurst, he grew impatient with his father's conservatism and overthrew him in a bloodless coup in 1970. He has since adopted liberal and expansionist policies, while maintaining his country's strict adherence to non-alignment, and has successfully resisted occasional incursions by Chinese-backed guerrillas.

QUESNAY, François
1694–1774

French economist, born Mérey. A former physician to **Louis XV**, he became famous as the leader of the physiocrats, who argued that land was the ultimate source of all wealth, and the author of several original and advanced economic theories. His *Tableaux Économiques* was a forerunner of the modern statistical tables of national income and expenditure.

QUEZON Y MOLINA, Manuel Luis
1878–1944

Filipino statesman, born Baler, Luzon. Following a six-year term as governor of Tayabas, he served as a commissioner in Washington, and returned in 1916 to become president of the senate, which office he held until 1935, when he was elected the Philippine Commonwealth's first President. He made courageous efforts to save his newly independent homeland from the Japanese invasion and to protect the defence forces of General MacArthur, but in response to a personal appeal by President **Franklin D. Roosevelt**, he eventually sought refuge in the USA in 1941 and died there three years later. The Phillipines capital from 1944 to 1976— Quezon City, near Manila—was named in his honour.

QUINCY, Josia
1772–1864

American politician, born Boston. The son of the New England revolutionary Josiah Quincy, he practised law before being elected a federalist member of the House of Representatives in 1804, where he campaigned vigorously against slavery, and was a senator from 1813 to 1820. He subsequently served as a member of the Massachusetts legislature and as mayor of Boston, and was a liberal and reforming president of Harvard from 1829 to 1845.

QUINET, Edgar
1803–75

French writer and politician, born Bourg. Elected to the National Assembly after taking an active part in the revolution, he aligned himself with the extreme left and was eventually exiled to Brussels, where he continued to write extensively and provocatively on the interaction of religion and politics. He returned to Paris after the downfall of **Napoleon III** to rally the patriots, and sat in both the Bordeaux and Versailles Assemblies. His prodigious output includes *La Republique* (1872) and *L'Esprit nouveau* (1874).

QUISLING, Vidkun (Abraham Lauritz Jonsson)
1887–1945

Norwegian diplomat and fascist leader, born Fyresdal. After army service, he worked as a League of Nations official, representing British interests in Russia, and was appointed Defence Minister in 1931. Two years later he founded the ultra right-wing National Unity Party as the equivalent of Hitler's national socialists, proclaimed himself Prime Minister following German occupation in 1940, and shortly afterwards was recognised by Berlin at least as Norway's administrative supremo, in which capacity he sent more than 1000 Jews to concentration camps. He was tried as a traitor in 1945 and executed.

RABIN, Itzhak
1922–

Israeli soldier and politician, born Jerusalem. He abandoned his agricultural education as a teenager and joined the Israeli Army, completing his training in Britain. He saw active service in the 1948–9 War of Independence, subsequently representing the Israeli Defence Forces at the Rhodes armistice. He was made IDF chief-of-staff in 1964, and took it to victory in the 1967 Six Day War. In 1968, he began a five-year term as ambassador to the USA, returning to Israel to become Labour party leader and Prime Minister (1974) and Defence Minister (1984).

RABUKA, Sitiveni
1948–

Fijian soldier and politician, born Drekeniwai, Sura. Educated at Queen Victoria School, he completed his army training at Sandhurst Military College in England, and then served with a UN peacekeeping force in the Lebanon, before returning to Fiji with the rank of colonel. When the 1987 elections produced an Indian-dominated coalition government, he engineered a coup that deposed the Prime Minister, Kamisese Mara, and established his own provisional Administration. In December 1987, he declared the country a republic and reinstated Mara as premier, while retaining control of the security forces and of internal affairs.

RADEK, Karl Bernardovich (K.B. Sobelson)
1885–1940

Russian author and politician, born Poland. Having made a start in his chosen career of journalism in his 20s, Radek was imprisoned several times for his support of the Social Democratic Party, fought in the Russian revolution, and tried unsuccessfully to organise a similar event in Germany in 1918. He joined the presidium of the Communist International the following year, but his influence waned with Comintern's failure, and in 1923 he began teaching at the Chinese University in Moscow. Accused of being a Trotskyite, he was expelled from the party in 1927, but was eventually rehabilitated and wrote frequently for *Izvestia*, as well as helping to draft the 1936 constitution. However, a year later he was found guilty of treason, and died in prison after serving four years of a 10-year sentence.

RAFSANJANI, Hojatoleslam Ali Akbar Hashemi
1934–

Iranian cleric and politician, born Rafsanjan, south-east Iran. Born into a wealthy farming family, he was tutored as a mullah by Ayatollah **Ruholla Khomeini** at the holy city of Qom from 1950, and his close friendship with his religious mentor brought him into conflict with Shah **Mohammed Reza Pahlavi** and brief imprisonment in 1963. During the 1970s, he became wealthy in his own right from his Teheran-based construction company, and remained in close contact with the exiled Ayatollah. With Khomeini's return to power in the 1979–80 Islamic Revolution, Rafsanjani became Speaker of the Iranian Parliament, in which capacity he was a moderating influence in reconciling the worst excesses of the fundamentalists with the needs of 20th-century international politics. A key figure in bringing an end to the 1980-8 war with Iraq, he was appointed President and his country's national leader on the death of Ayatollah Khomeini in August 1989.

RÁKOSI, Mátyás
1892–1971

Hungarian politician. First Secretary of the Communist Party from 1945 to 1956, his one-year term as Prime Minister from 1952 was characterized by his hard-line, Stalinist policies. He is credited with inventing the phrase 'salami tactics', to describe the technique of ideologically dividing one's political opponents, or of defeating political opposition little by little.

RAMPHAL, Sir Shridath Surrendranath ('Sonny')
1928–

Guyanan and Commonwealth lawyer and diplomat, born British Guiana. After studying law at King's College, London, he was called to the London Bar in 1951 and returned to British Guiana to work as a Crown Counsel, assistant attorney-general, and attorney-general, also serving as a draftsman, and assistant attorney-general for the West Indies. When his country achieved independence, he entered its National Assembly and subsequently held office as Minister for External Affairs (1967–72), and Foreign Minister (1972–3), and remained a member of the National Assembly until 1975, when he began a 14-year term as Secretary-General to the Commonwealth. His numerous published works on politics and the law include his early collected speeches *One World to Share* (1980), *Nkrumah and the Eighties* (1980), and *Inseparable Humanity* (1988).

RANJIT SINGH
1780–1839

Sikh ruler. Succeeding his father as head of his clan at 12 years of age, at 19 he led a victory over the Afghans to retrieve Lahore, and drove them from Amritsar two years later. By the time of his death, the Punjab's warring factions had been reconciled, and it had become India's most powerful state, due largely to his successful boundary negotiations with the British East India Company. *Ranjit Singh: Maharajah of the Punjab* (1962).

RASPUTIN, Grigori Efimovich
1871–1916

Russian peasant, charlatan, and royal adviser, born Pokrovskoye, Tobolsk. He achieved notoriety as a phony mystic who insisted that women could only achieve salvation through sexual intercourse with him (his name means 'debaucher'). His arrival in St Petersburg coincided with a fashion for mystical religion, and he soon engineered an introduction to the tsarina. His supposed ability to ease the bleeding of the haemophiliac crown prince and the tsar's preoccupation with World War I allowed Rasputin to exploit his place at court and to ensure the political advancement of his friends. Suspicious of Rasputin's growing influence, and appalled by stories of immorality involving the ladies of the court, a group of noblemen, led by Prince Felix Yusopov, resolved to take Rasputin's life. Their victim's size and strength reportedly made that far from easy, and it was necessary to have him poisoned, shot and then thrown into the River Neva to drown.

RATSIRAKA, Didier
1936–

Malagasy naval officer and politician, born Vatomandry. Educated for naval service in Madagascar and France, he was in the service from 1963 to 1970, when he was posted to Paris for two years to serve as a military attaché with the rank of lieutenant-colonel. In his absence, the traditional enmity between the country's two ethnic groups— the army-backed highland Merina and the *cotiers* (coast-dwellers), favoured by the Government—intensified, and martial law was imposed in 1975. Later that year, Ratsiraka was elected President under a new Constitution, and in 1976 founded the Advanced Guard for the Defence of the Malagasy Revolution, which formed the nucleus of his one-party system. Although AREMA retained overwhelming public support in the 1983 and 1989 Assembly elections, dislike of the Ratsiraka Government among the Merina has barely diminished.

RAU, Johannes
1931–

West German politician, born Wuppertal. The son of a Protestant pastor, he worked as a salesman for a church-music publisher before developing his interest in politics as a follower of Gustav Heinemann. He entered the Diet for the Social Democrats in 1958, chaired the SDP's parliamentary group between 1967 and 1970, and was Minister of Science and Research in 1978. As a progressive moderate, he was a popular choice as his party's deputy chairman in 1982, but his candidacy as chancellor in the 1987 Bundestag elections was blighted by the SPD's failing popularity, and he has since concentrated on his office as premier of his home state, which is the most populous in the country.

RAWLINGS, Flight-Lieutenant Jerry John
1947–

Ghanaian soldier and head of state, born Accra. As the leader of a bloodless coup in 1979, he supported a return to civilian government four months later, but threatened intervention if Ghana's political leaders again put their own interests before those of the country. In 1980, he was forced to retire from the army, but his personal popularity remained high among its lower ranks, and with their support he formed the Armed Forces Revolutionary Council, which seized power again at the end of 1981. Increasingly under pressure because of the unpopularity of his economic measures, he is faced with allowing greater democracy, or repressing dissent.

REAGAN, Ronald Wilson
1911–

Fortieth President of the USA, born Tampico, Illinois. The son of a bankrupted Irish immigrant shoe salesman, Reagan graduated in economics from Eureka College, Illinois, but drifted into broadcasting in 1932 as a radio sportscaster in Des Moines, and signed with Warner Brothers in 1937. He made his screen debut the same year in *Love is in the Air*, and went on to make another 53 films. As an admirer of **Franklin D. Roosevelt** and a liberal Democrat at first, he became interested in politics and served as president of the Screen Actors Guild between 1947 and 1952. The late 1950s saw a change in his political viewpoint, which coincided with his work as a presenter in programmes sponsored by the immutably conservative General Electric Corporation, and by 1962 he had declared himself a true Republican. His contribution to the Republicans' 1964 campaign was rewarded with the governorship of California two years later. He twice failed to win his party's presidential nomination in 1968 and 1976, but his highly successful stewardship of the sunshine state gave him the ticket in 1980, and he defeated **Jimmy Carter** in an election campaign that played on America's second-rate economy and defence programme. He survived an assassination attempt in 1981, and although the economy was still far from making a recovery, the American people—admiring his resolution during the successful Grenada invasion in 1983, and warming to his avuncular style— returned him to the White House with a record majority over the Democrats' **Walter Mondale** in 1984. His second term saw not only an upturn in the economy, but a change of philosophy from the hawkishness of his early days, and between 1985 and 1988 he attended four summit conferences with Soviet leader **Mikhail Gorbachev**, which resulted in the scrapping of intermediate nuclear forces. His Administration suffered a crisis of credibility over the 1986–7 Irangate scandal, but Reagan's personal reputation remained largely intact, to the extent that he devised the first trillion-dollar budget in 1987. His recovery from two cancer operations added to his public appeal, and he remained a popular public figure long after he nominated his Vice-President, **George Bush**, to succeed him in the 1989 election. In retirement, he has worked ceaselessly with his second wife, Nancy (1923–), at raising funds to establish the Ronald Reagan Library. His 1965 autobiography *Where's the Rest of Me?* was republished in 1981 as *My Early Life*. His later political life is described in *An American Life* (1990).

REDMOND, John Edward
1856–1918

Irish politician, born Dublin. The son of a Wexford MP, he was called to the London Bar in 1886 and entered Parliament in 1891. As an advocate of home rule, he led the Parnellite wing of the Nationalist Party from 1900 and supported Asquith's 1912–14 Bill, raising a volunteer force against Sir Edward Carson's resistance. Although he refused a seat in Asquith's 1915 wartime coalition, his strong support of the war lost him the support of the Irish electorate, and the Nationalists were trounced by Sinn Fein, whose violent methods to achieve Irish ambitions Redmond had always denounced.

REEVES, William Pember
1857–1932

New Zealand politician and reformer. As a progressive Minister of Education, Labour and Justice between 1891 and 1896, he initiated several significant labour reforms, which included arbitration and conciliation machinery. In 1905 he was posted to London as High Commissioner, and was director of the London School of Economics from 1908

until 1919. His published works include *The Long White Cloud: A History of New Zealand* (1898).

REGAN, Donald Thomas
1918–

American politician, born Cambridge, Massachusetts. The son of an Irish Catholic immigrant railway guard, Regan rose above his humble beginnings to study English and economics at Harvard, where his classmates included **John F. Kennedy**. At first a Democrat, he switched his loyalties to the Republicans in the 1940s, and in wartime service distinguished himself by becoming the youngest ever US marine line major. In 1946 he joined the brokers Merrill Lynch as a sales trainee, and by the time he became its president in 1968, the company was America's largest securities brokerage corporation. As an obvious worshipper of President **Ronald Reagan**'s supply-side economic creed, Regan was appointed Treasury Secretary in 1981 and implemented radical tax-cutting legislation that only succeeded in producing an escalating budget deficit. He became White House chief-of-staff in 1985 but was compelled to resign two years later, ostensibly over his role in the Irangate affair, though his controversial memoirs, *For the Record* (1988), which revealed Nancy Reagan's use of horoscopes in helping her husband to reach decisions on affairs of state, suggest that Donald Regan's growing disenchantment with the First Lady may also have been a factor in his dismissal.

REID, Sir George Houstoun
1845–1918

Australian politician and statesman, born Johnston, Renfrew. A resident first of Melbourne after his parents emigrated there in 1852, he moved to Sydney six years later, and after securing a junior appointment in the Treasury, he studied law, to become secretary to the Attorney-General of New South Wales in 1878. Two years later, he entered the state assembly, and in 1891 succeeded Sir Henry Parkes as Opposition leader. He was premier from 1894 to 1899, and joined the first federal Parliament in 1901, again as Opposition leader. He became Prime Minister of Australia in 1904, but was defeated a year later and retired from politics in 1908. In 1909, he was appointed Australia's first high commissioner to London, and when his posting ended in 1916, he remained in London and entered the Commons as MP for Hanover Square.

RENÉ, France-Albert
1935–

Seychelles politician. Educated in the Seychelles and Switzerland, and at King's College, London, he entered the Bar in 1957, and became active in politics on returning to the Seychelles in the early 1960s, founding the Seychelles People's United Party in 1964. Six years later, he strongly advocated complete independence, while his political opponent, James Mancham of the Seychelles Democratic Party, sought integration with the United Kingdom. When independence was achieved in 1976, the two leaders formed a coalition, with Mancham as President and Ren as Prime Minister. A year later, while Mancham was on a foreign trip, Ren seized control, proclaimed himself President, and declared a non-aligned one-party state.

RHEE, Syngman
1875–1965

Korean statesman, born Kaesong. As an early campaigner for constitutional reform, he was imprisoned from 1897 to 1904, spent some time in America, and returned to his Japanese-annexed homeland in 1910. Following the abortive 1919 uprising, he was appointed President of the provisional Government in exile, and returned in 1945 following the Japanese surrender that ended World War II. Three years later, he was elected President of the new Republic of South Korea, and in 1950 won United Nations backing to resist border invasions by the Communist forces of the North. The border was secured only after three years of costly fighting, led largely by General Douglas McArthur, and even then Rhee condemned the UN's 1953 peace treaty, which he viewed as appeasement rather than victory over the north. He was re-elected in 1956, and began his third term as head of state in March 1960—but a month later he was forced to leave office when leading members of his Cabinet resigned over his continuing and destructive attitude to partition, which had also triggered street riots by students sympathetic to the Communist regime. He spent his remaining years abroad. His published works include *Japan Inside Out* (1941).

RHODES, Cecil John
1853–1902

South African statesman, born Bishop's Stortford, England. The son of a vicar, he was a sickly child and was sent to Natal for the sake of his health. By his twenties, he had made a fortune at the Kimberley diamond diggings, and succesfully amalgamated several mining companies to form the De Beers Consolidated Mines Company in 1888. Meanwhile, he developed an interest in politics—sending **Parnell** £10000 to help advance the cause of home rule for Ireland—and on his return to England decided to advance his education, gained a degree at Oxford, and became a self-made millionaire. He next set about attempting to realise his ambition of a British-controlled Africa by promising protection to the Cape Dutch in return for allowing his northward advance, and inducing the British to declare a protectorate over Bechuanaland, as a means of extending the Transvaal. After purchasing the Matabele mining rights, he established the British South Africa Company in 1889 and Rhodesia soon after. Rhodes was Prime Minister from 1890 to 1896, during which time he granted the coloured population some say in their local government. He was bitter at his failure to negotiate a confederation with the South African Republic, whose recent discovery of gold made it economically independent, and gave President **Kruger** the confidence to become increasingly belligerent—refusing all political rights to the British and other foreigners. Rhodes's reaction was covertly to organize a disastrous raid in 1896, but his part in it was discovered, and the Boer War was triggered as a result. Forced to resign, Rhodes spent his remaining years nurturing his beloved Rhodesia, where he was buried. Part of his huge personal fortune was used to fund the Rhodes scholarships at Oxford University in perpetuity.

RIBBENTROP, Joachim von
1893–1946

German politician and diplomat. A wine merchant, he joined the National Socialists in 1932 and soon became **Hitler**'s foreign affairs adviser. From 1932 to 1936 he served as his country's London ambassador, and was appointed Minister in 1938—which post he held until he was taken into custody by the British at the end of World War II, tried for war crimes at Nuremberg, and executed.

RICARDO, David
1772–1823

English political economist, born London. After becoming a partner in the stockbroking firm owned by his father, and although Dutch-Jewish by birth, he became a Quaker in 1793 and converted to Christianity. Inspired by **Adam Smith**'s essay *The Wealth of Nations*, he argued for the supremecy of coinage over paper currency in a pamphlet published in 1809, which he followed with the *Principles of Political Economy and Taxation* (1817). He later abandoned its argument that the value of a commodity should be assessed by the amount of labour put into its production, but it was adopted by **Karl Marx** and so had lasting influence, as did his theory of comparative costs and their effect on international exchange, in helping to establish free trade. He sat in Parliament as a radical, for an Irish seat, from 1819 until his death. His country seat was Gatcombe Park, now the home of The Princess Royal, HRH Princess Anne. *David Ricardo: A Centenary Estimate* (1910).

ROBESPIERRE, Maximilien Marie Isidore de
1758–94

French revolutionary, born Arras, of Irish parentage. A successful advocate, he entered the Estates-General, later National Assembly, in 1789, and, by aligning himself with the extreme left and speaking virtually every sitting day, soon became immensely popular with the Paris commune and the extreme republican members of the Jacobin Club. In 1792, he resigned his office as public accuser and petitioned for a revolutionary tribunal and a new convention, and the murder of **Marat** the following year brought the proscription of the Girondists and Robespierre's election to the Committee of Public Safety. With real power at his disposal for the first time, he purged the National Assembly of ultra-revolutionaries, introduced strict economic control, and embarked on the establishment of a form of welfare state. However, Robespierre's growing autocracy coincided with a new era of ascendancy for the French army—resulting from successes such as that at the battle of Fleurus in 1794—that served to undermine the Reign of Terror's raison d'etre, and the prospect of Robespierre heading a dictatorship finally spurred his enemies into action. On 27 July 1794, he was denounced in the convention and a deputy called for his arrest. He was apprehended by the National Guard after being shot in the jaw, and the next day, he and 21 of his supporters were guillotined without trial.

ROBINSON, Arthur Napoleon (Ray)
1926–

Trinidad and Tobago politician. Educated in Trinidad and at Oxford, he qualified as a barrister, but turned to politics on returning home in the 1950s. When his country achieved independence in 1967, he was deputy leader of the moderate People National Movement, and in 1985 formed the breakaway National Alliance for Reconstruction. In the general election the following year, the NAR enjoyed a massive victory, and Robinson became Prime Minister.

ROBINSON, Mary
1944–

Irish President. A lawyer associated with human rights and civil liberties work, she was a member of the senate for 20 years. She stood twice for Labour but resigned from the Labour Party in 1985 in protest at the Anglo-Irish agreement. With a track record as an activist on behalf of homosexuals and illegitimate children, it was feared that she would be vulnerable during the presidential campaign to the charge of anti-family radicalism. In fact she polled very well among women even in rural areas. After the unexpected results of her election were announced on 7 November 1991 she attributed her victory to votes from the women of Ireland, who 'instead of rocking the cradle rocked the system'.

ROCARD, Michel
1930–

French politician, born Paris. The son of a nuclear scientist who worked on France's first atomic bomb, Rocard completed his education at the Ecole National d'Administration, where his classmates included **Jacques Chirac**, and joined the civil service as a finance inspector in 1958. In 1967, he was elected leader of the radical Unified Socialist Party, and stood as its presidential candidate in the 1969 election. On entering the National Assembly the same year, he joined the Socialist Party, and in 1973 emerged as leader of its moderate social-democratic faction, unsuccessfully challenging **François Mitterrand** for the 1981 presidential nomination. He served in Mitterrand's Administration as Planning and Agriculture Minister between 1983 and 1985, resigning over his Government's expedient introduction of proportional representation, but, in May 1988, benefiting from Mitterrand's need to nurture a wider span of support from within his own party, Rocard was appointed Prime Minister. However, his continuing moderacy brought an end to his premiership in 1991, when he was replaced by the left-winger **Edith Cresson**.

ROCKEFELLER, Nelson Aldrich
1908–79

American politician. The grandson of the fabulously wealthy industrialist John Davison Rockefeller, Snr (1839–1937), and the son of the philanthropist John Davison Rockefeller, Jnr (1874–1960), who donated to the United Nations the site that it occupies, Nelson served as Assistant Secretary of State for Latin American Affairs between 1944 and 1955, and as Health and Public Welfare Under-Secretary for one year from 1953. He was governor of New York from 1959 to 1973—the only Republican to enjoy a major victory in the 1958 election—and was Vice-President under **Gerald Ford** from 1974 to 1977.

RODGERS, William Thomas
1928–

British politician, born Liverpool. Educated in Liverpool and at Magdalen College, Oxford, he was general secretary of the Fabian Society between 1953 and 1960 before entering Parliament as the Labour Member for Stockon-on-Tees in 1962. He was a Trade and Treasury Minister in the Labour Administrations of the 1960s and mid 1970s, and was Transport Secretary from 1976 until his party's defeat in the 1979 general election. A strong supporter of Britain's membership of the Common Market at a time when that was not official Labour policy, Rodgers grew increasingly disenchanted with his party's isolationism and its growing dominance by the left, and resigned the Whip in 1981 to form with **Roy Jenkins**, **David Owen** and **Shirley Williams** the moderate Social Democratic Party. He lost his seat in the 1983 general election, but served the SDP in an administrative role, as its vice president, until

1987. Having nurtured the fading SDP's merger with the Liberal Party, he formally withdrew from national politics in 1987 to become director-general of the Royal Institute of British Architects. His books include an autobiography of Hugh Gaitskell, *The Politics of Change* (1982), and *Government and Industry* (1986).

ROH TAE WOO
1932–

South Korean politician, born Sinyong, Kyonsang. Educated at the Korean Military Academy from 1951 until 1955, where his classmates included a future president, Chun Doo-Hwan, Roh fought briefly in the Korean War and was a battalion commander in the Vietnam War. As commanding general from 1979, he used his position to help General Chun seize power in the coup of that year. Roh retired from the army in 1981 and held office in Chun's Administration as National Security and Foreign Minister (1981–2) and Home Affairs Minister (1982). He was elected chairman of the ruling Democratic Justice Party in 1985 and again in 1987, when, after responding to public demonstrations by drafting a package of political reform that restored democracy, he was also elected President. However, the increasing number of student demonstrations and growing street violence triggered by pro-communist students seeking reunification with the North has put his Administration under increasing pressure since the early 1990s.

ROOSEVELT, Franklin D(elano)
1882–1945

Thirty-second President of the USA, born Hyde Park, New York. America's most popular Democrat leader, with the possible exception only of **John F. Kennedy**, he triumped over paralysis from the waist down after contracting poliomyelitis in 1921, to become President in 1933 and the first to win re-election three times. Educated in Groton, Harvard and Colombia University Law School, he entered the state legislature in 1910 and was the Democrats' vice-presidential candidate in the 1920 campaign. After two terms as governor of New York, he defeated **Herbert Hoover** in the 1932 presidential race, and immediately confronted the task of rescuing his country from the economic ravages of the American Depression, using imaginative policies such as the

New Deal to stimulate agriculture, industry and employment. His landslide re-election in 1936 was followed by a term also characterized by domestic successes, though he failed to reform the Supreme Court. In 1940, he defeated Wendell Wilkie to achieved his presidential hat trick. With the outbreak of World War II, Roosevelt provided aid to the allies through lend-lease, and committed American forces to the conflict in 1941 after the Japanese bombing of Pearl Harbour. At the 1943 Casablanca conference, he devised with **Winston Churchill** and **Joseph Stalin** allied strategy for eastern and western Europe, and met them again two years later—having defeated Thomas E. Dewey in 1944 to begin his fourth presidential term—at the Yalta conference, which shaped the political map of post-war Europe. Roosevelt died in office, of a brain haemorrhage, on 12 April 1945. His wife Eleanor (1884–1962), whom he married in 1905, broke the mould of First Lady as social accessory, making a practical and valuable contribution to many aspects of her husband's Administrations. After his death, she served as US representative in the UN General Assembly from 1949 to 1952, and was then active in New York politics. She describes her life with and without Roosevelt in *This I Remember* (1948), *On My Own* (1958), and *The Autobiography of Eleanor Roosevelt* (1961).

ROOSEVELT, Theodore

1858–1919

Twenty-sixth President of the USA, born New York. Born into a wealthy family whose ancestors had emigrated from Holland in the 16th century, he entered the state legislature in 1881 and took an early stand against corruption, but left politics to become a rancher in North Dakota after the death of his wife in 1884 and because of his own poor health. In 1886, he remarried and resolved to make a political comeback, made an unsuccessful bid to be elected as mayor of New York, but accepted a post with the Civil Service Commission in 1889, which he left in 1895 to become president of New York City police board, redoubling his earlier efforts to break the links between the police and the underworld. In 1897 he was appointed assistant naval secretary, but resigned on the outbreak of war with Spain in 1898 to form the Rough Riders to fight in the Cuban campaign. Returning as a national hero, he was elected governor of New York in 1899,

and his ambitious programme of social reform brought him the vice-presidency in 1900, and the presidency on McKinley's assassination a year later. Re-elected in 1904, he promoted legislation against monopolies and the exploitation of child and female labour, and demonstrated America's power overseas through its intervention in the 1902 Venezuela and 1904 Dominica emergencies, and seizure of the canal zone to enable the building of the Panama Canal. His personal mediation in the Russo-Japanese War in 1905 brought him the Nobel Peace Prize the following year. His choice of his close friend **William Taft** as his running mate in 1908 proved to be one of Roosevelt's less successful moves, for Taft virtually engineered a conservative coup during his President's absence in Africa and Europe for most of 1909, to win the presidential nomination in 1912. Roosevelt stood as a candidate of a new Progressive Party, and **Woodrow Wilson** exploited the split to take the Democrats back into power. Roosevelt's popularity with the public remained undiminished, and at the time of his sudden death, he was still considered the leading Republican contender for the 1920 presidential race. *Theodore Roosevelt: An Autobiography* (1913).

ROSEBERY, Archibald Philip Primrose, 5th Earl of

1847–1929

British statesman, born London. Educated at Eton and Christ College, Oxford, he became Lord Rector of Aberdeen University in 1878, of Edinburgh in 1880, and of Glasgow in 1899, and from 1881 to 1883 served as a junior minister in the Home Office, then as commissioner of works. He was Foreign Secretary under Gladstone in 1886 and again from 1892 to 1894. In 1889–90 and again in 1892 he was chairman of London County Council, and assumed the Liberal premiership on Gladstone's retirement in 1894. He remained leader after his party's general election defeat the following year, but resigned in 1896. Thereafter, he advocated an imperial federation, contrary to official Liberal policy, and leaned increasingly towards Conservative policies in the first decade of the new century, but withdrew increasingly from political life to write political biographies and to indulge his love of horse racing. He was the owner of three Derby winners, in 1894, 1895, and 1905, and his contribution to the sport is commemorated still by the Rosebery Cup.

ROUSSEAU, Jean Jacques
1712–78

French political philosopher, educationist, and essayist, born in Geneva, Switzerland. Largely self-taught, he carried on a variety of menial occupations, until after he moved to Paris in 1741, where he came to know Diderot and the *encyclopédistes*. In 1754 he wrote *Discours sur l'origine de l'inégalité parmi les hommes* (1755, Discourse on the Origin and Foundations of Inequality Amongst Men), emphasizing the natural goodness of human beings, and the corrupting influences of institutionalized life. He later moved to Luxembourg (1757), where he wrote his masterpiece, *Du contrat social* (1762, The Social Contract), a great influence on French revolutionary thought, introducing the slogan 'Liberty, Equality, Fraternity'. The same year he published his major work on education, *Emile*, in novel form, but its views on monarchy and governmental institutions forced him to flee to Switzerland, and then England, at the invitation of David Hume. There he wrote most of his *Confessions* (published posthumously, 1782). He returned to Paris in 1767, where he continued to write, but gradually became insane. He died at Ermenonville.

ROWLING, Sir Wallace Edward
1927–

New Zealand politician, born Motueka, South Island. A graduate of Canterbury University, he served in the army education corp for several years, finally as assistant director of education, before becoming active in Labour politics and entering Parliament in 1962. He was Finance Minister until Norman Kirk's death in 1974, when Rowling succeeded him as Prime Minister until **Robert Muldoon**'s National Party returned to power in 1985, when Rowling accepted a posting as ambassador to the USA.

RUDDOCK, Joan Mary
1943–

British anti-nuclear campaigner and politician, born Pontypool, Wales. Educated in Wales and at Imperial College, London, she worked for Shelter, the national campaign for the homeless, between 1968 and 1973, and was then director of an Oxford housing aid centre. In 1977, she joined the Manpower Services Commission with special responsi-bilities for the young unemployed, and was chairperson of the Campaign for Nuclear Disarmament from 1981 until entering Parliament for Labour in 1987, almost immediately becoming a member of the Opposition Front Bench. Her published work includes *The CND Story* (1983), *CND Scrapbook* (1987), and *Voices for One World* (1988).

RUSHDIE, (Ahmed) Salman
1947–

British novelist. Educated at Cathedral School, Bombay and then at Rugby in England, he emigrated to Britain in 1965. After graduating from King's College, Cambridge, in 1968, he worked as an actor and a copywriter. His first novel, *Grimus*, published in 1975, was indifferently received, but *Midnight's Children* (1981), which takes as its subject India's independence, was hailed by the critics, won the Booker Prize, and became an international bestseller. *Shame* (1983), a satirical history of Pakistan and its leaders, was similarly well received. His fourth novel, *The Satanic Verses* (1988), was deemed incomprehensible by many critics, but it became instantly notorious for allegedly blaspheming Islam, and was instantly banned in India. The following year, Iran's spiritual leader, Ayatollah Khomeini, proclaimed a *fatwa*, or death sentence, against Rushdie and he went into hiding with constant police protection. However, improving relations with Iran in 1990–1, and Rushdie's declaration that he would not allow a paperback version of *The Satanic Verses* to be published, encouraged him to begin making public appearances again, even though the *fatwa* had not been officially lifted.

RUSK, Dean
1909–

American politician, born Cherokee County, Georgia. Educated at Davidson College, North Carolina, and St John's College, Oxford, he was appointed associate professor of government and dean of faculty at Mills College in 1934, and after army service in World War II, he held several Government posts between 1947 and 1951, including special assistant to the War Secretary, assistant Secretary of State for UN Affairs, and deputy Under-Secretary of State for Far Eastern Affairs. In 1952 he was appointed president of the Rockefeller Foundation, and from 1961 served as Secretary of State under **John F. Kennedy**, in which capacity he played a key rule in the 1962 Cuba missile crisis. He remained in office under the subsequent Administration of **Lyndon Baines Johnson**, retiring in 1969.

RUSKIN, John

1819–1900

English author and socialist, born London. The son of a wealthy wine merchant, he enjoyed a privileged upbringing and spent a great deal of his early life travelling and drawing, and his spirited defence of John Turner's work provided him with a new career as an art critic and lecturer. In his late 30s, he formulated the theory that great art required a society that embraced morality, high standards of education, and good social conditions. The views that he expressed in numerous publications—such as *Essays on Political Economy* (1862) and *Letters to the Workmen and Labourers of Great Britain* (1885–9) inspired the socialist movement of his time, and remain influential to this day.

RUSSELL, Bertrand Arthur William, 3rd Earl Russell

1872–1970

British philosopher, mathematician and author, born Trelleck, Gwent. Orphaned as a young child, he was brought up by his grandmother, the widow of Liberal Prime Minister Lord **John Russell**, finishing his education at Trinity College, Cambridge, where he got a first in mathematics and philosophy. In 1894, he was briefly with the staff of the British Embassy in Paris, but returned to England a year later to become a Fellow of Trinity and to marry. His first book, *German Social Democracy*, followed in 1896, and over the next 18 years he wrote several important academic works, including the hugely influential *The Principles of Mathematics*, and developed his theory of types and of descriptions. His accessible and entertaining layman's guide, *The Problems of Philosophy*, appeared in 1912, but his academic career came to a halt with the start of World War II, because of his vocal pacificism, which brought his imprisonment in 1918. While in gaol, he wrote *Introduction to Mathematical Philosophy*, which was published on his release a year later, when he began a series of lecture tours. His visit to

Russia, where he met **Lenin**, **Trotsky** and Gorky, sparked his interest in communism and inspired *Theory and Practice of Bolshevism* (1919). He married his second wife while lecturing in China in 1921, and on returning to England founded a progressive school near Petersfield at which they both taught, and produced *On Education* (1926) and *Education and the Social Order* (1932). The controversy surrounding his second divorce and remarriage, and the publication of *Marriage and Morals* (1932), led to the loss of his lectureship at City College, New York, but he subsequently won substantial damages for wrongful dismissal. He renounced pacifism at the start of 1939, and the rehabilitation that began with the award of an OM in 1944, and the restoration of his Trinity fellowship in 1945, was completed with an invitation to give the first Reith Lecture in 1949. He was awarded the Nobel Prize for Literature the following year. His output in that period included *An Enquiry into Meaning and Truth* (1940), *Human Knowledge: its Scope and Limits* (1938), and the best-seller *History of Western Philosophy* (1945). The 1950s saw Russell becoming increasingly identified with the movement for nuclear disarmament as a leading member of CND and the Committee of 100. In 1961, at 89 years of age, he was again imprisoned, with his fourth wife, for his part in a CND sit-down in Whitehall. His final years were spent in Wales, and his three-volume *Autobiography* (1967–9) provides evidence that he retained his extraordinary intellectual powers to the end.

RUSSELL, John, 1st Earl Russell

1792–1878

British statesman, born London. A graduate of the University of Edinburgh, he entered Parliament for the Liberals in 1813, and his untiring efforts to bring about social reforms helped to win many more seats for his party in the 1830 general election, driving the Duke of **Wellington** from office. Under Earl **Grey**, Russell became paymaster of the armed services, and was then entrusted with helping to draft the first (1832) Reform Bill, which he also presented to Parliament. He lost his office together with Melbourne in 1834, but returned to power on **Peel**'s downfall in 1835, first as Home Secretary, then Colonial Secretary and Leader of the Commons. In the 1841 election he was returned to represent the City of London, which seat he held until moving to the Lords. On the repeal of the Corn Laws in 1846, Peel was again defeated and Russell assumed the premiership at the head of the Whig Administration that lasted until 1852. He then joined Lord **Aberdeen**'s coalition as Foreign Secretary and Leader of the Commons, but his misjudged 1854 Reform Bill, together with his poor stewardship of the Crimean campaign and of the Vienna Conference, saw him leave office for four years. In 1859 he returned as Foreign secretary under **Palmerston**, and received an earldom in 1861. He became Prime Minister once again on Palmerston's death in 1865, but was defeated in his attempt to introduce yet another Reform Bill in 1865 and was forced to resign.

RYKOV, Alexei Ivanovich

1881–1938

Russian politician. A Social Democrat at first, he subsequently joined the Bolsheviks in 1905 and was imprisoned several times for associating with them. After the revolution, he headed the Supreme Economic Council until 1924, when he succeeded **Lenin** as USSR premier. He was removed by **Stalin** in 1930, but was allowed to return to the Government a year later after recanting his opposition to Stalin's policies. But his rehabilitation was short-lived, and in 1936 he was charged with complicity in a plot to murder Stalin and was executed.

RYZHKOV, Nikolai

1929–

Soviet politician, born in the Urals. He worked as a miner before studying engineering at the Urals Polytechnic in Sverdlovsk. He subsequently joined a local heavy-machinery manufacturing plant as a welding foreman, but eventually rose to head the Soviet Union's largest engineering conglomerate, Uralmash—which is also the country's biggest industrial enterprise. A CPSU member since the mid-1950s, he was invited to Moscow in 1975 to work as deputy Minister for Transport and Machinery, and four years later became first deputy chairman of the state purchasing organisation Gosplan. In 1982, **Yuri Andropov** recruited him as head of economic affairs, and in 1985, he was brought into the Politburo by **Mikhail Gorbachev** and appointed Prime Minister with a special brief to restructure the discredited state planning process. More cautious in his approach to reform than Gorbachev, and considerably less flamboyant than **Boris Yeltsin**, he is viewed as a steadying and stable influence in overcoming the economic and infrastructural problems that have blighted Gorbachev's new-look USSR since the end of the 1980s—and as a possible future Soviet leader. He was forced to step down as Prime Minister in 1991 due to ill health.

SABAH, Sheikh Jaber al-Ahmad al-Jaber al-

1928–

Emir of Kuwait, born Kuwait City. Educated at Almubarakiyyah School, Kuwait, and privately, as a member of the family that has ruled the country since the 18th century, he was appointed governor of the Ahmadi and oil areas in 1949, and in 1959 became president of the Kuwaiti department of finance and economy, and Minister of Finance, Industry and Commerce in 1963. He was made Prime Minister in 1965, and after being proclaimed Crown Prince in 1966, succeeded his uncle as Emir in 1978. When Iraqi dictator **Saddam Hussein** ordered the invasion of Kuwait in November 1991 following a dispute over oil revenues, the Emir, the Crown Prince, and other members of the royal family fled to Saudi Arabia to lead a government-in-exile. In April 1991, in his first public speech since returning to his country, the Emir announced that the first elections since Parliament was suspended in 1986 would be held within 12 months, and hinted also that women might be given the vote for the first time since Kuwait gained independence in 1962.

SABAH, Sheikh Saad al-Abdullah al-Salen al-

1930–

Crown Prince of Kuwait, born Kuwait City. Educated at schools in Kuwait and trained at Hendon Police College, England, he was appointed deputy chief of his country's police and public security department in 1959, and became its head two years later with the office also of Minister of the Interior. He was Minister of Defence from 1965 until 1978, when he was proclaimed Crown Prince and appointed Prime Minister. On returning to Kuwait after the 1991 Gulf War, he promised to re-enact the constitution implemented when the country gained independence in 1962 but suspended in 1986, which provided for an elected Parliament but would give only 62 000 of the country's 500 000 population the vote. Opposition parties were also disappointed by the membership of the Crown Prince's new Cabinet, for although it included 11 new faces, eight of the 22 Ministers are members of the Sabah family. The former Foreign and Defence Ministers were dismissed over their handling of the 1990 Gulf crisis, but were replaced by other members of the Sabah family. However, the Crown Prince, pledged, together with his father the Emir, a return to a limited form of parliamentary democracy—but one in which they will retain overall control.

SACHEVERELL, William
1638–91

English politician, born Marlborough. Known as the first Whig, he studied law and entered Parliament in 1670 as a member of the anti-Court party that, aided by his outstanding powers of oratory, overthrew the cabal ministry of **Charles II**. A supporter of the Exclusion Bill, he was fined by Judge Jeffreys for opposing the king's Nottingham charter and defeated in the 1685 election. He was returned to the Convention Parliament of 1689 that offered the throne to **William III**.

SACKVILLE, Thomas, 1st Earl of Dorset
1536–1608

English statesman and dramatist, born Buckhurst, Surrey. A barrister, he entered Parliament in 1558, and is probably the only MP ever to have his own dramatic work performed before the monarch, when his blank verse tragedy, *Ferrex and Porres* (later retitled *Gorbuduc*) was presented to Queen **Elizabeth I**. While on one of his many excursions abroad, he was imprisoned in Rome as a suspected spy, but on his safe return to England was given both a knighthood and a peerage by his queen, after which he served as a diplomat in France and the Netherlands. To him fell the duty of announcing to **Mary Queen of Scots** the death sentence that had been passed upon her. He subsequently held office as Lord High Treasurer, and was created Earl of Dorset in 1604.

SADAT, Muhammad Anwar
1918–81

Egyptian soldier and statesman, born in the Tala district. Commissioned in 1938, he was imprisoned during World War II for consorting with Nazi Germany in his efforts, as a fervent nationalist and Muslim, to overthrow the British-dominated monarchy, and in 1952 played a leading role in the Army coup that deposed King **Farouk**. Under **Gamal Abdel Nasser** he served from 1964 as one of four Vice-Presidents, becoming the sole holder of the office in 1969. He was elected President on Nasser's death in 1970, and subsequently temporarily assumed the office of Prime Minister, and that of military governor-general during the Arab-Israeli War of 1973. He relinquished the premiership the following year, and then worked unceasingly to achieve a negotiated end to the hostilities, culminating with his unprecedented peace trip to Israel and the Camp David settlement in 1978, for which he and Israeli leader **Menachim Begin** were awarded the Nobel Peace Prize. But his success at international diplomacy was overshadowed by a failing economy and domestic strife and, three years after becoming the first Arab to sign a peace treaty with Israel, he was assassinated by Muslim extremist officers while reviewing an Army parade. Sadat's autobiography, *In Search of Identity*, was published in 1978.

SAFAVIDS

A Kurdish dynasty that provided the shahs of Persia from 1501 to 1722. Its most prominent members were Shaykh Zamahid-i Gimalamanima, who founded the revolutionary Sumafima religious movement, which was strengthened under his successors by the Turkish tribesmen of Azerbaijan and eastern Anatolia; and Ismama'imal, who led the defeat of the Turkish confederation in 1501 and developed the form of Islam that is the prominent religion of modern Iran. The Safavids' influence waned under civil war and internecine disputes, but was rekindled under Abbamas the Great, whose military and social reforms outlasted his mediocre successors and enabled the state to resist the Ottomans and Uzbeks until it was overthrown by the Afghans in the 18th century.

SAINT LAURENT, Louis Stephen
1882–1973

Canadian politician, born Compton, Quebec. Already a distinguished lawyer, he entered the Dominion Parliament in 1941 as a Liberal, and served as Minister of Justice and

Attorney-general and Minister of External Affairs before becoming party leader and Prime Minister in 1948. He resigned the premiership after his party's defeat in the 1957 election.

SAINT–SIMON, Claude Henri
1760-1825

French social philosopher, born Paris. After fighting in the American War of Independence, he returned to France and imprisonment as an aristocrat, but subsequently made a new fortune through land speculation. But divorce and lavish living brought him poverty, which doubtless inspired his first work on Socialism, *L'Industrie*, in 1817. His simplistic but undeniably influential arguments for replacing his country's feudal and military system with an industrial order, and for entrusting its people's spiritual wellbeing to men of science rather than to the Church, were presented in four further works—the last and most important of which, *Nouveau Christianisme*, was published in the year of his death.

SAKHAROV, Andrei Dimitrievich
1921–89

Soviet physicist and dissident, born Moscow. Graduating from Moscow State University in 1942, he won a doctorate for work on cosmic rays and was instrumental in developing Russia's first hydrogen bomb, receiving the accolade of being the youngest member ever to be admitted to the Soviet Academy of Sciences. Over the next two decades, he agitated for international nuclear test-ban treaties and peaceful co-existence, and for more freedom of expression in his own country. His speeches and writings led in 1980 to his internal exile in Gorky with his wife. He endured several hunger strikes to draw attention to his wife's medical needs. Freed in 1986 on the personal orders of **Mikhail Gorbachev**, he was elected to the Congress of the USSR People's Deputies in 1989. His political works include *Intellectual Freedom* (1968) and *Alarm and Hope* (1978). His autobiography, *Memoirs*, was published posthumously in 1990.

SALANDRA, Antonio
1853–1931

Italian statesman, born Troia, Foggia. A lawyer and an expert in economics, he became a deputy of the rightist Liberals in 1886, and served in several senior Treasury posts under **Sidney Sonnino**. On his resignation in 1914, Salandra replaced him as Prime Minister, ensuring instant popularity by immediately announcing Italy's neutrality in World War I, which he rescinded the following year when Austria refused to reciprocate with territorial concessions. His belief that Italy's participation in hostilities would be short-lived proved erroneous, and his Government fell in 1916. When Luigi Facta's Administration collapsed in 1922, Salandra made an abortive attempt to form a Liberal-Nationalist coalition, and the mandate was instead offered to **Benito Mussolini**. In 1924, he resigned after two years as Italy's representative to the League of Nations, bitterly disillusioned by Mussolini's dictatorial ambitions. He was appointed to the Senate in 1928, but spent most of his remaining years writing autobiographical works, including *Ricordi e Pensieri* (1930) and *Memorie Politiche* (1951).

SALAZAR, Antonio de Oliveira
1889–1970

Portuguese dictator, born near Coimbra. A professor of economics, he joined **Antonio Carmona**'s administration as Finance Minister in 1928, rescuing the country from financial chaos. He became Prime Minister four years later. Serving also as both war and foreign minister from 1936 to 1944, he maintained Portuguese neutrality, and held the latter office until 1947. He suppressed overt political opposition and elections as support for his Government waned—as was evident in the 1959 elections. He suffered a stroke in 1968 and seemed unaware that he was no longer Prime Minister at the time of his death.

SALDANHA, João Carlos, Duke of
1790–1876

Portuguese soldier and statesman, born Arinhaga. After service at Buscao in 1810 and in Brazil's war against Montevideo between 1817 and 1822, he supported the constitutionalist forces of Don Pedro against Dom Miguel, and for a decade from 1846 was both a member of the Government and a leader of armed opposition. Given a dukedom in 1846, he was twice ambassador to Rome, Prime Minister in 1870, and ambassador to London from 1871.

SALEH, Ali Abdullah
1942–

North Yemeni soldier and politician. As an army colonel in the Yemen Arab Republic, he helped engineer Ibrahim al–Hamedi's 1974 coup to restore the monarchy, and on his assassination in 1977, supported his successor, Hussein al-Ghashmi, who was also murdered within a year of taking office. The country, sickened by violence and division, turned to Saleh to assume the presidency, and was repaid by his success in achieving the eventual reunification of North and South Yemen in 1990.

SALLUST (Gaius Sallustius Crispus)
86–34 BC

Roman historian and politician, born Amiternum. As a tribune, in 52 BC he was among those who avenged the murder of Claudius, but his almost unparalleled licentiousness brought him numerous expulsions from the Senate, though they may have had more to do with his support of **Caesar**'s party. Returning to the Senate in 50 BC, he was made Governor of Numidia after the African campaign, and used the the fruits of his corruption in that office to build splendid residencies at Nerva, Vespasian and Aurelian. In retirement, he drew on the model of Greek literature in writing his famous histories, *Bellum Catalinae, Bellum Iugurthinum*, and *Historiarum Libri Quinque*.

SALMOND, Alex
1955–

Scottish nationalist, born Linlithgow. He joined the Scottish National Party at 19 while still a student at St Andrews University, graduated in economics, and worked for the Scottish agricultural ministry and the Royal Bank of Scotland before winning Banff and Buchan for the SNP in the 1987 general election. He soon endeared himself to the left-wingers in his own party, and his potential appeal to disaffected Scottish Labour voters helped him to achieve a clear victory in the party's 1990 election of a successor to party leader Gordon Wilson.

SAMUEL, Herbert Louis, 1st Viscount Samuel
1870–1963

British politician and political philosopher. Educated at University College School and Bailliol College, Oxford, he entered Parliament in 1902 and between 1909 and 1932 held office as Chancellor of the Duchy of Lancaster, Postmaster-General and Home Secretary. He served as High Commissioner for Palestine from 1920 to 1925, and was ennobled in 1937. His books include *Belief and Action* (1937) and *In Search of Reality* (1957).

SANDS, Bobby
1954–81

Irish revolutionary, born Belfast. He had been a member of the IRA for only one year when, in 1973, he began a five-year gaol term for possessing firearms, and shortly after his release in 1977 he was found guilty of a bomb attack on a factory and sentenced to 14 years' imprisonment. In March 1981 he began a hunger strike in protest at the authorities' refusal to allow him and others found guilty of terrorist offences certain privileges usually accorded to political prisoners. The following month, he was elected to Parliament in the Fermanagh-South Tyrone by-election, but maintained his fast and died in May. His example was followed by nine other republican prisoners the same year.

SAN YU, U
1919–

Burmese soldier and politician, born Prome. After service in World War II under **Ne Win** and in the wake of the country's independence, he held several senior army posts and was a member of the revolutionary council that seized power in 1962. He subsequently served as Minister of Finance and of Defence, and as Army Chief of Staff, and was Secretary-General of the Burmese Socialist Programme Party (BSPP) from 1973 until he began a seven-year term as Ne Win's successor as State President in 1981. His resignation in 1988, and that of a number of senior BSPP figures, followed violent anti-government demonstrations in Rangoon.

SANDWICH, John Montagu, 4th Earl of
1718–92

English politician. Twice Lord of the Admiralty, his incompetence contributed much to British failures in the American War of Independence. He is better remembered for his corruptness and membership of the Hellfire Club, and for aiding the persecution of his former friend, **John Wilkes**. It is said that he created the snack that bears his name as a convenient way of satisfying his hunger during long sessions at the gaming table.

SANGUINETTI, Julio Maria
1936–

Uruguayan politician. Elected to the Assembly in 1962 as a member of the progressive Colorado Party, he headed the labour, industry and culture ministries, but was forcibly removed from office in 1972 under the oppressive military regime of Juan Maria Bordaberry. He was elected President of a government of national accord following the restoration in 1986 of democracy and the 1966 constitution.

SARNEY COSTA, José
1930–

Brazilian soldier and politician, born Maranhao state. Elected to the State Assembly at 20, he became governor in 1965 and President of the Social Democratic Party in 1970. With the introduction of open elections in 1985, he became deputy to Tancredo Neves, the country's first civilian leader for 21 years, but resumed the presidency on Neves's death a few months later.

SASSAU–NGUESSO, Denis
1943–

Congolese soldier and politician. Assuming the presidency in 1979 after his predecessor had been assassinated in a coup, he handed over real power to his own Congolese Labour Party's central committee. He has been successful in strengthening the Congo's relationship with France and the USA in preference to maintaining its traditional ties with the USSR, and his continuing popularity was reflected in his re-election in 1984.

SAVAGE, Michael Joseph
1872–1940

New Zealand politician. Born in Australia, he won a reputation as a moderate trade unionist after emigrating in 1907, and helped to form the country's Labour party in 1916. Elected to Parliament in 1919, he was made party leader in 1933 and was elected the country's first Labour premier in the 1935 election with a manifesto that favoured rural interests. His popularity was consolidated with re-election in 1938, but he died in office two years later after making his historic wartime pledge to Britain, 'Wherever she goes, we go—where she stands, we stand.'

SCANLON, Hugh
1913–

British trade union leader, born Stretford. Educated at Stretford Elementary School, on finishing his engineering apprenticeship he joined AEI in Trafford Park and soon became involved in union activities as a shop steward of the Amalgamated Engineering Union. He was the AEU's divisional organizer in Manchester from 1947 to 1963, when he was elected to the union's executive council, and in 1968 was appointed union president and a member of the TUC General Council. He was also a member of the National Economic Development Council (1971), Metrication Board (1973–8), National Enterprise Board (1977–9), and chaired the Engineering Industry Training Board from 1975 to 1982. Considered a moderate in comparison with many of the labour organization leaders of the 1960s and 1970s, in 1979 he was rewarded for his contribution to the union movement with a life peerage on the recommendation of **James Callaghan** when he lost office in that year's general election.

SCARFE, Gerald
1936–

English political and social caricaturist and cartoonist, born London. After studying at St Martin's School of Art, he contributed to several publications, but found his metier with the renaissance of political satire in the 1960s. The demand for his vicious and grotesques caricatures of public figures, which appeared frequently in *Private Eye* (several issues of which were banned by the distributors because of his work) and many other national newspapers and magazines, soon spread to America, and he has frequently contributed to *Esquire* and *Life*. His more commercial work includes the animated sequences used in the Pink Floyd rock concert *The Wall*, the most significant recent performance of which was staged at the Berlin Wall in 1990 as part of Germany's reunification celebrations. His book *Scarfeland* (1990) brilliantly depicts world leaders as different kinds of animals.

SCARGILL, Arthur
1938–

English trade union leader, born Yorkshire. A miner from the age of 18, he joined the

Young Communist League in 1955, Co-Operative Party in 1963, and Labour Party in 1966. He then became active in the National Union of Mineworkers, of which he was elected Yorkshire area president in 1973. In 1984, three years after becoming national president, he led his union in a year-long strike over pit closures, which proved to be the most violent and socially divisive to occur since the end of the war. The action was aimed partly at bringing down the Conservative government under **Margaret Thatcher**, in the same way that the miners had contributed to the industrial strife that lost **Edward Heath** the 1974 election. Thwarted by industry's greater reliance on other forms of fuel and coal stockpiling at power stations, and following sequestration of the NUM's assets and the formation of the moderate breakaway Union of Democratic Mineworkers, the strike collapsed. Scargill narrowly defeated a moderate candidate for another five-year term as president in 1988 after his predictions of closures and huge job losses proved correct, but two years later his leadership again came under threat over revelations that £1.4 million in strike funds donated by Soviet miners was still held by the Paris-based International Mineworkers Organization that he had founded, but he remained in office after arranging for the money to be transferred to the NUM.

SCARMAN, Lord

1911–

British judge and Law Lord, born London. Educated at Radley College and Oxford University, he was a Harmsworth Law Scholar before being called to the Bar in 1936, and served in the RAF Volunteer Reserve from 1940 to 1945. After being made a QC in 1956, he was appointed to the High Court of Justice in 1961, and was chairman of the Law Commission from 1965 to 1972. He was a Lord Justice of Appeal from 1973 until 1977, when he received a life peerage and was appointed a Lord of Appeal. One of the most independent-minded members of the judiciary, his 1981 report on the Brixton riots was praised by leaders of the capital's black community for its impartiality and criticism of some aspects of police reaction. He retired as a Lord of Appeal in 1986, but continues to contribute regularly to debates in the Upper House as a Cross-Bencher. His books include *Pattern of Law Reform* (1967), and *English Law—The New Dimension* (1974).

SCHARANSKY, Natan (Anatoly Borisovich)

1948–

Soviet academic and dissident, born Donetsk. The son of a Jewish writer, and a brilliant mathematician, his disillusionment with Soviet society and repeated denials by the authorities of his request to emigrate to Israel prompted him to join informal dissident groups and, in 1976, Yuri Orlov's Helsinki Watch Group, formed to monitor human rights violations. Less than a year later, Scharansky was sentenced to 13 years' hard labour for alleged espionage on behalf of the CIA, but an East-West spy exchange in 1986 brought him freedom. He was at last able to settle in his chosen homeland, and in 1989 was nominated as Israel's ambassador to the United Nations.

SCHEEL, Walter

1919–

West German statesman. After war service as a Luftwaffe pilot, he went into business and was elected to the Bundestag as a Free Democrat in 1953. He was made party Vice-Chairman in 1958, leading the policy review that led to the coalition with the Social Democratic Party in 1969. On his appointment as Foreign Minister the following year, he signed significant treaties with Russia and Poland, and held office also as Vice-Chancellor until 1974, when he began a five-year term as President.

SCHEIDEMANN, Philipp

1865–1939

German politician. A Socialist leader who served as finance and colonial minister in the 1918 provisional government, he became the republic's first Chancellor in 1919.

SCHIRACH, Baldur von

1907–74

Nazi politician, born Berlin. He founded the Hitler Youth in 1933, a year after entering the Reichstag, and remained its leader until 1940, when he was appointed Gauleiter of Vienna. Captured in 1945, he was found guilty at Nuremberg of the mass deportation of Jews and was imprisoned in Spandau for 20 years, being released in 1966.

SCHLEICHER, Kurt von
1882–1934

German general and politician, born Brandenburg. A member of the General Staff in World War I, he succeeded Franz von Papen as Chancellor in 1932, but his failure to appease both the Nazis and trade unions forced his resignation within a year, allowing **Adolf Hitler** to seize power. He was later murdered.

SCHLUTER, Poul Holmskov
1929–

Danish politician. After a successful early career in law, he became leader of the Conservative Youth Movement in 1944 and national leader seven years later. He joined the executive committee of the Conservative People's Party in 1964, and became chairman in 1972—10 years after his election to Parliament. His 1982 premiership of a centre-right coalition survived the 1987 election, after which he reconsituted the coalition with Liberal support.

SCHMIDT, Helmut (Heinrich Waldemar)
1918–

West German statesman, born Hamburg. A group leader in the Hitler Youth, his work in the Wehrmacht in World War II brought him the Iron Cross, and when peace came he studied at Hamburg University, becoming the first national chairman of the Socialist Student Leagues. He entered the Bundestag in 1953 as a rightist Social Democratic Party candidate, and consolidated his reputation by his proficiency as Senator of Domestic Affairs in coping with the 1962 Elbe floods. After serving as SPD parliamentary leader between 1969 and 1972, he held office as Defence Minister, and as Finance Minister from 1972 to 1974 laid the foundations for the two decades of growth that made it possible for the FDR to sustain the economic demands of the unification of the two Germanies in 1990.

SCHUMACHER, Kurt Ernst
1895–1952

German statesman, born Kilm, Prussia. A student of law and political science at Leipzig and Berlin universities, he joined the Reichstag as a Social Democrat in 1930. His criticism of the National Socialists was rewarded with 10 years' incarceration in Nazi concentration camps. On his release at the end of the war, he became party and parliamentary chairman, and was a strong opponent of Germany's integration with the other armed forces of Western Europe.

SCHUMAN, Robert
1886–1963

French politician, born Luxembourg. A resistance fighter in World War II, he became Prime Minister in 1947 and devised a scheme for pooling Western Europe's coal and steel resources to help ensure its post-war reconstruction. He was elected President of the European Assembly in 1958 and was a recipient of the Charlemagne Prize. He survived **Charles de Gaulle**'s electoral reforms, securing re-election to the National Assembly in 1958.

SCHURZ, Carl
1829–1906

German-American politician, born Cologne. After joining the revolutionary movement of 1849, he went to the USA where he worked as a journalist and lecturer, served as a major-general in the Civil War, and was a member of the Senate from 1869 to 1875. He held office as Minister of the Interior between 1877 and 1881. His autobiography, *Reminiscences*, was published posthumously in 1909.

SCHUSCHNIGG, Kurt von
1897–1977

Austrian statesman, born Riva. A decorated World War I veteran, he was elected a Christian Democrat deputy in 1927 and held office as Justice and Education Minister before becoming Chancellor on the murder of **Engelbert Dollfuss** in 1934. He was imprisoned by the Nazis until Austria's liberation in 1945, and spent his remaining years as a professor of political science at an American university. He wrote *Farewell Austria* (1938) and *Austrian Requiem* (1947).

SCHUYLER, Philip John
1733-1804

American revolutionary and politician, born Albany, New York. After fighting at Lake George in 1755, he joined the colonial assembly in 1768 and was a delegate to the continental congress of 1775 as one of the first four revolutionary major-generals. He was preparing to invade Canada in 1877 on **George Washington**'s instructions when ill health forced him to resign. He subsequently served as commissioner for Indian affairs, was a member of both the Congress and Senate, and a state surveyor. As a joint leader of the Federal party, he also helped to prepare New York State's constitution.

SCHWARZENBERG, Felix Ludwig Johann Friedrich

1800–52

Austrian statesman. A former diplomat, he became Prime Minister during the 1848 revolution, restoring order to the Hapsburg empire and establishing a new constitution that strengthened the emperor's power. He also thwarted Prussian ambitions to establish and dominate a union of German states.

SCHWARZKOPF, General H. Norman ('Stormin' Norman')

1935–

American general. Born into a military family with strong military ties, he became a cadet at the age of ten and entered the US Army after graduating from West Point Military Academy. Having given distinguished service during two tours of duty in the Vietnam War and in the 1986 US invasion of Grenada, he was given overall command of the coalition land forces in Operation Desert Shield Storm following the Iraqi invasion of Kuwait in November 1990. An inspiration to his 675000-strong infantry he masterminded the brilliant offensive that in just 100 hours brought an end to the war with minimal casualties among the coalition forces. On his return from the Gulf in June 1991, he confirmed that he would retire from the army later in the year, after 35 year's service, and was immediately invited by the Republicans to stand as Governor for Florida.

SCIASCIA, Leonardo

1921–89

Sicilian novelist and politician, born Racalmuto, the author of many influential works on the political, social and spiritual nature of Europe which have only recently reached a wider audience in translation. They include *Salt in the Wound*, *Candido* (1977), *The Council of Egypt* (1980) and *To Each His Own* (1989).

SCIPIO, Publius Cornelius

237–183 BC

Roman general. Regarded as Rome's greatest military leader before **Julius Caesar**, as general extraordinary to Spain, he first captured Nova Carthago, stronghold of the Carthaginians, in 209 BC, and went on to conquer the whole of the country, a year later sailing to Africa with a huge army to subjugate that continent. His successes prompted the Carthaginians to recall **Hannibal** from Italy, but Scipio triumped at Zama in 202 BC and a peace was concluded months later. He refused to accept the titles of consul and dictator for life, and in 190 served as legate under his brother Lucius in the war with Antiochus, but after seizing victory in the battle of Magnesia, they returned to face charges by the Senate of having been bribed by Antiochus to agree a lenient armistice. Popular support ensured his survival, but he soon retired from public life.

SCULZE–DELITZSCH, Hermann

1808–83

German economist and politician, born Delitzsch in Prussian Saxony. An advocate of constitutional and social reform, he founded the first people's bank on a co-operative basis, the success of which led to the concept being adopted throughout Europe.

SEAGA, Edward Philip George

1930–

American-born Jamaican politician. After studying at Harvard and teaching at the University of the West Indies, he joined the Jamaica Labour Party and entered the House of Representatives in 1962. He held several posts under Hugh Shearer before returning to lead the Opposition in 1974. He became premier after his party's surprise victory over **Michael Manley** in 1980, which he consolidated with a snap election in 1983 in which the JLP captured all the seats in the Assembly, but suffered a landslide defeat by Manley in the 1989 election.

SECKENDORFF, Veit Ludwig von

1626–92

German historian and statesman. A valued counsellor to the princes of Saxony and Brandenburg, he became chancellor of Halle university, and wrote a Latin compendium of church history and *De Lutheranismo* (1688).

SEDDON, Richard John
1845–1906

British-born New Zealand statesman, born Lancashire. Emigrating to Australia at 18, he found work in the goldfields and was elected to the House of Representatives as a Liberal in 1879, and succeeded John Ballance as Prime Minister a year later, which office he held until his death. His administration saw the normalizing of relations with Australia, troop support to Britain in the Boer War, and annexation of the Cook Islands. He also introduced state-controlled coal mining, fire insurance and housebuilding.

SELWYN–LLOYD, Baron (John) Selwyn Brooke
1904–78

English politician, born Liverpool. After graduating from Cambridge, he practised law and entered local politics, and was unsuccessful as a Liberal candidate in 1930 before moving to the Conservative party. He rose from staff officer to colonel, General Staff in World War II, and finally won election to Parliament in 1947. He held various ministerial appointments from 1951, and was Foreign Secretary under **Anthony Eden** during the 1956 Suez crisis until 1960, when he became Chancellor of the Exchequer, but was forced to resign in **Harold Macmillan**'s 'night of the long knives' in 1962. He continued to hold token office as Lord Privy Seal and Leader of the House of Commons before a successful term as Speaker from 1971 to 1976. He received a peerage in 1976.

SENECA (The Younger), Lucius Annaeus
4 BC–AD 65

Roman philosopher and politician, born Cordoba, Spain. Recalled by Agrippina after being exiled for 8 years for his adultery with Caligula's sister, he became tutor to **Nero** and, on his succession, one of the emperor's principal advisers. His influence gradually waned, and in semi-retirement he was implicated in Gaius Piso's conspiracy to depose Nero and chose suicide. As a philosopher, his prolific stoic, somewhat affected works, which included the biting satire *Apocolocyntosis divi Claudii* ('The Pumpkinification of the Divine Claudius'), were much imitated by later theorists.

SENGHOR, Léopold Sédar
1906–

Senegalese politician, Educated in Dakar and at the Sorbonne, he went on to teach in Paris and sat in the French National Assembly from 1946 to 1958. Returning to Senegal, he led the Senegalese Progressive Union and became President when Senegal achieved independence in 1960. He was instrumental in creating an opposition by encouraging the revival of the Senegalese Socialist Party in 1976, though the SPU was still the dominant political force when he retired four years later.

SERRANO, Francisco, Duke de la Torre
1810–85

Spanish statesman. A liberal at first favoured by Queen Isabella, he served in several Ministries but subsequently invoked his monarch's displeasure and was exiled in 1866. When Isabella was deposed two years later, he returned as Regent until the succession of Amadeus of Savoy in 1870. After success in the 1872 and 1874 campaigns against the Carlists, he was again Regent before relinquishing power to Alfonso XIII.

SEXTON, Thomas
1848–1932

Irish nationalist, born Ballygannon. A former railway clerk and leader writer, in 1880 he was elected MP for Sligo as a supporter of **Charles Parnell** and home rule, but lost his next seat in West Belfast, which he held from 1886 to 1892. He became MP for Kerry North the same year, but was again defeated in the next election. He went on to serve as mayor of Dublin, and to control the leading home rule daily newspaper, *Freeman's Journal*, from 1892 to 1912.

SEYMOUR, Edward, 1st Duke of Somerset
1506–52

English soldier and statesman. As the brother of Jane Seymour, on her marriage to **Henry VIII** he rapidly achieved high office, and led the devastating action by the English army against the Scots in 1543 when they refused to sanction marriage between the infant **Mary Queen of Scots** and the future Edward VII. With his succession on Henry's death in 1547, Seymour was, as Protector of England, the effective monarch. He waged another successful campaign against the Scottish army in 1547, and, as author of the first Book of Common Prayer (1549), he buttressed the Reformation. After his brother was executed for his overzealous attempts to marry the future Queen **Elizabeth I**, Seymour himself lost favour and was eventually executed.

SEYSS–INQUART, Artur von
1892–1946

Austrian Nazi collaborator, born in Sudetenland. Practising as a lawyer in Vienna, he became closely acquainted with **Kurt von Schuschnigg**, and—having served **Adolf Hitler** as a secret informer while a junior minister—replaced him as Nazi Chancellor after Austria's annexation. He was subsequently appointed Commissioner for the Netherlands, where his brutal treatment of slave labour brought him the death sentence at Nuremberg.

SFORZA, Carlo, Count
1873–1952

Italian statesman, born Montignoso. After a successful early career in the diplomatic service both before and after World War I, as Foreign Minister under **Giovanni Giolitti**, in 1921 he negotiated the Rapallo treaty, which returned the strategically important port of Fiume to Yugoslavia, ensuring his unpopularity with rightist extremists and demotion to ambassador to France, which post he resigned when **Mussolini** assumed power the following year. He continued to lead the anti-fascist opposition in the Senate until 1926, but then emigrated to France. In 1940 he fled the German occupation to live briefly in the UK and then the USA, where he cultivated his involvement in a post-war Administration, returning to his homeland after the war as a member of the provisional Government. He served as Foreign Minister again (despite strenuous British opposition) under **Alcide de Gasperi**, and was a strong advocate of NATO, until ill health forced his resignation in 1951. His writings include *European Dictatorships* (1931) and *Contemporary Italy* (1944).

SHAFTESBURY, Anthony Ashley Cooper, 3rd Earl of
1671–1713

English philosopher, politician and essayist, born London. Educated at Winchester College, he entered Parliament as a Whig in 1695 until succeeding to his earldom three years later, after which he sat in the House of Lords. Ill health forced his retirement from politics in 1702. Moving to Naples nine years later, he wrote on a number of social and cultural topics, frequently arguing against orthodox Christianity and promoting the concept of a naturally benevolent society in which all behave according to their intuitive distinction between right and wrong—he coined the term moral sense. His works, admired by Voltaire, Diderot and Lessing, were collected in three volumes entitled *Characteristics of Men, Manners, Opinions, Times* (1711, 1713).

SHAH OF PERSIA
See **Mohammad Reza Pahlavi**

SHAMIR, Yitzhak (Yitzhak Jazernicki)
1915–

Israeli politician, born in Poland. Educated at Warsaw University and the Hebrew University of Jerusalem, while barely out of his teens he joined the Stern Gang of Zionist terrorists that attacked British individuals and strategic targets in Palestine. Arrested in 1941 and exiled to Eritrea in 1946, he eventually found asylum in France and spent the next 20 years as a businessman. He was elected to the Knesset in 1973 and served as Speaker from 1977 to 1980, and then as Foreign Minister until 1983, when he succeeded **Menachem Begin** as leader of the right-wing Likud Party. The following year he lost the premiership but served again as Foreign Minister in an uneasy coalition with the Israel Labour Party of **Shimon Peres**. As Prime Minister again since 1986, he has consistently refused to enter into talks with the Palestine Liberation Organization to resolve the Israeli-Arab conflict, mainly on the somewhat paradoxical ground that he will not negotiate with terrorists.

SHASTRI, Lal Bahadour
1904–66

Indian politician, born Benares. Imprisoned by the British seven times after joining **Mohandas Gandhi**'s independence movement, he subsequently won a reputation as an inspired administrator as a Congress Party official and in regional politics, and joined **Pandit Nehru**'s Cabinet in 1952, heading the railways, transport and commerce Ministries, before becoming Home

Secretary in 1960. He resigned over inter-party differences in 1963 but the following year responded to a plea by Nehru, who had suffered a stroke, to serve him again, as Minister without Portfolio. He became Prime Minister on Nehru's death later the same year, and died suddenly in 1966 while in Tashkent for talks on the India-Pakistan dispute.

SHAWCROSS, Sir Hartley William, Baron Shawcross
1902–

British jurist, born Giessen, Germany. Educated at Dulwich College, he was called to the Bar in 1925 and was senior lecturer at Liverpool from 1927. After war service, he consolidated his reputation as an advocate at the Nuremberg trials, and held the post of Attorney-General in the first post-war Labour Government until 1951, when, as chief prosecutor in the **Fuchs** spy case, he set criteria for public espionage trials that are still applied today. He was appointed President of the Board of Trade by the Labour Government in 1951, but became disillusioned with his party's policies in opposition and resigned his seat in 1958. He received a life peerage the following year.

SHAW–LEFEVRE, Geroge John, Baron Eversley
1832–1928

English politician, born London. He served in Liberal ministeries (1881–4) and with Grote, Stephen and John Stuart Mill, he drafted legislation to protect common land from development, introduced sixpenny telegrams, and opened Hampton Court and Kew Palace to the public. He was given a peerage in 1906.

SHEFFIELD, John, 1st Duke of Buckingham and Normanby
1648–1721

English politician and author. After service in both the British Army and Royal Navy, he served **James II** as Lord Chamberlain and was a councillor to **William III**, and received a dukedom in 1703, but forfeited the Seal two years later for opposing **Godolphin** and the Duke of Marlborough. Under the Tories he was Lord Steward and Lord President, but lost office on Queen Anne's death and conspired to restore the Stuarts. His literary work includes two tragedies and essays on satire and poetry.

SHEIL, Richard Lalor
1791–1851

Irish dramatist and politician, born Drumdowney. With **Daniel O'Connell**, he formed the Catholic Association in 1825 and entered Parliament in 1839 under William Melbourne, serving in the Board of Trade and then becoming the first Catholic to be made a Privy Councillor. He was made Master of the Mint in 1846.

SHELBURNE, William Petty, 2nd Earl of (1st Marquess of Lansdowne)
1737–1805

English statesman, born Dublin. Two years after succeeding to his father's earldom in 1761, he was appointed President of the Board of Trade and, under Chatham, Secretary of State in 1766. He declined to form a Government when Lord North's Administration fell in 1782, instead continuing to serve Rockingham in the same office until his death the following year, when he was offered the Treasury by the king but nominated **William Pitt** for the office. A radical, he was a strong advocate of free trade and Roman Catholic emancipation. He was created Marquess of Lansdowne in 1784, and devoted his remaining years to amassing a splendid collection of paintings. His notable library of manuscripts was acquired by the British Museum shortly after his death.

SHEPILOV, Dmitri Trofimovitch
1905–

Soviet politician, born Ashkhabad. Educated at Moscow University, he served as a public prosecutor in Siberia before lecturing in political economy. Chief editor of *Pravda* from 1952, he joined the Supreme Soviet two years later and was made Foreign Minister in 1956. He was the victim of a party purge under **Nikita Khrushchev** and returned to teaching.

SHERBROOKE, Rupert Lowe, 1st Viscount
1811–92

English politician, born Birmingham. Educated at Winchester and Oxford, he successfully practised as a barrister in Australia, returning home to enter Parliament in 1852, and to serve as a Minister under the Earl of **Aberdeen** and Lord **Palmerston**. He established a payment-by-results educational system, and was prominent in disestablishing the Irish Church. He served as Chancellor of the Exchequer and Home Secretary under **William Gladstone**, and was ennobled in 1880.

SHERMAN, John
1823–1900

American statesman, born Lancaster, Ohio. The brother of the Civil War general who took Atlanta, as finance chairman in both houses of Congress he promoted Bills to achieve the reconstruction of seceded states, and, as Treasury Secretary from 1877, prepared a gold fund to raise the value of America's paper currency to par. In 1890, he introduced the enduring Anti-Trust Act to break monopolies and materials and transport cartels, but his legislation in the same year sanctioning the purchase by the Treasury of large silver reserves was repealed in 1893. He continued to serve in the Senate as its president, later as foreign relations chairman, and was appointed Secretary of State in 1897, resigning when war with Spain broke out the following year.

SHERMAN, Roger
1721–93

American statesman, born Newton, Massachusetts. A member of the state assembly from 1755, he also served as a Superior Court judge and as mayor of New Haven (both 1784–93). A signatory to the Declaration of Independence, he played a leading role in drafting the American Constitution.

SHEVARDNADZE, Eduard Ambrosievich
1928–

Soviet politician, born Mamti in Georgia. A history scholar, he joined the Communist Party in 1948, working in the Komsomol Youth League in the 1950s and in his republic's interior ministry during the 1960s, where he gained a reputation for quashing corruption. He was made Georgian party chief in 1972, and after successfully introducing innovative agricultural schemes was granted candidate status of the Politburo in 1978. A long-time associate of **Mikhail Gorbachev**, he was given full Politburo status and appointed Foreign Minister in 1985. Adept at acclimatizing himself to Western-style diplomacy, he was quickly accepted by European leaders at least as the most progressive and least duplicitous Soviet Foreign Minister to date. He excelled at maintaining Soviet credibility abroad in the

aftermath of the collapse of communism in Eastern Europe at the end of the 1980s and offered virtually unconditional support of the West in the 1990 Gulf crisis. He resigned in late 1990, expressing his fears of an imminent army-led right-wing reaction to perestroika. On 4 July 1991 he announced the formation of a new democratic reform movement and his resignation from the Communist Party. He refused to accept a post in the revamped Security Council following the abortive coup in August 1991.

SHINWELL, Baron Emanuel
1884–1986

British politician, born east London. Starting work in Glasgow at the age of 10, he became a political activist in his twenties and was imprisoned for inciting a workers' riot in 1921. Entering Parliament for Labour in 1923, he held junior ministerial posts before rising in his party's estimation after defeating **Ramsay MacDonald** in a bitterly-contested election battle for a Durham constituency in 1935. He helped **Clement Attlee** draft the manifesto that brought Labour's surprise victory in 1945, and as fuel and power Minister nationalised the mines a year later. Serving briefly as Minister of Defence, he gained the respect of both **Winston Churchill** and Viscount Montgomery. 'Manny' became party chairman, and even in his later years maintained his powers of oratory. He received a peerage in 1970, and in 1986, this one-time errand boy and street boxer became the oldest living peer in British history. He died shortly after celebrating his 98th birthday. He wrote three volumes of autobiography and memoirs, *Conflict Without Malice* (1955), *I've Lived Through it All* (1973), and *Lead With the Left* (1981).

SHORE, Peter David
1924–

British politician. Having joined the Labour party in 1948 after graduating from Cambridge, he ran its headquarters research unit, and was elected to Parliament in 1964. A former parliamentary private secretary to **Harold Wilson**, he held several ministerial posts before serving as Secretary of State for Economic Affairs (1967–9), Trade (1974–6), and the Environment (1976–9). After unsuccessfully contesting the party leadership in 1983, he was Shadow Leader of the Commons from 1983 to 1987 before returning to the Back-Benches.

SHULTZ, George Pratt

1920–

American statesman, born New York. Educated at Princeton, he served as an artillery officer in World War II, then taught labour economics at Massachusetts Institute of Technology and Chicago University. Between 1969 and 1974 he served **Richard Nixon** as Labour Secretary, Budget Director and Treasury Secretary. He then returned to a senior post in private industry but remained an economic adviser to **Ronald Reagan**, who called on Shultz to replace **Alexander Haig** as State Department Secretary in 1982, which post he held until the Reagan Administration ended in 1989. Considered a 'dove' in defence matters, he was a perfect foil to 'hawks' such as **Casper Weinberger** and Reagan himself, and was among the first to acclaim **Mikhail Gorbachev**'s new regime of glasnost. His negotiating skills resulted in the 1987 intermediate nuclear forces treaty that served as a springboard for the more extensive dismantling of East and West nuclear arsenals in the late 1980s. He abhorred terrorism in any cause, and endorsed his President's action in ordering the retaliatory bombing of Tripoli in 1986. He became professor of political economy at Stanford University in 1989.

SIBLEY, Henry Hastings

1811–91

American statesman, born Detroit. An agent of the American Fur Co. trading with the Sioux, he established himself in Mendota, Minnesota, became the first governor, and put down the Sioux uprising of 1862.

SIDMOUTH, Henry Addington, 1st Viscount

1757–1844

English statesman. Entering Parliament in 1783, he became Speaker six years later, and then briefly headed a government when **William Pitt** the Younger resigned in 1801. After receiving his viscountcy, he served in several Cabinets, and was a memorably repressive Home Secretary between 1812 and 1821, acting against Luddite rioters and being largely responsible for the 1819 Peterloo Massacre in Manchester, when 11 were killed in a cavalry charge against supporters of parliamentary reform who had peacefully assembled to hear Henry Hunt.

SIDNEY, Algernon

1622–83

English politician, born Penshurst. Fighting for the Parliamentarians, he was wounded in the decisive Civil War battle of Manston Moor, and despite later disenchantment with **Oliver Cromwell**'s corrupt use of power, he was forced into exile on the continent after the Restoration, returning to England in 1677. In 1683 he was falsely implicated with other Whigs, including the Duke of Monmouth and Lord Russell, in the Rye House plot to murder **Charles II**, and was beheaded. His innocence was officially proclaimed in 1689, in which year also his work on aristocratical republicanism, *Discourses Concerning Government*, was published.

SIGURDSSON, Jón

1811–79

Icelandic scholar and statesman, born Hrafnseyri. Educated in Copenhagen, where he lived the rest of his life, he worked as an archivist and produced several works on Iceland's history and law before leading the movement to secure its political and trade freedom from Denmark. He successfully persuaded King Kristian IX to reconstitute the Icelandic Parliament, the Althing, as a consultative assembly, and sat as one of its Members from 1845. Its probity under his influence secured for Iceland self-government in domestic affairs in 1874. The movement that he started achieved its ultimate aim when Iceland was granted full independence in 1944. His role as the father of modern Iceland is recognised each year by celebrating the country's National Day on his birthday, 17 June.

SIHANOUK, Prince Norodom

1922–

Cambodian politician. Educated in Vietnam and Paris, he was elected King of Cambodia in 1941 and achieved its independence from France in 1953, then abdicated two years later in favour of his father to become elected Prime Minister under the new constitution. He became head of state on his father's death in 1960, maintaining neutrality during the Vietnam War. In 1970, he fled to Peking after being deposed by Lt.Col Lon Nol in a US-backed right-wing coup. His resistance front, formed jointly with **Pol Pot**, removed Lon Nol in 1975, but after a year as head of state, Sihanouk was ousted by the Communist Khmer Rouge leadership. In exile in North Korea, he was elected head of a broader-based democratic government-in-waiting, but despite the withdrawal of Vietnamese troops that began in 1989, US reservations about Sihanouk's arrogance and vanity—his forays into screenwriting and composing have met with even less success than his attempts at controlling his country's destiny—make his restoration still far from certain.

SIKORSKI, Wladyslaw
1881–1943

Polish soldier and statesman, born Galicia. An engineering graduate, he joined the underground movement for Polish freedom from Tsarist rule, but was imprisoned by the Austrians on the signing of the Brest–Litovsk treaty. He commanded an infantry division during the Russo-Polish War, and, after successfully defending Warsaw in 1920, was Prime Minister for two years from 1922 and then War Minister, but temporarily retired to Paris to write military histories when **Józef Pilsudski** established his dictatorship in 1926. He returned to his homeland in 1938 advocating an alliance with Britain and France, but was refused office. He later fought in France, and headed a London-based government-in-exile from 1940, negotiating a treaty with the Soviet Union in 1941 that annulled the Russo-German partititon of Poland imposed at the beginning of the war, but the relationship soured after the discovery at Katyn in 1943 of a mass grave of Polish army officers thought to have been executed by Russian troops. In his play *Soldiers* (1966), German playwright **Rolf Hochhuth** suggested that **Winston Churchill** was guilty of complicity in Sikorkski's mysterious death in a helicopter crash over Gibraltar in July 1943.

SILAYEV, Ivan
1930–

Russian Federation Prime Minister. An engineer from Gorky he was appointed Deputy USSR Aircraft Industry Minister in 1974. After various other appointments he became USSR Duputy Prémier in 1985. A moderate reformer, in September 1990 he pledged to stabilize the economy by privatization, swingeing cutbacks in defence spending and a move to a market economy by breaking state monopolies and freeing up to 80% of prices, though those of basic commodities would be frozen.

SILIUS ITALICUS, Tiberius Catius Asconius
25–101

Latin poet and politician. A leading advocate in the Roman courts, he served as consul in 68 and proconsul in Asia in 77. In retirement, he became a patron of literature and the arts, and ended his own life by fasting after contracting an incurable disease. His epic 17-volume work on the second Punic War, *Punica*, is the longest Latin poem to have survived.

SIMMONDS, Kennedy Alphonse
1936–

St Christopher-Nevis physician and politician. After studying medicine at the University of the West Indies, he worked in hospitals in Jamaica, the Bahamas and the USA, returning home in 1964. He founded the centre-right People's Action Movement the following year, and after several unsuccessful attempts to defeat the Labour Administration, in 1980 his party won enough seats in the Assembly to form a coalition government with the Nevis Reformation Party, of which he became Prime Minister. The coalition was re-elected in 1984, having achieved the country's independence the previous year.

SIMON, John Allenbrook Simon, 1st Viscount
1873–1954

English jurist and statesman, born Bath. After graduating from Oxford and serving as a government junior counsel in the Alaska boundary dispute, he became a Liberal MP in 1906 and was appointed Solicitor-General four years later. Between 1913 and 1916 he was successively Attorney-General and Home Secretary, but resigned as a protest against World War I conscription, though himself going on to serve at the front. His political beliefs changed during his term as chairman of the Indian Statutory Commission from 1927 to 1930, and he was rewarded for his support of **Ramsay MacDonald**'s coalition government with his appointment as Foreign Secretary in 1931 and as leader of the National Liberals. He served again as Home Secretary from 1935, and as Chancellor of the Exchequer from 1937 to 1940, and was Lord Chancellor in **Winston Churchill**'s wartime coalition. He was made a viscount in 1940.

SIMON, Jules François
1814–96

French philosopher and statesman. A Sorbonne lecturer before entering politics, he refused the oath of allegiance after becoming a Deputy in 1848, making him a natural leader of left-wing republicans. He resigned in 1873 when, as Education Minister, his reforms came under attack, but his support allowed him at least a brief term as Prime Minister in 1876, until he resigned because of his justifiable suspicions of Macmahon's predisposition to the monarchy. Simon's published work included essays on political philosophy and biographical studies.

SINCLAIR, Sir Archibald Henry MacDonald, 1st Viscount Thurso
1890–1970

Scottish Liberal politician. Educated at Eton and Sandhurst, he entered Parliament in 1922 after Army service, and between 1930 and 1945 served as Chief Whip and party leader. During most of World War II, he was Secretary of State for Air in **Winston Churchill**'s wartime coalition Cabinet.

SINDIA, Daulat Rao Sindhia
1779–1827

Mahratta Prince of Gwalior. After taking Indore and Poona, he was defeated by Holkar in 1802, and then made himself the target of the East India Company. Routed at Assaye and Argaum by Sir Arthur Wellesley, later the Duke of **Wellington**, the Mahrattas were finally brought to accept defeat by Lord Lake's forces at Laswri, whereupon Sindia surrendered to the British all his territories in the Doab and on the right bank of the Jumna.

SINGH, V. P. (Vishwanath Pratap)
1931–

Indian statesman, born Allahabad. The son of a Raja, he was educated at Poona and Allahabad universities and elected to the Federal Parliament as a Congress Party representative in 1971. Between 1976 and 1987, he served under both **Indira Gandhi** and her son, **Rajiv Gandhi**, as Minister of Commerce, Finance and Defence, assiduously rooting out corruption to his eventual cost, being sacked from the government and Congress on exposing the Bofors arms scandal involving payments to senior officials closely associated with Rajiv Gandhi. He

made a comeback, however, as head of the Vanseta Dal coalition, and in 1990 defeated Rajiv to become Prime Minister. Singh's administration tried to promote a clean, consultative style of government, but it was plagued by factionalism and political crises. In November 1990 Singh was defeated on a vote of confidence and succeeded by Chandra Shekar.

SISULU, Walter Max
1912–

South African politician, born Transkei. As a youth he worked as a miner, factory hand and baker, and first showed his interest in politics by joining the African National Congress in 1940. He was subsequently secretary-general and treasurer, and his increasing outspokenness was rewarded in 1952 by a ban on making public appearances. He was charged with treason in 1956 and was in custody for five years before being acquitted. He was re-arrested in 1963 for inciting a strike, escaped briefly while on bail, and was sentenced to life imprisonment following his recapture later the same year. He was released in 1989 as part of the liberalizing reforms of **F.W. de Klerk** that brought freedom to **Nelson Mandela** the following year. His wife Nontsikelelo Albertina (1919–) has also been placed under house arrest on several occasions for her ANC activities, and in 1984 was jailed for three years. In 1989 she led a delegation of the United Democratic Front, of which she is president, to the USA and Britain.

SITHOLE, Reverend Ndabaningi
1920–

Zimbabwean cleric and politician. Educated in America, he worked as a teacher there and in his homeland, and first became active in the National Democratic Party and the Zimbabwe African People's Union (ZAPU) in the 1960s, and in 1963 was elected leader of the Zimbabwe National Union (ZANU), which was subsequently incorporated into the African National Congress. Shortly afterwards he was imprisoned for two years, and in 1969 was sentenced to six years' hard labour for incitement to murder Prime Minister **Ian Smith**. Released in 1974, he went into exile with ANC leader **Abel Muzorewa**, but became disillusioned with the organization's militancy and dissociated ZANU from it. He won a growing reputation even among white Rhodesians as a moderate and constructive proponent of majority rule and independence, and in 1978 reached agreement with Ian Smith on a constitutional settlement that was subsequently rejected by the Marxist leader **Robert Mugabe** and **Joshua Nkomo**, and deemed unworkable by the United Nations. His influence immediately suffered, and he returned to America to lecture after Mugabe achieved independence from Britain in 1979. His books include *Roots of a Revolution: Scenes from Zimbabwe's Struggle* (1977).

SKORZENY, Otto
1908–75

Austrian soldier, born Vienna. Personally chosen by **Hitler** to rescue **Mussolini** from internment, in September 1943 he led the detachment that landed by gliders on the Gran Sasso range and successfully rescued the Italian dictator, taking him by light aircraft to Hitler's headquarters in East Prussia. A year later, he infiltrated the citadel of Budapest, forcibly preventing Horthy from reaching a peace settlement with **Stalin** that would have endangered German forces. In December 1944, he masterminded numerous sabotage missions behind the allied lines during the Ardennes offensive, for which he was subsequently tried as a war criminal but acquitted.

SLANSKY, Rudolf
1901–52

Czechoslovakian politician. A lifelong Communist, he held several posts in local and national government service before being appointed secretary general at the end of World War II. He fell from favour in a Stalin-inspired anti-semitic purge and in 1951 he and nine other Jews prominent in the party were executed on wholly fabricated espionage charges. They were all posthumously absolved and honoured.

SMITH, Adam
1723–90

Scottish Economist and philospher, born Kirkcaldy. The posthumous son of a customs officer, he studied at Glasgow and Oxford, then joined the Edinburgh circle of fledgling intellectuals that included David Hume, John Home and Hugh Blair. Professor of logic, later of moral philosophy, at Glasgow from 1755 to 1764, he was subsequently tutor to the Duke of Buccleuch, meeting Quesnay,

Turgot, Necker and others on his travels. After moving to London, in 1776 he published a slim volume as the basis of a major work that would present the theory of society according to the traditions of Scottish moral philosophy, embracing natural theology, ethics, politics, and law. Entitled *Inquiry into the Nature and Causes of the Wealth of Nations*, it introduced original concepts such as the division of labour into specialist skills, individual enterprise, a common international currency, and what today is known as a market-led economy. His five-chapter book remains a cornerstone of contemporary economic thinking and practice. He returned to Edinburgh as customs commissioner in 1778, and was lord rector of Glasgow University in 1787.

SMITH, Alfred Emanuel
1873–1944

American politician, born New York. Typifying the rags-to-riches scenario that was a feature of turn-of-the-century America, he rose from newsboy to serve twice as New York State Governor between 1919 and 1928, but his political career came to an end when he was defeated as Democratic candidate in the 1928 presidential elections.

SMITH, Ian Douglas
1919–

Rhodesian politician, born Selukwe. Educated in Rhodesia and at Rhodes University, South Africa, he served with distinction as a fighter pilot in World War II and entered the Rhodesian Parliament in 1948. In 1961, he resigned from the United Federal Party to help found the Rhodesian Front, dedicated to achieving independence without majority rule. He was made Treasury Minister and Deputy Prime Minister the following year and succeeded Winston Field as premier in 1964, simultaneously holding the title of Minister of External Affairs and of Defence. The continuing failure of negotiations with the British government drove him, with reluctance, to make the famous Unilateral Declaration of Independence in November 1965. Sanction-busting by South Africa and other countries ensured the survival of Smith's rebel government, and further talks with **Harold Wilson** in 1966 and 1968 aboard HMS *Tiger* and HMS *Fearless* anchored off Gibraltar came to naught. When he at least ceded majority rule in 1979, he was made a minister without portfolio in Bishop **Muzore-wa**'s caretaker government, and was a member of the transitional council charged with preparing for the transfer of power. He was elected to the Zimbabwe Parliament in the subsequent open elections, but was suspended in 1987 on suspicion of collaborating with the South African Government and later resigned as leader of the white Opposition.

SMITH, John

1938–

Scottish politician. After graduating from Glasgow University, he was called to the Scottish Bar in 1967 and was made a Queen's Counsel in 1983. Elected to Parliament in 1970, he held junior Government posts under **Harold Wilson**, and in 1978 was appointed Secretary of Trade and Industry by **James Callaghan**. Since 1979, he has been Opposition front bench spokesman on trade, energy, and employment, consolidating his reputation on becoming Shadow Chancellor of the Exchequer in 1988. Unlike many of his front bench colleagues, he shines best at the dispatch box, combining considerable intellect and fluency with biting rhetoric, and his drive and forcefulness if anything increased after his recovery from a heart attack in 1989. Although his loyalty to **Neil Kinnock** is absolute, Smith—who topped the poll in the 1990 Shadow Cabinet election—is seen as his most obvious replacement in the event of another Labour general election defeat.

SMITH, William Henry

English bookseller and statesman, born London. He entered into partnership with his father in 1846, later taking control of the retail business that is today Britain's biggest chain of newsagents, booksellers and stationers. He became a Conservative MP in 1868 and served as Financial Secretary to the Treasury (1874–7), First Lord of the Admiralty (1877–80), and Secretary for War (1885), taking office again as First Lord of the Treasury in 1887 under Lord **Salisbury**, and as Leader of the Commons, until his death.

SMUTS, Jan Christian

1870–1950

South African statesman, born Malmesbury, Cape Colony. After graduating in law from Cambridge, he saw action in the Boer War as a leading member of the nationalist guerrilla movement under de la Rey. He became a member of the Assembly in 1907 and was Defence Minister and a member of Lloyd George's Imperial Cabinet during World War I before succeeding Louis Botha as Prime Minister of the Union of South Africa in 1919. He laid the foundations for his own United Party when, as Minister of Justice between 1933 and 1939 under J.B.M. Hertzog, he achieved a coalition with the nationalists. He assumed the premiership at the start of World War II when Parliament rejected Hertzog's policy of neutrality, and was made a field-marshal in 1941. In peacetime, he made a substantial contribution to establishing both the League of Nations and United Nations, and to improving relations between South Africans of Dutch and British descent, but the growing strength of the post-war nationalist movement brought his defeat in the 1948 election.

SNOWDEN, Philip Snowden, 1st Viscount

1864–1937

English politician, born Keighley. Invalided out of the customs service after being crippled in a cycling accident, he won election to Parliament for Labour in 1906, and was Chancellor of the Exchequer in both the 1924 and 1929 Administrations. His unwillingness to deviate from strictly orthodox fiscal policies in a Britain whose social and economic infrastructure had changed drastically since World War I triggered the 1931 crisis, and after receiving his title and being made Lord Privy Seal, he resigned in 1932 in protest at the coalition's abandonment of free trade. His memoirs, *Autobiography*, were published in 1934.

SOAMES, Arthur Christopher John Soames, Baron Soames

1920–87

English politician. Entering Army service after receiving his education at Eton and Sandhurst, he served with the Coldstream Guards in the Middle East, Italy and France during World War II, and in 1947 entered politics after marrying Sir **Winston Churchill**'s daughter, Mary. Elected an MP in 1950, he held junior posts under Churchill and Sir **Anthony Eden**, and in 1958 was appointed Secretary of State for Defence by **Harold Macmillan**. Between 1960 and 1977 he served as agriculture minister, ambassador to France, and a member of the European Commission. Given a peerage in 1979, he assumed the office of Lord President and Leader of the House of Lords, and was chosen by **Margaret Thatcher** to hold office as governor of Zimbabwe to oversee its independence in 1980.

SOCRATES
469–399 BC

Greek philosopher, born and died in Athens. Little is known of his early life. By **Plato**'s account, he devoted his last 30 years to convincing the Athenians that their opinions about moral matters could not bear the weight of critical scrutiny. His technique, the so-called Socratic method, was to ask for definitions of such morally significant concepts as piety and justice, and to elicit contradictions from the responses, thus exposing the ignorance of the responder and motivating deeper enquiry into the concepts. His profession to know none of the answers himself is ironic: he most likely held the doctrines that human excellence is a kind of knowledge; thus, that all wrongdoing is based on ignorance; that no one desires bad things; and that it is worse to do injustice than to suffer it. He was tried on charges of impiety and corruption of the youth by zealous defenders of a restored democracy in Athens. Found guilty, he was put to death by drinking hemlock. His personality and his doctrines were immortalized in Plato's dialogues; his influence on Western philosophy is incalculable.

SODDU, Ubaldo
1889–1949

Italian army officer and politician, born Salerno. After service in Libya in World War I, he held several senior military and governmental posts, and was Under-Secretary of War in 1939. He conspired with **Benito Mussolini** to undermine the king's credibility, refused Greek intervention that might have restored the authority of the monarchy, and after almost indecent rapid promotion to full general, took charge in Albania. Rattled by the progress made by Greek forces, he pleaded with Mussolini for political intervention and was replaced in Decmeber 1940. He retired from active service a month later.

SOLZHENITSYN, Aleksandr Isayevich
1918–

Russian writer and dissident, born Kislovodsk. A graduate of Rostov and Moscow universities in mathematics and physics, he was decorated for his distinguished service with the Red Army in World War II, but in 1945 was interned in an Arctic labour camp for eight years for criticizing the Soviet leadership's wartime conduct under **Joseph Stalin**. He was rehabilitated under **Nikita Khrushchev**'s anti-Stalinist regime and won acclaim for his 1962 prison-camp novel, *One Day in the Life of Ivan Denisovich*, but his subsequent criticism of Soviet censorship led to the authorities banning his two subsequent, semi-autobiographical works, *Cancer Ward* (1968-9) and *The First Circle* (1968). His expulsion from the Soviet Writers Union was swiftly followed by the award of the Nobel Prize for Literature in 1970. Translation of his work, including *August 1914* (1972), *The Gulag Archipelago* (1973), an account of the terrors of the Stalin regime, and *Lenin in Europe* (1974) continued to appear in the West. After accepting deportation to West Germany in 1974, he subsequently settled in the USA to write his memoirs, *The Oak and the Calf* (1980).

SOMARE, Michael Thomas
1936–

Papua-New Guinea politician. He worked as a teacher and journalist before founding the pro-independence Papua-New Guinea Party in 1967, and was elected to the House of Assembly the following year, becoming Chief Minister under Australian rule in 1972. When the country attained independence from Australia in 1972 he was Prime Minister of a coalition government, but resigned at the time of a corruption scandal in 1980. He returned as premier in 1982 but stepped down three years later, and in 1988 relinquished his leadership of the PNGP, continuing as Foreign Minister under Rabbie Namaliu.

SOMERS, John, 1st Baron
1651–1716

English Whig statesman, born Worcester. Educated at Oxford, he entered the law in 1676, and after helping to draft the Declaration of Rights, served after the Revolution as Solicitor-General, Attorney-General and Lord Keeper of the Great Seal, becoming Lord Chancellor in 1697. His loyalty to

William III brought him into disfavour and lost him the Seal in 1700, and the following year he was impeached by the Commons but cleared by the Lords, to serve Queen Anne as Lord President until 1710.

SONNINO, Baron Sidney
1847–1922

Italian statesman, born Pisa. After an early career in the law, he was elected as a centre-right member of the Chamber of Deputies in 1880, and was an advocate of universal suffrage, fairer taxation, and labour reforms—particularly in respect of the peasantry. He made a competent Treasury Ministry, but his ambitions for national reform were thwarted by **Giovanni Giolotti**'s domination of Parliament, which allowed him only a few months' office in his two terms as Prime Minister in 1906 and 1910. On Giolotti's resignation in 1914, he declined the premiership in favour of **Antonio Salandra**, and as his Foreign Minister he initially led the unsuccessful negotiations for territorial concessions by Austria in return for Italy's neutrality in World War I, but eventually achieved them by pledging his country's intervention to the Triple Alliance in the London Pact of 1915. He continued as Foreign Minister under **V.E. Orlando**, but attempts to modify the pact in favour of Yugoslavia at the 1919 Paris Peace Conference brought down his Government and Sonnino abandoned politics, never taking the honorific seat in the Senate that he was paradoxically given by his long-time political opponent, Giolotti. His *Discourse on Parliament* was published in three volumes in 1925.

SOREL, Georges
1847–1922

French social philosopher, born Cherbourg. Working initially as a civil engineer, from 1892 he devoted himself to studying philosophy and social theory, causing him to embrace extremes of political thought, from Marxism to royalism. His belief in the implicit violence of certain laws and institutions was propounded in his most significant work, *Reflexions sur la violence* (1908), which also advocated confrontation and revolution as the only means of attaining true Socialism. His theories were admired by such political opposites as **Lenin** and **Benito Mussolini**, and provided inspiration for the French student riots of the 1960s.

SORSA, (Taisto) Kalevi
1930–

Finnish politician, born Keuru. After graduating from Tampere University, he worked in publishing and with the UN in the Ministry of Education, then in 1969 became Secretary-General of the Social Democratic Party and its president in 1975. He was elected to the Eduskunta in 1970, and served two terms as Foreign Minister between 1977 and 1987. When the SPP formed a government with the conservative National Coalition Party in 1987, he became Deputy Prime Minister.

SOUPHANOUVONG, Prince
1902–

Laotian politician. Half-brother of Prince Souvanna Phouma, leader of the moderate Lao Issara Party for most of the period between 1951 and 1975, he studied engineering in Paris, returning to his home country in 1938 to enter nationalist politics. He founded the Lao Independence Front with Chinese backing to fight French rule and, in 1954, the ruling rightist Lao Issara. With the country's emergence as a Socialist republic in 1975 he was given the honorific post of State President, from which he retired in 1986.

SOUTHAMPTON, Sir Thomas Wriothesley, 3rd Earl of
1505–50

English statesman. An active dissolutionist under **Thomas Cromwell**, he avoided sharing his fate only by giving evidence against him and opposing the marriage of Anne of Cleves to **Henry VIII**, subsequently receiving a baronetcy as the author of a defensive treaty wth Spain. As Lord Chancellor for three years from 1544, he consolidated his reputation for brutality against reformists, personally taking part in their torture. He was created an earl by Edward VII, but his influence declined and he was deprived of the Great Seal soon after.

SPAAK, Paul Henri
1899–1972

Belgian statesman, born Brussels. After practising law, he was elected a Socialist Deputy in 1932, was Foreign Minister from 1936, and became his party's first Premier in 1938—but resigned a year later to return to his former post, which he held almost interruptedly until 1957. Between 1947 and

1949 he concurrently served a second term as Prime Minister. One of the founders of the United Nations, he was made its first president in 1946, and was later its secretary-general (1957–61). He was again Foreign Minister from 1961 until resigning from Parliament in 1966.

SPEER, Albert
1905–81

German Nazi Minister. An architect by training, he joined **Adolf Hitler**'s staff in 1934, having become a member of the National Socialist Party two years earlier. He served in the Reichstag from 1941 to 1945, and was appointed armaments and munitions Minister in 1942, bringing his flair for organization and technical innovation to the task of refining Germany's armoury and increasing weapons production. In the final months of the war he openly criticized Hitler and urged surrender, and at Nuremberg he was the only leading Nazi to acknowledge his war crimes. He was imprisoned in Spandau for 20 years, and after his release in 1966 wrote *Inside the Third Reich* (1970) and *Spandau: The Secret Diaries* (1976).

SPENCER, John Charles Spencer, 3rd Earl
1782–1845

English politician, born Althorp. Educated at Harrow and Trinity College, Cambridge, he served as a Whig Chancellor of the Exchequer and Leader of the House of Commons, and was largely responsible for steering the 1832 Reform Bill through Parliament, together with legislation for reforming the Irish Church. He resigned over the Irish Coercion Bill, but returned to the Government under Lord Melbourne. He was ennobled in 1834.

SPENGLER, Oswald
1880–1936

German historical philosopher. born Blankenburg. Educated at Halle, Munich and Berlin, he worked briefly as a mathematics tutor, and then engaged himself wholly in developing his theory, propounded in *Decline of the West* (1926–9), that all civilizations or cultures merely accord with a predictable cycle of growth and decay in observance of their organic destiny. His theories were warmly embraced by the Nazis as appearing to reinforce the inevitable destiny of the Third Reich to rule, apparently oblivious to the fact that their own organic decay would occur sooner rather than later.

SPERANSKI, Mikhail, Count
1722–1839

Russian reformer and statesman. As adviser to Tsar Alexander I, his advocacy of liberal constitutional reform and governmental reorganization according to the Napoleonic model inevitably brought his dismissal on **Napoleon**'s invasion in 1812. Rehabilitated under Nicholas I, he was responsible for the trial and conviction of the Decembrist conspirators in 1825, and in later life was a major influence in codifying pre-revolutionary Russian law.

STAËL, Anne Louise Germaine (Baroness of Staël–Holstein)
1766–1817

French writer, born Paris. Her precocious talent as a romantic novelist and dramatist, combined with her marriage to the Swedish ambassador and her numerous affairs, soon won her a reputation as one of the cleverest and most entertainingly scandalous women of her time, but her unwelcome attempts to include **Napoleon Bonaparte** among her conquests and his general distrust of intelligent women forced her to travel widely throughout Europe to escape his retribution. She was immediately adopted into the circle of emigrés that included **Talleyrand**, and wrote treatises in an attempt to save Marie Antoinette. The emperor permitted her to return to Paris in 1797, but their enmity remained undiminished and her continued association with dissidents such as Moreau and Bernadotte brought her second banishment from the capital. Moving to Germany after the death of her husband, she became an intimate of Schiller, Goethe and August Schlegel. Finding herself again surrounded by Napoleon's spies, she escaped to London, where she wrote *De l'Allemagne*, and her growing reputation as a novelist found her back in Paris at the invitation of Louis XVIII. Napoleon's return again forced her to flee the capital briefly, but she went back after her secret marriage to a French officer. Her unfinished *Considerations sur la Révolution Française* and autobiographical *Dix Années d'exil* were published posthumously.

STAHLBERG, Kaarlo Juho
1865–1952

Finnish politician. Having established his reputation as professor of law at Helsinki university, a judge, and a member of the Finnish Diet, in 1919 he drafted Finland's constitution and served as the republic's first president until 1925. Kidnapped by members of a pro-Fascist movement in 1930, he was narrowly defeated in the elections of 1931 and 1937.

STAIR, Sir John Dalrymple, 1st Earl of
1648–1707

Scottish judge and politician. Fined and imprisoned in 1667 after defying Claverhouse, he was rehabilitated under **James II**, serving as his advocate, which office he continued to hold under **William III**, later becoming Secretary of State and Minister in charge of Scottish affairs. He resigned after taking responsibility for the 1692 massacre of Glencoe, but subsequently played a key role in securing acceptance by the Scottish Parliament of the 1707 Act of Union.

STALIN, Joseph (Iosif Vissarionovich Dzhugashvili)
1879–1953

Soviet leader, born near Tiflis, Georgia. The son of a shoemaker, he joined the Bolshevik underground after being expelled from a seminary for propagating Marxism, and was soon transported to Siberia, whence he escaped, establishing the pattern of five subsequent internments. While at liberty, he organized strikes of oil workers, worked closely with **Lenin**, and wrote extensively on the rights of national minorities. At the start of the 1917 revolution, he was released from exile in Siberia and organized the second, Bolshevik, uprising later that year. By his influential interventions in the civil war, he irritated **Trotsky**, whose power he continued to undermine on being made general secretary of the Communist Party in 1922. After Lenin's death in 1924, Stalin's secret police began the ruthless purging of political and military opponents, real or imagined, while Stalin worked at establishing Russia as a powerful industrial nation and developing agricultural collectivization despite the oposition of the peasant population, 10 million of whom were victims of famine or of summary executions. Red Army forces were sent to support the Communist Government

in the Spanish Civil War, but in World War II, Stalin at first totally misread German intentions, though he successfully rallied his people after the 1941 invasion, and exploited allied aid while never publicly acknowledging its contribution to Russia's salvation. With Western leaders preoccupied with domestic rehabilitation, his blatantly opportunistic strategies and empty assurances at the Tehran and Yalta conferences went unchecked, leaving Stalin in control of half of post-war Europe. Three years after his death, Stalin was denounced by **Khrushchev** for his purges and cult of personality, and the 1961 party congress voted for the removal of Stalin's body from the Lenin Mausoleum. In 1988, **Mikhail Gorbachev**, while acknowledging Stalin's qualities as a wartime leader and the validity of collectivization, accused him of unforgivable crimes against the people and of corrupting the ideals of the Soviet political system.

STAMBOLOV, Stephen Nikolov
1854–95

Bulgarian statesman, born Trnova. Having taken an active part in the 1875–6 uprising, he was made chief of the Russophobe regency in 1886, and was premier from 1887 until his forced retirement in 1894. He was assassinated the following year.

STANHOPE, Charles, 3rd Earl of Stanhope
1753–1816

English politician and scientist, born London. After marrying a sister of **William Pitt** the Younger, he entered Parliament in 1790 but opposed his brother-in-law during the French Revolution, advocating peace with **Napoleon**. As an inventor, he developed the microscope lens and iron printing press that bear his name, and calculating machines. His scientific works include *Principles of Electricity*.

STANHOPE, James, 1st Earl
1673–1721

English soldier and statesman. After giving distinguished service to Marlborough in the war of the Spanish succession (1701–14), and helping to suppress the 1715 Jacobite uprising, he entered Parliament as a Whig and was responsible for foreign affairs before being made Chief Minister to George I in 1717.

STANSGATE, William Wedgwood Benn, 1st Viscount
1877–1960

English politician. First serving as a Liberal MP between 1906 and 1927, he then left the party and was elected as a Labour MP in 1928, taking office as secretary for India and for air. He had a distinguished military career, receiving a DSO and DFC in World War I and returned to the RAF during World War II. The viscountcy that he was given in 1941 was renounced by his son, **Tony Benn**, so that he could enter the Commons.

STANTON, Edwin McMasters
1814–69

American statesman, born Steubenville. A successful lawyer, he was chosen by **Abraham Lincoln** as his Minister for War, and when he was dismissed from that office by the much-despised Andrew Johnson, in 1867 the Senate reinstated him, grateful for the gift of the excuse that it needed to impeach the seventeenth President. But when Johnson was acquitted by one vote, Stanton resigned. He died a year later.

STASSEN, Harold Edward
1907–

American politician, born West St Paul, Minnesota. After studying law, at 31 he became the youngest senator in the state's history. Following war service, he twice failed to secure the Republican presidential nomination but became a foreign administrator under **Eisenhower**, and represented the USA at the 1957 London disarmament talks, subsequently resigning after disagreements with **John Foster Dulles**. Autobiography, *Where I Stand* (1947).

STAVISKY, Serge Alexandre
1886–1934

Russian-born French confidence trickster, born Kiev. Resident in Paris from early childhood, in adulthood he devoted himself to devising elaborate commercial frauds, which reached their zenith with a scheme involving the issue of worthless bonds representing the 500-million-franc assets of municipal pawnshops. The affair revealed widespread corruption and led to the Government's downfall and a lowering of public morale in the crucial pre-war period. Stavisky fled to Chamonix but was traced and committed suicide to avoid arrest.

STEEL, Sir David (Martin Scott)
1938–

Scottish politician, last leader of the Liberal Party. After working as a journalist and broadcaster, he became the House's youngest MP when elected in 1965, and sponsored abortion law reform and actively opposed apartheid before succeeding Jeremy Thorpe as leader in 1976. His pact (1977–8) with the Labour Government prolonged its survival after its shoestring victory in the 1974 election, and he subsequently formed an alliance with the Social Democratic Party, which helped win the two parties a quarter of the votes in the 1983 election but only 23 seats. After the 1987 general election, he advocated a merger of the two parties, which came in 1989, but withdrew from the leadership contest, which was won by **Paddy Ashdown**. He was awarded a knighthood the same year in recognition of his political services. Although unable to match the oratorical skills of **Jo Grimond** or Thorpe's flair for public if not private relations, Steel's immense popularity within his party and his obvious integrity, combined with a streak of gentle opportunism, helped rescue his party from the electoral doldrums and provided firm foundations for the Liberal Democrats' resurgence in the 1990s.

STEELE, Sir Richard
1672–1729

Irish politician and essayist. Educated at Charterhouse and Oxford, his disaffection with the military establishment after service in the Life Guards produced *The Christian Hero* (1701), and he went on to write stage comedies and to work as a gazetteer and in publishing, founding *The Tatler* in 1709, which, while poking fun at the pedants and coffee-house society of the day, also promoted Steele's Christian values and belief in the family. He entered Parliament in 1713 but was expelled a year later for writing a pamphlet supporting the House of Hanover. He was rehabilitated under George I as supervisor of the Drury Lane Theatre, and knighted. In 1718 he lost office after conflicting with **Joseph Addison** over constitutional procedure, and retired to Wales in near poverty in 1722.

STEIN, Heinrich Friedrich Carl, Baron von
1757–1831

Prussian statesman and German nationalist, born Nassau. His unremarkable presidency of the Westphalian Chamber in 1796 was followed by an equally undistinguished term as Secretary for Trade from 1804 to 1807, though his reappointment following the treaty of Tilsit brought inspired reforms that included the abolition of serfdom, and the establishment of peasant land ownership and municipal government, and extended to the Army under Gerhard Scharnhorst. **Napoleon** ordered his dismissal, but in exile in Austria, Stein formed a coalition against him, and, as the most effective proponent of aggressive nationalism from the battle of Leipzig to the Vienna Congress, served as a role model for the Nazis a century later.

STEINEM, Gloria
1934–

American feminist and writer, born Toledo, Ohio. One of the leading feminists to emerge in the 1960s, she was also active in organizing protests against the Vietnam War and racism. She helped establish the Women's Action Alliance in 1970 and co-founded *Ms* magazine.

STEPHENS, Alexander Hamilton
1812–63

American politician, born Crawfordsville, Georgia. A lawyer, he sat in Congress from 1843 to 1849 and was an advocate of the annexation of Texas. Initially an opponent of secession, be went on to become a Confederate Vice–President in 1861, serve another term in Congress, and become Governor of his home state.

STEPHENS, James
1825–1901

Irish nationalist, born Kilkenny. A railway engineer, he was still in his teens when he first became involved in the Young Ireland Party and active opposition to British rule. Wounded in the 1848 Ballingarry uprising, he went into hiding and then fled to France, returning in 1853. He then began the work of establishing the Fenians (Irish Republican Brotherhood), and founded the *Irish People* in 1863, the columns of which he used to incite armed rebellion. On returning from an American fund-raising tour in 1865, he was arrested by the British authorities, but escaped and returned to live in New York. He was deposed as Fenian leader in his absence, and his waning influence gave the British Government little reason to stop him returning to Ireland in 1891.

STEVENS, Siaka Probin
1905–89

Sierra Leonian politician. After working in the police force and industry, he was a trade union activist before entering politics, founding the moderate socialist All People's Congress in 1960, which, thanks partly to his mixed Christian and Muslim parentage, he led to victory in the 1967 general election. Army opposition forced him to resign the premiership, but he was returned to power the following year as Sierra Leone's first President under its new constitution. He ruled a one-party state until his retirement at 80.

STEVENS, Thaddeus
1792–1868

American politician, born Danville, Vermont. After developing a successful law practice, he was elected to Congress as a Republican in 1849, and, as a leading member of the anti-slavery lobby, he advocated penalties against the Southern states and chaired the impeachment trial of Andrew Johnson in 1868. Broken by Johnson's acquittal by one vote, Stevens died later the same year.

STEVENSON, Adlai Ewing
1900–65

American politician, born Los Angeles. The grandson of a Democratic Vice-President under **Grover Cleveland**, he was educated at Princeton and spent two years on the family newspaper before starting a Chicago law practice. From 1945 until 1948, when he was elected Governor of Illinois, he headed several State Department missions to Europe and played a significant role in the conferences that established the United Nations Organization. He stood against **Dwight D. Eisenhower** in the 1952 and 1956 presidential elections, but his intellectual style failed to capture America's middle ground. He served as America's permanent representative to the UN under both **John F. Kennedy** and **Lyndon B. Johnson**, and died of a heart attack while walking to the American

Embassy on a visit to London. His speeches were published in two volumes, *Call to Greatness* (1954) and *What I Think* (1956).

STEWART, Baron (Robert) Michael Maitland

1906–

British politician, born London. After graduating from Oxford, he entered teaching, and twice stood for Parliament as a Labour candidate, in 1931 and 1935, before winning a London seat in 1945. He entered the Cabinet in 1947, and held senior office in every subsequent Labour Administration. He became Foreign Secretary in 1968 on the resignation of **George Brown**, and in 1975 started a two-year term as head of the British delegation to the European Parliament. He continued to contribute his moderate and well-informed views as a member of the Upper House after receiving a peerage in 1979.

STEYN, Martinus Theunis

1857–1916

South African politician, born Winsburg. Orange Free State president from 1896, he aligned with the Transvaal in the 1889–1902 war and promoted the 1910 union, but subsequently encouraged Boer extremists and supported their 1914 rebellion.

STIMSON, Henry Lewis

1867–1950

American politician, born New York City. After studying law at Yale and Harvard, he joined the Bar in 1891 and was appointed a US Attorney in 1906. He came to the notice of **Theodore Roosevelt** for his success in prosecuting tax corruption by the railroad companies, which were deemed by Roosevelt to have shown contempt for the presidency. He failed to win the state governorship for the Republicans in 1910 but held office as Secretary of War under **William Taft** from 1911 to 1913, before serving as a colonel in World War I, then as governor-general of the Philippines from 1927 to 1929. As Secretary of War again under **Herbert Hoover** he produced the Stimson Doctrine on Japanese aggression in Manchuria, and while serving in the same capacity under **Franklin D. Roosevelt** for the whole of World War II, he was primarily responsible for persuading the reluctant President to use the atomic bomb to truncate the war with Japan—for which

action thousands of US servicemen at least owed him their lives. He retired shortly after grooming **Harry S. Truman** for the new era of Cold War international politics. *On Active Service in Peace and War* (1946) are memoirs of his most influential period.

STONEHOUSE, John Thompson

1925–1988

British politician, born Southampton. A student of the London School of Economics, he worked in the probation service and in the co-operative movement before election as a Labour MP in 1957. He held a number of junior posts under **Harold Wilson**, eventually winning promotion to Minister of Technology in 1967, and in 1968 began two years as Minister of Posts and Telecommunications. Complications in his financial affairs and private life led him to fake his death by drowning off a Miami beach in 1974, but he was identified in Australia a year later and returned to Britain, where he was tried and found guilty of fraud and embezzlement. In 1979, his exemplary conduct behind bars was rewarded with early release from his seven-year gaol sentence, and he married his secretary, Sheila Buckley, two years later. In joining the newly-formed Social Democratic Party in 1982, he may have had aspirations to make a political comeback, but Stonehouse eventually died in the obscurity that he had once so spectacularly sought.

STRACHEY, (Evelyn) John St Loe

1901–

English politician. Educated at Eton and Oxford, he became a Labour MP in 1929, but his extremist views prompted his resignation from the party two years later. After RAF war service, he was a junior Air Minister, and made a controversial Minister for Food from 1946 to 1950, through his involvement in the farcical Tanganyika ground-nuts and Gambia egg schemes, and his decision to prolong rationing, but partly retrieved his popularity as Minister for War during the Korean hostilities. His numerous works include *The Menace of Fascism* (1936), *Contemporary Capitalism* (1956), and *The Strangled Cry* (1962).

STRAFFORD, Thomas Wentworth, 1st Earl of

1593–1641

English politician, born London. At first an opponent of **Charles 1** after entering Parliament in 1614, he turned royalist and was a despotic ruler of Ireland from 1632 to 1639, when he served as the king's principal adviser, received an earldom and became Lord Lieutenant of Ireland. His brutal suppression of the monarch's opponents in the 1639–40 Bishops' War provided John Pym's Long Parliament with the excuse to attempt his impeachment, which was unsuccessful. But growing hostility to the queen compelled Charles to abandon his support for Strafford, and he was beheaded on the eve of the Civil War.

STRANGFORD, George Augustus Frederick Percy Sydney Smythe, 7th Viscount

1818–57

English politician. A member of **Benjamin Disraeli**'s New England Party, he was MP for Canterbury from 1841 but virtually retired from parliamentary life in 1846 by refusing to participate in debates. He survived what is reputed to be the last private duel fought in England, in 1852.

STRATFORD, John de

?–1348

English prelate and politician. Appointed bishop of Winchester in 1323 against the wishes of Edward II, he was among the conspirators who dethroned the king in 1327 and served Edward III as Chancellor for 10 years. He became Archbishop of Canterbury in 1333.

STRATHCONA, Donald Alexander Smith, 1st Baron

1820–1914

Canadian politician, born Forres, Scotland. As an immigrant, he progressed from working as a clerk for the Hudson's Bay Company to becoming its governor in 1889, and was the main promoter of the Canadian Pacific Railway, which was completed in 1885. In 1896 he was appointed Canadian High Commissioner for London, receiving a peerage the following year.

STRAUSS, Franz-Josef

1915–88

German politician, born Munich. A butcher's son, he was a soldier during World War II and in 1945 joined the rightist Christian Social Union and was elected to the Bundestag four years later. He assumed the leadership of the CSU in 1961, and between 1955 and 1969 headed the Nuclear Energy, Finance and Defence Ministries under **Konrad Adenauer**. His political career seemed finished in 1962 when he was forced to resign as Defence Minister after authorizing a security raid on the offices of the influential current affairs weekly *Der Spiegel* and the arbitrary arrests of its proprietor and editorial staff. Nevertheless, he maintained a high profile throughout the 1970s as a vociferous opponent of the Ostpolitik of the **Willy Brandt** and **Helmut Schmidt** Administrations, but was soundly defeated as CSU/Christian Democrat candidate for the federal chancellorship in 1980. But as Bavaria state governor from 1978, he continued to be a force in the Bundesrat and was an influential voice in the 1982 coalition led by **Helmut Kohl**.

STREICHER, Julius

1885–1946

German politician, born Bavaria. An early close associate of **Adolf Hitler** and supporter of the National Socialist Party, he played an active part in the 1923 putsch and applied his training as a journalist to found and edit the anti-Semitic newspaper *Der Stürmer* ('The Stormtrooper'), which was so extreme that it even offended some members of the Nazi high command. At Nuremberg, he was tried for war crimes that encompassed his term as Governor of Franconia from 1940 to 1944 and was executed.

STRESEMANN, Gustav

1878–1929

German statesman, born Berlin. He entered the Reichstag in 1907 as a National Liberal, led the party, and then after World War I founded its successor, the German People's Party. He was briefly Chancellor of the Weimar Republic in 1923, then served as a conciliatory Foreign Minister from 1923 to 1929, securing the Locarno Pact of mutual security with **Aristide Briand** and **Neville Chamberlain**. He took Germany into the League of Nations in 1926, for which he was awarded jointly with Briand the Nobel Peace Prize.

STRIJDOM, Johannes Gerhardus

1893–1958

South African statesman, born Willowmore, Cape Province. A farmer before starting a law practice in the Transvaal, he was elected to Parliament in 1929 and soon became leader of the extremist faction in the National Party, advocating apartheid and the establishment of an Afrikaner Republic outside the Commonwealth. He was Prime Minister from 1954 until shortly before his death.

STROESSNER, Alfredo
1912–

Paraguayan soldier and politician. Commissioned in 1932, he rose to Commander-in-Chief of the Army in 1951, and three years later engineered a right-wing coup that gave him the presidency under the token aegis of the Colorado Party. Despite his appalling human rights record, perhaps partly as a consequence of it, he secured re-election no fewer than seven times, but was finally ousted when General Andreas Rodriguez seized power in 1989.

STRUENSEE, Johann Friedrich, Count
1737–72

Danish statesman. As physician and confidante to Kristian VII, he had his and the queen's sponsorship in seeking to free Denmark from Russian influence and enter into an alliance with Sweden, but court jealousies thwarted his efforts and he was eventually tried for treason and executed.

SUCRE, Antonio José de
1793–1830

South American soldier and revolutionary, born Cumana, Venezuela. He became Bolivia's first President after its release from Spanish rule after the 1824 victory of Ayacucho, but resigned after the 1828 rebellion. He then fought for Colombia, and was victorious in the 1829 battle of Giron, but was assassinated after becoming President. Bolvia's original capital was named in his honour.

SUHARTO, General Raden
1921–

Indonesian soldier and politician, born Kemusu. After working as a bank clerk, he entered the Japanese-sponsored Indonesian Army in 1943 and became Chief-of-Staff in 1965. The same year, the Government of **Achmad Sukarno** survived an abortive communist-inspired coup thanks to his brutal tactics, but Suharto subsequently connived at achieving total power by drawing the attention of the Muslim population to the president's private life, and replaced him in 1967. Trusting in only a small circle of military officers and technocrats, he has courted both Japan and the West in achieving economic stability, made peace with Malaysia, seized the former Portuguese colony of East Timor, and fully exploited the country's oil assets. Despite the improvements that he has brought to Indonesia's infrastructure, the regime's political repression—which has ensured his re-election every five years since 1973—has increasingly triggered student riots, and a question mark must hang over Suharto's ability to remain in power much longer.

SUHRAWARDY, Husein Shaheed
1893–1963

Pakistani politician, born East Bengal. Oxford-educated, he entered the Bengal Assembly in 1921 and served as Minister of Law from 1954, before starting a two-year term as Prime Minister in 1956.

SUKARNO, Achmad
1902–70

Indonesian statesman, born Sarabaya, eastern Java. After forming the pro-independence Indonesian Nationalist Party in 1927, he was installed by the Japanese as the republic's first president in 1945, but widespread poverty and his Administration's corruption, combined with Sukarno's virulent anti-West policies, brought an abortive communist coup in 1965 and student riots. Increasing intervention by the army culminated in **Suharto**'s seizing power in 1967, with Sukarno remaining as president in name only until his death.

SULLA, Lucius Cornelius
138–78 BC

Roman general and statesman. After successes under Marius in the wars against the Mauretanians, Cimbri and Teutones, he restored Ariobarzanes to the Cappadocian throne, and triumphed again in the Social War of 91–89 BC. Resisting Marius's coalition with Sulpicius Rufus, he marched on Rome and seized power, and subsequently won further victories in the East, at Chaeronea and Orchomenus. After Marius's death in 86, he made peace with his old adversary Mithridates and returned to rule Italy after defeating the Samnites and Lucanians. He used his dictatorship constructively to return government control to the Senate and reform the criminal courts, but his constitutional reforms were undermined by the restoration of the tribunes in 70. He died a year after retiring in 78.

SUMMERSKILL, Baroness Edith
1901–80

English physician and politician, born London. Educated at King's College, she shared a medical practice with her husband before becoming a Labour MP in 1938. She served briefly as a junior Minister, and was party chairman from 1954 until she left Parliament the following year. She is best remembered as a vociferous defender of women's rights as a member of both Houses, having received a perage in 1961. Her daughter, Shirley, the subject of *Letters to My Daughter* (1957), also became a physician, MP and government minister.

SUMNER, Charles
1811–74

American statesman, born Boston. A Harvard law graduate, he practised in the US and Europe before helping to found the New Soil Party in 1848 to oppose the extension of negro slavery to new territories, and won election to Congress in 1851 with the support of Massachusetts Democrats. He was forced to retire from public life in 1856 for four years after receiving head injuries when attacked in the Chamber by a southern congressman. He subsequently promoted the admission of Kansas as a free state, and on the southern states' secession, which left the Republicans in total control of both houses, he was elected Senate foreign affairs chairman. He supported **Johnson**'s impeachment, and his criticisms of **Grant**'s Administration and support of Greeley's presidential ambitions finally brought his estrangement from the Republicans.

SUNDERLAND, Robert Spencer, 2nd Earl of
1641–1702

English politician, born Paris. Secretary of State to **Charles II**, he negotiated an abortive secret treaty with **Louis XIV** that would have given his monarch a pension in return for making England subservient to France. Despite subsequently failing with a similar scheme involving Spain, he survived to serve as principal adviser under **James II**. Displaying duplicity on a staggering scale even for his age, he represented himself as a devout Catholic, but as quite the opposite to **William of Orange**, who, on taking the throne, rewarded Sunderland with the office of Lord Chamberlain.

SUN YAT–SEN (Sun Wen, Sun Zhong Shan) See **Sun Yixian**

SUN YIXIAN
1866–1925

Chinese revolutionary, born Tsuiheng, near Xiangshan, Guangzhou (Canton). The son of a Christian farmer, he graduated in medicine in Hong Kong in 1892, and founded the New China Party (Hsin Chung Hui) in 1894, and, after leading an unsuccessful uprising against the Manchus a year later, lived in exile in Japan and America. Kidnapped while staying in London in 1896 and held at the Chinese legation, he was freed after the intervention of his former tutor, the distinguished surgeon Sir Edward Cantlie. Sun engineered a further 10 uprisings, finally seizing power in the 1911 revolution. The presidency went to General Yuan Shikai, who had forced the emperor's abdication, and, under his dictatorship, Sun again went into exile after leading an attempted coup. In 1923, he returned to Canton as president of the southern republic, and under **Jiang Jieshi** and Guandong with Russian aid, reorganized the Kuomintang and established a military academy. Acknowledged to be the father of the Chinese republic, his 1927 treatise on nationalism, democracy and social reform, *The Three Principles of the People*, inspired Jiang Jieshi in achieving Chinese unification three years after Sun's death.

SUSLOV, Mikhail Andreyevish
1902–82

Soviet politician. A graduate of the Moscow and Plekhanov economic institutes, he was made a member of the Central Committee in 1941 and was a ruthless administrator who wholly fulfilled **Joseph Stalin**'s concept of party and state loyalty. He served briefly as editor of *Pravda*, and in 1952 was appointed to the Praesidium. Suslov's reputation as a somewhat aloof academic and theorist did not stop him from getting his hands dirty as a member of the staunchly pro-Stalinist faction that despised **Nikita Khrushchev**'s liberalism and engineered his dismissal as Soviet premier in 1960.

SU TUNG–P'O
1037–1101

Chinese philosopher. Though from a peasant family, he excelled in most of the arts, including painting, calligraphy and poetry, and was briefly Prime Minister before being exiled for holding views too aesthetic and humanist to serve the needs of the pragmatic Sung dynasty, though in recent years his teachings at least have received official endorsement and are growing in popularity among Chinese cultural society.

SUZMAN, Helen
1917–

South African politician, born Germiston, in the Transvaal. An economics graduate, it was while working as a lecturer at Witwatersrand University in the late 1940s that she first publicly denounced apartheid, and in 1953 was elected to Parliament as a Democrat. Though black leaders may at first have suspected her motives, she eventually won the unqualified patronage of **Nelson Mandela**, and in 1978 received the UN Human Rights Award. She retired in 1989 after giving 36 uninterrupted years of parliamentary service.

SUZUKI, Zenko
1911–

Japanese politician, born Yamada, Honshu Island. A graduate of the Academy of Fisheries, he entered the Diet as Socialist Party deputy in 1947, but joined the Liberals two years later, and then in 1950 became a founder member of the Liberal Democratic Party. He subsequently held numerous ministerial and party posts, becomng LDP president and Prime Minister in 1980. His premiership, sullied by inter-party strife, unpopular defence measures and deteriorating US relations, lasted only two years.

SVOBODA, Ludwik
1895–1979

Czechoslovak soldier and politician, born Bratislava. After fleeing his Nazi-occupied homeland, he became a commanding general of the Czechoslovak army corp attached to the Red Army and from 1943 until the end of the war helped to liberate Kosice, Brno and Prague. He subsequently joined the Communist Party and served as Defence Minister until 1950. He managed to avoid the Stalinist purges of the 1950s, and under **Nikita Khrushchev** re-entered public life, succeeding **Antonin Novotny** as President in 1968. His liberalism was reflected in his support for **Alexander Dubcek**'s attempted reforms, and Moscow's respect for Svoboda allowed him to achieve

some relaxation of the occupying regime after the Soviet Union's initial intervention in 1968. He continued to hold office until poor health hastened his retirement in 1975.

SYKES, Sir Mark
1879–1919

English diplomat. Co-negotiator with Georges Picot of a secret 1916 agreement with France which, with Russian approval, provided for the post-war partition of the Turkish empire. The scheme was eventually abandoned, but its disclosure by the Russian revolutionary government caused an international outcry.

TAFAWA BALEWA, Alhaji, Sir Abu Bakar
1912–66

Nigerian politician, born northern Nigeria. Educated at Bauchi and Katsina College, he worked as a teacher and headmaster until 1944, when he won a scholarship to London University. On returning home he was appointed inspector of schools, sat in the northern House of Assembly, and was elected to the House of Representatives in 1952. He was subsequently Minister of Works (1954) and of Transport (1955), and was federal Prime Minister from 1957. Following the granting of independence in 1960, his country was plagued by growing disorder and disturbances, and in 1966 he was murdered in a coup by young army officers.

TAFT, William Howard
1857–1930

Twenty-seventh US President, born Cincinnati. After graduating from Yale and qualifying as a lawyer, he held a number of Government posts in Ohio and became Solicitor-General in 1890. In 1900 he was appointed president of the Phillipines Commission, and was made the islands' first civil governor a year later. From 1904 to 1908 he was Secretary of War, and in 1906 provisional governor of Cuba. In 1909 he was elected President for the Republicans but failed to win a second term, and from 1913 was professor of law at his old college. As Chief Justice from 1921 he made a number of useful reforms to the judiciary.

TAKESHITA, Noboru
1924–

Japanese politician, born Kakeyamachi, western Japan. After training as a kamikaze pilot in World War II, he attended university and worked as a school teacher before being elected to the House of Representatives for the Liberal Democratic Party in 1958. He served as Chief Cabinet Secretary (1971–2) and Minister of Finance (1982–6) before leading his own faction to become LDP president and Prime Minister in 1987. Though a conservative, he implemented a number of significant tax reforms, but his Government was undermined by the Recruit-Cosmos insider-dealing scandal dating back to 1986, which prompted the resignation of several of his Ministers, and of Takeshita himself in 1989.

TALLEYRAND-PÉRIGORD, Charles Maurice de, Prince of Benevento

1754–1838

French statesman, born Paris. After being Abbot of St Denis (1775) and agent-general to the French clergy (1780) he was nominated Bishop of Autun by **Louis XVI**, and in 1788 was elected by the clergy of his diocese to the States General, where he helped to draft the Declaration of Rights. In 1791 he was elected President of the Assembly, and after consecrating two new bishops, was excommunicated by Rome. In 1792 he was sent to London to conciliate **William Pitt**, but failed in his mission and was exiled to the United States in 1796. On the fall of **Robespierre** in 1796, he returned to Paris as Foreign Minister and established a close association with **Napoleon Bonaparte**, who made him consul for life in 1802. He successfully thwarted Britain's attempt to form a European coalition and organized the Confederation of the Rhine (1806) before temporarily retiring from public life. He lost favour with Bonaparte for opposing the invasion of Russia, and after the Spanish campaign mortally offended the emperor by making arrangements with Fouch for the succession. Through him, communications were opened with the allies and the Bourbons, and he dictated to the Senate the terms of Napoleon's deposition. As Minister of Foreign Affairs under Louis XVIII he negotiated new treaties that left France in possession of the boundaries of 1792, and ensured his country's participation in the Congress of Vienna. After the second restoration, he served briefly as Prime Minister, but his influence had waned by the time that Charles X took the throne. Nevertheless, he took office again as chief adviser to **Louis Phillipe**

at the July revolution, for which he was partly responsible, and on his appointment as ambassador to London reconciled the British Government and court to France. He retired in 1824.

TAMBO, Oliver

1917–

South African politician, born Bizana, Transkei. The son of a peasant farmer, at 16 he moved to Johannesburg to attend a missionary school, where his mentor was **Trevor Huddleston**. After graduating at Fort Hare University, he began a diploma course in teaching but was expelled for organizing student protests. In 1944 he joined the African National Congress and was vice-president of its youth league. His ambition to train for the priesthood under Huddleston was thwarted in 1956 when he was imprisoned for a year. As Secretary-General of the ANC when it was banned in 1960, he left South Africa to establish an overseas wing, becoming its acting president in 1967 and president in 1977. Since **Nelson Mandela**'s release in 1990, Tambo has worked closely with him in overcoming the traditional rivalry between the ANC and the Zulu faction in bringing about black equality under the more enlightened white leadership of President **F.W. de Klerk**.

TANAKA, Kakuei

1918–

Japanese politician, born Futuda, western Japan. After training as a civil engineer and establishing his own contracting business, he was elected to the House of Representatives in 1947, and rose swiftly within the Liberal Democratic Party to become Minister of Finance (1962–5) and Minister of International Trade and Industry (1971–2), before being elected party president and Prime Minister (1972–4). In 1976, he was found guilty of accepting bribes from the Lockheed Corporation during his premiership, and was sentenced to four years' imprisonment. His first appeal was rejected, but he lodged another, and meanwhile remained an influential faction leader, having resigned from the LDP in the year of his arrest.

TAUFA'AHAU (Tupouto Tungi) Tupou IV

1918–

King of Tonga. Educated at Newington College and Sydney University, he was

Minister for Education (1943) and for Health (1944–9) before being appointed Prime Minister under his mother, Queen Salote Tupou III. On succeeding to the throne on his mother's death in 1965, he shared power with his younger brother, Prince Fatafehi Tu'ipeleshake, who succeeded him as premier. In 1970, he negotiated independence within the Commonwealth, and continues to be the strongest supporter of the Western powers in the Pacific region.

TAWNEY, Richard Henry
1880–1962

English economic historian, born Calcutta. Educated at Rugby School and Balliol College, Oxford, of which he was elected a fellow in 1918. After working at the Toynbee Hall mission for the poor in the East End, he joined the Workers' Educational Association as a tutor in 1905. After being severely wounded in the Battle of the Somme (1916) while serving as a sergeant, he returned to work with the WEA, and was its president from 1928 to 1944. From 1931 to 1949 he was professor of economic history at London University. His published works, which represent a significant contribution to Christian socialist theory, include *The Acquisitive Society* (1926), *Religion and the Rise of Capitalism* (1926), *Equality* (1931) and *Business and Politics under James I* (1956).

TAYLOR, Helen
1831–1907

English women's rights activist. After the death of her stepfather, John Stuart Mill, in 1873, she entered politics in London, and as a radical member of the London School Board (1876–84) agitated for wide-ranging reforms of the capital's industrial schools. An advocate of land nationalization and taxation of land values, she founded the Democratic Federation in 1881 and campaigned for female suffrage, but after failing to be nominated to enter Parliament in 1885, she retired to Avignon. On returning to England in 1904, her ability as a public speaker was used to great advantage by the emerging suffragette movement.

TEBBIT, Norman Beresford

British politician, born Enfield, London. After a grammar-school education, he worked briefly as a journalist, and after National Service with the RAF became an airline pilot with BOAC (1953–70) and head of the British Airline Pilots Association. Soon after entering Parliament for the Conservatives in 1970, his outspoken observations about self-help established him as a leading member of the aggressive new right, earning him the sobriquet of 'The Chingford Skinhead'. He was appointed junior Trade Minister in **Margaret Thatcher**'s new 1979 Government and Minister of State for Industry (1981), before serving as a member of the Cabinet as Secretary of State for Employment (1981-3), for Trade and Industry (1983–5) and Chancellor of the Duchy of Lancaster (1985–7). Despite the injuries he sustained in 1984 when he was trapped in the debris of the Grand Hotel, Brighton, when it was bombed by the IRA during the Conservative national conference, the following year he took on the arduous job of party chairman and masterminded the Conservatives' 1987 election success. He retired from office soon after, partly because of his cooling relationship with Margaret Thatcher, but mainly to spend more time with his wife, who was permanently crippled in the Grand Hotel blast. In 1991 he announced his decision not to contest his seat at the next general election. His autobiography, *Upwardly Mobile*, was published in 1988.

TEMPLE (-BLACK), Shirley
1928–

American child actress and diplomat, born Santa Monica, California. Having achieved worldwide movie fame from the age of three and a half, she retired as an actress in adulthood, and after becoming involved in Republican politics, she was appointed US representative to the UN General Assembly in 1969, ambassador to Ghana (1974–6), and White House chief of protocol (1976–7).

THANT, U
1909–74

Burmese diplomat, born Pantanaw. After an early career as a teacher and headmaster of Pantanaw High School (succeeding the future Prime Minister, Thakin Nu), he worked as a government official, and in 1957 was appointed Burma's permanent representative to the United Nations. In 1961 he was elected acting Secretary-General after the death of **Dag Hammarskjöld**, and Secretary-General a year later. During the 1962 Cuban missile crisis, he headed a delegation that met **Fidel Castro**, devised the plan that ended the 1962 Congolese war, which ended the Katanga secession in 1963, and mobilized a UN peacekeeping force in Cyprus in 1964. He resigned in 1971.

THATCHER, Margaret Hilda
1925–

British politician, born Grantham. The daughter of a small-town greengrocer who, as a strict puritan and independent local councillor, laid the foundations for her own personal and political values, she took elocution lessons before entering Somerville College, Oxford, where she sat part of the exams that gave her a second-class science degree in a sanatorium after suffering a partial breakdown. She worked as a food analyst before twice unsuccessfully contesting a Kent constituency in 1950 and 1951 (Denis Thatcher was a member of the candidate selection panel), and then qualified as a tax lawyer before winning Finchley for the Conservatives in 1959. She was junior Minister for pensions and national insurance (1961–4), and was Shadow spokesman also for housing, economic affairs, power and transport before joining **Edward Heath**'s new Government as Secretary of State for Education and Science from 1970 until Labour's victory in the 1974 election, after which she served as Opposition spokesman on the environment and Treasury matters. In 1974, she deposed Heath in the first-ever parliamentary party elections for leader, and took the Conservatives back into power in 1979, to become Britain's first woman Prime Minister. The image of a softly-spoken housewife's friend that she had cultivated during her campaign for No. 10 was soon replaced by one of a tough, unbending, economic hard-liner, which was manna to cartoonists and political commentators, but came as a shock to the public. But just as her popularity was falling lower than any Prime Minister since opinion polls began, and with the jobless total the highest for 50 years, the 1982 Falklands War, and the opportunity it presented to display her resoluteness in a different light, came to her rescue, and in the following year's general election, the Conservatives added 56 seats to their parliamentary majority. Government by consensus, even within the Cabinet, now a thing of the past, she embarked on a huge programme of privatizing state utilities and Government agencies, and automatically broadened the party vote by creating an enhanced 'property-owning democracy'—at the same time undermining socialist support—by legislating for the sale of council houses at knockdown prices. Although the economic boom had largely passed by the time of the 1987 general election, Labour's internal squabbling ensured another victory for the Conservatives with the loss of only 20 seats. On the international stage, her particularly close friendship with **Ronald Reagan** survived the Americans' invasion of the British dependency of Granada in 1986, and she even won **Mikhail Gorbachev**'s admiration for her resoluteness—which, in respect of Northern Ireland, made her the prime target of the IRA bombing of the Grand Hotel, Brighton, headquarters of the 1984 Conservative Party conference, in which she narrowly escaped being killed. But by the late 1980s, the way in which Thatcher chose to display her unquestionable patriotism made alarm bells ring in Europe—not least because of her undisguised hostility towards the growing influence over the British economy of the western European member states of the EEC and their plans for monetary union and a single currency, which in 1989 triggered the resignation of Chancellor of the Exchequer **Nigel Lawson**. Shortly afterwards, fearful that her Foreign Secretary, Sir **Geoffrey Howe**, had 'gone native', she demoted him to Leader of the House of Commons, appointing **John Major** as his successor. Her continuing anti-European stance at the 1990 Rome summit brought Sir Geoffrey's resignation, and after he had made one of the most bitter personal attacks against a premier ever heard in the House of Commons, in October 1990, the annual formality of re-electing Thatcher as party leader gave her former Defence Secretary **Michael Heseltine** a chance to exploit the party split and to return from four years in the political wilderness. She immediately denounced Heseltine as being a crypto-Socialist and hinted at a national referendum on European monetary union, despite having described that option as 'a device of dictators and demagogues' when **Harold Wilson** suggested in 1975 that one be called on British membership of the EEC. On 22 November, only 12 hours after declaring 'I shall fight. I fight on', after failing to win a clear majority in the first round of MPs' votes for the leadership, Britain's longest-serving 20th-century Prime Minister made a U-turn and announced her resignation to the Cabinet—ironically, the first member of it to quit that way since Heseltine in January 1986, over the

Westland affair—effectively becoming the first Tory leader to be ousted by the party since it replaced Chamberlain with Churchill in 1940. Paradoxically, in Thatcher's 15 years in office, 11 of them as premier, her personal fate contradicted two of her most famous statements. As Education Secretary in 1973, she had said 'I do not think that there will be a woman Prime Minister in my lifetime,' and on the steps of No. 10, as Britain's new Prime Minister in 1979, she misquoted a prayer by St Francis of Assisi, saying, 'Where there is dispute, may we bring harmony.' In February 1991, her affinity with the US Republican Administrations that was a characteristic of her premiership was acknowledged when she received from President **George Bush** the Medal of Freedom—the country's highest civilian honour. In June 1991, days after making a further rousing Commons speech (but this time, as a Back Bencher) against a federal Europe, she announced her intention, after 32 years as an MP, not to stand at the next general election, and the imminent foundation—with multi-million pound backing—of the Thatcher Foundation to promote free enterprise, democracy, and 'all the things that I believe in' throughout the world, but particularly in the newly-democratized states of eastern Europe.

THERESA of CALCUTTA, Mother (Agnes Gonxha Bojaxhiu)

1910–

Albanian Roman Catholic nun and missionary to India, born Skopje, now part of Yugoslavia. She first went to India in 1928, where she joined an Irish order, the Sisters of Loretto, and taught at a Calcutta convent school. In 1948 she left to work in the slums, then received medical training in Paris before returning to open her first school for destitute children in Calcutta. She established her own sisterhood, the Order of the Missionaries of Charity, in 1950, opened her first House of the Dying in 1952, and in 1957 extended her work to the care of lepers. Her order now comprises 2000 sisters in 200 branches throughout the world. In 1971 she was awarded the Pope John XXIII Peace Prize, and in 1979 the Nobel Peace Prize.

THISTLEWOOD, Arthur

1770–1820

English conspirator, born Lincoln. After service in the army, he spent some time in America, where he developed his revolutionary ideas, and in 1820 led the Cato Street Conspiracy to murder Lord Castlereagh and other Ministers. He and the other plotters were arrested, and Thistlewood, with four others, was tried for high treason and hanged.

THOMAS, Dafydd Elis

1946–

Welsh nationalist leader, born Carmarthen. After an early career as a lecturer, writer and broadcaster, and as a self-proclaimed Marxist, in 1983 he was elected Plaid Cymru MP for Meirionnydd Nant Conway, and continued to lead the party until resigning in 1991 over growing criticism that he was moving to the right and ignoring the interests of traditional Welsh nationalists.

THOMAS, James Henry

1874–1949

British trade union leader and politician, born Newport. After working as an engine cleaner and fireman, he became president of the Amalgamated Society of Railway Servants (1905), and as assistant secretary led the national rail strike of 1911. He became assistant secretary of the National Union of Railwaymen in 1913, general secretary in 1917, and president of the Trades Union Congress in 1920. As National Labour MP from 1910 until 1931, his refusal to support extremist miners' leaders led to the failure of the triple alliance in 1921, but he failed to avert the 1926 general strike. He was appointed Colonial Secretary in 1924 and Lord Privy Seal, with special responsibilities for curbing unemployment, in 1929. In 1931, his decision to continue serving in the National Government as Dominions Secretary brought his expulsion from the party, and in 1936 he was the centre of further controversy for his unauthorized disclosure of Budget proposals.

THOMSON, Christopher Birdwood, 1st Baron Thomson

1875–1930

British soldier and politician, born Nasik, India. After serving in the South African war from 1899 until 1901, he worked in the War Office (1911), was military attache to Budapest (1915–17) and served in Palestine from 1917 until retiring from the army in 1919. After unsuccessfully standing for Parliament, he was made Secretary of State for Air in the first Labour Government and created a baron in 1924, and instigated a three-year programme of development that included the R100 and R101 airships. A year after returning to the Air Ministry when Labour took power again in 1929, he was killed in the R101 disaster at Beauvais, France.

THORNE, William (Will) James
1857–1946

British trade union leader and politician, born Birmingham. After working at the local brickyards from the age of six, he moved to London and found work at a gas works, establishing the National Union of Gasworkers and General Labourers in 1889, and as its general secretary until 1934 won an eight-hour working day for his members. He served as a member of the Trades Union Congress parliamentary committee (1894–1933), and was a Labour MP from 1906 until 1945.

THORPE, (John) Jeremy
1929–

British politician. Educated at Eton and Trinity College, Oxford (where he was president of the Union), he was called to the Bar in 1954, and carried on a family tradition by becoming a Liberal MP at his second attempt, in 1959. He was made party treasurer in 1965 and succeeded **Jo Grimond** as leader in 1967. His debonair style and wit did much to revive the party's public appeal, but he resigned the leadership in 1976, following allegations of his homosexuality, which he denied. He lost his seat in the general election and was soon after acquitted of charges of conspiracy and incitement to murder his alleged lover, Norman Scott. After failing to be appointed head of Amnesty International, he established in 1984 his own consultancy on third-world development. His published work includes *To All who are interested in Democracy* (1951) and *Europe: The case for going in* (1971).

TIBERIUS, Tiberius Claudius Nero Caesar Augustus
42 BC–37 AD

Second emperor of Rome. After the death of his father, **Nero**, when he was aged 9, Tiberius spent the first 20 years of his adulthood travelling with the Roman legions

in Spain, Armenia, Gaul, Pannonia and Germany, and returned to Rome in triumph after crushing the Dalmatian revolt of 9 BC. He then retired from public life, devoting himself to the study of astrology, but after the banishment of his wife, the daughter of **Augustus**, he was named as imperial heir and spent the next seven years on active service in north Germany, where he won several victories, returning in triumph in 12 AD, and becoming emperor two years later. A reluctant occupant of the throne, the positive aspects of the earlier years of his reign were overshadowed by the insecurity that followed, which brought the execution of his former loyal praetorian prefect, Sejanus, in 31 AD, whom he suspected of intending to seize power during his residency on Capri; the murder of Agrippa Postumus, the mysterious death in the East of the popular Germanicus, and the alleged poisoning of his own son, Drusus.

TIKHONOV, Nikolay Aleksandrovich
1905–

Soviet politician. After working as a train driver, he trained as a metallurgist at the Dnepropetrovsk Institute, where he met **Leonid Brezhnev**, and became a Communist Party organiser before being appointed Deputy Minister for the iron and steel industries (1955-7), Deputy Chairman of Gosplan (1963–5), and Deputy Chairman of the Council of Ministers (1965–80). He was made a full member of the Politburo in 1979, and was Prime Minister from 1980 until 1985, in which office his cautious, centralist policies did little to alleviate Soviet economic stagnation.

TITO, Josip Broz
1892–1980

Yugoslav statesman, born near Klanjec, Croatia. During service in the Hungarian army in World War I, he was taken prisoner and stayed in Russia to fight with the Red Army during the civil war. On returning to Yugoslavia, he helped to form its Communist Party and after being imprisoned for his activities (1928–34) spent some years in western Europe rallying support for the Spanish Civil War. In 1939 he returned to his homeland and led the partisans during the German occupation of 1941, conflicting with the royalist interests headed by General Mihailovich, but he was favoured by the allies and had his adversary executed at the end of the war, banished King Peter, and established a communist state. As head of state and President from 1953, he soon showed his independence from Moscow, opening trade links with the West and following a policy of positive neutrality. After becoming President for life in 1974, he established a system of rotating leadership, to make Yugoslavia the most enlightened of the communist states, and establishing a prototype that encouraged the westernization of others in eastern Europe in the late 1980s.

TOCQUEVILLE, Alexis Charles Henry de
1805–59

French historian, born Verneuil. After being called to the Bar in 1825, he was assistant magistrate at Versailles, and in 1831 was sent to America to report on its prison system. On his return, he published the influential study *De la Democratie en Amérique*, which argued that greater equality was the product of centralization and therefore diminished liberty. He paid his first visit to England in 1833, married an Englishwoman, and grew increasingly impressed by its national solidarity despite political dissention. In 1839 he returned to the Chamber of Deputies, becoming a formidable opponent both of the socialists and extreme republicans, and of **Napoleon**. In 1849 he was made Vice-President of the Assembly and Minister of Foreign Affairs. After the coup, he retired to his Norman estate to write *L'Ancien Régime et la Revolution* (1856), in which he argued that the revolution did not mark a break with the past but merely accelerated the natural trend of the centralization of authority.

TODD, Ron (Ronald)
1927–

English trade union leader, born Walthamstow, east London. The son of a market trader, he was a commando in the Far East, and in 1954 joined the Ford Motor Company as an assembly-line worker. He rose from shop steward to regional secretary and national organizer of the Transport and General Workers Union', Britain's largest labour organization, before becoming its General Secretary in 1985 with strong left-wing support. His personal commitment to unilateral disarmament, which is a policy shared by the TGWU, has occasionally brought Todd into conflict with the Labour Party and its leader, **Neil Kinnock**.

TOJO, Hideki
1885–1948

Japanese soldier, born Tokyo. After graduating from military college, he served as a military attache in Germany, then as chief of secret police and chief of staff of the Kwantung army in Manchuria, from 1937 to 1940. After a year as Minister of War, he became premier and dictator in 1941, but resigned in 1944. After his arrest, he was tried after attempting suicide and sentenced to death.

TONE, (Theobold) Wolfe
1763–98

Irish nationalist, born Dublin. After graduating from Trinity College, Dublin, he was called to the Bar in 1789, but soon developed an interest in politics, and in 1791 published *An Argument on Behalf of the Catholics of Ireland* and helped to found the Society of United Irishmen. In 1792 he was made secretary of the committee that worked for the Catholic Relief Act of 1793, but two years later he was forced to leave his country to avoid being tried for treason. In the USA from 1796, he campaigned for an American invasion of Ireland, and was a member of the small expeditionary force under General Hoche that never reached its destination. After Hoche's death, Tone made another attempt to seize his homeland with French support in 1798 but was captured. He was tried in Dublin and sentenced to death, but cheated the hangman by cutting his own throat while in prison awaiting execution.

TOOKE, John Horne
1736–1812

English politician, born London. A poulterer's son, his academic brilliance brought him an education at Eton and Cambridge University, and he practised briefly as a barrister before taking to travel as a tutor. In Paris, he met **John Wilkes**, and after failing to enter Parliament in 1771, he founded the Constitutional Society for Parliamentary Reform. He resumed his career as a lawyer in 1773, and after eventually being returned for Old Sarum in 1801 was excluded by a special Act of Parliament.

TREURNICHT, Andries Petrus
1921–

South African politician, born Piketberg. After studying theology at Cape Town and

Stellenbosch Universities, he was ordained a minister in the Dutch Reformed Church in 1946 and was elected to Parliament for the National Party in 1971. As Transvaal party leader from 1978, he served in several Cabinets under **P.W. Botha**, gaining a reputation as a hardliner opposed to his premier's policies of power-sharing with coloureds and Asians. In 1982, he resigned with 15 other leading National Party figures to form the right-wing Conservative Party, which, with its advocacy of a return to traditional apartheid and partitioning, has attracted the electoral support of more than a quarter of South Africa's white population.

TROTSKY, Leon (Lev Davidovich Bronstein)
1879–1940

Russian Jewish revolutionary, born Yanovka, Ukraine. After being expelled from Odessa University for his Marxist activities, at the age of 19 he was arrested and exiled to Siberia, but escaped in 1902 to join **Lenin** in London. After the abortive 1905 revolution, he returned to Russia as President of the first Soviet in St Petersburg (Leningrad), but was arrested and sent to Siberia again, and again escaped. In 1916, he was expelled from Paris for his pacifist propaganda, and after the March 1917 revolution returned to Russia, joined the Bolsheviks, and with Lenin organized the November revolution that put them in power. As Commissar for Foreign Affairs, he negotiated the Treaty of Brest-Litovsk (1918), and built up the 7000-strong Red Army to a force of more than five million soldiers. However, his doctrine that Bolshevism could only survive in Russia if revolutions were permanently staged in the West was unpopular with the party, and on Lenin's death in 1924, **Josef Stalin** was chosen to succeed him. Trotsky retaliated by organizing several political factions, for which he was expelled from the party in 1927 and exiled in 1929— after which 'Trotskyite' became a term of abuse for anyone whose loyalty to the official party line was in doubt. Trotsky spent some time in Turkey organizing dissident groups, then settled in Mexico in 1937. Three years later, he was murdered with an ice-pick by a Spaniard, Ramon Mercader, whose mother was the mistress of an NKVD general. His published work includes the three-volume *History of the Russian Revolution* (1932–4), *The Revolution Betrayed* (1937), *Stalin* (1948), and *Diary in Exile* (1959).

TRUDEAU, Pierre Elliott
1919–

Canadian politician, born Montreal. After being called to the Bar in 1943, he practised law in Montreal and founded the left-wing magazine *Cit Libre*, which advocated wide-ranging educational and electoral reform. In 1956, he was active in the short-lived group of leftist radicals known as the Rassemblement, and from 1961 until 1965 was associate professor of law at Montreal University. Having switched his support from the New Democratic Party to the Liberals, he won election to the House of Commons in 1966 and served as parliamentary secretary to the Prime Minister (1966). As Minister of Justice and Attorney-General (1967) he opposed the Quebec separatists, and in 1968 succeeded **Lester Pearson** as federal leader and Prime Minister. He immediately called a general election in which the Liberals won an overall majority, but his Government was defeated the following year. He was returned to power in 1981 but retired from active politics in 1984.

TRUJILLO, Molina Rafael Leonidas
1891–1961

Dominican dictator. After graduating from the republic's military academy in 1921, he was made chief of staff and President in 1930, maintaining dictatorial rule for the next 30 years. He operated a policy of conciliation with the US that allowed him to implement many worthwhile social and economic benefits, while amassing a huge personal fortune, which eventually gave rise to the discontent that brought his assassination in 1961, after which the rest of his family fled the country.

TRUMAN, Harry S.
1884–1972

Thirty-third President of the USA (1945-53), born in Lama, Missouri. After active service on the western front in World War I, he returned to work his farm, later becoming involved in an ill-fated retail venture. Despite exam failures putting an end to his ambition to become a lawyer, he was appointed a judge for Jackson County in 1922, which post he held until being elected to the Senate as a Democrat in 1934. His chairmanship of a defence committee after re-election in 1940 is reputed to have saved the Government $1 billion. He became Vice-President in the 1944 election and assumed the presidency on the death of **Franklin D. Roosevelt** a year later. He quickly demonstrated his strength of purpose and political courage to a nation devastated by Roosevelt's death, ordering the dropping of the world's first nuclear bombs on Hiroshima and Nagasaki, as well as instigating or encouraging important peacetime initiatives such as the Truman Directive, Marshall Plan, Fair Deal scheme, and NATO, though he was again compelled to invoke US military support as an element in the UN's attempts to resist the communist invasion of South Korea in 1950. His dismissal of General Douglas McArthur in 1951 for political interference was among his least popular actions. He defied the opinion polls to score a substantial victory over Dewey in 1948, survived an assassination attempt in 1950, but declined to stand again in 1952. In retirement at his home in Independence, Missouri, he wrote two volumes of memoirs, *Decisions* (1955) and *Years of Trial and Hope* (1956).

TSENDENBAL, Yumjaagiyn
1916–90

Mongolian dictator, born Davst, Uvs province. Born into a poor herdsman family, and despite being largely self-educated in his early years, he won admission to the Irkutsk Institute of Finance and Economics, and after graduating in 1938 worked as a teacher at the School of Finance in the Mongolian capital, Ulan Bator. A year later, he joined the only permitted political party, the Mongolian People's Revolutionary Party, and in the same year was appointed Finance Minister. In 1940, he was admitted to the party's central committee and praesidium, and was appointed secretary-general. From 1941 to 1945, Tsendebal served as deputy commander-in-chief and chief of the army's political directorate, and was rewarded with the Order of Lenin in 1944 for organizing aid to Russian troops in World War II. The folowing year he was further honoured by Moscow for the Mongolian army's part in helping Soviet forces to defeat the Japanese in northern China. In 1945, he was appointed deputy Prime Minister in the dictatorship of Marshal Horloogiyn Choybalsan, and assumed the premiership on Choybalsan's death in 1952. In 1954, he lost office to his second secretary, Dashiyn Damba, who improved relations with China, but his reinstatement as first secretary in 1958 saw a return to strongly pro-Soviet policies. In 1974, he resigned the premiership to be elected chairman of the People's Great Hural (national assembly), and in 1981 readopted the title of General Secretary. Under his increasingly autocratic leadership, dissenting Ministers and other leading party figures were removed from office, and in 1983 twice avoided an attempt by vice-president Jalan Aajay to overthrow him. The following year, while on a visit to Moscow, he was stripped of office and replaced by premier **Jambyn Batmunh**. After briefly returning to his homeland in 1984, Tsendenbal went back to Moscow, but in 1988 was denounced for allowing his country to suffer political and economic stagnation and was expelled from the Communist Party. He died while still in exile in Moscow.

TSHOMBE, Moïse Kapenda
1919–69

Congolese politician. As President of the important copper-producing Katanga province, he declared its independence in 1960 following that of the Belgian Congo, and United Nations troops were sent to the province at the invitation of **Patrice Lumumba**, for whose death in 1961 Tshombe was alleged by his opponents to be responsible. He went into exile in failing health in 1963, but was recalled by President **Kasavubu** to serve as Prime Minister in 1964. The following year, both were deposed in the military coup led by General **Sese Mobutu**. Tshombe took refuge abroad but was kidnapped and taken to Algiers, where he died.

TUDJMAN, Franjo
1922–

Croatian partisan and politician. As a young communist, he fought in World War II in the Yugoslav resistance army of **Josip Tito** against the Utashe fascist regime headed by the Nazi puppet premier Ante Pavelic, and rose to the rank of general, but subsequently he was twice imprisoned by Tito for his strong nationalist views. He remained on the political sidelines until the mid-1980s, when he became increasingly influential in the independence movement, and in 1990, as leader of the right-wing Christian Democratic Union, he won the Croatian presidency in the first free federal elections since the war. In his first year in office, there was little sign of the westernized economy that Tudjman had promised to introduce, the media remained stifled, and the traditional subjugation of the Serbs who account for 700 000 of the republic's otherwise mainly Catholic 5 million population continued. However, in June 1991 Tudjman proclaimed jointly with the Slovenian president, **Milan Kucan**, their respective country's independence, and civil war broke out when Croatia's hardline communist leader, President **Slobodan Milosevic**—having failed to mollify the rebel presidents by assenting to the immediate appointment of a Croatian, Stip Mesic, as federal president—ordered army units into both republics and air attacks on Slovenia's airport and its key military and communications targets. In July it was agreed that Solvenia should be allowed to secede but there was strong Serbian resistance to Croatia with its large Serbian population leaving the Yugoslav federation.

TURNER, John Napier
1929–

Canadian politician. After graduating from the University of British Columbia, he won a Rhodes Scholarship to read political science and jurisprudence at Oxford, and was called to the Bar. He later led the Bars of Quebec and Ontario, entered the House of Commons in 1962, and was a junior Minister under **Lester Pearson**, and Attorney-General and Minister of Finance under **Pierre Trudeau**. On his premier's retirement in 1984, Turner succeeded him as party leader and Prime Minister, but lost the general election the same year. He resigned as Opposition leader in 1989.

TUTU, Bishop Desmond Mpilo
1931–

South African Anglican prelate, born Klerksdorf. The son of a headmaster, he studied theology at the University of South Africa and London University, and after working briefly as a schoolteacher, was made a parish priest in 1960, rising rapidly in the Anglican hierarchy to become Bishop of Lesotho in 1977. In 1979, he was appointed Secretary-general of the South African Council of Churches, and was made Archbishop of Cape Town in 1986. He has frequently risked imprisonment for his criticisms of apartheid and calls for punitive sanctions against the South African Government, but has always condemned the use of violence and urged a negotiated reconciliation between his country's black and white communities. He received the Nobel Peace Prize in 1984.

TWEED, William Mercy
1823–78

American politician, born New York. Trained as a carpenter, he became an alderman in 1852 and sat in Congress (1853–5) and frequently in the state senate. In 1870 he was made commissioner of public works, and, as one of the most notorious bosses of the so-called Tammany Society, helped to control a ring of corrupt public officials whose massive frauds were exposed in 1871. After eventually being convicted, he fled to Cuba and Spain, but returned to New York in 1876 and died in jail while suits were pending against him for the recovery of $6 million.

TYLER, John
1790–1862

Tenth President of the USA, born Charles City County, Virginia. After qualifying as a lawyer, he sat in the state legislature (1811–16) and then in Congress, and in 1825 was elected Governor of Virginia and a senator the following year. In 1836, he resigned in protest at **Andrew Jackson**'s despotic control of the United States Bank, and after joining the new Whig Party formed by Jackson's opponents was elected Vice-President in 1840. On Harrison's death a month after taking office, Tyler became President. Chief features of his administration were the Ashburton Treaty and the 1845 annexation of Texas, and he remained one of Congress's strongest supporters of the Confederate cause until his death.

ULBRICHT, Walter
1893–1973

German politician, born Leipzig. Having held office as Communist deputy for Potsdam from 1928, he spent the war in Paris, Spain and Russia with **Adolf Hitler**'s rise to power, returning to his homeland in 1945 as Marshal **Zhukov**'s political adviser and head of East Germany's Communist Party. He was made premier of the GDR in 1950 and on his appointment as party secretary-general later the same year, began implementing the 'sovietization' of East Germany, which he consolidated by ordering the building of the Berlin Wall in 1961. He retired in 1971.

UMBERTO II
1904–83

Last King of Italy. On completing his military education, he inevitably rose rapidly to the rank of marshal, but the allies would not permit him to take front-line command of the Italian armies of liberation. In 1946, his father, compromised by his close association with the fascists in World War II, abdicated in favour of his son, hoping that would ensure the survival of the monarchy, but a national referendum one month later was over-whelmingly in favour of the establishment of a republican government. Umberto II went into voluntary exile in Portugal, but he and his descendants were subsequently banned from returning to Italy. That stricture has been lifted in recent years, and one of his three daughters now lives as a commoner in the country in which she might once have been a princess.

UNCLE SAM

A 19th-century caricature meant to personify the United States of America and its people. The name was originally used as a derogatory nickname for the federal government by New Englanders, disenchanted with the admin-istration's policies in the 1812 War, and *The Adventures of Uncle Sam* was published in 1816. The familiar depiction of Uncle Sam as a lean figure dressed in a tall hat, swallow-tail coat and striped trousers in the design of the American flag first appeared in cartoons by Thomas Nast in the 1870s.

USSHER, James
1581–1656

Irish churchman, born Dublin. Ordained in 1601, he drew up the articles of doctrine for the Irish Protestant Church four years later. As the author of a chronology of the scriptures, he was also famous for defining the year of the creation as 4004 BC. He was made Irish Privy Councillor in 1623 and Archbishop of Armagh in 1625, and settled in England following the 1641 rebellion. Though loyal to the Crown, he was favoured by **Cromwell** and was buried in Westminster Abbey

USTINOV, Sir Peter Alexander
1921–

British actor, writer and raconteur, born London. Of White Russian parentage, he made his first stage appearance in 1938 and has since appeared in numerous plays and films. As a playwright and screenwriter, his most successful works, such as *Love of Four Colonels* and *Romeo and Juliet*, mercilessly satirize national idiosyncracies, petty bureaucracy, and the political, social and literary pretensions of the European middle class. His autobiographical travel writings *My Russia* (1983) uncannily anticipated the coming of glasnost and perestroika two years before **Mikhail Gorbachev** took power. He has for many years served as a global ambassador for UNICEF, and was knighted in 1990.

VANUNU, Mordechai
1948–

Israeli nuclear technician. A relatively junior member of the previously undreamt-of tech-nical staff developing Israel's nuclear arsenal, Vanunu's disillusionment with the duplicity of his country's Government, which had always claimed that it would not be the first Middle East country to acquire atomic weapons, led him to resign his post in 1986, and later that year *The Sunday Times* published an interview with Vanunu in which he revealed that Israel had already stockpiled up to 200 atomic bombs at an underground factory in the Negev Desert. In September, he was abducted at Rome airport by agents of Mossad, the Israeli secret service, and returned to Jerusalem. After a secret trial, Vanunu was found guilty of treason and sentenced to life imprisonment in solitary confinement.

VAN RENSSELAER, Stephen
1765–1839

American soldier and politician. A federalist leader of New York state, his command on the northern frontier in the war of 1812 proved disastrous when his troops refused to cross the Niagara and the British recaptured Queenston Heights. He subsequently pur-sued a successful political career in Congress from 1823 to 1829, promoting the con-struction of the Erie and Champlain canals.

VANE, Sir Henry
1613–62

British statesman, born Hadlow, Kent. A staunch republican, he settled in New England in 1635 and served briefly as governor of Massachusetts before returning to England and entering Parliament in 1640.

A year later, he conspired to discredit and thus bring about the execution of **Thomas Strafford**, and headed the parliamentary government until 1653. For his part in Strafford's death, he was executed shortly after the restoration of **Charles II**—the only non-military figure to meet that fate.

VARGAS, Getulio Dorneles
1883–1954

Brazilian statesman, born Sao Boria. A federal deputy from 1923, and provincial governor from 1928, he was narrowly defeated in the 1930 national elections but seized power with the help of the military, promising new elections within two years. He embarked on an ambitious programme of economic and social rehabilitation embracing public works, schools construction, a 48-hour working week and minimum wages. He triumphed in the 1934 election, creating a new constitution that gave women the vote for the first time. He brutally suppressed a communist revolt led by Carlos Prestes and survived a subsequent coup ironically led by fascist elements, keeping power by skilfully mixing benevolent social reform with almost total repression of political opposition and trade unionism. He displayed the same duplicity in expanding Brazil's trading links with Germany and other fascist states while securing economic aid from the USA and aligning with the allies in World War II. He was deposed by a democratic military coup in 1945, but won a landslide victory in the 1954 elections. That same year, he was falsely implicated in the murder of an opposition newspaper editor and committed sucide rather than resign.

VASSILOU, Georgios Vassos
1931–

Cypriot president, born Famagusta. A self-made millionaire, his long-standing peripheral interest in politics and his belief that a wholly fresh approach was needed to solve his country's economic and social problems prompted him to stand as an independent candidate in the 1988 presidential election, in which, with the support of the Communist Party, he triumphed. Most of his efforts in the first years of his Administration have reflected his commitment to reunification of the island, but despite 100 hours of negotiations with **Rauf Denktas**, the Turkish Cypriot leader, in 1989–90, he has not yet achieved the federal settlement he desires.

VENIZELOS, Eleutherios
1864–1936

Greek statesman, born Canea, Crete. After studying law, he led the Liberals in the Chamber of Deputies and played a major role in the uprising against the Turks in 1896. He first served under Prince George as Minister of Justice, then led the guerrilla warfare against him, and was made Prime Minister in 1910. His rallying of the Balkan states against Turkey and Bulgaria (1912–13) served to extend the Greek territories, and his alignment with the British and French in World War I contrary to the sympathies of King Constantine I, whose wife was the German Emperor's sister, and his formation of an alternative Government, forced the monarch's abdication in 1917. Venizelos lost the 1920 election to the royalists, and remained out of office until 1928, by which time the monarchy had again been suspended. He remained Prime Minister until 1932, and in 1935 led an unsuccessful revolt against the restored king and died a year later in exile in Paris.

VERWOERD, Dr Hendrik Freusch
1901–66

South African politician, born Amsterdam. After emigrating to South Africa with his parents, his early career was spent as a sociology lecturer and in journalism, when, as editor of a new Afrikaans newspaper, he opposed his adoptive country's entry into World War II. He became vice-chairman of the National Party of Transvaal in 1946, was elected a senator in 1948, and took office as Minister of Native Affairs in 1950. His relentless support for apartheid ensured his selection as Nationalist Party leader in 1958, and as his country's sixth Prime Minister he pledged himself to the founding of a South African republic. He narrowly survived the first attempt on his life in 1960, and went on to take his country out of the Commonwealth in 1961, leaving him free to redouble his efforts to ensure the widest possible implementation of the most hateful aspects of racial discrimination. He was assassinated in the House of Assembly in Cape Town.

VICTOR EMANNUEL III
1869–1947

King of Italy, born Naples. Ascending to the throne in 1900 on the assassination of his father, he ruled as a constitutional monarch under the Administration of **Giovanni Giolitti**—whom he detested—and after Italy entered World War I in 1915, he remained at the front for the duration of the hostilities. When the fascists threatened to march on Rome in 1922, he offered the premiership to **Benito Mussolini**, and refused to remove him even after **Giacomo Matteotti** was assassinated by Mussolini's supporters. Thereafter, Victor Emmannuel was king in name only, permitting the establishment of a fascist dictatorship in 1925, Italy's involvement in the Ethiopian War, its intervention in the Spanish Civil War, and the 1939 invasion of Albania. In June 1940 he signed his country's declaration of war against the Allies. Following the invasion of Sicily and bombing of Rome in 1943, the king ordered Mussolini's arrest, and the allies allowed him to continue to rule on condition that he declared war against Germany. He effectively surrendered his throne in favour of his son after Rome was liberated in 1944, in which year his daughter died in a Nazi concentration camp. He formally abdicated in 1946 and died a year later in exile in Alexandria.

VICTORIA, Alexandrina
1819–1901

Queen of the United Kingdom, Empress of India, born Kensington Palace, London. Within a year of her coronation in 1837, the early maturity and strong will that were the product of a precocious childhood spent almost entirely in the company of adults denied the premiership to Sir **Robert Peel**, when in 1838 she refused to observe the convention of dismissing the (Whig) ladies of the bedchamber with the fall of Lord Melbourne's Administration, giving him a further two years in office. Melbourne was her closest confidant for many years, though she was at least equally influenced in later years by Prince **Albert**, whom she married in 1840. On his death in 1861 she went into virtual seclusion and lost much of her popularity, but her interest in controlling the fate of her empire was rekindled by **Benjamin Disraeli**, who, as Prime Minister from 1864, repaid her confidence in and affection for him by consolidating and extending her influence—acquiring for Britain a controlling interest in the Suez Canal, having Victoria proclaimed Empress of India in 1876, and annexing the Transvaal in 1877. He also won her special gratitude for skilful handling of the Russo-Turkish conflict which prevented a

European war. Victoria proved less at ease with premiers of a more radical persuasion, such as **Palmerston** and **Gladstone**, but there can be no doubt constitutional government was fully realized for the first time under her reign. At the same time she did not shrink from continuing fully to exercise the monarch's prerogative to prompt the government of the day when she saw fit, with an authority and effectiveness that has been equalled subsequently only by **Elizabeth II**. She is the subject of possibly more autobiographies than any modern monarch, but the most revealing insight into her reign is offered by her own collected *Letters*, published in three volumes between 1907 and 1932.

VIEIRA, Joao Bernardo
1939–

Guinea-Bissau politician, born Bissau. As a member of the African Party for the Independence of Portuguese Guinea and Cape Verde, he joined the political bureau during the 1964 war of independence, and when it was achieved in 1974, he joined the Government of Luiz Cabral, whom he deposed in a coup in 1980. He held the posts of chairman of the Council of Revolution and head of state until 1984, when constitutional changes combined the two offices in the new office of Executive President.

VILLIERS, Charles Pelham
1802–98

English statesman. A lawyer, he was a Member of Parliament for 60 years from 1835, first as a free trader and then as a Liberal Unionist. He moved motions against the Corn Laws every year until they were repealed in 1846, and between 1859 and 1866 had a place in the Cabinet as president of the Poor Law Board.

VIVIANI, René
1862–1925

French statesman, born Sidi-bel Abbès, Algeria. Prime Minister during World War I, he took the notable step of withdrawing French troops from the German border in 1915 as an indication of his country's peaceful intentions. He was appointed Minister of Justice the same year, and represented France at the League of Nations from 1920.

VOGEL, Hans-Jochen
1926–

West German politician, born Göttingen. After studying law, he became Social Democratic Party chairman of Bavaria and mayor of Munich in 1972, and was appointed housing minister in the same year. He was appointed Justice Minister by **Helmut Schmidt** in 1975, and in 1981 was given responsibility for overhauling the party machine in West Berlin. Elected SPD Bundestag leader in 1982, he remained on the sidelines after his party's resounding defeat in the 1983 federal election, but in 1987 replaced **Willy Brandt** as SPD chairman.

VOLSTEAD, Andrew Joseph
1860–1947

American politician, born Goodhue County, Minnesota. A lawyer, he entered Congress for the Republicans in 1903 and is best remembered as the author of the 1919 Prohibition Act, which forbade the manufacture, distribution and sale of alcoholic drinks. The purpose of the legislation, which remained in force until 1933, was to placate the influential temperance movement, which argued that alcohol contributed to crime and poverty, and to divert grain to food production in the wake of World War I. In fact, it proved impossible to enforce effectively, and did little other than to create enormous profits for bootleggers and speakeasies, and to provide Hollywood with the inspiration for countless gangster movies.

VOLTAIRE, François Marie Arouet
1694–1778

French writer, born Paris. Declining to emulate his father's career as a lawyer, he accepted a junior diplomatic post in Holland, but was sent back to Paris in disgrace for conducting an indiscreet affair with a French Protestant *emigrée* in The Hague. He was then banished from the capital for satirizing the regent, and for a second attack he was rewarded with a year in the Bastille, where he wrote a poem about Henri IV that was banned by the authorities for its advocacy of religious tolerance. He was subsequently exiled in Britain, where he became a favourite of the literary giants of the day and studied the work of Shakespeare, Milton, Dryden, **Addison**, and others. Permitted to return to France in 1729, he amassed a fortune from his shareholding in a

Government lottery and speculating in the corn trade. His new-found wealth and increasingly brilliant literary output ensured him a ready welcome in Court circles, and Madame de Pompadour sponsored his appointment as royal historian, but she too soon became a target for his satirical writings and in 1750 he took refuge in Berlin and then, having offended Frederick the Great too, in Prussia and Geneva. He next incurred the wrath of the French Parliament with a poem on natural religion, and by his efforts to prove the innocence of Jean Calas, accused of murdering one of his sons for wanting to become a Catholic. That and other efforts to counter and lampoon religious fanaticism made Voltaire hugely popular among the ordinary public, and together with many of his writings, which reflected his famous phrase, 'I may disapprove of what you say, but I will defend to the death your right to say it', did much to inspire the French Revolution, after which his remains were reinterred in the Pantheon.

VOROSHILOV, Klimenti Yefremovich
1881–1969

Soviet politician, born Dniepropetrovsk, Ukraine. A Bolshevik from 1903, he was exiled to Siberia for his political activities, but his military role in World War I and in the Civil War was rewarded with rapid promotion in the party hierarchy, and he served as defence commissar from 1925 until 1940. He was appointed marshal of the Soviet Union in 1935, and his modernization of the Red Army helped to ensure its victory over the Germans in 1941. His lack of success in the 1940 Finland campaign brought about his dismissal by **Joseph Stalin**, but on his death in 1953 Voroshilov succeeded him as President. After his failure to dislodge **Nikita Khrushchev** in 1957, he lost all influence and was finally compelled to resign from office in 1960.

VORSTER, Balthazar Johannes
1915–83

South African politician, born Jamestown. While a law student, he joined the Afrikaner nationalist movement in 1938, was interned between 1942 and 1944 for opposing the war effort, and after one unsuccessful attempt to enter the legislature in 1948, was elected as an extremist National Party MP in 1953. He was Justice Minister from 1961, and was elected Prime Minister following the assassination of

Dr **Verwoerd** in 1966. He remained loyal to his predecessor's commitment to absolute apartheid while maintaining effective trade and diplomatic links with black African states, but resigned in 1978 over the misappropriation of government funds for party propaganda purposes. He was immediately elected state president, but surrendered that office when an official inquiry held him partly responsible for the financial irregularities that had occurred during his premiership.

VYSHINKSY, Andrei Yanuarevich
1883–1954

Soviet jurist and politician, born Odessa. Forbidden from lecturing in law because of his Menshevik activities until 1921, he became Attorney-General in 1923 and rector of Moscow University in 1925. He prosecuted at many of the Stalinist purge trials of the 1930s, including those of **Bukharin**, **Zinoviev** and **Kamenev**. From 1940 he served as deputy Foreign Minister under **Molotov**, and was appointed the Soviet Union's permanent representative to the United Nations in 1944. He succeeded Molotov in 1949, losing office after **Stalin**'s death in 1953.

WADDINGTON, Lord David Charles
1929–

British politician. A barrister, he became a Conservative MP on his fourth attempt in 1968, and after holding several junior ministerships was appointed Chief Whip in 1987. As a right-winger, he was a natural choice for Home Secretary in the 1989 Cabinet reshuffle, in which office he openly advocated the return of the death penalty but showed restraint in his handling of the country's worst-ever prison riots. However, his curtness at the Dispatch Box did little to endear him to liberal Tory Back–Benchers, who, mindful of the need for the Government to develop a softer post-Thatcher image, were not sorry to see him leave the Commons in November 1990, on his appointment as Leader of the Lords in **John Major**'s first Cabinet.

WAITE, Terry (Terence Hardy)

British churchman, born Cheshire. After serving as an adviser to the Bishop of Bristol, Archbishop of Uganda between 1964 and 1971, he was appointed the Church of England's adviser to the Roman Catholic Church in 1972, and special adviser to Robert Runcie, Archbishop of Canterbury, in 1980. In his capacity as the prelate's special envoy to the Middle East, he was immediately successful in negotiating the return of British and American hostages held by Islamic Jihad terrorists in Beirut, but disappeared while on a similar mission in January 1987. The reinstatement of diplomatic relations with Iran in 1990 brought hopes that Waite and his fellow detainees would soon be released, but that development brought freedom the same year only for the Irish teacher Brian Keenan.

WALDHEIM, Kurt
1918–

Austrian statesman, born Vienna. After service as a diplomat in Paris (1948–51), he held several senior Foreign Ministry posts before being posted to Canada in 1955. In 1960, he returned to his old Ministry as director-general of political affairs, and became Austria's permanent representative to the United Nations in 1964. He remained there except for a two-year term as Foreign Minister (1968–70). In 1971 he made an unsuccessful bid for the Austrian presidency, and a year later succeeded **U Thant** as UN Secretary-General. He eventually achieved his ambition to win the presidency in 1986, but his standing in the international community suffered enormously following the allegations that he had served as a Nazi intelligence officer in World War II and was implicated in the transportation of Jews to concentration camps. He was banned from entering the USA as a result of these charges. His personal visit to **Saddam Hussein** in December 1990 was viewed by many as being more motivated by Waldheim's desire to retrieve his personal credibility than by any expectation that he could make a meaningful contribution to averting the Gulf War but it secured the release of 80 Austrian nationals.

WALESA, Lech
1943–

Polish trade unionist and statesman, born Popowo. An electrician at the Gdansk shipyard from 1966, at the start of the 1970s he galvanized his fellow workers into union activism and led the 1979 strike that resulted in his dismissal. The following year, he was re-employed and immediately founded his free trade union Solidarity (*Solidarnosc*). The series of strikes that followed secured several economic, political and social concessions, but in 1981 Solidarity was banned and Walesa arrested with the imposition of martial law by General **Jaruzelski**. He was released a year later, and in 1983 was granted an audience with **John Paul II**, who made a papal visit to his homeland later the same year. Despite subsequent attempts by the authorities to besmirch Walesa's personal and political integrity, his escalating political influence and strong support from his fellow Roman Catholics brought eastern Europe's first democratization of the decade, and in 1990 he was elected President in the country's first free elections for 45 years.

WALLACE, Colin
1937–

British Ulster-based Ministry of Defence press officer who was effectively dismissed after leaking intelligence information to a journalist supposedly without authority, and who subsequently claimed the existence of a dirty tricks campaign by MI5, codenamed Clockwork Orange, targeted at moderate Loyalist and Catholic politicians, as well as at members of the then Labour Government, including premier **Harold Wilson** and Home Secretary Merlyn Rees. Wallace also claimed that MI5 had covered up for eight years sexual abuses at the Kincora Boys' Home in Belfast by homosexuals who included at least one leading Loyalist. Wallace's campaign for a full inquiry and compensation was interrupted by 10 years' imprisonment for the murder of his wife's lover in 1976, for which crime he says he was framed by MI5. His allegations of a smear campaign against the Labour Government were supported by Wilson in 1977, and by former MI5 officer Peter Wright in *Spycatcher* (1987). Four years after Wallace's release, Prime Minister **Margaret Thatcher** announced in Parliament that she had been personally misled about the extent of the security service's black propaganda tactics in the Province in the 1970s, and after further revelations that an appeal tribunal had been improperly approached by Defence Ministry officials and that security papers mentioning a project named Clockwork Orange had been unearthed, in 1990 Wallace was awarded £30000 compensation for the loss of his MOD appointment.

WALPOLE, Sir Robert, Earl of Oxford
1676–1745

English statesman, born Houghton, Norfolk. After entering Parliament in 1701, he soon achieved high position in the Whig Admin-

istration, becoming First Lord of the Treasury and Chancellor of the Exchequer in 1715. Given that George I could not speak English and anyway was bored by parliamentary procedure, Walpole soon had a free rein in running the country, which from 1721 he did as the head of an inner-circle of his most trusted and competent Ministers that was the forerunner of the modern Cabinet—thus making Walpole Britain's first Prime Minister. He also established a record term of 21 years in that office, but was eventually brought down in 1742 by a vote of no confidence in the wake of his inept handling of the Spanish-Austrian War of Succession. He built Britain's economic strength by neglecting her armed forces and imposing instant taxation, and kept power by eventually presiding over a Cabinet of nonentities and buying the favours of those who could help or hinder him personally, once making the famous remark that 'Every man has his price.' The opposite of many British premiers after him, Walpole was strongest in dealing with domestic rather than foreign affairs, but he always sought expedient remedies rather than long-term policies.

WALTERS, Sir Alan (Arthur)
1926–

British economist. After graduating from Leicester University and obtaining an MA at Oxford, he lectured widely in Britain and the USA from 1958, and returned to Oxford as a visiting professor between 1982 and 1984, and then acted as economic adviser to the World Bank until 1986. As an apostle of the strict policies of monetary control that proved so appealing to **Margaret Thatcher**, he subsequently became her special adviser; his influence eventually brought about the threatened resignation of Chancellor of the Exchequer **Nigel Lawson** and Walters, adorned with a knighthood, resumed his academic career in the States. His works include *Money in Boom and Slump* (1970) and *Britain's Economic Renaissance* (1986).

WANG JINGWEI (Wang Ching-wei)
1883–1944

Chinese revolutionary, born Guangzhou (Canton). After some years in exile following his unsuccessful attempt to assassinate the Prime Minister in 1910, he failed in his bid to replace **Jiang Jieshi** for leadership of the Nationalist People's Party, and in 1927 briefly headed an alternative Government in

Wuhan. Reconciled with Jiang in 1932, he went on to head a puppet Japanese government but was eventually disgraced and died in obscurity.

WARD, Sir Joseph George
1856–1930

New Zealand statesman, born Melbourne, Australia. The last of the Liberal Prime Ministers, from 1870 he took his adoptive country through a period of immense social and economic development. He entered Parliament in 1887 and was premier from 1906 to 1912, and again from 1915, when he led a coalition government that brought New Zealand victory in World War I. He was briefly Prime Minister again from 1928 to 1930.

WARREN, Earl
1891–1974

American politician and jurist, born Los Angeles. After a successful early career as a lawyer, he served as California state governor for 10 years from 1943, and was Chief Justice of the US Supreme Court until 1969. A liberal, he campaigned actively for black human rights, an end to segregation in schools, and greater control over police treatment of suspects. He headed the commission that investigated the assassination of **John F. Kennedy** in 1963, and vehemently defended until his death its still-disputed finding that **Lee Harvey Oswald** acted alone and that there was no evidence of a conspiracy.

WASHINGTON, Booker Taliaferro
1856–1915

Black American educationalist, born Franklin Co, Virginia. Born into a slave family, he rose to become a respected teacher and a lecturer on negro problems, and in 1881 was appointed head of an Alabama institute founded to train black people in trades and professions. His published works include *Up from Slavery* (1901).

WASHINGTON, George
1732–99

American military leader and first President of the USA, born Bridges Creek, Virginia. Having inherited huge estates and vast wealth by his early twenties, he was given charge of the provincial militia and soon showed his courage and abilities as a tactician in his mission to flush out the threatening French settlements in Ohio which, although unsuccessful, was attempted without many casualties. In the years that followed, however, he lived almost as an English country gentleman, and in the period immediately prior to the war was a strong supporter of the colonists. His service as a delegate to the second Continental Congress in 1775 to decide future action was interrupted by the outbreak of hostilities, and immediately after their defeat at Bunker Hill in 1775, Washington was the revolutionaries' inevitable choice as commander-in-chief. He set about an ambitious programme of recruitment and training, and enjoyed early success in driving the British from Boston in 1776, but the next year he failed to hold New York and thereafter withdrew his troops for a year so that they could benefit from rest and further training. After joining with the French in 1778, Washington saw victory over Cornwallis at Yorktown in 1781, which proved to be the last decisive encounter, and America's independence was formally declared in the Treaty of Versailles in 1783. Washington subsequently presided over the 1787 Constitutional Congress, at which the 12 states unanimously chose him as their leader, and two years later he took office as the first President of the United States. He established a strong, multi-faceted Administration comprising men chosen for their abilities rather than acquiescence to Washington's interpretation of the constitution, and he encouraged the formation of new political parties. Among them, the Republicans expressed the most virulent personal criticism of Washington and he became a committed Federalist. He was re-elected unopposed in 1792, but, tiring of his political enemies, he refused to serve a third term and died at Mount Vernon on the Potomac in the last year of the century that effectively saw the birth of the world's greatest democratic power.

WAVERLEY, John Anderson, 1st Viscount
1882–1958

British politician, born Eskbank, Midlothian. After holding several senior posts in the home and colonial Civil Service, he was appointed Home Secretary in 1939 and devised the simple domestic air-raid shelter that took his name and saved countless lives in German bombing raids. As Chancellor of the Exchequer in 1943, he introduced the pay-as-you-earn system of collecting income tax suggested by his predecessor, Sir Kingsley Wood.

WEATHERILL, Sir (Bruce) Bernard
1920–

British politician and Speaker of the House of Commons. Following distinguished service in the Royal Dragoon Guards, Indian Army and the King's Lancers in World War II, he became managing director of his family's chain of menswear shops, and entered Parliament as a Conservative MP in 1964. He served as an Opposition Whip, then as a Treasury Minister, before being appointed Deputy Speaker in 1979, becoming Speaker on the retirement of George Thomas in 1983. Occasionally unpopular among some Tory Members during **Margaret Thatcher**'s premiership for being a little too even-handed, he also frequently voiced displeasure with her Ministers' habit of announcing major policy decisions to the press before formally presenting them to Parliament. With the televising of the Commons in 1989, his admonishing—and highly telegenic—gestures, particularly when dealing with the more unruly elements in the Chamber, have become as familiar to the viewing public as was the distinctive cry of 'Order, order' of his Welsh predecessor to radio listeners. In the spring of 1991, he announced his intention to leave the Commons at the next general election.

WEBB, Sidney James, Baron Passfield
and **(Martha) Beatrice** (1858–1943)
1859–1947

Social historians and economists, Sydney born London, Beatrice born near Gloucester. A graduate of London University, Sidney worked as a civil servant and barrister, and helped to found the Fabian Society in 1884 and the London School of Economics in 1895, where he lectured in public administration until 1927. He entered Parliament in 1927 and held office in two Labour Governments between 1924 and 1931. His wife wrote *The Co-operative Movement in Great Britain* (1891), and their joint works included *The History of Trade Unionism* (1894), the ten-volume *English Local Government* (1906–29), *The Decay of Capitalist Civilisation* (1921) and *Soviet Communism* (1935).

WEBSTER, Daniel
1782–1852

American orator and statesman, born Salisbury, New Hampshire. After qualifying as a lawyer, he sat in Congress briefly from 1813 but subsequently returned to the law and was notable for his advocacy in the infamous Dartmouth College case. He was also famous for his oration marking the bicentenary of the landing of the Pilgrim Fathers. He returned to Congress in 1823 and went to the Senate in 1827. With the Whigs' triumph in the 1840 election he took office as Secretary of State but resigned the office four years later and declined the presidential nomination in 1844. He was opposed to the war with Mexico, and, while professing to be anti-slavery, would not countenance splitting the Union in that cause. He was recalled to serve again as Secretary of State from 1850 to 1852 to settle differences with England. His collected speeches, including the two Bunker Hill orations of 1825 and 1843, and those made on the deaths of **John Adams** and **Thomas Jefferson**, were first published in 1851.

WEINBERGER, Caspar Willard
1917–

American politician, born San Francisco. He practised law for several years before entering Government service in 1952, first in California and then Washington. In 1975, after a brief period working in private industry, he was appointed Defence Secretary by **Ronald Reagan**, and headed a programme of military development that embraced the Strategic Defence Initiative, which was the target of Congressional criticism for its cost and because of the Pentagon's inefficiency in its implementation. As an opponent of rapprochement, he was deeply suspicious of the thawing of the cold war with the Soviets towards the end of the Reagan Administration and resigned in 1987. The following year, he was awarded an honorary British knighthood for his services to Britain, notably during the 1982 Falklands War.

WEIZMANN, Chaim
1874–1952

Jewish statesman, born Motol, Belorussia. While working as a chemistry lecturer in Switzerland and England, he campaigned extensively for the Zionist cause, and, while employed as an Admiralty biochemist, his development of a simple method for extracting explosive substances from maize proved crucial to Britain's World War I effort, brought him to the notice of the Prime Minister and resulted in the famous 1917 Balfour Declaration that promised Jews a national home in Palestine. He twice served as president of the World Zionist Organization (1920–30, 1935–46), and headed the Jewish Agency from 1929. On the establishment of the State of Israel in 1948, he was made its first President and held office until his death.

WEIZSÄCKER, Richard Freiherr, Baron von

1920–

West German politician, born Stuttgart. After wartime service in the Wehrmacht, he practised law and, as an active churchman, became president of the German Protestant Congress in 1964. As a Christian Democratic Unionist, he entered the Bundestag in 1968 and was its deputy chairman from 1972 to 1979. He was mayor of Berlin in 1981, and became president of the FDR in 1984. In a notable speech to the Bundestag in 1985 marking the 40th anniversary of the end of World War II, he urged his countrymen never to forget the lessons of the Nazi era. He was re-elected in 1989. In 1990, he was elected president of the new single state of Germany.

WELENSKY, Sir Roy (Roland)

1907–

Rhodesian politician, born Salisbury, Rhodesia. A one-time heavyweight boxing champion and barman, as a railway trade unionist he won election to Northern Rhodesia's Legislative Council in 1938 and joined its Executive Council the following year. In 1941, he founded the Northern Rhodesian Labour Party, and in 1953 was knighted for his part in the formation of the Federation of Rhodesia and Nyasaland the previous year. He served in the new Administration as Transport Minister, then as Prime Minister, from 1956 until the federation's dissolution in 1963.

WELLINGTON, Arthur Wellesley, 1st Duke of ('The Iron Duke')

1769–1852

Irish soldier and statesman, born Dublin. After a military education and working as

ADC to two lord-lieutenants of Ireland, he sat in the Irish Parliament from 1790 to 1795, and then resumed his active military career as a captain in campaigns in India. After entering the Commons and becoming Irish Secretary in 1807, he returned to the battlefield the same year to win victories over the Danes and over the French in Portugal in 1808 and again in 1812–14. Following his greatest military triumph, at the battle of Waterloo in 1815—for which he was rewarded with a dukedom and a magnificent house in Hyde Park (still correctly addressed as No. 1, London)—he returned to office in Lord **Liverpool**'s Administration and was made commander-in-chief for life in 1827. Only too aware that Britain no longer had the military strength to engage in foreign adventures, he resigned when **George Canning** ignored his counsel and committed Britain to joining forces with France and Russia in threatening the imposition by force of Greek autonomy on Turkey. On Canning's death in 1827, Wellington became Prime Minister. During his two years in office, he managed to offend the Liberals by resisting a broadening of the franchise, the Church of England by enacting Catholic emancipation in 1829, and members of his own party by refusing to intervene in the east after Navarino, which together brought about the fall of his Government in 1830. He was briefly Prime Minister again in 1834 and served in **Robert Peel**'s 1841–6 Cabinet as a Minister without Portfolio. He retired briefly in 1846, but, as Lord High Constable two years later, he organized the military against Chartist demonstrations in London. The scale of his ceremonial funeral remains unsurpassed, and he is buried in the crypt of St Paul's Cathedral.

WHITELAW, Viscount William (Stephen Ian)

1918–

British politician, born Nairn, Scotland. After distinguished service in the Scots Guards in World War II for which he received the MC, he entered Parliament as a Conservative MP in 1955, and was Secretary of State for Northern Ireland for one year from 1972, then Home Secretary for four years. Having achieved office under **Edward Heath**, he remained loyal to him when in 1975 the party leader was elected for the first time rather than being selected by senior Tories, but that did not stand in the way of his becoming one of **Margaret Thatcher**'s closest advisers throughout her Administration, particularly during the Falklands War and general election campaigns. He was made a Viscount in 1983—the first hereditary peerage to be created for 20 years—and was Leader of the Lords until 1988. His deceptively vague manner undoubtedly masks one of the great political survivors of the closing decades of the 20th century, though his ability to retain power and influence under two very different kinds of premier probably owed more to his lack of ambition than to cunning. *The Whitelaw Memoirs* (1989)

WHITLAM, (Edward) Gough
1916–

Australian statesman, born Melbourne. After war service with the RAAF, he practised as a lawyer and became a Labour MP in the New South Wales Parliament in 1952. He was made party leader in 1967, taking Labour to victory for the first time for 23 years in the 1972 general election, but failed to win an overall majority. In 1974, the Senate forced another election, when Labour took control of the House of Representatives but not the Senate, and his party's inability to enact meaningful legislation combined with inflation and high unemployment brought Whitlam's dismissal by the Governor-General the following year and Labour's defeat in the ensuing general election. He served as an ambassador to UNESCO from 1983 until 1986, and in 1988 retired from politics to take a chair at the National University in Canberra.

WILBERFORCE, William
1759–1833

English reformer, born Hull. After entering Parliament in 1780, he became close to **William Pitt** the Younger while never espousing his politics, and during a continental tour in 1784–5, he was converted to evangelical Christianity and later, with the support of the Quakers, embarked on a 19-year campaign for the abolition of British involvement in the slave trade, which he finally achieved in 1807. Meanwhile, he had helped to establish the Church Missionary Society (1798) and the Bible Society (1803). In 1825 he founded the Anti-Slavery Society with the aim of extending the ban to the Continent and then the world, but poor health forced his retirement from Parliament in 1825. He died eight years later—just a month before the Commons passed legislation that curtailed slavery in the British colonies.

WILHELM II
1859–1941

German Emperor and King of Prussia, born Berlin. Succeeding to the throne in 1888, his efforts to win the hearts of the working class soon brought him into conflict with **Bismarck**, whom he dismissed in 1890 for refusing to allow his Ministers audiences with the king except in his presence. Wilhelm exercised personal rule until 1908, when he suffered a nervous breakdown and began to exert much less influence over affairs of state. After adopting an anti-British stance in the Boer War, he made some attempts at reconciliation, but subsequently encouraged the development of a German Navy under Admiral von Tirpitz, and aligned with Turkey in excursions into the Middle East. Following the assassination of Archduke Franz Ferdinand in 1914, he made strenuous efforts to avoid war, but his failing intellect allowed the generals to take control, and the kaiser's part in fomenting and sustaining Germany's aggression in World War I was considerably less than popularly portrayed. Nevertheless, as the scapegoat for his country's defeat, Wilhelm was forced to abdicate in 1918 and he retired to Arnheim. His translated *Memoirs 1878–1918* were published in 1922.

WILKES, John
1727–1797

English politician, born London. As a member of Parliament from 1757, he was an outspoken critic of the king's Chief Minister, Lord Bute, and in the weekly newspaper that he founded, *The New Briton*, made his famous allegation that in the King's Speech for the state opening of Parliament, Ministers had put lies into the mouth of the monarch. He was acquitted of libel on the ground of parliamentary privilege, but was subsequently accused of obscenity for his *Essays on Women*, imprisoned for 22 months, and denied his seat in the Commons. He returned to public life in 1771 as Sheriff of Middlesex, and became Lord Mayor of London and an MP again in 1774.

WILLIAM I
1027–87

King of England, born Falaise, France. Although promised the English succession by Edward the Confessor in 1051, the crown was taken by Harold Godwinsson on the monarch's death in 1066. After successfully petitioning the Pope, William began his October invasion on the Kent coast, defeating the English in the confrontation at Battle, near Hastings, in which Harold was killed. William was crowned on Christmas Day, but the subsequent years of his reign were marked with revolts in the north and the west. Land entitlement was an important element in his form of feudal rule, and in 1086 he ordered the compilation of the Domesday Book. He suppressed further rebellions in the Fen Country and the north, and finally secured the allegiance of the Scottish king, Malcolm III, and conquered much of Wales. He died after falling from his horse after setting fire to Mantes in an action against the forces of his son, Robert, who had rebelled against him in Normandy. Ironically, Robert then automatically inherited the territory, and William's other surviving son was crowned King of England as William II.

WILLIAM III

1650–1702

Prince of Orange and King of Great Britain and Ireland, with Mary II. The posthumous son of William II of Orange, he first distinguished himself as commander-in-chief, by halting the 1672 French invasion of republican Holland, and achieving a negotiated peace in 1678. He married Mary (1631–94), the daughter of the future **James I**, but following the accession of his father-in-law in 1685, with his unpopular policy of Catholicization, William was invited by British Protestant notables to invade the country, and in 1688 his forces landed at Torbay in Kent. James soon fled to France, and William and Mary were proclaimed king and queen the following year. James's supporters held out in Scotland and Ireland, but were finally defeated in the battles of Killicrankie (1691), the Boyne (1690), and Limerick (1691). In peacetime, William refined the economic innovations, such as the establishment of a system of national debt, that had helped to finance the war, and established the Bank of England in 1694. During his reign also, control of the Army was vested in Parliament, and greater freedom of the press was permitted. He was killed in a riding accident, and was succeeded by Mary's sister, Queen Anne.

WILLIAMS, Shirley Vivien Teresa Brittain

1930–

British politician, born London. The daughter of the novelist Vera Brittain—whose *Testament of Youth* (1933) movingly describes her struggle to enter university—she was secretary of the Fabian Society from 1960 until entering Parliament in 1964, and was a junior Education and Home Office Minister before being appointed Secretary of State for Prices and Consumer Protection (1974–6) and Education and Science (1976–9). In 1981, she was one of the Gang of Four who founded the breakaway Social Democratic Party and became its first elected MP later the same year. After losing her seat in the 1983 general election, she switched her allegiance to the revamped Social and Liberal Democratic Party but never returned to Parliament. She moved to the USA following her second marriage to a Harvard professor, Richard Neustadt, in 1988. *Politics is for People* (1981), *A Job to Live* (1986).

WILLIS, Norman David

1933–

British trade unionist, born Ashord, Middlesex. Educated at Ruskin and Oriel colleges, Oxford, he worked briefly for the Transport and General Workers Union (1951–3) before national service, returning in 1954 to serve as personal assistant to its general secretary. In 1970, he was made head of the union's research and education unit, and in 1974 was appointed assistant general secretary of the Trades Union Congress, succeeding Len Murray as General Secretary in 1984. As a moderate, his measured approach to industrial relations has frequently provoked hostile reaction by leftist union leaders, notably for his failure to call a national strike in support of the deunionization on security grounds of the Government Communications Headquarters at Cheltenham in 1987.

WILSON, Sir (James) Harold, Baron Wilson of Rievaulx

1916–

British statesman, born Huddersfield. An economics lecturer at Oxford from 1937 to 1943, he worked briefly as a junior civil servant before entering Parliament for Ormskirk in 1945. He rapidly rose through junior ministerships to become President of the Board of Trade in 1947, but his opposition to **Clement Attlee**'s armament policies brought his resignation from office in 1951. He was returned to Parliament for Liverpool, Huyton in 1951 and 1955, and was a leading member of the Shadow Cabinet until 1963, when he succeeded **Hugh Gaitskell** as party leader, taking Labour to a narrow victory, with a majority of just 13 seats, in the 1964 general election. Despite the legacy of a neglected economy and the thinly disguised hostility of the financial establishment, Wilson rapidly won the electorate's approval as a premier whose verve and openness drew favourble comparisons with the style set by **John F. Kennedy**—and Labour was returned in 1966 with a landslide 96-seat majority in the Commons. Britain's worsening balance of payments, the devaluation of the pound, and the growing power of the trade unions brought defeat in the 1970 general election, but Wilson turned the tables again in 1974, and remained as Prime Minister for two years before resigning and naming **James Callaghan** as his successor. He was knighted in 1976 and made a life peer in 1983. Although Wilson cultivated a homely, pipe-smoking, man-of-the-people public image, he was one of the shrewdest political operators this century. Often dazzling in parliamentary debates, his astonishing ability to recollect in embarrassing detail his opponents' past speeches and pledges made him a devastatingly effective and unnerving Dispatch Box adversary. His books include *The Governance of Britain* (1976), *Final Term* (1979) and *Harold Wilson: Memoirs 1916–64* (1986).

WILSON, Thomas Woodrow

1856–1924

American statesman and twenty-eighth President of the USA, born Staunton, Virginia. After practising in Atlanta, he became a law lecturer at Princeton and became its president in 1902. As a Democrat, he won the Jersey state governorship in 1911, and was elected President in 1912 and 1916. His first term brought notable social innovations, such as worker compensation and child welfare. At the start of World War I he advocated neutrality, but could not resist the shift in public opinion that followed the sinking of the Lusitania and other American ships, and he took his country into the conflict in 1917. His famous but idealistic Fourteen Points for a just and lasting peace found few takers at the 1919 Paris Peace Conference, and the Senate subsequently refused to ratify the realistic resolution represented by the Treaty of Versailles. As a consequence, the League of Nations was established without American involvement. Wilson's continuing efforts to persuade the electorate to espouse a more sophisticated world role for America caused him in 1919 to suffer a heart attack from which he never recovered. His condition was, amazingly, kept secret from the public, and the Administration was run by his second wife, Edith Wilson (1872–1961), and his private secretary, Joseph Tumulty (1879–1954), until the President's death four years later.

WINGTI, Paias

1951–

Papua New Guinea politician. As an MP for the Papua New Guinea Party (Pangu Pati), he was Transport and then Planning Minister under **Michael Somare** during the 1970s and early 1980s, and then deputy Prime Minister, but resigned in 1985 to found the People's Democratic Movement, which headed the 1985 five-party coalition of which he became Prime Minister. Growing dissatisfaction with the country's economic problems and Wingti's style of premiership forced his resignation in 1988.

WOLSEY, Cardinal Thomas

1471–1530

English prelate and statesman, born Ipswich. After 19 years spent teaching in an Oxford seminary, he moved to Lymington in Somerset, and became secretary and chaplain to the Archbishop of Canterbury. He soon came to the notice of **Henry VII** and became his chaplain in 1507, and, by cultivating a friendship with the Lord Privy Seal and Royal Treasurer, he was entrusted with much of Henry's private business. He was rewarded with the deanery of Lincoln after his astute representation in Scotland and the Low Countries, and when **Henry VIII** took the throne, he used Wolsey's experience to agree terms with Francis I of France. Further lucrative appointments and gifts of land followed and Wolsey's unsurpassed influence at court soon made him the most powerful Minister since Thomas Becket. His downfall came with his vacillation over Henry's divorce from Catherine of Aragon, which irritated not only the king but widened Wolsey's already numerous circle of jealous enemies, and in 1529 he was deprived of the Great Seal. Impeachment and the forfeiture of his vast estates swiftly followed, and he died while awaiting trial for treason.

WOOD, Sir Kingsley
1881–1943

British statesman, born London. After an early career as a solicitor, he entered Parliament in 1918 for the Conservatives and held junior office in several Ministries before being made Minister of Health (1935–8) and Secretary of State for Air (1938–40). As Chancellor of the Exchequer until 1943, he devised the pay-as-you-earn system of personal tax collection.

WORNER, Manfred
1934–

West German politician, born Stuttgart. A former lawyer, he entered the Bundestag as a Christian Democratic Unionist in 1965 and on his appointment as Defence Minister in 1982 he oversaw the controversial deployment on German soil of USAF Pershing and cruise missiles, and introduced an unpopular extension of mandatory military service from 15 to 18 months to compensate for a declining birth rate. He succeeded Lord **Carrington** as Secretary-General of NATO in 1988.

WORRALL, Denis John
1935–

South African politician, born Benoni. After an early career as a lecturer in political science, he became a National Party senator in 1974 and an MP three years later, and accepted the sensitive posting of ambassador to the UK in 1984. On his return to South Africa three years later, he resigned from the NP and stood unsuccessfully as an independent in that year's general elections. In 1988 he founded the Independent Party, which soon merged with other opposition groups to form the Democratic Party, which advocates an end to apartheid and universal suffrage. He was elected co-leader of the DP and returned to Parliament in 1989.

WYSZYNSKI, Stepan
1901–81

Polish prelate and cardinal, born Warsaw. A member of the resistance movement during the German occupation, he became Bishop of Lublin in 1946 and Archbishop of Warsaw and primate of Poland in 1949. In 1953, he was suspended and then imprisoned for criticizing the Communist regime for its actions against the Church. Gaining freedom after the bloodless 1956 revolution, he worked to reconcile Church and state under the liberal regime of **Wladyslaw Gomulka**, but without much success, and the national celebrations in 1966 of 1000 years of Christianity in Poland were viewed by the authorities as gross provocation. A further attempt at co-existence failed with the strikes of the early 1970s. The subsequent emergence of Solidarity and Poland's eventual democratization were in no small part inspired by Wyszynksi's constructive defiance.

XERXES I
519–465 BC

King of Persia. On succeeding his father, Darius I, in 486 BC, he first subdued the Egyptians and then raised a huge army. With the use of a fleet provided by the Phoenicians, he devised a bridge of boats across the Hellespont, cut a canal through Mount Athos, and arrived in Sardis in 481 BC. His army marched into Greece the following year, defeated Leonides, and, on arriving in Athens and finding it deserted, destroyed the city. On withdrawing, he was defeated at sea, and the remains of his army perished at Plataea in 479 BC. The remaining years of his reign were spent peacefully, but he died at the hands of a traitor.

XIMENES DE CISNEROS, Francisco
1436–1517

Spanish prelate and statesman, born Castile. Ordained in Rome, his papal nomination was refused by the Archbishop of Toledo and Ximenes was imprisoned for six years. On his release, he went into seclusion, but his great learning and piety reached the ears of Queen Isabella of Castile, who invited him to become her confessor. Three years later he replaced the Archbishop of Toledo who had once incarcerated him, and on Isabella's death, and in the absence of her husband, Ferdinand of Aragon, he wielded enormous influence over the country's affairs. He introduced centralised monarchical authority and beneficial fiscal reforms, but his obsession with persecuting the Moors was counterproductive. When Ferdinand died in 1516, Ximenes became regent but died travelling to meet his new emperor, Charles V, for the first time. His writings include the great scholarly work known as the Complutensian Polyglot Bible.

YAHYA KHAN, Agha Muhammad
1917–80

Pakistani soldier and politian, born Chakwal, Jhelum. Educated in India, he fought with the British 8th Army in World War II and by 1957 had been promoted to chief of general staff. A confidant of General **Ayub Khan**, he helped ensure the success of his 1958 coup, and was appointed commander-in-chief in 1966. Three years later, he replaced Ayub Khan as the country's military ruler and sanctioned the first free national elections in 1970. His inability to assuage the Bangladeshi separatists triggered a civil war and led to the republic's fragmentation in the aftermath of the war with India in 1971. Yahya Khan then resigned and was placed under house arrest for five years.

YAMAGATA, Prince Aritomo
1838–1922

Japanese general and politician, born Hagi. War Minister from 1873 and chief of staff from 1878, he modernised Japan's military system to ensure his country's emergency as a world force by the beginning of the 20th century. He served twice as Prime Minister between 1889 and 1900, was chief of staff in the 1904 Russo-Japanese war, and president of the Privy Council the following year. He received an honorary OM in 1906.

YAMANI, Sheikh Ahmed Zaki
1930–

Saudi Arabian politician, born Cairo. Educated in New York and at Harvard, he graduated as a lawyer and practised law before entering politics in the 1950s. In 1962, he was appointed Minister of Petroleum with responsibility also for his country's mineral resources, and came to public prominence as the chief spokesman of the OPEC countries during the 1973 oil crises. A resourceful and personable moderate, he always cautioned the organization's other members against using their countries' most valuable natural resource to hold western nations to ransom in times of diplomatic discord or economic difficulty. In 1986, he founded the Centre for Global Energy Studies.

YANAYEV, Gennady
1937–

Soviet statesman, born in the Gorky region of Russia. He helped lead the Komsomol, the Communist youth league, and went on to become head of the Committee on Soviet Youth Organisations. From 1980 he was leader of the Union of Soviet Societies for Friendship and Cultural Relations with Foreign Countries, moving on to the official trade union movement in 1986. He became chairman of the Central Council of Trade Unions in 1990, but left the post when he entered the Central Committee Secretariat and Politburo in July of the same year. He pledged to back **Gorbachev**'s reform programme but was opposed to the shock of radical economic reform. Nominated for the Vice-President's post by Gorbachev in December 1990, and strongly supported by him, he attempted to replace Gorbachev as president in the unsuccessful August coup, but was in hospital 'with high blood pressure' before Gorbachev's reinstatement.

YANG SHANGKUN
1907–

Chinese politician. Educated in Moscow, he took part in the 1934 Long March and the liberation war (1937–49), and joined the Chinese Community Party's secretariat in 1956. A victim of the Cultural Revolution purges of 1966–9, he was rehabilitated in 1978 and was made a member of the CCP's politburo in 1982, and elected President in 1988. It was under his authority that the 27th Army troops carried out the Tiananmen Square massacre in June 1989.

YELTSIN, Boris Nikolayevich
1931–

Soviet politician, born Sverdlovsk. As a construction worker, he joined the Soviet Communist Party of the Soviet Union (CPSU) in 1961 and was appointed regional secretary in 1976. His abilities came to the attention of **Mikhail Gorbachev**, who sponsored his appointment to the CPSU in 1985. He worked briefly under **Nikolai Ryzhkov** before being made Moscow party chief later the same year. He immediately set himself the task of rooting out corruption in the Moscow party machine. His success was such that by 1987 anti-reformist conservatives whom he had accused of sabotaging perestroika engineered his dismissal from high office. However, Gorbachev's electoral reforms saw Yeltsin—always popular with the people—returning to public life in 1990 as a Deputy to the new USSR Congress. In the same year he became Chairman of the Russian Federation Supreme Soviet, giving him a power base from which to criticize Gorbachev. In the autumn of 1990, having grown increasingly impatient with his former mentor's lack of progress, Yeltsin advocated a radical reform programme for Russia embracing property ownership, anti-monopoly laws, taxes, banking and credit, and extensive consitutional reforms. However, when a crippling strike by miners seeking higher pay to meet burgeoning food prices threatened army intervention and Gorbachev's reformist Administration, Yeltsin helped to bring the dispute to an end. In 1991 he consolidated his personal power base by winning the election for the Russian presidency and establishing his international credibility with foreign visits to meet world leaders, including President **George Bush**. His international standing and domestic power were increased further by his high-profile resistance to the failed attempt to depose **Mikhail Gorbachev** as president. A struggle for control between the two men seemed inevitable after Gorbachev resumed the presidency, at a time when the USSR looked in danger of fragmenting.

YOSHIDA, Shigeru
1878–1967

Japanese politician, born Tokyo. Ambassador to Italy and to London between 1930 and 1938, and having been imprisoned for his anti-extremist views in World War II, he was made Foreign Minister with the allies, approval in 1945 and shortly after being elected the first chairman of the Liberal Party in 1946, he formed a Government and implemented a new constitution. He won re-election in 1948, resigning in 1954.

YOUNG, David Ivor, Baron Young of Graffham
1932–

British politician. After qualifying as a solicitor, he entered commerce and industry, and was made director of the Centre for Policy Studies, a ring-wing think-tank, by **Margaret Thatcher** in 1979. He was subsequently appointed chairman of the Manpower Services Commission, and received a peerage and joined the Cabinet in 1984, becoming Employment Secretary the follow-

ing year. He supplanted **Norman Tebbit** as Thatcher's closest adviser during the 1987 general election campaign, but gradually lost influence and returned to commerce in 1989.

YUAN SHIKAI
1859–1916

Chinese dictator, born Henan province. After army service, he was appointed an imperial adviser and held ministerial office with responsibility for Korea from 1885 until 1894. Banished as governor of Shantung after the death of the Empress in 1908, he was recalled and given supreme command in the 1911 revolution. He managed to engineer both the abdication of the young emperor and the resignation of the recently elected president, **Sun Yixian** (Sun Yat Sen), assumed power, and abolished the newly formed Parliament, but he grew over-ambitious and his attempts to become emperor in 1915 resulted in his downfall and death in mysterious circumstances.

ZAGHLUL, Saad
1857–1927

Egyptian politician, born Cairo. As a co-founder in 1918 of the nationalist Wafd Party, he was arrested by the British, but with the granting of limited independence in 1924 he was made Prime Minister for a brief term before being forced to resign, though he remained a strong background influence until his death.

ZHAO ZIYANG
1918–

Chinese politician, born Henan province. A member of the Communist Party underground during the 1937–49 liberation war, he held senior party posts between 1951 and 1962, but as a supporter of the reforming **Liu Shaoqi**, he was purged in the 1966-9 Cultural Revolution. With **Zhou Enlai**'s rise to power, he was rehabilitated in 1973 and appointed secretary of Sichuan, the country's largest province, in 1975. The success of his market-led reforms brought him full membership of the Politburo in 1979 and his appointment as prime minister in 1980. He relinquished that office in 1987 on replacing the disgraced **Hu Yaobang** as General Secretary, but was dismissed over his liberal handling of the 1989 student demonstrations.

ZHIVKOV, Todor
1911–

Bulgarian statesman, born Sofia. A Communist Party member since 1932, in World War II he fought in the resistance movement that in 1944 overthrew the pro-German Sofia regime. He was made party secretary in 1954 and Prime Minister in 1962, and, as chairman of the Council of State from 1981, he was effectively the republic's President. In 1989 Zhivkov was replaced by Petur Mladenov as leader of the Bulgarian Communist Party, and in 1990 he was indicted on charges of 'especially gross embezzlement'. When his trial began in February 1991 he pleaded not guilty, complaining that the trial was 'a farce'.

ZHOU ENLAI
1898–1976

Chinese politician, born Jaingsu province. As a student in Paris between 1920 and 1924, he co-founded the Chinese Communist Party's first overseas branch, and, on returning to his homeland, he established several communist cells in Shanghai and organized an abortive coup in Nanchang in 1927. He supported **Mao Zedong**'s election as party leader in 1935, and between 1936 and 1946 liaised between the CCP and the nationalist government of **Jiang Jeshi**. He was elected Prime Minister in 1949, which office he held until his death, and was concurrently Foreign Minister until 1958. An influential figure in his country's foreign affairs, his negotiations with **Kosygin** in 1969 averted a border war with the Russians, and throughout the 1970s he improved détente with the USA to counterbalance Soviet influence in Asia.

ZHU DE
1886–1976

Chinese soldier and statesman, born Sichuan province. As an activist in the 1911 **Sun Yixian** (Sun Yat-sen) revolution, he achieved the rank of brigadier-general by 1911, but soon after became addicted to opium. By 1922 he was cured and went to study in Germany, but was expelled from the country for his communist activities. Returning to China, he obtained a command in a military training school and took part in the 1927 army uprising against **Jiang Jeshi** (Chiang Kai-shek), helping to establish the Red Army the following year. As commander-in-chief, he led the Long March (1934–6), successfully

devised and deployed guerrilla tactics against the Japanase until 1945, and headed the People's Army until 1954. He was Vice-President from 1949 to 1959, and acting head of state in 1975.

ZHUKOV, Georgi Konstantinovich
1896–1974

Russian soldier and politician, born Strelkovka, Kaluga. A former member of the Red Army, in World War II he commanded Soviet tanks in Outer Mongolia, ended the siege of Moscow in 1941 and liberated Stalingrad in 1943, going on to capture Warsaw and Berlin. In 1945, he accepted the German surrender on behalf of the Soviet high command, and subsequently became commander-in-chief of the Russian sector. He was made Minister of Defence in 1955, and despite supporting **Nikita Khrushchev** in the move to oust him in 1957, later that year Zhukov was dismissed as a potential rival for the leadership.

ZIA, Begum Khaleda
?–

Bangladeshi. politician. The widow of General **Ziaur Rahman** who was president of Bangladesh from 1977 until his assassination in 1981, she became leader of the Bangladesh Nationalist Party (BNP) in 1982. In 1990 elections were called for when President **Hossein Mohammad Ershad** was forced to resign. The BNP's main contestant was the Awami League led by Sheikh Hasina Wajed but in the event they only gained 30 per cent of the seats and in 1991 Begum Zia became the first woman Prime Minister of Bangladesh.

ZIA (UL–HAQ), General Mohammed
1924–88

Pakistani soldier and politician, born Jaladnhar. The son of a middle-class Muslim family, he was educated in India and fought in Burma, Malaya and Indonesia during World War II. Following officer training in the USA, he held a number of senior commands in the 1950s and 1960s before being appointed chief-of-staff in 1976. A year later, he led the coup against **Zulfikar Ali Bhutto**, and proclaimed himself President in 1978. He introduced new Islamisation and free-market policies, and his opposition to the Soviet invasion of Afghanistan in 1979 brought him support from the the USA and other western powers. However, his ruthless suppression of political opposition at home and Bhutto's execution in 1979 brought international condemnation. He moved towards the introduction of a civilian government in 1981 and lifted martial law in 1985, but he was killed when the military aircraft in which he was a passenger crashed in south-eastern Punjab three years later.

ZIAUR RAHMAN
1935–81

Bangladeshi soldier and politician. As a major in the 1971 insurrection and the civil war, he played a key role in the emergence of Bangladesh as an indendent state, and was appointed chief-of-staff after the assassination of Sheik **Mukibur Rahman** in 1975. Military rule continued even after the 1978 election that brought him the presidency, but he remained a popular ruler, surviving several attempted coups, but was eventualy assassinated.

ZIMMERMANN, Arthur
1864–1940

German politician, born East Prussia. After diplomatic service in China, he was briefly Foreign Secretary in 1917, and was the author of the famous telegram to the German Minister in Mexico suggesting that an attack on the USA be launched from that country with German and Japanese assistance and which finally took America into World War I.

ZINOVIEV, Grigory Evseyevich
1883–1936

Russian politician, born Elisavetgrad, Ukraine. A prominent member of the government between 1817 and 1926, a letter allegedly written by him in 1924 suggesting an insurrection in Britain helped bring down **Ramsay MacDonald**, but he was expelled from the party for aligning with **Leon Trotsky**. He was the victim of one of the first big purge trials and executed in 1936 for conspiring with Trotsky and **Lev Kamenev** to murder **Sergey Kirov** and **Joseph Stalin**. He was posthumously rehabilitated by the Soviet Supreme Court in 1988.

Quotations

ACHESON, Dean

1893–1971   American politician

I will undoubtedly have to seek what is happily known as gainful employment, which I am glad to say does not describe holding public office.

On resigning as Secretary of State in 1952 to resume his career as a lawyer.

Great Britain has lost an Empire and not yet found a role. The attempt to play a separate power role — that is, a role apart from Europe, based on a special relationship with the United States, on being the head of the Commonwealth — is about to be played out. Her Majesty's Government is now attempting, wisely in my opinion, to re-enter Europe.

Speech at West Point military academy, December 1962.

ACTON, Lord

1834–1902   British historian

Power tends to corrupt, and absolute power corrupts absolutely. Great men are almost always bad men. There is no worse heresy than that the office sanctifies the holder of it.

Letter to Bishop Mandell Creighton, 5 April 1887.

ADAMS, John Quincy

1735–1826   2nd US President

The second day of July 1776 will be the most memorable epoch in the history of America. It ought to be solemnised with pomp and parade, with shows, games, sports, guns, bells, bonfires and illuminations from one end of this continent to the other — from this time forward, for ever more.

Letter to his wife dated 3 July 1776, on the vote of Congress for independence from Britain.

What a poor, ignorant, malicious, short-sighted, crapulous mass is Tom Paine's common sense.

Letter to Thomas Jefferson dated 22 June 1819, referring to the republican's treatise on independence entitled Common Sense.

ADDINGTON, Henry (Viscount Sidmouth)

1757–1844   British Prime Minister

I hate liberality. Nine times out of ten it is cowardice — and the tenth time, lack of principle.

Attrib.

ADENAUER, Konrad

1876–1967   West German Chancellor

We must free ourselves from thinking in terms of nation states. The countries of western Europe are no longer in a position to protect themselves individually. Not one of them is any longer in a position to salvage Europe's culture.

Speech, May 1953.

ADDISON, Joseph

1672–1719   English essayist

We are always doing something for posterity, but I would fain see posterity do something for us.

The Spectator

AGNEW, Spiro T

1918–90   American Vice-President

To some extent, if you've seen one city slum, you've seen them all.

Election campaign speech, Detroit, 18 October 1968.

In the United States today we have more than our fair share of the nattering nabobs of negativism. They have formed their own Four H Club – the hopeless, hysterical, hypochondriacs of history.

Speech decrying media pundits, September 1970.

ALEXANDER I

1777–1825   Tsar of Russia

Napoleon thinks that I am a fool, but he who laughs last laughs longest.

Letter to his sister, 8 October 1808.

ALEXANDER II

1818–81   Tsar of Russia

It is better to abolish serfdom from above than to wait for it to abolish itself from below.

Speech, 30 March 1856.

AMERY, Julian

1919–   British politician

We have suffered the inevitable consequences of a combination of unpreparedness and feeble counsel.

On the Falklands crisis, House of Commons, 3 April 1982.

AMERY, Leo

1873–1955   British statesman

Cromwell said to the Long Parliament when he thought it was no longer fit to conduct the affairs of the nation, 'You have sat too long here for any good you have been doing. Depart, I say, and let us have done with you. In the name of God, go!'

Remark addressed to Prime Minister Neville Chamberlain, House of Commons, 7 May 1940.

Speak for England, Arthur!

Shouted to Arthur Greenwood, Labour Opposition spokesman, as he began a House of Commons speech on 2 September 1939, immediately preceding the declaration of World War II.

AMIN, Idi

1925–   Ugandan soldier and President

Your experience will be a lesson to all of us men to be careful not to marry ladies in very high positions.

Unsolicited advice to Lord Snowdon on the ending of his marriage to Princess Margaret.

ANNE

1665–1714   Queen of Great Britain

I have changed my Ministers but I have not changed my measures. I am still for moderation, and I will govern by it.

Addressing her new Tory Administration, January 1711.

ANTHONY, Susan B.

1820–1906   American journalist and feminist

The true Republic: men, their rights and nothing more; women, their rights and nothing less.

The Revolution

There will never be complete equality until women themselves help to make laws and to elect lawmakers.

The Arena

APPIUS CAECUS

4th-3rd century BC   Roman statesman

Sed res docuit id verum esse, quod in Carminibus Appius ait, fabrum esse suae quemque fortunae.

But the cast has proved that to be true which Appius says in his songs, that each man is the architect of his own fate.

APPLETON, Edward

1892–1965   British physicist

You must not miss Whitehall. At one end you will find a statue of one of our kings who was beheaded; at the other, a monument to the man who did it. That is just one example of our attempts to be fair to everybody.

Speech, Stockholm, 1 January 1948.

ARIOSTO, Ludovico

1474–1533   Italian poet

Nature made him, and then broke the mould.

Orlando Furioso

ARISTOTLE

384–322 BC   Greek philosopher

Man is by nature a political animal.

Politics

ARMSTRONG, Sir Robert

1927–   British civil servant

I was being economical with the truth.

On being cross-examined at the Spycatcher secrets trial, Australia, November 1986.

ARNOLD, Matthew
1822–88   British poet, critic and essayist

But that vast portion, lastly, of the working class that, raw and half-developed, has long lain half-hidden amidst its poverty and squalor, and is now issuing from its hiding place to assert an Englishman's heaven-born privilege of doing as he likes, and is beginning to perplex us by marching where it likes, meeting where it likes, bawling what it likes, breaking what it likes — to this vast residium we may with great propriety give the name of populace.
Culture and Anarchy

ASHDOWN, Paddy
1941–   British politician

Neil Kinnock has travelled the road to Damascus so often, I hear that he has decided to buy himself a season ticket.
Liberal Democratic Party conference, September 1990.

The ringmaster has altered, but the circus remains the same.
On John Major's election as Conservative Party leader, The Observer, 2 December 1990.

ASQUITH, Herbert Henry
1852–1928   British Prime Minister

We shall never sheathe the sword, which we have not lightly drawn, until Belgium receives in full measure all and more than all that she has sacrificed; until France is adequately secured against the menace of aggression; until the rights of the smaller nationalities of Europe are placed upon an unassailable foundation; and until the military domination of Prussia is wholly and finally destroyed.
Speech, Guildhall, 9 November 1914.

It is fitting that we should have buried the unknown Prime Minister by the side of the Unknown Soldier.
Remark at the Westminster Abbey funeral of Bonar Law, 5 November 1923.

ASQUITH, Margot
1865–1945   Wife of H. H. Asquith

If Kitchener is not a great man, he is, at least, a great poster.
Portrait of an Imperialist

David Lloyd George could not see a belt without hitting below it.
Quoted by Baroness Asquith in a TV interview, April 1967.

Stafford Cripps has a brilliant mind, until he makes it up.
The Wit of the Asquiths

F. E. Smith is very clever, but sometimes he lets his brains go to his head.
Ib.

ASTOR, Viscountess Nancy
1879–1964   American-born British MP

You will never get on in politics, my dear, with *that* hair.
Attributed remark addressed to Shirley Williams.

ATATURK, Kemal
1880–1938   Founder of the Turkish republic

It was necessary to abolish the fez, emblem of ignorance, negligence, fanaticism and hatred of progress and civilisation, to accept in its place the hat — the headgear worn by the whole civilised world.

From his six-day speech, Turkish Assembly, October 1927.

ATTLEE, Clement
1883–1967   British statesman

We believe in a League system in which the whole world should be ranged against an aggressor . . . We do not think that you can deal with national armaments by piling up national armaments in other countries.

House of Commons, 11 March 1935.

One cannot divide peace in Europe. One must have peace running right through. I think that we ought to give up altogether the old traditional doctrine of the balance of power — that balance of armed strength that we used to support for so many years. That is obsolete now. The way to get peace is not through the balance of power but through the League.

House of Commons, 26 March 1936.

We have seen today a gallant, civilized and democratic people betrayed and handed over to a ruthless despotism.

House of Commons speech on Czechoslovakia, 3 October 1938.

I count our progress [in the Labour Party] by the extent to which what we cried in the wilderness five and thirty years ago has now become part of the assumptions of the ordinary man and woman . . . It is better to argue from what has been done to what may be done, rather than to suggest that very little has been accomplished.

Letter to H. J. Laski, 1 May 1944.

I have been very happy . . . serving in a state of life to which I had never expected to be called.

Autobiography

Russian communism is the illegitimate child of Karl Marx and Catherine the Great.

Speech, 11 April 1956.

Democracy means government by discussion, but it is only effective if you can stop people talking.

Quoted in Anatomy of Britain.

The House of Lords is like a glass of champagne that has stood for five days.

Attrib.

ATTWOOD, Thomas
1783–1856   English radical

All that these honest men said was that the Members of that House of Commons by birth, parentage, habits of life, wealth, and education had not shown that anxiety to relieve the sufferings, and redress the wrongs, of the working classes, which they believed to be their rights as enjoying the privileges of British subjects. Therefore, they had adopted the extreme course of entering upon their separate path, with the view of endeavouring to recover those ancient privileges that they believed to form the original and constitutional right of the Commons of England.

Introducing the Chartist petition, House of Commons, 14 June 1839.

AUBREY, John
1626–97   English antiquary

Neither will it be that a people overlaid with taxes should ever become valiant and martial.
Of the True Greatness of Kingdoms

AUDEN, W. H.
1907–73   British poet

Political history is far too criminal and pathological to be a fit subject of study for the young. Children should acquire their heroes and villains from fiction.
A Certain World

The true men of action in our time, those who transform the world, are not the politicians and the statesmen but the scientists. Unfortunately, poetry cannot celebrate them, because their deeds are concerned with things, not persons — and are, therefore, speechless.
The Dyer's Hand

AUSTIN, Warren R.
1877–1962   American diplomat

It is better that aged diplomats be bored than for young men to die.
On soporifically-lengthy debates at the United Nations.

Jews and Arabs should settle their differences like good Christians.
Attrib.

BABEUF, François-Emile
1760–97   French socialist

The French Revolution is merely the herald of a far greater and much more solemn revolution, which will be the last . . . The hour has come for founding the Republic of equals — that great refuge open to every man.
Conjuration des Égaux

BACON, Francis
1561–1626   English philosopher

It is as hard and severe a thing to be a true politician as it is to be truly moral.
Advancement of Learning

The French are wiser than they seem, and the Spaniards seem wiser than they are.
Of Seeming Wise

BAER, George
1842–1914   American industrialist

The rights and interests of the laboring man will be protected and cared for, not by the labor agitators, but by the Christian men to whom God, in his infinite wisdom, has given control of the property interests of the country.
Letter to press during the 1902 Pennsylvanian miners' strike.

BAGEHOT, Walter
1826–77   British economist and journalist

No man has come so near to our definition of a constitutional statesman — the powers of a first-rate man and the creed of a second-rate man.
Historical Essays: The Character of Sir Robert Peel

A severe though not unfriendly critic of our institutions said that the cure for admiring the House of Lords was to go and look at it.
The English Constitution

It is said that England invented the phrase, Her Majesty's Opposition.
Ib.

The best reason why monarchy is a strong government is that it is an intelligible government. The mass of mankind understand it, and they hardly anywhere in the world understand any other.
Ib.

BAILLIE, Robert
1599–1662   Scottish Presbyterian leader

The Parliament of England cannot have on earth so strong pillars and pregnant supporters of all their privileges as free protestant assemblies established by law, and kept in their full freedom from the lowest to the highest — from the congregational eldership to the general synod of the nation.
A Dissuasive from the Errors of the Time

BALDWIN, James
1924–87   American writer

It is a great shock at the age of five or six to find that in a world of Gary Coopers, you are the Indian.
Speech to Cambridge Union, 17 February 1965.

BALDWIN, Stanley
1867–1947   British statesman

A lot of hard-faced men who look as if they had done very well out of the war.
On the first post-World War I Parliament, quoted in **Economic Consequences of the Peace.**

I met Curzon in Downing Street, and received the sort of greeting a corpse would give an undertaker.
On his rival for the premiership, Lord Curzon, on the death of Bonar Law in 1923.

When the call came to me to form a Government, one of my first thoughts was that it should be a Government of which Harrow would not be ashamed.
Attrib.

The work of a Prime Minister is the loneliest job in the world.
Speech, 9 January 1927.

BALDWIN, Stanley *(contd.)*

The papers conducted by Lord Rothermere and Lord Beaverbrook are not newspapers in the ordinary acceptance of the term. They are engines of propaganda for the constantly-changing policies, desires, personal wishes, and personal likes and dislikes of two men. What the proprietorship of those papers is aiming at is power, and power without responsibility — the prerogative of the harlot throughout the ages.
Speech, March 1931.

When you think about the defence of England, you no longer think of the chalk cliffs of Dover. You think of the Rhine. That is where our frontier lies today.
House of Commons, 30 July 1934.

There is a wind of nationalism and freedom blowing round the world, and blowing as strongly in Asia as elsewhere.
Speech, December 1934.

You will find in politics that you are much exposed to the attribution of false motives. Never complain and never explain.
To Harold Nicholson, 1943, quoting Disraeli.

BALFOUR, Arthur James
1848–1930   British statesman

I thought that [Winston Churchill] was a young man of promise, but it appears that he was a young man of promises.
*Quoted in **Winston Churchill**, Volume 1.*

I look forward to a time when Irish patriotism will as easily combine with British patriotism as Scottish patriotism combines now.
Speech, Glasgow, December 1889.

His Majesty's Government looks with favour upon the establishment in Palestine of a national home for the Jewish people.
The Balfour Declaration, made in a letter to Lord Rothschild, 2 November 1917.

The General Strike has taught the working classes more in four days than years of talking could have done.
House of Commons, 7 May 1926.

There are three groups that no British Prime Minister should ever provoke: the Vatican, the Treasury, and the miners.
Attrib.

I would rather be an opportunist and float, than go to the bottom with my principles around my neck.
Attrib.

Nothing matters very much, and very few things matter at all.
Attrib.

It has always been desirable to tell the truth, but seldom if ever necessary to tell the whole truth.
Attrib.

BAKUNIN, Mikhail
1814–76   Russian anarchist

From each according to his faculties, to each according to his needs; that is what we wish, sincerely and energetically.

Anarchists' 1870 declaration

BANDA, Hastings
1906–   Malawi statesman

I wish that I could bring Stonehenge to Nyasaland, to show that there was a time when Britain had a savage culture.

The Observer, *10 March 1963.*

BARNUM, Phineas
1810–91   American showman

There's a sucker born every minute.

Attrib.

BARRIE, J. M.
1860–1937   Scottish novelist and dramatist

I have always found that the man whose second thoughts are good is worth watching.

What Every Woman Knows

BARUCH, Bernard
1870–1965   American financier and presidential adviser

Let us not be deceived. We are today in the midst of a cold war.

Speech to the South Carolina legislature, 16 April 1947.

BATES, Katharine Lee
1859–1929   American poet

O beautiful for spacious skies,
For amber waves of grain,
For purple mountain majesties
Above the fruited plain!
America! America!
God shed His grace on thee.
And crown thy good with brotherhood
From sea to shining sea.

America the Beautiful

BAXTER, Beverley
1891–1964   British politician

A great many persons are able to become Members of this House without losing their insignificance.

House of Commons, 1946.

Beaverbrook is so pleased to be in the Government that he is like the town tart who has finally married the mayor.

Remark attributed to Beverley Baxter by Sir Henry Channon.

BEAVERBROOK, Lord (Max Aitken)

1879–1964   Canadian-born British newspaper proprietor and politician

David Lloyd George did not care in which direction the car was travelling, so long as he was in the driver's seat.

The Decline and Fall of Lloyd George

He has all the qualities that go to the making of a leader of the Conservative Party. He is not stupid, but he is very dull. He is not eloquent, but he talks well. He is not honest, politically, but he is most evangelical. He has a little money, but not much. He always conforms to the party policy.

Commenting on Sir Samuel Hoare's appointment as Foreign Secretary in 1935.

Churchill on top of the wave has in him the stuff of which tyrants are made.

Politicians and the War

With the publication of [Earl Haig's] private papers in 1952, he committed suicide 25 years after his death.

Men and Power

BEHAN, Brendan

1923–64   Irish playwright

Other people have a nationality. The Irish and the Jews have a psychosis.

Richard's Cork Leg

BELLOC, Hilaire

1870–1953   French-born British writer

I am a Catholic. As far as possible I go to Mass every day. As far as possible I kneel down and tell these beads every day. If you reject me on account of my religion, I shall thank God that he has spared me the indignity of being your representative.

Election campaign speech, Salford, 1906.

They died to save their country, and they only saved the world.

The English Graves

BENN, Tony

1925–   British politician

The House of Lords is the British Outer Mongolia for retired politicians.

Speech made during his campaign to disclaim his hereditary peerage, 11 February 1962.

It is beginning to dawn on people that the influence of a nation is not measured by the size of its military budget, but by its industrial strength.

The Independent, 18 April 1991

The dependence of London on Washington for the supply of our so-called independent nuclear weapons is all that remains of the 'special relationship' and . . . it is really a ball and chain limiting our capacity to play a more positive role in the world.

Ib.

BENN, Tony *(contd.)*

As the debate about 'constitutional reform' proceeds, a fundamental change will be called for that converts Britain from a monarchy to a republic — or commonwealth — that is secular, federal, and democratic; ending our jurisdiction in Northern Ireland, giving women absolutely equal representation in Parliament, replacing patronage by election, making the judiciary, police and security services accountable, and restoring and entrenching civil liberties in a charter of rights.

Ib.

BENNETT, Arnold
1867–1931   British writer

Mr Lloyd George spoke for 117 minutes, in which period he was detected only once in the use of an argument.

Things That Have Interested Me

Journalists say a thing that they know isn't true, in the hope that if they keep on saying it long enough it will be true.

The Title

BENSON, A. C.
1862–1925   British writer

Land of Hope and Glory, Mother of the Free,
How shall we extol thee, who are born of thee?
Wider still and wider shall thy bounds be set;
God who made thee mighty, make thee mightier yet.

Land of Hope and Glory

BENTHAM, Jeremy
1748–1832   English political theorist

The greatest happiness of the greatest number is the foundation of morals and legislation.

The Commonplace Book

BENTLEY, Nicholas
1907–78   British cartoonist and writer

Henry Campbell-Bannerman is remembered chiefly as the man about whom all is forgotten.

An Edwardian Album

BERKELEY, Bishop
1685–1753   Irish philosopher and churchman

It is impossible that a man who is false to his friends and neighbours should be true to the public.

Maxims Concerning Patriotism

BEVAN, Aneurin
1897–1960   British politician

The worst thing that I can say about democracy is that it has tolerated the right honourable gentleman [Neville Chamberlain] for four and a half years.

House of Commons, 23 July 1929.

BEVAN, Aneurin *(contd.)*

We have been the dreamers. We have been the sufferers. Now we are the builders. We want the complete political extinction of the Tory Party — and 25 years of Labour Government, for we cannot do in five years what requires to be done.
Labour Party conference, Blackpool, 18 May 1945.

No amount of cajolery, and no attempts at ethical or social seduction, can eradicate from my heart a deep and burning hatred for the Tory Party that inflicted those experiences on me. So far as I am concerned, they are lower than vermin.
Speech on the inter-war depression, made at the inauguration of the National Health Service, 5 July 1948.

Winston Churchill . . . does not like the language of the 20th century; he talks the language of the 18th century. He is still fighting Blenheim all over again. His only answer to a difficult diplomatic situation is to send a gunboat.
Labour Party conference, Scarborough, 2 October 1951.

In Place of Fear
Title of his 1952 book about disarmament.

We know what happens to people who stay in the middle of the road. They get run over.
The Observer, December 1953.

I am not going to spend any time whatsoever attacking the Foreign Secretary. Quite honestly, I am beginning to feel extremely sorry for him. If we complain about the tune, there is no reason to attack the monkey when the organ grinder is present.
Expressing his wish to address Prime Minister Harold Macmillan rather than Selwyn Lloyd on the Suez crisis, House of Commons, May 1957.

If you carry this resolution, you will send a Foreign Secretary — whoever he may be — naked into the conference chamber. You call that statesmanship. I call it an emotional spasm.
Labour Party conference speech against unilateral disarmament, October 1957.

Politics is a blood sport.
Quoted in Jennie Lee's biography, My Life with Nye.

BEVERIDGE, Lord
1879–1963 British economist

The trouble in modern democracy is that men do not approach to leadership until they have lost the desire to lead anyone.
The Observer, 15 April 1934.

BEVIN, Ernest
1881–1951 British politician

The most conservative man in the world is the British trade unionist, when you want to change him.
Speech to Trade Union Congress, 8 September 1927.

If you open that Pandora's box, you never know what Trojan 'orses will jump out.
On his doubts about the value of the Council of Europe on its formation in 1949.

If you recognize anyone, it does not mean that you like him. We all, for instance, recognize the honourable Member for Ebbw Vale.
Said of him by Sir Winston Churchill in a House of Commons debate on 1 July 1952 on British recognition of communist China

BIKO, Steve
1946–77   South African Black civil rights activist

Whites must be made to realise that they are only human, not superior. It's the same with Blacks. They must be made to realise that they are also human, not inferior.
Boston Globe, 26 October 1977.

BIRKENHEAD, Lord
1872–1930   British politician

The world continues to offer glittering prizes to those who have stout hearts and sharp swords.
Rectorial address, Glasgow, 7 November 1923.

BISMARK, Count Otto von
1815–98   German Chancellor

The great questions of our day cannot be solved by speeches and majority votes but by iron and blood.
Speech to the Prussian Chamber, 30 September 1862. He later altered the concluding words to the more commonly quoted 'blood and iron'.

Politics is not an exact science.
Speech to the Prussian Chamber, 18 December 1863.

Anyone who has ever looked into the glazed eyes of a soldier dying on the battlefield will think hard before starting a war.
Speech, Berlin, August 1867.

If we are to negotiate, I envisage that we shall play an essentially modest role; that of an honest broker who really intends to do business.
Speech to the Reichstag, 19 February 1878, on preventing war in Europe.

If there is ever another war in Europe, it will come out of some damned silly thing in the Balkans.
Deathbed remark attributed by Ballen.

BOILEAU, Nicolas
1636–1711   French writer

Often, the fear of one evil leads us into inflicting one that is worse.
L'Art poétique

BOLINGBROKE, Henry St John, Viscount
1678–1751   British writer and politician

Faction is to party what the superlative is to the positive. Party is a political evil, and faction is the worst of all parties.
The Patriot King

BONHAM-CARTER, Lady Violet
1887–1968   British society hostess

Harold Macmillan held his party together by not allowing his left wing to see what his right wing was doing.
Attrib.

BOOTHBY, Sir Robert
1900–86   British politician

Of all the pygmies, Samuel Hoare was the pygmiest.

BORAH, William Edgar

1865–1940 American politician

A democracy must remain at home in all matters that affect the nature of her institutions. They are of a nature to call for the undivided attention and devotion of the entire nation. We do not want the racial antipathies or national antagonisms of the Old World transformed to this continent — as they will, should we become a part of European politics. The people of this country are overwhelmingly for a policy of neutrality.

Radio broadcast, 22 February 1936.

BORGES, Jorge Luis

1899–1986 Argentinian writer

The Falklands thing was a fight between two bald men over a comb.

Time, February 1983.

BOTHA, Pik

1932– South African Foreign Minister

We simply could not go on with policies that were a failure economically and internationally, and which we could not morally justify. To allocate rights and privileges on the basis of a physical characteristic was tantamount to sinning against God. In the new Constitution, there cannot possibly be any threat because of colour, race, or what have you. The chairman of my own branch of the National Party will probably be black. But what worries me is, unless President de Klerk can say to the whites, sooner rather than later, 'What I've done is to your advantage', we shall be in trouble.

Interviewed by Donald Woods, BBC TV, February 1991.

BRADLEY, Omar

1893–1981 American general

The wrong war, at the wrong place, at the wrong time — and with the wrong enemy.

At the 1951 Senate inquiry into proposals to escalate the Korean war into China.

BRECHT, Bertolt

1898–1956 German dramatist

The finest plans have always been spoiled by the littleness of those who should carry them out. Even emperors cannot do it all by themselves.

Mother Courage

If there are obstacles, the shortest line between two points may be the crooked one.

Galileo

BREZHNEV, Leonid

1906–82 Soviet statesman

Whatever may divide us, Europe is our common home. A common fate has linked us through the centuries, and it continues to link us today.

Speech while visiting the Federal Republic of Germany, 23 November 1981.

[Margaret Thatcher] is trying to wear the trousers of Winston Churchill.

Speech, 1979.

BRIGHT, John
1811–89   British radical politician

The Angel of Death has been abroad throughout the land. You may almost hear the beating of his wings.
Referring to the Crimean War, House of Commons, 23 February 1855.

This regard for the liberties of Europe, this care at one time for the protestant interest, this excessive love for the balance of power, is neither more nor less than a gigantic system of outdoor relief for the aristocracy of Great Britain.
Speech, Birmingham, 29 October 1858.

England is the mother of Parliaments.
Speech, 18 January 1865.

There is no nation on the continent of Europe that is less able to do harm to England, and there is no nation on the continent of Europe to whom we are less able to do harm, than Russia. We are so separated that it seems impossible that the two nations, by the use of reason or common sense at all, could possibly be brought into conflict with each other.
Speech, Birmingham, 13 January 1878.

BRONOWSKI, Jacob
1908–74   British scientist

Ask an impertinent question, and you are on the way to the pertinent answer.
The Ascent of Man

BROWN, George (later George-Brown, Baron)
1914–85   British politician

Most British statesman have either drunk too much or womanised too much. I never fell into the second category.
The Observer, *November 1974.*

BROWN, John
1800–59   American slave abolitionist

I am as content to die for God's eternal truth on the scaffold as in any other way.
Letter to his children on the eve of his execution, 2 December 1859.

BROWNE, William
1692–1774   English physician

The King to Oxford sent a troop of horse,
For Tories own no argument but force:
With equal skill to Cambridge books he sent,
For Whigs admit no force but argument.
Literary Anecdotes

BRUYERE, Jean de la
1645–96   French satirist

Party loyalty lowers the greatest of men to the petty level of the masses.
Les Caractères

There are some who speak one moment before they think.
Ib.

BUCHANAN, James
1791–1869   US President

All the friends that I loved and wanted to reward are dead, and all the enemies that I hated and I had marked out for punishment are turned to my friends.
On finally achieving his country's highest political office in 1857, at the age of 65.

If you are as happy, my dear Sir, on entering this house as I am on leaving it and returning home, you are the happiest man in the country.
Said on welcoming his successor, Abraham Lincoln, to the White House in 1861.

BUCKINGHAM, Duke of
1628–87   English politician

The world is made up for the most part of fools and knaves.
To Mr Clifford, on his Human Reason

BUCK, Pearl
1892–1973   American novelist

Nothing and no one can destroy the Chinese people. They are relentless survivors. They are the oldest civilised people on earth. Their civilisation passes through phases, but its basic characteristics remain the same. They yield, they bend to the wind — but they never break.
China, Past and Present

BULLOCK, Alan
1914–   British historian

Hitler showed surprising loyalty to Mussolini, but it never extended to trusting him.
Hitler: A Study in Tyranny

The people Hitler never understood, and whose actions continued to exasperate him to the end of his life, were the British.
Ib.

BULMER-THOMAS, Ivor
1905–   British politician

If he ever went to school without any boots, it was because he was too big for them.
Responding at the 1949 Conservative Party conference to remarks by Harold Wilson about his humble upbringing.

BULWER-LYTTON, Edward George
1803–73   British writer and politician

Beneath the rule of men entirely great, the pen is mightier than the sword.
Richelieu

BUNYAN, John
1628–88   English writer

Hanging is too good for him.
The Pilgrim's Progress

BURKE, Edmund
1729–96   English statesman

The greater the power, the more dangerous the abuse.
House of Commons, 7 February 1771.

Parliament is a deliberative assembly of one nation. You choose a Member indeed; but when you have chosen him, he is not the Member for Bristol, but he is a Member of Parliament.
Speech to Bristol voters, 1774.

All government, indeed every human benefit and enjoyment, every virtue, and every prudent act, is founded on compromise and barter.
On conciliation with America, House of Commons, 22 March 1775.

The use of force alone is but temporary. It may subdue for a moment, but it does not remove the necessity of subduing again — and a nation is not governed that is perpetually to be conquered.
Ib.

If any man ask me what a free government is, I answer that for any practical purpose, it is what the people think it so.
Letter to the sheriffs of Bristol 1777

Individuals pass like shadows, but the Commonwealth is fixed and stable . . . The people are the masters.
House of Commons, February 1780.

He was not merely a chip off the old block, but the old block itself.
Commenting on William Pitt the Younger's maiden speech in the House of Commons, 26 February 1781.

A state without the means of some change is without the means of its conservation.
Reflections on the Revolution in France *(1790)*

And having looked to Government for bread, on the very first scarcity they will turn and bite the hand that fed them.
Thoughts and Details on Scarcity 1797

BUSH, George
1924–   41st US President

The United States is the best and fairest and most decent nation on the face of the earth.
Speech, May 1988.

A new breeze is blowing — and a nation refreshed by freedom stands ready to push on. There is new ground to be broken, and new action to be taken.
Inaugural speech, 20 January 1989.

The coalition will give Saddam Hussein until noon Saturday to do what he must do, begin his immediate and unconditional withdrawal from Kuwait. We must hear publicly and authoritatively his acceptance of these terms . . . Saddam Hussein risks subjecting the Iraqi people to further hardship unless the Iraqi Government complies fully with the terms of the statement.
White House statement, 22 February 1991.

BUSH, George *(contd.)*

Yesterday . . . Saddam Hussein was given one last chance, set forth in very explicit terms, to do what he should have done more than six months ago — withdraw from Kuwait without condition or further delay, and comply fully with the resolutions passed by the United Nations Security Council. Regrettably, the noon deadline passed without the agreement of the Government of Iraq to meet the demands of United Nations Security Council Resolution 660 . . . to withdraw unconditionally from Kuwait.

To the contrary, we have seen a redoubling of Saddam Hussein's efforts to destroy completely Kuwait and its people. I have therefore directed General Norman Schwarzkopf, in conjunction with coalition forces, to use all forces available, including ground force, to eject the Iraqi army from Kuwait. Once again, that decision was made only after extensive consultations within our coalition partnership. The liberation of Kuwait has now entered a final phase. I have complete confidence in the ability of the coalition forces swiftly and decisively to accomplish their mission. Tonight, as this coalition of countries seeks to do that which is right and just, I ask only that all of you stop what you were doing and say a prayer for all the coalition forces, and especially for our men and women in uniform, who, this very moment, are risking their lives for their country and for all of us. May God bless and protect each and every one of them, and may God bless the United States of America.

National TV broadcast, 23 February 1991.

BUTLER, Rab

1902–82   British politician

After all, it is not every man who nearly becomes Prime Minister of England.

Commenting in January 1957 on being passed over as Harold Macmillan's
successor in favour of Alec Douglas-Home.

Politics is the art of the possible.

The Art of the Possible

BUTLER, Samuel

1835–1902   British politician

The wish to spread those opinions that we hold conducive to our own welfare is so deeply rooted in the English character that few of us can escape its influence.

Erewhon

Justice is being allowed to do whatever I like. Injustice is whatever prevents my doing it.

Notebooks

BYRON, Lord George Gordon

1788–1824   English poet

Never under the most despotic of infidel Governments did I behold such squalid wretchedness as I have seen since my return, in the very heart of a Christian country. And what are your remedies? After months of inaction, and months of action worse than inactivity, at length comes forth the grand specific — the never-failing nostrum of all state physicians from the days of Draco to the present time; death. Is there not blood enough upon your penal code that more must be poured forth to ascend to Heaven and testify against you?

Maiden speech, House of Lords, 27 February 1812, against a proposal
to introduce the death penalty for machine-wrecking.

CABELL, James Branch
1879–1958 American writer

The optimist proclaims that we live in the best of all possible worlds, and the pessimist fears that is true.
The Silver Stallion

CALHOUN, John Caldwell
1782–1850 American Vice-President

The Government of the absolute majority, instead of the Government of all the people, is but the Government of the strongest interests; and when not efficiently checked, it is the most tyrannical and oppressive that can be devised.
Speech, US Senate, 15 February 1833.

CALIGULA
12–41 AD Roman emperor

Utinam populus Romanus unam cervicem haberet!
Would but the Roman people had but one neck!
Life of Caligula

CALLAGHAN, James
1912– British Prime Minister

A lie can travel halfway round the world before the truth has got its boots on.
House of Commons, November 1976.

Britain has lived for too long on borrowed time, borrowed money, and even borrowed ideas.
The Observer, 3 October 1976.

Crisis? What crisis?
Newspaper headline alluding to his remark on returning from the Guadaloupe summit in 1979 to be confronted by widespread strikes. His actual words were: 'I don't think that other people in the world would share the view that there is mounting chaos.'

CAMUS, Albert
1913–60 French writer

Politics and the fate of mankind are shaped by men without ideals and without greatness. Men who have greatness within them do not go in for politics.
Notebooks 1935–42

CARLYLE, Thomas
1795–1881 Scottish historian and essayist

The seagreen incorruptible.
*Referring to Robespierre in **The History of the French Revolution.***

The public is an old woman. Let her maunder and mumble.
Journal, 1835.

All reform except a moral one will prove unavailing.
Corn Law Rhymes

A man willing to work, and unable to find work, is perhaps the saddest sight that fortune's inequality exhibits under the sun.
Chartism

CARROLL, Lewis (Reverend Charles Dodgson)
1832-98   British writer

'If everybody minded their own business,' the Duchess said in a hoarse growl, 'the world would go round a deal faster than it does.'
Alice's Adventures in Wonderland

CARSON, George Nathaniel
1859–1925   British politician

The British flag has never flown over a more powerful or a more united empire. Never did our voice count for more in the councils of nations, or in determining the future destinies of mankind.
House of Lords, 18 November 1918.

CARTER, Jimmy
1924–   39th US President

Why not the best?
Presidential campaign slogan.

I am convinced that UFOs exist, because I have seen one.
TV interview, 16 June 1976.

We have been shaken by a tragic war abroad, and by scandals and broken promises at home. Our people are searching for new voices and new ideas and new leaders.
Acceptance speech after receiving the Democratic presidential nomination, New York, 14 July 1976.

I have looked on a lot of women with lust. I have committed adultery in my heart many times. God recognises I will do that, and forgives me.
Playboy interview, November 1976.

CARTER, Mrs Lillian
1898–1983   Mother of President Carter

Sometimes when I look at my children, I say to myself, 'Lillian, you should have stayed a virgin.'
Woman, *9 April 1977*

CARTWRIGHT, John
1740–1824   British writer

One man shall have one vote.
People's Barrier Against Undue Influence .

CASTLE, Ted (later, Lord Castle)
British journalist

In Place of Strife.
Title of 1969 Government White Paper on industrial relations suggested to his wife, Barbara Castle.

CASTRO, Fidel
1926–   Cuban revolutionary

We are not politicians. We made our revolution to get the politicians out.
*Speech on assuming the presidency in 1961, two years after overthrowing
the Batista regime.*

A man who does not believe in human beings is not a revolutionary.
Speech, 29 January 1967.

I was a man lucky enough to have discovered a political theory, a man who was
caught up in the whirlpool of Cuba's political crisis long before becoming a fully-
fledged communist. Discovering Marxism was like finding a map in a forest.
Speech, Chile, 18 November 1971.

CICERO
106–43 BC   Roman statesman

Salus populi suprema est lex.
The good of the people is the chief law.
De Legibus

CECIL, Robert Arthur Talbot Gascoyne, 3rd Marquess of Salisbury
1830–1903   British statesman

Peace without honour is not only a disgrace, but, except as a temporary respite, it is
a chimera.
Quarterly Review, *April 1864.*

Under a more heroic Minister, and in a less self-seeking age, it is probable that
England would have preferred the risk, whatever its extent, to the infamy of
betraying an ally whom she had enticed into peril. But our Ministry is not heroic; and
our generation, though not indifferent to glory, prefers it when it is safe and cheap.
*On Palmerston's failure to defend Denmark against Prussia, Quarterly
Review, July 1864.*

English policy is to float lazily downstream, occasionally putting out a diplomatic
boathook to avoid collisions.
Remark attributed by his daughter, 1877.

The commonest error in politics is sticking to the carcasses of old policies.
Speech, Hatfield, 25 May 1877.

We are part of the community of Europe, and we must do our duty as such.
Speech, Caernarvon, 10 April 1888.

It is a superstition of an antiquated diplomacy that there is any necessary antagonism
between Russia and Great Britain.
Speech, London Guildhall, 9 November 1896.

One may roughly divide the nations of the world as the living and the dying. The
weak states are becoming weaker and the strong states are becoming stronger. For
one reason or another — from the necessities of politics or under the pretence of
philanthropy — the living nations will gradually encroach on the territory of the
dying, and the seeds and causes of conflict among civilised nations will speedily
appear.
Ib.

CECIL, Robert Arthur James Gascoyne, 5th Marquess of Salisbury
1893–1972   British politician

The Colonial Secretary [Iain Macleod] has been too clever by half. I believe that he is a very fine bridge player. It is not considered immoral, or even bad form, to outwit one's opponent at bridge. It almost seems to me as if the Colonial Secretary, when he abandoned the sphere of bridge for the sphere of politics, brought his bridge technique with him.
House of Lords, 1961.

CERVANTES, Miguel de
1547–1616   Spanish novelist and dramatist

There are but two families in the world, as my grandmother used to say – the Haves and the Havenots.
Don Quixote

CHALMERS, Patrick Reginald
1872–1942   British writer

What's lost upon the roundabouts we pulls up on the swings!
Green Days and Blue Days

CHAMBERLAIN, Sir Austen
1863–1937   British Foreign Secretary

I yield to no one in my devotion to this great League of Nations, but not even for this will I destroy that smaller but older league of which my own country was the birthplace, and of which it remains the centre . . . Beware how you so draw tight the bonds, how you so pile obligation on obligation and sanction on sanction, lest at last you find that you are not living nations but dead states.
Speech, League of Nations Assembly, Geneva, 9 September 1927.

CHAMBERLAIN, Joseph
1836–1914   British statesman

Lord Salisbury constitutes himself the spokesman of a class, of the class to which he himself belongs, who 'toil not neither do they spin'.
Speech, 30 March 1883.

The day of small nations has long passed away. The day of empires has come.
Speech at Birmingham, May 1904, advocating preferential trade within the British Empire as a means of ensuring Britain's security.

CHAMBERLAIN, Neville
1869–1940   British Prime Minister

In war, whichever side may call itself the victor, there are no winners — but all are losers.
Speech, Kettering, 3 July 1938.

How terrible, fantastic, and incredible it is that we should be digging trenches and trying on gas masks because of a quarrel in a faraway country, between people of whom we know nothing.
Radio broadcast on Germany's invasion of Czechoslovakia, September 1938.

CHAMBERLAIN, Neville *(contd.)*

This morning I had another talk with the German Chancellor, Herr Hitler, and here is the paper that bears his name upon it as well as mine: 'We regard the agreement signed last night and the Anglo-German naval agreement, as symbolic of the desire of our two people never to go to war with one another again.'
Speech on the signing of the Munich Agreement, Heston airport,
30 September 1938.

My good friends, this is the second time in our history that there has come back from Germany to Downing Street peace with honour. I believe that it is peace for our time. Go home and have a nice, quiet sleep.
To the crowds on his return to Downing Street from signing the Munich
Agreement, 30 September 1938.

This morning, the British ambassador in Berlin handed the German Government a final note stating that, unless we heard from them by 11 o'clock, that they were prepared at once to withdraw their troops from Poland, a state of war would exist between us. I have to tell you that no such undertaking has been received, and that consequently this country is at war with Germany.
Radio broadcast, 3 September 1939.

Hitler has missed the bus.
House of Commons, 4 April 1940.

CHAMFORT, Sebastien Roch Nicholas
1741–94   French writer and Jacobin

Society is composed of two large classes; those who have more dinners than appetites, and those who have more appetites than dinners.
Maximes

CHANNON, Henry (Chips)
1897–1958   British politician

How are the mighty fallen!
Responding to the complaints of Tory ladies, including Clementine
Churchill, that they had been denied their traditional favoured view of the
State Opening on 15 August 1945, having been crowded out by the
spouses of the huge intake of new Labour MPs.

This afternoon I slept for two hours in the Library of the House of Commons. A deep House of Commons sleep. There is no sleep to compare with it — rich, deep, and guilty.
Attrib.

I love the House of Commons so passionately that were I to be offered a peerage, I should be tempted to refuse it. Only tempted, of course.
Attrib.

CHARLES, Elizabeth
1828–96   British writer

To know how to say what others only know how to think is what makes men poets or sages; and to dare to say what others only dare to think makes men martyrs or reformers — or both.
Chronicle of the Schönberg-Cotta Family

CHARLES I
1600–49   King of Great Britain and Ireland

Never make a defence or an apology before you be accused.
Letter to Lord Wentworth, 3 September 1636.

This is very true — for my words are my own, and my actions are my Ministers'.
Riposte to The King's Epitaph
See also ROCHESTER.

CHARTER 88

We call for a new constitutional settlement that will:
1. Enshrine, by means of a Bill of Rights, such civil liberties as the right to peaceful assembly, to freedom of association, to freedom from discrimination, to freedom from detention without trial, to trial by jury, to privacy, and to freedom of expression.
2. Subject executive powers and prerogatives, by whomsoever exercised, to the rule of law.
3. Establish freedom of information and open government.
4. Create a fair electoral system of proportional representation.
5. Reform the Upper House of Lords to establish a democratic, non-hereditary second chamber.
6. Place the executive under the power of a democratically renewed Parliament and all agencies of the state under the rule of law.
7. Ensure the independence of a reformed judiciary.
8. Provide legal remedies for all abuses of power by the state and by officials of central and local government.
9. Generate an equitable distribution of power between the nations of the United Kingdom and between local, regional, and central government.
10. Draw up a written constitution, anchored in the idea of universal citizenship, that incorporates these reforms.

CHATHAM, 1st Earl of (William Pitt the elder)
1708–78   British Prime Minister

The atrocious crime of being a young man, which [Walpole] has, with such spirit and decency, charged upon me, I shall neither attempt to palliate nor deny; but content myself with wishing that I may be one of those whose follies cease with their youth, and not of those who continue ignorant in spite of their age and experience.
House of Commons, 6 March 1741.

It is now apparent that this great, this powerful, this formidable kingdom is considered only as a province of a despicable electorate.
House of Commons, 10 December 1742.

I know that I can save this country and that no one else can.
In conversation with one of his private secretaries, November 1756.

I was called by my sovereign and by the voice of the people to assist the State when others had abdicated the service of it. That being so, no one can be surprised that I will go on no longer, since my advice is not taken. Being responsible, I will direct — and will not be responsible for nothing that I do not direct.
Said on informing his Cabinet of his resignation, 3 October 1761.

Where law ends, there tyranny begins.
House of Lords, 9 January 1770.

CHATHAM, 1st Earl of *(contd.)*

The spirit that now resists your taxation in America is the same that formerly opposed loans, benevolences and ship-money in England; the same spirit that called all England on its legs, and by the Bill of Rights vindicated the English constitution; the same spirit that established the great fundamental, essential maxim of your liberties — that no subject of England shall be taxed but by his own consent. The glorious spirit of Whigism animates three million in America, who prefer poverty with liberty to gilded chains and sordid affluence; and who will die in defence of their rights as men, as free men.
House of Lords, 20 January 1775.

As an American, I would recognize to England her supreme right of regulating commerce and navigation; as an Englishman by birth and principle, I recognize to the Americans their supreme, unalienable right to their property — a right that they are justified in the defence of to the last extremity. To maintain that principle is the common cause of the Whigs on the other side of the Atlantic and on this...In that great cause they are immovably allied; it is the alliance of God and nature — immutable, eternal, fixed as the firmament of Heaven.
Ib.

CHESTERFIELD, Earl of

1694–1773   English statesman

Whatever is worth doing at all is worth doing well.
Letter to his son dated 10 March 1746.

I recommend you to take care of the minutes, for hours will take care of themselves.
Letter to his son dated 6 November 1747.

George I's views and affections were singly confined to the narrow compass of the electorate. England was too big for him.
Letters.

CHESTERTON, G. K.

1874–1936   British writer

Democracy means government by the uneducated, while aristocracy means government by the badly educated.
Quoted in New York Times, 1 February 1931.

'My country, right or wrong' is a thing that no patriot would think of saying, except in a desperate case. It is like saying, 'My mother, drunk or sober.'
The Defendant

The madman is not the man who has lost his reason. The madman is the man who has lost everything except his reason.
Orthodoxy

All conservatism is based upon the idea that if you leave things alone, you leave them as they are — but you do not. If you leave a thing alone, you leave it to a torrent of change.
Ib.

Compromise used to mean that half a loaf was better than no bread. Among modern statesmen, it really seems to mean that half a loaf is better than a whole loaf.
What's Wrong with the World

CHURCHILL, Lord Randolph
1849–95   British politician

Ulster will not be a consenting party. Ulster, at the proper time, will resort to the supreme arbitrament of force; Ulster will fight and Ulster will be right.
Letter, 7 May 1886.

This monstrous mixture of imbecility, extravagance and political hysteria, better known as the Bill for the future Government of Ireland — this farrago of superlative nonsense, is to be put in motion for this reason and no other: to gratify the ambition of an old man in a hurry.
Pamphlet attacking Gladstone's Home Rule Bill, June 1886.

The duty of an Opposition is to oppose.
Remark attributed by his son, Winston Churchill.

CHURCHILL, Sir Winston Spencer
1874–1965   British statesman

If Ulster is to become a tool in party calculations; if the civil and parliamentary systems under which we have dwelt so long, and our fathers before us, are to be brought to the rude challenge of force; if the Government and the Parliament of this great country and greater Empire are to be exposed to menace and brutality; if all the loose, wanton and reckless chatter we have been forced to listen to these many months is, in the end, to disclose a sinister and revolutionary purpose, then I can only say to you, 'Let us go forward together and put these grave matters to the proof.'
Speech during the Irish crisis, 14 March 1914.

Of all tyrannies in history, the Bolshevik tyranny is the worst, the most destructive, the most degrading. Every British and French soldier killed last year was really done to death by Lenin and Trotsky — not in fair war, but by the treacherous desertion of an ally without parallel in the history of the world.
Speech, London, 11 April 1919.

The day must come when the nation's whole scale of living must be reduced. If that day comes, Parliament must lay the burden equally on all classes.
Speech as Chancellor of the Exchequer, House of Commons, 7 August 1925.

The loss of India would mark and consummate the downfall of the British Empire. That great organism would pass at a stroke out of life into history. From such a catastrophe there could be no recovery.
Speech to Indian Empire Society, London, 12 December 1930.

It is alarming and odious to see Mr Gandhi, a seditious Middle Temple lawyer, now posing as a fakir of a type well-known in the East, striding half-naked up the steps of the vice-regal palace, while he is still conducting a defiant campaign of civil disobedience, to parley on equal terms with the representative of the King-Emperor.
Speech, 23 February 1931.

I cannot forecast to you the action of Russia. It is a riddle wrapped in a mystery inside an enigma. But perhaps there is a key; that key is Russian national interest.
Radio broadcast, 1 October 1939.

You ask what is our aim. I can answer in one word — victory. Victory at all costs, victory in spite of all terror, victory, however long and hard the road may be.
Ib.

CHURCHILL, Winston Spencer *(contd.)*

We shall fight on the beaches, we shall fight on the landing grounds, we shall fight in the fields and in the streets, we shall fight in the hills. We shall never surrender.
House of Commons, June 1940, after the Dunkirk evacuation.

Never in the field of human conflict was so much owed by so many, to so few.
House of Commons, August 1940, on the Battle of Britain pilots.

Here is the answer that I will give to President Roosevelt. Give us the tools, and we will finish the job.
Radio broadcast, February 1941.

You do your worst, and we will do our best.
Addressed to Hitler in a speech made on 14 July 1941.

No one has been a more consistent opponent of Communism than I have for the last 25 years. I will unsay no word that I have spoken about it, but all that fades away before the spectacle that is now unfolding. The past, with its crimes, its follies, and its tragedies, flashes away. I see the Russian soldiers standing on the threshold of their native land, guarding the fields that their fathers have tilled from time immemorial. Any man or state who fights on against Nazidom will have our aid. Any man or state who marches with Hitler is our foe.
Radio broadcast on the German invasion of Russia, 22 June 1941.

What kind of people do they think we are?
Referring to the Japanese in a speech to Congress, December 1941.

When I warned the French that Britain would fight on alone, General Weygand told their Prime Minister and his divided Cabinet that in three weeks England will have her neck wrung like a chicken. Some chicken, some neck!
Speech to the Canadian Parliament, 30 December 1941.

I have not become the King's First Minister in order to preside over the liquidation of the British Empire.
Mansion House speech, November 1942.

Now this is not the end. It is not even the beginning of the end. But it is, perhaps, the end of the beginning.
Ib.

I have only one purpose — the destruction of Hitler, and my life is much simplified thereby. If Hitler invaded Hell, I would make at least a favourable reference to the Devil in the House of Commons.
The Grand Alliance

The Bomb brought peace, but man alone can keep that peace.
House of Commons, 16 August 1945.

If this is a blessing, it is certainly very well disguised.
On his defeat in 1945 in the first post-war general election, quoted in Richard Nixon's memoirs.

From Stettin in the Baltic to Trieste in the Adriatic, an iron curtain has descended across the Continent.
Speech at Fulton, Missouri, March 1946.

Would a special relationship between the United States and the British Commonwealth be inconsistent with our overriding loyalty to the world organisation?
Ib.

CHURCHILL, Winston Spencer *(contd.)*

In war, resolution. In defeat, defiance. In victory, magnanimity. In peace, good will.
The Second World War

I am ready to meet my maker. Whether my maker is ready for the ordeal of meeting me is another matter.
Speech, November 1949.

Perhaps it is better to be irresponsible and right than to be responsible and wrong.
Radio broadcast, 26 August 1950.

Talking jaw is better than going to war.
White House speech, June 1954.

I have never accepted what many people have kindly said — that I inspired the nation. It was the nation and the race dwelling round the globe that had the lion heart. I had the luck to be called upon to give the roar.
Speech to both Houses of Parliament in Westminster Hall, November 1954, on the occasion of his 80th birthday.

Do not criticise your Government when out of the country. Never cease to do so when at home.
Attrib.

Those who can win a war well can rarely make a good peace, and those who could make a good peace would never have won the war.
My Early Life

Democracy is the worst form of government, except for all the others.
Attrib.

In Franklin Roosevelt there died the greatest American friend we have ever known and the greatest champion of freedom who has ever brought help and comfort from the New World to the Old.
The Second World War

When I look back on all these worries, I remember the story of the old man who said on his deathbed that he had a lot of trouble in his life, most of which had never happened.
Their Finest Hour

I am so bored with it all.
Attributed last words.

CLAUSEWITZ, Karl von
1780–1831   Prussian general

War is the continuation of politics by other means.
Vom Kriege

CLEMENCEAU, Georges
1841–1929   French politician

War is too serious a business to be left to the generals. My home policy? I wage war? My foreign policy? I wage war. Always, everywhere, I wage war. And I shall continue to wage war until the last quarter of an hour.
Speech to the Chamber of Deputies, 8 March 1918.

It is far easier to make war than to make peace.
Speech, 14 July 1919.

CLEMENCEAU, Georges *(contd.)*

We have won the war. Now we have to win the peace — and that may be more difficult.
Quoted in D. R. Watson's autobiography.

America is the only country in history that miraculously has gone directly from barbarism to degeneration without the usual interval of civilisation.
Attrib.

CLEVELAND, Grover
1837–1908   22nd and 24th US President

His whole carcass seemed to be made of iron. There was no give in him – no bounce, no softness. He sailed through American history like a steel ship loaded with monoliths made of granite.
Said of him by H. L. Mencken.

CLIVE, Robert
1725–74

By God, Mr Chairman — at this moment I stand astonished at my own moderation!
Said at a 1773 parliamentary inquiry into his rapacious policies on India.

COBDEN, Richard
1804–65   British politician

Is it that war is a luxury? Is it that we are fighting — to use a cant phrase of Mr Pitt's time — to secure indemnity for the past and security for the future? Are we to be the Don Quixotes of Europe — to go about fighting for every cause where we find that someone has been wronged?
Referring to the Crimean War, House of Commons, 22 December 1854.

The progress of freedom depends more upon the maintenance of peace, the spread of commerce, and the diffusion of education than upon the labours of Cabinets and Foreign Offices.
House of Commons, 26 June 1850.

COKE, Sir Edward
1552–1634   English politician

A man's house is his castle.
Institutes

We have a saying in the House of Commons; that old ways are the safest and surest ways.
Speech, London, 8 May 1628.

COLTON, Charles Caleb
1780–1832   British clergyman and writer

When you have nothing to say, say nothing.
Lacon

Men will wrangle for religion; write for it; fight for it — anything but live for it.
Ib.

Imitation is the sincerest form of flattery.
Ib.

CONFUCIUS
551-479 BC   Chinese philosopher

The people may be made to follow a course of action, but they may not be made to understand it.

Analects

Man has three ways of acting wisely. First, on meditation; that is the noblest. Secondly, on imitation; that is the easiest. Thirdly, on experience; that is the bitterest.

Ib.

CONNELL, James
1852–1929   British socialist

The people's flag is deepest red;
It shrouded oft our martyred dead.
And ere their limbs grew stiff and cold,
Their heart's blood dyed its every fold.
Then raise the scarlet standard high!
Within its shade we'll live or die.
Tho' cowards flinch and traitors sneer,
We'll keep the red flag flying here.

The Red Flag, Official anthem of the Labour Party.

CONNOLLY, James
1870–1916   Irish republican leader

It is an axiom enforced by all the experience of the ages, that they who rule industrially will rule politically.

Socialism made Easy

CONNOR, Sir William Neil
1909–67   British journalist

As I was saying when I was interrupted, it is a powerful hard thing to please all of the people all of the time.

*On resuming his Cassandra column in the **Daily Mirror** in September 1946, after the end of World War II.*

COOK, A. J.
1885–1931   British trade unionist

Not a penny off the pay; not a minute on the day.

1926 miners' strike slogan.

COOLIDGE, Calvin
1872–1933   30th US President

There is no right to strike against the public safety by anybody, anywhere, at any time.

Telegram to the president of the American Federation of Labour in 1919, while Governor of Massachusetts during the Boston police strike.

The business of America is business.

Speech to the Society of Newspaper Editors, 17 January 1925.

Prosperity is only an instrument to be used, not a deity to be worshipped.

Speech, Boston, 11 June 1928.

COOLIDGE, Calvin *(contd.)*

Perhaps one of the most important accomplishments of my Administration has been minding my own business.
Press conference, March 1929.

Patriotism is easy to understand in America. It means looking out for yourself while looking out for your country.
Attrib.

COUSINS, Norman

1915–   American newspaper editor

President Nixon's motto was, if two wrongs don't make a right, try three.
The Daily Telegraph, *17 July 1979.*

CRIPPS, Sir Stafford

1889–1952   British politician

There is only a certain sized cake to be divided up, and if a lot of people want a larger slice they can only take it from others who would, in terms of real income, have a smaller one.
Speech, Trades Union Congress, 7 September 1948.

There but for the grace of God, goes God.
Said of him by Sir Winston Churchill.

CRITCHLEY, Julian

1930–   British MP

I was told when a young man that the two occupational hazards of the Palace of Varieties were alcohol and adultery. The hurroosh that follows the intermittent revelation of the sexual goings-on of an unlucky MP has convinced me that the only safe pleasure for a parliamentarian is a bag of boiled sweets.
The Listener, *June 1982.*

CROKER, John Wilson

1780–1857   British Tory politician

We are now, as we have always been, decidedly and conscientiously attached to what is called the Tory, and which might with more propriety be called the Conservative party.
Quarterly Review, *January 1830.*

CROMWELL, Oliver

1599–1658   English soldier and statesman

The state, in choosing men to serve it, takes no notice of their opinions. If they be willing faithfully to serve it, that satisfies.
Said before the battle of Marston Moor, 2 July 1644.

I beseech you, in the bowels of Christ, think it possible you may be mistaken.
Letter to the General Assembly of the Church of Scotland, 3 August 1650.

Take away that fool's bauble — the Mace.
On dismissing the Rump Parliament, 20 April 1653.

It is not fit that you should sit here any longer. You shall now give place to better men.
Ib.

CROSSMAN, Richard
1907–74   British politician

My Minister's room is like a padded cell, and in certain ways I am like a person who is suddenly certified a lunatic and put safely into this great, vast room, cut off from real life. Of course they don't behave *quite* like nurses, because the Civil Service is profoundly deferential — 'Yes, Minister! No, Minister! If you wish it, Minister!'
The Diaries of a Cabinet Minister 1964–70

CURRIE, Edwina
1946–   British politician

My message to the businessmen of this country when they go abroad on business is that there is one thing above all that they can take with them to stop them catching AIDS — and that is the wife.
Speech as a junior Health Minister, February 1987.

The strongest possible piece of advice that I could give to any young woman is: Don't screw around, and don't smoke.
The Observer, 3 April 1988.

Most of the egg production in this country, sadly, is now infected with salmonella.
Radio interview as junior Health Minister on 3 December 1989, which outraged both the domestic poultry industry and those of her own Back- Benchers who represented agricultural constituencies, forcing her resignation two weeks later.

CURTIS, Lionel
1872–1955   British writer

In private conversation [Winston Churchill] tries on speeches like a man trying on ties in his bedroom, to see how he would look in them.
Letter to Nancy Astor, 1912.

CURZON, Lord George Nathaniel
1859–1925   British statesman

It is only when you get to see and realise what India is — that she is the strength and the greatness of England — that you feel that every nerve a man may strain, every energy he may put forward, cannot be devoted to a nobler purpose than keeping tight the cords that hold India to ourselves.
Speech at Southport, 15 May 1893.

I never knew that the lower classes had such white skins.

Remark made during a visit of front-line British troops in World War I, after observing some of them bathing in old beer barrels.

I hesitate to say what the functions of the modern journalist may be, but I imagine that they do not exclude the intelligent anticipation of the facts even before they occur.
House of Commons, 29 March 1898.

DARROW, Clarence
1857–1938   American lawyer

When I was a boy, I was told that anybody could become President. I'm beginning to believe it.
Attrib.

DAUGHERTY, Harry

1860–1941   American politician

A group of senators, bleary eyed for lack of sleep, will have to sit down at about two o'clock in the morning around a table in a smoke-filled room in some hotel, and decide the nomination.

*On the Republicans' failure to choose a presidential candidate at their
1920 convention.*

DAVIS, Jefferson

1808–89   President of the rebel Confederate States

All we ask is to be let alone.

Inaugural address, 18 February 1861.

DAYAN, Moshe

1915-81   Israeli soldier and politician

Whenever you accept our views, we shall be in full agreement with you.

*Remark to US envoy Cyrus Vance during the Arab-Israeli negotiations,
Quoted in **The Observer**, 14 August 1977.*

DE COUBERTIN, Baron Pierre

1863–1937   French founder of the modern Olympics

The most important thing in the Olympic games is not winning but taking part — just as the most important thing in life is not the triumph but the struggle. The essential thing in life is not conquering but fighting well.

Speech to Olympic Games Officials, London 24 July 1908.

DEAN, John

1938–   White House adviser to President Nixon

I am convinced that we are going to make the whole road and put this thing in the funny pages of the history books.

Taped conversation with the President, February 1973.

We have a cancer within, close to the presidency, that is growing. It is growing daily.

Ib. March 1973.

DECATUR, Stephen

1779–1820   US naval officer

Our country! In her intercourse with foreign nations, may she always be in the right; but our country, right or wrong.

Speech made in Norfolk, Virginia, April 1816.

DEFFAND, Marquise du

1697–1780   French noblewoman

The distance does not matter; it is only the first step that counts.

Letter dated 7 July 1763.

DE GAULLE, Charles
1890–1970   French soldier and President

Nothing great will ever be achieved without great men — and men only become great if they are determined to be so.
Le Fil de l'Épée (1934)

France has lost a battle, but France has not lost the war.
Proclamation, June 1940.

The French will only be united under the threat of danger. How else can one govern a country that produces 246 different types of cheese?
*Speech, 1951, quoted in **Les Mots du Général** (1962).*

I myself have become a Gaullist only little by little.
The Observer, *29 December 1963.*

I respect only those who resist me, but I cannot tolerate them.
New York Times, *12 May 1966.*

When I want to know what France thinks, I ask myself.
Sons of France

Politics is too important to be left to the politicians.
Attrib.

Treaties are like roses and young girls — they last while they last.
Attrib.

In order to become the master, the politician poses as the servant.
Attrib.

DERBY, 14th Earl of (Edward Geoffrey Smith Stanley)
1799–1869   British statesman

The foreign policy of the noble Earl, Lord Russell, may be summed up in two truly expressive words: meddle and muddle.
House of Lords, February 1884, referring to the Prime Minister's policy on the American Civil War.

DICKENS, Charles
1812–70   British novelist

Now, what I want is Facts . . . Facts alone are wanted in life.
Hard Times

DISRAELI, Benjamin
1804–81   British statesman

Though I sit down now, the time will come when you will hear me.
On being barracked during his maiden speech in the House of Commons, 28 February 1845.

If a traveller were informed that such a man was Leader of the House of Commons, he may well begin to comprehend how the Egyptians came to worship an insect.
Attributed remark about Lord John Russell.

The Continent will not suffer England to be the workshop of the world.
House of Commons, 15 March 1838.

DISRAELI, Benjamin *(contd.)*

I am neither a Whig nor a Tory. My politics are described in one word, and that word is England.
Speech, House of Commons, 1844.

Consider Ireland. Thus you have a starving population, an absentee aristocracy, and an alien Church — and in addition, the weakest executive in the world. That is the Irish Question.
House of Commons, 16 February 1844.

The right honourable gentleman caught the Whigs bathing and walked away with their clothes.
House of Commons speech, February 1845, attacking Prime Minister Sir Robert Peel for bullying his Back-Benchers into supporting the Government's action in intercepting the private mail of radical MPs.

Posterity will do justice to that unprincipled maniac Gladstone — an extraordinary mixture of envy, vindictiveness, hypocrisy and superstition and with one commanding characteristic. Whether Prime Minister or Leader of the Opposition, whether preaching, praying, speechifying, or scribbling — never a gentleman. He is so vain that he wants to figure in history as the settler of all the great questions; but a parliamentary Constitution is not favourable to such ambitions. Things must be done by parties, not by persons using parties as tools.
Referring to Sir Robert Peel in a letter to Lord John Manners, 17 December 1846.

England does not love coalitions.
House of Commons, 17 December 1852.

His temper, naturally morose, has become licentiously peevish. Crossed in his Cabinet, he insults the House of Lords and plagues the most eminent of his colleagues with the crabbed malice of a maundering witch.
Said of Lord Aberdeen, whose disagreements with his Whig-Peelite coalition over the Crimean war eventually forced his resignation in 1855.

The question is this: is man an ape or an angel? I am on the side of the angels.
Speech, 25 November 1864.

Assassination has never changed the history of the world.
From a speech paying tribute to Abraham Lincoln made in May 1865, following the American President's assassination in Washington on 14 April.

I have climbed to the top of the greasy pole.
On becoming Prime Minister in 1868.

Gladstone, like Richelieu, cannot write. Nothing can be more unmusical, more involved, or more uncouth than all his scribblement.
Letter dated 3 October 1877.

Lord Salisbury and myself have brought you peace — but a peace, I hope, with honour.
Declaration on returning from the 1878 Berlin Congress and the guarantees it had produced of continuing peace in Europe.

I am dead: dead, but in the Elysian fields.
On his elevation to the House of Lords.

DISRAELI, Benjamin *(contd.)*

Little things affect little minds.
Sybil

Every woman should marry — and no man.
Lothair

DOUGLAS-HOME, Sir Alec (later, Lord Home of the Hirsel)
1903–   British Prime Minister

When I read economic documents, I have to have a box of matches and start moving them into position, to illustrate and simplify the points to myself.
The Making of the Prime Minister

There are two problems in my life. The political ones are insoluble, and the economic ones are incomprehensible.
Speech, January 1964.

DRIBERG, Tom
1905–76   British politician

Sincerity is all that counts is a widespread modern heresy.
Think again. Bolsheviks are sincere. Fascists are sincere. Lunatics are sincere. People who believe that the earth is flat are sincere. They can't all be right. Better make certain first that you have something to be sincere about, and with.
Daily Express, 1937.

DRUMMOND, Thomas
1797–1840   British statesman

Property has its duties as well as its rights.
Letter to the Earl of Donoughmore, 22 May 1838.

DRYDEN, John
1631–1700   British poet and dramatist

If by the people you understand the multitude, the hoi polloi, 'tis no matter what they think. They are sometimes in the right, sometimes in the wrong; their judgment is a mere lottery.
Essay of Dramatic Poesy

Beware the fury of a patient man.
Absalom and Achitophel

Politicians neither love nor hate.
Ib.

For present joys are more to flesh and blood than a dull prospect of a distant good.
The Hind and the Panther.

DULLES, John Foster
1888–1959   American Secretary of State

The ability to get to the verge without getting into the war is the necessary art. If you cannot master it, you invariably get into war. If you try to run away from it, if you are scared to go to the brink, you are lost. We've had to look at it square in the face ... We walked to the brink and we looked it in the face.
Life Magazine, January 1956.

DUMAS fils, Alexandre
1824–95   French writer

All generalisations are dangerous, even this one.
Attrib.

DUNNING, John
1731–1820   British lawyer and politician

The influence of the Crown has increased, is increasing, and ought to be diminished.
From his motion passed by the House of Commons in 1780.

DURANT, Will
1885–1981   American historian

There is nothing in Socialism that a little age or a little money will not cure.

DÜRRENMATT, Friedrich
1921–90   Swiss writer

What was once thought can never be unthought.
The Physicists

EDEN, Sir Anthony
1897–1977   British Prime Minister

Everybody is always in favour of general economy and particular expenditure.
The Observer, *17 June 1956.*

We best avoid wars by taking even physical action to stop small ones. Everybody knows that the United Nations is not in a position to do that . . . We must face the fact that the United Nations is not yet the internal equivalent of our own legal system and rule of law. Police action must be to separate the belligerents and to prevent a resumption of hostilities.
House of Commons, 1 November 1956.

We are not at war with Egypt. We are in armed conflict.
On the Suez crisis, House of Commons, 4 November 1956.

EDEN, Lady Clarissa
1920–   Wife of Sir Anthony Eden

During the past few weeks, I felt sometimes that the Suez canal was flowing through my drawing room.
Speech, November 1956.

EDWARD VII
1842–1910   King of Great Britain

Because a man has a black face and a different religion from our own, there is no reason why he should be treated as a brute.
Letter from India to Lord Granville, 30 November 1875.

EDWARD VIII
1894–1972   British sovereign

I have found it impossible to carry the heavy burden of responsibility, and to discharge my duties as King as I would wish, without the help and support of the woman I love.
Radio broadcast to the nation, 11 December 1936, following his abdication to marry Wallis Simpson.

EINSTEIN, Albert
1879–1955 German physicist

If only I had known, I would have become a watchmaker.
On his part in developing the atom bomb, **New Statesman**, *16 April 1955.*

Everything should be made as simple as possible, but not simpler.
Attrib.

EISENHOWER, Dwight D.
1890–1969 American soldier and statesman

The eyes of the world are upon you. The hopes and prayers of liberty-loving people everywhere march with you.
Despatch to US forces on D-Day, 6 June 1944.

I shall go to Korea, to try to end the war.
Presidential campaign pledge, October 1952

Neither a wise man nor a brave man lies down on the tracks of history to wait for the train of the future to run over him.
Time, *6 October 1952.*

History does not long entrust the care of freedom to the weak or the timid.
Inaugural address, 20 January 1953.

You have a row of dominoes set up. You knock over the first one, and what will happen to the last is that it will go over very quickly.
Explaining the domino theory in relation to South-East Asia, April 1954.

There can be no law if we were to invoke one code of international conduct for those who oppose us and another for our friends.
Speech on the Suez crisis, 31 October 1956.

If the United Nations once admits that international disputes can be settled by using force, we will have destroyed the foundation of the organisation and our best hope of establishing a world order.
Address to the nation on Israel's invasion of Egypt, 20 February 1957.

In the councils of government, we must guard against the acquisition of unwarranted influence, whether sought or unsought, by the military-industrial complex. The potential for the disastrous rise of misplaced powers exists and will persist.
Farewell address, January 1961.

There's one thing to be said about being President — nobody can tell you when to sit down.
Speech, 1964.

ELIZABETH I
1533–1603 Queen of England

I know that I have the body of a weak and feeble woman, but I have the heart and stomach of a king — and a king of England too.
Address at Tilbury on the approach of the Spanish Armada, 1588.

ELIZABETH II
1926– Queen of Great Britain

I think that people will concede that, on this of all days, I should begin my speech with the words, 'My husband and I'.
Speech at a banquet to celebrate her silver wedding anniversary,
20 November 1972.

Experience shows that great enterprises seldom end with a tidy and satisfactory flourish. Together, we are doing our best to re-establish peace and civil order in the *Gulf* region, and to help those members of civil and ethnic minorities who continue to suffer through no fault of their own. If we succeed, our military success will have achieved its true objective.
Commenting on the aftermath of the Gulf War in the first address by a
British monarch to Congress, 16 May 1991.

ENGELS, Friedrich
1820–95 German communist

The first act in which the state really comes forward as the representative of society as a whole — the taking possession of the means of production in the name of society — is at the same time its last independent act as a state. The state is not 'abolished'; it withers away.
Anti-Dühring

The British Labour movement is today, and for many years has been, working in a narrow circle of strikes that are looked upon, not as an expedient, and not as a means of propaganda, but as an ultimate aim.
Letter to Eduard Bernstein, 17 June 1878.

ERASMUS, Desiderius
1466–1536 Dutch scholar

Let a king recall that it is better to improve his realm than to increase his territory.
Querela Pacis

FALKLAND, Viscount (Lucius Cary)
1610–43 English soldier and politician

When it is not necessary to change, it is necessary not to change.
House of Commons, 22 November 1641.

FARQUHAR, George
1678–1707 Irish dramatist

There's no scandal like rags, nor any crime so shameful as poverty.
The Beaux' Stratagem

FAWKES, Guy
1570–1606 English conspirator

A desperate disease requires a dangerous remedy.
Questioned after his arrest on 5 November 1605.

FEIFFER, Jules

1929– American cartoonist

I used to think I was poor. Then they told me I wasn't poor, I was needy. They told me it was self-defeating to think of myself as needy, I was deprived. Then they told me underprivilege was over-used. I was disadvantaged. I still don't have a dime. But I have a great vocabulary.

Cartoon caption, 1956.

FERDINAND I

1503–64 Holy Roman Emperor

Let justice be done, though the world may perish.

Attrib.

FIELD, Frank

1942– British politician

The House of Lords is a model of how to care for the elderly.

The Observer, 24 May 1981.

FISHER, Geoffrey Francis

1887–1972 Archbishop of Canterbury

The long and distressing controversy over capital punishment is very unfair to anyone meditating murder.

The Sunday Times, 24 February 1957.

FISHER, H. A. L.

1865–1940 British historian and politician

Men wiser and more learned than I have discerned in history a plot, a rhythm, a predetermined pattern. Those harmonies are concealed from me. I can see only one emergency following upon another, as wave follows upon wave; only one great fact with respect to which, since it is unique, there can be no generalizations. Only one safe rule for the historian: that he should recognize in the development of human destinies the play of the contingent and the unforeseen.

History of Europe

FOOT, Michael

1913– British politician

[Aneurin Bevan] was the only man I knew who could make a curse sound like a caress.

Aneurin Bevan 1897–1945

A Royal Commission is a broody hen sitting on a china egg.

House of Commons, 1964.

The members of our secret service have apparently spent so much time looking under the bed for Communists that they haven't had time to look in the bed.

Attributed comment on the Profumo scandal, 1963.

Men of power have not time to read; yet men who do not read are unfit for power.

Debts of Honour

FORD, Gerald R.
1913–   38th US President

I am a Ford, not a Lincoln. My addresses will never be as eloquent as Mr Lincoln's, but I will do my very best to equal his brevity and plain speaking.
Speech on becoming Vice-President, December 1973.

The political lesson of Watergate is this: never again must America allow an arrogant, elite guard of political adolescents to bypass the regular party organisation and dictate the terms of a national election.
New York Times, 31 March 1974.

I cannot imagine any other country in the world where the opposition would seek, and the Chief Executive would allow, the dissemination of his most private and personal conversations with his staff — which, to be honest, do not exactly confer sainthood on anyone concerned.
Speech, University of Michigan, 4 May 1974.

Truth is the glue that holds Government together — not only our Government but civilisation itself. Our long national nightmare is over. Our Constitution works. Our great republic is a government of laws and not of men. Here, the people rule.
On being sworn in as President after Richard Nixon's resignation,
9 August 1974.

There is no Soviet domination of eastern Europe — and there never will be under a Ford administration.
TV confrontation with Jimmy Carter, 1976.

FORD, Henry
1863–1947   American industrialist

History is more or less bunk. It's tradition.
*Interview, **Chicago Tribune**, May 1916.*

FORGY, Howell Maurice
1908–83   US naval chaplain

Praise the Lord and pass the ammunition.
Said at Pearl Harbour, 7 December 1941.

FORSTER, E.M.
1879–1970   British novelist

If I had to choose between betraying my country and betraying my friend, I hope that I should have the guts to betray my country.
Two Cheers for Democracy

We are now concerned with the very poor. They are unthinkable, and only to be approached by the statistician or the poet.
Howards End

FOX, Charles James
1744–1806   English Whig

Kings govern by popular assemblies only when they cannot do without them.
House of Commons, 31 October 1776.

The worst of a revolution is a restoration.
House of Commons, 10 December 1785.

FRANCIS I
1768–1835   Austrian emperor

But is he a patriot for me?
On being assured of the loyalty of a candidate for high office, 1822.

FRANK, Hans
1900–46   Governor-General of Poland

A thousand years will pass and the guilt of Germany will not be erased.
Statement before his execution for World War II crimes.

FRANKLIN, Benjamin
1706–90   US scientist and statesman

Some punishment seems preparing for a people who are so ungratefully abusing the best Constitution and the best king that any nation was ever blessed with.
Said in London during the Wilkes riots of May 1768.

There never was a good war or a bad peace.
Letter, 11 September 1773.

We must indeed all hang together or, most assuredly, we shall all hang separately.
Said on signing the Declaration of Independence, 4 July 1776.

In this world, nothing can be said to be certain except death and taxes.
Letter, 13 November 1789.

No nation was ever ruined by trade.
Essays

FRASER, Keith
1867–1935   British politician

I never met anyone in Ireland who understood the Irish question, except one Englishman who had been there only a week.
House of Commons, May 1919.

FREDERICK THE GREAT
1712–86   King of Prussia

My people and I have come to an agreement that satisfies us both. They are to say what they please, and I am do what I please.
Attrib.

FREDERICK II
1194–1250   Holy Roman emperor

Our work is to present things that are as they are.
De Arte Venandi cum Avibus

FREDERICK II
1712–86   King of Prussia

It is a political error to practise deceit, if deceit is carried too far.
Antimachiavel

FREEMAN, Edward Augustus
1823–92   British historian

History is past politics, and politics is present history.
Methods of Historical Study

FRIEDMAN, Milton
1912– American economist

There is no such thing as a free lunch.

Lecture, 1973.

FROST, Robert
1874–1963 American poet

Good fences make good neighbours.

North of Boston

FROUDE, James Anthony
1818–94 British historian

Wild animals never kill for sport. Man is the only one to whom the torture and death of his fellow-creatures is amusing in itself.

Oceana

FRYE, David
1934– American comedian and impressionist

Gerald Ford looks like the guy in a science-fiction movie who is the first to see the creature.

FUENTES, Carlos
1928– Mexican novelist and dramatist

What America does best is to understand itself. What it does worst is to understand others.

Time, *16 June 1986.*

FULBRIGHT, James William
1905– American politician

We have the power to do any damn fool thing we want to do, and we seem to do it every 10 minutes.

Time, *4 February 1952.*

GAITSKELL, Hugh
1906–63 British Labour Party leader

Some of us will fight and fight again to save the party we love. We will fight and fight again to bring back sanity and honesty and dignity, so that our party, with its great past, may retain its glory and its greatness.

Denouncing unilateralists trying to gain control of the party, national conference October 1960.

Let us not forget that we can never go farther than we can persuade at least half the people to go.

Labour Party conference, October 1961.

[Joining the European Community] does mean the end of Britain as an independent European state. It means the end of a thousand years of history.

Labour Party conference speech 1962.

GALBRAITH, John Kenneth

1908– Canadian-born US economist

In the affluent society, no useful distinction can be made between luxuries and necessities.

The Affluent Society

Few things are as immutable as the addiction of political groups to the ideas by which they have once won office.

Ib.

There are times in politics when you must be on the right side and lose.

The Observer, *11 February 1968.*

Politics is not the art of the possible. It consists in choosing between the disastrous and the unpalatable.

Ambassador's Journal

Nothing is so admirable in politics as a short memory.

A Guide to the 99th Congress

GALLUP, George Horace

1901–84 American public-opinion pollster

Polling is merely an instrument for gauging public opinion. When a president or any other leader pays attention to poll results, he is, in effect, paying attention to the views of the people. Any other interpretation is nonsense.

NBC News, 1 December 1979.

GALSWORTHY, John

1867–1933 British author

Nobody tells me anything.

The Man of Property

GALTIERI, Leopoldo

1926– Argentine President

Why are you telling me this? The British won't fight.

Responding to a warning from US Secretary of State Alexander Haig in April 1982 about the consequences of the Argentinian invasion of the Falkland Islands.

GANDHI, Mahatma

1869–1948 Indian leader

Non-violence is not a garment to be put on and off at will. Its seat is in the heart, and it must be an inseparable part of our very being.

*Non-violence in **War and Peace**.*

What do I think of Western civilisation? I think that it would be a good idea.

Attrib.

GANDHI, Indira

1917–84 Indian Prime Minister

Even if I die in the service of this nation, I would be proud of it. Every drop of my blood, I am sure, will contribute to the growth of this nation and make it strong and dynamic.

Speech at Orissa, 31 October 1984, the day before being assassinated by one of her own bodyguards.

GARIBALDI, Giuseppe
1807–82   Italian revolutionary

England is a great and powerful nation, foremost in human progress, enemy to despotism, the only safe refuge for the exile, friend of the oppressed. If ever England should be so circumstanced as to require the help of any ally, cursed be the Italian who would not step forward with me in her defence.
Letter, 12 April 1854.

GARNER, John Nance
1868–1937   US Vice-President

The vice-presidency isn't worth a pitcher of warm piss. It doesn't amount to a hill of beans.
Attrib.

GEDDES, Sir Eric
1875–1937   British politician

I have no doubt that we will get everything out of Germany that you can squeeze out of a lemon and a bit more. I will squeeze her until you can hear the pips squeak. I would strip Germany as she has stripped Belgium.
Speech at Cambridge Guildhall, December 1918.

The Germans, if this Government is returned, are going to pay every penny. They are going to be squeezed as a lemon is squeezed — until the pips squeak. My only doubt is not whether we can squeeze hard enough, but whether there is enough juice.
Speech at Beaconsfield, December 1918.

GELDOF, Bob
1954–   Irish musician and humanitarian

Irish Americans are about as Irish as Black Americans are African.
The Observer, *22 June 1986.*

'GEORGE, Daniel' (pseudonym of D. G. Bunting)
1890–1967   British author and critic

O Freedom, what liberties are taken in thy name!
The Perpetual Pessimist

GEORGE III
1738–1820   King of Great Britain

I can never suppose this country so far lost to all ideas of self-importance as to be willing to grant America independence; if that could ever be adopted, I shall despair of this country being ever preserved from a state of inferiority, and consequently falling into a very low class among the European states.
Letter to Lord North, 7 March 1780.

I was the last to consent to the separation, but the separation having been made, and having become inevitable, I have always said that I would be the first to meet the friendship of the United States as an independent power.
Letter to John Adams, first US ambassador to England, 1 June 1785.

GEORGE V
1865–1936   King of Great Britain

Today 23 years ago, dear Grandmama [Queen Victoria] died. I wonder what she would have thought of a Labour Government.
*Diary entry, 22 January 1924, on having invited Ramsay Macdonald to
form the first Labour Administration.*

I will not have another war. If there is another and we are threatened with being brought into it, I will go to Trafalgar Square and wave a red flag myself sooner than allow this country to be brought in.
To David Lloyd George, 10 May 1935.

GEORGE VI
1895–1952   King of Great Britain

The British Empire has advanced to a new conception of autonomy and freedom, to the idea of a system of British nations, each freely ordering its own individual life, but bound together in unity by allegiance to one Crown, and co-operating in all that concerns the common weal.
*Opening, as Duke of York, the first Australian Parliament to assemble in
Canberra, 9 May 1927.*

GIBBON, Edward
1737–94   British historian

Corruption, the most infallible symptom of constitutional liberty.
The Decline and Fall of the Roman Empire

All that is human must retrograde if it does not advance.
Ib.

The principles of a free constitution are irrevocably lost when the legislative power is nominated by the executive.
Ib.

GIBBONS, Stella
1902–89   British writer

Something nasty in the woodshed.
Cold Comfort Farm

GILBERT, Sir William Schwenck
1836–1911   British librettist

The House of Peers, throughout the war,
Did nothing in particular,
And did it very well.
Iolanthe

GILMOUR, Sir Ian
1926–   British politician

It does no harm to throw the occasional man overboard, but it does not do much good if you are steering full speed ahead for the rocks.
The Times, *after he was sacked by Margaret Thatcher for publicly
criticizing her anti-European stance.*

GLADSTONE, William Ewart
1809–98   British statesman

It is upon those who say that it is necessary to exclude forty-nine fiftieths of the working classes [from the vote] to show cause, and I venture to say that every man who is not presumably incapacitated by some consideration of personal unfitness or of political danger, is morally entitled to come within the pale of the Constitution.
House of Commons, 11 May 1864.

One cannot fight against the future. Time is on our side.
On the Reform Bill, House of Commons, 1866.

Remember the rights of the savage, as we call him. Remember that the happiness of his humble home, remember that the sanctity of life in the hill villages of Afghanistan, among the winter snows, is as inviolable in the eye of Almighty God as can be your own.
Speech, Dalkeith, 26 November 1879.

England's foreign policy should always be inspired by the love of freedom. There should be a sympathy with freedom, a desire to give it scope, founded not upon visionary ideas but upon the long experience of many generations within the shores of this happy isle, that in freedom one lays the firmest foundations both of loyalty and order.
Speech, West Calder, 27 November 1879.

If it shall ever appear that there is still to be fought a final conflict in Ireland, between law on the one side and sheer lawlessness upon the other; if the law purged from defect and from any taint of injustice is still to be repelled and refused; and the first conditions of political society to remain unfulfilled, then I say without hesitation that the resources of civilisation against its enemies are not yet exhausted.
Speech, Leeds, October 1881.

All the world over, I will back the masses against the classes.
Speech, Liverpool, 28 June 1886.

We are part of the community of Europe, and we must do our duty as such.
Speech, 10 April 1888.

GOEBBELS, Joseph
1897–1945   Nazi Minister of Propaganda

Should the German people lay down arms, the Soviets would occupy all eastern and south-eastern Europe, together with the greater part of the Reich. Over all this territory, which, with the Soviet Union included, would be of enormous extent, an iron curtain would at once descend.
Das Reich, *23 February 1945.*

GOERING, Hermann
1893–1946   Nazi Air Marshal

Our movement took a grip on cowardly Marxism, and from it, extracted the meaning of socialism. It also took from the cowardly, middle-class parties their nationalism. Throwing both into the cauldron of our way of life there emerged, as clear as crystal, the synthesis — German National Socialism.
Speech, Berlin, 9 April 1933.

Guns will make us powerful; butter will only make us fat
Radio broadcast, 1936.

GOERING, Hermann *(contd.)*

I herewith commission you to carry out all the preparations with regard to . . . a total solution of the Jewish question, in those territories of Europe that are under German influence.

Directive to the Nazi High Command, quoted in **The Rise and Fall of the Third Reich** *by William Shirer.*

GOLDMARK, Peter C.
1937– American Budget director

Welfare is hated by those who administer it; mistrusted by those who pay for it; and held in contempt by those who receive it.

New York Times, *24 May 1977.*

GOLDSMITH, Oliver
1730–74 Irish-born British writer

Silence has become his mother tongue.

The Good-Natured Man

GOLDWATER, Barry M.
1909– American politician

Extremism in the defence of liberty is no vice, and moderation in the pursuit of justice is no virtue.

Speech to the Republican convention, 16 July 1964.

In your heart, you know I'm right.

Presidential campaign slogan, 1964.

GOOCH, George Peabody
1873–1968 British historian and politician

We can now look forward with something like confidence to the time when war between civilised nations will be considered as antiquated as a duel.

History of Our Time

GORBACHEV, Mikhail
1931– Soviet statesman

Some comrades apparently find it hard to understand that democracy is just a slogan.

The Observer, *1 February 1987.*

The Soviet people want full-blooded and unconditional democracy.

Speech, July 1988.

Life is making us abandon established stereotypes and outdated views; it is making us discard illusions.

Speech, United Nations, 7 December 1988.

If the Russian word 'perestroika' has easily entered the international lexicon, it is due to more than just interest in what is going on in the Soviet Union. Now the whole world needs restructuring; that is, progressive development, a fundamental change.

Perestroika

Mitterrand has 100 lovers. One has AIDS, but he doesn't know which one. Bush has 100 bodyguards. One is a terrorist, but he doesn't know which one. Gorbachev has 100 economic advisers. One is smart, but he doesn't know which one.

The Sunday Times, *9 December 1990.*

GRANT, Ulysses S.
1822–85   18th US President

I know no method to secure the repeal of bad or obnoxious laws so effective as their stringent execution.
Inaugural address, 4 March 1869.

GRAYSON, Victor
1881–1920   British politician

Never explain. Your friends don't need it, and your enemies won't believe it.
Attrib.

GREGORY VII
1020–85   Pope

I have loved justice and hated iniquity; therefore, I die in exile.
Attributed last words, May 1085.

GRELLET, Stephen
1773–1855   French-born US missionary

I expect to pass through this world but once. Any good thing, therefore, that I can do, or any kindness that I can show to any fellow-creature, let me do it now...for I shall not pass this way again.
Attrib.

GRENVILLE, George
1712–70   British Prime Minister

It is clear that both England and America are now to be governed by the mob.
On the repeal of the Stamp Act, July 1765.

GREY, Sir Edward
1862–1933   British politician

If there is war, there will be Labour Governments in every country — and quite right too.
In conversation with the Italian Ambassador, July 1914.

In 1914, Europe had arrived at a point at which every country except Germany was afraid of the present, and Germany was afraid of the future.
House of Lords, 24 July 1924.

The lamps are going out all over Europe. We shall not see them lit again in our lifetime.
*Remark made in August 1914, on the eve of World War I, in his room at the Foreign Office, recounted in **Twenty-Five Years** (1925).*

GROMYKO, Andrei
1909–89   Soviet statesman

Every night, whisper 'Peace' in your husband's ear.
Said to Nancy Reagan at a White House reception, 28 September 1984.

This man, Comrades, has a nice smile, but he has iron teeth.
Speech to the Supreme Soviet on proposing Mikhail Gorbachev as the new party leader, 1985.

HAIG, Alexander Meigs, Jr
1924– US Secretary of State

As of now, I am in control here in the White House.

Said immediately after the attempted assassination of President Ronald Reagan, 30 March 1981, in Vice-President George Bush's absence from Washington DC.

HAIG, Douglas (1st Earl Haig)
1861–1928 British Field Marshal

Every position must be held to the last man; there must be no retirement. With our backs to the wall, and believing in the justice of our cause, each one of us must fight on to the end.

Order to British troops, 12 April 1918.

HAILE SELASSIE
1891–1975 Emperor of Ethiopia

Throughout history it has been the inaction of those who could have acted, the indifference of those who should have known better, the silence of the voice of justice when it mattered most, that has made it possible for evil to triumph.

Address to a special session of the UN General Assembly, 4 October 1963, making him the first head of state to address both that organisation and the League of Nations.

HAILSHAM, Lord (Quintin Hogg)
1907– British politician and Lord Chancellor

A great party ought not to be brought down because of a squalid affair between a woman of easy virtue and a proved liar.

On the Profumo affair, BBC TV, 13 June 1963.

If the British public fall for this, I say that it will be stark, staring bonkers.

Press conference on Labour election manifesto, 12 October 1964.

HALDANE, John Burdon Sanderson
1892–1964 Anglo-Indian biologist

My suspicion is that the universe is not only queerer than we suppose, but queerer than we can suppose.

Possible Worlds

HALE, Nathan
1755–76 US revolutionary

I only regret that I have but one life to lose for my country.

Said at his execution, 22 September 1776.

HALIFAX, 1st Marquis of (George Savile)
1633–95 English politician

Men are not hanged for stealing horses, but that horses may not be stolen.

Political Thoughts and Reflections

When the people contend for their liberty, they seldom get anything by their victory but new masters.

Ib.

HALIFAX, Viscount (Edward Frederick Lindley Wood)
1881–1959   British Foreign Secretary

I often think how much easier the world would have been to manage if Herr Hitler and Signor Mussolini had been at Oxford.

Speech, York, 4 November 1937.

HALL, Professor Stuart
1932–   British sociologist

It is a question of globalisation, reconceptualising its own questions in a global framework. I mean, interdependencies. We are too intricated, one society with another, for national sociologies to be any longer the case.

*Asked whether the nature of sociology should change, on the 40th anniversary of the subject's recognition by British academics, **The Sunday Times**, 17 February 1991.*

HAMILTON, Alexander
1755–1804   American statesman

To model our political systems upon speculations of lasting tranquillity is to calculate on the weaker springs of the human character.

Federalist Papers

HAMMARSKJOLD, Dag
1905–61   UN Secretary-General

Never let success hide its emptiness from you; achievement its nothingness; toil its desolation. Keep alive the incentive to push on further, that pain in the soul that drives us beyond ourselves. Do not look back, and do not dream about the future either. It will neither give you back the past, nor satisfy your other daydreams. Your duty, your reward, your destiny are here and now.

Markings

HAMPTON, Christopher
1946–   British writer

I always divide people into two groups. Those who live by what they know to be a lie, and those who live by what they believe, falsely, to be the truth.

Philanthropist

If I had to give a definition of capitalism, I would say: the process whereby American girls turn into American women.

Savages

HARDIE, James Keir
1856–1915   Scottish socialist

From his childhood onwards, this boy will be surrounded by sycophants and flatterers . . . In due course, following the precedent that has already been set, he will be sent on a tour of the world, and probably rumours of a morganatic marriage alliance will follow, and the end of it will be that the country will be called upon to pay the bill.

Opposing a motion congratulating Queen Victoria on the birth of the future Edward VIII, House of Commons, 28 June 1894.

HARDING, Warren Gamaliel
1865–1923   29th US President

America's present need is not heroics but healing; not nostrums but normalcy; not revolution but restoration.

Speech, Boston, June 1920.

HARRINGTON, James
1611–77   English writer

No man can be a politician except he first be an historian or a traveller; for except he can see what must be, or what may be, he is no politician.

The Commonwealth of Oceana

HART, Gary
1936–   American politician

This is one Hart that you will not leave in San Francisco.

Said after his failed bid for the 1984 presidential nomination at the Democratic National Convention in San Francisco.

HAUGHEY, Charles
1925–   Irish statesman

It seems that the historic inability in Britain to comprehend Irish feelings and sensitivities still remains.

The Observer, *February 1988.*

HAVERS, Sir Michael
1923–   British politician and Attorney-General

[Blunt] maintained his denial. He was offered immunity from prosecution. He sat in silence for a while. He got up, looked out the window, poured himself a drink, and after a few minutes confessed. Later he co-operated, and he continued to co-operate. That is how the immunity was given and how Blunt responded.

House of Commons, November 1979, on the immunity from prosecution offered to the Soviet spy, Sir Anthony Blunt.

HAY, Ian
1876–1952   British writer

What do you mean, funny? Funny peculiar, or funny ha-ha?

The Housemaster

HAYES, Rutherford B.
1822–93   19th US President

He serves his party best who serves his country best.

Inaugural address, 5 March 1877.

HEALEY, Denis
1917–   British Labour politician

That part of his speech was rather like being savaged by a dead sheep.

Responding to a speech by Chancellor of the Exchequer Sir Geoffrey Howe, House of Commons, June 1978.

For the past few months, [Margaret Thatcher] has been charging about like some bargain-basement Boadicea.

The Observer, *7 November 1982.*

HEATH, Edward
1916– British Prime Minister

It would not be in the interests of the European Community that its enlargement should take place except with the full-hearted consent of the Parliament and people of the new member countries.

Speech to the Franco-British Chamber of Commerce in Paris, May 1970.

I cannot promise to stop roaring inflation overnight, but I will give it priority.

Election broadcast, 27 May 1970.

This would, at a stroke, reduce the rise in prices, increase productivity, and reduce unemployment.

Statement on proposed tax cuts and a price freeze by nationalized industries, June 1970.

We were returned to office to change the course of history of this nation — nothing less. If we are to achieve that task, we will have to embark on a change so radical, a revolution so quiet and yet so total, that it will go far beyond the programme for a Parliament to which we are committed, and on which we have already embarked. Far beyond the decade and well into the 1980s.

Conservative Party conference, May 1973.

It is the unpleasant and unacceptable face of capitalism, but one should not suggest that the whole of British industry consists of practices of this kind.

House of Commons, 15 May 1973, referring to the Lonrho affair.

If you want to see the acceptable face of capitalism, go out to an oil rig in the North sea.

Election campaign speech, 18 February 1974.

We are the trade union for pensioners and children; the trade union for the disabled and the sick; the trade union for the nation as a whole.

Election campaign speech, 20 February 1970.

HEGEL, Georg Wilhelm
1770–1831 German philosopher

Political genius consists in identifying oneself with a principle.

Constitution of Germany

Experience and history teaches us that people and Governments have learnt nothing from history, nor acted on principles deduced from it.

The Philosophy of History

In England, even the poorest of people believe that they have rights; that is very different from what satisfies the poor in other lands.

The Philosophy of Right

HELLMAN, Lillian
1905–84 American dramatist

I cannot, and will not, cut my conscience to this year's fashions.

Letter to House Committee on Un-American Activities, 19 May 1952.

HENDERSON, Leon
1895–1986 American economist

Having a little inflation is like being a little pregnant.

Attrib.

HENLEY, W.E.
1849–1903   British writer

I am the master of my fate:
I am the captain of my soul.
Echoes

HENRY VIII
1491–1547   King of England

We at no time stand so highly in our estate royal as in the time of Parliament, wherein
we as head, and you as members, are conjoined and knit together into one body
politic, so as whatsoever offence or injury is offered to the meanest member of the
House is to be judged as done against our person and the whole Court of Parliament.
Address to a deputation from the House of Commons, 31 March 1543.

HERBERT, George
1593–1633   English poet

He that makes a good war makes a good peace.
Outlandish Proverbs

HERRICK, Robert
1591–1674   English poet

'Twixt kings and tyrants there's this difference known:
Kings seek their subjects' good; tyrants their own.
Hesperides

HERZEN, Alexander
1812–70   Russian writer

There is a certain basis of truth in the fear that the Russian Government is beginning
to have of communism, for communism is Tsarist autocracy turned upside down.
My Past and Thoughts

HESELTINE, Michael
1933–   British politician

It is the only time that I can ever remember the Prime Minister reading out the
conclusions of a meeting that did not take place. They were already written before
it started.
*On the Cabinet meeting in January 1986 on the Westland affair at which
he resigned as Defence Minister.*

I can foresee no circumstances in which I would allow my name to be put forward
for the leadership of the Conservative Party.
Said on numerous occasions in the Autumn of 1990.

I am persuaded now that I have a better prospect than Mrs Thatcher of leading the
Conservatives to a fourth electoral victory and preventing the ultimate calamity of
a Labour Government.
On announcing his decision to stand for the leadership, November 1990.

HEWART, Gordon
1870–1943   British barrister

Justice should not only be done, but should manifestly and undoubtedly be seen to be done.

Case of Rex v. Sussex Justices, 9 November 1923.

HICKSON, William Edward
1803–70   British educator

If at first you don't succeed,
Try, try again.

Try and Try Again

HIPPOCRATES
460–377 BC   Greek physician

Life is short and art is long.

Aphorisms

HITLER, Adolf
1889–1945   Nazi leader

In the big lie, there is always a certain force of credibility. In the primitive simplicity of their minds, the great masses of the people will more easily fall victim to a big lie than to a small one . . . The broad masses of a population are more amenable to the appeal of rhetoric than to any other force.

Mein Kampf

Before us stands the last problem that must be solved, and will be solved. It is the last territorial claim that I have to make in Europe, but it is the claim from which I will not recede and which, God willing, I will make good. With regard to the problem of the Sudeten Germans, my patience is now at an end.

Speech at the Berlin Sportpalast, 26 September 1938.

As England, despite her hopeless military position, still shows no sign of willingness to come to terms, I have decided to prepare, and if necessary carry out, a landing operation against her. The aim of this enterprise is to eliminate the English mother country as a base for continuance of the war against Germany.

Directive, 16 July 1940.

All coalitions in history have disintegrated sooner or later...We will fight until we get a peace that secures the life of the German people for the next 50 or 100 years; a peace that, above all, does not shame our honour a second time, as in 1918.

Military conference, 31 August 1944.

In starting and waging a war, it is not right that matters but victory.

In The Rise and Fall of the Third Reich by William Shirer.

HOBBES, Thomas
1588–1679   English philosopher

They that are discontented under monarchy call it tyranny; and they that are displeased with aristocracy call it oligarchy: so also, they which find themselves grieved under a democracy call it anarchy, which signifies the want of government; and yet I think no man believes that want of government is any new kind of government.

Leviathan

HOBHOUSE, John Cam (Baron Broughton)
1786–1869   British statesman

It is said to be hard on His Majesty's Ministers to raise objections to this proposition. For my part, I think it no more hard on His Majesty's Opposition to compel them to take this course.

*First recorded use of the term 'His Majesty's Opposition', House of
Commons, 27 April 1826.*

HOBY, Sir Edward
1560–1617   English politician

On the 5th November, we began our Parliament, to which the King should have come in person but refrained, through a practice but that morning discovered. The plot was to have blown up the King...at one instant and blast to have ruined the whole estate and kingdom of England.

*Letter dated 19 November 1605 to the British Ambassador to Brussels,
describing the Gunpowder Plot.*

HOGGART, Simon
1946–   British writer

The nanny seemed to be extinct until 1975, when, like the coelacanth, she suddenly and unexpectedly reappeared in the shape of Margaret Thatcher.

Vanity Fair, August 1983.

HOLME, Richard
1936–   British electoral reformer

[Margaret Thatcher] is the Enid Blyton of economics. Nothing must be allowed to spoil her simple plots.

Liberal Party Conference, 10 September 1980.

HOLMES, Oliver Wendell
1809–94   US writer

A moment's insight is sometimes worth a life's experience.

Breakfast Table

HOOVER, Herbert
1874–1964   31st US President

When the war closed, we were challenged with a peacetime choice between the American system of rugged individualism and the European philosophy of diametrically-opposed doctrines — doctrines of paternalism and state socialism.

Presidential campaign speech, 22 October 1923.

We are nearer today to the ideal of the abolition of poverty and fear from the lives of men and women than ever before in any land.

Ib.

The grass will grow in the streets of a hundred cities, a thousand towns; the weeds will overrun the fields of millions of farms if [tariff protection] is taken away.

Ib.

Honour is not the exclusive property of any political party.

Christian Science Monitor, 21 May 1964.

HORACE
65–8 BC   Roman poet

Dulce et decorum est pro patria mori.
It is a sweet and seemly thing to die for one's country.
Epistles

Carpe diem. (Seize the day.)
Ib.

HORSLEY, Samuel
1733–1806   English bishop

In this country...the individual subject has nothing to do with the laws but to obey them.
House of Lords, 13 November 1795.

HOWE, Sir Geoffrey
1926–   British politician

Megaphone diplomacy leads to a dialogue of the deaf.
*Quoted in **The Observer**, 29 September 1985.*

If some of my former colleagues are to be believed, I must be the first Minister in history to have resigned because he was in full agreement with Government policy.
Personal statement on his resignation as Deputy Prime Minister, over
Margaret Thatcher's continuing hostility towards European monetary
union, House of Commons, 13 November 1990.

I do not regard the Delors report as some kind of sacred text...I do not regard the Italian presidency's management of the Rome summit as a model of its kind...I do not regard it as in any sense wrong for Britain to make criticisms of that kind plainly and courteously...But it is crucially important that we should conduct those arguments upon the basis of a clear understanding of the true relationship between this country, the Community, and our Community partners. And it is here, I fear, that my right honourable Friend the Prime Minister increasingly risks leading herself and others astray in matters of substance as well as of style.
Ib.

How on earth are the Chancellor of the Exchequer and the Governor of the Bank of England...to be taken seriously against that kind of background noise? It is rather like sending your opening batsmen to the crease, only for them to find, the moment the first balls are bowled, that their bats have been broken before the game by the team captain.
Ib.

HOWE, Julia Ward
1819–1910   US writer

Mine eyes have seen the glory of the coming of the Lord:
He is trampling out the vintage where the grapes of wrath are stored.
Battle Hymn of the Republic

HOWE, Louis McHenry
1871–1936   US diplomat

You can't adopt politics as a profession and hope to remain honest.
Speech, Colombia University, 17 January 1933.

HUBBARD, Elbert
1856–1915 US writer

One machine can do the work of 50 ordinary men. No machine can do the work of one extraordinary man.
Reflections

Little minds are interested in the extraordinary; great minds in the commonplace.
Ib.

Life is just one damned thing after another.
1001 Epigrams

HUGHES, Richard
1900–76 British writer

A politician rises on the backs of his friends...but it is through his enemies that he will have to govern afterwards.
The Fox in the Attic

HUGHES, William Morris
1864–1952 Australian Prime Minister

Without the Empire we shall be tossed like a cork in the cross-current of world politics. It is at once our sword and our shield.
Speech, Melbourne, 1926.

HUNT, Sir Rex
1926– Governor of the Falkland Islands

It is very uncivilised to invade British territory. You are here illegally.
*Attributed remark to an Argentinian general, quoted in **Life**, January 1983.*

HUSSEIN, ibn Talal
1935– King of Jordan

After all the doors were shut, our region is facing a deep abyss after the turning of the Gulf crisis into an imminent catastrophe. We have not left a door that we did not knock on, or a road that we did not take to find a political settlement of this crisis.
On his attempts to intercede for peace in the Gulf War, January 1991.

HUSSEIN, Saddam
1937– Iraqi leader

There is no other course but the one we have chosen, except the course of humiliation and darkness, after which there will be no bright sign in the sky or brilliant light on earth . . . All this will make us more patient and steadfast, and better prepared for the battle which God blesses and which good men support. Then there will only be a glorious conclusion, where a brilliant sun will clear the dust of battle, and where the clouds of battles will be dispelled . . . Iraq seeks to establish peace . . . that will open the door to a comprehensive and equitable solution that achieves a real and permanent peace in the region in its entirety — foremost in Palestine.
Baghdad Radio broadcast, 21 February 1991.

HUTCHESON, Francis
1694–1746 British philosopher

That action is best, which procures the greatest happiness for the greatest numbers.
Concerning Moral Good and Evil

HUXLEY, Aldous
1894–1963   British writer

Facts do not cease to exist because they are ignored.
Proper Studies

That all men are equal is a proposition to which, at ordinary times, no sane individual has ever given his assent.
Ib.

I am afraid of losing my obscurity. Genuineness only thrives in the dark. Like celery.
Those Barren Leaves

The propagandist's purpose is to make one set of people forget that certain other sets of people are human.
The Olive Tree

Idealism is the noble toga that political gentlemen drape over their will to power.
Quoted in his New York Herald Tribune obituary, 24 November 1963.

HUXLEY, Thomas Henry
1825–95   British biologist

It is the customary fate of new truths to begin as heresies and to end as superstitions.
The Coming of Age of the Origin of the Species

IBARRURI GOMEZ, Dolores ('La Pasionaria')
1895–1989   Spanish politician

It is better to die on your feet than to live on your knees.
Speech, Paris, 3 September 1936.

IBSEN, Henrik
1828–1906   Norwegian dramatist

The minority is always right.
An Enemy of the People

You should never put on your best trousers when you go out to fight for freedom and truth.
Ib.

INGE, William Ralph
1860–1954   British churchman

The enemies of freedom do not argue; they shout and they shoot.
The End of an Age

A nation is a society united by a delusion about its ancestry and by a common hatred of its neighbours.
Sagittarius and George

INNOCENT III
1160–1216   Pope

This [Magna Carta] has been forced from the King. It constitutes an insult to the Holy See, a serious weakening of the royal power, a disgrace to the English nation, a danger to all Christendom, since this civil war obstructs the crusade. Therefore . . . we condemn the charter and forbid the King to keep it, or the barons and their supporters to make him do so, on pain of excommunication.
Papal Bull, 24 August 1215.

IRISH REPUBLICAN ARMY

Tiocfaidh Ar La ('Our day will come')
Slogan of the Movement, founded in 1919.

Thatcher will now realise that Britain cannot occupy our country, torture our prisoners, and shoot our people in their own streets and get away with it. Today we were unlucky. But remember, we have only to be lucky once. You will have to be lucky always.
Message to the British Government telephoned to a Dublin radio station following the bombing of the Grand Hotel, Brighton, during the Conservative Party conference in October 1984.

JACKSON, Jesse

1941–   American politician

I cast my bread on the waters long ago. Now it is time for you to send it back to me — toasted, and buttered on both sides.
Addressing black voters, New York, 30 January 1984.

My constituency is the desperate, the damned, the disinherited, the disrespected, and the despised.
Democratic National Convention, San Francisco, 17 July 1984.

Our flag is red, white and blue, but our nation is a rainbow — red, yellow, brown, black and white – and we are all precious in God's sight . . . America is not like a blanket – one piece of unbroken cloth, the same colour, the same texture, the same size. America is more like a quilt – many patches, many pieces, many colours, many sizes; all woven and held together by a common thread.
Launching his 'rainbow coalition', ib.

JAMES, Clive

1939–   Australian writer and broadcaster

[Margaret Thatcher] sounded like the book of Revelations read out over a railway station public-address system by a headmistress of a certain age wearing calico knickers.
The Observer, *1979.*

JAURES, Jean

1859–1914   French socialist

There is, then, over the affairs of the army a universal conspiracy of silence, of childlike mysteries, of clannishness, routine and intrigue.
L'Armée Nouvelle

JAY, Sir Antony

1930–   British writer

From now on you can keep the lot.
Take every single thing you've got,
Your land, your wealth, your men, your dames,
Your dream of independent power,
And dear old Konrad Adenauer,
And stick them up your Eiffel Tower.
On France's rejection of British membership of the Common Market,
Time, *8 February 1963.*

JAY, Peter
1937–   British Ambassador to US

[Prince Charles] is entitled to be as underwhelmed by the prospect of reigning over a fourth-class nation as the rest of us are by the prospect of living in it.
London Illustrated News, April 1986.

JEFFERSON, Thomas
1743–1826   3rd US President

The tree of liberty must be refreshed from time to time with the blood of patriots and tyrants. It is its natural manure.
Letter to W.S. Smith, 13 November 1787.

A bill of rights is what the people are entitled to against every Government on earth, general or particular, and what no just Government should refuse or rest on inference.
Letter to James Madison, 20 December 1787.

Equal and exact justice to all men...freedom of religion, freedom of the press, freedom of the person under the protection of the habeas corpus; and trial by juries impartially selected — these principles form the bright constellation that has gone before us.
Inaugural address, 4 March 1801.

When a man assumes a public trust, he should consider himself as public property.
Letter to Baron von Humboldt, 1807.

Some men look at Constitutions with sanctimonious reverence and deem them like the Ark of the Covenant — too sacred to be touched.
Letter to Samuel Kercheval, 12 July 1816.

JIANG QING
1914–91   Chinese politician, member of the Gang of Four

Man's contribution to human history is nothing more than a drop of sperm.
Newsweek, 20 February 1984.

JOHN PAUL II
1920–

The command 'Thou shall not kill' must be binding on the conscience of humanity if the terrible tragedy and destiny of Cain is not to be repeated.
Speech, Drogheda, 29 September 1979.

Violence is a lie, for it goes against the truth of our faith, the truth of our humanity . . . Violence is a crime against humanity, for it destroys the very fabric of society. On my knees I beg you to turn away from the paths of violence.
Ib.

JOHNSON, Hiram
1866–1945   US politician

The first casualty when war comes is truth.
Speech, US Senate, 1917.

JOHNSON, Lyndon Baines

1908–73   36th US President

Until justice is blind to colour, until education is unaware of race, until opportunity is unconcerned with the colour of men's skins, emancipation will be a proclamation but not a fact.
Gettysburg Memorial Day address, 30 May 1963.

All I have, I would have given gladly not to be standing here today.
Speech to Congress on assuming the presidency in November 1963 after the assassination of John F. Kennedy.

We are not about to send American boys 9000 or 10 000 miles away from home to do what Asian boys ought to be doing for themselves.
National broadcast on the war in Vietnam, October 1964.

I am going to build the kind of nation that President Roosevelt hoped for, President Truman worked for, and President Kennedy died for.
The Sunday Times, 27 December 1964.

The vote is the most powerful instrument ever devised by man for breaking down injustice and destroying the terrible walls that imprison men because they are different from other men.
On signing the Voting Rights Bill, 6 August 1965.

A rioter with a Molotov cocktail in his hand is no more fighting for civil rights than a Klansman with a sheet on his back and a mask over his face.
Speech, Washington DC, 20 August 1965.

You let a bully come into your front yard, and the next day he'll be on your porch.
Time Magazine, April 1964.

It is true that a house divided against itself is a house that cannot stand. There is a division in the American house now, and believing that as I do, I have concluded that I should not permit the presidency to become involved in the partisan divisions that are developing in this political year. Accordingly, I shall not seek, and I will not accept, the nomination of my party for another term as your President.
National broadcast, March 1968.

I'd much rather have [J. Edgar Hoover] inside my tent pissing out, than outside my tent pissing in.
The Guardian Weekly, 18 December 1971.

[Gerald Ford] can't fart and chew gum at the same time.
A Ford, Not a Lincoln

JOHNSON, Philander Chase

1866–1939   US journalist

Cheer up — the worst is yet to come.
Shooting Stars

JOHNSON, Samuel

1709–84   British lexicographer and writer

I would not give half a guinea to live under one form of government rather than another. It is of no moment to the happiness of an individual.
Life of Johnson

JOHNSON, Samuel *(contd.)*

Patriotism is the last refuge of the scoundrel.

Ib.

Politics are now nothing more than a means of rising in the world.

Ib.

A wise Tory and a wise Whig will agree. Their principles are the same, though their modes of thinking are different.

Ib.

JUNG, Carl Gustav

1875–1961   Swiss psychiatrist

The pendulum of the mind oscillates between sense and nonsense; not between right and wrong.

Memories, Dreams, Reflections

JUNIUS (Sir Philip Francis)

1740–1818

There is a holy mistaken zeal in politics as well, as in religion. By persuading others, we convince ourselves.

Letters of Junius

JUVENAL

60–130 AD   Roman satirist

Duas tantum res anxius optat, panem et circenses.
Only two things does he worry about or long for — bread and the big match.

Satires

KAFKA, Franz

1883–1924   Czech-born Austrian writer

It is often safer to be in chains than to be free.

The Trial

KEATS, John

1795–1821   British poet

Fanatics have their dreams, wherewith they weave
A paradise for a sect.

The Fall of Hyperion

Negative Capability; that is, when a man is capable of being in uncertainties, mysteries, doubts, without any irritable reaching after fact and reason.

Letter to G. and T. Keats, 21 December 1817.

KEENAN, Brian

1947—   Irish teacher

I'm going to visit every country in the world, eat all the food of the world, drink all the drink of the world — and, I hope, make love to every woman in the world. Then I might get a good night's sleep.

Said on his release after six years as an Iranian hostage, BBC TV,
25 August 1990.

KENNAN, George Frost
1935–   US diplomat

The best that an American can look forward to is the lonely pleasure of one who stands at long last on a chilly and inhospitable mountain top where few have been before, where few can follow, and where few will consent to believe that he has been.
On negotiating with the Soviets, The Wise Men.

KENNEDY, Edward F.
1932–   American politician, brother of John F. Kennedy

For me, a few hours ago this campaign came to an end. For all those whose cares have been our concern, the work goes on, the cause endures, the hope still lives, and the dream shall never die.
Speech to the Democratic Convention, August 1980.

I don't mind not being President. I just mind that someone else is.
Speech, Washington, 22 March 1986.

KENNEDY, John Fitzgerald
1917–63   35th US President

We stand today on the edge of a new frontier. But the new frontier of which I speak is not a set of promises. It is a set of challenges. It sums up not what I intend to offer the American people, but what I intend to ask of them. It appeals to their pride, not their pocketbook — it holds out the promise of more sacrifice instead of more security.
On accepting the Democratic Convention's presidential nomination, 15 July 1960.

I hope that no American . . . will waste his franchise and throw away his vote by voting either for me or against me on account of my religious affiliations. It is not relevant.
Time, 25 July 1960.

Let the word go forth from this time and place, to friend and foe alike, that the torch has been passed to a new generation of Americans, born in this century, tempered by war, disciplined by a hard and bitter peace, proud of our ancient heritage, and unwilling to witness or permit the slow undoing of those human rights to which this nation has always been committed, and to which we are committed today at home and around the world. Let every nation know, whether it wishes us well or ill, that we shall pay any price, bear any burden, meet any hardship, support any friend, oppose any foe, to assure the survival and success of liberty.
Let us never negotiate out of fear, but let us never fear to negotiate. Together let us explore the stars.

All this will not be finished in the first 100 days, nor will it be finished in the first 1000 days, nor in the life of this Administration — nor even, perhaps, in our lifetime on this planet. But let us begin.

And so, my fellow Americans, ask not what your country can do for you. Ask what you can do for your country.
Inaugural address, Washington, 20 January 1961.

I believe that this nation should commit itself to achieving the goal, before this decade is out, of landing a man on the moon and returning him safely to earth.
State of the Union message to Congress, May 1961.

KENNEDY, John Fitzgerald *(contd.)*

[Winston Churchill] mobilised the English language and sent it into battle.
Conferring honorary US citizenship on Sir Winston Churchill, April 1963.

All free men, wherever they may live, are citizens of Berlin, and therefore, as a free man, I take pride in the words, 'Ich bin ein Berliner.'
Speech at Berlin City Hall, June 1963.

History teaches us that enmities between nations ... do not last for ever. We must conduct our affairs in such a way that it becomes in the communists' interests to agree on a genuine peace ... to let each nation choose its own future, so long as that choice does not interfere with the choices of others. If we cannot now end our differences, at least we can help make the world safe for diversity.
Speech, American University, Washington DC, 10 June 1963.

I look forward to ... a future in which our country will match its military strength with our moral restraint; its wealth with our wisdom; its power with our purpose.
Last major public speech, Amherst College, 26 October 1963.

KENNEDY, Joseph P.

1888–1969   American politician, father of John F. Kennedy

Don't get mad, get even.
Conversations with Kennedy

KENNEDY, Robert F.

1925–68   American politician, brother of John F. Kennedy

One fifth of the people are against everything all the time.
The Observer, May 1964.

My thanks to you all — and now it's on to Chicago, and let's win there.
Last public remark after winning the California primary for the Democratic presidential nomination in Los Angeles, before being assassinated as he left the rally, 4 June 1968.

KENT, Bruce

1929–   Campaigner for nuclear disarmament

Preparing for suicide is not a very intelligent means of defence.
Speech, 1989.

KEY, Francis Scott

1779–1843   US lawyer

'Tis the star-spangled banner; O long may it wave
O'er the land of the free, and the home of the brave.
The Star-Spangled Banner

KEYNES, John Maynard

1883–1946   British economist

England still stands outside Europe. Europe's voiceless tremors do not reach her. Europe is apart, and England is not of her flesh and body.
The Economic Consequences of Peace

319

KEYNES, John Maynard *(contd.)*

Worldly wisdom teaches us that it is better for the reputation to fail conventionally than to succeed unconventionally.
The General Theory of Employment

Practical men, who believe themselves to be quite exempt from any intellectual influences, are usually the slaves of some defunct economist. Mad men in authority, who hear voices in the air, are distilling their frenzy from some academic scribbler of a few years back.
Ib.

If Enterprise is afoot, Wealth accumulates whatever may be happening to Thrift; and if Enterprise is asleep, Wealth decays, whatever Thrift may be doing.
Treatise on Money

When David Lloyd George is alone in a room, there's no one there.
Attributed by Baroness Asquith on BBC TV, April 1967.

KHRUSHCHEV, Nikita S.
1894–1971   Soviet leader

Those who wait for the USSR to reject Communism must wait until a shrimp learns to whistle.

Whether you like it or not, history is on our side. We will bury you.
The Times, quoting a remark made to western diplomats, November 1956.

Politicians are the same all over. They promise to build a bridge even where there is no river.
Press conference, New York, October 1960.

When you are skinning your customers, you should leave some skin on to grow so that you can skin them again.
Speech to British industrialists, May 1961.

They talk about who won and who lost. Human reason won. Mankind won.
On the ending of the Cuban missile crisis, November 1962.

We had no use for the teachings of the Gospels; if someone slaps you, just turn the other cheek. We had shown that anyone who slapped us on our cheek would get his head kicked off.
Khrushchev Remembers

KING, Martin Luther
1929–68   American civil rights leader

I have a dream. I have a dream that my four little children will one day live in a nation where they will not be judged by the colour of their skin but by the content of their character.
Washington civil rights rally, 15 June 1963.

Discrimination is a hellhound that gnaws at negroes in every waking moment of their lives, to remind them that the lie of their inferiority is accepted as truth in the society dominating them.
Christian leadership conference, Atlanta, 16 August 1967.

KING, Martin Luther *(contd.)*

I've been to the mountain top. I've looked over, and I've seen the promised land. I may not get there with you, but I want you to know tonight that we as a people will get to the promised land. So, I'm happy tonight. Mine eyes have seen the glory of the coming of the Lord.
Speech at Memphis, 3 April 1968, the day before he was assassinated.

If a man hasn't discovered something that he would die for, he isn't fit to live.
Strength to Love

KINNOCK, Neil
1942– British politician

We cannot remove the evils of capitalism without taking its source of power: ownership.
Tribune, *1975.*

I want to retire at 50. I want to play cricket in the summer and geriatric football in the winter, and sing in the choir.
The Times, *28 July 1980.*

Like Brighton pier — all right as far as it goes, but inadequate for getting to France.
On Conservative European policy, House of Commons, 2 February 1981.

Proportional representation is fundamentally counter-democratic.
Marxism Today, *1983.*

The idea that there is a model Labour voter — a blue-collar council-house tenant who belongs to a union and has 2.4 children, a five-year-old car and a holiday in Blackpool — is patronising and politically immature.
Speech, 1986.

KIPLING, Rudyard
1885–1936   British writer

Oh, East is East, and West is West, and never the twain shall meet.
The Ballad of East and West

If you can keep your head when all about you
Are losing theirs and blaming it on you.
Gunga Din

KIRKPATRICK, Jean Duane Jordan
1926–   US Ambassador to the United Nations

Democrats can't get elected unless things get worse — and things won't get worse unless they get elected.
Time, *17 June 1985.*

A Government isn't legitimate just because it exists.
On the Sandinista regime, ib.

KISSINGER, Henry
1923– American diplomat and Secretary of State

It is not often that nations learn from the past — even rarer that they draw the correct conclusions from it. For the lessons of historical experience, as of personal experience, are contingent. They teach the consequences of certain actions, but they cannot force a recognition of comparable situations.
A World Restored

Power is the ultimate aphrodisiac.
New York Times, January 1971.

No foreign policy, no matter how ingenious, has any chance of success if it is born in the minds of a few and carried in the heart of none.
Speech to International Platform Association, 2 August 1973.

There can't be any crisis next week. My schedule is already full.
Time, January 1977.

We are all the President's men, and we must behave accordingly.
On the Cambodian invasion, alluding to the nursery rhyme Humpty Dumpty. The phrase was used in the title of the book by Washington Post reporters Bob Woodward and Carl Bernstein on the Watergate scandal.

High office teaches decision-making, not substance. It consumes intellectual capital; it does not create it. Most high officials leave office with the perceptions and insights with which they entered: they learn how to make decisions, but not what decisions to make.
The White House Years

The statesman's duty is to bridge the gap between his nation's experience and his vision.
Years of Upheaval

Nixon had three goals: to win by the biggest electoral landslide in history; to be remembered as a peacemaker; and to be accepted by the establishment as an equal. He achieved all those objectives at the end of 1972 and the beginning of 1973. And he lost them all two months later — partly because he turned a dream into an obsession.
Ib.

The nice thing about being a celebrity is that when you bore people, they think that it's their fault.
Reader's Digest, April 1985.

Whatever must happen ultimately should happen immediately.
*On the Iran–Contra scandal, **Time**, 8 October 1986*

KOESTLER, Arthur
1905–83 Hungarian-born British writer

The most persistent sound that reverberates through men's history is the beating of war drums.
Janus: A Summing Up

KOROLEV, Sergei
1918– Chief designer for the early Soviet space programme

Just wait. In five years' time, there will be trade union-subsidised flights into space.
Said to Yuri Gagarin as he entered Vostok 1 for the world's first manned Earth orbit.

KOSSUTH, Lajos
1802–94   Hungarian revolutionary

Despotism and oppression never yet were beaten except by heroic resistance. I hope that the people of the United States will remember that in the hour of their nation's struggle, it received from Europe more than kind wishes. It received aid from others in times past, and it will, doubtless, now impart its mighty agency to achieve the liberty of other lands.
Speech on arriving on Staten Island, 5 December 1851.

KUBRICK, Stanley
1928–   US film director

The great nations have always acted like gangsters, and the small nations like prostitutes.
The Guardian, *1963.*

LABOUCHERE, Henry
1831–1912   British radical

Nothing has conduced more to shake that decent respect for the living symbol of the state that goes by the name of royalty than the ever-recurring rattle of the money box.
Fortnightly Review, *February 1884.*

LABOUR PARTY
British socialist political organization

To secure for the workers by hand or by brain the full fruits of their industry and the most equitable distribution thereof that may be possible upon the basis of the common ownership of the means of production, distribution or exchange.
Clause 4 of the Party's 1926 Constitution.

LAMARTINE, Alphonse Marie Louis de
1790–1869   Poet and revolutionary

France is revolutionary or she is nothing at all. The revolution of 1789 is her political religion.
Histoire des Girondins

At its birth, the republic gave voice to three words — Liberty, Equality, Fraternity! If Europe is wise and just, each of those words signifies Peace.
A Manifesto to the Powers, 4 March 1848.

LANG, Andrew
1844–1912   British poet

Politicians use statistics in the same way that a drunk uses lamp-posts — for support rather than illumination.
Speech, 1910.

LAW, Andrew Bonar
1858–1923   British Prime Minister

I can imagine no length of resistance to which Ulster can go in which I should not be prepared to support them, and in which, in my belief, they would not be supported by the overwhelming majority of the British people.
Said during the Irish home rule crisis, 27 July 1912.

LAZARUS, Emma
1849–87   American poet

Give me your tired, your poor,
Your huddled masses yearning to breathe free,
The wretched refuse of your teeming shore,
Send these, the homeless, tempest-tossed to me;
I lift my lamp beside the golden door.

Verse inscribed at the foot of the Statue of Liberty, New York harbour, 1886.

LEASE, Mary Elizabeth
1853–1933   American reformer

The farmers of Kansas must raise less corn and more hell.

Speech, 1890.

LEES-SMITH, H.B.
1878–1941   British politician

Security can only be obtained by a scheme by which the nations of Europe and outside agree together that all will guarantee each, and each will guarantee all. The purposes of the war will be attained if there is a League of Nations with an absolute and decisive veto upon any mere aggression, and consideration of any legitimate claims that any of the countries engaged in the war may be able to make good.

House of Commons, 21 October 1916.

LEMAY, Curtis E.
1906–   American general and air force chief

My solution to the problem would be to tell them that they've got to draw in their horns, or we're going to bomb them into the Stone Age.

*On the North Vietnamese, quoted in **Mission with LeMay**.*

LENIN, Vladimir
1870–1924   Russian revolutionary

A small, compact core, consisting of reliable, experienced and hardened workers, with responsible agents...connected by all the rules of strict secrecy with the organisations of revolutionists, can, with the wide support of the masses and without an elaborate set of rules, perform all the functions of a trade-union organisation.

What Is to be Done?

One Step Forward, Two Steps Back

Title of book, 1904.

I greet you as the advance guard of the world proletarian army. The hour is not far off when . . . the German people will turn their weapons against their capitalist exploiters. The sun of the socialist revolution has already risen.

Speech, Petrograd, 16 April 1917.

[Bernard Shaw] is a good man fallen among Fabians.

*Quoted in **Six Weeks in Russia in 1919**.*

LENTHALL, William
1591–1662   Speaker of the House of Commons

May it please Your Majesty, I have neither eye to see nor tongue to speak in this place, but as this House is pleased to direct me, whose servant I am.

To Charles I, on his arrival in the Chamber to arrest five Members, House of Commons, 4 January 1642.

LESLIE, David
1601–82   Scottish parliamentarian

How glorious it would be in the eyes of God and men, if we managed to hunt the Catholics from England, follow them to France, and, like the bold King of Sweden, rouse the Protestants in France, plant our religion in Paris by agreement or force, and go from there to Rome to chase the Antichrist and burn the town whence superstition comes.

Said to Lord Hume, Council of Scottish Nobles, August 1643.

LIGNE, Prince Charles-Joseph de
1735–1814   Austrian diplomat

One could forgive the fiend for becoming a torrent, but to become an earthquake was really too much.

Said of Napoleon I, 1814.

LINCOLN, Abraham
1809–65   16th US President

No man is good enough to govern another man without that other's consent.

Speech, Peoria, 16 October 1854.

'A house divided against itself cannot stand': I believe that this Government cannot endure permanently half-slave and half-free. I do not expect the Union to be dissolved. I do not expect the house to fall — but I do expect it will cease to be divided. It will become all one thing, or all the other.

Speech, Springfield, 16 June 1858.

You can fool some of the people some of the time, and some of the people all the time, but you cannot fool all the people all of the time.

Speech, Clinton, 8 September 1858.

What is conservatism? Is it not adherence to the old and tried, against the new and untried?

Speech, New York, 27 February 1860.

Let us have faith that right makes might; and in that faith let us to the end dare to do our duty as we understand it.

Ib.

Four score and seven years ago our fathers brought forth upon this continent a new nation, conceived in liberty and dedicated to the proposition that all men are created equal . . . we here highly resolve that the dead shall not have died in vain; that this nation, under God, shall have a new birth of freedom; and that government of the people, by the people, and for the people, shall not perish from the earth.

Dedication address, Gettysburg National Cemetery, 19 November 1863.

With malice toward none; with charity for all; with firmness in the right, as God gives us to see the right.

Second inaugural address, 4 March 1865.

LIPPMAN, Walter
1899-1974   American writer

Successful politicians . . . are insecure and intimidated men. They advance politically only as they placate, appease, bribe, seduce, bamboozle, or otherwise manage to manipulate the demanding and threatening elements in their constituencies.

The Public Philosophy

LLOYD-GEORGE OF DWYFOR, David Lloyd George, 1st Earl
1863–1945   British Liberal Prime Minister

This is the trusty mastiff that is to watch over our interests, but which runs away at the first snarl of the trade unions. A mastiff? It is the right honourable gentleman's poodle. It fetches and carries for him. It barks for him. It bites anybody that he sets it on.
Speech to the House of Commons, 21 December 1908, referring to the
obstructive Conservative majority in the House of Lords exploited by the
then Tory leader, A.J. Balfour.

There are no credentials. They do not even need a medical certificate. They need not be sound either in body or mind. They only require a certificate of birth — just to prove that they were the first of the litter. You would not choose a spaniel on those principles.
Referring to the House of Lords, Budget speech, March 1909.

We are placing the burdens on the broadest shoulders. I made up my mind that, in forming my Budget, no cupboard should be barer, no lot should be harder to bear.
Speech on the People's Budget, London, 30 July 1909.

Four spectres haunt the poor — old age, accident, sickness, and unemployment. We are going to exorcise them. We are going to drive hunger from the hearth. We mean to banish the workhouse from the horizon of every workman in the land.
Speech, Reading, 1 January 1910.

We have been too comfortable and too indulgent — many, perhaps, too selfish — and the stern hand of fate has scoured us to an elevation where we can see the great everlasting things that matter for a nation; the great peaks we had forgotten, of honour, duty, patriotism, and, clad in glittering white, the great pinnacle of sacrifice pointing like a rugged finger to Heaven. We shall descend into the valleys again, but as long as men and women of this generation last, they will carry in their hearts the image of those great mountain peaks, whose foundations are not shaken, though Europe rock and sway in the convulsions of a great war.
Speech, London, 19 September 1914.

What is our task? It is to make Britain a fit country for heroes to live in.
Speech at Wolverhampton at the end of World War I, November 1918.

Every man has a House of Lords in his own head. Fears, prejudices, misconceptions — those are the peers, and they are hereditary.
Speech, Cambridge, 1927.

It is the old trouble — too late in dealing with Czechoslovakia, too late with Poland, and certainly too late with Finland. It is always too late, or too little, or both. That is the road to disaster.
House of Commons, 13 March 1940.

A politician is a person with whose politics you don't agree; if you agree with him, he is a statesman.
Attrib.

The world is becoming like a lunatic asylum run by lunatics.
Attrib.

LOCKE, John
1632–1704   English philosopher

Government has no other end but the preservation of property.
Second Treatise on Civil Government

Freedom of men under government is to have a standing rule to live by, common to every one of that society, and made by the legislative power vested in it; a liberty to follow my own will in all things, when the rule prescribes not, and not to be subject to the inconstant, uncertain, unknown, arbitrary rule of another man.
Ib.

A sound mind in a sound body is a short but full description of a happy state in this world. He that has those two, has little more to wish for; and he that wants either of them will be little the better for anything else.
Thoughts Concerning Education

LONGWORTH, Alice Roosevelt
1884–1980   American political hostess

You can't make a soufflé rise twice.
On Thomas Dewey's second nomination in 1948, after he had been defeated by Franklin D. Roosevelt in the 1944 presidential election.

LOUIS IX
1214–70   King of France

I would rather have a Scot come from Scotland to govern the people of this kingdom well and justly, than that you should govern them ill in the sight of all the world.
Said to his son, Louis, at Fontainebleau, 1244.

LOUIS XI
1423–83   King of France

I have chased the English out of France more easily than my father ever did, for my father drove them out by force of arms, whereas I have driven them out with venison pies and good wine.
Said after the signing of the Treaty of Picquigny, September 1475.

LOUIS XIV
1638–1715   King of France

Everyone knows how much trouble your meetings have caused in my State, and how many dangerous results they have had. I have learnt that you intend to continue them. I have come here expressly to forbid you to do this, which I do absolutely.
Address to the Parlement of Paris, 13 April 1655.

The function of kings consists primarily of using good sense, which always comes naturally and easily. Our work is sometimes less difficult than our amusements.
Mémoires for the Instruction of the Dauphin

Every time that I fill a high office, I make one hundred men discontented and one ungrateful.
Attrib.

When you are considering the State, you are working for yourself; the good of the one becomes the glory of the other. When the State is happy, famous and powerful, the King is glorious.
Manuscript found after his death.

LOUIS PHILIPPE
1773–1850   King of the French

Died, has he? Now I wonder what he meant by that.
Said on the death of Talleyrand, 18 March 1838.

LOVELESS, George
1805–40   English trade unionist

If we have violated any law it was not done intentionally. We have injured no man's reputation, character, person, or property. We were meeting together to preserve ourselves, our wives, and our children from utter degradation and starvation.
Statement to the Dorchester Assizes on behalf of the Tolpuddle martyrs,
March 1833.

LUCE, Clare Boothe
1903–87   American writer

Communism is the opiate of the intellectuals, with no cure except as a guillotine might be called a cure for dandruff.
Newsweek, 24 January 1955.

LUTHER, Martin
1483–1546   German theologian

I cannot and will not recant anything, for to go against conscience is neither right nor safe.
Diet of Worms, 18 April 1521.

The Devil knows that I would have gone into Worms though there were as many devils as tiles on the roof. I would ride into Leipzig now, though it rained Duke Georges for nine days.
Letter to Frederick, Elector of Saxony, 1522.

Anyone who can be proved to be a seditious person is an outlaw before God and the Emperor; and whoever is the first to put him to death does right and well. Therefore, let everyone who can, smite, slay and stab, secretly or openly, remembering that nothing can be more poisonous, hurtful or devilish than a rebel.
Against the Robbing and Murdering Hordes of Peasants.

It is better that all of these peasants should be killed rather than that the sovereigns and magistrates should be destroyed, because the peasants take up the sword without God's authority.
Letter to Nicholas von Ansdorf, 30 May 1525.

MACARTHUR, Douglas
1880–1964   American General

A great tragedy has ended. A great victory has been won. A new era is upon us . . . We have had our last chance. If we do not devise some greater and more equitable system, Armageddon will be at our door.
National radio broadcast on the surrender of Japan, 2 September 1945.

Like the old soldier of the ballad, I now close my military career and just fade away; an old soldier who tried to do his duty as God gave him the sight to see that duty.
Address to Congress, 19 April 1951.

MACAULAY, Lord (Thomas Babington)

1800-59   British historian and Whig politician

We know of no spectacle so ridiculous as the British public in one of its periodical fits of morality.

Edinburgh Review, 1828.

Dark and terrible beyond any season within my remembrance of political affairs was the day of their flight. Far darker and far more terrible will be the day of their return.

On the defeat of the Tory Government, House of Commons, 20 September 1831.

We hardly know any instance of the strength and weakness of human nature so striking, and so grotesque, as the character of this haughty, vigilant, resolute, sagacious blue-stocking — half Mithridates and half Trissotin, bearing up against a world in arms, with an ounce of poison in one pocket, and a quire of bad verses in the other.

Historical Essays: Frederick the Great

I hardly know which is the greater pest to society: a paternal Government; that is to say, a prying meddlesome Government, which intrudes itself into every part of human life and which thinks that it can do everything for everybody better than anybody can do for himself, or a careless, lounging Government, which suffers grievances, such as it could at once remove, to grow and multiply, and which to all complaint and remonstrance has only one answer, 'We must let things take their course, we must let things find their own level.'

House of Commons, 22 May 1846.

Persecution produced its natural effect on them. It found them a sect; it made them a faction.

Ib. (On the Puritans).

The history of England is emphatically the history of progress.

Ib.

MACDONALD, J. Ramsay

1866–1937   British Prime Minister

The League of Nations grows in moral courage. Its frown will soon be more dreaded than a nation's arms, and when that happens, you and I shall have security and peace.

Speech, London, 9 November 1929.

MACHIAVELLI, Niccolò

1469–1527   Italian politician

It never or rarely happens that a republic or monarchy is well constituted, or its old institutions entirely reformed, unless it is only done by one individual.

Discourses on First Ten Books of Livy

MACLEOD, Iain

1913–70   British politician

We now have the worst of both worlds — not just inflation on the one side or stagnation on the other, but both of them together. We have a sort of stagflation situation.

House of Commons, November 1965.

MACMAHON, Maurice de
1808–93   Marshal of France

Here I am, here I stay.
Said on capturing Malakoff Fort, 8 September 1855.

MACMILLAN, Harold (1st Earl of Stockton)
1894–1986   British statesman

We have not overthrown the divine right of kings to fall down for the divine right of experts.
Speech, Strasbourg, 16 August 1950.

Forever poised between a cliché and an indiscretion.
*On the role of a Foreign Secretary, quoted in **Newsweek**, April 1956.*

I thought that the best thing to do was to settle up these little local difficulties, and then turn to the wider vision of the Commonwealth.
On departing for a Commonwealth conference, after sacking several members of his Cabinet in his Night of the Long Knives, January 1956.

Let us be frank about it. Most of our people have never had it so good. Go around the country, go to the industrial towns, go to the farms, and you will see a state of prosperity such as we have never had in my lifetime — nor indeed ever in the history of this country.
Speech, Bedford, 20 July 1957.

At home, you always have to be a politician. When you are abroad, you almost feel yourself to be a statesman.
Speech, 17 February 1958, during the first visit of a British Prime Minister to Australia.

Tradition does not mean that the living are dead; it means that the dead are living.
__Manchester Guardian__, 18 December 1963.

The most striking of all the impressions that I have formed since I left London a month ago is of the strength of African national consciousness. In different places it may take different forms, but it is happening everywhere. The wind of change is blowing through this continent. Whether we like it or not, the growth of national consciousness is a political fact.
Speech to the South African Parliament, 3 February 1960.

Are we so sure that with 15 representatives . . . in NATO, acting under the unanimity rule, the deterrent would continue to deter? There may be one finger on the trigger, but there will be 15 fingers on the safety catch.
House of Commons, 30 May 1960.

I was determined that no British Government should be brought down by the action of two tarts.
On the Profumo scandal, referring specifically to Christine Keeler and Mandy Rice Davies, July 1963.

I have never found, in a long experience of politics, that criticism is ever inhibited by ignorance.
__Wall Street Journal__, 13 August 1963.

A man who trusts nobody is apt to be the kind of man whom nobody trusts.
__New York Herald Tribune__, 17 December 1963.

MACMILLAN, Harold *(contd.)*

There is a growing division in our comparatively prosperous society between the south and the north and midlands, which are ailing, that cannot be allowed to continue. There is a general sense of tension. The old English way might be to quarrel and have battles, but they were friendly. I can only describe as wicked the hatred that has been introduced, and which is to be found among different types of people today. Not merely an intellectual but a moral effort is required to get rid of it.

Maiden speech as the Earl of Stockton (60 years after first entering the House of Commons), House of Lords, 13 November 1984.

First of all the Georgian Silver goes, and then all that nice furniture that used to be in the salon. Then the Canalettos go.

Speech to a private dinner of the Tory Reform Group, 8 November 1985

Margaret Thatcher is a brilliant tyrant surrounded by mediocrities.

Newsweek, 12 October 1986.

If people want a sense of purpose, they should get it from their archbishop, they should certainly not get it from their politicians.

*Quoted in **The Life of Politics**.*

MADISON, James

1751–1836   4th US President

The diversity in the faculties of men, from which the rights of property originate, is not less an insuperable obstacle to a uniformity of interests. The protection of those faculties is the first object of government.

Federalist Papers, November 1787.

What is government itself but the greatest of all reflections on human nature? If men were angels, no government would be necessary. If angels were to govern men, neither external nor internal controls on government would be necessary.

Ib. January 1788.

MAINTENON, Françoise de

1635–1719   Wife of Louis XIV

You must make use of people according to their abilities, and realise that absolutely no one is perfect.

Letter to Count d'Aubigne, 25 September 1679.

MAJOR, John

1943–   British Prime Minister

I am grateful for the enormous achievements that I inherit from Margaret Thatcher. I think that history will record that she was a towering Prime Minister who left our country in a far better position than she found it 11 years ago. I hope in the next few years to build on those achievements. I certainly hope in those years to build a society of opportunity. By opportunity, I mean an open society — a society in which what people fulfil will depend upon their talent, their application, and their good fortune. What people achieve should depend particularly on those things, and I hope increasingly in the future that that will be the case.

Address on entering No. 10 Downing Street for the first time as Prime Minister, 27 November 1990.

MAJOR, John *(contd.)*

We have seen in the last few years the remarkable ending of the Cold War and the bringing together of nations in a fashion that no one would have imagined just a few years ago. We have in front of us the building and development of an entirely new Europe, in which this country will play an important part and leading role.

Ib.

Saddam Hussein is a man without pity. Whatever his fate may be, I for one will not weep for him.

House of Commons, February 1990.

I think that we had better start again, somewhere else.

Attributed remark when the Cabinet Room was rocked by an IRA mortar attack on No. 10 Downing Street, 7 February 1991.

It will not be a long conflict, but it may be a fierce one. There is no doubt in my mind that it is an absolutely justifiable conflict, and that we will win it.

On the Gulf War, February 1991

The war has been won. Now we have to set about establishing a durable peace . . . Such a peace has many facets. It must provide for the security of Kuwait and of other countries in the Gulf. Also, it must deal with the other problems of the region – above all, that of the Palestinians. We should be clear that our quarrel has been with the Iraqi leadership, not the Iraqi people, who are themselves victims of the war to which Saddam Hussein condemned them.

Ib.

When I have talked of a classless society or opportunity society, I mean that it just does not matter whether you come from a tiny, scruffy back-to-back in a pretty poor housing area or from one of the best mansions in one of the best parts of the United Kingdom. We should have a society that opens up the same opportunities that you can achieve for oneself, whatever one's own particular abilities, aptitudes, hard work and talents enable one to achieve.

BBC Radio 1, 16 April 1991.

MAJOR, Patricia

1931–   Sister of John Major

He isn't God. I see him as the runny-nosed boy I've always known . . . I sometimes wonder if he is devious and cunning enough to be a great Prime Minister.

Daily Mirror, 16 April 1991.

MAKWETU, Clarence

1931–   President, Pan-Africanist Congress

We are determined to confront the oppressor with one voice.

Addressing the first formal joint meeting of the PAC and the rival African National Congress for 30 years, 15 April 1991.

MALTHUS, Thomas Robert

1766–1843   English economist

Population, when unchecked, increases in a geometrical ratio. Subsistence only increases in arithmetical ratio.

The Principle of Population

MANCHESTER, William
1922–   American author

It would be inaccurate to say that Churchill and I conversed. Like Gladstone speaking to Victoria, he addressed me as though I were a one-man House of Commons.
The Last Lion

MANDELA, Nelson
1918–   South African Black rights leader; Deputy President, African National Congress

We are not a political party. We have not changed at all. On the contrary, the ANC is a Government in waiting.
Interviewed by Donald Woods, BBC TV, February 1991.

MANNING, Cardinal Henry Edward
1808–92   Archbishop of Westminster

To put labour and wages first and human or domestic life second is to invert the order of God and of nature.
On the 1889 London dock strike.

MANSFIELD, Lord
1705–93   Lord Chief Justice

We must not regard political consequences, however formidable they may be. If rebellion was the certain consequence, we are bound to say, 'Justitia fiat, ruat coelum' (Let Justice be done, though the skies may fall).'
Judgement against the sentence imposed on John Wilkes for publishing the North Briton, 28 April 1758.

Every man who comes to England is entitled to the protection of the English law, whatever oppression he may heretofore have suffered, and whatever may be the colour of his skin, whether it is black or whether it is white.
Judgement on the Somersett slavery case, May 1772.

MAO ZEDONG
1893–1976   Chinese revolutionary

A single spark can start a forest fire. Our forces, although small at present, will grow rapidly.
Letter, 5 January 1930.

If you want to know the taste of a pear, you must taste the pear by eating it yourself. If you want to know the theory and methods of revolution, you must take part in revolution. All genuine knowledge originates in direct experience.
Address, Anti-Japanese Military and Political College, July 1937.

China has stood up.
Proclaiming the establishment of the Chinese People's Republic, 1 October 1949.

All the so-called powerful reactionaries are paper tigers, for they are cut off from their people. Was not Hitler a paper tiger, and was he not overthrown? US imperialism has not yet been overthrown, and it has atomic bombs — but I believe that it too will be overthrown. It, too, is a paper tiger.
Speech to Communist International Congress, Moscow, November 1957.

MAO ZEDONG *(contd.)*

People of the world, unite and defeat the US aggressors and all their running dogs.
Speech, July 1958.

Every Communist must grasp the truth that political power grows out of the barrel of a gun.
Quotations from Chairman Mao Zedong.

Politics is war without bloodshed; war is politics with bloodshed.
Ib.

MARSH, Sir Edward Howard
1872–1953 British civil servant and scholar

In war, resolution; in defeat, defiance; in victory, magnanimity; in peace, good will.
Epigram on World War I; usually wrongly attributed to Winston Churchill, whom Sir Edward Marsh served in several offices until retiring in 1937.

In defeat, unbeatable; in victory, unbearable.
Ib. (Said of General Montgomery of Alamein)

MARX, Karl
1818–83 German political theorist

Religion is the sigh of the oppressed creature, the feelings of a heartless world, and the spirit of conditions that are unspiritual. It is the opium of the people.
A Critique of Hegel's Philosophy of Right

A spectre is haunting Europe — the spectre of communism. All the powers of old Europe have entered into a holy alliance to exorcise this spectre: Pope and Tsar, Metternich and Guizot, French Radicals and German police spies.
The Communist Manifesto

The history of all hitherto existing society is the history of class struggles.
Ib.

Let the ruling classes tremble at a communist revolution. The proletarians have nothing to lose but their chains. They have a world to win. Working men of all countries, unite!
Ib.

What I did that was new was to prove that the existence of classes is only bound up with particular, historic phases in the development of production; that the class struggle necessarily leads to the dictatorship of the proletariat; and that dictatorship itself only constitutes the transition to the abolition of all classes and to a classless society.
Correspondence of Marx and Engels

The centralisation of the means of production and the socialisation of labour reach a point where they prove incompatible with their capitalist husk. The knell of private property sounds; the expropriators are expropriated.
Das Kapital

Only in a higher phase of communist society . . . can the narrow horizon of bourgeois right be crossed in its entirety, and society inscribe on its banners, 'From each according to his ability, to each according to his needs!'
Critique of the Gotha Programme, May 1875.

MARY
1867–1953   Queen Consort of Great Britain, wife of George V

God grant that we may not have a European war thrust upon us, and for such a stupid reason too. No, I do not mean stupid — but to have to go to war on account of tiresome Serbia beggars belief.
Letter to her aunt, the Grand-Duchess of Mecklenburg, 28 July 1914.

MASARYK, Tomas
1850–1937   First President of Czechoslovakia

Our whole history inclines us towards the democratic powers. Our renaissance is a logical link between us and the democracies of the west.
Inaugural address, 23 December 1918.

MAZARIN, Cardinal Jules
1602–61   Italian-born Minister to Louis XIV

The French are nice people. I allow them to sing and to write, and they allow me to do whatever I like.
Attributed by the Duchess of Orléans in a letter dated 25 October 1715.

MAZZINI, Giuseppe
1805–72   Italian republican

A nation is the universality of citizens speaking the same tongue.
La Giovine Italia

McCARTHY, Joseph Raymond
1909–57   American Senator

While I cannot take time off to name all the men in the State Department who have been named as members of the Communist Party and members of a spy ring, I have here in my hand a list of 205 that were known to the Secretary of State as being members of the Communist Party, and who nevertheless are still working and shaping the policy of the State Department.
Speech, 9 February 1950, that marked the beginning of the McCarthy 'witch hunts'.

McCarthyism is Americanism with its sleeves rolled up.
Re-election campaign slogan, 1952.

McGOVERN, George Stanley
1922–   American politician

To those who charge that liberalism has been tried and found wanting, I answer that the failure is not in the idea but in the course of recent history. The New Deal was ended by World War II. The New Frontier was closed by Berlin and Cuba almost before it was opened. And the Great Society lost its greatness in the jungles of Indochina.
Lecture at Oxford University, 21 January 1973.

McLUHAN, Marshall
1911–80   Canadian writer

The new electronic independence recreates the world in the image of a global village.
The Gutenberg Galaxy

McLUHAN, Marshall *(contd.)*

Television brought the brutality of war into the comfort of the living room. Vietnam was lost in the living rooms of America, not on the battlefields of Vietnam.
*Quoted in **Montreal Gazette**, May 1975.*

McNAMARA, Robert Strange
1916–   US Secretary of Defense

Neither conscience nor sanity itself suggests that the United States is, or should or could be the global gendarme.
Speech to American newspaper editors, 19 May 1966.

MELBOURNE, 2nd Viscount (William Lamb)
1779–1848

I wish that I were as cocksure of anything as Tom Macaulay is of everything.
Attributed by Earl Cowper, 1889.

MENCKEN, H. L.
1880–1956   American journalist

No one ever went broke underestimating the intelligence of the American people.
American Leader, 1931.

He slept more than any other President, whether by day or by night. Nero fiddled, but Coolidge only snored. He had no ideas, and he was not a nuisance.
American Mercury, 1933.

MENZIES, Sir Robert
1894–1978   Australian Prime Minister

Considering the company that I keep in this place, that is hardly surprising.
*Riposte on being accused by an Opposition MP of having a superiority complex, quoted in **Time**, May 1978.*

Never forget posterity when devising a policy. Never think of it when making a speech.
The Measure of the Years

METTERNICH, Clement
1773–1859   Austrian Chancellor

When Paris sneezes, Europe catches cold.
Letter, 26 January 1830.

Italy is a geographical expression.
Letter, 6 August 1847.

MILL, John Stuart
1806–73   English philosopher

If all mankind minus one were of one opinion, and only one person were of the contrary opinion, mankind would no more be justified in silencing that one person than he, if he had the power, would be justified in silencing mankind.
On Liberty

A party of order or stability, and a party of progress or reform, are both necessary elements of a healthy state of political life.
Ib.

MILL, John Stuart *(contd.)*

Everyone who receives the protection of society owes a return for the benefit, and the fact of living in a society renders it indispensable that each should be bound to observe a certain line of conduct towards the rest. That conduct consists . . . in each person bearing his share of the labours and sacrifices incurred for defending the society or its members from injury and molestation.
Ib.

The worth of the State, in the long run, is the worth of the individuals composing it.
Representative Government

MILLER, Henry Valentine
1891–1980   American writer

One has to be a lowbrow, a bit of a murderer, to be a politician; ready and willing to see people sacrificed, slaughtered, for the sake of an idea — whether a good one or a bad one.
Writers at Work

MILNER, Alfred, 1st Viscount
1854–1925   British Conservative peer

If we believe a thing to be bad, and if we have a right to prevent it, it is our duty to try to prevent it and damn the consequences.
Speech at Glasgow in November 1909, on the blocking by the Conservative majority in the House of Lords of the Liberal Government's Budget.

MILTON, John
1608–74   English poet and pamphleteer

The power of kings and magistrates is nothing else but what is only derivative; transformed and committed to them in trust from the people to the common good of them all, in whom the power yet remains fundamentally, and cannot be taken from them without a violation of their natural birthright.
The Tenure of Kings and Magistrates

MIRABEAU, Count (Honoré Gabriel)
1749–91   French revolutionary

To administer is to govern; to govern is to reign. That is the problem.
Memorandum, 3 July 1790.

MONDALE, Walter Frederick
1928–   American politician

I don't want to spend the next two years in Holidays Inns.
On withdrawing from the 1976 presidential campaign.

In our system, at about 11.30 pm on election night, they just push you off the edge of the cliff — and that's it. You might scream on the way down, but you're going to hit the bottom, and you're not going to be in office.
*On losing to Ronald Reagan in the 1984 election, **New York Times**, 4 March 1984.*

MONROE, James
1758–1831   5th US President

The American continents, by the free and independent condition that they have assumed and maintain, are henceforth not to be considered as subjects for future colonisation by any European powers . . . In the wars of the European powers in matters relating to themselves, we have never taken any part; nor does it comport with our policy to do so.

The Monroe Doctrine, *2 December 1823.*

MONTAGU, Alexander V.E.P.
1906–   Conservative Politician

Lord Hailsham said the other day that the machinery of Government was creaking. My Lords, it is not even moving sufficiently to emit a noise of any kind.

House of Lords, 20 April 1963, said shortly before disclaiming his peerage for life.

MOORE, Major-General Jeremy
1928–   British Army commander

The Falkland Islands are once more under the Government desired by their inhabitants. God save the Queen.

Message from Port Stanley to London, 14 June 1982.

MORAN, Lord (Richard John McMoran Wilson)
1924–   British diplomat

Courage is a moral quality; it is not a chance gift of nature, like an aptitude for games. It is a cold choice between two alternatives; the fixed resolve not to quit, an act of renunciation that must be made not once but many times by the power of the will.

The Anatomy of Courage

MORITZ, Karl Philipp
1756–93   German Lutheran

When you see how in this happy country the lowest and poorest member of society takes an interest in all public affairs; when you see how high and low, rich and poor, are all willing to declare their feelings and convictions; when you see how a carter, a common sailor, a beggar is still a man, nay, even more, an Englishman — then, believe me, you find yourself very differently affected from the experience you feel when staring at our soldiers drilling in Berlin.

Letter to a friend after observing a London by-election, 1782.

MORRIS, William
1834–96   English socialist

The Socialist papers . . . came out full to the throat of well-printed matter . . . admirable and straightforward expositions of the doctrines and practice of Socialism, free from haste and spite and hard words . . . with a kind of May-day freshness amidst the worry and terror of the moment.

News from Nowhere

Between complete socialism and communism there is no difference whatever in my mind. Communism is in fact the completion of socialism; when that ceases to be militant and becomes triumphant, it will be communism.

Addressing Hammersmith Socialist Society, 1893.

MORTON, Rogers
1931– American Republican politician

I have no intention of rearranging the furniture on the deck of the Titanic.
On declining to rescue President Ford's disastrous 1976 election campaign.

MOUNTBATTEN of BURMA, 1st Earl(Louis Francis Victor Albert Nicholas)
1900–79 British viceroy and admiral

As a military man who has given half a century of active service, I say in all sincerity that the nuclear arms race has no military purpose. Wars cannot be fought with nuclear weapons; their existence only adds to our perils because of the illusions that they have generated. The world now stands on the brink of the final abyss. Let us all resolve to take all possible practicable steps to ensure that we do not, through our own folly, go over the edge.
Speech at the Council of Europe in Strasbourg, 11 May 1979.

MÜNSTER, Count Georg
1794–1868 Hanoverian diplomat

An intelligent Russian once remarked to me, 'Every country has its own Constitution. Ours is absolutism moderated by assassination.'
Political Sketches of the State of Europe 1814–1867

MURROW, Edward (Edgar) Roscoe
1908–65 American political commentator

The politician is trained in the art of inexactitude. His words tend to be blunt or rounded, because if they have a cutting edge they may later return to wound him.
Murrow

MUSSOLINI, Benito
1883–1945 Italian dictator

I could have transformed this grey assembly hall into an armed camp of Blackshirts, a bivouac for corpses. I could have nailed up the doors of Parliament.
Inaugural speech to the Lower House as Prime Minister, 16 November 1922.

If I advance, follow me. If I retreat, kill me. If I die, avenge me.
Said to senior officials after an attempt on his life, 6 April 1926.

The keystone of Fascist doctrine is its conception of the State — of its essence, functions, and aims. For Fascism, the State is absolute, individuals and groups relative.
Fascism, Doctrine and Institutions

NAPOLEON I
1769–1821 Emperor of the French

Power is my mistress. I have worked too hard in conquering her to allow anyone to take her from me, or even to covet her.
The Journal of Roederer

Wisdom and policy dictates that we must do as destiny demands and keep pace with the irresistible march of events.
Said to Alexander I of Russia, 2 February 1808.

France has more need of me than I have of France.
Speech to Corps Législatif, Paris, 31 December 1813.

NAPOLEON I *(contd.)*

An army marches on its stomach.
Attributed while in exile on St Helena.

England is a nation of shopkeepers.
Ib.

NAPOLEON III
1808–73   Emperor of the French

For too long, society has resembled a pyramid that has been turned upside down and made to rest on its summit. I have replaced it on its base.
Speech to the Legislative Assembly, 29 March 1852.

We must not seek to fashion events, but let them happen of their own accord.
In conversation with Bismarck, Biarritz, 4 October 1865.

NEHRU, Jawaharlal
1889–1964   First Prime Minister of India

Stalin . . . that great lover of peace, a man of giant stature who moulded, as few other men have done, the destinies of his age . . . The occasion is not merely the passing away of a great figure but perhaps the ending of an historic era.
Tribute, Indian Parliament, 9 March 1953.

NELSON, Viscount (Horatio)
1758–1805   English admiral

Before this time tomorrow, I shall have gained a peerage, or a place in Westminster Abbey.
Said on the eve of the Battle of the Nile, 31 July 1798.

I wish to say Nelson confides that every man will do his duty.
To the flag officer on HMS Victory, 21 October 1805. The signal was amended to begin, 'England expects . . .'.

NICHOLAS II
1868–1919   Last Tsar of Russia

There are senseless dreams of the participation of local government representatives in the affairs of internal administration. I shall maintain the principle of autocracy just as firmly and unflinchingly as it was upheld by my own, ever to be remembered dead father.
Declaration, 17 January 1896.

NIETZSCHE, Friedrich Wilhelm
1844–1900   German philosopher

I teach you the Superman. Man is something to be surpassed.
Also Sprach Zarathustra

NIXON, Richard Milhous
1913–   37th President of the United States

I don't believe that I ought to quit because I am not a quitter.
National TV broadcast, September 1952, after allegations that he was financing his vice-presidential candidacy from a secret fund.

NIXON, Richard Milhous *(contd.)*

We cannot learn from one another until we stop shouting at one another; until we speak quietly enough so that our words can be heard as well as our voices. For its part, Government will listen. We will strive to listen in new ways to the voices of quiet anguish, to voices that speak without words, to the voices of the heart, to the injured voices, and to the anxious voices, and the voices that have despaired of being heard.

Inaugural address, 20 January 1969.

This is the greatest week in the history of the world since the Creation.

On the landing of the first American spacecraft on the moon, 20 July 1969.

And so, tonight, to you — the great silent majority of my fellow Americans — I ask for your support.

TV broadcast seeking support for his Vietnam peace plan, November 1969.

Those who scoff at balance-of-power democracy on the world scene should recognise that the only alternative to a balance of power is an imbalance of power — and history shows us that nothing so drastically escalates the danger of wars as such an imbalance.

White House press conference, 25 June 1972.

I don't give a shit what happens. I want you all to stonewall . . . plead the Fifth Amendment, cover-up, or anything else. If that will save it, save the plan.

From the White House tapes relating to the Watergate scandal, recorded March 1973.

There will be no whitewash in the White House.

Statement on the Watergate affair, 17 April 1973.

In your business, you have a way of handling problems like this. Somebody leaves a pistol in the drawer. I don't have a pistol.

Said to General Alexander Haig in August 1974, quoted in **The Final Days.**

When the President does it, that means that it is not illegal . . . But I brought myself down. I gave them a sword and they stuck it in and they twisted it with relish. And I guess that if I had been in their position, I'd have done the same thing.

Interviewed by David Frost, May 1977.

A man is not finished when he is defeated. He is finished when he quits. You've got to survive a defeat. That's when you develop character.

Dallas Times-Herald, *10 December 1978.*

NORTH, Colonel Oliver

1943–   American soldier

I don't think that there's another person in America that wants to tell this story as much as I do.

Invoking the Fifth Amendment at the House Committee investigating arms sales to Iran, 10 December 1986.

I thought that using the Ayatollah's money to support the Nicaraguan resistance . . . was a good idea.

Ib., 8 July 1987.

NORTHCLIFFE, Lord (Alfred Harmsworth)

1865–1922   British newspaper proprietor

I know Palestine. It is rather a poor country. There's a lot of unemployment there now. The danger is that you may get too many people down there to fit the conditions.

Addressing prominent Zionists, New York, 1921.

O'BRIEN, Conor Cruise

1917–   Irish historian and politician

The United Nations cannot do anything, and never could. It is not an animate entity or agent. It is a place, a stage, a forum and a shrine . . . a place to which powerful people can repair when they are fearful about the course on which their own rhetoric seems to be propelling them.

New Republic, 4 November 1985.

O'CONNELL, Daniel

1775–1847   Irish nationalist leader

Let us never tolerate the slightest inroad on the discipline of our holy Church. Let us never consent that she should be made the hireling of the Ministry. Our forefathers would have died — nay, perished in hopeless slavery – rather than consent to such degradation.

Speech, Dublin, 23 February 1814.

OLLIVIER, Emile

1825–1913   French Prime Minister

One is never weaker than when one appears to have everybody's support.

Letters, 1870.

ORMSBY GORE, (Francis) David (Lord Harlech)

1918–85   British diplomat

It would indeed be the ultimate tragedy if the history of the human race proved to be nothing more noble than the story of an ape playing with a box of matches on a petrol dump.

Christian Science Monitor, 25 October 1960.

ORWELL, George

1903–50   British novelist

All animals are equal, but some are more equal than others.

Animal Farm

The great enemy of clear language is insincerity. When there is a gap between one's real and one's declared aims, one turns instinctively to long words and exhausted idioms — like a cuttlefish squirting out ink.

The Lion and the Unicorn

Big Brother is watching you.

1984.

(Attlee) reminds me of nothing so much as a recently-dead fish before it has had time to stiffen.

Diary, May 1942.

OVERTON, Robert
fl. 1642-63   English radical printer

Whatever our forefathers were, or whatever they did or suffered, or were enforced to yield unto, we are the men of the present age, and ought to be absolutely free from all kinds of exorbitancies, molestations, or arbitrary power.

Remonstrance to the House of Commons, 1646.

OWEN, Dr David
1938–   British politician

We are fed up with fudging and nudging, with mush and slush.

Speech to Labour's national conference, October 1980, shortly before leaving the party to found the Social Democratic Party.

PAINE, Thomas
1737–1809   English radical writer

Government, even in its best state, is but a necessary evil; in its worst state, an intolerable one. Government, like dress, is the badge of lost innocence; the palaces of kings are built upon the bowers of paradise.

Common Sense

There are times that try men's souls.

The Crisis

Man is not the enemy of Man, but through the medium of a false system of government.

The Rights of Man

To establish any mode to abolish war, however advantageous it might be to nations, would be to take from such Government the most lucrative of its branches.

Ib.

That as he rose like a rocket, [Burke] fell like a stick.

Letters to the Addressers on the late Proclamation, 1792.

PALMERSTON, 3rd Viscount (Henry Temple)
1784–1865   English statesman

Half the wrong conclusions at which mankind arrive are reached by the abuse of metaphors, and by mistaking general resemblance of imaginary similarity for real identity.

Letter to Henry Bulwer, 1 September 1839.

We have no eternal allies, and we have no perpetual enemies. Our interests are eternal, and it is our duty to follow them.

House of Commons, 1 March 1848.

Large republics seem to be essentially and inherently aggressive.

Letter to the British Ambassador to Paris, 5 March 1848.

You may call it coalition, you may call it the accidental and fortuitous concurrence of atoms . . . but when gentlemen are in the habit of finding themselves in the same Lobby, it is not unnatural to suppose that they may, under certain circumstances, be ready to unite themselves together for the purpose of forming an Administration and becoming responsible for the opinions that they severally entertain.

Speech on the rumoured Palmerston-Disraeli coalition, 5 March 1858.

PALMERSTON, 3rd Viscount *(contd.)*

England is one of the greatest powers of the world. No event or series of events bearing on the balance of power, or on probabilities of peace or war, can be matters of indifference to her, and her right to have and to express opinions on matters thus bearing on her interests is unquestionable.

Letter to Queen Victoria, 23 August 1859.

PANKHURST, Emmeline
1858–1928   British suffragette leader

There is something that Governments care for far more than human life, and that is the security of property. So it is through property that we shall strike the enemy . . . Be militant each in your own way . . . I incite this meeting to rebellion.

Speech, Royal Albert Hall, 17 October 1912.

What is the use of fighting for the vote if we do not have a country to vote in? With that patriotism that has nerved women to endure torture in prison for the national good, we ardently desire that our country shall be victorious.

Declaring a truce on suffragette activities for the duration of World War I, 10 August 1914.

PARKES, Sir Henry
1815–96   Australian statesman

Why should not the name of an Australian be equal to that of a Briton . . . to that of a citizen of the proudest country under the sun? Make yourselves a united people, appear before the world as one, and the dream of going 'home' will die away.

Speech to the Australian Federation Conference, February 1880.

PARNELL, Charles Stewart
1846–91   Champion of Irish Home Rule

When a man takes a farm from which another has been evicted, you must show him on the roadside when you meet him; you must show him in the streets of the town; you must show him in the fair and the market place; and even in the house of worship, by leaving him severely alone — by putting him into a moral Coventry, by isolating him from his kind as if he were a leper of old. You must show him your detestation of the crimes that he has committed.

Speech, Ennis, 19 September 1880, that established the practice of boycotting.

No man has a right to fix the boundary of the march of a nation. No man has a right to say to his country, 'Thus far thou shalt go and no further.'

Speech, Cork, 21 January 1885.

PAVLOV, Valentin
1923—   Soviet Prime Minister

Privatization must come after the liberalization of prices . . . How on earth can you privatize or denationalize anything if you have no means of assessing the value of assets before offering them on the market?

*Interview, **The Independent**, 18 April 1991.*

It is no use making revolutionary cavalry charges against the problems that we are facing.

On Boris Yeltsin's proposals for economic republican autonomy, ib.

Civil war is impossible in the Soviet Union.

Ib.

PAZWAK, Abdul Rahman
1902– Afghanistan statesman

Few, if any, calamities in our time have befallen the world without some advance notice
. . . from this rostrum. Thus, if fools and folly rule the world, the end of man in our time
may come as a rude shock, but it will no longer come as a complete surprise.

Final address to the UN General Assembly on retiring as its president,
19 September 1967.

PEARSON, Lester Bowles
1897–1972   Canadian Prime Minister

Politics is the skilled use of blunt objects.

Quoted in Canadian Broadcasting Corporation tribute, 1972.

PEEL, Sir Robert
1788–1850   British Prime Minister

If the spirit of the Reform Bill implies merely a careful review of institutions, civil
and ecclesiastical, undertaken in a friendly temper, combining with the firm
maintenance of established rights the correction of private abuses and the redress of
real grievances, I can for myself and my colleagues undertake to act in such a spirit
and with such intentions.

The Tamworth Manifesto, *1834.*

During my tenure of power, my earnest wish has been to impress the people
of this country with a belief that the legislature was animated by a sincere desire
to frame its legislation upon the principles of equity and justice . . . Deprive
me of power tomorrow, but you can never deprive me of the consciousness
that I have exercised the powers committed to me from no corrupt or
interested motives, from no desire to gratify ambition, or to attain any personal
object.

On the repeal of the Corn Laws, House of Commons, 15 May 1846.

PÉTAIN, Philippe
1856–1951   Marshal of France

I was with you in the days of glory. At the head of the Government, I shall remain
with you during the days of darkness. Stay by my side.

Radio broadcast announcing his intention to seek an armistice, 20 June 1940.

PHILIP, Prince
1921–   Duke of Edinburgh

I have very little experience of self-government. In fact, I am one of the most
governed people in the world.

New York Times, *30 December 1959.*

We are suffering a national defeat comparable to any lost military campaign, and
what is more, it is self-inflicted . . . It is about time that we pulled our fingers out . . .
The rest of the world most certainly does not owe us a living.

Speech to British industrialists, London, 17 October 1961.

PINOCHET UGARTE, General Augusto
1915– Chilean dictator

I am not a dictator. It's just that I have a grumpy face.
Attrib.

PITT, William (the younger)
1759–1806 British statesman

Amid the wreck and the misery of nations it is our just exaltation that we have continued superior to all that ambition or despotism could effect; and our still higher exaltation ought to be that we provide not only for our own safety but hold out a prospect for nations now bending under the yoke of tyranny of what the exertions of a free people can effect.
House of Commons, 25 April 1804.

Europe is not to be saved by any single man. England has saved herself by her exertions, and will, as I trust, save Europe by her example.
Speech, London Guildhall, 9 November 1805.

I think that I could eat one of Bellamy's veal pies.
Attributed last words, 23 January 1806.

PLEHVE, Viacheslav Konstantinovich
1846–1904 Russian Minister

Russia has been made by bayonets, not by diplomacy; and we must decide the questions at issue with China and Japan with bayonets and not through the pens of diplomats.
Russian Imperial Council, 7 May 1903.

POBEDONOSTSEV, Konstantin
1827–1907 Russian jurist

Parliaments are the great lie of our time.
Moskovskii Shornik

POINDEXTER, John Marlan
1936– US Rear Admiral

I made a very deliberate decision not to ask the President, so that I could insulate him from the decision and provide some future deniability for him if it ever leaked out.
On his action in diverting funds from arms sales at Iran-Contra hearings, 15 July 1987.

POPE, Alexander
1688–1744 English poet

For forms of government let fools contest,
Whate'er is best administered is best.
An Essay on Man

POTTER, Henry Codman
1835–1908 American churchman

If there be no nobility of descent in a nation, it is all the more indispensable that there should be nobility of ascent; a character in them that bear rule, so fine and high and pure, that as men come within the circle of its influence, they involuntarily pay homage to that which is the one pre-eminent distinction — the royalty of virtue.
Washington centennial address, 30 April 1889.

POWELL, Enoch
1912–   British politician

As I look ahead, I am filled with foreboding. Like the Roman, I seem to see 'the River Tiber foaming with much blood.'
Speech at Birmingham, April 1968, on racial tension in Britain.

I was born a Tory, am a Tory, and shall die a Tory. I never yet heard that it was any part of the faith of a Tory to take the institutions and liberties, the laws and customs that his country has evolved over centuries, and merge them with those of eight other nations into a new-made artificial state — and, what is more, to do so without the willing approbation and consent of the nation.
Speech against Britain's entry into the Common Market, Shipley,
25 February 1974.

All political lives, unless they are cut off in mid-stream at a happy juncture, end in failure, because that is the nature of politics and of human affairs.
Biography of Joseph Chamberlain

PROFUMO, John
1915–   British politician

There was no impropriety whatsoever in my acquaintanceship with Miss Keeler . . . I shall not hesitate to issue writs for libel and slander if scandalous allegations are made or repeated outside the House.
House of Commons, March 1963.

PROUDHON, Pierre-Joseph
1809–65   French socialist

Property is theft.
Qu'est-ce que la Propriété

RAINBOROWE, Thomas
1598–1648   English radical soldier

The poorest He that is in England hath a life to live as well as the greatest He, and therefore, truly Sirs, I think that every man that is to live under a Government ought first, by his own consent, to put himself under that Government.
Said to Cromwell during the Army Debates, Putney, 29 October 1647.

REAGAN, Ronald
1911–   40th US President

To sit back hoping that some day, some way, someone will make things right is to go on feeding the crocodile, hoping that he will eat you last — but eat you he will.
CBS News, 7 November 1974.

Middle age is when you're faced with two temptations and you choose the one that will get you home by 9 o'clock.
On his 66th birthday, quoted in Washington Post, 7 February 1977.

His foreign policy is like the sorry tapping of Neville Chamberlain's umbrella on the cobblestones of Munich.
Said of President Carter following Russia's 1980 invasion of Afghanistan.

REAGAN, Ronald *(contd.)*

Never before in our history has America been called upon to face three grave threats to its very existence — any one of which could destroy us. We face a distressing economy, a weakened defence, and an energy policy based on the sharing of scarcity.
Presidential nomination acceptance speech, Detroit, 17 July 1980.

Recession is when your neighbour loses his job. Depression is when you lose yours. And recovery is when Jimmy Carter loses his.
Election campaign speech, Jersey City, 1 September 1980.

I was alarmed at my doctor's report. He said that I was as sound as the dollar.
Ib.

We all need to be reminded that the Federal Government did not create the states — the states created the Federal Government.
Inaugural address, 20 January 1981.

I can tell a lot about a fellow's character by the way that he eats jelly beans.
Daily Mail, January 1981.

Please tell me you're Republicans.
*To surgeons as he entered the operating room after being shot by John
W. Hinckley Jnr in Washington, 7 February 1977.*

The founders of the United Nations sought to replace a world at war with a world of civilised order. They hoped that a world of relentless conflict would give way to a new era; one where freedom from violence prevailed . . . But the awful truth is that the use of violence for political gain has become more, not less, widespread in the last decade.
*Addressing the UN General Assembly after the Soviet shooting down of
a Korean passenger plane, 26 September 1983.*

What happened to the dreams of the United Nations' founders? What happened to the spirit that created the United Nations? The answer is clear: Governments got in the way of the dreams of the people.
Ib.

My fellow Americans, I am pleased to tell you that I have signed legislation to outlaw Russia for ever. We begin bombing in five minutes.
Said during a microphone test prior to a radio broadcast, August 1984.

This is not the end of anything. This is the beginning of everything.
On his re-election, quoted in Time, November 1984.

The only weapon that we have is MAD – Mutual Assured Destruction. Why don't we have MAS instead – Mutual Assured Security?
*Announcing his Strategic Defence Initiative, quoted in New York Times,
12 February 1985.*

We are not going to tolerate these attacks from outlaw states, run by the strangest collection of misfits, looney tunes and squalid criminals since the advent of the Third Reich.
Speech on terrorist attacks by Shi'ite Muslims, July 1985.

Do you remember when I said that bombing would begin in five minutes? When I fell asleep during my audience with the Pope? Those were the good old days.
Dinner speech, Washington, 28 March 1987.

Since I came to the White House, I got two hearing aids, a colon operation, skin cancer, a prostate operation, and was shot. The damn thing is, I've never felt better in my life.
Ib.

REDMOND, John
1856–1918   Irish politician

The Government may tomorrow withdraw every one of their troops from Ireland. Ireland will be defended by her armed sons from foreign invasion, and for that purpose the armed Catholics in the south will be only too glad to join arms with the armed Protestant Ulsterman. Is it too much to hope that out of this situation a result may spring that will be good not merely for the Empire but for the future welfare and integrity of the Irish nation?
House of Commons, 3 August 1914.

RED STAR
Soviet Ministry of Defence publication

The Iron Lady of British politics is seeking to revive the Cold War.
Issue dated 23 January 1976.

REED, John
1887–1920   American author

Ten Days That Shook the World
Title of his 1919 book on the Bolshevik Revolution.

REES-MOGG, Lord William
British newspaper editor and head of the Broadcasting Standards Council

Information, free from interest or prejudice, free from the vanity of the writer or the influence of a Government, is as necessary to the human mind as pure air and water to the human body.
***Christian Science Monitor**, 22 September 1970.*

RENAN, Ernest
1823–92   French historian

War is a condition of progress; the whip-cut that prevents a country from going to sleep and forces satisfied mediocrity to shake off its apathy.
La Réforme Intellectuelle et Morale

RHODES, Cecil
1853–1902   Founder of Rhodesia

Remember that you are an Englishman, and have consequently won first prize in the lottery of life.
*Quoted by Peter Ustinov in **Dear Me**.*

RICARDO, David
1772–1823   English political economist

The interest of the landlord is always opposed to the interests of every other class in the community.
Principles of Political Economy and Taxation

The natural price of labour is that price which is necessary to enable the labourers, one with another, to subsist and to perpetuate their race, without either increase or diminution.
Ib.

RICE, Sir Stephen
1637–1715   Head of the Irish Exchequer

I will drive a coach and horses through the [Irish] Act of Settlement.
Attrib.

RICHELIEU, Cardinal de (Armand Jean Duplessis)
1585–1642   French statesman

Not least among the qualities in a great King is a capacity to permit his Ministers to serve him.
Testament Politique

Secrecy is the first essential in the affairs of State.
Ib.

When the people are too comfortable, it is not possible to restrain them within the bounds of their duty . . . They may be compared to mules who, being accustomed to burdens, are spoilt by rest rather than labour.
Ib.

Wounds inflicted by the sword heal more easily than those inflicted by the tongue.
Ib.

ROCKEFELLER Jnr, John Davison
1874–1960   Oil magnate and philanthropist

The rendering of useful service is the common duty of mankind, and that only in the purifying fire of sacrifice is the dross of selfishness consumed and the greatness of the human soul set free.
Credo engraved in Rockefeller Centre Plaza, New York.

ROGERS, General Bernard Williams
1921–   NATO Supreme Allied Commander Europe

The last thing that we want to do is to make Europe safe for a conventional war.
Time, *16 March 1987.*

ROOSEVELT, (Anna) Eleanor
1882–1962   American humanitarian, wife of Franklin D. Roosevelt

Where, after all, do human rights begin? They begin in small places, close to home — so close and so small that they cannot be seen on any map of the world.
New York Times, *26 December 1965.*

ROOSEVELT, Franklin D.
1882–1945   32nd US President

I pledge you, I pledge myself, to a New Deal for the American people.
Speech accepting the Democratic Convention's presidential nomination, Chicago, 2 July 1932.

Let me assert my belief that the only thing that we have to fear is fear itself — nameless, unreasoning, unjustified terror that paralyses needed efforts to convert retreat into advance.
Inaugural address, 4 March 1933.

In the field of world policy, I would dedicate this nation to the policy of the good neighbour.
Ib.

ROOSEVELT, Franklin D. *(contd.)*

Better the occasional faults of a Government that lives in a spirit of charity than the consistent omissions of a Government frozen in the ice of its own indifference.
Renomination acceptance speech, Philadelphia, 27 June 1936.

When peace has been broken anywhere, the peace of all countries everywhere is in danger.
Radio broadcast, 3 September 1939.

A conservative is a man with two perfectly good legs who has never learned to walk forwards. A reactionary is a somnambulist walking backwards. A radical is a man with both feet planted firmly in the air.
Radio broadcast, October 1939.

I have told you once and I will tell you again — your boys will not be sent to any foreign wars.
Election speech, 1940.

We must be the great arsenal of democracy.
Radio broadcast, 29 December 1940.

In the future days, which we seek to make secure, we look forward to a world founded upon four essential freedoms. The first is freedom of speech and expression, everywhere in the world. The second is the freedom of every person to worship God in his own way, everywhere in the world. The third is freedom from want . . . The fourth is freedom from fear.
Third inaugural address, 6 January 1941.

Yesterday, December 7 1941 — a date that will live in infamy — the United States of America was suddenly and deliberately attacked by naval and air forces of the Empire of Japan.
Message to Congress on the attack on Pearl Harbour, 8 December 1941.

ROOSEVELT, Theodore
1858–1919   26th US President

There is a homely adage that runs, 'Speak softly and carry a big stick, and you will go far.' If the American nation will speak softly and yet build, and keep at a pitch of the highest training, the Monroe Doctrine will go far.
Vice-presidential speech, September 1901.

In the western hemisphere, the adherence of the United States to the Monroe Doctrine may force the United States, however reluctantly, in flagrant cases of wrongdoing or impotence, to the exercise of an international police power.
Message to Congress, 6 December 1904.

The men with the muck-rakes are often indispensable to the well-being of society, but only if they know when to stop raking the muck.
House of Representatives, 14 April 1906.

I stand for the square deal . . . not merely for fair play under the present rules of the game, but for having those rules changed, so as to work for a more substantial equality of opportunity and of reward for equally good service.
Speech, Osawatomie, 31 August 1910.

Do not hit at all if it can be avoided, but never hit softly.
Autobiography

ROOSEVELT, Theodore *(contd.)*

Practical efficiency is common, and lofty idealism is not uncommon; it is the combination that is necessary, and that combination is rare.

Ib.

We have room in this country but for one flag, the Stars and Stripes. We have room for but one loyalty, loyalty to the United States. We have room for but one language, the English language.

Message to American Defense Society, 3 January 1919, two days before his death.

ROSEBERY, 5th Earl of (Archibald Philip Primrose)

1847–1929   British politician

It is beginning to be hinted that we are a nation of amateurs.

Rectorial address, Glasgow University, 16 November 1900.

For the present at any rate, I must proceed alone. I must plough my own furrow alone — but before I get to the end of that furrow, it is possible that I may not find myself alone.

On breaking from the Liberal Party, July 1901.

ROUSSEAU, Jean-Jacques

1712–78   French political theorist

Man is born free; and everywhere he is in chains.

Contrat Social

The English people imagine themselves to be free, but they are wrong. It is only during the election of Members of Parliament that they are so.

Ib.

ROYDEN, Agnes Maude

1887–1967   Congregationalist Minister

The Church of England should be no longer satisfied to represent only the Conservative Party at prayer.

Address to the Life and Liberty Movement, London, 16 July 1917.

RUNCIE, Robert Alexander

1924–   Archbishop of Canterbury

Royalty puts a human face on the operations of government.

*Sermon at a service to mark the Queen Mother's 80th birthday, St Paul's
Cathedral, 15 July 1980.*

Those who dare to interpret God's will must never claim Him as an asset for one nation or group rather than another. War springs from the love and loyalty that should be offered to God being applied to some God substitute — one of the most dangerous being nationalism.

*Sermon at Thanksgiving Service after the Falklands War, St Paul's
Cathedral, 26 July 1982.*

RUSHWORTH, John

1610–90   Clerk to the House of Commons

His Majesty entered the House, and as he passed up towards the Chair, he cast his eye on the right hand near the Bar of the House, where Mr Pym used to sit; but His Majesty, not seeing him there (knowing him well) went up to the Chair and said, 'By your leave, Mr Speaker, I must borrow your chair a little.'

*His account of the attempt by Charles I to arrest five Members of
Parliament on 4 January 1642.*

RUSK, Dean
1909– US Secretary of State

We're eyeball to eyeball — and I think that the other fellow just blinked.
*On the Cuban missile crisis, **Saturday Evening Post**, 8 December 1962.*

Communications today puts a special emphasis on what happens next, for an able, sophisticated and competitive press knows that what happens today is no longer news — it is what is going to happen tomorrow that is the object of interest and concern.
Time's 40th anniversary dinner, 17 May 1963.

RUSKIN, John
1819–1900 English writer

Men don't and can't live by exchanging articles, but by producing them. They don't live by trade, but by work. Give up that foolish and vain title of Trades Unions; and take that of Labourers' Unions.
Open Letter to English Trades Unions, 29 September 1880.

RUSSELL, Bertrand
1872–1970 British philosopher

This idea of weapons of mass extermination is utterly horrible, and is something that no one with a spark of humanity can tolerate. I will not pretend to obey a Government that is organising a mass massacre of mankind.
Speech urging civil disobedience in support of nuclear disarmament, Birmingham, 15 April 1961.

RUSSELL, Lord John
1792–1878 British Prime Minister

If peace cannot be maintained with honour, it is no longer peace.
Speech, Greenock, 19 September 1853.

SAMUEL, Lord (Herbert Louis)
1870–1963 British statesman

The House of Lords must be the only institution in the world that is kept efficient by the persistent absenteeism of its members.
American News Review, 5 February 1948.

Hansard is history's ear, already listening.
House of Lords, December 1949.

SANDBURG, Carl
1878–1967 American poet

Sometime they'll give a war and nobody will come.
The People, Yes

SANTAYANA, George
1863–1952 Spanish-born American philosopher

Those who cannot remember the past are condemned too repeat it.
The Life of Reason

SARTRE, Jean-Paul
1905–80   French writer

Man is condemned to be free.
Existentialism is a Humanism.

Hell is other people.
In Camera

SCARGILL, Arthur
1938–   British miners' leader

My father still reads the dictionary every day. He says that your life depends on your power to master words.
The Sunday Times, *10 January 1982.*

I speak of that most dangerous duo – President Ray-Gun and the plutonium blonde, Margaret Thatcher.
Quoted in **Time**, *3 December 1984.*

SCHACHT, Hjalmar
1877–1970   German banker

I wouldn't believe that Hitler was dead, even if he told me himself.
Attributed remark, 8 May 1945.

SCHARANSKY, Natan (Anatoly Borisovich)
1948–   Soviet mathematician and dissident

All the resources of a superpower cannot isolate a man who hears the voice of freedom; a voice that I heard from the very chamber of my soul.
Speech, New York, 11 May 1986, shortly after his release following nine years in a Soviet labour colony.

SCHLESINGER, Arthur Meier Jr
1917–   American historian

Television has spread the habit of instant reaction and has stimulated the hope of instant results.
Newsweek, 6 July 1970.

SCHLESINGER, James
1932–   US Secretary of Defence

The notion of a defence that will protect American cities is one that will not be achieved, but it is that goal that supplies the political magic in the President's vision.
Senate Foreign Relations Committee, 6 February 1987.

SCHROEDER, Patricia
1937–   US Congresswoman

I was cooking breakfast this morning for my kids and I thought, 'He's just like Teflon. Nothing sticks to him'.
On President Ronald Reagan, **Boston Globe**, *24 October 1984.*

SCHUMACHER, E.F.
1911–77   German-born British economist

Small is Beautiful
Title of his 1973 book.

SCHWARZKOPF, General Norman 'Stormin' Norman'

1934– American commander-in-chief, 1991 Gulf War.

We are not going after Saddam Hussein. If I can eliminate his ability to communicate with his forces, I would be entirely satisfied with that result.

Press briefing on the start of the Gulf War, 15 January 1991.

I asked you to be the thunder and lightning of Desert Storm. You were all of that and more.

Message to US units on the cease-fire that ended the 1991 Gulf War.

SCHWEITZER, Albert

1875–1965 Alsatian theologian and philosopher

An optimist is a person who sees a green light everywhere, while the pessimist sees only the red stop-light. The truly wise person is colour-blind.

Quoted in CBS News tribute, 14 January 1965.

SCOTT, C.P.

1846–1932 British newspaper editor

Comment is free, but facts are sacred.

The Manchester Guardian, 5 May 1921.

SEELEY, Sir John

1834–95 British historian

We seem to have conquered and peopled half the world in a fit of absence of mind.

The Expansion of England

SELDEN, John

1584–1654 English historian

Ignorance of the law excuses no man; not that all men know the law, but because 'tis an excuse every man will plead, and no man can tell how to confute him.

Table-Talk

Those that govern most make least noise.

Ib.

SELLAR, Walter Carruthers

1898–1951 British humorist

[Gladstone] spent his declining years trying to guess the answer to the Irish Question. Unfortunately, whenever he was getting warm, the Irish secretly changed the question.

1066 And All That

The National Debt is a very Good thing, and it would be dangerous to pay it off for fear of Political economy.

Ib.

SENIOR, W. Nassau

1790–1864 English political economist

This barbarous feeling of nationality... has become the curse of Europe.

Diary, 20 May 1850.

SERVICE, Robert W.
1874–1958 Canadian poet

Ah! The clock is always slow;
It is later than you think.
Spring

SHAW, George Bernard
1856–1950 Irish playwright and critic

[The Red Flag] is the funeral march of a fried eel.
Quoted by Winston Churchill in **Great Contemporaries**.

[Lord Rosebery] was a man who never missed an occasion to let slip an opportunity.
Ib.

You see things, and you say, 'Why?' But I dream things that never were; and I say 'Why not?'
The Serpent

Assassination is the extreme form of censorship.
Maxims for Revolutionaries

Democracy substitutes election by the incompetent many for the appointment by the corrupt few.
Ib.

Liberty means responsibility. That is why most men dread it.
Ib.

The worst sin towards our fellow creatures is not to hate them, but to be indifferent to them; that's the essence of inhumanity.
The Devil's Disciple

Nothing is ever done in this world until men are prepared to kill one another if it is not done.
Major Barbara

An Englishman thinks he is moral when he is only uncomfortable.
Man and Superman

Do not do unto others as you would they should do unto you. Their tastes may not be the same.
Ib.

Idiots are always in favour of inequality of income (their only chance of eminence), and the really great in favour of equality.
The Intelligent Woman's Guide to Socialism and Capitalism

[To Helen Keller] I wish that all Americans were as blind as you.
Quoted by H. Pearson in **Bernard Shaw**.

If all the economists in the world were laid end to end, they would not reach a conclusion.
Attrib.

SHAWCROSS, Lord (Hartley William)
1902–   British jurist and Attorney-General

We are the masters at the moment, and not only at the moment, but for a very long time to come.

Alluding to Labour's victory in the 1945 general election, House of Commons, 2 April 1946.

The so-called new morality is too often the old immorality condoned.

The Observer, *17 July 1963.*

SHEVARDNADZE, Eduard Ambrosievich
1928–   Soviet reformist Foreign Minister

Democrats are fleeing in all directions. Reformers are going into hiding. A dictatorship is beginning, and no one knows what shape it will take or who will come to power.

On the increasing disarray in the USSR caused by failing Soviet reforms, rivalry between the Gorbachev and Yeltsin factions, and unrest in the Baltic states, **The Sunday Times**, *23 December 1990.*

SHINWELL, Lord Emanuel ('Manny')
1884–1986   British Labour politician

We know that you, the organised workers of the country, are our friends . . . As for the rest, they do not matter a tinker's curse.

Trade union conference, 7 May 1947.

SIDNEY, Algernon
1622–83   English politician

Liars ought to have good memories.

Discourses concerning Government

SIEYES, Abbot Emmanuel Joseph
1748–1836   French revolutionary

Who will dare deny that the Third Estate contains within itself all that is needed to constitute a nation? . . . What would the Third Estate be without the privileged classes? It would be a whole in itself, and a prosperous one. Nothing can be done without it, and everything would be done far better without the others.

Qu'est-ce que le Tiers État?

SIKORSKY, Igor Ivan
1889–1972   Russian-born American aeronautical engineer

The work of the individual still remains the spark that moves mankind ahead, even more than teamwork.

Quoted in **New York Times** *obituary, 27 October 1972.*

SIMON, Sir John
1873–1954   British Foreign Secretary

If Joan of Arc had been born in Austria and worn a moustache, she might have conveyed much the same impression.

Letter to George V, referring to his first meeting with Adolf Hitler, 27 March 1935.

'SIMPLE, Peter' (Michael Wharton)

1913– Newspaper columnist

Rentacrowd Ltd – the enterprising firm that supplies crowds for all occasions, and has done so much to keep progressive causes in the public eye.
The Daily Telegraph, *1962.*

SKELTON, Noel

1880–1935 British politician

To state as clearly as may be what means lie ready to develop a property-owning democracy, to bring the industrial and economic status of the wage-earner abreast of his political and educational status, to make democracy stable and four-square.
The Spectator, *19 May 1923.*

SKINNER, Burrhus Frederic

1904– American psychologist

Education is what survives when what has been learnt has been forgotten.
New Scientist, *21 May 1964.*

SLOGANS

Balfour must go.
British press, 1905.

Ban the Bomb.
Used by American nuclear disarmament movement from 1953.

Berlin by Christmas.
British press, 1914.

Better Red than dead.
Used by British nuclear disarmament movement from 1958.

Black is beautiful.
US, 1966.

Black power.
American black civil rights slogan coined by Stokely Carmichael, 1966.

Bombs away with Curtis LeMay.
Used by US anti-Vietnam demonstrators, 1967.

Britain can take it.
1940

Burn, baby, burn!
Coined by American black extremists, 1965.

Burn your bra!
US feminists' slogan, 1970.

Ein Reich, ein Volk, ein Führer (One realm, one people, one leader)
Nazi slogan, 1934.

Export or die.
British Board of Trade, 1940s.

GOTCHA!
*Headline in the **Sun**, on the sinking of the Argentine cruiser, the General Belgrano, during the Falklands War, 4 May 1982.*

SLOGANS *(contd.)*

Hearts and minds.
Used by US Defence Department official with regard to winning public support for its Vietnam policy.

Hey, hey, LBJ! How many kids did you kill today?
US anti-Vietnam war demonstrators, 1966.

I like Ike.
Dwight D. Eisenhower's campaign slogan from 1947.

I'm Backing Britain.
Coined by publisher Robert Maxwell in 1968 to encourage the public to buy British-made goods.

Labour isn't working.
Used by the Conservative Party in its 1979 general election campaign, referring to high unemployment under the then Labour Government.

Let's get America moving again.
John F. Kennedy's 1960 presidential election slogan.

Life's better with the Conservatives . . . don't let Labour ruin it.
Conservative Party general election slogan, 1959.

Make love, not war.
Flower Power movement, mid-1960s.

Nation shall speak unto nation.
First motto of the BBC, 1927.

Never again.
Jewish Defence League, 1960s.

On yer bike!
Catchphrase derived from Norman Tebbit's Conservative Party conference speech, 1981.

Out of the closets and into the streets.
US Gay Liberation Front, 1969.

Power to the people.
US Black Panther movement, 1969.

Safety first.
Conservative Party general election slogan, 1929.

Send them a message.
Governor George Wallace's presidential election slogan, 1972.

Stop The World, I Want to Get Off
From the 1961 musical by Leslie Bricusse and Anthony Newley.

That Was The Week That Was
Title of satirical BBC TV series, 1962–3.

Thirteen wasted years.
Labour Party general election slogan, 1964.

Votes for Women.
British suffragette movement, 1905.

SLOGANS *(contd.)*

Walls have ears.
Ministry of Defence, 1940s.

We shall overcome.
US black civil rights movement, 1946.

When you've got it, flaunt it.
Braiff Airlines, 1969.

Who dares, wins.
Motto of the Special Air Service, 1940s.

Winston's back.
Admiralty signal on Winston Churchill's reappointment as First Lord, 3 September 1939.

Yesterday's men.
Labour Party general election slogan, referring to the Conservative leadership, 1970.

Your country needs you!
British World War I recruiting slogan, first used 1914.

SMILES, Samuel
1812–1904   British writer

The healthy spirit of self-help created among working people would, more than any other measure, serve to raise them as a class; and this, not by pulling down others, but by levelling them up to a higher and still advancing standard of religion, intelligence, and virtue.
Self-Help

He who never made a mistake never made a discovery.
Ib.

A place for everything, and everything in its place.
Thrift

SMITH, Adam
1723–90   British economist

To found a great Empire for the sole purpose of raising up a people of customers, may at first sight appear a project fit only for a nation of shopkeepers. It is, however, a project altogether unfit for a nation of shopkeepers; but extremely fit for a nation that is governed by shopkeepers.
The Wealth of Nations

SMITH, Alfred E.
1873–1944   American politician

Nobody shoots Santa Claus.
Denouncing criticisms of the US aid programme, 1936.

No matter how thin you slice it, it's still baloney.
Election campaign speech, October 1936.

SMITH, Sir Cyril
1928–   British Liberal politician

If the fence is strong enough, I'll sit on it.
The Observer, 15 September 1974.

SMITH, F.E.
1872–1930   British lawyer and politician

[Winston Churchill] has devoted the best years of his life to preparing his impromptu speeches.
Attrib.

SMITH, Ian
1919–   Rhodesian Prime Minister

We have the happiest Africans in the world.
The Observer, 28 Nov 1971.

Let me say again, I don't believe in black majority rule ever in Rhodesia. Not in a thousand years.
Radio broadcast, 20 March 1976.

SMITH, Sydney
1771–1845   British essayist

[Macaulay] has occasional flashes of silence that make his conversation perfectly delightful.
Lady Holland, Memoirs.

The moment that the very name of Ireland is mentioned, the English seem to bid adieu to common feeling, common prudence, and common sense, and to act with the barbarity of tyrants and the fatuity of idiots.
Peter Plymley Letters

SMUTS, Jan Christian
1870–1950   Prime Minister of South Africa

Perhaps it is God's will to lead the people of South Africa through defeat and humiliation to a better future and a brighter day.
Speech at the Vereeniging peace talks, 31 May 1902.

Europe is being liquidated, and the League of Nations must be the heir to that great estate. The peoples left behind by the decomposition of Russia, Austria and Turkey are mostly untrained politically. Many of them are either incapable of self-government. They are most destitute, and will require much nursing towards economic and political independence.
The League of Nations: A Practical Solution.

What was everybody's business in the end proved to be nobody's business. Each one looked to the other to take the lead, and the aggressors got away with it.
Explaining the failure of the League of Nations to the Empire Parliamentary Association, London, 25 November 1943.

SNOW, Lord C.P.
1905–80   British novelist and scientist

The official world, the corridors of power, the dilemmas of conscience and egotism — she disliked them all.
*Homecomings, later used as the title of his 1964 novel, **Corridors of Power**.*

SNOWDEN, 1st Viscount (Philip)
1864–1937   British socialist politician

The Labour Party's election programme . . . is the most fantastic and impracticable programme ever put before the electors. This is not socialism. It is bolshevism run mad.
Radio broadcast, 17 October 1931.

SOLZHENITSYN, Alexander
1918–   Soviet novelist and dissident

You only have power over people so long as you do not take everything away from them. But when you have robbed a man of everything, he is no longer in your pocket — he is free.
The First Circle

In our country the lie has become not just a moral category but a pillar of the State.
*Quoted in **The Observer**, 29 December 1974.*

For us in Russia, communism is a dead dog, while, for many people in the West, it is still a living lion.
The Listener, 15 February 1979.

SOMOZA, Anastasio
1925–80   Nicaraguan dictator

You won the elections. But I won the count.
The Guardian, 17 June 1977.

SOULE, John Babsone Lane
1815–91   American writer

Go West, young man, go West!
Terre Haute Express

SPARK, Muriel
1918–   British novelist

Every communist has a fascist frown, every fascist a communist smile.
The Girls of Slender Means

SPENCER, Herbert
1820–1903   British sociologist

No one can be perfectly free until all are free; no one can be perfectly moral till all are moral; no one can be perfectly happy till all are happy.
Social Statics

The liberty that the citizen enjoys is to be measured not by the governmental machinery that he lives under, whether representative or otherwise, but by the paucity of restraints that it imposes upon him.
The Man Versus the State

The republican form of government is the highest form of government; but because of this, it requires the highest type of human nature — a type nowhere at present existing.
The Americas

SPRING-RICE, Sir Cecil
1858–1918   British diplomat and poet

I vow to thee, my country — all early things above —
Entire and whole and perfect, the service of my love.
I Vow To Thee, My Country

STALIN, Joseph

1879–1953   Soviet leader

In the name of the Constitution, Cromwell took up arms, executed the king, dissolved Parliament, imprisoned some, and beheaded others.
In conversation with H.G. Wells, Moscow, 1934.

To attempt to export revolution is nonsense.
Said to Roy Howard, American newspaper proprietor, 1 March 1936.

Communism fits Germany as a saddle fits a cow.
In conversation with the Polish politician, Stanislaw Mikolajcik, August 1944.

He who is not with us is against us.
Attrib.

STEEL, Sir David

1938–   British politician

[Margaret Thatcher] has turned the British bulldog into a Reagan poodle.
Time, 28 April 1986.

STEFFENS, Lincoln

1866–1936   American journalist

I have seen the future and it works.
*On his visit to the Soviet Union in 1919, **Autobiography**.*

STEVENSON, Adlai

1900–65   American statesman

Eggheads of the world unite; you have nothing to lose but your yolks.
Presidential election campaign speech, 1952.

A lie is an abomination unto the Lord, and a very present help when in trouble.
Speech, Washington, January 1951.

It is often easier to fight for principles than to live up to them.
Speech, New York, 27 August 1952.

My definition of a free society is a society in which it is safe to be unpopular.
Speech, Detroit, October 1952.

Man has wrested from nature the power to make the world a desert or to make the deserts bloom. There is no evil in the atom — only in men's souls.
Speech, Connecticut, 18 September 1952.

When political ammunition runs low, inevitably the rusty artillery of abuse is wheeled into action.
Speech, New York, 22 September 1952.

You will find that the truth is often unpopular and the contest between agreeable fancy and disagreeable fact is unequal. For, in the vernacular, we Americans are suckers for good news.
Speech, Michigan, 8 June 1958.

Freedom is not an ideal; it is not even a protection, if it means nothing more than the freedom to stagnate.
Putting First Things First

STEVENSON, Adlai *(contd.)*

We have confused the free with the free and easy.
Ib.

It will be helpful in our mutual objective to allow every man in America to look his neighbour in the face and see a man — not a colour.
New York Times, 22 June 1964.

An independent is a guy who wants to take the politics out of politics.
The Art of Politics

A politician is a statesman who approaches every question with an open mouth.
Attrib.

The Republican Party needs to be dragged kicking and screaming into the 20th century.
Quoted by Kenneth Tynan in **Curtains.**

In America, any boy may become President. I suppose that's just one of the risks that he takes.
Attrib.

STEVENSON, Robert Louis
1850–94   British writer

To travel hopefully is a better thing than to arrive, and the true success is to labour.
An Apology for Idlers

Politics is perhaps the only profession for which no preparation is thought to be necessary.
Familiar Studies of Men and Books

STOPPARD, Tom
1937–   British dramatist

The House of Lords [is] an illusion to which I have never been able to subscribe — responsibility without power; the prerogative of the eunuch throughout the ages.
Lord Malquist and Mr Moon.
See also BALDWIN.

It's not the voting that's democracy; it's the counting.
Jumpers

War is capitalism with the gloves off.
Travesties

STRAFFORD, 1st Earl of (Thomas Wentworth)
1593–1641   Chief Minister to Charles I

Divide not between Protestant and Papist. Divide not nationally, betwixt English and Irish. The King makes no distinction betwixt you.
To the Irish Parliament, 15 July 1634.

I would desire that every man would lay his hand on his heart, and consider seriously whether the beginnings of the people's happiness should be written in letters of blood.
At his execution, 12 May 1641.

SUN, Yixian (Yat Sen)
1867–1925   Chinese revolutionary

The foundation of the government of a nation must be built upon the rights of the people, but the administration must be entrusted to experts. We must not look upon those experts as stately and grand presidents and ministers, but simply as our chauffeurs, guards at the gate, cooks, physicians, carpenters, or tailors.
The Three Principles of the People

SWIFT, Jonathan
1667–1745   Irish-born writer

Promises and pie-crust are made to be broken.
Polite Conversation

SZENT-GYORGYI, Albert
1893–1986   Hungarian-born US biochemist

Discovery consists of seeing what everybody has seen and thinking what nobody has thought.
The Scientist Speculates

TAAFE, Count Eduard von
1833–95   Austrian Prime Minister

As a Minister, it is my policy to keep all the nationalities within the Habsburg monarchy in a balanced state of well-modulated dissatisfaction.
Letters, 1881

TACITUS, Cornelius
55–120   Roman historian

Solitudinem faciunt pacem appellant.
They make a wilderness and call it peace.
Agricola

TALLEYRAND, Charles Maurice de
1754–1838   French statesman

The allies are too frightened to fight each other, too stupid to agree.
Congress of Vienna, November 1814.

TAWNEY, R.H.
1880–1962   English economic historian

The instinct of mankind warns it against accepting at their face value spiritual demands that cannot justify themselves by practical achievements. The road along which the organised workers, like any other class, must climb to power starts from the provision of a more effective economic service than their masters, as their grip upon industry becomes increasingly vacillating and uncertain, are able to supply.
The Acquisitive Society

As long as men are men, a poor society cannot be too poor to find a right order of life; nor a rich society too rich to have need to seek it.
Ib.

TAYLOR, Professor A.J.
1906–90   British historian

History gets thicker as it approaches recent times.
English History 1914–1945

Human blunders usually do more to shape history than human wickedness.
The Origins of the Second World War

Like most of those who study history, Napoleon learned from the mistakes of the past how to make new ones.
BBC radio broadcast, 6 June 1963.

TAYLOR, Professor Laurie
1927–   British sociologist

My students are more interested in dolphins than the proletariat.
On 40 years of British sociology as an academic subject, and its historical image as a breeding ground for Marxism.

TEBBIT, Norman
1931–   British Conservative politician

He didn't riot. He got on his bike and looked for work, and he kept looking till he found it.
Speaking of his father after criticism of high unemployment under the Conservative Government, party conference, 15 October 1981.

TENNYSON, Alfred (Lord)
1809–92   British poet

He makes no friend who never made a foe.
Idylls of the King

The old order changeth, yielding place to new,
And God fulfils himself in many ways.
Ib.

Our little systems have their day;
They have their day and cease to be.
Ib.

TERENCE
185–159 BC   Roman dramatist

Fortis fortuna adiuvat.
Fortune favours the brave.
Phormio

Quot homines tot sententiae.
There are as many opinions as there are people.
Ib.

TERESA, Mother
1910–   Yugoslavian missionary

To keep a lamp burning, we have to keep putting oil in it.
Time, *29 December 1975.*

TERTULLIAN

160–225 AD   Carthaginian writer

Certum est quia impossible est.
It is certain because it is impossible.
De Carne Christi

THATCHER, Margaret Hilda

1925–   British Prime Minister

No woman in my time will be Prime Minister or Chancellor of the Exchequer or Foreign Secretary — not the top jobs. Anyway, I would not want to be Prime Minister; you have to give yourself 100 per cent.
*On her appointment as a junior Education Minister, **The Sunday Telegraph**, 26 October 1969.*

I owe nothing to Women's Lib.
*Quoted in **The Observer**, 1 December 1974.*

In politics, if you want anything said, ask a man. If you want anything done, ask a woman.
People, *15 September 1975.*

Let our children grow tall, and some taller than others if they have it in them to do so.
Speech, October 1975.

I stand before you tonight in my green chiffon evening gown, my face softly made up, my fair hair gently waved . . . the Iron Lady of the Western world? Me? A Cold War warrior? Well, yes–if that is how they wish to interpret my defence of values and freedoms fundamental to our way of life.
*Speech, Dorking, 31 January 1976, alluding to the title bestowed upon her by the Soviet defence journal, **Red Star.***

We want a society in which we are free to make choices, to make mistakes, to be generous and compassionate. That is what we mean by a moral society — not a society in which the State is responsible for everything, and no one is responsible for the State.
Speech, Zurich University, 14 March 1977.

Let us make this country safe to work in. Let us make this a country safe to walk in. Let us make it a country safe to grow up in. Let us make it a country safe to grow old in.
General election party broadcast, 30 April 1979.

Unless we change our ways and our direction, our greatness as a nation will soon be a footnote in the history books, a distant memory of an offshore island, lost in the mist of time like Camelot, remembered kindly for its noble past.
General election campaign speech, Bolton, 2 May 1979.

Where there is discord, may we bring harmony. Where there is error, may we bring truth. Where there is doubt, may we bring faith. Where there is despair, may we bring hope.
Said on entering No. 10 Downing Street for the first time as Prime Minister, 4 May 1979; a misquotation of St Francis of Assisi.

THATCHER, Margaret Hilda *(contd.)*

Any woman who understands the problems of running a home will be nearer to understanding the problems of running a country.
*Interviewed by **The Observer**, 8 May 1979, four days after becoming Britain's first woman Prime Minister.*

Is he one of us?
Attributed comment on considering a candidate for office in her new Government.

There is no easy popularity, in that I believe that people accept that there is no alternative.
On her Government's stringent economic policies, Conservative Women's Conference, 21 May 1980.

To those who wait with bated breath for that favourite media catchphrase, the u-turn, I have only this to say. You turn if you want to. The lady's not for turning.
Conservative Party Conference, 1980.

Pennies do not come from heaven. They have to be earned here on earth.
*Quoted in **The Sunday Telegraph**, 1980.*

This is the day that I was meant not to see.
Said on attending church the Sunday after she had narrowly escaped being killed in the IRA bomb explosion at the Grand Hotel, Brighton, October 1984.

I like Mr Gorbachev. We can do business together.
Said on her first meeting with him, before he became premier, 17 December 1984.

Democracies must try to find ways to starve the terrorist and the hijackers of the oxygen of publicity on which they depend.
Speech to the American Bar Association meeting in London, 15 July 1985, referring in particular to increasing British press coverage of IRA terrorist activities.

I have made it clear that a unified Ireland was one solution that is out. A second solution was a confederation of the two states. That is out. A third solution was joint authority. That is out — that would be derogation of sovereignty.
New York Times, 20 November 1985.

I always cheer up immensely if an attack is particularly wounding because . . . it means that they have not a single political argument left.
The Daily Telegraph, 21 March 1986.

I don't mind how much my Ministers talk — as long as they do what I say.
The Times, 1987.

If one leads a country such as Britain — a strong country that has taken a lead in world affairs in good times and in bad, that is always reliable, then you must have a touch of iron about you.
Ib.

If you want to cut your own throat, don't come to me for a bandage.
*Said to Robert Mugabe, Prime Minister of Zimbabwe, when he pressed for sanctions against South Africa, quoted in **Time**, 7 July 1986.*

THATCHER, Margaret Hilda *(contd.)*

To wear your heart on your sleeve isn't a very good plan. You should wear it inside, where it functions best.
Interview, ABC TV, 18 March 1987.

After three general election victories, leading the only party with clear policies, resolutely carried out, I intend to continue.
On Michael Heseltine's challenge for the leadership of the Conservative Party, The Sunday Times, 18 November 1990.

It's not time to write memoirs yet. I shall be in No. 10 at the end of this week — and a little bit longer than that.
On the eve of the voting by Conservative MPs for the leadership, 19 November 1990.

I shall fight. I will fight on.
To reporters, on learning that she had not won the necessary majority to secure her re-election as party leader, 21 November 1990; two days before announcing her decision to step down.

If you are guided by opinion polls, you are not practising leadership — you are practising followship.
American TV interview, 5 March 1991.

THIERS, Adolphe
1797–1877   First President of the Third French Republic

The Republic will be conservative, or it will be nothing.
Presidential address to the French National Assembly, November 1872.

THOMAS, J. Parnell
1895–1970   American politician

Are you now, or have you ever been, a member of the Communist Party?
Stock question to those called before the House of Representatives Committee on Un-American Activities, 1947–57.

THOMSON, E.P.
1924–   British historian

This going into Europe will not turn out to be the thrilling mutual exchange supposed. It is more like nine middle-aged couples with failing marriages meeting in a darkened bedroom in a Brussels hotel for a group grope.
On Britain's entry into the EEC, The Sunday Times, 27 April 1975.

THOMSON, James
1700–48   British poet

Rule, Britannia, rule the waves:
Britons never will be slaves.
Alfred: a Masque

THORNEYCROFT, Lord (George Edward) Peter
1909–   British statesman

The choice in politics isn't usually between black and white. It is between two horrible shades of grey.
The Sunday Telegraph, 11 February 1979.

THORNEYCROFT, Lord Peter *(contd.)*

Some men go through life absolutely miserable because, despite the most enormous achievements, they just didn't do one thing — like the architect who didn't build St Paul's. I didn't quite build St. Paul's, but I stood on more mountain tops than possibly I deserved.
Ib.

THORPE, Jeremy
1929–   British politician

Greater love hath no man that this, that he lay down his friends for his life.
On Harold Macmillan's sacking of several Cabinet members, House of Commons, 1962.

Looking around the House, one realises that we are all minorities now.
On the absence of a clear party majority, House of Commons, 6 March 1974.
See also *SHAWCROSS*.

TODD, Ron
1927–   British trade union leader

You don't have power if you surrender all your principles — you have office.
Speech, London, June 1988.

TOYNBEE, Arnold
1852–83   English economic historian

The Industrial Revolution.
Title of Oxford lectures, 1880-81, published posthumously in 1884.

TOYNBEE, Arnold Joseph
1889–1975   British historian

No annihilation without representation.
Advocating greater British representation at the United Nations, 1947.

America is a large, friendly dog in a very small room. Every time it wags its tail, it knocks over a chair.
Letter, 26 October 1949.

Civilisation is a movement and not a condition; a voyage and not a harbour.
Reader's Digest, *October 1958.*

TREDINNICK, David
1950–   British politician

History will relate that while President Bush fiddled, Kurdistan burned.
On US Government policy over the Iraqi persecution of the Kurds, House of Commons, 15 April 1991.

TREVELYAN, George Macaulay
1876–1962   British historian

Disinterested intellectual curiosity is the life-blood of real civilisation.
English Social History

TROLLOPE, Anthony
1815–82   British novelist

Nobody holds a good opinion of a man who has a low opinion of himself.
Orley Farm

TROTSKY, Leon
1879–1940   Russian revolutionary

In a country that is economically backward, the proletariat can take power earlier than in countries where capitalism is advanced.
Permanent Revolution

Marxism is, above all, a method of analysis.
Ib.

The end may justify the means, as long as there is something that justifies the end.
An Introduction to his Thought

TRUDEAU, Pierre Elliott
1919–   Canadian Prime Minister

The state has no business in the bedrooms of the nation.
On divorce law reform, New York Times, 16 June 1968.

Living next to [the US] is like sleeping with an elephant. No matter how friendly and even-tempered is the beast, one is affected by every twitch and grunt.
Ib.

NATO heads of state and of Governments meet only to go through the tedious motions of reading speeches drafted by others, with the principal objective of not rocking the boat.
On receiving the Albert Einstein International Peace Prize, 14 November 1984.

TRUMAN, Harry S.
1884–1972   33rd US President

When I first came to Washington, for the first six months I wondered how the hell I ever got here. For the next six months, I wondered how the hell the rest of them ever got here.
Speech, April 1940.

Every segment of our population, and every individual, has a right to expect from his Government a Fair Deal.
Speech to Congress, 6 September 1945.

I like old Joe Stalin. He's a good fellow, but he's a prisoner of the Politburo. He would make certain agreements but they won't let him keep to them.
News Review, 24 June 1948.

If you can't stand the heat, get out of the kitchen.
Time, 28 April 1952.

In 1945 we did much more than draft an international agreement among 50 nations. We set down on paper the only principles that will enable civilised human life to continue to survive on this globe.
On the 10th anniversary of the United Nations, 24 June 1955.

I never give them hell. I just tell the truth and they think it is hell.
Interview, Look, 3 April 1956.

A politician is a man who understands government, and it takes a politician to run a Government. A statesman is a politician who has been dead 10 or 15 years.
New York World Telegram, 12 April 1958.

TRUMAN, Harry S. *(contd.)*

It's a recession when your neighbour loses his job; it's a depression when you lose yours.
The Observer, 13 April 1958.
See also REAGAN.

[Nixon] is one of the few in the history of this country to run for high office talking out of both sides of his mouth at the same time, and lying out of both sides.
An Oral History of Harry S. Truman

[Eisenhower] wasn't used to be criticised, and he never did get it through his head that is what politics is all about. He was used to getting his ass kissed.
Ib.

The buck stops here.
Motto displayed on his desk in the Oval Office.

TUCHMAN, Barbara
1912–   American historian

No more distressing moment can ever face a British Government than that which requires it to come to a hard and fast and specific decision.
August 1914

TUTU, Bishop Desmond
1931–   Bishop of Johannesburg

Be nice to whites. They need you to rediscover their humanity.
New York Times, 19 October 1984.

I am not interested in picking up crumbs of compassion thrown from the table of someone who considers himself to be my master. I want the full menu of rights.
NBC News, 9 January 1985.

We don't want apartheid liberalized. We want it dismantled. You can't improve something that is intrinsically evil.
Speech, March 1985.

TWAIN, Mark
1835–1910   American writer

Always do right. This will gratify some people, and astonish the rest.
Speech, Brooklyn, 16 February 1901.

Man is the only animal that blushes. Or needs to.
Following the Equator

UNITED NATIONS CHARTER
26 June 1945   Drafted by John Foster Dulles, Field Marshal Jan Smuts, and others.

We the Peoples of the United Nations, determined to save succeeding generations from the scourge of war, which twice in our lifetime has brought untold sorrow to mankind, and to reaffirm faith in fundamental human rights, in the dignity and worth of the human person, in the equal rights of men and women and of nations large and small, and to establish conditions under which justice and respect for the obligations arising from treaties and other sources of international law can be maintained, and to promote social progress and better standards of life in larger freedom, and for

UNITED NATIONS CHARTER *(contd.)*

these ends, to practice tolerance and live together in peace with one another as good neighbours, and to unite our strength to maintain international peace and security, and to ensure by the acceptance of principles and the institution of methods, that armed force shall not be used, save in the common interest, and to employ international machinery for the promotion of the economic and social advancement of all peoples, have resolved to combine our efforts to accomplish these aims.

UNESCO CONSTITUTION

1946

Since wars begin in the minds of men, it is in the minds of men that the defences of peace must be constructed.

Preamble

USTINOV, Peter

1921–   British playwright and raconteur

A diplomat these days is nothing but a head waiter who's allowed to sit down occasionally.

Romanoff and Juliet

VACHELL, Horace Annesley

1861–1955   British writer

In nature there are no rewards or punishments; there are only consequences.

The Face of Clay

VERGNIAUD, Pierre

1753–93   French revolutionary

There is reason to fear that the Revolution may, like Saturn, devour each of her children one by one.

Said at his trial, November 1793.

VICTORIA, Queen

1819–1901   Queen of Great Britain

This mad, wicked folly of 'Women's Rights' with all its attendant horrors, on which her poor sex is bent, forgetting every sense of womanly feeling and propriety. Lady Amberley ought to get a good whipping.

Letter to Sir Theodore Martin, 29 March, 1870, concerning the feminist views of Lady Amberley, mother of Bertrand Russell.

Oh, if the Queen were a man, she would like to go and give those Russians, whose word one cannot believe, such a beating! We shall never be friends again till we have it out.

Letter to Lord Beaconsfield, 10 January 1878.

Please understand that there is no one depressed in this house. We are not interested in the possibilities of defeat; they do not exist.

To A.J. Balfour, on British casualties in the Boer War, December 1899.

[Gladstone] speaks to Me as if I were a public meeting.

Attributed by G.W.E. Russell in **Collections and Recollections**.

VIRGIL
70-19 BC   Roman poet

timeo Danaos et dona ferentis.
I fear the Greeks even when they bring gifts.
Aeneid

Bella, horrida, bella,
Et Thybrim multo spumantem, sanguine cerno.
I see wars, horrible wars, and the Tiber foaming with much blood.
Ib.
See also POWELL.

Latet anguis in herba.
There is a snake hidden in the grass.
Eclogue

VOLTAIRE
1694–1778   French writer

In this country [England] it is good to kill an admiral from time to time, to encourage the others.
Candide, *referring to Admiral Byng's execution on 14 March 1757.*

All is for the best in the best of possible worlds.
Ib.

If God did not exist, it would be necessary to invent him.
A l'Auteur du Livre des Trois Imposteurs

They say that God is always on the side of the big battalions.
Letter to Le Riche, 6 February 1770.

God is on the side not of the big battalions, but of the best shots.
Notebooks

I disapprove of what you say, but I will defend to the death your right to say it.
Attrib.

VORSTER, John (Balthazar Johannes)
1915–83   Prime Minister of South Africa

As far as criticism is concerned, we don't resent that unless it is absolutely biased — as it is in most cases.
The Observer, *9 November 1969.*

WAITE, Terry
1939–   Envoy to the Archbishop of Canterbury

Politics come from man. Mercy, compassion, and justice come from God.
The Observer, *13 January 1985.*

Freeing hostages is like putting up a stage set — which you do with the captors, agreeing on each piece as you slowly put it together. Then you leave an exit through which both the captor and the captive can walk with sincerity and dignity.
Interviewed on ABC News, 3 November 1986.

WALESA, Lech
1943– President of Poland

He who once became aware of the power of Solidarity and who breathed the air of freedom will not be crushed.

Nobel Peace Prize lecture, read on his behalf, 11 December 1983.

The English are all right. They're quiet, they're slow, they count things carefully, they hesitate — and I'm switching to their track.

The Times, 17 April 1991, on the eve of his state visit to London.

The Soviet Union remains a superpower in the military and nuclear sense — only its economy is in difficulty. People want me to lead the troops out or to chuck them over the border, but I have neither the strength nor the will to do it.

Ib.

WALLACE, George
1919– American politician

Segregation now, segregation tomorrow, and segregation for ever.

Inaugural speech as Governor of Alabama, 19 January 1963.

WALLACE, Henry
1888–1965   US Vice-President

The century on which we are entering, the century that will come out of this war, can be and must be the century of the common man.

Speech, New York, 8 May 1942.

WALLACE, William Ross
1819–81   American poet

The hand that rocks the cradle
Is the hand that rules the world.

John o'London's Treasure Trove

WALPOLE, Horace (Earl of Orford)
1717–97   English political commentator

All the sensible Tories that I ever knew were either Jacobites or became Whigs; those that remained Tories remained fools.

Memoirs of the Reign of George III

The world is a comedy to those that think, a tragedy to those that feel.

Letter to the Countess of Upper Ossory, 16 August 1776.

WALPOLE, Sir Robert (Earl of Orford)
1676–1745   English statesman

They may ring their bells now; before long, they will be wringing their hands.

Remark on hearing church bells celebrating the declaration of war against Spain, 19 October 1739.

I have lived long enough in the world to know that the safety of a Minister lies in his having the approbation of this House. Former Ministers neglected that and therefore they fell; I have always made it my first study to obtain it, and therefore I hope to stand.

House of Commons, 21 November, 1739.

WALPOLE, Sir Robert *(contd.)*

Patriots spring up like mushrooms. I could raise 50 of them within the four and twenty hours. I have raised many of them in one night. It is but refusing to gratify an immeasurable or insolent demand, and up starts a patriot.
House of Commons, 13 February 1741.

All those men have their price.
Memoirs of Sir Robert Walpole

WASHINGTON, George
1732–99   First President of the United States

Father, I cannot tell a lie. I did it with my little hatchet.
On admitting in childhood to vandalizing a cherry tree, attributed by his biographer, Mason Weems, in 1880.

I can answer for but three things: a firm belief in the justice of our cause, close attention in the prosecution of it, and the strictest integrity.
On being elected Commander of the Unionist Army commander, 19 June 1775.

It is our true policy to steer clear of permanent alliance with any portion of the foreign world.
Farewell address to the nation, 17 September 1796.

WATERHOUSE, Keith
1929–   British writer

I cannot bring myself to vote for a woman who has been voice-trained to speak to me as though my dog has just died.
Attributed comment on Margaret Thatcher, 1978.

WEATHERILL, Sir (Bruce) Bernard
1920–   Speaker of the House of Commons

Mine is one of the jobs that, if you want it, you will never get it — and if you're seen to want it, you will certainly never get it.
The House Magazine, January 1991.

WEBB, Sidney
1859–1947   English socialist

No philosopher now looks for anything but the gradual evolution of the new order from the old . . . History shows us no example of the sudden substitutions of Utopian and revolutionary romance.
Fabian Essays

How anyone can fear that the British electorate, whatever mistakes it can make or may condone, can ever go too far or too fast is incomprehensible . . . The Labour Party, when in due course it comes to be entrusted with power, will naturally not want to do everything at once. Once we face the necessity of putting our principles into execution from one end of the kingdom to the other, the inevitability of gradualness cannot fail to be appreciated.
Labour Party Conference, 26 June 1923.

WEBSTER, Daniel
1782–1852   American statesman

[Alexander Hamilton] smote the rock of the national resources, and abundant streams of revenue gushed forth. He touched the dead corpse of the public credit, and it sprang upon its feet.
Speech, New York, 10 March 1831.

There is always room at the top.
Attributed remark on being advised against joining the overcrowded
legal profession.

WEIGHELL, Sidney
1922–   British trade union leader

If you . . . believe in the philosophy of the pig trough — that those with the biggest snouts should get the largest share — I reject it.
Labour Party Conference, 6 October 1978.

I don't see how we can talk with Mrs Thatcher . . . I will say to the lads, "Come on, get your snouts in the trough."
Speech, London, 10 April 1979.

WEILL, Simone
1909–43   French philosopher

The word 'revolution' is a word for which you kill, for which you die, for which you send the labouring masses to their deaths; but which does not possess any content.
Oppression and Liberty.

The future is made of the same stuff as the present.
On Science, Necessity, and the Love of God.

WEIZSÄCKER, Richard Freiherr
1920–   German President

There were many ways of not burdening one's conscience, of shunning responsibility, looking away, keeping silent. When the unspeakable truth of the Holocaust became known at the end of the war, all too many of us claimed that they had not known anything about it, or even suspected anything . . . Whoever refuses to remember the inhumanity is prone to new risks of infection . . . Seeking to forget makes exile all the longer; the secret of redemption lies in remembrance.
*On the 40th anniversary of the end of World War II, **New York Times**,*
12 May 1985.

WELLINGTON, Duke of (Arthur Wellesley)
1769–1852   British general and statesman

There is nothing worse than a battle won except a battle lost.
To Philip von Neumann, 11 January 1821.

Beginning reform is beginning revolution.
Attributed remark, 7 November 1830.

There is no such thing as a little war for a great nation.
House of Lords, 16 January 1838.

Don't quote Latin; say what you have to say, and then sit down.
Advice to a new Member of Parliament.

There is no mistake; there has been no mistake, and there shall be no mistake.
Wellingtoniana

WELLS, H.G.
1866–1946   British novelist

In the country of the blind the one-eyed man is king.
The Country of the Blind

WENTWORTH, Peter
1530–96   English parliamentarian

In this House, which is termed a place of free speech, there is nothing so necessary for the preservation of the Prince and State as free speech; and without it, it is a scorn and a mockery to call it a Parliament House, for in truth it is none but a very school of flattery and dissimulation, and so fit a place to serve the devil and his angels in, and not to glorify God and benefit the Commonwealth.
House of Commons, 8 February 1576.

WEST, Rebecca
1892–1983   British novelist

Margaret Thatcher's great strength seems to be that the better people know her, the better they like her. But she has one great disadvantage — she is a daughter of the people and looks trim, as the daughters of the people desire to be. Shirley Williams has such an advantage over her because she is a member of the upper-middle class and can achieve that kitchen-sink revolutionary look that one cannot get unless one has been to a really good school.
*Interviewed in **The Sunday Times**, 25 July 1976.*

WHATELY, Richard
1787–1863   English churchman

Preach not because you have to say something, but because you have something to say.
Apophthegms

Happiness is no laughing matter.
Ib.

WHISTLER, James McNeill
1834–1903   American artist

I am not arguing with you — I am telling you.
The Gentle Art of Making Enemies

WHITBREAD, Samuel
1758–1815   Radical Whig

In a political point of view, nothing can possibly afford greater stability to a popular Government than the education of the people.
House of Commons, 19 February 1807.

The nation suspects that the regular ministerial majorities in Parliament are bought, and that the Crown has made a purchase of the House with the money of the people. Hence the ready, tame and servile compliance to every royal verdict issued by Lord North . . . It is almost universally believed that this debt has been contracted in corrupting the representatives of the people.
House of Commons, 16 April 1777.

WHITE, Theodore H.
1926– American political commentator

The best time to listen to a politician is when he is on a street corner, in the rain, late at night, when he's exhausted. Then he doesn't lie.

New York Times, 5 January 1969.

WHITEHEAD, A.N.
1861–1947 British philosopher

What is morality in any given time or place? It is what the majority then and there happen to like, and immorality is what they dislike.

Dialogues

WHITELAW, Viscount (William)
1918– British politician

I do not intend to prejudge the past.

Said on arriving in Ulster for the first time as Secretary of State for Northern Ireland, 2 December 1973.

[Harold Wilson] is going around the country stirring up apathy.

Said during 1974 general election campaign.

A short, sharp shock.

Said as Home Secretary, on the need for more effective treatment of young offenders, Conservative Party Conference, 10 October 1979.

WHITLAM, Gough
1916– Australian Prime Minister

I do not mind the Liberals, still less do I mind the Country Party, calling me a bastard. In some circumstances, I am only doing my job if they do. But I hope that you will not publicly call me a bastard, as some bastards in the Caucus have.

Speech to the Australian Labour Party, 9 June 1974.

We may say 'God Save the Queen', because nothing will save the Governor-General ... Maintain your rage and your enthusiasm for the election now to be held and until polling day.

On the Governor-General's action in dissolving the Australian Parliament, 11 November 1975.

WILDE, Oscar
1854–1900 Irish-born British dramatist and poet

Yet each man kills the thing he loves,
By each let this be heard,
Some do it with a bitter look
Some with a flattering word.
The coward does it with a kiss,
The brave man with a sword.

The Ballad of Reading Gaol

We are all in the gutter, but some of us are looking at the stars.

Lady Windermere's Fan

[A cynic is one] who knows the price of everything and the value of nothing.

Ib.

WILDE, Oscar *(contd.)*

A little sincerity is a dangerous thing, and a great deal of it is absolutely fatal.
The Critic as an Artist

There is no sin except stupidity.
Ib.

WILHELM II, Kaiser
1859–1941   German Emperor

We fought for our place in the sun and won it. Our future is on the water.
Speech, Elbe regatta, June 1901.

We draw the sword with a clean conscience and with clean hands.
Address from the throne, Berlin, 4 August 1914.

The machine is running away with him as it ran away with me.
Said of Adolf Hitler to Sir Robert Bruce-Lockhart, 27 August 1939.

WILLIAM III
1650–1702   King of Great Britain and Ireland

People in Parliament occupy themselves with private animosities and party quarrels, and think little of the national interest. It is impossible to credit the serene indifference with which they consider events outside their own country.
Letter, January 1699.

The eyes of all Europe are upon this Parliament. If you do in good earnest wish to see England hold the balance of Europe and to be indeed at the head of the Protestant interest, it will appear by your right improving the present opportunity.
State Opening, 31 December 1701.

WILLIAMS, Shirley
1930–   British politician

The British Civil Service . . . is a beautifully-designed and effective braking mechanism.
Speech, Royal Institute of Public Administration, 11 February 1980.

WILSON of RIEVAULX, Lord (Harold Wilson)
1916–   British Prime Minister

The school that I went to in the north was a school where more than half the children in my class never had any boots or shoes to their feet. They wore clogs, because they lasted longer than shoes of comparable price.
Speech, Birmingham, 28 July 1948.
See also BULMER-THOMAS.

All the little gnomes in Zurich and other finance centres.
Speech, House of Commons, 12 November 1956.

Every time that Mr Macmillan comes back from abroad, Mr Butler goes to the airport and grips him warmly by the throat.
Attributed comment, 1957.

We are redefining and restating our socialism in terms of the scientific revolution . . . the Britain that will be forged in the white heat of this revolution will be no place for restrictive practices or outdated methods on either side of industry.
Labour Party Conference, 1 October 1963.

WILSON of RIEVAULX, Lord *(contd.)*

The selection has been through the machinery of an autocratic cabal. I am worried to know how a scion of an effete establishment can understand the scientific revolution. After half a century of democratic advance, the whole process has ground to a halt with the 14th Earl.
Said of Lord Alec Douglas-Home's selection as Harold Macmillan's successor as Prime Minister, Manchester, 19 October 1963.

The Labour Party is a moral crusade, or it is nothing.
Scottish Labour Party Conference, 5 September 1964.

We are going to need something like that which President Kennedy had after years of stagnation — a programme of a hundred days of dynamic action.
General election campaign speech, 1964.

Smethwick Conservatives can have the satisfaction of having topped the poll, of having sent a Member who, until another election returns him to oblivion, will serve his time here as a parliamentary leper.
On the success of a Conservative MP who fought his campaign largely by exploiting racial issues, House of Commons, 4 November 1964

A week is a long time in politics.
Said to Lobby correspondents, October 1964.

The cumulative effect of the economic and financial sanctions against Rhodesia might well bring the rebellion to an end within a matter of weeks rather than months.
Commonwealth Prime Ministers' Conference, Lagos, 12 January 1966.

Given a fair wind, we will negotiate our way into the Common Market, head held high, not crawl in . . . Negotiations? Yes. Unconditional acceptance of whatever terms we are offered? No.
Speech, Bristol, 20 March 1966.

In a recent interview, I was asked what, above all, I associated with socialism in this modern age. I answered that if there was one word I would use to identify modern socialism, it was 'Science'.
Speech, 17 June 1967.

From now on the pound abroad is worth 14 per cent or so less in terms of other currencies. That does not mean, of course, that the pound here in Britain — in your pocket or purse, or in your handbag — has been devalued.
National broadcast, 19 November 1967.

We are creating a Britain of which we can be proud, and the world knows it. The world's tourists are coming here in their millions...because the new Britain is exciting. Yes, Britain with a Labour Government is an exciting place.
Labour Party Conference, 30 September 1969.

One man's wage rise is another man's price increase.
The Observer, 11 January 1970.

The greatest asset that a head of state can have is the ability to get a good night's sleep.
BBC Radio 4, 16 April 1975.

WILSON of RIEVAULX, Lord *(contd.)*

The party must protect itself against the activities of small groups of inflexible political persuasion — the extreme so-called left and, in a few cases, the extreme so-called moderates — having in common only their arrogant dogmatism. Those groups are now what this party is all about. Infestation of that kind thrives only in minuscule local parties . . . I have no wish to lead a party of political zombies.
Labour Party Conference, 30 September 1975.

A constant effort to keep a party together, without sacrificing either principle or the essentials of basic strategy, is the very stuff of political leadership. Macmillan was canonised for it.
The Labour Government 1974–76

The main essentials of a successful Prime Minister are sleep and a sense of history.
The Governance of Britain

WILSON, (Thomas) Woodrow
1856–1924   28th US President

The feelings with which we face this new age of right and opportunity sweep across our heartstrings like some air out of God's own presence, where justice and mercy are reconciled, and the judge and the brother are one.
Inaugural address, 4 March 1913.

Human rights, national integrity, and opportunity as against material interests . . . are the issues that we now must face. I take this occasion to say that the United States will never again seek one additional foot of territory by conquest.
Speech, Alabama, 27 October 1913.

The people of the United States are drawn from many nations, and chiefly from the nations now at war. Some will wish one nation, others another, to succeed in this momentous struggle. I venture to speak a solemn word of warning. The United States must be neutral in fact as well as in name during these days that are to try men's souls. We must be impartial in thought as well as in action.
Message to the Senate, 19 August 1914.

American cannot be an ostrich, with its head in the sand.
Speech, New Mexico, 1 February 1916.

Nations should with one accord adopt the doctrine of President Monroe as the doctrine of the world; that every people should be left free to determine its own policy, its own way of development, unhindered, unthreatened, unafraid — the little along with the great and powerful. Those are American principles, American policies. We could stand for no others. They are also the principles of mankind, and must prevail.
Speech to the Senate, 22 January 1917.

The world must be safe for democracy. Its peace must be planted upon trusted foundations of political liberty.
Address to Congress, 2 April 1917.

It is not an army that we must train for war; it is a nation.
Speech, Washington, 12 May 1917.

In this war, we demand nothing that is peculiar to ourselves; only that the world be made fit and safe to live in. The programme of the world's peace, therefore, is our programme.
The Fourteen Points speech to Congress, 8 January 1918.

WILSON, Woodrow *(contd.)*

Peoples and provinces must not be bartered about from sovereign to sovereign as if they were chattels, or pawns in a game. Self-determination is not a mere phrase. It is an imperative principle, which statesmen will henceforth ignore at their peril.
Address to Congress, 11 February 1918.

People call me an idealist. That is how I know that I am an American. America is the only idealistic nation in the world.
Speech, Sioux Falls, 8 September 1919.

WITTE, Serge

1849–1915   First Prime Minister of Russia

The world is in flames today for a cause that interests Russia first and foremost; a cause that is essentially the cause of the Slavs, and which is of no concern to France or to England.
Said to the French Ambassador, 10 September 1914.

WITTGENSTEIN, Ludgwig

1889–1951   Austrian philosopher

Whereof one cannot speak, thereon one must remain silent.
Tractatus Logico-Philosophicus

WOLFE, Tom (Thomas Kennerley)

1931   American author

The idea was to prove at every foot of the way up...that you were one of the elected and anointed ones who had the right stuff and could move higher and higher and even — ultimately, God willing, one day — that you might be able to join that special few at the very top, that elite who had the capacity to bring tears to men's eyes, the very Brotherhood of the Right Stuff itself.
The Right Stuff

WOODS, Donald

1933–   South African editor and Black civil rights campaigner

When I left South Africa, I arrogantly predicted that within seven years, apartheid would be gone. It has taken a bit longer than that. There is naturally concern abroad about the continuing violence, but there is a perception that it comes from problems of recovery — whereas the violence of past years came from the problems of decline.
BBC TV, February 1991.

When I left South Africa, only a handful of Whites could contemplate majority rule. Today, most of them, however reluctantly, accept that it is coming. For Whites, this is the last stopping place in Africa. As one African country after another has achieved independence, those Whites wanting to stay in Africa, while avoiding Black rule, moved ever southward — from Kenya, Zambia, Mozambique, and Zimbabwe. But South Africa is where that trek stops. This is where they must decide finally whether they are indeed Africans, and to accept all that implies.
Ib.

WOTTON, Sir Henry

1568–1639   English poet

An ambassador is an honest man sent to lie abroad for the good of his country.
Izaak Walton, Life

WYCLIFFE, John

1318–84   English religious leader

Christ during His life upon earth was of all men the poorest, casting from Him all worldly authority. I deduce from these premises...that the Pope should surrender all temporal authority to the civil power and advise his clergy to do the same.

Dismissing an order to appear before the Papal Court, 1384.

YELTSIN, Boris

1931–   Russian reformer

The West has not lived through totalitarianism, with a single ideology for 70 years. We are escaping from the burden of the past, and only after we have done that will we be ready to integrate with Europe — and Europe needs Russia.

Addressing socialist MEPs in Strasbourg, 15 April 1991.

Perestroika has transformed and deformed society...but it is not the Soviet Union that is falling apart but the system — and Gorbachev started the process.

Ib.

ZANGWILL, Israel

1864–1926   British dramatist

America is God's Crucible, the great Melting Pot where all the races of Europe are melting and re-forming . . . God is making the American.

The Melting Pot

ZHIVKOV, Todor

1911–   Bulgarian statesman

If I had to do it over again, I would not even be a communist. And if Lenin were alive today, he would say the same thing.

The Sunday Times, *9 December 1990.*

ZHOU ENLAI

1898–1976   Chinese Prime Minister

For us, it is all right if the talks succeed; and it is all right if they fail.

On President Nixon's visit, 5 October 1971.

Glossary

abat-voix [*French*] a sounding board; a test of public opinion.

à bras ouverts [*French*] with open arms; widely welcomed.

ab uno disce omnes [*Latin*] judge them all alike; one person or policy is much like another.

abusus non tollit usum [*Latin*] the abuse of a right or treaty cannot invalidate its basic integrity.

Achilles' heel the weakest point of an argument or of a person's character.

acid rain an environmental hazard that can inflict lasting harm on the earth's **ecosystems**, caused by the release into the atmosphere of toxic gases generated by industrial processes.

Act of Parliament a new or amended law that is the product of the legislative process. In the British Parliament it typically consists of a formal First Reading of the Bill; a general debate on Second Reading of its principles and objectives; detailed consideration and amendment in Standing Committee; and further debate and possible amendment at Report stage and again on Third Reading. At this point, a Bill introduced in the Commons must be sent to the Lords to undergo the same substantive stages of scrutiny, and vice versa. The Bill is then returned to the originating House, with or without suggested amendments—though the Lords are not permitted to alter **Money Bills**. The Upper House can also delay the progress of Commons legislation that it dislikes, but cannot prevent it eventually becoming law. Once a Bill has been considered by both Houses and receives Royal Assent—the formal approval of the monarch—its provisions pass into law.

acte gratuit [*French*] an impulsive and pointless or motiveless act.

ADB (Asian Development Bank) formed in 1966 by the 32 member countries that comprise the ESCAP region and 15 others, with the aim of attracting private and public development funding.

ad captandum vulgus [*Latin*] an argument or policy appealing to popular prejudice.

ad crumenam [*Latin*] an argument or policy whose appeal is of a financial nature.

addled Parliament the second Parliament of **James I** (April-June 1614), so called because it was dissolved without passing any Acts.

ad hoc [*Latin*] improvisational; a committee or other body convened, sometimes hastily, for a special purpose.

ad hominem [*Latin*] an argument or policy appealing to personal prejudices.

ad interim [*Latin*] of a provisional or temporary nature.

ad rem [*Latin*] to the matter at hand; to use debating points of worth and relevance, rather than those whose only purpose is to humiliate one's opponent.

ad valorem [*Latin*] a tax or penalty bearing a relationship to the value or extent of the goods, service or misdemeanour involved.

Afrikaner Bond [*Afrikaans*] political league formed in 1880 to promote unity and independence among South Africans.

agrogorod [*Russian*] a Soviet agricultural new town.

air superiority as defined in the 1991 Gulf War: the freedom to use the skies unhindered by hostile aircraft because the enemy has chosen not to deploy them, or has withdrawn them from battle for a prolonged period.

air supremacy the state of being totally in control of the skies because the enemy's air force has been destroyed or permanently withdrawn from battle.

à la guerre comme à la guerre [*French*] one must take the rough with the smooth.

Aldermaston An Atomic Weapons Research Establishment in Berkshire that served as the rallying point for those who took part in the Ban-the-Bomb marches organized every Easter between 1958 and 1963 by the Committee of 100—the precursor of CND.

Al-Fatah Palestinian resistance group co-founded in 1966 by **Yasser Arafat**.

All the President's Men the account by *Washington Post* journalists Bob Woodward and Carl Bernstein of their role in uncovering the **Watergate** scandal. The title borrows from **Henry Kissinger**'s remark at the time of the 1970 Cambodian invasion, 'We are all the President's men, and we must act accordingly.'

Amazonia the 2.4 million sq km/1.5 million sq ml plain in Brazil through which the River Amazon flows to the sea. The effect on the world's ecosystems of the escalating destruction of its rain forests since the 1970s is a cause of increasing concern to environmentalists.

Amen Corner a part of the corridor in New York's Fifth Avenue Hotel where Republican Party managers congregated to discuss policies and tactics.

American Civil War the 1861–5 conflagration between the agricultural and slave-owning southern states and the abolitionist northern states, fuelled by disagreements over the way in which the nation should develop as it expanded in the west. The original breakaway confederacy of South Carolina, Georgia, Mississippi, Florida, Alabama, Louisiana and Texas was soon joined by Virginia, Tennessee and North

Carolina. Fighting between the Union and Confederate armies, having strengths of 2.5 million and 1 million respectively, began in April 1861, and the four years of fighting claimed more than 600000 lives—a high proportion of those killed being the victims of disease. The organizational supremacy of the Union army, combined with its superior weaponry as a product of its industrial developments brought the surrender of the south in April 1865.

American Congress the federal legislature of the United States of America, founded in 1789. It consists of the House of Representatives, which has 435 seats, and of the Senate, 100 seats. Elections to the lower chamber are held every even-numbered year, with each state returning to the House of Representatives an allotted number of members proportional to the size of its population. Senators are also chosen in elections in each even-numbered year, but only one third of them enter the upper chamber, over which the Vice-President presides, at any one time.

American Constitution the articles of governance drawn up in September 1787 and implemented in June 1788, and deemed to be the most significant constitution in modern history. Its most successful innovation was to partition those who made the laws in Congress from those who interpreted them (the judiciary in the Supreme Court) and from the Executive or President responsible for their administration, thus ensuring a balance of power and pre-empting the abuse of central authority.

American Pacific Islands also known as Micronesia; the former Japanese colonies in the Pacific held under US trustee-ship.

American presidential elections candidates for the most important and powerful political office in the world must be natural-born American citizens, at least 35 years old, and have resided in the US for a minimum of 14 years. The victor serves a four-year term not only as head of state but Commander-in-Chief of the Armed Forces and Chief Executive of the United States Government—a post equivalent to Prime Minister.

Amnesty International British-based pressure group that campaigns for the release of any person detained for their political or religious beliefs or who has been injustly imprisoned for any other reason.

amor patriae [*Latin*] affection for one's homeland; patriotism.

Anatolia the Asian and therefore the major part of Turkey, once known as Asia Minor.

ANC (African National Congress) The most important of the Black South African organizations opposed to the Pretoria regime. It began life in 1912 as the South African Native National Congress, and under the influence of Gandi organized passive resistance to White power. Banned by the South African goverment in 1961,

it began a campaign of industrial and economic sabotage through its military wing. This campaign was not particularly successful, and in the 1980s the ANC started attacking persons as well as property. Based in Zambia for several years, it is estimated to have a force of 6000 guerrillas. It was unbanned in February 1990.

ancien régime [*French*] pre-revolutionary France; the way things were.

Andean Group (Andean Pact) formed in 1969 to promote the harmonious economic and social development of Bolivia, Chile, Colombia, Ecuador, Peru and Venezuela. Chile withdrew in 1977. Its Parliament, which assembles occasionally in each country in turn, comprises five delegates from each member state.

Andersonstown a district of west Belfast, Northern Ireland, which is an IRA stronghold, but which was also the birthplace in 1976 of the People's Peace Movement.

Anglo-Polish Pact an alliance entered into between **Neville Chamberlain** and Poland in March 1939, following Germany's occupation of Prague in contravention of the **Munich Agreement**. Its observance following the invasion of Poland on 1 September 1939 took Britain into World War II.

angst [*German*] anxiety or anguish; an unjustifiable disquiet. Spirit soul 'mind'.

animus [*Latin*] breadth of vision; animosity or malice.

annus mirabilis [*Latin*] a remarkable year.

Anschluss [*German*] the joining of Austria with Germany, particularly under the Nazi regime; a forced union.

anti-Semitism active discrimination against, or the persecution of, Jews because of their origin or religious beliefs. Its most extreme manifestation was the Nazis' 'Final Solution', which resulted in 6 million Jews being executed or sent to their deaths in concentration camps.

antithesis [*Greek*] the complete opposite; one notion compared with another to demonstrate their dissimilarity.

ANZUS (Anzus Treaty) a commitment to co-ordinate collective defence in the Pacific area, signed in 1951, and ratified in 1962, by Australia, New Zealand, and the USA.

apartheid [*Afrikaans*] separation; an Afrikaans word to describe the reviled system of segregation of the South African Republic's white, black and coloured population, popularized by the Nationalist Party in the 1948 elections. The system was the cause of South Africa's social and economic isolation from the rest of the West throughout the 1960s and 1970s, but the country seemed set for rehabilitation following the dismantling in 1990 and 1991 of apartheid under **F. W. de Klerk**'s Government and his willingness to recognize formally outlawed black political parties such as the African National Congress.

aperçu [*French*] intuitive or inspired comprehension.

apologia [*Greek*] strictly, a written justification for holding a certain view or taking a particular action, though popular usage embraces the oral equivalent also.

apparatchik [*Russian*] a member of the Soviet bureaucracy, usually used disparagingly.

appeasement in modern history, any endeavour to avoid hostilities by concessionary negotiations. The term generally fell into disrepute in the wake of **Neville Chamberlain**'s efforts to pacify Nazi Germany at any price.

a priori [*Latin*] from cause to effect; deductive reasoning.

a quattr' occhi [*Italian*] literally, between four eyes; a face-to-face confrontation.

Arabia the modern states of Saudi Arabia, Yemen, Oman, Bahrain, Qatar, and the United Arab Emirates.

Arab-Israeli conflict a general term used to describe the continuing hostilities between neighbouring Arab states and Israel following the country's emergence as an independent state, which served to exacerbate the Palestinian problem, in 1948. The two most significant manifestations of it were the **Six Day War** (1967) and **Yom Kippur War** (1973).

Arab Monetary Fund a body aimed at achieving economic integration among the Arab states, formed in 1977 by Algeria, Bahrain, Egypt, Iraq, Jordan, Kuwait, Lebanon, Libya, Mauritania, Morocco, Oman, PLO, Qatar, Saudi Arabia, Somalia, Sudan, Syria, Tunisia, United Arab Emirates, Yemen Arab Republic, and Yemen People's Democratic Republic.

à rebours [*French*] contrarily; perversely against the grain.

argot [*French*] slang or jargon affected by the members of a particular class, social group, or occupation.

ariston metron [*Greek*] the middle course is to be preferred.

Armageddon in the Book of Revelations, the place where the last, decisive battle between good and evil will take place. In modern usage, it evokes a terrible threatened conflagration, such as that which might involve the use of nuclear weapons.

arrière-pensée [*French*] a hidden and perhaps unworthy ulterior motive.

artel [*Russian*] a Russian workers' co-operative.

ASEAN (Association of South-East Asian Nations) founded in 1967 by Brunei, Indonesia, Malaysia, Philipines, Singapore and Thailand, to promote their collective economic and political stability.

Asia Minor the western peninsula of Asia covering an area of 518000 sq km/199999 sq ml, and its principal land link with Europe.

assassins a fanatical Islamic sect founded at the end of the 11th century, whose murderous followers terrified the Crusaders and other religious rivals for more than 200 years, until defeated by the Tatar prince Hulagu, and in Syria by the Egyptian sultan Baybars. Their name derived from the practice of rewarding those returning from successful missions with gifts of hashish.

ataraxia [*Greek*] passiveness; a serenity achieved through indifference.

ataxia [*Greek*] disorder; a lack of social order.

Atlantic Charter a joint declaration of the requirements for a post-war settlement made in August 1941 by **Franklin D. Roosevelt** and **Winston Churchill**. It enshrined eight principles of personal and national liberty, including 'freedom from fear and want'.

atomic bomb, A-bomb the name given to the earliest form of nuclear weapon.

attaché [*French*] a member of an ambassador's staff.

au courant [*French*] well-informed of current affairs; up to date with the topics of the day.

audi alteram partem [*Latin*] heeding the other argument; hearing both sides of a case.

Aufklärung [*German*] age of reason; a period of moderation or of reconstruction.

aurea mediocritas [*Latin*] the golden mean; a happy compromise, often used in a disparaging sense.

Ausländer [*German*] a foreigner; an unsophisticated interloper.

Australasia strictly, the south-west Pacific Ocean regions of Australia and New Zealand, but often extended to include their nearby islands, Micronesia and Polynesia. Alternatively, it may be used to describe collectively Australia, New Zealand, Fiji, and Western Samoa.

auto-da-fé [*Portuguese*] an act of faith; strictly, the burning at the stake of supposed heretics during the Spanish Inquisition, but now more broadly used to suggest any extreme action or commitment.

autres temps, autres mœurs [*French*] other days, other ways; circumstances or solutions change with the times.

axis powers the signatories to the 1936 alliance between Berlin and Rome, which led to the German-Japanese-Italian pact of 1937.

ayatollah a divine interpreter of Muslim law; a Shiite leader.

Baha'i faith a religion founded in Persia in 1867 by Baha-Ullah that lays emphasis on the underlying truths of all creeds and the unity of all peoples of the world. It has no set priesthood or rituals, but daily private prayer is compulsory. Baha'is in the Middle East have frequently been subjected to political persecution and secular violence.

baksheesh, buckshee [*Persian*] free; a bribe, something for nothing.

balance of payments a precise record of a country's net transactions with the rest of the world over a specific period, including trade, services, capital movements, unilateral transfers, and invisible exports.

balance of trade a monetary record of a country's net imports and exports of actual goods.

Balkans the countries of the mountainous peninsula in south-eastern Europe. The modern Balkans comprise Yugoslavia, Romania, Albania, Bulgaria, the European part of Turkey, and Greece.

Baltic states the Soviet republics of Estonia, Latvia and Lithuania bordering the east coast of the Baltic sea. Russian troops occupied all three in January 1991 on the pretext of apprehending draft dodgers, but in truth to discourage further moves towards independence from the USSR. Lithuania had declared its independence in March 1990; Estonia and Latvia declared theirs following the failed attempt to depose Gorbachev in August 1991. All three were recognized as independent immediately by the EC, Russia, Poland, Sweden, Czechoslovakia, Finland and Panama.

banana republic once widely used as a derisory name for any Central or South American country whose economy relied heavily on fruit exports to the US, it is now more likely to be used to describe any state having an unsophisticated economy or administration.

Bangladesh War the devastation of Pakistan's eastern province by a cyclone in 1970 and the Dacca government's ineffectual response to the disaster—which claimed 220000 lives and countless homes and crops—triggered fighting the following year, which developed into a full-scale border war in 1971. Pakistan surrendered the territory only months later, following military intervention by India, which had accepted huge numbers of Bangladeshi refugees, and the independent republic of Bangladesh was created. It joined the Commonwealth a year later.

Bank of England Britain's premier financial institution, founded in 1694 as a private bank by Whigs, in return for lending the Government £1.2 million to finance the war against the French. It soon became the central repository for the nation's gold reserves, and under the Bank Charter Act 1844, it was empowered to control the country's money supply as the sole source of paper currency. It was nationalized in 1946.

bathos [*Greek*] descending from the sublime to the ridiculous; an unsatisfactory conclusion.

Battle of Britain the name given to the series of air battles between fighter planes of the German Luftwaffe and the Royal Air Force between July and September 1940. Despite the Luftwaffe's numerical strength the RAF's system of five fighter commands and its early-warning radar network, caused it heavy losses. In October 1940, Operation Sea Lion was abandoned and the German invasion fleet was dispersed.

beatae memoriae [*Latin*] of blessed memory; often used ironically when recalling adversaries from the recent past.

beati pacifici [*Latin*] blessed are the peacemakers; the opening words of the eighth beatitude from the Sermon on the Mount, according to Matthew.

belle époque [*French*] the fine period; a way of life that has disappeared or been destroyed.

Benelux the countries that comprise an informal economic union formed in 1948; namely, Belgium, the Netherlands and Luxembourg.

bene qui latuit bene vixit [*Latin*] he who lives in obscurity is more likely to survive; sometimes, it is best to adopt a low profile.

becquerel a unit of measurement per sq centimetre of radioactivity. In laboratories, the level at which work is immediately abandoned and decontamination procedures triggered is 3 becquerels per sq cm. In the **Chernobyl** disaster, levels of as high as 150 becquerels were still being recorded in the immediate vicinity four years after the incident.

Berlin Congress territorial negotiations held in June–July 1878, in which Russia gained territory from the Turks as a consequence of intervention to protect the Christian population of Bulgaria, and Britain gained Cyprus—which served to stabilize the Balkans until the 1912–13 war.

Berlin Wall The two-metre-high wall between East Germany and West Berlin built in August 1961, for the purpose of preventing the population of the communist German Democratic Republic from crossing into the Federal Republic of Germany. Countless would-be escapees were shot dead by East German border guards during the wall's 28 years of existence. It was finally breached by joyous East and West Germans in November 1989, when the Berlin checkpoints were thrown open as a precursor to German reunification the following year.

Berufsverbot [*German*] a ban on political undesirables from entering public service.

Bessarabia a region occupied briefly by Romania after World War II but ceded to the Soviet Union in 1947. Most of the territory is part of Moldavia.

Bhopal capital of Madya Pradesh, India, and the location of a Union Carbide plant that leaked methyl isocyanate into the atmosphere in December 1984, bringing death and long-term sickness to thousands of the city's inhabitants.

Big Bang the deregulation of the London Stock Exchange in October 1986, whereby foreign organizations could become members for the first time, and share dealings were no longer the prerogative of stockbrokers but could be transacted by jobbers too.

Big Ben nickname for the 13 tonne bell that chimes the hours from the clock tower of the British Parliament. It alludes to Sir Benjamin Hall, commissioner of works at the time of the bell's installation in 1859.

Big Brother the omnipotent and tyrannical unseen demagogue, meant as a representation of Stalin, in **George Orwell**'s 1947 futuristic novel, *1984*, whose two central dissenting characters are constantly reminded by huge posters and TV broadcasts that 'Big Brother is watching you'.

Bill a document containing the terms of a new law, or of amendments to existing legislation. A Public Bill is presented by the Government of the day and will usually reflect either policies first advanced in the **manifesto** on which it was elected, or the contents of any subsequent **Queen's Speech**. It is often preceded by a White Paper describing the general scope of the proposed legislation, which can be the subject of influential debate before the Bill itself goes before Parliament. A private Member's Bill can be introduced by an MP of any party, and usually concerns social topics. Such Bills seldom survive beyond Committee stage without cross-party support. A Private Bill can be promoted for reasons of self-interest by an individual or body outside Parliament, but it must attract the sponsorship of one MP and the support of several others, who pilot the Bill through Parliament on the promoter's behalf.

Bill of Rights (1) A Bill to enact the **Declaration of Rights**, it asserted that **James VII** and **II** had abdicated, established **William III** and Mary **II** as monarchs, forbade Roman Catholics from ever taking the throne, and declared illegal grievances, such as the maintenance of an army in peacetime. (**2**) The first ten amendments to the US Constitution, adopted 1791.

bis dat qui cito dat [*Latin*] he gives twice who gives quickly; the value of a quick response is doubled.

black economy that portion of a country's trade in goods and services that illegally avoids taxation.

black market informal trading in prohibited or regulated goods or currencies by individuals or small groups.

Black Power an initially benign but later aggressive pressure group that arose in America in the 1960s, whose leaders, who included **Malcolm X**, asserted that black equality would only be achieved by the use of force against the white establishment.

blackshirts name adopted by supporters of the British Union of Fascists (1932-6) under the leadership of **Oswald Mosley**. It alluded to the style of their uniform, which was meant as an equivalent to the brown shirts worn by Germany's National Socialists.

blasé [*French*] world-weary; disaffected.

Blick ins Chaos [*German*] a glimpse into hell; a forewarning of the consequences of social collapse.

Blitzkrieg [*German*] lightning war; a surprise attack, extreme corrective action.

Bloody Sunday the escalation of a demonstration by the unemployed into violent rioting in Trafalgar Square on 13 November 1887, which prompted William Booth and others to campaign for better living conditions for London's jobless and lower classes.

blue laws a set of absurdly stringent laws, printed on blue paper, imposed by the 17th-century Puritan establishment on New Englanders. In modern usage, the term has come to be applied to any unreasonable or unwarranted legislation.

Blut und Eisen [*German*] blood and iron; the use of military force to achieve a specific end; slogan of the Nationalist Socialist Party.

Body of Liberties a colonial governmental code for Massachusetts introduced in 1641 that incorporated many tenets of English law, it ranks with the **Magna Carta** and American **Bill of Rights** as an exposition of fundamental constitutional and personal freedoms.

Boer [*Afrikaans*] South African farmer, especially in the Transvaal.

bolsheviks [*Russian*] bigger; followers of the extreme left-wing Russian socialists led by **Lenin** that seized power in 1917.

Boston tea party a famous demonstration by colonists on 16 December 1773, in which they dumped the cargo of three tea ships into Boston harbour in protest at the East India Company's monopoly over exports to America of the commodity.

bourgeois [*French*] middle-class; usually used disparagingly to describe indifference to socialist principles.

Bourse (de Commerce) the French stock exchange.

Bretton Woods agreement the terms for a post-war international monetary system that resulted in the creation of the **International Monetary Fund** and the **World Bank**, named after the place in New Hampshire, USA, where it was negotiated.

brinkmanship the art of assessing the ultimate point to which a potentially threatening political or military situation can be exploited before it irretrievably escalates. In recent history, brinkmanship was epitomized by **John F. Kennedy**'s handling of the **Cuban missile crisis**.

British North American Act the 1867 legislation that established Canada as a federation, initially of Quebec, Ontario, Nova Scotia and New Brunswick.

brouhaha [*French*] fuss or uproar.

brutum fulmen [*Latin*] an empty threat, a meaningless stricture imposed without the power or authority to enforce it.

Budget the annual forecast of the nation's revenue and expenditure, and the set of fiscal measures designed to balance the two. The Budget is devised by the **Chancellor of the Exchequer**, who will be subjected to furious lobbying from his Cabinet colleagues on behalf of their Ministries on the one hand, and from the Treasury, urging maximum probity, on the other. The Chancellor presents his Budget to the House of Commons each March, and its provisions—particularly those affecting excise duty—may be implemented literally overnight.

Bundesbank [*German*] the Frankfurt-based German central bank.

Bundesrepublik [*German*] the Federal Republic of Germany; the name given to West Germany prior to reunification in 1990.

Bundestag [*German*] the lower house of the federal German Parliament.

Bundeswehr [*German*] permitted German armed forces under Supreme Allied Command formed by the 1955 Treaty of Paris.

Burkina Faso West African republic, formerly Upper Volta.

cabal an elite, powerful and secretive group; the term was derived from the initials of the Ministers of **Charles I**'s Ministers of 1667–73—Clifford, Arlington, Buckingham, Ashley-Cooper, and Lauderdale.

Cabinda an autonomous enclave within Angola, West Africa.

CACM (Central American Common Market) formed in 1960, and ratified in 1963, to liberalize inter-regional and free trade and customs harmonization. Its members are Costa Rica, Guatemala, El Salvador, Honduras, and Nicaragua.

cachet [*French*] a seal of authority; kudos.

cadmean [*Greek*] an empty triumph; a victory achieved at too great a cost.

cadre [*French*] framework; a body of key men; a member of a Communist unit.

camaraderie [*French*] a friendly association; an intimate political group.

camarilla [*Spanish*] a conspirational group.

Cambodia a south-east Asian state, re-named under various governments and regimes as the Khmer Republic in 1970; Democratic Kampuchea in 1975; and the People's Republic of Kampuchea in 1979.

Cambridge mafia the generation of 1950s and 1960s right-wing Cambridge students that produced eight members of post-1979 Conservative Cabinets: Sir Leon Brittan, Kenneth Clarke, Norman Fowler, John Selwyn Gummer, Michael Howard, David Howell, Norman Lamont and John Nott.

Camelot an amazing ironic kingdom; the name sardonically applied to the White House during the presidency of **John F. Kennedy**.

camino real [*Spanish*] the royal route; the most effective way of reaching an objective.

canaille [*French*] the common people.

canard [*French*] a false report; a misleading assertion or argument.

Cape Verde Islands a republic off the west coast of Africa comprising 15 islands in two groups that were Portuguese territory until 1975.

capitalism a social order whereby the means of production, and therefore the main source of a nation's wealth and economic well-being, is in private hands.

CARICOM (Caribbean Community) formed in 1973 to co-ordinate economic and foreign policy, by Antigua and Barbados, Bahamas, Belize, Dominica, Grenada, Guyana, Jamaica, Montserrat, St Christopher and Nevis, Saint Lucia, St Vincent and the Grenadines, Trinidad and Tobago.

carpe diem [*Latin*] seize the day; take the opportunity while it exists.

carte-blanche [*French*] complete freedom, acting at will.

cartel [*French*] an agreement for the exchange of prisoners of war; an unlawful commercial accord, usually for the purpose of controlling prices or supplies.

caste [*Portuguese*] pure; a religious or social grouping.

casus belli [*Latin*] an act justifying war; the grounds for a dispute.

casus omissus [*Latin*] an event or circumstances not envisaged by a law or treaty.

catastasis [*Greek*] drama; the height of the action.

Catch-22 an unresolvable dilemma; taken from the Joseph Heller novel of that name published in 1961, in which the central character, Captain Yossarian, is thwarted in his attempt to get out of flying more World War II bombing missions by pleading insanity, when a doctor tells him that a man would be crazy to fly more missions and sane if he didn't, but if he was sane, he had to fly them. If he flew them he was crazy and didn't have to; but if he didn't, he was sane and had to.

cathexis [*Greek*] a burst of mental energy prompted by a particular notion.

catholicon [*Greek*] an all-embracing remedy; a universal solution.

Cato Street conspiracy a plot devised in 1820 by the followers of the socialist radical Thomas Spence (1750-1814), to assassinate all the members of **Lord Liverpool**'s Government and to declare a republic. After the group was infiltrated by spies, its leaders were arrested and hanged.

caudillo [*Spanish*] leader; the popular name for General **Franco**.

causa movens [*Latin*] the motive behind a particular action.

cause célèbre [*French*] an event of great public interest, usually of some notoriety.

caveat (emptor) [*Latin*] a warning or reservation; let the buyer beware.

cedant arma togae [*Latin*] from arms to the toga; the replacement of military by civil rule.

census [*Latin*] an official demographic and social survey of the population. The first British census was commissioned in 1801, and one has been undertaken every 10 years ever since.

central rate the exchange rate against the **ecu** adopted by each currency within the **European monetary system** that links contributory currencies to the EMS **exchange rate mechanism.**

cercle privé [*French*] closed circle; a private group.

c' est la guerre [*French*] such is war; a philosophical acceptance of the inevitable consequences of a policy or action.

ceteris paribus [*Latin*] all else being equal.

chacun à son goût [*French*] each to his own taste.

chagrin [*French*] annoyance, frustration.

Chancellor of the Exchequer in the British Cabinet, the office held by the Government's chief financial Minister, having overall responsibility for developing and implementing fiscal and general economic policies, and for devising the annual Budget. The **Prime Minister**'s additional title of First Lord of the Treasury acknowledges the importance of the Treasury, but the Chancellor's authority there is supreme.

Chappaquiddick an exclusive summer resort on the island of Martha's Vineyard, Massachusetts, where in 1969 a Democratic Party campaign worker, Mary Jo Kopechne, met her death by drowning as the only passenger in a car driven by Senator Edward Kennedy which ran off a small bridge. After an attempted cover-up and a closed inquest at which the senator was exonerated, a report released by the presiding magistrate implied negligence on Kennedy's part, and the scandal put an end to his aspirations to stand for the presidency.

chargé d'affaires [*French*] an ambassadorial representative; one who delegates for the senior envoy in his absence.

Chartists a group of English reformers, comprising mainly industrial workers and radical intellectuals, active between 1838 and 1849. Their principal objectives were universal male suffrage, voting by secret ballot in parliamentary elections, the abolition of property ownership qualifications for the franchise, and remuneration for Members of Parliament—all of which had been adopted by the early 20th century.

Checkpoint Charlie the Berlin crossing point between the East and West that came to epitomize Germany's geographical and political division. The famous border guard-house was dismantled in November 1990, shortly after the country's reunification.

cherchez la femme [*French*] look for the lady; a suggestion that a woman is really the power behind the throne—or that a romantic or scandalous entanglement is the cause of a man's untypical behaviour.

Chernobyl an industrial complex in the Ukranian republic of Belorussia, and the site of the world's first known nuclear power plant disaster, on 26 April 1986. During a routine shutdown, a malfunction caused the release into the atmosphere of radiation measured at up to 150 times the accepted safe level. Subsequent worldwide monitoring disproved the Politburo's claim that radiation was confined to a 30 km/18 ml radius of Chernobyl. It has been estimated that the number killed outright was 10 times the official toll of 31, and that as many as 2 million inhabitants of Belorussia, including 800000 children, were at risk of developing leukaemia from immediate direct exposure, while millions more could contract it after consuming contaminated crops. For years after the incident deformed babies were still being born to women who had been living near Chernobyl at the time of the incident. In April 1991, Soviet scientists revealed that the concrete sarcophagus erected around the reactor to contain the 135 tonnes of radioactive material remaining—having a life of 25000 years—was crumbling, giving rise to the risk of further contamination of the atmosphere.

che sarà, sarà [*Italian*] what will be, will be; fate will take its own course.

chicane [*French*] a trick or deception; hence chicanery—cunning scheming or underhanded action.

Chiltern Hundreds a notional Crown office for which a British MP must apply if he wants to leave Parliament at any time other than on its dissolution. Members are technically forbidden from resigning, but applying for stewardship of the Chiltern Hundreds has the convenient effect of bringing automatic disqualification from sitting as an MP.

chimera [*Greek*] a grotesque figment of the imagination; an illusory perception of the true facts; an impossible aspiration.

China Support British-based group that campaigns against the deportation of Chinese refugee dissidents from Europe and America and their forced repatriation to China, including those who fled persecution after the **Tiananmen Square massacre**.

Christian Socialists a group of moderate reformers who attempted unsuccessfully to mediate between the radical demands of the **Chartists** with the traditional institutions of the state.

Circumlocution Office derisory name for public offices used by Charles Dickens in *Little Dorritt* (1855), which savagely attacks bureaucracy. It alludes to public departmens in which civil servants employ delaying tactics to avoid taking decisions or to evade personal responsibility.

civil disobedience the staging of non-violent but disruptive demonstrations against political or military policies or social injustices. The term was first used as the title of an 1849 essay by David Thoreau, in which he asserted that 'government is best which governs least.' The concept inspired **Mohandas Gandhi**'s strategy of passive resistance.

civil rights the claim of individuals or the social or ethnic groups to which they belong to enjoy fundamental liberties, including non-discrimination on the grounds of race, colour, or creed;

equality before the law; freedom of speech; and the absence of press censorship.

claque [*French*] a group of sychophantic supporters; originally, those paid to lead the applause at theatrical events.

cliché [*French*] an overworked or timeworn expression or argument.

clique [*French*] an association of those holding similar views or interests—usually used disparagingly.

cloud-cuckoo-land the supposed abode of any person whose beliefs or policies are ridiculously out of touch with reality. It was the name given by Aristophanes in his play *The Birds* to a city in the sky built by feathered creatures.

CND, (Campaign for Nuclear Disarmament) an organization formed in 1958 to agitate against the development of Britain's nuclear arsenal. Its most effective demonstrations were the annual **Aldermaston** marches. It successfully persuaded the Labour Party to declare a policy of unilateral disarmament in 1960, only to see it effectively reverse that decision a year later. Paradoxically, CND's public appeal and its raison d'etre declined in the wake of the non-proliferation pacts of the 1980s.

coalition an alliance between two or more political parties for the purpose of forming a viable Government in the absence of a clear electoral mandate; or for the purpose of achieving national unity at a time of difficulty—typically, for the duration of a war.

cockpit of Europe the name given to Belgium due to its historical vulnerability as a buffer state between France and Germany,

COCOM (Co-ordinating Committee for Multi-lateral Export Controls) a Paris-based body that compiles lists of goods and services considered to be of strategic importance, and therefore not to be supplied by the West to the eastern bloc.

Coercive Acts legislation passed by the British Parliament in 1774 by way of retaliation for the **Boston tea party**, which closed the port and installed troops there, exercised greater control of the Massachusetts administration, and ordered several officials to be sent for trial. The Acts precipitated the American War of Independence.

cognoscente [*Italian*] experts in a particular subject or field of endeavour; those in the know.

Cold War a state of estrangement or tension between two or more nations, particularly that which existed between the Soviet Union and the West from the mid-1950s until the 1980s.

Colombo Plan an agreement originally between seven Commonwealth countries, later joined by 19 others, to promote economic and social development in the Asian and Pacific region.

Combination Acts legislation enacted in 1790 ostensibly for the purpose of imposing trade restrictions, but which had the effect of outlawing trade unions. Even after they were repealed in 1824, unions were liable to prosecution for breach of contract or for taking strike action.

Combined Loyalist Military Command an umbrella organization for Protestant paramilitary groups in Northern Ireland, formed in 1991.

COMECON (Council for Mutual Economic Assistance) a Moscow-based organization established in 1949 to co-ordinate and accelerate the economic development of eastern bloc countries, Cuba, and Vietnam.

comitadji [*Turkish*] a revolutionary secret society, or a member of it, of the kind active in the Balkans at the end of the 19th century.

comme ci, comme ça [*French*] you win some and lose some.

comme il faut [*French*] as is necessary; the correct response.

commissar [*Latin*] a senior Soviet official.

Common Market the popular name for the **European Economic Community**.

Commonwealth of Nations an association of 49 independent countries accounting for about one quarter of the world's population, comprising the United Kingdom and its former dependencies, and those of Australia and New Zealand. The precondition to observe allegiance to the same monarch was waived with India's entry as a republic in 1950. Heads of state meet for informal debate at the Commonwealth Conference, which is held at a different capital every two years. The American Commonwealth comprises Kentucky, Massachussetts, Pennsylvania, and Virginia, which prefer not to style themselves states.

communard [*French*] a member of the post-revolutionary Parisian administration; one who believes in the extension of local municipal power.

communiqué [*Latin*] an official report or announcement—often used ironically to suggest its dubious veracity.

communism a social order whereby all of a nation's means of production and its property is owned by the working class or proletariat (but effectively by the state), and the wealth that they produce is distributed to the common good. The first communist manifesto was produced by **Karl Marx** in 1848,

Communist Party of Great Britain formed in 1920 through the merger of various leftist groups, it acknowledged from its inception the authority of Moscow. Its fortunes improved with Soviet intervention in World War II, but it never won more than four seats in Parliament, and the 1956 Hungarian revolution saw many of its supporters defect to the new left of the Labour Party. The changing political climate and Moscow's waning influence led to the party undergoing a transformation in 1990, with a new emphasis on social reform.

Communist Party of the United States of America founded shortly after the Russian revolution, it started as a loose alliance of secret pro-union groups, such as those organized by Indians and Finns working in the mining and steel industries. Although it had already moved away from the Moscow model by the 1930s, it became an obvious target for patriotic extremism once America had entered World War II, which continued with the notorious House of Un-American Activities Committee of the early 1950s. Later that same decade, it abandoned the hammer and sickle and ended expulsions of those disinclined to adhere strictly to the party line. The CPUSA began the 1990s with a claimed card-carrying membership of 20000 and the unofficial support of half a million American citizens.

Comoros an archipelago in the Indian Ocean; three of the four islands that comprise the territory—Great Comoro, Anjouan and Moheli—secured independence from France in 1975, but Mayotte decided in a referendum to remain part of the French republic.

compos mentis [*Latin*] of sound mind; a proper awareness.

concordat [*French*] an understanding between Church and state relating to ecclasiastical privileges; an agreement between nations of less significance than a treaty.

condottiere [*Italian*] a leader of mercenaries; an unprincipled political opportunist.

conjunctis viribus [*Latin*] a united effort; two or more powers working towards a common goal.

consensus [*Latin*] the opinion of most or of the majority. Hence, the phrase 'the general consensus' is tautological.

consensus gentium [*Latin*] global unanimity; near-perfect agreement.

Conservative and Unionist Party Although the ideology of the modern Conservative Party was enshrined as long ago as 1790, in **Burke**'s *Reflections on the Revolution in France*, it took more tangible political form under **Pitt the Younger**, whose notions of a party that protected the interests of the ruling establishment while embracing industrial and social development were first effectively realized by **Benjamin Disraeli**. Having exploited the Liberal split over Irish home rule, he laid the foundations for more than 30 years of Tory dominance, aided by a switch of allegiance from the newly-affluent in the traditional pockets of Liberal supremacy and the support of the working class in the industrial North, where a new social order was beginning to emerge as a consequence of the industrial revolution. The Conservatives' record of ideological cohesion remained unblemished for three decades, until the row over tariff reform that brought an end to three decades of power in 1906. The period in Opposition that followed allowed the party to redefine its objectives and settle internal strife, and Liberal prevarication

over the Irish issue and Britain's stance in World War I assured Conservatives a place in **Asquith**'s 1915 coalition. Their appeal to the electorate was consolidated in the 1918 and 1926 elections, and under **Stanley Baldwin** the Conservatives were seen increasingly as the representatives of business interests and of the middle classes, while improvements to welfare provisions brought them added popularity among those lower down the social scale. **Neville Chamberlain**'s disastrous efforts at appeasement saw the party at its lowest ebb as Britain entered World War II, and not even **Winston Churchill**'s huge personal popularity could surpress the electorate's resentment at the country having been dragged into hostilities by default, and its justifiable belief that Labour had been the most effective partner in the coalition. The five years in Opposition following the party's 1945 election defeat again gave it an opportunity to reorganize and to structure a new mixed economy to vie with Labour's platform, which it implemented with considerable success after returning to power in 1951. Although the Suez fiasco evoked for some the same complacency and unpreparedness that was seen in 1940, the party won a new lease of life under **Harold Macmillan**, who combined Edwardian probity with progressive fiscal policies to such good effect that it was with some justification that he told the country in the 1959 election that 'You've never had it so good'. In the wake of the **Profumo scandal**, the safe choice of **Alec Douglas-Home** as Macmillan's successor in 1963 must have seemed a good idea at the time, but Britain was now into the swinging 60s, and **Harold Wilson** and the socially flexible Labour Party offered an irresistible alternative—not least to the post-war baby boomers who had never known anything but life under the Conservatives. But Labour's inability to grapple with a worsening economic climate and the the social disruption caused by the growing power of the unions brought disaffection, though **Edward Heath**'s two Administrations were notable more for their success in breaking Britain free of her international isolationism and for taking her into the **Common Market** than by any success at reconciling an increasingly polarized society. The party's choice of **Margaret Thatcher** as leader in 1975 can be seen retrospectively as an inspired choice. Her strong nationalistic tendencies and unflinching espousement of high rewards for personal effort captured the imagination of an electorate that had become bored waiting for Labour to make something happen. The two years that followed her 1979 election success were undistinguished, but her successful stewardship of the 1982 **Falklands War** restored her personal popularity, and from then on the Conservative Party *was* Margaret Thatcher. Any damage to the party caused by the mediocrity of many of her Ministers was eclipsed by her own sureness of touch, and the party's successive election victories owed everything to manifestos that were indisputably the product of her personal vision. Her removal from the leadership in 1990, following the Cabinet split over European economic policy, undoubtedly dismayed the party faithful, but in **John Major** the Conservatives struck lucky again, in choosing a successor who was not only sure to sustain the most appealing aspects of the Thatcher doctrine but who—like Thatcher in 1982—had an early opportunity to establish his credentials as a statesman of international standing on the outbreak of the Gulf War only three months into his premiership.

contra bonos mores [*Latin*] contrary to good morals; against the interests of society.

contra mundum [*Latin*] against the world; wholly contrary to international opinion.

contrat de majorité [*French*] a parliamentary undertaking, commonly in a coalition, to support a Government's policies for a prescribed length of time.

contretemps [*French*] against time; an unfortunate event; an upset.

co-operatives a social order whereby, typically, small farmers collectively market their produce direct to the customer; co-operative societies operate a retail system in which members of the public are members of the establishments that they patronize and enjoy a share of the profits by way of a dividend on their purchases.

cordon sanitaire [*French*] the containment or isolation of a politically sensitive territory or subject.

corps diplomatique [*French*] the diplomatic representatives or staff of an embassy.

corpus delicti [*Latin*] the manifestation of a crime; proof of a dreadful deed.

corpus juris [*Latin*] a nation's body of laws.

coterie [*French*] an exclusive or intimate group.

couleur du temps [*French*] the colour of the weather; the current public or political climate.

Council of Europe a body formed in 1949 by 10 European states, for the purpose of promoting economic growth and social development and harmonizing foreign policy. Membership had grown to 23 countries by 1989. Its parliamentary assembly, which meets three times a year in Strasbourg, comprises delegations of varying sizes, whose members are appointed by the political parties of their own national assemblies in proportion to their respective representational strengths in them.

coup de grâce [*French*] the final blow; the last action needed to achieve dominance.

coup d'état [*French*] the removal by violence of the established political order, be it a democracy or a dictatorship.

cri de coeur [*French*] a cry from the heart; an emotional plea.

Crimean War Anglo-French war against the Russians from 1854 to 1856, prompted partly by the threat to British interests in Turkey as a consequence of Russian aggression there but also as a way of admonishing the power for its suppresson of the 1848 revolutions. Britain's incompetent handling of the hostilities brought the fall of Lord **Aberdeen**'s Government in 1855. The conflict was notable only because it marked the British Army's use of the rifle for the first time, and the development of field nursing techniques by Florence Nightingale.

crise de combat [*French*] a turning point in war; the moment when victory is assured.

crux [*Latin*] a crucial difficulty; the most significant point of an argument.

CSCE (Conference on Security and Co-operation in Europe) a series of negotiations between the 34 member countries of the then **Warsaw Pact** and **NATO** on conventional arms limitation. It began in Helsinki in 1978 and culminated with the signing in Paris on 19 November 1990 of the Conventional Forces in Europe treaty that scrapped 250000 weapons, effectively bringing an end to the **Cold War**.

Cuban missile crisis the 1962 strategic emergency that arose when American spy planes detected that Russia was shipping nuclear missiles to the island, which had achieved independence from America in 1959 after the revolution led by **Fidel Castro**. Warnings by President **John F. Kennedy** of immediate retaliatory measures forced a stand down by Soviet leader **Nikita Khrushchev** and the armaments were removed. The incident is judged to be the closest that the West has ever come to initiating a nuclear war.

cui bono? [*Latin*] who stands to benefit?; what is the real motive for a particular action or policy?

cypres [*French*] as closely as possible; the implementation of a law or policy according to the intentions or sentiments behind it rather than to the letter, where that is not possible.

Cyprus emergency a British territory since 1878, the agitation for union (Enosis) with Greece in the early 1950s erupted in 1955 into two years of intensive and effective guerilla warfare by EOKA against the British and the Turkish minority, which sought partition. Subsequent negotiations with **Makarios** and Denktash led to the founding of a joint republic in 1960 under the Greek leader's stewardship, but it collapsed after Makarios was deposed in 1975, and its partition followed Turkey's subsequent invasion.

dark continent a disparaging and defunct name for Africa, used by 19th-century colonialists in alluding to the then unexplored continent and its dark-skinned inhabitants.

débâcle [*French*] a complete breakdown, an utter fiasco.

Declaration of Independence the document dated 4 July 1776 that proclaimed the colonies' right to become free and independent states owing no allegiance to the British Crown or to and its political system. Its adoption is celebrated on 4 July each year.

Declaration of Rights a document drawn up by the English Parliament in 1689 that nullified the Acts of **James VII** and **II** against which the **Glorious Revolution** had been directed. Its provisions were subsequently embodied in the **Bill of Rights**.

Declaratory Act 1766 legislation reasserting the right of the English Parliament to legislate for the American colonies.

decolonization Britain's programme of independence for many of her colonial territories undertaken in the 1960s.

Defence of the Realm Acts a series of statues passed during World War I to allow governmental control over industry and individuals, and used to suppress the industrial unrest that followed the end of hostilities.

deflation a fall in the prices of consumer goods and services and of raw materials caused by a contraction of money supply and credit, usually accompanied by a fall in output and rising unemployment.

déjà vu [*French*] the sensation of having previously encountered an identical occurrence or predicament.

de jure [*Latin*] sanctioned by law.

demi-monde [*French*] half-world; a class of dubious reputation or worth.

democracy a political system in which the populace are free to choose who should govern them, and have the freedom periodically to change the nature of their government in free elections.

Democratic Forum predominantly leftist Kuwaiti opposition umbrella group formed after the 1991 **Gulf War.**

democratization a term that gained popularity in the 1980s to describe the ending of Russian dominance over eastern bloc countries and their transformation into independent republics.

dénouement [*French*] the unravelling of a plot; the final outcome.

depression a prolonged period of low economic activity accompanied by a fall in personal wealth and high unemployment.

de profundis [*Latin*] out of the depths of despair; an inspired solution prompted by adversity.

de rigueur [*French*] strictly to convention; the required standard.

descamisados [*Spanish*] the shirtless ones; the followers of **Eva** and **Juan Peron**.

détente [*French*] relaxation; an easing of political tension.

deus ex machina [*Latin*] a god out of the machine; an unexpected and helpful intervention; a providential event.

Deuxième Bureau the French Department of Military Intelligence, comparable to Britain's MI5.

devaluation an official downgrading of a currency's value and hence its realistic exchange rate.

devil's advocate one who argues against a proposition only to display its weaknesses.

diaspora [*Greek*] fragmentation, dispersal; specifically, that of the Jewish people from Israel following the Romans' destruction of Jerusalem.

diplomatic immunity a convention under international law whereby diplomats and their households are exempt from tax and customs duties and are immune from prosecution for minor criminal offences.

dirigisme [*French*] direct state intervention; bureaucratic inteference.

dirigiste [*French*] one who favours state planning or central Government control.

disarmament the process of surrendering or limiting military strength. In modern times, the term is applied almost exclusively to nuclear disarmament, which was to some extent achieved by the non-proliferation pacts entered into by the Soviet Union and western powers in the late 1980s.

disinflation a slowing down of the speed at which prices have been rising, either through governmental intervention or naturally as a consequence of economic **depression**.

divide et impera [*Latin*] divide and rule; the ploy of fomenting disagreement between parties to overcome their collective strength.

doukhobors [*Russian*] religious conscientious objectors, many of whom fled to Canada from Russia at the end of the 19th century.

Dow-Jones index a barometer of the buoyancy or otherwise of the American stock-market, based on the average price of 30 blue chip shares, mainly industrial, traded on the New York Stock Exchange.

Downing Street a thoroughfare off Whitehall, just north of the Houses of Parliament, and the location, at No. 10, of the official residence of the First Lord of the Treasury (**Prime Minister**) since Walpole's 1721–42 Administration. No. 11 is the official home of the **Chancellor of the Exchequer**. Unrestricted public access to the street came to an end in the 1970s with the growth of international terrorism and London street riots, and in 1989 the Whitehall entrance was fortified with the erection of high security gates.

dramatis personae [*Latin*] the players in a drama; familiar or predictable participants in an event.

Drang nach Osten [*German*] an impulse to achieve an eastward extension of territorial boundaries.

Druzes an Islamic sect common to Syria, Lebanon and Israel that is an offshoot of Shia Muslims, but which borrows also from Christianity, Judaism and other middle eastern religions.

Duce, Il [*Italian*] the leader; the Italian fascists' affectionate name for **Benito Mussolini**.

dukka the Buddhist belief that everything, however superficially wonderful, leads to suffering.

Easter Rising the climax of the 20th-century Irish constitutional crisis, when 2 000 Irish Nationalists rose in revolt in Dublin on Easter Monday

1916 and seized several public buildings, but were defeated six days later by British forces in the absence of the expected support from Germany. The execution of several **Sinn Fein** leaders only served to win increasing support for the movement and to fuel increasing violence, culminating in the 1922–3 civil war, and the establishment of the south's first separate Government in 1932.

ébauche [*French*] the first draft; a rough outline of an idea.

é buon orator chi a se persuade [*Italian*] he is a good speaker who persuades himself; convince yourself, and you can convince the world.

EC (European Community) a community of twelve states in W Europe, it comprises three communities: the *European Steel and Coal Community* (1952) established under the Treaty of Paris by France, West Germany, Italy, Belgium, the Netherlands, and Luxembourg; the *European Economic Community* and the *European Atomic Energy Community* (1958) established by the six states under the Treaty of Rome which provided for collaboration in the civilian sector of nuclear power. Six members have been added to the original six: Denmark, Ireland, and the UK (1973); Greece (1981): and Portugal and Spain (1986). Turkey is seeking to become a member.

échange de vues [*French*] an exchange of views; a declaration of principles made before the start of formal negotiations.

éclaircissement [*French*] clarification; elucidation of a particular point.

economic indicators statistics that reflect accurately a country's trade, inflation, and unemployment.

ECOWAS (Economic Community of West African States) a body formed in 1975 by the Treaty of Lagos to promote economic, social and cultural advancement of its 16 member countries. The treaty provides for compensation where trade liberalization adversely affects import duties, and embodies a commitment to abolish obstacles to the free movement of people, services and capital.

ecu (*pl.* ecu), European currency unit; a largely notional currency whose value is based on a basket of 10 European currencies, and which is at the heart of the **European monetary system**. Each currency's share in the basket is determined according to the output of the state from which it originates. The hard ecu favoured by Britain in its negotiations to enter into full membership of the EMS provides for the ecu's value to be fixed, rather than to fluctuate according to the economic strength of the contributing economies. The 17th-century écu was a silver coin of equivalent value to the English crown or French 5 franc piece.

EEC (European Economic Community) the Common Market an association within the European Community essentially a customs union, with a common external teriff and a common market with the removal of barriers to trade among the members. There are common policies for fisheries, regional development, industrial intervention, and economic and social affairs.

EFTA (European Free Trade Association) a body founded in 1960 to encourage free trade in industrial products and increased trade in agricultural goods between its member countries. Denmark, the UK and Portugal left EFTA on achieving membership of the European Community. Its current members are Austria, Finland, Iceland, Norway, Sweden, and Switzerland.

égarement [*French*] an unfortunate blunder; lack of purpose.

EIB (European Investment Bank) a non-profit making bank created in 1958 by the founder members of the European Community, for the purpose of financing regional development and projects of common interest to a group of member states or the Community as a whole. The bank is funded mainly by borrowings in the form of public or private bond issues, which totalled more than 7600 million ecu in 1988.

eile mit Weile [*German*] more haste, less speed; make progress at leisure.

ein Mann, ein Wort [*German*] one man, one word; a pledge that will be honoured.

einmal ist keinmal [*German*] once is not for ever; the exception proves the rule.

Einsamkeit [*German*] solitude; cultural or political isolation.

Einwohnerwehr [*German*] an early 20th-century civil guard, long since discarded; hence, a redundant form of defence.

Eisen und Blut [*German*] blood and iron; the use of military might to secure a specific purpose; used by **Bismarck** in a speech to the Prussian Parliament in 1862.

Eldorado [*Spanish*] a legendary country supposedly rich in gold, believed by the conquistadors to exist on the Upper Amazon.

Emancipation Proclamation the announcement made by President **Abraham Lincoln** on 1 January 1863 that all slaves held in rebel areas were deemed to be free men, but not those in border states or those subject to military occupation. Slavery was not completely abolished until the 13th amendment to the American Constitution was adopted in 1865.

embargo [*Spanish*] arrest; originally, an order forbidding the free passage of shipping between two countries; a prohibition on trade between two nations as a measure of displeasure, such as that which operated against South Africa from the 1960s until it officially began to be eased following moves to end **apartheid** and segregation in 1990/1.

embarras de choix [*French*] an embarrassment of choices; an abundance of options that makes it difficult to arrive at the right choice.

EMF (European Monetary (Co-operation) Fund) a body that exists to settle claims by Community central banks on one another made as a consequence of intervention under the **European Monetary System.**

emir [*Arabic*] a military commander.

Empfindung [*German*] sensitivity; a perception of the public will.

EMS (European Monetary System) an apparatus for maintaining the comparable values of the subscribing European currencies, one against another, so that member states may enjoy maximum mutual trade without the disadvantages of widely varying exchange rates. The system revolves around a notional central unit of currency, the **ecu** (European currency unit) and the **exchange rate mechanism** (ERM), which limits the extent of any fluctuation between the values of member currencies to 2.25 per cent. (with the exception of the lire, which is allowed to deviate by up to 6 per cent). When most or all of the member countries decide that adherence to the central rate is imposing too great a strain on their domestic economies, they agree jointly to modify it.

en cabochon [*French*] a polished gem but one without facets; hence, a slick argument that owes more to cosmetic appeal than its worth.

en connaissance de cause [*French*] fully conversant with the subject; well informed.

en Dieu est ma fiance [*French*] in God I trust.

en flagrant délit [*French*] caught red-handed.

enosis [*Greek*] reunification, particularly as applied to that sought by Greece in respect of Cyprus.

en passant [*French*] in passing; incidentally.

en plein [*French*] in the thick of it; completely implicated.

Enquiry Concerning Political Justice, An the title of a 1793 treatise by the English novelist and theorist William Godwin (1756–1836), which held that all monarchy is corrupt and all government inhibits the development of mankind. It urged the abolition of every man-made social and political institution, including state control, law, wealth, and marriage, arguing that man's own perfectibility would naturally produce a viable society.

en revanche [*French*] in return; by way of retaliation.

ense et aratro [*Latin*] with sword and plough.

entente (cordiale) [*French*] an understanding; a cordial agreement; a state of friendly association between two nations, particularly that enjoyed by France, England and Russia between 1904 and 1908.

entre chien et loup [*French*] between dog and wolf; the inability to distinguish between good and bad.

entre deux guerres [*French*] between the (two world) wars.

entre quatre yeux [*French*] between four eyes; a confidential discussion between only two people.

entremetteur/entremetteuse [*French*] a go-between; an intermediary who serves to reconcile those in conflict.

e pluribus unum [*Latin*] one out of many; strength through unification; the motto of the United States of America.

Equality State the nickname given to Wyoming because of its pioneering attitude to women's suffrage.

Erin go bragh] [*Irish*] Ireland for ever; an ancient battle cry.

erlaubt ist was gefällt [*German*] what a man likes, he thinks is right; the belief that any action, however selfish, is permissible if it is self-serving.

ERM (exchange rate mechanism) the key component of the **European monetary system**, whereby the maximum fluctuation of member currencies against each other is limited to 2.25 per cent (with the exception of the Italian lira, which can shift by as much as 6 per cent).

ersatz [*German*] an inferior substitute for an article or condition when the genuine article is not available.

Erskine May the familiar name for the single-volume guide to the law, privileges, proceedings and usage of both Houses of Parliament, first published in 1832. The 21st edition, edited by Clifford Boulton, Clerk of the House of Commons, was published in 1989.

erst wägen, dann wagen [*German*] consider first, then venture; act with caution.

escamotage [*French*] sleight of hand; a deception.

esclandre [*French*] a public quarrel; an open scandal.

espérance en Dieu [*French*] trust in God.

Esperanto an artificial common world language invented by a Polish philosopher, L.L. Zamenhof (1859–1917), to aid international understanding and thus contribute to world peace. More than 100000 people worldwide speak the language, and the British Parliamentary Esperanto Group has 200 members from both Houses.

esprit borné [*French*] narrow-minded; of limited vision.

esprit de corps [*French*] the collective spirit; the loyalty that exists within a particular body of people.

esprit de parti [*French*] the party spirit; acquiescing to the general mood.

esprit d'escalier [*French*] staircase wit; the witty rejoinder that only comes to mind when the appropriate moment to utter it has passed.

esprit de suite [*French*] consistency; acting according to type.

esprit fort [*French*] a free thinker; one who claims to rise above common prejudice.

Establishment a contemptuous name for the British ruling classes—and particularly those members of the aristocracy, government, and the judiciary who strive to maintain the existing social order, so as to protect their power and wealth at the expense of the lower classes. In the 1960s, the Establishment Club in Soho served as a professional springboard for satirists such as Peter Cook, David Frost, and Dudley Moore.

est brevitate opus [*Latin*] firmness is needed; terseness may be the best way to achieve results.

étatisme [*French*] state control; the extension of bureaucratic power over the individual.

Ethiopia on 28 May 1991 the forces of the Ethiopian People's Revolutionary Democratic Front (EPRDF) entered Addis Ababa, meeting little opposition. Meles Zenawi, the leader of the EPRDF, announced the formation of a transitional government in consultation with other groups pending elections. The separatist Eritrean People's Liberation Front (EPLF) announced the setting up of its own provisional government in Eritrea, although it agreed to co-operate with the EPRDF in Addis Ababa.

etiam quod esse videris [*Latin*] be what you seem to be; do not act out of character.

et nunc et semper [*Latin*] now and for always.

Eurasia the continents of Europe and Asia, taken as a single land mass. A Eurasian is a person of mixed European and Asian blood.

European Commission of Human Rights a body formed within the Council of Europe in 1950, charged with examining complaints by a contracting party, individuals, social groups, and non-governmental organizations of abuses of the **European Convention on Human Rights**. Cases that cannot be resolved informally are referred to the European Court of Justice.

European Convention on Human Rights a protocol governing the protection and development of all human rights. Formulated in 1950 by the **Council of Europe**, it was extended in 1989 to cover torture and loss of liberty. Observance of the convention is monitored by an independent panel of experts, who are empowered to visit any place where they suspect that it is being abused.

European Council a body comprising the heads of state from all the member countries of the European Community, which meets twice a year to discuss matters of general interest to the Community and to review the decisions taken at the quarterly meetings of Foreign Ministers.

European Council of Ministers a body consisting of nominated representatives of every member state of the EEC, which meets approximately 60 times during the course of the year to discuss foreign affairs, economics, and agriculture. Policy is decided by a simple majority, qualified majority, or unanimity, with the number of votes available to each country ranging from just two for Luxembourg to 10 each for the UK, France, Germany, and Italy. Since 1987, qualified majority voting was introduced to curb the use of the veto and to allow faster progress to be made with the removal of trade barriers. However, certain measures—such as those relating to indirect tax harmonization, health and environmental safety—must still secure unanimous approval.

European Court of Justice a judicial body composed of 13 judges and six advocates-general, who are appointed by the European Community's member states to serve a six-year term. The president of the court is elected by his peers to serve for three years. Matters of major importance are decided by the full bench, and the remainder are entrusted to one of six chambers.

European Parliament the assembly of the European Community's member states. Members of the European Parliament (MEPs) are selected in national elections held in their respective countries, and sit in the European Parliament according to their political, not national, affiliations. In the third direct elections held in June 1989, the Socialists took 180 of the 518 seats, and the Christian Democrats and aligned parties took 121 seats. Britain returns 81 MEPs, in common with France, Germany and Italy. The Parliament is controlled by a president and 14 vice-presidents, who are elected by secret ballot every 30 months, and its 12 annual sessions—each of one week's duration—are usually convened in Strasbourg.

Eurostat the **European Community's** central statistics office, based in Luxembourg.

eventus stultorum magister [*Latin*] the result is the tutor of fools; the injudicious will learn the hard way.

ex animo [*Latin*] from the soul; with all sincerity.

ex cathedra [*Latin*] from the throne; speaking with the force of unquestionable authority.

exchange controls measures that restrict or prevent foreign currency transactions, particularly by individuals, for the purpose of protecting the national economy and the integrity of the currency affected.

exchange rate the rate at which one country's currency is exchangeable for another.

exempli gratia, eg [*Latin*] for example.

ex gratia [*Latin*] by favour rather than by legal right; such as a payment made out of respect or for services rendered.

exitus acta probat [*Latin*] the ends justify the means; all's well that ends well.

ex more [*Latin*] according to custom.

ex nihilo nihil fit [*Latin*] nothing comes out of nothing; inaction cannot be expected to produce results.

Exodus [*Greek*] going out; the escape of the Jewish people from Egyptian bondage in 1200 BC, to begin their search for the promised land; the title of Leon Uris's 1958 novel about the founding of the modern state of Israel.

ex officio [*Latin*] by virtue of one's office; the status of an unelected member of a committee or other body, who may serve mainly in an advisory capacity rather than share in decision-making.

ex parte [*Latin*] in the interests of only one faction. For example, an ex parte injunction is a court instruction often secured in the absence of the person who must observe it.

ex silentio [*Latin*] (an argument arising) from silence; the contention that, for example, a defence exists because of the omission from a statute of provision that it might be expected to contain.

extra modum [*Latin*] beyond measure; incapable of being assessed or quantified.

Fabian Society an association formed by middle-class socialist intellectuals in London in 1884, to encourage the spread of socialism by peaceful, not revolutionary, means. Founder members included George Bernard Shaw and Sidney and Beatrice Webb. Quintus Fabius (275–203 BC) was the Roman General who out-manoeuvred Hannibal by stealth rather than violence.

facile largire de alieno [*Latin*] it is an easy matter to build on that which already exists; there is little merit in embellishing another's ideas.

façon de parler [*French*] as a manner of speaking; a remark or argument used purely for effect and having no intrinsic worth.

facta non verba [*Latin*] action, not words.

faeces populi [*Latin*] the dregs of society; the general rabble.

faire bonne mine [*French*] to put a good face on it; being amenable despite one's personal reservations.

faire une trouée [*French*] to find the gap in an argument; to make one's point.

faiseur de mots [*French*] a word-spinner; one who can speak or write endlessly but conveys practically nothing of value.

fait accompli [*French*] a feat already accomplished; pre-emptive action that is difficult to reverse.

Falklands War the hostilities between Argentina and Britain that were triggered when Argentine forces invaded and occupied the long-disputed Falkland Islands, or the Malvinas, on 2 April 1982. When Argentina failed to respond to UN Resolution 502 calling for the immediate withdrawal of her troops, a British task force left for the Falklands and initial landings on 1 May coincided with aerial bombardment by RAF Vulcans based on Ascension Island. The enemy warship *General Belgrano* was sunk the following day, and the Royal Navy lost the *Sheffield* on 4 May. A successful full-scale landing at San Carlos began on 21 May, at the cost of the HMS *Ardent*, *Antelope*, *Coventry*, and *Atlantic Conveyor*. The decisive battle of Goose Green began on 28 May, but that success was eclipsed by the catastrophic bombing of the HMS *Sir Galahad* and *Tristram*, with the loss of 51 lives. The battle of Port Stanley began on 11 June, and the British accepted Argentina's surrender three days later. Criticism of the Foreign Office for not anticipating the Argentine invasion brought the resignation of Foreign Secretary Lord **Carrington**, but the wave of patriotism that the war engendered returned **Margaret Thatcher** from her lowest ebb as Prime Minister and the so-called Falklands factor was considered a major element in her next general election success.

Falls Road the thoroughfare that runs west from Belfast city centre to Andersonstown, through the main area of Catholic population and an IRA stronghold.

falsa lectio [*Latin*] a wrong reading; a misinterpretation of the facts.

fama nihil est celerius [*Latin*] nothing travels faster than rumour; a warning that action must be taken quickly to counter the deliberate or inevitable dissemination of false information.

FAO (Food and Agriculture Organization) a Rome-based United Nations body concerned with improving world agriculture, fishing, and forestry, through the provision of technical assistance, statistical information, and forecasts.

fardé [*French*] disguised; a cosmetic explanation; a glossing over of the facts.

Far East the countries of eastern Asia, including China, Japan, Korea, eastern Siberia, the Malay archipelago and Indo-China. Sometimes it is taken to include the Indian subcontinent.

fascism an extreme right-wing ideology or style of government that is characterized by a one-party, authoritarian state, totalitarian control of economic and social activity, and a strong military force for the purpose of achieving domestic stability and acquiring extra territories. Individual expression and liberty is supplanted by unquestioning acceptance of, and obedience to, a hierarchal society, with a dictator at its head.

Fascista [*Italian*] a member of the nationalistic and anti-radical movement that developed in Italy at the end of World War I.

fas est ab hoste doceri [*Latin*] one can learn even from one's enemies.

father of his country affectionate name given to **George Washington**, 1st President of the USA, first used on a 1778 calendar published in Pennsylvania.

father of the Constitution name given to **James Madison**, 4th President of the USA, who helped draft both the **American Constitution** and the **Bill of Rights**.

Fat Man the 4.5 tonne atomic bomb, equivalent to 20000 tonnes of high explosive, dropped by the USAF superfortress B-52 Bockscar on Nagasaki at 11 am on 9 August 1945. Plutonium-based, it was potentially even more destructive than **Little Boy**, dropped on **Hiroshima** three days earlier, but the hills surrounding Nagasaki served to contain the blast with in a comparatively small area. Nevertheless, Fat Man obliterated 8 sq km/3 sq ml north of the city and claimed more than 80000 victims. The cumulative horror of Hiroshima and Nagasaki, combined with Russia's successful invasion of Manchuria within hours of Fat Man being dropped, brought Japan's formal surrender on 2 September 1945.

fatwa [*Arabic*] religious ruling; sometimes of an extreme nature and even taking the form of a death sentence—as in the case of the Iranian fatwa passed on **Salman Rushdie**.

faute de mieux [*French*] done for want of anything better; a last resort.

faux pas [*French*] an embarrassing social error; a mistake for which one feels ashamed.

Federal List collective title for the series of 85 essays published between in 1787–8—most of them written by **Alexander Hamilton**—for the purpose of convincing New Yorkers that the proposed Constitution would ensure effective government that accorded with republican principles.

Federal reserve system (the Fed) the United States's central banking system, comprising 12 federal reserve banks controlling as many districts under the Federal Reserve Board in Washington.

fendre un cheveu en quatre [*French*] literally, to split a hair into four; to be absurdly over-critical.

Fenians an association of Irish Nationalists founded in New York in 1857, derived from Fionn MacCumhail, the semi-mythical hero of Ireland. The movement spread throughout America, where Fenian congresses were held between 1863 and 1872, and then to Ireland, where it absorbed the nationalist Phoenix Society and eventually developed into the Irish Republican Brotherhood—a forerunner of the **IRA.**

fiat [*Latin*] let it be; a command; a sanction having the full weight of authority.

fiat justitia (ruat caelum) [*Latin*] let justice be done (though the heavens fall); the proper action must be taken, however unpleasant may be the consequences.

fifth column the name given to any group of enemy sympathizers engaged in sabotage. The term was originally applied to the pro-**Franco** inhabitants of Madrid who attacked from the rear loyalists who were attempting to defend the capital against General Mola's four columns of infantry. In World War II, it was applied to German sympathizers in the USA; but its modern usage includes small politically motivated groups that attempt to create disorder by, for example, infiltrating trade unions or ethnic groups and fomenting unofficial strikes or street violence.

fin de non-recevoir [*French*] the contention that a point, even if valid in itself, is not relevant to the matter in hand.

fin de race [*French*] the end of the human race; more generally, a characteristic that is held to

blame for the misfortunes of a particular nationality or social class.

fin de siècle [*French*] characteristic of the closing years of a century, particularly the late 1800s; hence a period of decadence.

finem respice [*Latin*] bear in mind the outcome; consider the consequences.

fiscal drag the effect that increased taxation has on higher incomes, in reducing disposable income despite wage rises.

fixed exchange rate the exchange value of central rates with gold, the US dollar, or other currencies.

flagrante bello [*Latin*] at the height of the battle; in the midst of hostilities.

fléchette [*French*] one of hundreds of small darts, sometimes tipped with poison, which fill a warhead that is dropped from an aircraft and explodes above ground level, inflicting fatalities over a wide area.

Flixborough disaster the explosion at a chemical plant near Scunthorpe in June 1974 that took the lives of 29 people and first drew public attention to the hazards of the large-scale manufacture and storage of inflammable products. The plant reopened in 1979, but closed two years later.

flower power the influence exerted by the so-called flower children who originated in San Francisco in the mid-1960s. They were the prime movers in the anti-Vietnam war movement, holding huge peace rallies, or 'love-ins', at which the dominant slogan was 'Make love, not war', and the all-pervading aroma that of marijuana.

fluctuat nec mergitur [*Latin*] she is tossed by the waves but does not sink; the motto of Paris.

Foggy Bottom a metaphor for the US Department of State, from its location in downtown Washington DC.

Folketing [*Danish*] the Lower House of the Danish Parliament.

fonctionnaire [*French*] a minor public servant; a petty official.

fons vivus [*Latin*] the living spring; an everlasting source of inspiration or influence.

force de frappe [*French*] the striking force; the military strength assured by ownership of nuclear weaponry.

force majeure [*French*] a significant force; an irresistible power.

foreign exchange rate the number of units of one currency needed to buy another.

fortes fortuna juvat [*Latin*] fortune favours the brave; the greater the risk, the bigger the reward.

Fort Knox the repository of all the US Government's gold reserves, near Louisville in northern Kentucky.

Fourierism a social system devised by the French economist François Marie Charles Fourier (1772–1837), whereby—under a form of republican government—society would comprise groups of 1600 persons living in common buildings called phalansteries, with labour receiving the largest share of the products resulting from their economic activity. Fourierism features in several of George Sand's novels, and was introduced into America in 1842, where it also failed to capture the public's imagination.

Fourteen Points the statement of American peace aims made by President **Woodrow Wilson** in an address to Congress on 8 January 1918. They included the proposal for a League of Nations, which was among several of the 14 points included in the **Treaty of Versailles.**

fourth estate, the the name given to the press, attributed variously to **Edmund Burke** and **Thomas Macaulay**. The three traditional estates are the Lords, spiritual and temporal, and the Commons.

Franc zone a monetary union comprising France and 14 central and West African and other countries whose currencies are linked with the French franc at a fixed rate of exchange.

Franglais [*French*] a form of French that incorporates English words not always common to both languages, often for comic effect.

fraus est celare fraudem [*Latin*] it is fraudulent to conceal a fraud; those who condone or choose to ignore deception are as despicable as those who practise it.

frondeur [*French*] one who always finds fault; a rebellious critic.

Fronde [*French*] a political group of malcontents (Frondists) who violently opposed the French court during the minority of **Louis XIV.**

front à front [*French*] face-to-face; a direct confrontation.

frontis nulla fides [*Latin*] it is unsafe to judge from appearances; a plea to look beyond the obvious.

fuero [*Spanish*] statute law; an official direction.

Führer [*German*] leader, chief; the name adopted by **Adolf Hitler**.

Führerprinzip [*German*] the doctrine that dictatorship is an efficient and desirable form of government.

furor arma ministrat [*Latin*] rage supplies arms; unendurable provocation will lead to war, however unrealistic initiating that action may be.

G5 (group of five) the five most important members of the group of 10: the USA, Japan, West Germany, France, and Britain.

G7 (group of seven) the group of five, plus Canada and Italy.

G10 (group of 10) actually 11 of the most significant industrialized nations within the **International Monetary Fund**. They are Belgium, UK, Canada, France, Germany, Italy, Japan, Netherlands, Sweden, Switzerland, and the USA.

Gang of Four (1) the group of right-wing conspirators led by **Jiang Qing**, widow of **Mao Zedong**,

who in the mid-1970s were tried for treason and other crimes against the state. The others were Zhang Chunqiao, a political organizer in the Cultural Revolution; Wang Hogwen, a youth activist; and Yao Wenyuan, a journalist. The death penalty passed on them was subsequently commuted to life imprisonment. (2) the group of disenchanted senior Labour MPs led by **Roy Jenkins** who in 1981 formed the Social Democratic Party. The others were former Foreign Secretary **David Owen**, **Shirley Williams**, and **William Rodgers**.

garde de nuit [*French*] a nightwatchman; a precautionary measure; a military force installed to keep the peace.

gardez la foi [*French*] keep the faith; remain constant.

GATT (General Agreement on Tariffs and Trade) a framework established in Geneva in 1948, aimed at minimizing international trade barriers by eliminating quotas or reducing tariffs.

Gauleiter [*German*] the rank of provincial leader in Nazi Germany; hence a little dictator; a petty-minded official who abuses what little power is at his disposal.

Gaza Strip the 160 sq km/100 sq ml Mediterranean coastal area inhabited by 250000 Arabs and surrounded almost entirely by Israel, but administered by Egypt from 1949 until it was lost to the Israelis in the 1967 war. A 1978 Egyptian-Israeli agreement provided for five years of self-government followed by negotiations to determine its future status, but the region remains a isolated Arab outpost with no prospect of self-determination.

GDP (gross domestic product) the value of all goods and services produced by an economy over a given period of time, excluding net exports.

Geist [*German*] spirit; a motivating force or principle.

gemach [*German*] comfortable; complacent; an entreaty to act without haste.

generalia [*Latin*] general concepts; first principles

Geneva Convention a set of four conventions, the first of which was submitted by the International Committee of the Red Cross to a diplomatic conference in Geneva in 1864, governing the conduct of war and the treatment of prisoners of war.

gens de peu [*French*] the little people; a section of society that is of no account.

Germanice [*Latin*] in the German manner; according to strict convention.

gerrymandering the altering of electoral boundaries to the advantage of a particular politician or political party; a practice first overtly used by a Governor Gerry of Massachussetts.

Gettysburg Address a speech made by President **Abraham Lincoln** on 19 November 1863, at the dedication of the national cemetery at Gettysburg—the place of a battle from 1–3 June 1863 that was considered to be the turning point in the **American Civil War.**

ghazi [*Arabic*] a Moslem hero; one who triumphs over infidels.

Gipper, the nickname for US President **Ronald Reagan**, from the 1940 movie *Knute Rockne— All American*, based on the life of the American football star George Gipp.

glasnost [*Russian*] openness; the policy of greater political permissiveness that was encouraged by **Mikhail Gorbachev** on assuming the Soviet leadership in 1985, and which allowed the publication of previously suppressed political works and public criticism of the communist system, and brought the release of several political prisoners.

Gleichschaltung [*German*] the violent liquidation of political opposition, such as that practised by the National Socialists in the 1930s.

Gleneagles Agreement an undertaking entered into by Commonwealth Heads of Government in 1977, meeting in Scotland, to discourage sporting links with South Africa, as a way of exhibiting international disapproval of **apartheid** and segregation.

gli assenti hanno tortu [*Italian*] the absent are always deemed to be guilty; those who do not defend themselves can expect to suffer the consequences.

Glorious Revolution the term applied by the English Whigs to the period from 1688–9 in which **James II** was driven from the throne and the Crown was offered to **William of Orange** and Mary.

gnomes of Zurich a derisory name coined by **Harold Wilson** for the Swiss bankers and financiers, whose disaffection with his 1963 Labour Government undermined the country's economic credibility internationally and eventually forced it to devalue sterling.

GNP (gross national product) the value of all goods and services produced by an economy over a given period of time, including net exports.

gold precious metal against which the value of many world currencies is gauged. Some 80 per cent of gold comes from South Africa and the Soviet Union. Jewellery accounts for 50 per cent of world consumption, and industrial usage for 10 per cent.

gospodar [*Russian*] a noble or master in pre-revolutionary Russia.

goy, *pl.* **goyim** [*Hebrew*] a gentile; a follower of the Christian faith.

gradatim [*Latin*] step-by-step; success by degrees; victory by stealth.

grand monde [*French*] a marvellous world; an ideal society.

Grand Old Man (of British politics) name given to **William Gladstone**, who served four terms as a Liberal Prime Minister.

gratis dictum [*Latin*] only an assertion; an argument bereft of substance or authority.

graviora manent [*Latin*] there is worse to come; the present predicament is only the tip of the iceberg.

green currency an artificial exchange rate reflecting the value of an **EC** state's currency in respect of its agricultural output, used to implement common agricultural policy rates, or green rates.

Greenham Common Royal Air Force in Berkshire that provided a base for US cruise nuclear missiles and was thus chosen in the 1980s as the site of a permanent all-female peace camp, which finally disbanded when the missiles were removed in 1989.

green ribbon men the 17th-century anti-monarchy Whig politicians who met in coffee houses and taverns, and who wore a green ribbon in their hats to help identify one another. Green was a colour associated with opposition since Cromwell's day.

Greens supporters of any of the otherwise apolitical parties, such as the Green Party in the UK, whose policies relate mainly to conservation and to environmental protection in general.

Grenada a small island in the Caribbean that has been an independent republic in the British Commonwealth since 1974. The USA briefly sullied its so-called special relationship with Britain when American troops landed on the island in 1983 to suppress an attempted Marxist coup, without apparently consulting the UK Government.

Grenzgänger [*German*] one who crosses a physical political boundary; a political refugee.

Grub Street an 18th-century London street that was the address of many of the most famous, and infamous, struggling writers and literary hacks of the day, including Pope, Byron and Swift. In modern usage, the term is used to describe (disparagingly) and collectively journalists and political correspondents.

Gründerzeit [*German*] the period of reckless economic and financial speculation that followed the 20th-century Franco-Prussian War.

guberniya [*Russian*] a provincial territory within the USSR.

guerrilla [*Spanish*] warfare waged by small groups of irregular troops, usually operating from an adjacent country and armed and funded by a third power having an interest in displacing the existing order.

guistamente [*Italian*] with absolute precision; attention to detail.

Gulag Archipelago, The a three-volume work by Alexander Solzhenitsyn taking the form of an autobiographical analysis of life inside Soviet prison camps as they existed between 1918 and 1956. The discovery of the manuscript by the KGB led to the author's expulsion from the Soviet Union, but the book was subsequently published in Paris between 1973 and 1978.

Gulf Co-operation Council formed in 1981 for the purpose of co-ordinating economic, social and cultural organization and co-ordination, its most significant activity is the harmonization of operations concerned with petroleum, investment, and customs duties. Its member states are Bahrain, Kuwait, Oman, Qatar, Saudi Arabia, and United Arab Emirates.

Gulf States, The collective name for the eight oil-producing countries of the Persian Gulf: Bahrain, Iran, Iraq, Kuwait, Qatar, Oman, Saudi Arabia, and United Arab Emirates.

Gulf War the conflict that followed Iraq's invasion of Kuwait on 2 August 1990 and its continuing occupation of that country. The United Nations called in Security Council Resolution 660, passed on the day of the invasion, for Iraq's immediate withdrawal, and Baghdad's failure to respond resulted in Resolution 678, which directed whatever action may be necessary to restore peace and security to the region, in the absence of Iraq's withdrawal by 15 January 1991. Coalition forces led by American and British troops based in Saudi Arabia began the offensive almost immediately the deadline passed, the Iraqis responding with the firing of Scud missiles at cities in Saudi Arabia and Israel. With the allies soon gaining air superiority, the first three weeks of the war saw devastating bombing and missile raids against Baghdad and nuclear, chemical and military bases throughout Iraq. Mid-February saw a change of tactics, with air attacks on the Republican Guard's forward troop positions, convoys, tanks, and gun emplacements. On 19 February, in Moscow, Russian premier **Mikhail Gorbachev** presented a peace plan to Iraqi Foreign Minister Tariq Aziz, which provided for Iraq's withdrawal but not the removal from power of **Saddam Hussein** or the payment of reparations. In the absence of any response, on 22 February President **Bush** warned of an impending invasion, and following a wave of systematic executions by Iraqi troops in Kuwait City the next day, on 24 February Operation Desert Storm began with a ground offensive by coalition forces along a 125-mile front. Within 48 hours, Saddam Hussein announced on Baghdad Radio that all Iraqi forces were withdrawing from Kuwait and that it was no longer considered Iraqi territory. Coalition forces entered Kuwait City the next day, and by 05.00 GMT on 28 February, President Bush had announced a ceasefire and Baghdad unconditionally accepted all 12 UN Security Council resolutions. However, Iraqi forces left a final legacy of blazing Kuwait oil wells, and within days, Saddam Hussein had turned for revenge on his country's Kurdish population, who were forced to flee in their tens of thousands to the Turkish and Iranian borders.

Gunpowder Plot a plan devised by a Catholic convert, **Guy Fawkes**, to explode a huge quantity of gunpowder in a cellar below the Chamber of the House of Lords during the State Opening of Parliament in November 1605, with the aim of killing not only King **James I** and his Ministers but a sizeable number of the Protestant establishment. The conspirators, led by Robert Catesby, first obtained the tenancy of a house that abutted the Lords, and began the task of digging a connecting tunnel. That work was abandoned when they learnt of the existence of an empty cellar immediately below the Chamber, which one of them, using his connections at Court, was able to lease. A week before the State Opening, a Catholic peer, Lord Monteagle, received an anonymous warning to stay away from Parliament on 5 November. The letter was passed to **Robert Cecil**, Secretary of State, who guessed the significance of its reference to 'a big blow', and during a second search of Parliament only hours before the State Opening, Fawkes was caught red-handed in the cellar, which was stacked to the roof with barrels of gunpowder. Some of the intriguers managed to escape, and Fawkes refused to reveal their identity even after two days of being tortured. In January 1606, he and seven of his co-conspirators were part-hung, then decapitated and their heads set on spikes. Every year since, the cellars of the Lords are ritually searched at midnight on 4 November, and the anniversary of the Gunpowder Plot's discovery is marked throughout the kingdom by the burning of effigies of Guy Fawkes, and, in more recent times, by private and public firework displays. Some historians point to the ease with which the plotters were able to secure the best possible vantage point and install huge amounts of explosive undetected, to support their contention that the conspiracy was organized, or at least encouraged, by Cecil, to stir up more hatred of the Catholics and to increase his own standing in the king's eyes.

hamartia [*Greek*] a tragic or disastrous error of judgment or flaw in a person's character.

handwriting on the wall a warning of impending disaster; from the handwriting on the wall of Belshazzar's palace proclaiming the loss of his kingdom.

Hansard familiar name for the *Official Report*— the verbatim report of the proceedings of the British Parliament. It alludes to Thomas Curson Hansard, son of Luke Hansard, the Government printer who, with William Cobbett, produced the first reliable reports of parliamentary proceedings from 1803.

Hanseatic League a 13th-century confederacy of northern German towns designed to defend trade routes. By the 14th century, it reached the height of its political and trade influence, having extended to most of Germany and to several Dutch cities, but was disbanded in 1669.

hara-kiri [*Japanese*] ritual self-disembowelment; now more generally applied to any reckless course of action in which self-preservation is apparently not a consideration.

hard currency a strong currency that can easily be exchanged for others, usually at advantageous rates.

haute politique [*French*] high politics; diplomatic activity at the most senior level.

hauteur [*French*] exhibiting unbearable arrogance; adopting a lofty or detached attitude.

hauts faits [*French*] great accomplishments; meritorious deeds.

Heimat [*German*] one's actual or spiritual homeland.

Heimweh [*German*] nostalgia; a longing for the old order.

Helsinki process the series of **Conferences on Security and Co-operation in Europe (CSCE)** that began in Helsinki in 1978, and which led to the East-West nuclear non-proliferation pacts signed in the late 1980s.

Herrenvolk [*German*] the master race; a term adopted by the National Socialists to signify their pre-ordination to rule the world.

hic et nunc [*Latin*] here and now; without prevarication or delay.

Hillsborough Stadium disaster Britain's worst-ever sports disaster, in which 84 people were killed and 169 were seriously injured during the Liverpool and Nottingham Forest FA cup-final on 16 April 1989. The tragedy was blamed on police admitting thousands of Liverpool supporters just as the match began, whose extra numbers crushed to death those already on a section of the terraces, who were unable to escape because of the fencing erected to stop vandals gaining access to the field. A Government inquiry led to the introduction of revised policing methods and to the installation of safety gaps at grounds where anti-vandal fencing was installed.

Hinduism the religion of the majority of Indians, it has no founder, single creed or set of beliefs, or common scriptures—though the *Bhagavad gita*, from the Mahabharata, is widely followed. Hinduism embraces a great many gods, and frequently borrows and absorbs new concepts and divinities—for example, Jesus is venerated by its adherents. Common to all Hindus is observance of four castes and their sub-castes, for those outside them (the untouchables) are forbidden to take part in the religion and its rituals. Most Hindus belong to one of three sects; Shaivite (worshippers of Shiva), Vaishnavite (worshippers of Vishnu or Krishna), or Durga (the mother goddess).

Hiroshima Japanese coastal conurbation chosen as the target for **Little Boy**, the first atomic bomb ever dropped (on 6 August 1945), because of its importance as a centre of military and supply bases, shipyards, and industrial plants.

hodie mihi, cras tibi [*Latin*] your turn today, mine tomorrow; reciprocity.

hoi polloi [*Greek*] the multitude; a disparaging term to describe the masses.

holistics the practice of examining a system in its entirety for the purpose of gaining a proper understanding of one or more of its constituent parts.

hominis est errare [*Latin*] to err is human; man's fallibility is inevitable.

homme d'état [*French*] a statesman.

homo nullius coloris [*Latin*] a man of no party; an individual outwith the existing political establishment; a politician who owes allegiance only to his conscience.

honi soit qui mal y pense [*French*] shame to him who thinks evil of it; do not look for an ulterior motive, because none exists.

honneur et patrie [*French*] honour and country; the motto of the Legion of Honour.

honoris causa [*Latin*] for the sake of honour; face-saving.

honos habet onus [*Latin*] honour has its responsibilities; status imposes its own burdens.

horribile dictu [*Latin*] dreadful to tell; horrible to admit.

horribile visu [*Latin*] a dreadful thing to see; an awful event to witness.

hors de combat [*French*] out of the battle; no longer a significant participant or threat.

hors de jeu [*French*] out of the game; unrealistic politics.

hors de prise [*French*] safely out of danger; beyond harmful reach.

hors de propos [*French*] not suitable for the purpose; irrelevant.

hospodar [*Russian*] the title of princes of certain pre-revolutionary Russian territories.

hostis humani generis [*Latin*] an enemy of the human race; a threat to the whole world.

House of Commons the UK's elected constitutional assembly. The modern Lower House has its origins in the 1265 Parliament summoned by Simon de Montfort, which included borough representatives for the first time. Within 60 years, the Commons and Lords were acknowledged instruments of government, and their status was enhanced by **Thomas Cromwell**'s use of them to break with Rome. The conflict between the Lower House and **James I** and **Charles I** over the extent of the Commons' powers led to the 1642–51 Civil War and the establishment of republican government under **Oliver Cromwell**. The restoration of the monarchy in 1660 and **James II**'s attempt to rule absolutely triggered the **Glorious Revolution** of 1688 and, subsequently, the Commons' effective ascendency over the Crown. The 18th century saw the emergence of party politics in the Commons, and the Reform Acts passed between 1832 and 1884 took further power from the Upper House, which finally lost its right of veto in the Parliament Act 1911. Today's House of Commons returns Members of Parliament for 523 English constituencies, 38 Welsh constituencies, 72 Scottish constituencies, and 17 Northern Ireland constituencies, making a total of 650 MPs. Regular televising of the proceedings of the House of Commons began in 1988.

House of Lords the unelected Upper House of the UK's legislative assembly. The Lords originated from the 13th-century King's Court at which the monarch consulted with his barons. The membership of the modern House of Lords comprises the Lords Spiritual, in the form of two archbishops and 24 bishops, and the Lords Temporal—23 dukes, 27 marquesses, 158 earls and countesses, 102 viscounts, 24 bishops, and 850 barons and baronesses. There are also four royal peers. Although membership of the Lords numbers nearly 1200, only about half that number register their intention to attend at some time during a Session (the one-year parliamentary cycle). Unlike MPs, ordinary peers receive no salary but only an attendance fee for every day that they actually make an appearance in the Chamber—though Cabinet and junior Ministers and the Leader of the Opposition are remunerated in the same way as their counterparts in the Commons.

House of Representatives the Lower House of the American Congress, whose 435 seats are allocated according to the size of each state's population, and whose members are elected every two years. Only the House of Representatives can initiate money Bills and call for the impeachment of the President.

How to Win Friends and Influence People the title of a 1924 book on self-improvement based on the teachings of the American lecturer Dale Carnegie (1880–1958). The title has itself become synonymous with the adoption by political leaders of shallow or superficial solutions or attitudes to serious social, economic, and international problems.

hubris [*Greek*] insolence; an arrogant disregard for accepted conventions or established moral codes.

hurler à la lune [*French*] to howl at the moon; a futile attempt to complain about a higher authority.

hurler avec les loups [*French*] to howl with the wolves; slavishly to copy the actions of others.

hyperinflation rapidly escalating inflation that spirals upward beyond control, and which may trigger economic collapse.

IBEC (International Bank for Economic Co-Operation) A Moscow-based fund formed in 1963, to promote economic development and co-operation among its 10 member states, which include Cuba and Vietnam.

ICFTU (International Confederation of Free Trade Unions) a Brussels-based organization formed in 1949 to promote the interests of working people, defend fundamental human and trade union rights, and to reduce the gap between rich and poor. It is composed of 142 labour organizations in 97 countries, representing more than 85 million trade unionists.

ich dien [*German*] I serve; the motto of the Prince of Wales.

ICM (Islamic Constitutional Movement) Kuwaiti opposition group.

iconoclast [*Greek*] image-breaker; one who questions or criticizes attitudes and perceptions that are generally held as correct and justified out of tradition rather than by objective examination.

ICRC (International Committee of the Red Cross) an independent and wholly neutral worldwide humanitarian organization formed in 1863, for the purpose of alleviating general suffering and providing medical care in war. Its representatives are also charged with ensuring adherence to certain requirements of the **Geneva Convention**, such as those concerning prisoners of war. Its sister organizations, the League of Red Cross and Red Crescent Societies, operate in peace time, and mainly at a national level.

IDB (Inter-American Development Bank) a monetary union formed in 1959 to promote the individual and collective development of the economies and social infrastructures of its member states, which now total 45, including the UK, Canada, France, Germany, most South American countries, and the USA. Loans are repayable over a period of up to 40 years, and are backed by the provision of technical assistance to ensure the effective realization of the projects to which they relate. IDB loans in 1988 totalled more than $2360 million.

idée fixe [*French*] a fixed idea; intransigence.

idée reçue [*French*] generally accepted principle; conventional attitude.

idem [*Latin*] identical to the foregoing; precisely the same.

id est, ie [*Latin*] that is to say; by way of further explanation.

IFC (International Finance Corporation) an affiliate of the **World Bank**, founded in 1966 to encourage the economic development of its 128 member countries through investment in private enterprises.

ignorantia legis neminem excusat [*Latin*] ignorance of the law excuses nothing.

Ike the nickname since his schooldays of **Dwight D. Eisenhower**, 34th President of the USA. His 1953 election campaign used the slogan 'I Like Ike'.

il faut attendre le boiteux [*French*] wait for the lame man; the pace of progress is determined by the least able.

ILO (International Labour Organization) a body founded in 1919 under the Treaty of Versailles for the purpose of achieving lasting peace by improving social justice and working conditions throughout the world.

ils ne passeront pas [*French*] they shall not pass; the rallying cry of the French infantry at Verdun in World War I.

imam [*Arabic*] the title conferred on certain Moslem leaders, both spiritual and temporal.

imbada [*Zulu*] a meeting of South African tribal factions.

IMF (International Monetary Fund) a specialized agency of the United Nations established under the **Bretton Woods agreement** that provides short-term loans according to certain conditions of need and policy—typically to help overcome balance of payments problems.

im Jahre (der Welt) [*German*] in the year of the war.

impasse [*French*] a blind alley; an unresolvable difficulty; the point at which further negotiation becomes impossible.

imperium et libertas [*Latin*] empire and liberty; freedom and country.

imperium in imperio [*Latin*] one absolute authority within another; a sovereignty within a sovereignty.

in camera [*Latin*] held secretly; court proceedings held in private.

incartade [*French*] a crude insult; a personal attack completely lacking in sophistication.

in curia [*Latin*] in open court; a public examination.

indictum sit [*Latin*] it is best left unsaid.

Indochina the mainland of south-east Asia between India and China, comprising Burma, Cambodia, Laos, Malaya, Thailand, Vietnam, and Singapore.

in esse [*Latin*] actually in existence; not a figment of the imagination.

in flagrante delicto [*Latin*] in the very act; caught red-handed.

inflation a general trend of upward price movements, usually coupled with a fall in purchasing power.

infra dig(nitatem) [*Latin*] below one's dignity; not worth troubling about.

in genere [*Latin*] in kind; a comparable exchange.

Inkatha Freedom Party extremist South African black rights movement, whose supporters violently opposed the African National Congress for its conciliatory approach, resulting in the death of more than 4000 blacks in fighting between the two factions in Natal alone in the five years before the release of **Nelson Mandela** in 1990. On 29 January 1991, Mandela and Inkatha leader Chief **Buthelezi** signed a treaty to end the conflict between the two organizations. In July 1991 it was disclosed that Inkatha had been secretly funded by the South African Government. Dubbed Inkathagate, two Government ministers were demoted as a consequence.

in loco [*Latin*] in the proper place; in the right circumstances.

in medio [*Latin*] the middle course; the least radical approach.

in ocolus civium [*Latin*] in the public eye; out in the open.

in perpetuum [*Latin*] everlasting; for the rest of time.

in rem [*Latin*] a rightful legal action.

in tenebris [*Latin*] in a doubtful state; uncertainty.

inter alia [*Latin*] among other things.

inter arma leges silent [*Latin*] in war, the laws are silent.

Intergovernmental Conference on European Union a standing body charged with expanding the constitutional, security and commercial basis of the 1958 Treaty of Rome.

in terminis [*Latin*] in precise terms; unequivocably.

International Investment Bank a Moscow-based organization founded in 1970 for the purpose of providing medium and long-term funding for up to 15 years of projects related to the international socialist division of labour. Its 10 member countries include Cuba and Vietnam.

interregnum [*Latin*] a suspension of authority; the period of provisional government that occurs between the reigns of successive rulers.

intervention the action taken by a central bank to influence exchange rates or market stability; within the EEC, the purchase by member states of agricultural produce, in order artificially to maintain market prices at predetermined levels.

intifada [*Arabic*] uprising; the continuing revolt by Palestinians on the West Bank and **Gaza Strip** following the occupation of those territories by Israeli forces in December 1967 in the wake of the **Six Day War**.

in toto [*Latin*] the whole; in its entirety.

intra vires [*Latin*] falling within the powers (of).

intrigant [*French*] a conspirator, one who chooses to become involved in intrigues.

IOC (International Olympic Committee) the Swiss-based final authority on all matters concerning the Olympic Games and the Olympic movement. Its network of 167 National Olympic Committees throughout the world represent their respective countries' interests in, and arrange their representation at, the Games of the Olympiad, which are held every four years—Seoul (1988); Barcelona (1992). From 1994, when the venue will be Lillehammer, the Olympic Winter Games will be held in the second calendar year following that in which the Olympiad is staged.

IOM (International Organization for Migration) a non-political and humanitarian Geneva-based organization formed in 1950 to promote the sympathetic and orderly resettlement of refugees, persecuted minorities, and other displaced persons. It is composed of 35 full member countries, including Australia, Germany, Israel, Italy, and the USA. The 16 nations having observer status include the UK, Canada, France, and Spain.

IPE (International Petroleum Exchange) Paris-based organization formed in 1973 by 21 of the

West's most significant oil consuming nations, in the wake of that year's oil crisis.

IPLA (Irish People's Liberation Army) an off-shoot of Irish National Liberation Army (itself an **IRA** breakaway group) that once had left-wing pretensions, but which in the 1980s became identified more with drug dealing—an activity forbidden to IRA supporters and punishable by execution.

ipse dixit [*Latin*] he himself uttered it; an assertion supported by indisputable evidence.

ipso facto [*Latin*] by that very fact; a necessary consequence.

ipso jure [*Latin*] under the law itself; in accordance with existing provisions.

IPU (Inter-Parliamentary Union) founded in 1889 by two parliamentarians—one a member of the House of Commons, the other a member of the French Assembly—the IPU exists to resolve international disputes by peaceful means through its network of Back-Benchers in 113 countries, who provide an informal channel of communication between their respective Governments, even when they have formally broken off diplomatic relations.

IRA (Irish Republican Army) Irish nationalist organization founded in 1919 that successfully fought the British for independence between 1919 and 1921, and which continued to press for a wholly-independent republic after the signing of the subsequent treaty. The IRA, which was declared illegal in 1923, embarked on its first bombing campaign in 1939, and terrorist attacks in the North grew in intensity between 1956 and 1962. Over the past 20 years, IRA sectarian violence—which has often been reciprocated by outlawed loyalist groups—has been supplemented with the killing of British troops and suspected informers, together with outrages on the British mainland. In 1969, the organization and its political wing, **Sinn Fein**, split into the Official IRA, which seeks a socialist 32-county republic, and the Provisional IRA, whose avowed aim is to expel the British from the Province. A third faction, the Irish National Liberation Army, aims to achieve both objectives solely by terrorism. From the mid-1980s, the IRA adopted a policy of attacking only political and military targets on the mainland and abroad, so as not to alienate British public opinion—but that tactic appeared to have been abandoned with the London bombings of Paddington and Victoria railway stations in February 1991, which occurred shortly after the mortar attack on No.10 Downing Street during a meeting of the **Gulf War** Cabinet.

Irangate the 1986–7 scandal that threatened **Ronald Reagan**'s second presidential term, centring on the illegal sale of arms to Iran, partly to help ensure the return of American hostages, but also to fund anti-Marxist Contra guerilla fighters in Nicaragua. It brought the resignations of White House chief-of-staff Donald Regan and

National Security Adviser Rear-Admiral **John Poindexter**. In May 1989, White House aide Colonel **Oliver North** was convicted of misleading Congress and of accepting an illegal gift, but was cleared on nine other counts.

Irish Free State the name by which the Republic of Ireland was known between 1921 and 1937.

Iron Chancellor the name given to Prince **Otto Bismarck**, first Chancellor of the German Empire, from his famous remark to the Prussian Parliament in 1886 that his policy was one of 'Blut und Eisen'—blood and iron.

iron curtain the philosophical divide between the communist east and the democracies of western Europe, physically represented by the post-war border that separated East Germany, Czechoslovakia, Hungary and Yugoslavia from the West. The phrase was made famous by **Winston Churchill** in an address to an American college in 1946, but it was first used to describe an impenetrable barrier in 1817, and to describe Soviet isolationism in Ethel Snowden's 1920 book, *Through Bolshevik Russia*. The term largely became redundant with the democratization of several eastern European countries in 1989 and 1990.

Iron Duke the name given to Arthur Wellesley, 1st Duke of **Wellington**, soldier and Prime Minister, which alluded not only to his great strengths as a military commander but the iron gates that he erected around his London home, Apsley House, to repel rioters angry at his opposition to the Reform Bill.

Iron Lady the name used by the Russian newspaper *Red Star* to describe Prime Minister **Margaret Thatcher** in 1976, alluding to her strong anti-communist stance at that time.

irredentism [*Italian*] a policy of forceful acquisition of adjacent territories, exemplified by the efforts of the 19th-century Italian irredentists.

Islam [*Arabic*] the religion founded by Muhammad in Saudi Arabia in the sixth century, which has 600 million followers, or Muslims, worldwide. Its doctrine is enshrined in the Koran, or Holy Qu'ran, which records the teachings that Muhammad received from the angel Gabriel, as well as the prophet's own words (Hadith) and practices (sunna). Islam holds that there is only one God (Allah), that Mohammad is the only true messenger of God because the Torah and Bible distort the teachings of Moses and Jesus, and that it is the duty of Muslims to spread the faith throughout the world, by violent means if necessary. Mainstream Muslims are **Sunnis**; the members of the persecuted breakaway sects are known as **Shiites**.

Islamic Development Bank a Jeddah-based international financial institution founded in 1973 to encourage the economic development and social progress of its 45 member countries, sometimes by the provision of interest-free loans. Funding for 1986–7 totalled nearly 600 million dinars.

Islamic Jihad (for the Liberation of Palestine) one of several pro-Iranian **Shiite** groups whose tactics have included kidnapping Europeans to use as hostages in negotiating the release of Lebanese Shiites held in southern Lebanon and elsewhere.

Jacobins extreme French republicans led by **Maximilien Robespierre** and others, from 1780 to 1795.

Jacobites supporters of the claim to the British throne of the deposed **James VII** and **II** and his son, James, who were concentrated mainly in Scotland after the 1691 conquest of Ireland.

jacta est alea [*Latin*] the die is cast; there is no turning back.

Jamaica Agreement a 1976 **International Monetary Fund** agreement to abolish the official gold price and to change the system of fixed rates on which IMF rules were formerly based, in favour of one allowing for greater flexibility.

Janata Dal (S) Indian political party that formed a minority Government in 1990–1 with the support of the much larger Congress (I) Party.

januis clausis [*Latin*] behind closed doors; in secret.

Jarrow crusade the 1936 march by dock workers from Jarrow on Tyneside to London, in protest at the closure of Palmer's shipyard under a rationalization programme, which made two-thirds of the town's work force unemployed.

ja, wohl [*German*] most certainly; quite so.

j curve a graphic interpretation of the characteristic pattern that follows devaluation, in which the trade balance initially worsens as import prices rise, but then recovers as exports improve as a consequence of their lower prices to overseas buyers.

je maintiendrai [*French*] I will maintain; the motto of the Netherlands.

je ne sais quoi [*French*] I do not know what it is; a certain something; an indefinable yet definite quality—usually applied to people rather than objects.

jeu de hasard [*French*] a game of chance; a risky course of action.

je vis en espoir [*French*] one lives in hope.

jihad [*Arabic*] striving; any Muslim war or action against the enemies of Islam; a campaign motivated by a strongly-held belief, rather than by the prospect of territorial gains.

John Bull a once-popular but now outdated graphic personification of the British character, perhaps inspired by the minor 17th-century organist of that name who composed a national anthem. He first appeared in print in John Arbuthnot's 1712 political satire, *The History of John Bull*, and lent his name to a weekly journal published in 1906. John Bull is usually depicted as cheerful and rotund, dressed in garments whose design borrows from the Union Jack, and accompanied by a British bulldog.

Judaism the religion of the Jewish race—the descendants of the ancient Israelites and Hebrews. Jews hold that there is only one God, and their four main festivals—Passover, Pentecost, Tabernacles and Chanukah—are based largely on historical events. Also important is the festival of repentance, Rosh Hashanah, and the Day of Atonement, or Yom Kippur. Jewish teachings are taken from the laws recorded by Moses in the Torah, and the early rabbis' interpretation of them in the Talmud. The past century has seen the traditional orthodox majority supplemented by progressive groups—who even worship in separate synagogues—such as the conservatives, liberals and reformists.

Judendeutsch [*German*] Jewish-German, Yiddish.

Judenhetze [*German*] the persecution of Jews, specifically that practised in Nazi Germany.

junta [*Spanish*] a self-elected and usually dictatorial body, such as a military regime.

jure non dono [*Latin*] by right (under the law); not a concession.

jus gentium [*Latin*] the common law of nations; values shared by all civilized peoples.

juste milieu [*French*] the just mean; a fair form of government that avoids taking extreme measures.

Kampf der Anschauugen [*German*] a difference of opinion; a dispute.

Kampf ums Dasein [*German*] a struggle for existence.

Kapital, Das a three-volume critical and systematic study of the capitalist system by **Karl Marx** (1818–83), according to the principles of his Communist Manifesto. The first volume was published in 1867, and the second and third, completed by **Friedrich Engels** from Marx's notes, appeared between 1885 and 1894.

Kellogg-Briand Pact an international pledge to observe perpetual friendship negotiated by US Secretary of State **Frank B. Kellogg** (1856–1937) and French Foreign Minister **Aristide Briand** (1862–1932), and signed in Paris in 1928 by 15 nations and, later, by 48 others. It succeeded only in dealing with some South American disputes, but was clearly of little value when invoked against the Japanese invasion of Manchuria in 1931, Italy's 1938 action against Ethiopia, or the start of Hitler's territorial aggression.

Kennedy round the round of **GATT** industrial tariff cuts achieved between 1964 and 1967, largely brought about by the US Trade Expansion Act introduced by President **John F. Kennedy**.

Kenya emergency the state of emergency that existed in Kenya between 1952 and 1956, during which anti-colonial Kikuyu tribal militants, the Mau Mau, massacred 100 Europeans and 2000 African loyalists, at a cost of 11 000 rebel lives.

KGB Committee of State Security; the Soviet secret police concerned with internal security and international intelligence operations. It was formed in 1954 to replace the even more sinister and brutal MGB (Ministry of State Security) that operated between 1946 and 1953 under Laventi Beria; many of its leaders were accused of implication in the failed attempt (Aug 1991) to remove **Gorbachev** from power.

khaki election the 1900 general election victory enjoyed by the Conservatives on the tide of patriotism engendered by the second Boer War; more generally, any electoral success owing to similar circumstances.

kibbutz [*Hebrew*] an Israeli collective farm.

Knesset [*Hebrew*] the Israeli Parliament.

kolkhoz [*Russian*] a Russian collective farm.

Komeito the Clean Government Party of Japan, which achieved the power of veto over the traditional ruling Social Democratic Party by winning 20 seats in the Upper House in the 1989 elections, following revelations about Government corruption. Komeito is an offshoot of Soka Gakkai, a born-again Buddhist cult founded in 1930 but based on the teachings of a 13th-century holy man. In World War II, Soka Gakkai's leader was jailed by Japan's thought police and starved to death. The organization was unbanned in 1964 and formed Komeito as its political wing, but six years later the party broke its secular links to broaden its appeal.

Korean War the period of hostilities between the country's communist northern territories and the south that began when Soviet-backed North Korean troops crossed the 38th parallel on 25 June 1950 at the start of a full-scale invasion. US forces under the command of General **Douglas MacArthur** came to the aid of the south soon after, but MacArthur was dismissed after a year for defying President **Truman** by publicly advocating the escalation of the war to China. The war ended with an armistice that partitioned the country, which was signed on 27 July 1953 during **Eisenhower**'s first term as president.

Kremlin the 12th-century Moscow citadel that now contains the former Imperial Palace, three cathedrals, and a number of Government offices. It is popularly if inaccurately used to signify the centre of Soviet power, in the way that No. 10 Downing Street and the White House are taken to be representative of their countries' respective Governments.

Krieg [*German*] war.

Ku Klux Klan a name encompassing two American secret societies. The first was formed by ex-Confederates in 1866 to discourage the newly enfranchised blacks from using their votes, but was outlawed by Congress and disbanded in 1871. In 1915, the society was revived in Georgia with the avowed aim of achieving 'pure' Americanism and white supremacy, and the Klan's estimated 20 million supporters in the southern states persecuted blacks, Catholics, Jews, and

pacifists, and vilified Darwinism, birth control, and the repeal of prohibition. Newspaper campaigns against the Klan's terrorist activities—exemplified by lynchings of blacks and arson attacks on the homes of blacks and whites who sympathized with them—saw its decline in the 1920s, but it enjoyed renewed popularity at the end of World War II and in the 1960s, as a reaction to **John F. Kennedy**'s civil rights legislation.

Kultur [*German*] racial or nationalistic arrogance; the imposition of one's own values on other nations.

kulturny [*Russian*] the propagation of Marxism.

Kuomintang [*Chinese*] the radical People's National Party, founded by **Sun Yixian** (Sun Yat-sen) in 1912.

kurzem [*German*] in brief; to summarize.

Labour Party political body formed in 1899 (known initially as the Labour Representation Committee) by the Trades Union Congress that linked the existing Independent Labour Party, trade unions, and other socialist organizations for the purpose of securing working class representation in Parliament, which it achieved in 1901 with the return of three Labour MPs. In the 1906 general election, LRC (Labour Representation Committee) secretary **Ramsay MacDonald** made a secret pact with the Liberals that provided for a straight contest between Labour and Tory candidates in certain seats to win 29 seats for the new faction, which thereafter was known as the Labour Party. In 1909, the miners' federation switched its support from the Lib-Lab pact to back the Labour Party exclusively, which, together with Labour participation in the wartime Government, the extension of the franchise in 1918, and the Liberals' failing appeal, helped to secure 57 Labour seats in the 1918 election—more than doubling to 142 in 1922, in which year MacDonald became party leader. Continuing division among the Liberals permitted him to form a minority Government the following year, and again in 1929, but its adherence to Liberal finance and foreign policies during a world depression and inter-party disputes over cuts in welfare benefits, together with the loss of MacDonald and other key figures to the National Government, saw the number of Labour MPs fall from 288 to 52 in 1931–2. By 1935, the party's fortunes had recovered to the extent that it was able successfully to field 154 candidates in that year's general election, and its subsequent role in the wartime coalition, coupled with its promotion of welfare reform and support for its now clearly-defined social and economic policies brought triumph for **Clement Attlee** in the 1945 election, with Labour taking 394 seats against the Conservatives' 213. However, the new Administration's ambitious programme of nationalization and its establishment of the National Health Service did little to placate public discontent with continuing austerity, and 1951 brought the first of three successive general election defeats for the party, whose public appeal was hardly helped by splits between the ideological left and the pragmatists typified by its new leader, **Hugh Gaitskell**. However, those rifts had healed, or were successfully disguised, by 1963 when Gaitskell's successor, **Harold Wilson**, embarked on an inspired vote-catching campaign that, while reassuring the socialist traditionalists, exploited the new god of technology and the mood for change among baby boomers who had never known anything but a Conservative-controlled state. His narrow 1964 general election majority improved to 96 in 1966, and while Labour fulfilled many of its manifesto promises, it failed lamentably—not least because of a often hostile domestic financial establishment—to grapple with the country's economic difficulties, and suffered a singular lack of success in acting as a positive influence in foreign affairs (typified by its passive stance over Vietnam, the Rhodesia fiasco, and inter-party squabbling over Common Market membership). Together with a rash of union disputes triggered by the Government's need to control inflation, the electorate had all the excuses that they needed to return to a Conservative Government under **Edward Heath** in 1970, but it fared little better and Wilson returned to Downing Street by a whisker in February 1974. A second election in October gave the party a safe working majority under its new leader, **James Callaghan**, but his narrow approach to the country's economic problems, increasing party divisions, further union disruption, and Britain's declining influence as a world power saw the electorate turn again to the Conservatives in the 1979 election, with Labour holding only 251 seats. Growing personal prosperity and the emergence of the middle-way Social Democratic Party-Liberal alliance further eroded Labour's representation to 209 in the 1983 election, but it recovered slightly in 1987 to take another 20 seats—most of them from the Conservatives. Under the leadership of **Neil Kinnock** since 1983, Labour has worked hard to broaden its appeal to the middle classes, not least by soft-pedalling or even abandoning its former hardline policies on renationalization and nuclear disarmament and outlawing Militant Tendency. By the start of the 1990s, and buttressed by its highly effective and popular opposition to the **poll tax**, it consistently pulled far enough ahead in the opinion polls to suggest certain victory in any imminent general election, but the Conservatives enjoyed an immediate reversal of fortune with the resignation of **Margaret Thatcher** and her replacement by **John Major**, which he consolidated with his impressive handling of Britain's involvement in the 1991 **Gulf War**, the scrapping of the poll tax, and his upbeat first Budget—with the result that with the next general election on the horizon, Labour was consistently being beaten by the Liberal Democrats in by-elections in which it should have made some headway, and was running neck-and-neck with the Conservatives in the opinion polls.

Labourer's statute a law passed in 1351 in an attempt to stabilize the English economy in the wake of the Black Death, it represented the first ever attempt to control wages and prices by freezing wages and the prices of manufactured articles, and by restricting the movement of labour. Like most subsequent attempts, it failed abysmally to achieve its aims and contributed largely to the 1381 **peasants' revolt.**

Lady's Not for Burning, The 1949 verse play by Christopher Fry whose title was famously borrowed by **Margaret Thatcher** at the 1980 Conservative party conference, for a speech reasserting her Government's continuing strict adherence to their proclaimed economic policies.

lacuna [*Latin*] a hiatus; a gap or failing in an argument or proposition.

lagadoism ludicrous initiatives; the commissioning of pointless schemes; from Jonathan Swift's *Gulliver's Travels*, in which the wise men of Lagado busy themselves with useless endeavours such as converting ice into gunpowder and distilling sunbeams from cucumbers.

LAIA (Latin American Integration Association) a body of 11 Latin American countries established in 1980, to replace the Latin American Free Trade Association that operates a flexible system of tariff preferences between its member states.

laisser-aller [*French*] *without constraint; excessive lack of control.*

laisser-faire [*French*] let do; the principle that problems should be allowed to resolve themselves without state intervention; a casual or passive attitude to the difficulties of others.

lama [*Tibetan*] Buddhist monk or priest of Tibet.

Last Man name given to **Charles I** by parliamentarians, fondly imagining that he would be the last English monarch.

latet anguis in herba [*Latin*] a snake in the grass; a hidden peril.

LDCs (less-developed countries) those nations that are in the process of achieving a better level of economic and social development.

League of Arab States (Arab League) Tunis-based voluntary association of 22 sovereign Arab states established in 1945 to co-ordinate their trade and political activities. In 1976 it established the Arab Deterrent Force to supervise efforts to bring peace to Lebanon, with Saudi Arabia, Kuwait, United Arab Emirates and Qatar meeting 65 per cent of the costs and the league's other members making up the balance.

League of Nations formed in 1920 under the **Treaty of Versaille**, to encourage open diplomacy rather than the secret covenants and treaties that preceded it. Dominated initially by Britain and France because of America's failure to ratify its membership, the league was influential in social innovations such as the **International Labour Organization**, but in the absence of any military strength of its own was unable to intercede effectively against Japan or Italy in World War II and was eventually dissolved in 1946, to be replaced by the **United Nations**.

Lebensraum [*German*] room for living; making sufficient provision for an increasing population; a Nazi slogan.

Légion d'Honneur [*French*] Napoleonic order founded in 1802 to acknowledge civil or military distinction.

Leipzig, Battle of also called the Battle of the Nations, it brought the defeat in October 1813 of **Napoleon Bonaparte**'s army by the combined Prussian, Austrian, Swedish and Russian forces.

Leitmotiv [*German*] a recurring theme or argument. The popular alternative spelling sometimes offered of leitmotif is understandable but incorrect.

Leninism a variant of the theories of **Karl Marx**, including the doctrine that capitalism contains the seeds of its own downfall but that that should not be a cause of complacency among the working class, and that every era presents revolutionary opportunities that should be acknowledged and seized by the workers. He held also that imperialism is the highest form of capitalism, and that although every revolution must have the working class as its motive force, the party is a necessary element in ensuring its success and administering the new society that results.

lèse-majesté [*French*] working against the interests of the sovereign or nation; unjustified superiority, or the exercise of unwarranted control.

lettre de marque [*French*] a royal warrant giving authority to carry out reprisals against a hostile state.

levée en masse [*French*] the state mobilization of all persons capable of bearing arms in a civil war or at the start of hostilities against another nation.

Levellers (1) ultra-republican group active between 1647 and 1649, consisting mainly of soldiers in the parliamentary army during the English Civil War, whose followers advocated the vote for all men and an end to class distinctions. It was led by John Swinburne (1614–57); (2) illegal 18th-century association of Irish agitators, also known as the Whiteboys.

Liberal Party British political organization that began to emerge in 1859 from a combination of Whig and radical parliamentarians, including **William Gladstone**, Lord **John Russell** and John Bright, and which consolidated itself as the main opposition to the Conservatives with its success in the 1868 election, which was fought mainly on the issue of the disestablishment of the church of Ireland. However, its early popularity was short lived, and Gladstone hardly helped to restore its fortunes by fighting shy of **Joseph Chamberlain**'s efforts to establish a formal manifesto, believing

that the Liberals should appeal to the country on broad moral issues that avoided the risk of dividing the party. His policy proved sound enough to return the Liberals to power for a year in 1885, but his continued resistance to Whig initiatives and his stance on Irish home rule finally compelled the Whigs to seek an alliance with the Conservatives, bringing Gladstone's defeat in 1886. The Liberals' fortunes improved slightly over the next five years, but the leadership crisis that followed Gladstone's departure denied them office again in 1895. Over the next few years, the party continued to flourish fitfully and in disarray, suffering from the split between the Rosebery wing, which sought educational and social reforms and which was prepared to co-operate with the Conservatives in achieving them, and the radicals. The turn of the century brought a change of policy direction more in tune with the working-class electorate, not least as a reaction to the growing appeal of the newly-emerged Labour Party, which won its first three seats in 1903. Whatever the influence, it brought the Liberals a landslide victory in 1906, and thereafter it changed from being a largely sectarian and regional party to one that espoused class representation, exemplified by **Asquith**'s trade union and social reforms. The divisiveness that had dogged the party since its inception showed itself again during World War I, especially after **Lloyd George** had assumed the premiership in 1916, and the loss of more than 100 seats in the 1918 election was only a foretaste of its catastrophic performance in 1924, when only 40 Liberals were returned. Despite Lloyd George's efforts at Keynesian reform, the party's support dipped still further, until in 1945 it had only 12 MPs. It managed to retain even that tiny representation only with Conservative help through the 1950s, but by the early 1960s, under the leadership of **Jo Grimond**, it began to enjoy a new measure of public support as a steadying influence in what had long been a two-party system, and was given new impetus in 1962 when Eric Lubbock (later Lord Avebury) overturned the safe Tory seat of Orpington. Throughout the next two decades, under both **Jeremy Thorpe** and **David Steel**, the Liberals consistently performed well in general elections, often pushing the Labour candidate into third place—which understandably prompted their increasing agitation for proportional representation. A brief flirtation with Labour allowed **Callaghan**'s Administration to retain power at the end of the 1970s but did little to endear the Liberals to the electorate, and from the early 1980s the party concentrated on cultivating its image as the honest broker of British politics. It broadened its appeal still further by eventually absorbing the remnants of the Social Democratic Party, and after two name changes emerged as the Liberal Democratic Party in 1990 with **Paddy Ashdown** as its leader. Its stunning by-election successes in the Tory strongholds of Eastbourne (1990) and Ribble

Valley (1991), together with an ever-improving showing in the opinion polls, suggested that the next general election would be one of the best ever for a party that had dwelt so long in the political doldrums.

Libertins French 17th- and 18th-century free thinkers and sceptics who questioned the validity and morality of all received religions and the societies that they produce.

liberty cap a small red felt cap presented to a Roman slave on being given his liberty; it was adopted by the French revolutionaries as a symbol of their freedom from the authority of the throne.

lictor [*Latin*] an officer in ancient Rome who attended upon a dictator, consul, or magistrate, responsible for enforcing his superior's judgements and carrying out executions.

Likud Israeli right-wing political party.

Lillibulero 17th-century political marching song, with music by Henry Purcell and lyrics by Thomas Wharton, that satirized **James II** and the Catholics, and the title of which was ironically used by Irish Catholics as the password during their 1641 massacre of Protestants.

lingua franca [*Italian*] Frankish tongue; the mixed-language, simplified Italian, once used in the Levant—hence a common form of communication or implied agreement between different nationalities.

Lion of Judah the Ethiopian people's respectful and affectionate name for **Haile Selassie**, emperor of Ethiopia from 1930 until his dethronement in 1974.

Lisle letters a 1981 selection of correspondence from Viscount Lisle, illegitimate son of Edward IV and courtier of **Henry VIII**, which gives a vivid insight into political and domestic life in 16th-century England.

littera scripta manet [*Latin*] the written word survives; it is better to have it in writing.

Little Boy the four-ton atomic bomb, equivalent to 12 700 tons of high explosive, dropped by the USAF B-29 superfortress, Enola Gay, on **Hiroshima** at 8.15 am on 6 August 1945. Exploding 580m above ground level, it vaporized the area immediately below at temperatures in excess of 5000C, flattened 10 sq km 6 sq ml of the city, and created a 10000m-high mushroom-shaped cloud that spread fallout over a much wider area. An estimated 100000 of the city's 290000 population were killed instantly and another 160000 died within five years from radiation sickness. Despite this 'peep into hell', as it was described by one of the Enola Gay's crew, Japan surrendered only after **Fat Man** was detonated over Nagasaki three days later.

Little Englander derisory name originally applied to the Victorians who opposed British imperialism and colonization, believing that their country could be self-sufficient; more recently used to describe those who resist closer economic and social ties with the other member states of the **European Community.**

Little Red Book media nickname for a collection of the communist doctrinaire sayings of Chinese leader **Mao Zedong** published in 1966 as part of the Cultural Revolution.

local government elections a fragmented electoral scheme for electing British local authorities. In 1991, for example, all English and district councils held elections. The non-metropolitan 'shire' districts have the right to choose between all-out elections every four years, or elections by thirds three years out of four. The fourth year is set aside for county elections, last held in 1989. Local autority areas are divided into wards, each represented by two or three councillors. In 1991, no elections were held in London, Scotland or Northern Ireland.

Locarno Pact a series of agreements initiated at Locarno in October 1925 and ratified in London on 1 December which guaranteed the existing borders between Germany and France and Germany and Belgium, and the signing of which by Germany gained her admission to the **League of Nations**. The pact was formally denounced by **Hitler** in 1936, shortly before he sent troops into the Rhineland.

Lockerbie disaster the world's worst terrorist attack on an in-flight aircraft, when a bomb exploded aboard a Pan Am Boeing 747 flight from Frankfurt to America via London on 22 December 1988, killing all 258 passengers and crew. Another 17 people people died when the flaming fuselage and other wreckage fell on the Scottish village of Lockerbie. An official inquiry blamed the attack on the Liberation of Palestine General Command led by Aimed Jimbril, and criticized Pan Am's lack of effective security measures and procedures.

locus standi [*Latin*] the established position; an acknowledged state of affairs.

Lollards ('mumblers') [*Dutch*] originally the nickname for a group of 14th-century Dutch Franciscans who disputed the authority of Rome; and later, to describe the followers of the 14th-century English ecclesiastical reformer John Wycliffe—who by the time of his death in 1395 were said to number one man in every two. The movement was suppressed by the House of Lancaster and died out by the 16th century, though to some extent it can be said to have inspired the English Reformation.

Lomé Convention an agreement made between the **EEC** and a number of developing nations in Africa, the Caribbean and the Pacific, that covered development assistance and preferential trade terms.

Long March the 6000-mile/9600-km trek by **Mao Zedong** and his followers from south-east to north-west China between 1934 and 1935, after they had incurred the displeasure of **Jiang Jieshi**.

Long Parliament the assembly of November 1640 that followed the dissolution of the **Short Parliament**, which impeached the Earl of **Strafford**; cited the unconstitutional acts of **Charles I** and demanded reform; and ultimately conducted the Civil War against the king's forces. In 1648, the Long Parliament expelled those of its members who were willing to reach a compromise with Charles, with those remaining constituting the **Rump Parliament** that was forcibly dissolved by **Oliver Cromwell** in 1653 but twice recalled in 1659. The following year, the Rump Parliament sat again, briefly, with the members expelled in 1648, before declaring its own dissolution.

Lonrho affair the award of high salary increases to the directors of Tiny Rowlands' Lonrho multinational in 1973, at a time when **Edward Heath**'s Conservative Government was urging workers and management to contain pay awards in the interests of the economy, and which prompted Heath's famous comment about the 'unacceptable face of capitalism'.

Lord Haw-Haw name coined by *Daily Express* radio critic Jonah Barrington, to describe the British traitor William Joyce (1906–46), who broadcast Nazi propaganda from Germany during World War II, for which he was eventually executed.

Lord Porn media nickname for the Catholic convert Earl of **Longford** (Frank Pakenham), for his vigorous 1970s campaigns against pornography and sexual licence.

lost generation the American generation of rootless, disillusioned men and women who reached maturity between World War I and the Great Depression of the 1930s.

lotus eaters those who stand aside from the realities of life while enjoying a luxurious or privileged existence themselves, from the Greek belief that eating the fruit of the lotus tree produced a state of happy forgetfulness.

Louisiana purchase the 1803 acquisition from France for $15 million of the 1332000 sq km/828000 sq ml lying between the Mississippi River and the Rocky Mountains, which doubled the then area of the United States.

Louvre Accord a currency agreement made between G5 countries and Canada in Paris in 1987 to help halt the decline of the dollar and re-establish a better balance of trade, and to encourage world economic growth without inflation.

Luddites name given to those who resist technical innovations because of their effect on working practices and as a cause of redundancies; from the name given to the 19th-century workers who rioted against the mechanization of the farming and the textile industries, whose ringleaders included a Leicestershire farm hand, Ned Ludd.

Lumpenproletariat [*German*] term coined by **Karl Marx** to describe the common people; those without culture, influence or wealth.

Machtpolitik [*German*] power politics.

Machtübernahme [*German*] attaining power by force, particularly as practised by the National Socialist Party in Germany in 1933.

macroeconomics the overall study of a nation's activity and prosperity as measured against its level of national income, employment, wages and prices, consumption, and investment.

mad cow disease (bovine spongiform encephalopathy, BSE) a neural disorder found mainly in British cattle and similar to Creutzfeldt-Jakob disease in sheep, thought to be caused by infected feedstuff. Its increasing incidence in 1990 caused widespread public concern, and despite Government assurances that the health risk to humans and to pets from consuming meat from infected animals was neglible, 2000 school canteens stopped serving domestic beef products, home sales fell sharply, and Britain's £300 million export market was hit by bans or restrictions imposed by America, West Germany, Bahrain, Australia, and New Zealand.

Mad Mitch nickname for a British Army officer, Lieutenant-Colonel Colin Mitchell (1925–), for his audacious and courageous tactics in the 1967 Aden uprising, and who subsequently served briefly as a Conservative MP.

Mad Monk name first applied to **Grigori Rasputin**, notorious for his bogus piety and sway over the last Russian Tsarina, Alexandra; the nickname awarded by the British satirical magazine *Private Eye* to Sir **Keith Joseph**, in his capacity as a close friend of and adviser to **Margaret Thatcher** during her premiership.

Mae West factor a pollsters' term for the tendency among uncommitted members of the electorate to vote in general elections for the party in Opposition on the ground that it could not be worse than the current Administration. It borrows from the quip by the American actress that when choosing between two evils, she always favoured the one that she had not yet tried.

magisterium [*Latin*] the authoritative teachings of the Church.

Magna Carta the document signed by King John at Runnymede in 1215 that marked the beginnings of English democracy by permanently limiting by law the king's powers. Insisted upon by feudal barons embittered by the monarch's high taxation, uninspired government, and persecution of possible rivals for the throne, the charter required the consent of a counsel of the realm before the imposition of taxation, and that a free man could not be imprisoned or deprived of his property without being judged by his peers.

mal du siècle [*French*] pessimism of the state of the world; weary of life.

mañana [*Spanish*] there is always tomorrow; an excuse for inaction.

Manhattan Project code name for the work of designing and constructing America's first atomic bomb, which began at Colombia University in Manhattan in 1942 under the control of US Army engineer Brigadier General Leslie R. Groves, with Robert Oppenheimer as scientific director. Two years earlier, **Albert Einstein** tried to persuade President **Franklin D. Roosevelt** to sanction the development of an A-bomb, based on the physicist's own theory of relativity as applied to the work of the Hungarian-born physicist Leo Szilard and and the Italian-born physicist Enrico Fermi—both victims of Jewish persecution who fled to America—and the all-important successful experiments in nuclear chain reaction by two German physicists, Otto Hahn and Fritz Strassman, who had taken refuge in Britain. Roosevelt initially resisted the project, but relented after the Japanese attack on Pearl Harbour on 7 December 1941. Work continued at a special laboratory at Los Alamos, New Mexico, with production of the alternative fissile components uranium 235 and plutonium undertaken at a factory in Oak Ridge, Tennessee, and at a nuclear reactor at Hanford, Washington State, respectively. The $2000 million programme culminated in the world's first nuclear test, using a plutonium-based device, in the Mexico desert on 16 July 1945. Three weeks later, **Little Boy** was dropped on **Hiroshima**.

manifesto [*Italian*] a public declaration of intent; the statement of policy traditionally issued by political parties as the basis of their appeal to voters before any general election.

man of steel popular name for the Soviet leader **Joseph Stalin**, whose hardline political beliefs were coincidentally reflected by his surname, which is the Russian word for 'steel'.

man on the Clapham omnibus a description of the ordinary citizen, or the average member of the electorate, whose heart and mind are the traditional targets of British politicians. The term was first used in 1903 by Lord Bowen in giving his judgement on a case of negligence.

Mansfield judgement the 1772 ruling by Lord Justice Mansfield in a case involving a runaway black slave that slavery was neither allowed nor approved under English law, and which effectively abolished slavery in England and Wales.

maquisard [*French*] a World War II French freedom fighter.

Marconi scandal the furore that resulted from unfounded accusations made in 1912 by Conservative politicians and anti-Semitic journalists that Liberal Ministers, including **David Lloyd George** had speculated in the shares of the Marconi Wireless Company at the time that it was granted an empire-wide contract for its radio system.

marje name given to the world spiritual leader of Shiite Muslims.

Marshall aid financial programme of European reconstruction devised by US General George Marshall in 1945, and implemented with the support of British Foreign Secretary **Aneurin Bevan**, which resulted in 16 European nations—other than Finland, Spain, and the Communist states, which refused assistance—receiving aid totally $13000 million plus $1000 million in low-interest loans. The scheme was wound up in 1951.

Marxism see **communism**.

Mau Mau the name given to the Kikuyu militants who during the Kenya emergency that lasted from 1952 until 1956 murdered at least 100 Europeans and 2000 African loyalists, and lost 11000 of their own forces.

May Day a public holiday observed by many countries, usually on the first Monday in May, to celebrate international socialism.

MCA (monetary compensatory amount) a differential, calculated weekly, between **green currencies** and the real foreign exchange value of EC currencies. It serves as an import subsidy for countries having a weak currency, but at the same time makes their farm exports more costly. It has the opposite effect on countries having a strong currency, but ensures that the prices paid to their farmers do not fall.

Medicins sans Frontières French charity that specializes in providing neutral medical personnel in war zones.

medio tutissimus ibis [*Latin*] pass safely in the middle; the moderate course is the safest.

Mein Kampf ('My Struggle'); the title of **Adolf Hitler's** 1924 book (the English translation of which was published in 1940), which combines autobiographical passages with anti-Semitic rantings and a chillingly accurate forecast of the way that Hitler intended to transform central Europe.

me judice [*Latin*] in my opinion.

mêlée [*French*] a disorganized, hostile confrontation; a heated argument.

menshevik [*Russian*] smaller; a moderate faction within the Russian Socialist Party that came to prominence at the 1903 congress.

MER (multiple exchange rate) a system of differential values applied to foreign currencies according to their genesis, with that applying to tourists, raw materials and foreign investment perhaps more favourable than that applied in the case of non-essential imports.

mercantilism state trade controls of a nationalistic and protectionist nature of the kind widely imposed by Britain in the 17th and 18th centuries.

metropolitan districts the six largest British local authorities, which replaced metropolitan counties in 1986. They have responsibility for running county-wide social services, education and libraries, as well as for the housing, leisure, environmental health and planning services run by district councils.

Mexican War the period of hostilities between 1846 and 1848 triggered by Mexican resentment of US annexation.

MFA (multi-fibre arrangement) an agreement reached in 1973 by more than 50 GATT countries that provides a framework for international trade in textile products made of wool, cotton, and man-made fibres.

microeconomics the study of the prosperity of a particular industrial or social category as a measure of a nation's economic development.

Midlothian campaign the by-election campaign masterminded by **William Gladstone** in 1879–80 to win the seat from the Tories. Fought largely on the issue of **Benjamin Disraeli**'s foreign policies, it was notable for borrowing aggressive electoral techniques of the kind already common in American politics but never before used in Britain.

milieu [*French*] the existing social environment or intellectual climate.

Militant Tendency an extreme left-wing faction within the British Labour Party that gained a reputation for violently escalating trade union disputes and demonstrations, and whose activities led Labour in the mid-1980s to expel Militant Tendency members from the party.

millisieverts a unit of measurement of ionizing radiation. In 1991 the Ministry of Defence announced a new safety limit for its military and civilian personnel of whole-body exposure not exceeding 100 millisieverts over any consecutive five-year period.

minute de vérité [*French*] the moment of truth.

minutia *pl.* **minutiae** [*Latin*] the tiniest detail; a minor characteristic.

mirabile dictu [*Latin*] wonderful to relate—frequently used sarcastically.

mirabilia [*Latin*] wondrous matters; things marvellous to behold.

Mirage jet the most commercially successful and durable European-built fighter aircraft ever, with more than 1400 sales to 20 air forces since its production by Dessault-Breguet in France began in 1960. The current version, Mirage III, has a maximum speed of Mach 2.2 (2335 kph) at its ceiling of 17000m, and carries two 30mm cannon, bombs, or air-to-air missiles. Like all early designs of tailless deltas, the Mirage requires a long runway, and the unmodified craft suffers speed loss on sustained turns.

MLR (minimum lending rate) the lowest figure at which the Bank of England used to lend to the discount market, but from 1981 used only in exceptional circumstances to influence a change in direction of interest rates.

modus vivendi [*Latin*] way of living; a workable arrangement for co-existence where other irreconcilable differences exist.

moment critique [*French*] the instant of significance; the critical moment.

moment de défaillance [*French*] a moment of weakness; a temporary aberration.

monetarism the doctrine that strict control of a country's money supply—typically, by the imposition of import controls, high interest rates, and cuts in public expenditure—is its best weapon against inflation.

Money Bills British legislation of a fiscal nature and whose enactment the House of Lords may delay but cannot prevent. They were brought into being by the Parliament Act 1911, which itself was the result of the constitutional crisis that was triggered by the People's Budget of 1909.

money supply the sum of a nation's total money stock according to one of six definitions. They range from M1—the narrowest—which takes into account only cash and bank deposits, through to M5, which includes all other reserves redeemable in the short, medium and long term. Britain uniquely also defines M0 as being the state's currency and operational liabilities, including the value of all coins and notes in circulation.

Monroe doctrine the declaration of US foreign policy presented to Congress by President **James Monroe** in 1823, largely inspired by British Foreign Secretary **George Canning**'s argument that the two countries should issue a joint warning against the restoration of Spanish rule in the newly independent republics of South America. Monroe's statement asserted that in return for non-interference with existing European colonies in America or in Europe's internal affairs, the US would not countenance any extension of Europe's political system to the western hemisphere.

monstre sacré [*French*] sacred monster; a public figure whose eccentrities only add to his or her popular appeal.

montant forfaitaire [*French*] agreed amount; the internal trading or economic preference that exists between members of the **EEC**.

moral rearmament a movement founded in 1938 by Frank Buchman to promote strict Christian values in every aspect of religious and personal life, and the observance of the highest moral codes by those in public life, as the only means of ensuring a general improvement in the human condition.

moratorium [*Latin*] originally, the postponement of a debt; in modern usage, the suspension of any action or obligation pending the outcome of negotiations or some other development.

more majorum [*Latin*] according to custom.

mores [*Latin*] the accepted customs of a place, historical period, or particular society.

Mossad Israel's external secret service.

muckrakers a group of early 20th-century American reformers who saw it as their duty to draw the public's attention to political and business corruption, often in articles for leading mass-circulation magazines of the day, such as *Colliers*, *McClure's*, and *Cosmopolitan*. The word was first used by **Theodore Roosevelt**, who likened the group to the character in *Pilgrim's Progress* who was so preoccupied raking mud that he did not perceive the celestial crown above him.

mujaheddin [*Arabic*] fighters; the name given to the Islamic fundamentalist guerillas of Afghanistan and Iran.

multum in parvo [*Latin*] much out of little.

Munich agreement the concession by British Prime Minister **Neville Chamberlain** in September 1938 that followed **Adolf Hitler**'s demands for incorporation into Germany of the German-speaking Sudetenland region that had been acceded to Czechoslovakia as part of the **Treaty of Versailles**. Chamberlain, failing to anticipate Hitler's grander ambitions, permitted the annexation in return for an undertaking that Germany would respect the autonomy of the remaining Czechoslovakian territories, thus believing that he had achieved 'peace in our time'. Chamberlain's appeasement encouraged Hitler's subsequent move against Poland, which in turn brought the start of World War II.

Muslim [*Arabic*] to be submissive to God; the name given to a member of the Islamic faith; a follower of Muhammad.

mutatis mutandis [*Latin*] subject to appropriate changes; a phrase implying that a principle or agreement must be altered to meet a new set of circumstances.

Mutiny Acts legislation passed by the English Parliament annually between 1689 and 1879 that granted the state's military right to enforce discipline in peacetime and thus to establish a standing army.

mythopoeia [*Greek*] myth-making; to advance arguments that defy credulity.

National Front extreme right-wing, neo-Nazi British movement formed in 1967 by a merger of John Tyndall's British Movement and A.K. Chesterton's League of Empire Loyalists. It enjoyed a measure of electoral success in the 1970s through its anti-immigration stance, when its marches through areas in the Midlands and London having a high ethnic population was redolent of those staged by **Oswald Mosley**'s British fascists in the 1930s.

National Government the Administration established by **Ramsay MacDonald** and three members of his Labour Cabinet in 1931 but which was in essence a Conservative coalition. It enjoyed success in three general elections under MacDonald, **Stanley Baldwin** (1935–7) and **Neville Chamberlain** (1937-40).

nationalization the disposal of a state utility or agency to the public so that it effectively passes into private ownership.

NATO (North Atlantic Treaty Organization) collective defence organization founded in 1949 under the North Atlantic Treaty. The original membership of 10 European states, the USA and Canada subsequently admitted Greece and Turkey (1952), Federal Republic of Germany (1955), and Spain (1982). France withdrew from NATO in 1966 while remaining a member of the Atlantic Alliance.

Nazi the German national socialist party developed in the 1920s by **Adolf Hitler** and Ernst Roehm; abbreviated from the first word of the organization's full title, Nationalsozialistische Deutsche Arbeiterpartei.

nem(ine) con(tradicente) [*Latin*] without contradiction.

ne plus ultra [*Latin*] no more beyond; the ultimate limit.

neue Sachlichkeit [*German*] the new realism.

New Deal two-part programme of economic and social reform initiated by President **Franklin D. Roosevelt**. The first phase, from 1933 to 1935, aimed at alleviating the Depression that followed the Wall Street crash of 1929, by regulating banks, introducing currency controls, raising farm prices, and stimulating industrial recovery to cut unemployment. The second phase, from 1935 to 1939, introduced further labour and social reforms, including the right to collective bargaining; unemployment benefits; old-age pensions; a minimum wage; and a maximum working week.

new economic policy a brief return to capitalist trade and activity in the Soviet Union during the early 1920s to restore the country's war-torn economy.

New Liberalism the collectivist ideology that was embraced by the Liberal Party between 1900 and 1914.

nexus [*Latin*] a cluster of related ideas or arguments; a causal link or connection.

nihilism [*Latin*] nothing; extreme late-19th-century Russian revolutionary movement, which held that real world reform could only be achieved by wholesale anarchy and the complete overthrow of all existing state, legal and social institutions. Nihilism was rejected by **Karl Marx** but received some encouragement from **Nikolai Bulganin**.

Nikkei the Tokyo stock exchange.

nil desperandum [*Latin*] never despair; do not falter.

Nimitz the class of eight US Navy nuclear-powered, multirole aircraft carriers that are the most powerful surface warships in the world. The 72700 ton Nimitz—which has a length of 333m and a beam of 41m—carries a crew of 3300, air-wing personnel totalling 330, and at least 90 aircraft, which launch from a 77m-wide flight deck.

1984 1949 futuristic satirical novel by **George Orwell** that depicts a politically emasculated society in which there is no place for truth, historical records are destroyed, and factual information is replaced by propaganda, and in which 'Big Brother'—meant to represent Stalin—'is watching you'.

1992 refers to the Single European Act passed in 1986, allowing for the completion of the process of creating a common market within the Community by 1992. This will generate further competition among the industries of member states.

1922 Committee powerful group of Conservative Back-Benchers who meet regularly to redefine or reassert party policy, mostly according to right-wing principles, and to influence Ministers accordingly. It was formed after the party's decision in October 1922 to withdraw from **David Lloyd George**'s coalition.

Nobel Peace Prize one of several annual awards made under the terms of the will of Alfred Bernard Nobel (1833–96), the Swedish inventor of dynamite, who was stung into establishing a $9 million fund for the purpose before his death after reading a prematurely-published obituary that described him as 'a merchant of death'.

noblesse oblige [*French*] nobility has its obligations; the higher aristocracy are expected to behave according to their class.

nolens volens [*Latin*] unwilling, willing; regardless, willy-nilly.

non placet [*Latin*] it does not please me; a negative vote.

non-tariff barriers obstacles to foreign imports other than conventional customs tariffs, including import levies and price controls.

Nordic Council an association formed by Denmark, Iceland, Norway and Sweden in 1952 to promote co-operation between their respective Parliaments and Governments. They were joined by Finland in 1955, the Faeroe Islands and Aland Islands in 1970, and Greenland in 1984.

Nordic Council of Ministers a voluntary association of the Governments of Denmark, Finland, Iceland, Norway and Sweden formed in 1962 to promote economic co-operation and trade preferences.

nostrum [*Latin*] a remedy that has the recommendation only of the person who devised it.

Notting Hill riots a series of violent demonstrations in north-west London in 1958, directed at coloured immigrants living there, that brought immigration into the British political arena for the first time, and led eventually to the introduction by a Conservative Government in 1962 of the Commonwealth Immigration Act, which cut entry into the UK by nine-tenths; Labour's establishment of the anti-discrimination Race Relations Board in 1965; and its introduction of additional controls on Kenyan Asians with British passports in 1968.

nous [*Greek*] intellect; shrewdness, acumen.

nulli secundis [*Latin*] second to none.

nuncio [*Italian*] a permanent papal diplomatic representative.

OAPEC (Organization of Arab Petroleum Exporting Countries) Kuwaiti-based association of 10 petroleum-exporting nations established in 1968 to determine its member states' production and marketing strategy. Egypt's membership was suspended in 1979 but restored in 1989, and Tunisia participation was suspended in 1987.

OAS (Organization of American States) a voluntary association of 32 South American countries and the USA to promote peace, security and co-operation among all the nations of the western hemisphere.

OAU (Organization of African Unity) Addis Ababa-based inter-governmental organization created in 1963 to promote economic, trade and solidarity and independence among African states and to co-ordinate their defence.

ob majorem cautelam [*Latin*] with greater caution; to allow for every contingency.

obscurum per obscurius [*Latin*] to attempt to explain the arcane or obscure by reference to something even more impenetrable.

October Revolution the successful Bolshevik coup d'etat in October 1917 (November by the western calendar), led by **Vladimir Lenin**, who became head of the Soviet state, and retained that office until his death in 1924.

OECD (Organization for Economic Co-operation and Development) Paris-based institution established in 1961 for the purpose of expanding world trade. Its 24 full members include all **EEC** and **EFTA** members, the USA, Canada, Japan, Australia, New Zealand, and Turkey.

official reserves the foreign exchange fund held by a nation's treasury to ensure that it can honour fully all immediate and imminent claims, and which is counted as an asset in a country's balance of payments.

OIC (Organization of the Islamic Conference) a body founded in 1971 to promote Islamic solidarity, consolidate economic and social development, eliminate racial segregation and discrimination, promote international peace and security, and to advance the Palestine cause. Its 44 member states include Afghanistan, whose membership was suspended in 1980 but was effectively restored by the admission in 1989 of delegates of the self-declared Mujaheddin Government.

Olympic Games massacre the killing of 11 Israeli athletes by Palestinian terrorists at the 1972 games in Munich.

Omani official Iraqi news agency.

ombudsman [*Swedish*] an independent arbiter in disputes between official agencies and the individual.

OPEC (Organization of Petroleum Exporting Countries) Vienna-based organization established in 1960 that sets the price for its members states' crude oil products. As they account for more than 30 per cent of world oil production, OPEC's pricing tends to dictate world oil prices.

opinion polls sociologically-based surveys of local and national voting intentions pioneered in the USA by George S. Gallup in America in the 1940s and first used in a British general election in 1945. The three other main polling organizations are National Opinion Poll (1957), Opinion Research Centre (1965) and Harris Polls (1969).

Orangemen members of the Orange Order, founded in Ulster in 1795, for the purpose of maintaining the Protestant constitution; named in honour of William of Orange, later **William III**, who defeated the Catholic army of the exiled **James II** at the 1690 battle of the Boyne.

orders in council subordinate or secondary measures enacted by a committee of the Privy Council with the authority of the Cabinet.

overheating a consequence of an over-active and ostensibly buoyant economy, whereby pressure on production capacity only serves to promote high interest rates and to fuel inflation.

Owenism name given to the form of British pioneer socialism developed by Welsh-born **Robert Owen** (1771–1858), who from humble origins became a millionaire who offered exemplary social conditions to the workers at his Scottish mill, including the first infant school and adult education classes. The unsuccessful application of his co-operative ideals in the USA cost him most of his fortune, but he returned to England to continue promoting them until his death at 87.

oxymoron a rhetorical device often used to great effect by political orators, consisting of a deliberate contradiction in terms created by the use of a conflicting adjectival phrase—such as 'a fully-realized non-sequitur' or 'a winning defeat'.

pacifism the moral or religious belief that violence should never be used as a means of resolving conflicts. The pacifist movement, which took form with the establishment of American peace societies in the mid-19th century, developed internationally in the years following World War I with the support of numerous political and religious organizations, with students at American and English universities vowing not to fight in any war declared by their Governments, and Congress proclaiming US neutrality. By the start of World War II, both countries had enacted legislation allowing for conscientious objectors, and the pacifist ideal was successfully furthered by national political figures as disparate as **Gandhi** and **Martin Luther King**. Pacifism again manifested itself in the anti-**Vietnam War** peace movement of the 1960s and 1970s, but its influence appeared to wane towards the end of the century, to the point where it had only a neglible effect on public opinion in the 1991 **Gulf War**.

panacea [*Greek*] all-healing; the daughter of the Greek god of medicine; in modern usage, a universal remedy.

Pandora's box in Greek mythology, a vessel (actually a jar) from Zeus containing all the evils that afflict man, which were unleashed when opened by Pandora's husband, or perhaps by her out of curiosity; hence, anything that is ostensibly of benefit but which really disguises a curse.

panem et circenses [*Latin*] bread and circuses; food and entertainment—or anything else—that is thought will placate the masses.

papàbile [*Italian*] eligible for election as Pope; hence, deemed suitable for appointment to any high office.

pariah [*Tamil*] a member of the lowest Indian caste; a social outcast.

pari passu [*Latin*] with equal progress; in step, at the same rate of progress.

Paris Club an informal forum under the auspices of the French Treasury that provides a channel of communication between senior treasury officials of western countries in overseeing government-to-government loans.

parish councils the lowest tier of local authority representation (also known as town councils) of which there are 10 200 in England and 790 in Wales, where they are known as community councils. They have the power to maintain local amenities such as footpaths and playing fields, and to consider local planning applications, which they finance from a small charge that is included in the district authority's community charge (from 1993, council tax).

Parliament, British the legislative assembly for England, Wales, Scotland and Northern Ireland that originated from formalized meetings of the monarch, barons and leading prelates in the 13th century, and which achieved a permanent place in the British constitution in 1688. The English House of Commons took form in 1649 with the abolition of the monarchy and of the House of Lords, and its power and influence was consolidated with the passing of the **Bill of Rights** and Act of Settlement, which established annual sessions and permitted the emergence of political parties. It was further strengthened with the forced union of Scotland between 1653 and 1660, though after 1688 the Scottish Parliament again enjoyed full independence. Consolidation was again achieved under **Walpole**, and in 1800 legislative union with Ireland was enacted. Reform was finally achieved in the agitation that preceded the 1832 **Reform Bill**, under which patronage and privilege gave way to a broader franchise. The 1867 and 1884 Reform Bills brought further liberalizing measures, and secret voting was introduced by the 1872 Ballot Act. The Lords' power to veto fiscal legislation was removed by the Parliament Act 1911; Members of Parliament were first paid a salary in 1912; and the right of women aged over 30 to vote in municipal elections was extended to parliamentary elections in the 1918 Reform Bill. (The age limit for women was reduced to 21 in 1928). Life peerages were introduced in 1958, and in

1969 the voting age for both sexes was reduced to 18. Today's House of Commons has 650 seats—523 for England, 38 for Wales, 72 for Scotland, and 17 for Northern Ireland—while membership of the Upper House numbers just under 1200. In Britain, a Government may serve a maximum five-year term before calling a general election, when MPs campaign to hold their seats over the course of a three-week campaign, during which—unlike their counterparts in the US House of Representatives, for example—their expenditure is strictly controlled within pre-determined limits, to ensure that candidates having great financial resourcs do not enjoy an unfair advantage over their rivals.

parliamentary novels, the Anthony Trollope's series of novels concerned with political life whose central character is a young Irishman, Phineas Finn. They include *Phineas Redux* (1874) and *The Prime Minister* (1876).

Parnellites the followers of the Irish MP and nationalist leader **Charles Stewart Parnell**, who gained the support of **William Gladstone** and the Liberal Party in his ceaseless campaign for Irish home rule.

parti pris [*French*] one-sided; a preconceived or prejudiced opinion.

patois [*French*] a local or regional dialect that is geographical rather than class-based.

Patriot American ground-to-air missile introduced in 1970, but which first achieved fame for its success in defeating Iraqi Scud rocket attacks on Saudi Arabia and Israel in the 1991 **Gulf War**.

pax Britannica [*Latin*] phrase invented by Joseph Chamberlain to describe British authority in India; the peace enforced within the British empire.

Pays Bas [*French*] the low countries; Belgium and Holland.

pays sans frontière [*French*] a land without frontiers; an open, international community.

PCBs (polychlorinated biphenyls) toxic substances used in the manufacture of capacitors and other electronic components, which, if discharged into rivers by manufacturing plants, can cause skin and liver damage. PCBs are also believed to act as carcinogenic agents. Their use is to be banned in Europe by 1999.

peasants' revolt a series of violent uprisings throughout England between May and July 1381, triggered by excessive poll taxes, poor government, and the vicissitudes of the 100 years war. Rebel mobs led by Wat Tyler and Jak Strawe entered London where they lynched Chancellor Sudbury and the Treasury Minister. A pardon promised at their meeting with Richard II at Smithfield after Tyler had been killed by a sword blow by the Lord Mayor of London was later revoked, leading to fresh riots, but by the end of the summer the uprising had been suppressed.

Pelion and Ossa in Greek mythology, the giant sons of Poseidon, whom he planned to heap on Mount Olympus to conduct their continuing quarrel with the gods; hence the phrase 'piling Pelion on Ossa' means to add difficulty to difficulty.

People's Budget the programme of fiscal measures that included higher income tax, death duties, and tax on unearned income that was introduced by **David Lloyd George** in 1909 to finance the building of Dreadnought battleship and to pay for old-age pensions. The Budget enraged the Conservative majority in the House of Lords, whose refusal to pass it created a constitutional crisis and prompted the Parliament Act 1911, which removed the Upper House's power to veto Money Bills.

per ardua ad astra [*Latin*] to the stars through difficulties; great achievements are possible only by conquering adversity.

peredyshka [*Russian*] a breathing space; time to reflect.

perestroika [*Russian*] reconstruction, restructuring of society; advocated and developed by **Mikhail Gorbachev** from 1985 onwards.

perfide Albion [*French*] treacherous England; an archaic but not altogether obsolete expression of the low opinion that, it is said, the French traditionally have of the English nation.

per incuriam [*Latin*] by negligence; with an absence of care.

peripeteia [*Greek*] a rapid and unexpected change in circumstances or change of fortune.

periphrasis pl. **periphrases** [*Greek*] circumlocution; avoiding the point.

per pro(curationem) [*Latin*] by authority; a suffix (usually abbreviated to **per pro**) added to the initials or signature of a person signing a document on behalf of the individual whose name it bears.

per saltum [*Latin*] at a stroke; unhindered by any intermediate stages.

per se [*Latin*] in itself; without reference to anything else.

persona non grata [*Latin*] a person whose presence is no longer desired by the authorities, such as a discredited diplomat; a political or social outcast.

petite bourgeoisie [*French*] the lower middle classes; a derogative description for those having limited social or intellectual horizons.

petrodollars the surplus funds created by a country's sale for American dollars of its oil products.

pièces justificatives [*French*] documentary proof of the truth of an assertion or argument.

pis aller [*French*] one worse; the last resort; the only action remaining when no other remedy is available.

placet [*Latin*] it pleases me; a positive vote or indication of assent.

Plaza Accord an agreement made in 1985 between the **Group of Five** members to lower the value of the American dollar.

plebs [*Latin*] the common people of ancient Rome; the working classes.

plus ça change, plus c'est la même chose [*French*] everything changes but nothing alters; the more that things appear to change, the more they really remain the same.

pocket boroughs British parliamentary constituencies that, before the passing of the 1832 **Reform Bill**, were effectively 'in the pocket' of patrons who had it in their power to give or sell the seats to favoured candidates.

Pocket Dictator nickname given to the Austrian Chancellor **Englebert Dolfuss**, on account of his diminutive stature and his attempts to harangue the country's politial parties into uniting against the Nazi menace.

pogrom [*Russian*] destruction; the persecution or massacre of a specific class or other element in society, particularly of the Jews in eastern Europe, particularly in Russia.

point d'appui [*French*] fulcrum; a pivotal point or argument.

point d'honneur [*French*] point of honour; a matter of principle.

politico [*Spanish*] an opportunist; one who engages professionally in politics to achieve personal power.

poll tax the familiar name for the community charge system of local taxation, whereby a payment towards local services is made by every eligible individual registered on the electoral role. Its introduction in England and Wales in 1989 (having been imposed in Scotland a year earlier) produced many anomalies—and in most cases a liability per household substantially higher than that which existed under the old rates system, which led to widespread public criticism, high levels of non-payment, and serious rioting. As a key factor in successive Conservative by-election losses, the Government introduced in their 1991 Budget higher central subsidies to reduce poll tax bills, and shortly afterwards announced that they would by 1993 replace the community charge by a scheme owing more to the old rating system.

pons asinorum [*Latin*] literally, the bridge of asses; a difficulty or problem that only the stupid find insurmountable or impossible to overcome.

Popular Front the notional pre-World War II alliance between the capitalist democracies of the USA and Great Britain and the USSR that took concrete form after the German invasion of Russia in June 1941. The term has since been adopted as part of the title of progressive political parties worldwide.

Populist Party American political organization founded in 1892 by farmers and labourers in the West who had become disenchanted with the economic and commercial policies imposed by the East. Their first presidential candidate, James B. Weaver, took more than 1 million votes in 1892, but at the next election, the populists endorsed the Democratic nominee, and by the end of the century the party had disappeared as a political entity.

populus vult decipi (ergo decipiatur) [*Latin*] the people prefer to be deceived (so let them).

pork barrelling American political term meaning an action undertaken because of its appeal to the electorate rather than because there is any real need for it.

post facto [*Latin*] after the event; retrospectively.

postiche [*French*] a false embellishment; an inappropriate addition.

potential GNP the maximum output that a country can theoretically achieve given full employment.

Poulson scandal local government contracts corruption scandal exposed in 1972, in which the leading figure was T. Dan Smith.

pourparler [*French*] informal, preliminary discussions.

praetor [*Latin*] one of ancient Rome's eight magistrates, of equivalent power to an English High Court or US Supreme Court judge.

pragmatism a philosophy introduced by the American logician C.S. Peirce and developed by William James in his book *Pragmatism: A New Name for Some Old Ways of Thinking* (1907). The doctrine holds that the only real test of philosophical principles or theoretical remedies is their practical results, and that the integrity of all truths change according to the extent that their practical utility increases or decreases.

presidium [*Latin*] the executive committee of the Supreme Soviet of the USSR.

prima facie [*Latin*] on the face of it; at first glance; a good enough reason to justify further investigation or action.

Prime Minister the most senior member of the British Cabinet. The term was first applied to **Walpole**, but was not officially recognized until 1905 with **Campbell-Bannerman**'s formal appointment to that office.

primum mobile [*Latin*] prime mover; the motive force; the original cause of activity.

primus inter pares [*Latin*] first among equals; enjoying limited precedence.

Private Eye British anti-establishment fortnightly launched on a shoestring in 1962 by a small group of satirical writers and performers, including **Richard Ingrams** (who served as editor from 1963 until 1986), Peter Cook, and William Rushton. It has frequently, and justifiably, been the target of successful libel actions, but has just as frequently presented accurate exposés of corrupt practices by state agencies, commerce, and public figures. It has long since inherited the reputation that **Punch** once enjoyed as a breeding ground for brilliant new cartoon talent.

Privy Council an informal group of parliamentary advisers whose counsel is available to the monarch. MPs who are privy councillors are distinguished by the courtesy title of 'Right Honourable' as a prefix to their names.

pro bono publicus [*Latin*] for the public good; for the benefit of the masses.

Profumo scandal the revelations that followed the denial in the House of Commons by Defence Secretary **John Profumo** in 1962 that his affair with dancer and club hostess **Christine Keeler**, whose other entanglements included a diplomat at the Russian Embassy in London, had endangered the nation's security. He resigned in 1963 for having misled the House and turned to charitable works, for which he was awarded the CBE in 1975.

prolepsis [*Greek*] anticipation; something that has yet to come into existence.

pro re nata [*Latin*] for that which is to happen; making provision for an unexpected event or development.

protectionism in general, the imposition of trade barriers, such as high import quotas, on imports to protect domestic manufacturers from cheap competition. Currency protectionism is any measure designed to allow a nation's economy to develop unhindered by disruptive external influences.

protocolaire [*French*] one who insists on diplomatic niceties.

PSBR (public sector borrowing requirement) the difference between the British Treasury's total income and its expenditure, including grants to regional and local authorities.

pump priming expenditure by the state in an attempt to stimulate the recovery of a particular commercial or industrial sector or region with a view to restoring full employment.

Punch English satirical weekly journal founded in 1841, which quickly became the most important medium for the caricaturists, humorists and political commentators of the day, but which in recent years has exhibited a blandness that has helped to assure a continuing place for *Private Eye, Viz*, and other less conservative publications.

Puritans radical Protestants who broke from the Church of England during the reign of **Elizabeth I** to rid their faith of its heritage of Catholic doctrines and ritual, to return to the purist teachings of the Bible. Persecution compelled them to emigrate in the 17th century to America and Europe.

Putsch [*Swiss German*] a revolution; the violent overthrow of political opponents, such as the abortive Munich Putsch led by **Adolf Hitler** in 1923.

QED, quod erat demonstrandum [*Latin*] that which was to be proved.

Quakers nickname for members of the pacifist Religious Society of Friends, and one much disliked by them, as it was sarcastically conferred by a Derby magistrate at the 1650 blasphemy trial of founder George Fox (1624–91), after he had warned the Bench that it should 'Tremble and quake at the name of the Lord'.

Queen's Speech the address given by the monarch at the annual State Opening of Parliament, which announces the Government's proposed legislative programme for the coming Session. The speech is not of course written by the Queen but mainly by the **Prime Minister** of the day in consultation with the senior members of the Cabinet.

quid pro quo [*Latin*] in exchange for another; a fair trade-off.

quis custodiet ipsos custodes? [*Latin*] who is to control those who control us?

quisling a traitor or collaborator; after **Vidkun Quisling**, the former Defence Minister who headed Norway's puppet government under Nazi occupation, for which he was executed in 1945.

quo jure? [*Latin*] by what authority?; who says that must be so?

quota [*Latin*] a trade limit on the import or export of a particular category of manufactured goods, which may apply to one or more countries. Also, the name given to a country's subscription to the **International Monetary Fund**, 25 per cent of which is made in special drawing rights and the balance in its own currency.

radicals a general term to describe members of the political left of the late 18th and early 19th centuries, and those who adopted middle-class, laissez-faire attitudes. More recently, the term has come to be applied to any faction that has socialist, pacifist, or anti-cleric leanings.

raison d'état [*French*] a cause related to the security of the state; an excuse for autocratic action.

raison d'être [*French*] the reason for being; the justification or purpose for an action.

rappel à l'ordre [*French*] to return to the issue in question; back to basics.

rapporteur [*French*] one charged by a council or committee to investigate and report on a specific matter.

rapprochement [*French*] reconciliation; a convergence of ideals leading to better relations.

rara avis [*Latin*] a rare bird; something seldom encountered.

ratio decidendi [*Latin*] the crux of the matter; the rationale for arriving at a particular judgement.

rationale [*Latin*] a reasoned explanation; the logical basis for an argument or action.

reactionary one who adheres to conservative and usually outmoded economic and social policies and resists changes.

realpolitik [*German*] realistic policies as opposed to idealism; a practicable principle.

rebus sic stantibus [*Latin*] matters being as they are; given the prevailing circumstances.

recession a decline in a country's business activity and national wealth, characterized by low consumer and public spending, a high level of company closures, and increasing unemployment.

recherché [*French*] far-fetched; beyond reasonable bounds.

Red Dean media nickname for Dr Hewlett Johnson (1874–1965), Dean of Canterbury from 1931, who argued that the Communist ideal was akin to Christian ethics.

Red Flag the anthem of international socialism. The version having lyrics by Jim Connell is used by the British Labour Party.

Red Ken media nickname for **Ken Livingstone**, newt-keeping Marxist leader of the Greater London Council before it was dismantled by the Conservative Government in 1986. He became a Labour MP in 1987.

Red Robbo media nickname for militant trade unionist Derek Robinson (1937–), who was sacked by British Leyland chairman Sir Michael Edwardes in 1976, alleging that Robinson's activities had cost the car plant £200 million.

red shirts name applied to the volunteer force raised by **Giuseppe Garibaldi** in the 1860s war for Italian freedom against the Austrians and French.

reductio ad absurdum [*Latin*] to an absurd extreme; demonstrating the weakness of a proposition by suggesting the consequences of adopting it.

referendum [*Latin*] a means of testing the views of the electorate on a matter of national importance that is not necessarily binding on the Government who initiate it.

reflation the concerted and controlled rehabilitation of a country's economy in which the aim is to stimulate demand while not triggering inflation.

Reform Bills the 1832, 1867 and 1884 Acts of Parliament that extended the franchise, and brought an end to parliamentary corruption with the abolition of pocket and rotten boroughs. Their tenets were supplemented by further legislation in 1918, 1928, 1948 and 1971, which introduced the vote for women and then lowered the eligible voting age to 21, ended plural voting by abolishing university seats and business votes, and lowered the voting age to 18.

Reform League an organization formed by working-class radicals in 1863 to extend manhood suffrage, and whose 1866 demonstrations against the fall of the second **Reform Bill**

compelled the subsequent Administrations of Lord **Derby** and **Benjamin Disraeli** to introduce some of its proposals. It won the support of the Liberals in their 1868 election campaign, but was dissolved soon after.

refusniks young Soviet dissidents in general; in particular, conscripts from the Baltic states who refused to report for duty with the Russian army following their countries' moves to independence in 1990.

régime [*French*] a period of government, often of an oppressive nature, associated with a particular head of state or Admnistration.

regimen [*Latin*] a way of living; a strict economic or social code.

regulations the most powerful instrument of the **European Community**, equivalent to national legislative Acts, and which are absolutely binding on, and directly applicable to, all its member states.

Reich [*German*] empire; Nazi Germany's name for all the areas of Europe that it considered to be its own territory.

renversement [*French*] a reversal of fortune; a complete change of circumstances, usually for the worst.

reserve currency an internationally acceptable currency that can be used by central banks to meet their foreign commitments.

res ipsa loquitur [*Latin*] it speaks for itself; something so obvious that it hardly needs emphasizing.

res nullius [*Latin*] a trifling matter; something of little significance.

Restoration the period that followed the collapse of the Commonwealth, that brought the return of the Stuart dynasty, and saw **Charles II** take the throne in 1660. In contrast to the puritanical era that preceded it, it was a time of frivolity and social licence, but also saw significant accomplishments in the arts, as well as in philosophical and·religious advancement.

(la/le) Reyne/Roy le veult [*Old French*] the Queen/King wishes it; the monarch's formal assent to a parliamentary Bill that transforms it into an Act of Parliament.

Rhodesia crisis the series of events that began with the declaration by Prime Minister **Ian Smith** of a Unilateral Declaration of Independence on 11 November 1965, following the Rhodesian Government's failure to agree with successive British Administrations on a consitutional independence settlement that ensured the continuance of white supremecy. The British Government was successful in gaining United Nations support for sanctions while ruling out the use of force, and in 1966 and 1968, Smith met with premier **Harold Wilson** in unsuccessful attempts to resolve the crisis. An agreement was reached with **Edward Heath**'s Conservative Government in 1971, but it was ruled out after an independent fact-finding mission determined that it would be unacceptable to the black majority. The growing influence of the African National Congress, and the withdrawal of the Portuguese from Angola and Mozambique served to remind Smith of his isolationism, and in 1977 he announced that he was willing to enter into new talks on a one-man, one-vote basis and released nationalist leaders **Ndabaningi Sithole** and **Joshua Nkomo** as a sign of good faith. However, they initially refused to participate in negotiations, and the escalation of terrorist activities continued unabated despite Smith having reached in 1978 an internal settlement, providing for multiracial government, with the moderate Sithole and Bishop **Abel Muzorewa**. The return of a Conservative Government in 1979 provided the springboard for fresh talks and a new settlement, leading to elections in 1980 that were won by the former Marxist guerilla leader, **Robert Mugabe**.

Rights of Man, The the 1792 pro-republican work by **Thomas Paine** that defended the French Revolution, arguing that civil government can survive only by a consensus in which the rights of the individual are safeguarded and that revolution is permissible if they are abused. The uproar that followed its publication forced Paine to flee first to France, and he was found guilty of treason in his absence.

Rishon massacre the murder in March 1991, at a labour market in Rishon le Zion, of seven Arab workmen from the **Gaza Strip** by a 22-year-old Israeli, Ami Popper, which served to refocus political attention on the conditions of Palestinians under Israeli occupation after the distraction of the 1991 **Gulf War**.

risorgimento [*Italian*] resurrection; the period of Italian nationalism between 1815 and 1870, typified by aspirations of unity and independence.

Roman empire the period of worldwide Roman influence that began with Octavius's formal installation as emperor in BC 27, and which ended in the west in AD 476, and in the east in AD 1491, though the Byzantine empire lasted until 1453, when Constantinople fell to the Turks.

rond-de-cuir [*French*] circle of leather; a petty official, derived from the name given to the leather-topped stool that was once standard issue for French civil servants.

rotten boroughs the name given to ancient boroughs that, despite having small populations and having no economic or social infrastructure, returned Members of Parliament prior to the 1832 **Reform Bill**.

roundheads the puritan forces of **Charles I** and later of **Oliver Cromwell**. The name alludes to their habit of keeping their hair cut short, by comparison with the cavaliers' flowing locks.

royal prerogative the largely undefined discretion that the monarchy was once permitted to exercise over the nation's economic, foreign, administrative and religious policy that was the subject of disputes with Parliament throughout the 17th century, and which finally came to an end in the 19th century when the monarch's right to choose Ministers was relinquished.

RPI (retail price index) a monthly indicator of changes in retail prices that usually excludes luxury goods.

ruat caelum [*Latin*] though the heavens may fall; whatever happens, the outcome is certain.

Rump Parliament the assembly that survived the 1648 purge of the **Long Parliament**, and whose 60 members voted for the execution of **Charles I**.

Russian Revolution the events that brought an end to tsarist rule and established the modern Communist state, that bregan with the abdication of Tsar **Nicholas II** in March 1917 and concluded with the Bolsheviks, led by **Vladimir Lenin** seizing power the following November. After signing a peace treaty with Germany, the new regime's Red Army set to routing the loyal White Army infantry massed in the Volga, the south, and western Siberia, but the civil war did not come to an end in 1920, with the defeat of the pro-tsarist forces in the Crimea.

Sacco-Vanzetti case a famous 1921 murder trial in which two Italian anarchists, Nicola Sacco and Bartolomeo Vanzetti, were condemned to death for two killings that occurred during the course of a wages snatch from a Massachusetts shoe factory. International disquiet that the men were convicted mainly because of their political sympathies brought them several stays of execution, but in 1927 an independent committee upheld the original verdict and both men were executed later that year. Exactly 50 years later, the Governor of Massachusetts declared that the trial was unfair and ordered that no stigma or disgrace should be endured by the men's descendants.

Sacheverell case the 1710 impeachment of Henry Sacheverell for preaching that the Church of England was in danger and challenging the Whigs' interpretation of the **Glorious Revolution**. He was found guilty, but pamphleteering and rioting gave him the moral victory.

sachlich [*German*] a realist; one who is objective.

SADCC (Southern African Development Co-ordination Conference) a voluntary assembly of nine South African states, which convenes at least twice a year to promote their mutual development and to review the extent of their dependency on South Africa. The member states are Angola, Botswana, Lesotho, Malawi, Mozambique, Swaziland, Tanzania, Zambia, and Zimbabwe.

Saigon the capital of the republic of South Vietnam until the country fell to the communist north in 1973, when it was renamed Ho Chi Minh City.

Sajudis Lithuanian anti-Soviet popular front.

saltus [*Latin*] an abrupt change or break in continuity; a sudden transformation.

salus populi suprema est lex [*Latin*] the well-being of the masses is the supreme authority; the will and good of the people above all else.

samizdat [*Russian*] a privately-printed manuscript that is circulated without the knowledge or approval of the authorities; any subversive or banned literature.

samurai [*Japanese*] a member of the Japanese military caste.

sancta simplicitas [*Latin*] saintly simplicity; genuine innocence.

sang froid [*French*] cool-blooded; self-possessed.

sansculotte [*French*] without breeches; a peasant republican in the French revolution; a member of the lowest class in any revolutionary or anarchic movement.

sans façon [*French*] without ceremony; abruptly, done in the absence of diplomatic or social niceties.

sans-gêne [*French*] wholly unrestrained; without any regard for ordinary good manners or accepted standards of behaviour.

sans phrase [*French*] bluntly; straight to the point.

satyagraha [*Sanskrit*] loyal obstinacy; the policy of passive resistance.

sauve-qui-peut [*French*] every man for himself; a disorderly retreat from calamitous circumstances.

savoir faire [*French*] the quality of knowing almost instinctively the correct response or course of action, whatever the circumstances; a stylish and worldly manner.

Scandinavia collective term for Denmark, Finland, Norway, Iceland, and Sweden.

scenario [*Italian*] outline; the way in which it is anticipated that a conflict or policy will develop.

Schadenfreude [*German*] malicious enjoyment of the embarrassment or discomfiture of others.

Schlachtruf [*German*] battle cry; the signal to attack.

schlemozzle/schemozzle/shemozzle [*Yiddish*] a quarrelsome entanglement; a row, or a fuss over nothing.

scholium [*Latin*] an explanatory footnote or a supplementary comment.

Schrecklichkeit [*German*] frightfulness, dread; the committing of atrocities as a means of subjugating enemies.

Schwerpunkt [*German*] centre of gravity; the main thrust or point of attack.

scintilla [*Latin*] spark; a tiny glimmer of understanding or hope.

scire facias [*Latin*] so to inform; warning of the imminent application of a judgment.

Scottish National Party founded in 1927 as the National Party of Scotland, in 1934 it merged with the more right-wing Scottish Party, which had been formed only a year earlier. Popular support for the SNP and its policy of self-determination for Scotland grew rapidly in the 1960s and 1970s, but it lost 9 seats in the 1979 general election after the failure of a referendum on a Scottish Assembly. The party has regained some ground over the past decade, with electoral successes over the Conservative and Labour candidates in local and national elections.

scrutin de liste [*French*] a system of proportional representation whereby each eligible member of the electorate may vote for as many candidates as there are constituencies in a predetermined group.

SDI (strategic defence initiative) a scheme devised by the United States in the late 1970s for putting into fixed orbit over Earth space weaponry capable of detecting and destroying missiles launched anywhere in the world.

séance d'essais [*French*] practice session; a dry run, a preliminary examination.

Secretary of State for Scotland first instigated in 1707, the office was abolished in 1746 but revived in 1885. In 1926, the post was raised to Cabinet stature, and between 1941 and 1945 the Secretary of State's powers were increased significantly in respect of Scottish agriculture, education and social services—and further widened under the 1964–70 Labour Administrations.

secret de Polichinelle [*French*] an open secret; a confidence that is actually public knowledge.

secularist one who questions all forms of worship and religious belief and holds that state education policies should provide either for multidenominational religious teaching or none at all.

secundum quid [*Latin*] in only one respect; having a particular application.

securus judicat orbis terrarum [*Latin*] the verdict of the whole world must be valid; not everyone can be wrong.

Sehnsucht [*German*] nostalgia; a yearning for the old order.

Sellafield nuclear reprocessing plant in Cumbria, and the first (under its old name of Windscale) to suffer a radioactive leak.

semper eadem [*Latin*] always the same; the motto of Queen **Elizabeth II** and of the Princess Royal.

semper fidelis [*Latin*] forever faithful; always to be trusted.

seriatim [*Latin*] one by one; an orderly, sequential succession.

Sertões, Os a classic of Brazilian literature by Euclides da Cunha (1866–1909), published in 1902. It can be read both as a political, sociological and geographical treatise, and as a fast-moving novel, based on the conditions and events that led to the 1896–7 uprising against the central government. An English translation, *Rebellion in the Backlands* was published in 1944 and reprinted in 1970.

Settlement, Act of the 1701 legislation that nominated the descendants of Sophia of Hanover as heirs to the throne in the event of **William III** and Queen Anne dying without issue. It also imposed restrictions on the future monarch in respect of religious and judicial matters and foreign affairs.

seven seas a term meaning either the major oceans of the north and south Atlantic, north and south Pacific, Indian, Arctic and Antarctic; or the principal trade and navigation routes of the Arabian sea, Atlantic ocean, Bay of Bengal, Mediterranean sea, Persian gulf, Red sea, and South China sea.

Seven Years War the hostilities between 1756 and 1763 in which Britain allied with Prussia against Austria, France and Russia which established British supremacy in North America (through its victories in Canada) and India.

Shankill Road a Protestant stronghold that runs west from Belfast city centre, parallel to the Catholic Falls Road.

Sheffield disturbances an outbreak of violence against non-unionized labour in the cutlery trade in 1866-7 that prompted the Government to establish the first ever Royal Commission on trade unionism.

sheik [*Arabic*] an elder; the head of an Arab family or tribe.

shibboleth [*Hebrew*] any word whose mispro- nunciation is used to detect a foreigner or a person's geographical or class roots; a catchword or slogan used by members of a secret group or sect to recognize one another.

Shiites members of the minority Shia sect within Islam, which broke from the Sunni majority in the seventh century. Shiites are to be found mainly in Iran and Yemen.

Short Parliament the brief session that assembled in 1640 ostensibly to vote money for the Bishops Wars, but which was exploited by Scottish Members and **John Pym** to rally support against the Government of **Charles I**—who by promptly dissolving the Parliament, only added to their sense of grievance.

Siberia the sparsely-populated region of north and north-east Asia—much of it north of the Arctic Circle—that includes most of the Soviet Union east of the Urals.

siccum lumen [*Latin*] dry eye; a failure to display grief or regret when such is called for.

sic itur ad astra [*Latin*] the way to the stars; the route to fame and immortality.

sick man of Europe name bestowed upon the Turkish empire by the German emperor Kaiser **Wilhelm**, but nowadays often applied by other **EEC** members to Britain, as well as by British politicians themselves occasionally, in alluding to its economic vicissitudes.

sic semper tyrannis [*Latin*] such be the fate of all tyrants; the words uttered by John Wilkes Booth as he assassinated **Abraham Lincoln**.

sic transit gloria mundi [*Latin*] so the glory of the world passes away; an expression of the transient nature of material success.

siffleur [*French*] one who is paid to hiss and boo at a public performance; a lackey, or one promised a reward by another for lending his support to criticisms of a third party.

silent leges inter arma [*Latin*] laws are silenced by armed force; at a time of war, legislation is made useless.

simplesse [*French*] phoney simplicity; artful or feigned innocence.

simplex munditiis [*Latin*] wholly unadorned; sweet and simple.

simpliciter [*Latin*] unconditionally; without reser- vation in any respect.

simpliste [*French*] just too simple; too good to be true.

sine die [*Latin*] postponed; held back indefinitely.

sine qua non [*Latin*] without which, nothing; a person or element absolutely necessary if a particular action is to be accomplished.

Singapore, fall of the loss of Singapore to the Japanese on 15 February 1942, which was blamed on British over-reaction to the enemy's inadequate but fast-moving forces—and which was viewed by the rest of the empire as the incident that marked the beginning of the end of British colonial rule.

Sinn Fein [*Irish*] we ourselves; the movement for Irish independence and self-government founded by Arthur Griffith in 1905, mainly for the purpose of establishing a parallel parlia- mentary assembly (the Dáil), whether or not home rule was achieved. It enjoyed an over- whelming electoral victory in 1918, but was split by party differences 20–3, and again in 1969 in the wake of the **Ulster emergency**. Since 1969, Sinn Fein has consisted of the official and legal Marxist element, and the militant and outlawed Provisionals, which ostensibly serve as the political wing of the **IRA**.

Sittlichkeit [*German*] morality; a sense of proper standards.

si vis pacem, para bellum [*Latin*] if you seek peace, prepare for war; the doctrine that counsels against disarmament in peacetime.

six counties an alternative name for Northern Ireland, which consists of the counties of Antrim, Armagh, Derry, Down, Fermanagh, and Tyrone.

Six Day War the short, violent but highly successful offensive by Israel in 1967 that gained for her the whole of Jerusalem, the West Bank area of Jordan, Sinai Peninsula in Egypt, and the Golan Heights in Syria.

1600 Pennsylvania Avenue a synonym for the American presidency, being the proper address of the White House.

skyjacking the mid-flight abduction of an aircraft by terrorists who intend to use its passengers as hostages, or by individuals seeking political asylum.

Smith Square the location near the House of Commons of the Conservative Party headquarters (No. 32), and formerly also of the Labour Party at Transport House, now the headquarters of the Transport and General Workers Union..

social compact, social contract an understanding between a government and organized labour in particular that in return for wages restraint, the Administration will sustain a desirable infrastructure that supports the main elements of a welfare state.

Social Democratic Federation founded in 1881, it adopted Marxist policies in 1884, and through its amalgamation with other associations, developed by 1911, into the British Socialist Party, which in turn spawned in 1920 the Communist Party of Great Britain. The SDF retained its autonomy, but was finally dissolved in the late 1950s.

soi-disant [*French*] self-styled; deceitful pretence.

solvitur ambulando [*Latin*] remedy by action; the solution lies in practical experiment.

sottise [*French*] a stupid observation or careless remark.

sousentendu [*French*] a hidden meaning; a concealed truth.

South Sea bubble a period of wild speculation in 1720 in the shares of the South Sea Company, whose directors took over three-fifths of the national debt. The venture crashed within months, causing thousands of investors to lose their fortunes. The name is still invoked in cautioning against injudicious fiscal or economic policies.

south-east Asia the territory that comprises Burma, Thailand, Cambodia, Laos, Vietnam, Malaysia, Singapore, Indonesia, Brunei, the Philippines, as well as the islands to the south and east known as the Malay Archipelago.

South Pacific Forum an assembly of the heads of state of 15 independent and self-governing territories of the region that first met in August 1971. It allows for informal debate on a wide range of economic, social and cultural matters, with agreement reached by consensus rather than as a result of formal voting.

soviet [*Russian*] a governing council of the kind that, from local to national level, was installed after the 1917 revolution.

Soviet Union a shorthand term for the Union of Soviet Socialist Republics, the largest of which is Russia.

sovkhoz [*Russian*] a farm owned by the state, rather than by a collective.

Spanish-American War 1898 hostilities between the USA and Spain triggered by reports of atrocities on Spanish-held Cuba, in which America had long had a political and economic interest. War was finally declared after an explosion aboard a US battleship moored in Havana harbour that killed 260 of its crew. American successes led to Spain agreeing to Cuba's independence and to selling the Philippines, Puerto Rico and Guam to the US for $20 million.

Spanish Civil War the savage hostilities between fascist and republican forces that began in July 1936 and ended in March 1939. It was triggered by the election of a left-wing Government in February 1936, causing the fascist General **Francisco Franco** to raise an army in Morocco, from which he launched an offensive supported by Germany and Italy, with Mexico and Russia, together with the idealistic but largely untrained International Brigade aiding the democratically-elected Government. Bilbao was the first major city to fall to the rebels, in June 1937, and the surrender of Government forces in Barcelona and Madrid in January and March 1939 brought an end to the war, which had the effect of isolating Spain from world affairs and prolonging the poverty of the majority of her people for another quarter of a century.

SPC (South Pacific Commission) an organization established in 1948 by Australia, France, the Netherlands, New Zealand, the UK and the USA for the purpose of providing technical advice and training, and economic, social and cultural assistance to the countries of the South Pacific region. The SPC now has 27 member states.

Speaker, Mr an office created in 1376, mainly for the purpose of designating a senior parliamentarian to represent the views of the Commons to the Crown and the Lords. As its influence in those spheres declined, Mr Speaker's value in controlling the rowdy debates of the day grew, and in the modern Parliament, he is now viewed as indispensable in ensuring that Members representing all shades of political opinion enjoy a fair hearing. Parliament's 185th Speaker, **Bernard Weatherill** was the first to be chosen by MPs of all parties, and was also the first holder of the office to be regularly televised at work.

Speaker's Corner a place in Hyde Park, London, where any citizen is permitted to exercise the right of freedom of speech by regaling passers-by with his views on any topic of his choosing. It is known also as Soapbox Corner, because of the makeshift platforms from which speakers often address their audience.

special drawing rights an international reserve asset created by the **International Monetary Fund** in 1969, and which from 1981 has comprised the five most widely-traded currencies—the US dollar, deutschmark, British pound, French franc, and Japanese yen.

spes ultima gentis [*Latin*] the last hope of his kind; a term implying the outmoded nature of attitudes or policies of the individual to whom it is applied.

sputnik [*Russian*] a fellow traveller; the name of the first artificial satellite, launched by the USSR in 1957.

Stagg Field the birthplace of the atomic age; a converted squash court in Chicago where scientists engaged in the Manhattan Project achieved the world's first self-sustaining nuclear chain reaction, on 2 December 1942.

Stalhelm [*German*] steel helmet; nationalist ex-service organization formed after World War 1.

Stamp Act legislation passed in 1765 for the purpose of making the American colonies self-financing through the imposing of affixing revenue stamps to a wide range of publications and documents. The measure, which provoked the colonists' famous slogan, 'No taxation without representation', was repealed within a year.

Star Chamber the king's judicial office in the Palace of Westminster in medieval times and which, despite its corruption, survived until 1641. The name derived from the room's decorative blue ceiling.

Stars and Stripes familiar name for the United States flag, first used in John Philip Sousa's 1897 march, *Stars and Stripes Forever*. It was subsequently adopted also during both world wars as the name of the US Army newspaper.

Star Spangled Banner United States national anthem, originally written as a poem by Francis Scott Key (1779–1843) in 1814 during the British bombardment of Fort McHenry, and eventually sung to the tune of an English hymn, *To Anacreon in Heaven*. It was formally declared the country's national anthem by a 1931 Act of Congress.

star wars media nickname for the strategic defence initiative.

stentorian the quality that is ascribed to one having a particularly loud (but not necessarily authoritative) voice, after the Greek herald, Stentor, in Homer's *Iliad*, who was said to have the vocal power of 50 men.

Stimmung [*German*] a received mood; the quality of being in harmony with one's fellow men.

Strangelove, Dr a crazed presidential adviser (played by Peter Sellars) in Stanley Kubrick's 1963 nuclear age *film noir*. The name is still used sometimes, by senior Government officials in particular, in referring disparagingly to any outsider—crazy or otherwise—who has penetrated their defences and gained direct access to their Minister.

subbotnik [*Russian*] a voluntary but organized public service project.

sub rosa [*Latin*] in strict confidence; wholly secret.

Sudentenland the territory along Czechoslovakia's northwest border with Germany and Poland whose annexation by **Adolf Hitler** in 1938 on the pretext that it was inhabited mainly by German-speaking peoples led ultimately to World War II. In 1945, most of the its German inhabitants were expelled and the territory was returned to Czechoslovakia.

Suez crisis the announcement by Egyptian leader **Gamil Nasser** in July 1956 that he was nationalizing the Suez canal and the subsequent farcical invasion by British and French forces, in collusion with the Israelis, in November. The incident signalled the end of British imperialism and brought the resignation of Sir **Anthony Eden**—as despite minimal casualties, the inconclusive outcome served to leave a shadow over Britain's credibility as a conventional fighting force that was lifted only after the **Falklands War**.

suggestio falsi [*Latin*] deliberate misrepresentation falling just short of an outright lie.

sui juris [*Latin*] in one's own right; capable of managing one's own affairs.

summum bonum [*Latin*] the supreme good; the purpose that lies behind all rational effort.

Sunnis the majority sect within Islam, to which more than nine out of 10 Muslims belong. The Sunnis hold that they, not the Shiites, adhere to the true faith (Sunna) handed down by Muhammad, and the Islamic leadership must always come from the tribe to which he belonged.

Supermac media nickname for Prime Minister **Harold Macmillan**, which originated in a 1958 newspaper cartoon that depicted him as Clark Kent's alter ego.

Supper Club a group of left-wing and otherwise disenchanted British Labour MPs who meet occasionally over dinner to formulate alternative strategy and policy to that advocated by their party leader, **Neil Kinnock**. The group's existence had remained a secret until an agenda for their post-prandial and controversially pacifist-oriented deliberations was accidentally left in a House of Commons photocopier at the height of the 1991 **Gulf War**.

suppressio veri [*Latin*] the suppression of truth; the concealment of that which should be made public knowledge.

sur le tapis [*French*] on the carpet; the matter under discussion.

swaraj [*Sanskrit*] the self-government demonstrations that preceded India's independence.

Swing riots the agrarian equivalent of the **Luddite** disturbances, consisting of a series of arson attacks and the destruction of threshing machines in 1830 by farm labourers in southern and eastern England. The uprising was ruthlessly put down by the Whig Government, resulting in 19 executions and nearly 500 transportations—but the labourers eventually won wage concessions and delayed the introduction of mechanization and its effect on unemployment.

syndicalism a form of trade unionism that originated in France in the early 1900s, which anticipated worker control of major industries being achieved by a series of widespread strikes. The concept was evident to some degree in the British industrial rest that preceded World War I.

système D [*French*] self-preservation; to extricate oneself from difficulties regardless of the consequences for others.

tableau d'ensemble [*French*] the overall picture; the general situation.

tabula rasa [*Latin*] blank tablet; a person ignorant of a specified subject and receptive to information; an open mind.

Taff Vale judgment a momentous 1901 ruling that absolved railway workers involved in a dispute with their employer from liability for the costs incurred. The decision greatly encouraged the emerging Labour Party, and it was eventually enshrined in legislation, in the Trade Disputes Act 1906.

Tag [*German*] the big day; the day that marked the outbreak of World War I, which was eagerly anticipated by the German military.

Taiping rebellion Chinese rebellion in which as many as 30 million people are thought to have perished in actions orchestrated by the Government through General Gordon and other British officers, who exploited their involvement to bring China under British influence eventually.

Talmud historical rabbinical teachings that encompass many aspects of Jewish private and public life, and the faith's highest legal authority after the five original books of the Torah.

Tammany Hall the former Democratic Party headquarters for New York City and New York State that gained a reputation for abuses of the party organization. The name has since become synonymous with municipal malpractice or local government corruption in general.

Tamworth manifesto the pledges made in an 1834 election address by Sir **Robert Peel**, including the promise that the Tories would embrace the 1832 **Reform Bill** and become the party of conservative revisionism.

tanist [*Irish*] heir apparent; the title given to the deputy Prime Minister of the Republic of Ireland.

Taoiseach [*Irish*] chieftain; the title given to the Prime Minister of the Republic of Ireland.

Tariff Reform League the 1903 campaign spearheaded by **Joseph Chamberlain** to revive trade protectionism for industry, which served only to split the Cabinet and to give the Liberals a landslide victory in 1906 on a free trade ticket.

TD (Teachta Dála) the Irish Parliament's equivalent of a British MP.

témoignage [*French*] testimony; an unbiased account, and unprejudiced report.

terra incognita [*Latin*] unfamiliar territory; an unknown quantity.

tertium quid [*Latin*] having a relationship to, but distinct from, two ideas or actions; a happy medium.

Test Act 1673 a measure requiring all civil and military officers to take the oath of allegiance and to receive the sacraments of the Church of England designed to detect Roman Catholics and Protestant dissenters, which was repealed in 1828. Similar legislation affecting undergraduates and dons was repealed in 1856 and 1871 respectively.

third world the name applied by the so-called developed nations, be they of a capitalist or communist persuasion, to the mainly non-aligned countries of Africa, Asia and South America; in general, it is a somewhat patronizing collective euphemism for the under-developed countries.

Tiananmen Square massacre Student demonstrations in many Chinese cities against a return to the strict Maoist regime following the death of liberal reformer **Hu Yaobang** in April 1989 culminated with a peaceful mass rally of 200 000 young people in Tiananmen Square, in the capital Beijing (Peking) on 27 April. Initially, the authorities turned a blind eye to the protestors, who enjoyed massive public support and were encouraged by the promise made by party chief **Zhao Ziyang** to 'enhance democracy, oppose corruption, and expand openness' and the meeting between **Mikhail Gorbachev** and Chinese premier **Deng Xiaoping** in Moscow on 16 May. However, the Chinese Government's failure to assuage the scepticism of student leaders prompted Prime Minister **Li Peng** to impose martial law on 20 May. With no end to the demonstration in sight and embarrassed by world attention, on 4 June, on the orders of leadership, units of the People's Liberation Army brought the students' occupation of the square to a violent end. An estimated 3000 were killed and 12 000 injured as tanks crushed barricades and demonstrators alike and troops fired indiscriminately at others trying to escape from the carnage. Hundreds more are thought to have been imprisoned or executed after summary trial. The brutality of the event reversed the improving relations between China and the West, and renewed fears for the future security of British and other nationals in Hong Kong, and for the survival of its democratic infrastructure, when the colony reverts to Chinese rule in 1997.

tiers état [*French*] third estate; the status held by the commoners in the pre-revolutionary French National Assembly.

tirailleur [*French*] a soldier trained to act independently; a dangerous loner.

Tobacco Road 1932 novel by Erskine Caldwell (1903-87) that centres on the tragi-comic plight of a Georgia sharecropper, Jeeter Lester, and the effect of his degeneracy on his family. The name is sometimes invoked as a symbol of avoidable poverty.

tohu-bohu [*Hebrew*] formless and void; total confusion.

Tolpuddle martyrs a group of six Derbyshire farm labourers who were transported to Australia in 1834 on a charge of administering 'illegal oaths'—declarations of loyalty to the ideals of organized labour—in the year in which Britain's first trade union was formed. Public outrage at the sentence brought their pardon two years later.

Tories contemptuous 16th and 17th century nickname for dispossessed Irish Roman Catholic outlaws who attacked English soldiers and settlers, from the Irish word for 'pursuers'. The name was subsequently applied to those who opposed the succession of the Catholic **James VII** and **II** to the English throne, and a significant number of Tories sat in the Parliaments of **William III** and Queen Anne. The Tories developed into the ruling party by 1710, but the party virtually ceased to exist after 1714 for its alleged support of the **Jacobites**. The name regained its respectability 70 years later under **Peel** and **Disraeli**, and by the mid-19th century had become better known as the reactionary Conservative Party. The old name is still widely used today, but usually disparagingly.

toujours de l'audace [*French*] fearless always; audacity has its rewards.

tout comprendre, c'est tout pardonner [*French*] to understand is to forgive; comprehension brings compassion.

tout court [*French*] with nothing added, implying that something more is required for the sake of accuracy or protocol.

tout ensemble [*French*] the general effect; an achievement considered overall rather than in detail.

trade unions labour organizations that serve as a channel for collective bargaining on wages and working conditions, the first of which, the Grand National Consolidated Trade Union, was formed in 1834. Its avowed aim of bringing down the capitalist system by staging a general strike led to unionism being effectively outlawed by the mid-19th century, to be replaced by **Chartism**, but the social pressure for bodies representing the skilled workers who were a product of the Industrial Revolution produced the Trades Union Congress in 1868 and the repeal of suppressive legislation between 1871 and 1875. The first trade union Members of Parliament—both Liberals—were elected in 1868, and the subsequent Lib-Lab pact further strengthened the movement's development, as did the successful 1889 dock strike, the emergence of the Labour Party at the turn of the century, and the **Taff Vale judgment**. In Parliament, the Liberals secured in 1906 legislation that enshrined in the statute the unions' basic representational rights and their freedom from financial penalties, and a Bill establishing the legality of the political levy payable to the Labour Party was passed in 1913.

British trade union membership doubled during World War I, and Labour started emerging as the main opposition after the Liberals' postwar collapse. The failure of the 1926 general strike encouraged **Walter Citrine** and **Ernest Bevin** to adopt a less confrontational stance, and to work more closely both with the Labour Party and employers in improving the lot of the working class. Membership rose significantly again during World War II, and the unions' increasing numerical power brought in the 1950s a series of disruptive union actions—many of them taking the form of wildcat strikes fomented by local militants — which were eventually outlawed under a Labour Government. The application in the 1970s and 1980s of new technologies and the revised working practices saw the emergence of inter-union disputes—the most notable of which was that between the traditionally militant graphic trades unions and the right-wing, white-collar Electrical Trades Union, whose members were happy to perform skills that were previously the province of print workers. Protracted strikes, such as that by the miners and power workers which brought down the **Heath** Government, led to the anti-union legislation that was a characteristic of much of **Margaret Thatcher**'s 15 years as party leader, and the failure of the 1986 miners' strike, falling employment levels, and the general industrial malaise brought about by the recession that marked the beginning of the 1990s found the union movement again forming a constructive and occasionally joint anti-Government alliance with the employers.

tranche [*French*] one of several payments or instalments.

Tribune Group group of left-wing Labour MPs whose founders were followers of **Aneurin Bevan**, and whose views were reflected in the weekly paper that he founded in 1936, *The Tribune*.

trickle-down theory the always contentious and now largely discredited doctrine embraced by some American and British economists in the 1980s that if the better-off in society are permitted to enjoy an even higher standard of living, so too will the lot of the underclass improve.

tricoteuse [*French*] the women who busied themselves with knitting between watching victims of the French Revolution being guillotined; one who witnesses unpleasant or horrific incidents unperturbed.

Triennial Acts legislation passed in 1641, 1664 and 1694 requiring Parliament to assemble at least once every three years, as a reaction to the personal rule of **Charles I**. The 1694 Act also limited the life of each Parliament to three years.

triple alliance the pact between unions representing miners, dockers and railwaymen to threaten a national strike in the autumn of 1914. The miners attempted unsuccessfully to rekindle the alliance in 1921, and it was eventually dissolved by the failure of the 1926 general strike.

triple-headed monster disparaging nickname for the American Government, alluding to its legislative, judicial, and executive functions.

troika [*Russian*] a state body administered and controlled by three different authorities.

Trotskyism the doctrine developed by **Leon Trotsky** from the writings of **Karl Marx**, which re-emphasized the concept of a permanent revolution spreading communism from one country to another, as opposed to the centrism and isolationism encouraged under Stalinism—which Trotsky bitterly criticized, at the cost eventually of his own life.

trouvaille [*French*] a windfall; a happy discovery, or a lucky find.

Trucial States the name given to seven Arab emirates of the Persian Gulf prior to their full independence from Britain in 1971, and now known as the United Arab Emirates. They are Abu Dhabi, Ajman, Dubai, Fujairah, Ras el Khaimah, Sharjah, and Umm al Quaiwain.

tuan [*Malayan*] master; courtesy title used by Malayans when addressing Europeans.

tu quoque [*Latin*] you also; a riposte meant to imply that an accusation levelled by the speaker can equally well be made against him.

TW3 (That Was The Week That Was) weekly live satirical review of the week broadcast by the BBC between 1963 and 1965, whose lampooning of political and other public figures marked the start of a new era of British comedy. The show also served as a launchpad for the talents of David Frost, William Rushton, Ned Sherrin, and many other performers and scriptwriters who were later to achieve individual fame.

Übermensch [*German*] superman; a merciless superior being.

uberrima fides [*Latin*] in all good faith; the presumption that all the relevant circumstances or facts in a matter will be divulged.

ubi jus, ibi remedium [*Latin*] where right exists, there is a remedy to be found.

udarnik [*Russian*] emergency worker; a member of a special but non-military task force.

uitlander [*Dutch*] a South African settler, especially in the Transvaal.

ukase [*Russian*] an edict or decree; any arbitrary proclamation or ruling.

Ulster emergency the escalation of violence in Northern Ireland from 1968 that was triggered by police brutality against civil rights marches drawing attention to the housing and voting inequalities suffered by the Province's Catholic population. The promise of reforms by the Ulster premier **Terence O'Neill** lost him the confidence of loyalists in his Unionist Party and the indecisive 1969 election brought his resignation. The implementation by his successor, James Chichester-Clark, of many of the reforms

promised by O'Neill served only to foment rioting between Protestants and Catholics and an increase in specific acts of sectarian violence, resulting in 1970 in the imposition of internment without trial for Catholics only under **Brian Faulkner**'s Administration. Anti-British Army feeling among the Catholics and mainland **IRA** attacks increased markedly after the deaths of 13 young Catholics in the Bloody Sunday demonstrations of 30 January 1972, Direct rule was imposed in March, and the following year saw the election of a Fine-Gael-Labour Government less sympathetic to republicanism. In December 1973, the British, Ulster and Irish Governments signed the power-sharing Sunningdale Agreement, which provided for representation in the Province's government of both the Catholic and Protestant populations, but continuing resistance to the concept by Unionist loyalists, reflected in the results of the February 1974 election, and a general strike by Protestant workers brought the collapse of the Stormont executive on 28 May. The remainder of the 1970s and the 1980s saw no diminution in sectarian killings, and IRA mainland attacks continued, the most notable being the bombing of the Old Bailey, Harrods, and a British Army music school in Dover. Individual political targets included **Ian Gow**, a close parliamentary colleague and personal friend of **Margaret Thatcher**, who was killed by a car bomb in 1990. His murder marked the start of a new mainland campaign by the IRA, apparently in an attempt to re-establish its influence as new initiatives by Secretary of State for Northern Ireland, Peter Brooke, appeared to be bringing the British and Dublin Governments and Ulster Unionists closer than ever before to achieving a peace formula—and thus wholly undermine terrorist activities both by Catholic and Protestant extremists that seemed to many to have long ceased to have any political justification.

Ulster Volunteer Force Northern Ireland Protestant paramilitary organization.

ultima ratio [*Latin*] the final argument; the use of force after all other means of resolving a conflict have failed.

ultra vires [*Latin*] beyond authority; exceeding the authority of the individual or body concerned.

Umschwung [*German*] an abrupt reversal; a sudden change of opinion or climate.

UN (United Nations) successor body to the **League of Nations** that was developed during World War II and whose charter was finally ratified by the USA, USSR, China and the UK in October 1945. Its New York-based General Assembly consists of representatives from all member countries, supplemented by a Security Council of 15 members, five of whom are permanent representatives. The United Nations' perceived and actual value and influence has varied considerably through the decades that followed its establishment, but any doubts about its value as an instrument of international power were wholly dispelled during the 1991 **Gulf War**.

Uncle Sam the personification of the United States of America, he first appeared in cartoons in the 1830s but was not recognized by Congress as the country's official symbol until 1961. The figure depicted is an avuncular figure, wearing breeches, a waistcoat and tailcoat patterned with the stars and stripes of the American flag. The name is also used in a derogatory sense by unfriendly powers in alluding to US capitalism and its efforts to exert its influence abroad.

UNESCO (United Nations Educational, Scientific and Cultural Organization) a voluntary association of 158 countries established in 1946 for the purpose of advancing international peace through the educational, scientific and cultural relations of the peoples of the world.

UNIDO (United Nations Industrial Development Organization) a separate, specialized group formed in 1986 to promote industrial development in developing countries, for the purpose of establishing a new world economic order.

Unification Church a religion founded by Sun Myung Moon in Korea 1954 that is an amalgam of Christian and Taoist teachings, and which sees all history as a struggle between good and evil. It is strongly anti-communist and so is active mainly in South Korea.

Union, Act of (Ireland) legislation passed by **William Pitt**'s Government in 1800, in the face of stiff Irish opposition, to provide 100 Irish seats in the House of Commons and 32 in the Lords; immediate ecclesiastical union; gradual fiscal integration and contiguous free trade.

Union, Act of (Scotland) the 1707 legislation that gave Scotland 45 seats in the House of Commons and 16 in the House of Lords in return for acknowledging the Hanoverian succession. The Scots also accepted common fiscal, coinage and weights and measures systems, free trade, and a common flag but retained its distinctive legal system.

Union Jack the national flag of the United Kingdom of Great Britain and Northern Ireland.

Union of Democratic Control organization founded by Liberals and socialists at the start of World War I to defeat the tradition of secret diplomacy that they believed had brought it about, and which provided a springboard for the **League of Nations**.

Untergang des Abendlandes [*German*] the decline of the West; the erosion of the values of modern western civilization.

untouchables those at the bottom of the Hindu caste system that persists despite being outlawed after Indian independence in 1947, prompting many untouchables to convert to the caste-free Buddhism of Islam.

urbanisme [*French*] municipal planning; the proper orderly organization of urban life.

Utopia an imaginary realm enjoying perfect government described in Sir **Thomas More**'s 1516 work of that name; an exemplary society or an unattainable ideal.

Utrecht, Treaty of recognition by Britain and France in 1713 of Spain's sovereignty over its traditional territories in the Americas by way of compensating for her loss in the Spanish War of Succession of Gibraltar, Naples, Milan, Sicily and Spain's last vestiges of influence in the Netherlands. In 1769, Spain successfully routed small British and French forces that had broken the treaty by reoccupying one of the territories affected, the Falkland Islands, in 1764 and 1765. A British presence was re-established in 1770 after an agreement reaffirming Spanish jurisdiction over the islands, which survived until the collapse of Spain's empire in the New World and the colonization of the Falklands by Argentina in 1820. The British retook the islands by force in 1833, and continued to occupy them more or less peacefully for 150 years, until the 1982 **Falklands War**.

variatim [*Latin*] in different ways; by a variety of methods.

Vatican City an independent state enclave within the city of Rome, whose palace is the official residence of the Pope.

vécu [*French*] lived; a work of fiction; an argument or policy advanced by one who has no real experience of the circumstances to which it relates.

V-Effekt [*German*] surreal; a state of unreality.

vendetta [*Italian*] blood feud; a concerted and often unjustifiable attack.

ventre à terre [*French*] at full gallop; full speed ahead.

verbatim [*Latin*] word for word; a highly accurate account.

verbum sapienti sat est [*Latin*] one word suffices if one is wise; there is no need to labour the point.

Versailles, Treaty of the instrument signed on 28 July 1919 that formally ended World War I. The treaty was signed in Paris by **Georges Clemenceau**, **Woodrow Wilson**, **David Lloyd George** and German representatives. The severity of the reparations and territorial losses to Czechoslovakia, France, Lithuania and Poland that it imposed fuelled **Adolf Hitler**'s rise to power, and was eventually conceded by Britain and reflected in its initial policy of appeasement towards Germany's aspirations in respect of Sudentenland.

veto [*Latin*] forbid; to exercise one's right to prohibit a political act.

via media [*Latin*] the middle course; a compromise.

viet armis [*Latin*] by force and by armed power; through the display of military superiority.

Vietnam War the most serious and protracted armed conflict since World War II, it had its origins in the collapse of the French colonial regime in 1954, when the country was divided along the 17th parallel into North Vietnam, having the support of China, the Soviet Union, and other communist countries, and the USA-backed South Vietnam. In 1957, Vietcong guerillas from the north began a brilliantly conceived and conducted campaign to take the south, and American involvement escalated through the 1960s as a result of US fears that if the communist forces were allowed to go unchecked, other countries would effectively come under Moscow's control. America's huge budgetary and military investment peaked under the Administration of **Lyndon Baines-Johnson**, but US forces continued to make little headway at the cost of an ever-increasing death toll. World public criticism of napalm bombing and growing civilian casualties conveniently gave **Richard Nixon** all the political justification he needed to extricate America from its worst-ever military adventure, and in January 1973 America and the Vietnamese agreed to a ceasefire, although fighting only ended with the fall of Saigon in 1975.

volenti non fit injuria [*Latin*] no injury is caused to one who consents; one should not complain about the consequences of one's own actions.

vox et praeterea nihil [*Latin*] a voice and nothing more; an unseen critic of no account, insignificant opposition.

vox populi [*Latin*] the voice of the people; public opinion.

Wafd [*Arabic*] deputation; the Egyptian National Party founded in 1919.

Wailing Wall a holy shrine in Jerusalem, said to be part of Herod's temple and to contain stones from the original temple of Solomon. Before 1967, when Jerusalem was not wholly part of Israel, Jews would assemble there to lament the diaspora.

Wall Street a Manhattan thoroughfare that is famous as the address of the New York Stock Exchange and of the US Treasury, and which is also the home of countless stockbrokers and bankers. The name has become synonymous with American big business.

Walworth Road a euphemism for the headquarters of the Labour Party, which in 1981 moved to their new South London address from Transport House in Smith Square–now the headquarters of Britain's biggest labour organization, the Transport and General Workers Union.

Warsaw Pact a treaty signed in May 1955 and twice extended (most recently in 1975, for 20 years), for the purpose of extending military and technical assistance–most of it provided by Moscow–to Bulgaria, Czechoslovakia, East Germany, Hungary, Poland, and Romania. However, the rapid secession from USSR control that marked the last half of the 1980s made the pact redundant, and it was formally scrapped in April 1991.

Watergate affair the burglarizing and bugging of the Democratic Party's national campaign headquarters in the Watergate Hotel, Washington DC in June 1972 by members of **Richard Nixon**'s re-election team. The subsequent discovery of the White House tapes implicated the President in a plot of which he had previously denied all knowledge and in the subsequent attempted cover-up. He pre-empted calls for his impeachment by resigning the presidency in August 1974, the first holder of his office ever to do so. The following year he was pardoned by his successor, **Gerald Ford**, after more than 60 individuals had been convicted of criminal charges in connection with the Watergate escapade.

Watts Los Angeles residential district that won notoriety for the six days of rioting, ostensibly for black rights, that occurred there in August 1965, resulting in 34 deaths and more than 1000 injuries, as well as widespread property destruction.

WCC (World Council of Churches) Protestant organization formed at the end of World War II to encourage interdenominational collaboration, to allow the leaders of all faiths and sects to speak with one voice on the spiritual, moral or political challenges facing mankind. The Roman Catholic Church has never been a member of the council, though the Eastern Orthodox Churches have joined.

WCL (World Confederation of Labour) the name given in 1968 to the organization formerly known as the International Federation of Christian Trade Unions, which was founded in 1920. Today's WCL represents 15 million trade union and federation members in 78 countries.

Wealth of Nations outstandingly influential work on economics published by **Adam Smith** in 1776, which laid much of the groundwork for modern free economy thinking.

Wehrwirtschaft [*German*] wartime economy.

Weimar Republic the postwar political system that was drafted and adopted at Weimar—a German city known mainly for its cultural associations—and which was in force from 1919 until **Adolf Hitler** took power in 1931.

welfare state a term coined in the 1930s to describe the already defined concept whereby the Government of the day intervenes in the provision of a basic infrastructure from which all members of society, regardless of class, can benefit. It should include adequate education, health and social services; subsidized rented housing for those who cannot afford to purchase their own homes; and a proper standard of care for the handicapped and infirm and other disadvantaged members of the community. A free national health service, state benefits as of right without means testing, and family allowances were all introduced by the 1945 Labour Government, and ambitious programmes of municipal housing were implemented by both Labour and Conservative Administrations in the 1950s and 1960s. The next two decades brought increasing pressures on the wholesale operation of a welfare state, to which were added from 1979 a philosophical disinclination by the Conservative Government even to maintain high state subsidies of the housing, education and health sectors, let alone fund the increase that was needed.

Weltbürger [*German*] a worldly person; a man of the world.

Weltpolitik [*German*] international politics.

Weltschmerz [*German*] concern at the state of the world.

Weltverbesserungswahn [*German*] a fixation with improving the state of the world.

Wendepunkt [*German*] a crucial turning point; a sensational development.

West Bank the territory to the west of the River Jordan and the Dead Sea that belonged to Jordan until its annexation by Israel in 1967.

Western European Union Paris-based voluntary association formed in 1955, based on the 1948 Brussels Treaty, for the purpose of harmonizing defence and security among its member states of Belgium, France, Germany, Italy, Luxembourg, Netherlands, Portugal, Spain, and the UK.

Westland affair When Britain's only military helicopter manufacturer hit financial problems in 1985 and the Government refused aid, the company devised a rescue package involving its US competitor Sikorski that was favoured by **Margaret Thatcher**, but opposed by both British Secretary of State for Defence **Michael Heseltine** and Trade Secretary Sir Leon Brittan, initially, who wanted a European partner. The issue blew up in January 1986 when a letter from the Defence Ministry to the European consortium's bankers was alleged in an ostensibly secret memorandum from the Solicitor-General to Heseltine to contain 'material inaccuracies'. When it was discovered that the memo had been leaked to the press by Brittan with Downing Street approval to damage Heseltine's case, the Trade Secretary resigned—as did Heseltine the same month, when Thatcher denied him the opportunity to put his case fully to the Cabinet.

wets a derisory term that was originally applied to any member of **Margaret Thatcher**'s Cabinet who opposed her hardline monetarist or social policies, but which later encompassed even Back-Benchers who publicly wavered from the party line.

WFTU (World Federation of Trade Unions) Prague-based organization founded in 1945, and which represents the 214 million membership of 94 organizations in 82 countries.

Whigs the nickname awarded by **James II**'s supporters to those parliamentarians who opposed the Restoration. There are several versions of the origin of its political usage (it was also the name given to Scottish raiders and Presbyterians), though the most likely seems to be that it is an acronym of the covenanters' motto, 'We hope in God.' By the 18th century, the Whigs, with their emphasis on industrial enlightenment, social reform, and the curbing of the powers of the throne, had developed into the Liberal Party.

Whip parliamentary business manager who is responsible for ensuring the best possible representation of his party in Divisions, particularly when they concern contentious issues.

white man's grave a nickname for West Africa in the days of colonial rule, because of the high death rate from tropical diseases suffered by European settlers. Nowadays, the term is more widely applied to any African or Asian state in whose domestic politics Europeans are best-advised not to become involved.

WHO (World Health Organization) formed in 1948 to function as a central agency for directing health programmes in its 166 member countries particularly those classed as belonging to the third world.

Windscale former name of the Sellafield nuclear reprocessing plant in Cumbria, which has produced plutonium for Britain's nuclear arsenal since 1952. The name was changed in 1981 as part of a PR programme that was the aftermath of Britain's first serious radioactive leak.

Winter War the 15-week Russian invasion of Finland that began in November 1939 after the Nordic state had resisted Soviet demands to establish military bases there and to annex part of the south-eastern Karelian isthmus. Defeated, Finland ceded 43000 sq km/26718 sq ml of territory, which it attempted to reclaim by joining with Nazi Germany in attacking the USSR. An armistice between the two countries was signed in 1944.

Wirtschaftswunder [*German*] economic miracle; West Germany's postwar economic recovery.

woolsack the cushion stuffed with wool from countries of the British Commonwealth that serves as the Lord Chancellor's seat in the House of Lords. It was introduced in the 1300s to symbolize the importance of wool to the English economy.

World Bank, International Bank for Reconstruction and Development the main international agency through which mainly medium-term aid funds to developing countries are channelled. The bank, which was established in 1944 under the **Bretton Woods agreement** that also founded the **International Monetary Fund**, may also channel private funds and make loans of its own, using moneys raised by the sale of bonds on the world market.

Wunderkind [*German*] a child prodigy; a whiz-kid.

yankee originally the nickname for a resident of New England, it was later broadened to describe a southerner living in a northern state. British soldiers from the war of independence onwards have traditionally used the term to describe any American, but in the Civil War, it was used by confederates in referring exclusively to the union soldiers of the north.

Yom Kippur War the hostilities that broke out in 1974, towards the end of **Golda Meir**'s last term as Israeli premier, when an attack by Egypt and Syria coincided with Yom Kippur, the holiest day in the Jewish calendar. A cease-fire was reached after three weeks of fighting in which there were heavy losses on both sides.

Young Englanders a small group of well-intentioned but somewhat optimistic Tory politicians headed by **Benjamin Disraeli**, who between 1837 and 1840 attempted to forge an alliance between the aristocracy and the working class to achieve social reforms as an alternative to the middle-class liberalism promoted by the Tories' opponents.

Young Ireland an organization of young intellectuals under the leadership of **William Smith O'Brien** (1803–64), who broke away from the moderate Catholic Association believing that violent opposition to English rule was the only way to reverse the deprivations that were the result of the still raging potato famine. However, the readiness of the group's brightest members to articulate their strategies resulted in Smith O'Brien and other leaders being arrested in 1848 before any rebellion could be staged, and thereafter the organization went into decline.

Yugosalvia crisis 1991 Following the death of Marshal **Josip Tito** in 1980, the leaders of Yugoslavia's six republics devised a collective, revolving federal presidency, to ensure that the Belgrade Government fairly represented their respective states' varying forms of communism and ethnic mix. Towards the end of the 1980s, however, the democratization of several eastern bloc countries, and the move towards independence by the **Baltic states**, prompted a new wave of nationalism among the largely Catholic anti-communist populations of Slovenia and Croatia. On 24 June 1991, Slovenia and Croatia declared their independence. On the pretext of safeguarding Yugoslavia's borders **Slobodan Milosevic**, the Serbian president, immediately ordered federal infantry into the breakaway states. The inclusion met with fierce resistance, and, after European Commission intervention, a fragile three-week ceasefire pending further peace talks was agreed at a meeting of the federal presidents on the Adriatic island of Brioni on 7 July. It was agreed that Slovenia should be allowed to secede because it had no Serb minority, thus paving the way for the creation of the first new European country since WWI. With Slovenia indepedent, Serbia had greater energy to resist demands for independence from Croatia with its large Serb minority.

zamstvo [*Russian*] provincial local government council; hence, any small, officious body.

Zeitgeist [*German*] the spirit of the times; the current climate of opinion.

Zinoviev letter a letter purported to have been written by the president of Communist International and advocating revolutionary disruption in Britain that came to light just before the 1924 general election, which Labour lost. The British secret service attested to the letter's authenticity, but Labour has always maintained that the communication was a forgery designed to cost it vital votes.

Zionism the political movement to establish and develop a national homeland for the Jewish people, founded in the 19th century by Theodor Herzl, and which was lent credence in 1917 when the British Government—then supervising Palestine—agreed in principle to the need for a Jewish state. Public sympathy for the Jewish people following the atrocities committed against them in World War II led to the establishment of the modern state of Israel in 1948.

Zollverein [*German*] a customs agreement between German states that erects tariff barriers only on other countries.

zugzwang [*German*] checkmate; a counteraction that will always frustrate one's opponent.